THE
EARLY VERSIONS
OF THE
NEW TESTAMENT

THE
EARLY VERSIONS
OF THE
NEW TESTAMENT

*Their Origin, Transmission, and
Limitations*

BY

BRUCE M. METZGER

*George L. Collord Professor of
New Testament Language and Literature
Princeton Theological Seminary*

CLARENDON PRESS Oxford
1977

Oxford University Press, Walton Street, Oxford OX2 6DP

OXFORD LONDON GLASGOW NEW YORK
TORONTO MELBOURNE WELLINGTON CAPE TOWN
IBADAN NAIROBI DAR ES SALAAM LUSAKA ADDIS ABABA
KUALA LUMPUR SINGAPORE JAKARTA HONG KONG TOKYO
DELHI BOMBAY CALCUTTA MADRAS KARACHI

British Library Cataloguing in Publication Data

Metzger, Bruce Manning
    The early versions of the New Testament: their origin, transmission, and limitations.
    Index.
    ISBN 0 19 826170 5
    1. Title
    225.4   BS 2325
    Bible – New Testament – Criticism, interpretation, etc.

Library of Congress Catalogue Card Number: 77-30047

Printed in the United States of America

TO

THE EVANGELICAL THEOLOGICAL FACULTY

OF THE UNIVERSITY OF MÜNSTER

IN WESTPHALIA

AS A TOKEN OF GRATITUDE

FOR CONFERRING ON THE AUTHOR

THE HONORARY DEGREE OF

DOCTOR OF THEOLOGY

Preface

THE importance of the early versions of the New Testament is hard to overestimate. The Church historian, for example, can learn not a little from them concerning the spread of Christianity in the ancient world, and by identifying the parent text-type from which a given version was made it is possible to ascertain the headquarters and direction of missionary activity. Furthermore, since every translation is in some measure a commentary, one can trace the history of the exegesis of disputed passages as disclosed in successive modifications of a given version. Moreover, the additions and omissions in the transmitted text can tell us something about the doctrinal, liturgical, or ascetical interests of those who made and used such translations.

The philologist also is grateful for what are often the chief (or sometimes the only) remains of an ancient literature. A notable example is the codex Argenteus of the Gospels, which is the principal extant witness of the Gothic language, once spoken throughout nearly a third of Europe but preserved today in only a handful of documents. As recently as 1970 another chapter was added to the romantic fortunes of this famous codex when there was found in a chest of relics in the Cathedral of Speyer what turned out to be the final leaf of the manuscript—a manuscript which in 1648 was taken from Prague to Sweden as booty at the end of the Thirty Years War, was subsequently lost for a short time in a shipwreck on the Zuider Zee, and later was mutilated when ten leaves were stolen—but eventually returned by the repentant thief on his death-bed!

It is the textual critic, however, for whom the early versions of the New Testament are of prime importance. Earlier in the twentieth century F. C. Burkitt went so far as to argue that a reading supported by the Old Latin k and the Sinaitic Syriac deserved much respect as one witnessed by B and ℵ. Although the subsequent discovery of early Greek papyri (such as $\mathfrak{p}^{66}$ and $\mathfrak{p}^{75}$, which antedate B and ℵ by more than a century) has required a reassessment of Burkitt's views, the textual critic must still give serious attention to readings that are supported by a combination of unrelated versional witnesses. How far such coincidence of reading should be taken as proof of the existence of early bilingual or even trilingual manuscripts (as H. C. Hoskier, H. A. Sanders, and A. C. Clark supposed) will be estimated differently by different scholars. In any case, however, the versions of the New Testament, along with scriptural quotations made by patristic writers, provide diversified evidence concerning the geographical spread of individual readings as well as the boundaries of textual families.

The scope of the present volume is somewhat broader than might perhaps have been expected from the title. By 'early' versions of the New Testament is meant all the versions, whether surviving or not, that were made before about A.D. 1000. An account is given also concerning the Persian version, though the date of this version is not precisely known and may well be considerably after the year 1000. In the sub-title the word 'origin' refers, of course, to the historical circumstances during the expansion of Christianity which resulted in the translation of part or all of the New Testament into a local vernacular. Sometimes the identity of the translator is known; more often it is not. Under the rubric 'transmission' are included such items as a list of the earliest surviving manuscripts of a given version, noteworthy printed editions, and an account of the history of scholarly investigation and textual analysis of the version. In this connection an attempt has been made to report all significant bibliographical data relating to the progress of research on each version. The section on the 'limitations' of a version is devoted not so much to personal and theological idiosyncrasies of the translator as to features of the language of the version that prevent a literal rendering of the Greek text into that language. Here the author was assisted by specialists in the several languages: for Armenian, Dr. Erroll F. Rhodes of the Library Research Staff, American Bible Society, New York City; for Coptic, J. Martin Plumley, Herbert Thompson Professor of Egyptology, University of Cambridge; for Ethiopic, the Revd. Dr. Josef Hofmann, Hofendorf, Niederbayern, Germany; for Georgian, the late Canon Maurice Brière, honorary professor at l'Institut catholique de Paris; for Gothic, Dr. George W. S. Friedrichsen, Washington, D.C.; for Latin, Fr. Bonifatius

Fischer, O.S.B., formerly at the Monastery of Beuron and now at Mariendonk, Kempen, Germany; for Old Church Slavonic, Horace G. Lunt, Samuel Hazzard Cross Professor of Slavic Languages and Literatures, Harvard University; and for Syriac, Dr. Sebastian P. Brock, Lecturer in Aramaic and Syriac, Wolfson College, Oxford. It was suggested to each that he might consider the subject of limitations under the headings of phonetics, morphology, and syntax, but in every case freedom was granted to organize and to develop the section as seemed best. The users of the volume will join the author in expressing gratitude to these collaborators for dealing with important aspects of the early versions that have seldom been given sustained attention.

Thanks are due also to John A. Lygre for translating into English the contributions of Brière, Fischer, and Hofmann, and to Helmuth Egelkraut for going over the translation of Fischer's material. The author is grateful to the following scholars, each of whom kindly read a section and made a variety of suggestions and corrections: Dr. J. Neville Birdsall (the Georgian version), Dr. Donald Davies (the Ethiopic version), Dr. Ernst Ebbinghaus (the Gothic version), Professor Richard A. Frye (the Sogdian, Persian, and Caucasian Albanian versions), Dr. John A. Thompson (the Arabic versions), and Professor Horace G. Lunt and Dr. Marshall Winokur (the Old Church Slavonic version). The last-named scholar also checked and standardized the transliteration of the titles of Russian and other Slavic bibliography, following the system used in *The American Bibliography of Slavic and East European Studies*. The indexes were compiled by Lincoln D. Hurst and Charles D. Myers, Jr.

The work of collecting material for the present volume extended over many years; the writing of a major part of it was finished during the author's sabbatical leave during the first half of 1974, while he was a Member of the Institute for Advanced Study at Princeton and subsequently while a Visiting Fellow at Clare Hall in the University of Cambridge. In addition to drawing upon the extensive resources of the several libraries in Princeton, the author has consulted monographs and manuscripts in the Widener Library at Harvard University, in the Bodleian, in the British Museum, and in the libraries of Cambridge University and of the Papal Biblical Institute in Rome.

Finally, I should like to express my gratitude to the Delegates of the Oxford University Press for their acceptance of my book for publication. I am also indebted to the readers of the Press for their customary care and painstaking vigilance in correcting the proofs.

BRUCE M. METZGER

Princeton, New Jersey
February 1975

Contents

Contents xiii

Contents

Abbreviations

AB	*Analecta Bollandiana* (Brussels).
AbhBer	*Abhandlungen der (königlich) preussischen* [from 1947 *deutschen*] *Akademie der Wissenschaften zu Berlin* (philosophisch-historische Klasse).
AbhHeid	*Abhandlungen der Heidelberger Akademie der Wissenschaften* (philosophisch-historische Klasse).
AbhMainz	*Abhandlungen der Akademie der Wissenschaften und der Literatur* (Geistes- und Sozialwissenschaftlichen Klasse, Mainz).
AbhMn	*Abhandlungen der königlichen bayerischen Akademie der Wissenschaften* (philosophisch-philologisch-historische Klasse, Munich).
AJA	*American Journal of Archaeology* (Baltimore).
AJP	*American Journal of Philology* (Baltimore).
AJSL	*American Journal of Semitic Languages and Literatures* (Chicago).
AJT	*American Journal of Theology* (Chicago).
AO	*Acta Orientalia* (Utrecht).
ASP	*Archiv für slavische Philologie* (Berlin).
ATR	*Anglican Theological Review* (Evanston).
BASP	*Bulletin of the American Society of Papyrologists* (Urbana).
BBC	*Bulletin of the Bezan Club* (Leiden).
BedK	*Bedi Kartlisa* (Paris).
Bib	*Biblica* (Rome).
BibT	*The Bible Translator* (London).
BJRL	*Bulletin of the John Rylands Library* (Manchester).
BSOAS	*Bulletin of the School of Oriental and African Studies* (London).
Byslav	*Byzantinoslavica* (Prague).
Byz	*Byzantion* (Paris–Liège).
ByzZ	*Byzantinische Zeitschrift* (Munich).
BZ	*Biblische Zeitschrift* (Paderborn).
CBQ	*Catholic Biblical Quarterly* (Washington).
CC	*Civiltà cattolica* (Rome).
CQR	*Church Quarterly Review* (London).
CSCO	*Corpus Scriptorum Ecclesiasticorum Orientalium* (Louvain).
CSEL	*Corpus Scriptorum Ecclesiasticorum Latinorum* (Vienna).
EB	*Estudios bíblicos* (Madrid).
ES	*Englische Studien* (Leipzig).

Exp	*Expositor* (London).
ExpT	*Expository Times* (Edinburgh).
Greg	*Gregorianum* (Rome).
HA	*Handes Amsorya* (Vienna).
HSS	*Harvard Slavic Studies* (Cambridge, Mass.).
HTR	*Harvard Theological Review* (Cambridge, Mass.).
JA	*Journal asiatique* (Paris).
JAOS	*Journal of the American Oriental Society* (Baltimore).
JBL	*Journal of Biblical Literature* (Missoula, Mont.).
JEA	*Journal of Egyptian Archaeology* (London).
JEGP	*Journal of English and Germanic Philology* (Urbana).
JES	*Journal of Ethiopian Studies* (Addis Ababa).
JNES	*Journal of Near Eastern Studies* (Chicago).
JR	*Journal of Religion* (Chicago).
JRAS	*Journal of the Royal Asiatic Society of Great Britain and Ireland* (London).
JRS	*Journal of Roman Studies* (London).
JSL	*Journal of Sacred Literature* (London).
JSS	*Journal of Semitic Studies* (Manchester).
JTS	*Journal of Theological Studies* (Oxford).
KhV	*Khristianskij Vostok* (St. Petersburg).
Mu	*Muséon* (Louvain).
NovT	*Novum Testamentum* (Leiden).
NTS	*New Testament Studies* (Cambridge).
NZMRW	*Neue Zeitschrift für Missions- und Religionswissenschaft* (Schöneck–Beckenried).
OC	*Oriens Christianus* (Wiesbaden).
OCP	*Orientalia christiana periodica* (Rome).
OS	*L'Orient syrien* (Paris).
PG	*Patrologia Graeca* (Paris).
PL	*Patrologia Latina* (Paris).
PO	*Patrologia Orientalis* (Paris).
PS	*Palestinskij sbornik* (Leningrad).
RB	*Revue biblique* (Paris).
RBén	*Revue Bénédictine* (Abbaye de Maredsous).
RÉA	*Revue des études arméniennes* (Paris).
RÉS	*Revue des études slaves* (Paris).
RHE	*Revue d'histoire ecclésiastique* (Louvain).
RHR	*Revue de l'histoire des religions* (Paris).
ROC	*Revue de l'Orient chrétien* (Paris).

RQH	*Revue des questions historiques* (Paris).
RSE	*Rassegna di studi etiopici* (Rome).
RSO	*Rivista degli studi orientali* (Rome).
RSR	*Recherches de science religieuse* (Paris).
SbBer	*Sitzungsberichte der (königlich) preussischen* [from 1948 *deutschen*] *Akademie der Wissenschaften zu Berlin* (phil.-hist. Klasse).
SbHeid	*Sitzungsberichte der Heidelberger Akademie der Wissenschaften* (phil.-hist. Klasse).
SbWien	*Sitzungsberichte der Kaiserlichen* (after 1948 *Österreichischen*) *Akademie der Wissenschaften in Wien* (philosophisch-historische Klasse).
SEER	*Slavonic and East European Review* (London).
SO	*Symbolae Osloenses* (Oslo).
SR	*Slavic Review* (Menasha, Wisconsin).
SS	*Studia Slavica* (Budapest).
ThRu	*Theologische Rundschau* (Tübingen).
TLZ	*Theologische Literaturzeitung* (Leipzig).
TQ	*Theologische Quartalschrift* (Tübingen).
TSK	*Theologische Studien und Kritiken* (Gotha).
TU	*Texte und Untersuchungen zur Geschichte der altchristlichen Literatur* (Leipzig).
VC	*Vigiliae Christianae* (Amsterdam).
WS	*Welt der Slaven* (Wiesbaden).
ZÄS	*Zeitschrift für ägyptische Sprache und Altertumskunde* (Berlin).
ZAW	*Zeitschrift für die alttestamentliche Wissenschaft* (Berlin).
ZDA	*Zeitschrift für deutsches Altertum und deutsche Literatur* (Wiesbaden).
ZDMG	*Zeitschrift der Deutschen Morgenländischen Gesellschaft* (Wiesbaden).
ZDP	*Zeitschrift für deutsche Philologie* (Stuttgart).
ZKG	*Zeitschrift für Kirchengeschichte* (Stuttgart).
ZMRW	*Zeitschrift für Missionswissenschaft und Religionswissenschaft* (Münster).
ZNW	*Zeitschrift für die neutestamentliche Wissenschaft* (Berlin).
ZSG	*Zeitschrift für Semitistik und verwandte Gebiete* (Leipzig).
ZSP	*Zeitschrift für slavische Philologie* (Leipzig).
ZTK	*Zeitschrift für Theologie und Kirche* (Tübingen).
ZVS	*Zeitschrift für vergleichende Sprachforschung auf dem Gebiete der indogermanischen Sprachen* (Göttingen).

PART ONE

The Early Eastern Versions
of the New Testament

I

The Syriac Versions

Of all the early versions of the New Testament, those in Syriac have raised more problems and provoked more controversies among modern scholars than any of the others. The reasons lie partly in the multiplicity of translations and revisions of the Syriac Scriptures, and partly in the ambiguity of evidence concerning their mutual relationship. At the same time, that five or six separate versions in Syriac were produced during the first six centuries of the Christian era is noteworthy testimony to the vitality and scholarship of Syrian churchmen. In fact, as Eberhard Nestle has reminded us, 'No branch of the Early Church has done more for the translation of the Bible into their vernacular than the Syriac-speaking. In our European libraries we have Syriac Bible MSS from Lebanon, Egypt, Sinai, Mesopotamia, Armenia, India (Malabar), even from China.'[1]

The several Syriac versions that fall to be considered in the present chapter begin with the earliest translation of the Gospels. Whether this was Tatian's Diatessaron, a harmony of the four Gospels prepared about A.D. 170, or the Old Syriac version of the separate Gospels, is a question that scholars have debated for many years without reaching any generally accepted solution. How much of the rest of the New Testament was included in the Old Syriac version is difficult to ascertain. In any case, toward the close of the fourth or at the beginning of the fifth century a version of twenty-two books of the New Testament was available in a translation which came to be called at a later date the Peshitta[2] Syriac version. This translation, like Jerome's production of the Latin Vulgate text amid competing Old Latin translations, was intended to supply a standardized version and to bring to an end the confusion and variety of readings in earlier Syriac texts. The Peshitta, however, was unable to satisfy Syrian scholars who desired a more literal rendering than those already

---

[1] 'Syriac Versions', Hastings's *Dictionary of the Bible*, iv (1902), 645.
[2] For definitions of the term 'Peshitta' see p. 48 below.

available, and at the beginning of the sixth century Philoxenus, bishop of the Jacobite (or Monophysite) branch of the Syrian church, commissioned his rural bishop, Polycarp, to make another version. A century later the Philoxenian version, in turn, seems to have formed the basis for yet another revision made by one who designated himself as 'Thomas, a poor sinner', and who is no doubt correctly identified by an unknown Syriac writer as Thomas of Heraclea (Harkel). Finally, in addition to these several versions,[1] all of which are in the 'classical' Syriac dialect of Aramaic used at Edessa and generally throughout Syrian communities, there is also the so-called Palestinian Syriac version, which makes use of a form of western Aramaic similar to that used by Galilean Jews in the Old Testament Targums.

I. THE INTRODUCTION OF CHRISTIANITY INTO SYRIA AND THE TRANSLATION OF THE NEW TESTAMENT

It was at Antioch of Syria, the third-largest city of the Roman Empire, that the followers of Jesus were first called Christians (Acts xi. 26). Situated on the Orontes River, north of the Lebanon range, the city was a melting-pot where persons of many races met and mingled.[2] The leading classes were of Hellenic background and, along with some of the indigenous populace, spoke Greek. At the beginning of the second century Ignatius of Antioch,[3] while *en route* to Rome, wrote several letters in Greek.

[1] It is no longer customary to reckon among the Syriac versions the Karkaphensian materials, which are a kind of Syriac Massorah whose authors attempted to preserve what was regarded as the best traditions of the orthography and pronunciation of the more important and difficult words of the Syriac Bible. This Massorah was extant in two forms, corresponding to the two main branches of the Syrian Church. The Jacobite manuscripts greatly predominate in quantity over the Nestorian manuscripts. See J. P. P. Martin, *Tradition karkaphienne ou la Massore chez les Syriens* (Paris, 1870; Eng. tr. in *Hebraica*, ii (1885–6), 13–23); G. H. Gwilliam, 'The Materials for the Criticism of the New Testament, with Specimens of the Syriac Massorah', *Studia biblica et ecclesiastica*, iii (Oxford, 1891), 56–65 and 93–100; William Wright, *A Short History of Syriac Literature* (London, 1894; repr. from *Encyclopaedia Britannica*, 9th edn., vol. xxii, 1887), pp. 20–4; and F. H. A. Scrivener, *A Plain Introduction to the Criticism of the New Testament*, 4th edn., ii (London, 1894), 34–6.

[2] Among many monographs on Antioch mention may be made of George Haddad's dissertation *Aspects of Social Life in Antioch in the Hellenistic-Roman Period* (University of Chicago, 1949), and especially Glanville Downey's *A History of Antioch in Syria, from Seleucus to the Arab Conquest* (Princeton, 1961).

[3] Ignatius describes himself as bishop of Syria (*Ep. ad Rom.* ii. 2).

Near the close of the second century the bishopric at Antioch was occupied by a certain Theophilus who, though born near the Euphrates, received a Hellenistic education and produced in Greek a considerable body of writings, including a harmony of the Gospels.[1] Throughout the first two centuries it appears that Antiochian Christians, at least those whose writings have survived, were accustomed to make use of the Old and New Testaments in Greek.

Outside the gates of Antioch, that 'fair city of the Greeks', as Isaac of Antioch[2] described the metropolis, Syriac was the language of the people. The early history of the growth of the Syriac-speaking Church is to a certain extent a matter of conjecture and inference. The historical sources are scanty, and most of the accounts of the earlier periods that we possess leave much to be desired. Despite such limitations, however, we can trace at least the main outlines of the development in Syria of a Christianity possessing a national cast.

The native Syrian Church appears to have had two starting-points, Edessa and Arbela. Edessa,[3] called by the natives Urhai (the modern Urfa in Turkey), was a town in northern Mesopotamia east of the Euphrates, the capital of an independent buffer state (Osrhoëne) between the Roman and the Parthian Empires. According to local tradition, reported by Eusebius,[4] Christianity came to Edessa in the apostolic age as the result of the labours of Thaddaeus, one of the seventy disciples, who preached to King Abgar Ukkama ('the Black'). Another form of the same tradition is preserved in the so-called *Doctrine of Addai*,[5] a Syriac document which dates from the latter half of the fourth century. Here the labours of the apostolic emissary to Edessa, Addai by name, are described in detail, including his work of preaching, baptizing, and building the first church in Edessa.

---

[1] Of these treatises all that have survived are Theophilus' three books *To Autolycus*. On his harmony, cf. Jerome, *Ep.* cxxi. 6, 15 (ed. Hilberg, iii. 24–5): 'Theophilus, Antiochenae ecclesiae septimus post Petrum apostolum episcopus, qui quattuor evangelistarum in unum opus dicta conpingens ingenii sui nobis monumenta demisit...'   [2] *Carmen*, xv.

[3] The earlier work of J. P. P. Martin, *Les Origines de l'église d'Édesse et des églises syriennes* (Paris, 1889) has been superseded by A. F. J. Klijn's *Edessa, de stad van de Apostel Thomas* (Baarn, 1963; German trans., *Edessa, die Stadt des Apostels Thomas* (Neukirchen-Vluyn, 1965)), and J. B. Segal's *Edessa 'the Blessed City'* (Oxford, 1970).   [4] *Hist. eccl.* I. xiii. 1–20.

[5] Ed. by G. Phillips (London, 1876).

Apart from such quasi-legendary accounts, the earliest substantial evidence we have suggests that by the second half of the
second century Christianity took root in Edessa. To be sure, the
doctrinal cast of the earliest form of the new faith was apparently
characterized by a mixture of astrological and gnostic specu-
lations, later denounced as heretical. Tatian, for example, after
spending some time in Rome as a disciple of Justin Martyr, in
the year 172 was excommunicated for doctrinal aberrations[1]
(the exact nature of which is unclear) and returned to the East,
where he died. During this period Tatian's Harmony of the
Gospels (the Diatessaron) began to be circulated in Syria.

About the same time the Church at Edessa obtained a notable
convert in the person of Bar Daisān (Greek Βαρδησάνης).[2] Born
at Edessa about A.D. 155, he is said to have been educated in
philosophy by a pagan priest at Hierapolis (Mabbûg) and to
have become a Christian about 180. The first Syrian, so far as we
know, who wrote learned treatises in his own tongue and, with
his son Harmonius, composed hymns in the same, Bardesanes
earned for himself an ambivalent reputation. On the one hand,
Eusebius[3] speaks highly of him, praising him as a powerful
defender of the faith and a most skilful opponent against heretics.
Orthodox Syrians of the following period, on the other hand, have
nothing but scorn for him, reckoning him among the gnostic
heretics.

Toward the close of the second century the cause of orthodoxy
at Edessa was forwarded by the consecration of Bishop Palut,
which took place at Antioch about the year 190 at the hands of
Serapion. About Palut Burkitt writes, 'Though those outside
might at first call his followers Palutians, as if they were a new
sect, he or his immediate successors soon became the undisputed
presidents of the Catholic Church in Edessa.'[4] A variety of kinds
of testimony suggests the continued growth of the Church.
Mention of the destruction of a 'Christian temple' at Edessa in

---

[1] Eusebius, *Chronicle*, ed. by R. Helm (Berlin, 1956), p. 206.

[2] On Bardesanes see F. J. A. Hort, 'Bardaisan', in Wm. Smith and H. Wace,
Dictionary of Christian Biography, i (London, 1877), 250–60; H. H. Schaeder, 'Bardesanes von Edessa', *ZKG* li (1932), 21–74; and H. J. W. Drijvers, *Bardaiṣan of
Edessa* (Assen, 1966); cf. Walter Bauer, *Orthodoxy and Heresy in Earliest Christianity*,
ed. by Robert A. Kraft and Gerhard Krodel (Philadelphia, 1971), pp. 24–33.

[3] *Hist. eccl.* IV. xxx. 1–2.

[4] F. C. Burkitt, *Early Eastern Christianity* (London, 1904), p. 35.

the flood of 201[1] (which happens to be the earliest reference to
a church building) may be taken as evidence of a certain degree
of ecclesiastical organization. With even greater assurance the
same conclusion can be drawn from a comment by Eusebius[2]
concerning a synod convened near the close of the second century,
probably at Edessa, and made up of 'parishes in Osrhoëne and
the cities there', for the purpose of discussing the question concerning the date when Easter should be observed. That the royal
house was converted to Christianity in the second century and
that the new faith was soon after established as the state religion
have often been accepted as facts;[3] both remain, however, open
to question.[4]

The other main centre of early Syrian Christianity was located
at Arbela, situated east of the Tigris in the region of Adiabene.
A chronicle of the city is extant, composed about A.D. 550, which
contains a series of hagiographical biographies along the lines of
the Acts of Martyrs.[5] The compiler dates the introduction of
Christianity into Arbela during Trajan's reign (98–117) through
the evangelistic work of Addai. Inasmuch as the Jewish population of Arbela was particularly influential—in fact, during the
reign of Claudius (41–54) King Izates of Adiabene and other
members of the royal house were converted to Judaism[6]—it is
probable that the Jewish community provided the starting-point
for the Christian missionaries. It is significant that not a few
early Syrian bishops have Jewish names.

Several pieces of evidence suggest that the young Syrian
Church was not limited to cities, but from the beginning concerned itself with the evangelization of country-folk also. The

[1] *Edessene Chronicle*, 86 (= 1465, ed. L. Hallier); English trans. by B. H. Cowper
in *JSL* v (1864), 28 ff. Bauer (op. cit., pp. 13–14) erroneously questions the reliability of the account.   [2] *Hist. eccl.* V. xxiii. 4.

[3] Most recently by J. B. Segal in *Edessa 'the Blessed City'*.

[4] Cf., besides Bauer (op. cit., pp. 12–16), I. Ortiz de Urbina, 'Le origini del
cristianesimo in Edessa', *Greg.* xv (1934), 86–91.

[5] Eduard Sachau, *Der Chronik von Arbela. Ein Beitrag zur Kenntnis des ältesten
Christentums im Orient* (*AbhBer*, Nr. 6; Berlin, 1915), p. 42; cf. idem, *Zur Ausbreitung
des Christentums in Asien* (ibid., Nr. 1, 1919). The historicity of the accounts of the
earlier periods is open to serious doubts; cf. G. Messina, 'La cronaca di Arbela',
CC lxxxiii, 3 (1932), 362–76, and I. Ortiz de Urbina, 'Intorno al valore storico
della cronaca di Arbela', *OCP* ii (1936), 5–32. On J. M. Fiey's arguments that the
work is a modern forgery (*OS* xii (1967), 265–302), see S. Brock, *BJRL* l (1967),
199–206, and *JTS* n.s. xix (1968), 308 n. 1.

[6] Josephus, *Ant.* XX. ii. 1–5.

presence of Christians in the plain of Syria between Nisibis and the Euphrates is implied by the well-known inscription of Bishop Abercius, dating from the second half of the second century.[1] By A.D. 224/5, when the Sassanid dynasty came to power in Persia, more than twenty bishoprics are known to have existed in the Tigris–Euphrates valley and on the borders of Persia.[2] The congregations seem usually to have been small and occasionally subject to active resistance from leaders of rival religions. We hear, for example, of repeated persecutions during the lives of the early bishops of Arbela.[3] The faith continued, however, to gain strength. One of the persecuted bishops, in a time of enforced exile, is said to have won the entire population of the village in which he took refuge.

In turning now to consider the question when, where, and by whom the earliest translation into Syriac was made of the New Testament and of other early Christian literature, we find that next to nothing is known with certainty, and problems and learned disputes multiply without end. It is generally agreed that at least by the latter part of the second century the practical needs of the Church would have necessitated the production of a Syriac version of the Gospel story, though what form it took is debated (i.e. a harmony or the separate Gospels). Whether other Christian literature may have become available in Syriac at a still earlier date is a question to which quite diverse answers have been given. Haase, for example, supposed that the earliest Syrian Christians used a series of pericopes translated for liturgical purposes.[4] Others have attempted to connect the forty-two Odes of Solomon with early Syrian Christianity, but without being able to persuade a majority of other scholars.[5]

---

[1] καὶ Συρίης πέδον εἶδον καὶ ἄστεα πάντα Νίσιβιν, Εὐφράτην διαβὰς πάντῃ δ' ἔσχον συνομήμους (lines 10–11; for the final word, cf. W. M. Calder, *JRS* xxix (1939), 2–4). ² Sachau, *Der Chronik*, pp. 61–2. ³ Ibid., p. 62.

[4] F. Haase, 'Zur ältesten syrischen Evangelienübersetzung', *TQ* ci (1920), 270.

[5] The widest variety of scholarly opinion has been expressed concerning the authorship of the Odes of Solomon and their date (between A.D. 80 and 210). Harnack (followed by Diettrich, Grimme, Charles, Bacon, and Goguel) thought that he could detect two stages in their composition, that of a Jewish *Grundschrift* and the later modifications and additions made by a Christian redactor. Most investigators, however, have been impressed by the unity of style throughout the Odes (especially after Kittel's research), and regard them as the product of (*a*) a Jewish Christian (so Harris, Leipoldt, Bartlet, Abbott, Charlesworth), (*b*) an orthodox Christian who emphasized sacramental mysticism (Bernard, Lake, Plooij, Selwyn), (*c*) a paganized Christian (Bousset, Reinach, Labourt, Loisy,

Vööbus, on the basis of a passage in Eusebius, has suggested that in the earliest stages the Syrian Churches used the Gospel according to the Hebrews.[1] It must be acknowledged, however, that the text of the passage is uncertain,[2] and requires emendation in order to provide the desired support.

More recently it has been suggested that the earliest Gospel account to circulate in Syriac was the Gospel of Thomas, some thirty or forty years before the Diatessaron.[3] Although it may be, as a number of scholars have argued,[4] that the Gospel of Thomas discloses features that connect it with Syria (e.g. the presence of what are taken to be Aramaisms or Syriacisms; the agreement of

Guidi, Connolly), (*d*) a full-fledged Gnostic (Gunkel, Gressmann, Clemen, Abramowski, Ehlers), or (*e*) a Montanist (Conybeare, Fries). Others, seeking to identify the author more precisely, have suggested (*f*) a disciple of John (P. Smith), (*g*) or Bardesanes (Sprengling, Newbold). Several scholars regard Edessa as the place of their origin (de Zwaan, R. M. Grant, Klijn). For bibliographical references to most of these scholars, see the present writer's article 'Odes of Solomon', *Twentieth Century Encyclopedia of Religious Knowledge*, ed. by L. A. Loetscher, ii (Grand Rapids, 1955), 812, supplemented by J. H. Charlesworth, *The Odes of Solomon* (Oxford, 1973).

[1] Arthur Vööbus, *Studies in the History of the Gospel Text in Syriac* (*CSCO* cxxviii; Louvain, 1951), pp. 18–20.

[2] *Hist. eccl.* IV. xxii. 8, ἔκ τε τοῦ καθ' Ἑβραίους εὐαγγελίου καὶ τοῦ Συριακοῦ καὶ ἰδίως ἐκ τῆς Ἑβραΐδος διαλέκτου τινὰ τίθησιν, which H. J. Lawlor and J. E. L. Oulton render as follows: '[Hegesippus] sets down certain things from the Gospel of the Hebrews and the Syriac [Gospel] and, in particular, from [writings in] the Hebrew tongue.' They acknowledge, however, that they do not know what is meant by the 'Syriac Gospel', and mention Harnack's suggestion (*Chronologie*, i. 639 f.) that 'the Gospel of the Hebrews' indicates a Greek translation and 'the Syriac' the original text of the same. In view of the difficulty of the text A. C. McGiffert, followed by other scholars, prefers to emend by deleting καί after εὐαγγελίου, so as to give the meaning 'from the Syriac Gospel according to the Hebrews he quotes some passages in the Hebrew tongue'.

[3] H. S. Pelser, 'The Origin of the Ancient Syriac New Testament Texts— A Historical Study', *De fructu oris sui: Essays in Honour of Adrianus van Selms*, ed. by I. H. Eybers, *et al.* (*Pretoria Oriental Series*, ed. by A. van Selms, ix; Leiden, 1971), pp. 161–2.

[4] So, e.g., H.-C. Puech, 'Das Thomas-Evangelium', in Hennecke–Schneemelcher, *Neutestamentliche Apokryphen*, 3te Aufl. i (Tübingen, 1959), 207, English trans. by R. McL. Wilson, i (Philadelphia, 1963), 287; J. E. Ménard, 'Le Milieu syriaque de l'Évangile selon Thomas et de l'Évangile selon Philippe', *RSR* xlii (1968), 261–6; L. W. Barnard, 'The Church in Edessa during the First Two Centuries A.D.', *VC* xxii (1968), 161–75; J. E. Ménard, 'Syrische Einflüsse auf die Evangelien nach Thomas und Philippus', *ZDMG* Suppl. I, 2 (1969), 385–91; and A. F. J. Klijn, 'Christianity in Edessa and the Gospel of Thomas', *NovT* xiv (1972), 70–7. On the name Judas Thomas, see Klijn, 'John XIV 22 and the Name Judas Thomas', *Studies in John, Presented to J. N. Sevenster* (*Supplements to Novum Testamentum*, xxiv; Leiden, 1970), pp. 88–96.

words and ideas with passages in Syriac authors; the ascriptions of the document to the apostle Judas Thomas, whose double name is common in Syriac writings), none of these demands a date prior to Tatian.[1]

II. THE DIATESSARON OF TATIAN

1. WITNESSES TO TATIAN'S DIATESSARON

Except for a single fragment of Tatian's Diatessaron (διὰ τεσσάρων, 'through [the] four [Gospels]') preserved in Greek,[2] all other witnesses are of secondary or tertiary character. These witnesses, which range widely as to century and geographical area, can be conveniently divided into two groups, one Eastern and the other Western. The Eastern group (items *b* to *e* below) is represented by lemmata incorporated in Ephraem's Commentary on the Diatessaron, several manuscripts of two forms of an Arabic harmony, a Persian harmony translated from a Syriac *Vorlage*, and traces of Tatianic readings preserved in Gospel quotations included in the works of various Eastern writers. The Western group (items *f* to *k* below) comprises the Latin codex Fuldensis, several medieval German harmonies, several medieval Dutch (Flemish) harmonies, two Old Italian harmonies, a Middle English harmony, and the harmonized text presupposed by several medieval writers. All these differ from one another, and from the presumed Latin original from which they are derived.

---

[1] On the other hand, for what can be said against connecting the Gospel of Thomas with Edessa see, e.g., the vigorous objections set forth by Barbara Ehlers, 'Kann das Thomasevangelium aus Edessa stammen? Ein Beitrag zur Frühgeschichte des Christentums in Edessa', *NovT* xii (1970), 284–317.

[2] The leaf from a papyrus codex containing the Greek text of portions of Matt. xviii and xix, which its editor, Otto Stegmüller, believed to be a fragment of the Greek Diatessaron (see his article, 'Ein Bruchstück aus dem griechischen Diatessaron (P. 16, 388)', *ZNW* xxxvii (1938), 223–9), is probably nothing more than a Greek text which contains several Tatianic readings (so Curt Peters, 'Ein neues Fragment des griechischen Diatessaron?', *Bib*, xxi (1940), 68–77). The selections from Matthew and John in Greek which Agnes Smith Lewis published as 'Fragments of a Greek Harmony of the Gospels' (in *Codex Climaci Rescriptus* (1909), pp. xxvii–xxx) were drawn up in accord with a different plan from that of Tatian's Diatessaron and the two have no connection (so Ian A. Moir, *Codex Climaci Rescriptus Graecus* (*Texts and Studies*, n.s. ii; Cambridge, 1957)). A. Salac thought that the choice and order of the subjects of certain epigrams in the Palatine Anthology were influenced by the Greek Diatessaron (see his article, 'Quelques épigrammes de l'Anthologie palatine et l'iconographie byzantine' *Byslav*, xii (1951), 1–29, especially 9–12), but the resemblances are few and inconsequential.

Whether any of them are grandsons or merely great-nephews of Tatian's work, or whether they bear no discernible relationship at all, are questions on which there is no unanimity among scholars.

(*a*) A parchment fragment of the Diatessaron, measuring about four inches square and containing on one side the greater part of fourteen lines of Greek writing, came to light in 1933 during excavations on the site of the ancient Roman fortress-town of Dura-Europos on the lower Euphrates.[1] Inasmuch as the town fell to the Persians under King Shapur I in A.D. 256–7, the fragment cannot be more than about eighty years removed from the autograph.

The left-hand margin of the parchment has suffered damage, and the first half-dozen or so letters at the beginning of each line are lacking. Most of them, however, can be restored with almost perfect confidence. In the following English translation the restorations are enclosed within square brackets and the modern Scripture references within parentheses. (For a discussion of the debate whether the Greek fragment represents the original text of the Diatessaron, or is a translation of an original Syriac or Latin original, see pp. 30–2 below.)

[. . . the mother of the sons of Zebed]ee (Matt. xxvii. 56) and Salome (Mark xv. 40) and the wives [of those who] had followed him from [Galile]e to see the crucified (Luke xxiii. 49b–c). And [the da]y was Preparation; the Sabbath was daw[ning] (Luke xxiii. 54). And when it was evening (Matt. xxvii. 57), on the Prep[aration], that is, the day before the Sabbath (Mark xv. 42), [there came] up a man (Matt. xxvii. 57), be[ing] a member of the council (Luke xxiii. 50), from Arimathea (Matt. xxvii. 57), a c[i]ty of [Jude]a (Luke xxiii. 51b), by name Jo[seph] (Matt. xxvii. 57), g[o]od and ri[ghteous] (Luke xxiii. 50), being a disciple of Jesus, but se[cret]ly, for fear of the [Jew]s (John xix. 38). And he (Matt. xxvii. 57) was looking for [the] k[ingdom] of God (Luke xxiii. 51c). This man [had] not [con]sented to [their] p[urpose] (Luke xxiii. 51a) . . .

It is evident that Tatian went about composing his Diatessaron with great diligence. Probably he worked from four separate

---

[1] The fragment was edited by Carl H. Kraeling, *A Greek Fragment of Tatian's Diatessaron from Dura* (*Studies and Documents*, iii; London 1935), and re-edited, with a few minor corrections, by C. Bradford Welles, *et al.*, in *The Parchments and Papyri* (*The Excavations at Dura-Europos* . . . , *Final Report*, vol. 2, part 1 (New Haven, 1959)), pp. 73–4.

manuscripts, one for each of the Gospels, and, as he wove together phrases, now from this Gospel and now that, he would no doubt cross out those phrases in the manuscripts from which he was copying. Otherwise it is difficult to understand how he was able to combine so successfully phrases from four documents into a remarkable cento which reminds one of delicate filigree work.

The most noteworthy reading preserved in the fragment is near the beginning. Although it rests partly on a restoration, and although none of the secondary or tertiary witnesses to Tatian exhibits the reading, it is probable that Tatian referred to 'the wives of those who had followed' Jesus from Galilee. This phrase, which is without parallel in the text of Luke xxiii. 49 in any known Greek witness, finds an echo in the Palestinian Syriac Lectionary (MSS. A and C) and in the Old Latin MS. *c*.[1]

Eastern Witnesses

(*b*) The commentary on the Diatessaron written by St. Ephraem (d. A.D. 373) is of primary importance for the portions of the Diatessaron that he quotes, but it obviously was not his intention to cite and comment upon every word of the Diatessaron. The commentary is preserved in its entirety in an Armenian translation, which has been edited from two manuscripts, both of which date from A.D. 1195.[2] They represent two different

---

[1] In Syriac the difference between 'the wives of those who had followed him' and 'the women who had followed him' is the presence or absence of the letter *dalath*. Whether the omission was accidental, thus producing the generally accepted reading (so Plooij, *ExpT* xlvi (1934–5), 471–6, and A. F. J. Klijn, *A Survey of the Research into the Western Text of the Gospels and Acts* (Utrecht, 1949), p. 101), or, whether Tatian, in order to remove all trace of what could become the basis of slanderous attack, introduced the expanded reading (so Lagrange, *Critique textuelle*; ii, *La Critique rationnelle* (Paris, 1935), p. 631, and E. C. Colwell, *Studies in Methodology in Textual Criticism of the New Testament* (Leiden and Grand Rapids, 1969), pp. 38–9), is still *sub judice*.

[2] The Armenian text of one of the manuscripts was first published in 1836 by the Mechitarists of San Lazzaro in Venice (*Srboyn Ephraemi matenagrouthiunk'*, ii). Soon afterward a second manuscript was discovered, and a Latin translation, making use of both manuscripts, was prepared by the Mechitarist father J.-B. Aucher. Although Aucher's work was finished in 1841, it was not until 1876 that Prof. G. Moesinger of Salzburg published the work (*Evangelii Concordantis Expositio facta a Sancto Ephraemo Doctore Syro* (Venice, 1876)).

The Armenian text has been re-edited by Dom Louis Leloir, *Saint Éphrem, Commentaire de l'Évangile concordant, version arménienne* (*CSCO* cxxxvii, *Scriptores Armeniaci*, 1; Louvain, 1953); Leloir provides a Latin translation, op. cit., vol. cxlv, *Scriptores armeniaci*, 2 (1954).

recensions, one (MS. A) of the Old Armenian type, particularly as regards the scriptural citations, and the other (MS. B) of the newer Armenian type, with the scriptural citations conformed to the Armenian vulgate (or, as Harris has put it, 'de-Ephraemized').

Since 1963 about three-fifths of Ephraem's commentary has been available in the original Syriac, preserved on sixty-five folios of a manuscript acquired by Sir Chester Beatty and dated by its editor to the late fifth or early sixth century.[1] A comparison of the Syriac and Armenian texts discloses that the latter represents, on the whole, a reliable rendering of the original. It apparently was not made from a form of text identical with that preserved in the Beatty manuscript, for occasionally the latter presents supplementary paragraphs involving both lemmata and commentary, and occasionally it lacks material present in the Armenian translation. In view of the considerable lacunae in the Beatty manuscript, the Armenian version as well as patristic quotations are still indispensable for gaining more complete knowledge of the contents of Tatian's Diatessaron.

One folio of Syriac text of Ephraem's commentary has turned up in the collection of the Seminario de Papirología at San Cugat del Vallés (Barcelona).[2] Although the dimensions of the leaf (P. Palau Rib 2) do not coincide with those of the Beatty codex, the editor of the former believes, on the basis of a comparison of the style of the script in the two, that the stray folio was once part of the codex. By comparing the Syriac text with the Armenian version it can be deduced that the folio originally stood as no. 10 in the complete codex.

---

[1] *Saint Éphrem, Commentaire de l'Évangile concordant, texte syriaque* (*Manuscrit Chester Beatty 709*), ed. and trans. [into Latin] by Dom Louis Leloir (*Chester Beatty Monographs*, no. 8; Dublin, 1963). Leloir also provides a French translation of the Syriac and Armenian texts in *Sources chrétiennes*, no. 121: *Éphrem de Nisibe: Commentaire de l'évangile concordant ou Diatessaron . . .* (Paris, 1966). For an examination of differences between the Syriac and Armenian witnesses, see Leloir, 'Divergences entre l'original syriaque et la version arménienne du Commentaire d'Éphrem sur le Diatessaron', *Mélanges Eugène Tisserant* (*Studi e testi*, ccxxxii; Vatican City, 1964), pp. 303–31. For an examination of the textual affinities of Ephraem's text as revealed in the Beatty manuscript, see G. A. Weir, 'Tatian's Diatessaron and the Old Syriac Gospel; the Evidence of MS. Chester Beatty 709' (Diss., University of Edinburgh, 1969–70).

[2] Pedro Ortiz Valdivieso, 'Un nuevo fragmento siríaco del Comentario de san Efrén al Diatésaron', *Studia papyrologica*, v (1966), 7–17, with two plates and a Spanish translation.

Another small fragment of Ephraem's Commentary (MS. Borgia syriaca 82, now in the Vatican Library) was identified and transcribed by Baarda, who also added an instructive discussion of its significance.[1]

(*c*) The Arabic translation of Tatian's Diatessaron is preserved in five more or less complete manuscripts and in three stray folios. These, with the siglum commonly used to designate each, are as follows.

(1) MS. A (Vatican arab. 14), brought from the East to the Vatican Library by Joseph S. Assemani about 1719, is usually dated to the twelfth or beginning of the thirteenth century, though Kahle assigned it to the thirteenth or fourteenth century. It originally contained 125 folios, but fols. 17 and 118 are missing and fols. 1–7 are not well preserved.

(2) MS. B (Vatican Borg. arab. 250) was given in 1896 by its owner, Ḥalīm Dōs Ghālī, a prominent Catholic Copt in Cairo, to the Museum Borgianum de Propaganda Fide in Rome. After an Introduction to the Gospels (fols. 1–85), the Arabic Diatessaron follows on fols. 96–353. The manuscript is usually dated to the fourteenth century, but Kahle,[2] on the basis of the style of decoration, thought that it could certainly not be older than the sixteenth century.

(3) MS. E (no. 202 of the Library of the Coptic Patriarchate in Cairo), consisting of 114 folios, is dated A.D. 1795. The scribe was rather careless, and dozens of instances of sub-standard vocalization occur on almost every page.

(4) MS. O (Oxford, Bodl. arab. e. 163) contains three Christian texts: an Introduction to the Gospels (fols. 5–31), a compendium of Christian truth (fols. 41–139), and the Arabic Diatessaron (fols. 140–288). The manuscript is dated A.D. 1806, and its text agrees more often with E than with A or B.

(5) MS. 1020 of the Library of Paul Sbath (Cairo), written A.D. 1797–8, has not received as much attention as the others.

---

[1] Tj. Baarda, 'A Syriac Fragment of Mar Ephraem's Commentary on the Diatessaron', *NTS* viii (1961–2), 287–300.

[2] Paul E. Kahle, *The Cairo Geniza* (London, 1947), p. 213; 2nd edn. (Oxford, 1959), p. 300.

(6) What are commonly called the Beirut Fragments of the Arabic Diatessaron are three folios from a manuscript that was finished in July A.D. 1332. They present a form of text which agrees generally with that of codex A.[1]

The *editio princeps* of the Arabic Diatessaron was published toward the close of the nineteenth century by Agostino Ciasca[2] (later Cardinal Ciasca), on the basis of manuscripts A and B. Ciasca's Latin translation of the Arabic text is not altogether satisfactory, for he frequently adopts the familiar Vulgate wording instead of making a literalistic rendering of the original. Translations into English, accompanied by critical introductions and notes, were published by Hill[3] and Hogg,[4] and into German, by Preuschen.[5]

A more recent edition of the Arabic text, prepared by A.-S. Marmardji,[6] is based on MS. E, along with variant readings from manuscripts A and B. Unfortunately the edition leaves something to be desired,[7] for Marmardji frequently corrects the sub-standard vocalization of MS. E, but it is often impossible to determine from his apparatus whether the printed text is that of the manuscript or is his idea of what the manuscript ought to read. It must also be added that Marmardji's French translation of the Arabic cannot always be relied upon for strict accuracy.[8]

The manuscripts of the Arabic Diatessaron present two forms of the text. One form has the genealogies of Jesus near the beginning of the harmony: the genealogy of Matt. i stands in chap. 2 of the Diatessaron, and that of Luke iii in chap. 4 of the Diatessaron. The other form has them at the end, as a kind of appendix. In one form the Evangelists are quoted by the first two

---

[1] Edited by Georg Graf in Sebastian Euringer, *Die Überlieferung der arabischen Übersetzung des Diatessaron* (*Biblische Studien*, xvii, 2; Freiburg i. B., 1912), pp. 61–71.

[2] *Tatiani Evangeliorum harmoniae arabice* (Rome, 1888; repr. 1930).

[3] J. Hamlin Hill, *The Earliest Life of Christ ever Compiled from the Gospels, Being the Diatessaron of Tatian* (Edinburgh, 1894).

[4] Hope W. Hogg, 'The Diatessaron of Tatian', *The Ante-Nicene Fathers*, ix (New York, 1896), 33–138.

[5] Erwin Preuschen, *Tatians Diatessaron aus den Arabischen übersetzt*. Mit einer einleitenden Abhandlung und textkritischen Anmerkungen herausg. von A. Pott (Heidelberg, 1926).

[6] *Diatessaron de Tatien. Texte arabe établi, traduit en français, collationné avec les anciennes versions syriaques, suivi d'un évangéliaire diatessarique syriaque* . . . (Beirut, 1935).

[7] For a sharp criticism, see Baumstark in *OC* xxxiii (1936), 235–48.

[8] See D. S. Margoliouth, *JTS* xxxviii (1937), 76–9.

letters of their names; in the other, by single letters. On the basis of these criteria, MS. A and the Beirut Fragments belong to the first form, while B E O, and apparently Sbath's 1020, belong to the second form.

Many are the problems connected with the origin and relation of the two forms of Arabic Diatessaron.[1] After discussing previous research on the subject, Kahle concluded:

> We cannot derive one of these forms from the other and cannot reconstruct an 'Urtext' of the Arabic Diatessaron from them. They must be dealt with separately. Ciasca's attempt to publish a mixed text from both these forms was a mistake. Marmardji's attempt to create a 'new' text on the basis of these two forms by improving the Arabic and adapting it to the text of the Peshitta, which he supposed to be the Syriac original, shows that he had not any real understanding of the actual problems.[2]

From the point of view of the textual critic who wishes to ascertain whether a given reading stood originally in Tatian's Diatessaron, most scholars have considered the Arabic Diatessaron to be worthless, either because it had been translated from a Syriac Diatessaron which was almost completely assimilated to the Peshitta text, or because the Arabic translation itself had been accommodated to the Peshitta. On the other hand, Baumstark[3] in his review of Marmardji's edition dissented from this commonly held opinion, finding it contradicted by the presence of not a few disagreements between the Arabic Diatessaron and the Peshitta as well as agreements of the Arabic and syr[s,c] against the Peshitta.[4] According to Higgins, the main reason that the Arabic Diatessaron has been thought to be so closely in conformity with the Peshitta as to be of little or no value in ascertaining Tatian's text is that reliance has usually been placed on Ciasca's printed text as representing the text of the Arabic Diatessaron. But since MS. A (on which Ciasca relied) in

---

[1] See, e.g., A. J. B. Higgins, 'The Arabic Version of Tatian's Diatessaron', *JTS* xlv (1944), 187–99; id., 'Tatian's Diatessaron' [a summary of his doctoral dissertation at the University of Manchester], *Journal of the Manchester University Egyptian and Oriental Society*, xxiv (1942–5, published 1947), 28–32; and Paul E. Kahle, *The Cairo Geniza* (London, 1947), pp. 211–28; 2nd edn. (Oxford, 1959), pp. 297–313. [2] Ibid., p. 227; 2nd edn., p. 313.

[3] *OC*, 3rd Ser., xi (1936), 241 f.

[4] An opinion shared also by Marmardji, who regarded the text of the Arabic Diatessaron as 'purement et simplement celui de la Pšiṭṭâ' (op. cit., p. xxxix).

several respects shows itself to be farther removed from Tatian and more closely assimilated to the Peshitta than the other witnesses, the correct methodology is to seek Tatian's text in B E O.[1] When one or more of these witnesses implies a Syriac text different from the Peshitta, particularly when such readings agree with the Old Syriac and/or with other Diatessaric witnesses, we may with some measure of confidence regard such readings as genuine Tatianic remnants.

(*d*) A Persian Harmony of the Gospels,[2] made from a Syriac original, is the latest extensive Tatianic text to be given attention by New Testament scholars. Although the manuscript (Florence, Laurentian Lib. XVII (81)) was described by Assemani[3] as long ago as 1742, and again by Italo Pizzi[4] in 1886, it was not until the middle of the twentieth century that Giuseppe Messina made the text available, with an Italian translation and an extensive introduction.[5] A colophon gives the information that the manuscript, which contains 128 numbered folios (the first folio is lacking) was copied in the year 1547 by a Jacobite priest, Ibrahīm ben Shammas 'Abdullāh, in the city of Ḥiṣn Kaif on the Tigris River, from a parent manuscript dating probably from the thirteenth century. This earlier Persian Diatessaron appears to have been translated (not always quite accurately) from a Syriac

---

[1] Higgins, *JTS* xlv (1944), 195 f. For further investigations of the Arabic and the Persian Harmonies, see Higgins in *Studia Evangelica*, ed. by K. Aland *et al.* (*TU* lxxiii; Berlin, 1959), pp. 793–810, and in *Studies in New Testament Language and Text*, ed. by J. K. Elliott (Leiden, 1976), pp. 246–61.

[2] For a fuller discussion of the Persian Harmony, reference may be made to the present writer's volume, *Chapters in the History of New Testament Textual Criticism* (Leiden and Grand Rapids, 1963), pp. 103–20, parts of which have been used here.

[3] *Bibliotheca Mediceae Laurentianae et Palatinae codicum MSS. orientalium catalogus* (Florence, 1742), p. 59.

[4] *Cataloghi dei codici orientali di alcune biblioteche d'Italia*, iii (Florence, 1886), p. 301.

[5] *Diatessaron Persiano*, i. *Introduzione*; ii, *Testo e traduzione* (*Biblica et orientalia*, N. 14; Rome, 1951). This edition, excellent though it is, does not render obsolete Messina's earlier volume, *Notizia su un Diatessaron Persiano tradotto dal siriaco* (Rome, 1943). For a fuller discussion of certain stylistic features (e.g. conflate readings) and evidence bearing on the history of the Persian manuscript and its translator, including the complete text and translation of one of the chief colophons, one must refer to the earlier volume. It is a cause for regret also that, although Messina indicates the location and length of sporadic comments interspersed in the Harmony (some of which extend to a column or more in length), yet in the interests of saving space he neither transcribes nor translates any of them. One cannot but wonder whether these comments might reveal or corroborate some characteristic of the Harmonist. To learn even a modicum as to his methods of exegesis would contribute to a fuller understanding of his background and mental processes.

base by a Jacobite layman of Tabriz who calls himself Īwānnīs 'Izz al-Dīn, that is, 'John, Glory of the Religion'. Although Īwānnīs undoubtedly wished the reader to believe that he had himself composed the Harmony *de novo*, Messina found reasons to believe that in preparing the Persian work he utilized two slightly divergent Harmonies already existing in Syriac.[1]

The Persian Harmony is divided into four main divisions, containing respectively 71, 61, 60, and 58 paragraphs. When the sequence of the sections is compared with Tatian's work, represented in codex Fuldensis (see below, pp. 20–1) and the Arabic Diatessaron, only relatively few sections are found to be in the same order, and these can be explained on the basis of independent coincidence.

An early date for the composition of the underlying Syriac *Vorlage* was argued by Messina on the grounds of (*a*) the presence of numerous agreements with the Old Syriac and divergences from the Peshitta; and (*b*) the inclusion of a certain amount of non-canonical matter proving that the Harmony was composed when the New Testament canon was still fluid. But such reasons are quite inconclusive, for there is growing evidence that the Peshitta version did not immediately supplant all Old Syriac readings, and there is ample evidence that even in the Middle Ages authors of a somewhat similar type of literature, namely devotional lives of Christ, did not feel themselves at all inhibited by a universally recognized canon of the New Testament from introducing into their works more than one incident not reported in the New Testament.[2]

Another type of argument supporting a very early date for the *Vorlage* of the Persian Diatessaron has been advanced on the basis of iconography. According to a preliminary study by Nordenfalk, the miniatures contained at the end of the Persian codex suggest a second-century archetype.[3] The supporting evidence, however, was subjected to detailed scrutiny by other art historians,[4] and subsequently Nordenfalk modified his views

---

[1] *Diatessaron Persiano*, pp. xxi f.

[2] For further discussion of the points made in the text, see Metzger, *Chapters in the History of New Testament Textual Criticism*, pp. 107 ff.

[3] Carl Nordenfalk, 'An Illustrated Diatessaron', *Art Bulletin*, l (1968), 119–40.

[4] Meyer Schapiro and Seminar, 'The Miniature of the Florence Diatessaron (Laurentian MS Or. 81): Their Place in Late Medieval Art and Supposed Connection with Early Christian and Insular Art', *Art Bulletin*, lv (1973), 494–531.

concerning the high antiquity of the original of the Persian Diatessaron.[1]

By way of conclusion one can say that the Persian Harmony, though its structure and several other features bear no discernible connection with Tatian's Diatessaron, is still of great interest to the textual critic of the New Testament in view of the presence of many readings that are of undoubted Tatianic ancestry.[2] It deserves further investigation, particularly in relation to the Oxford manuscript (Bodl. Poc. 241) which provided the text for the Persian version in Walton's Polyglot Bible, and which presents a good number of affinities with the text of the Persian Diatessaron.[3]

(*e*) Other witnesses to the Eastern tradition of Tatian have been found in a wide variety of sources, among which are the following:

(1) Quotations from the Gospels found in the writings of such Syriac and Armenian writers as Aphraates, the *Liber Graduum*, Ephraem (in writings other than his commentary on the Diatessaron), Rabbula, Agathangelos, Eznik, Marutha Maipherkatensis, as well as in the Armenian Breviary and Ritual, and the Acts of the Persian Martyrs;[4]

---

[1] Nordenfalk has acknowledged the force of some of Schapiro's arguments, but still thinks it probable that 'in one way or another a copy of an illustrated Diatessaron reached Iona about the time the Book of Durrow was made [i.e. about A.D. 675]'. ('The Diatessaron Miniatures Once More', ibid., pp. 532–46, esp. p. 544.)

For the theory that the mural decorations in the Christian chapel at Dura-Europos were taken from an illustrated copy of Tatian's Diatessaron, see Clark Hopkins, *JNES* vii (1948), 97.

[2] For a list of about 100 such readings, found in the first of the four sections of the Persian Harmony, see Metzger, *Chapters in the History of New Testament Textual Criticism*, pp. 109–17.   [3] See Messina, op. cit., pp. lxxxv–xcii.

[4] For indexes to such quotations, see Louis Leloir, *L'Évangile d'Éphrem d'après les œuvres éditées* (*CSCO* clxxx, *Subsidia*, xviii; Louvain, 1958); idem, *Le Témoignage d'Éphrem sur le Diatessaron* (op. cit., vol. ccxxvii, *Subsidia*, xix; Louvain, 1962); and Ignatius Ortiz de Urbina, *Vetus Evangelium Syrorum, et exinde excerptum Diatessaron Tatiani* (*Biblia Polyglotta Matritensia*, ser. vi; Madrid, 1967). On the rather serious limitations of the last-mentioned work, see Robert Murray, 'Reconstructing the Diatessaron', *Heythrop Journal*, x (1969), 43–9.

For analyses of the nature and extent of Tatianic influence in Aphraates and in the *Liber Graduum*, see two unpublished theses: Owen Ellis Evans, 'Syriac New Testament Quotations in the Works of Aphraates and Contemporary Sources', M.A. thesis, University of Leeds (1951), esp. pp. 70 ff., and Fiona Joy Parsons, 'The Nature of the Gospel Quotations in the Syriac *Liber Graduum*', Ph.D. thesis, University of Birmingham (1969), esp. pp. 188 f.

(2) The Old Armenian and the Old Georgian versions of the Gospels (see pp. 166–7 and 191–3 below);

(3) A number of Arabic manuscripts of the Gospels and of liturgical texts in karshunic;[1]

(4) Citations in Manichaean texts;[2]

(5) The text of Matt. xix in the Jacobite marriage ritual, preserved in the Old Osmanic language;[3]

(6) Fragments of a lectionary in Sogdian (see pp. 280–1 below).

It has sometimes been thought that the Harclean Passiontide Harmony,[4] extant in more than two dozen manuscripts, preserves traces of Tatian's Diatessaron, but the most recent research on the subject suggests that the two are entirely independent (see pp. 74–5 below).

Western Witnesses

(*f*) The principal Latin evidence for the sequence of Tatian's Diatessaron is codex Fuldensis,[5] now in the Landesbibliothek at Fulda. This manuscript, a leading witness to the Vulgate (see p. 335 below), was written between 541 and 546 at Capua by the order of Victor, the bishop of that see. Later the manuscript was acquired by St. Boniface, who presented it in 745 to the

---

[1] For a list, see Curt Peters, *Das Diatessaron Tatians* (Rome, 1939), pp. 48–62.

[2] Anton Baumstark, 'Ein "Evangelium"-Zitat der manichäischen Kephalaia', *OC*, 3rd ser., xii (1937), 169–91; Peters, *Das Diatessaron Tatians*, pp. 125–32; and G. Quispel, 'Mani et la tradition évangélique des Judéo-Chrétiens', *RSR* lx (1972), 143–50.

[3] W. Heffening and C. Peters, 'Spuren des Diatessarons in liturgischer Überlieferung. Ein Türkischer und ein karšuni-Text', *OC*, 3rd ser., x (1935), 225–38.

[4] See J. P. P. Martin, *Introduction à la critique textuelle du Nouveau Testament*, Partie pratique, iii (Paris, 1885), pp. 121–44, and 'Le Διὰ τεσσάρων de Tatien', *RQH* xxxiii (1883), 374–78; H. H. Spoer, 'Spuren eines syrischen Diatessaron', *ZDMG* lxi (1907), 850–59; G. A. Barton and H. H. Spoer, 'Traces of the Diatessaron of Tatian in Harclean Syriac Lectionaries', *JBL* xxiv (1905), 179–95; and the appendix in Marmardji, op. cit., 'Évangélaire diatessarique syriaque', pp. 1*–75*. According to a note in a Syriac manuscript discovered by A. Mingana, this Passiontide Lectionary was drawn up by Rabban Daniel, of the village of Beth Bātīn near Ḥarran, and his disciple, Isaac (*BJRL* xv (1931), 178).

[5] The standard edition is still that of Ernst Ranke, *Codex Fuldensis. Novum Testamentum Latine interprete Hieronymo ex manuscripto Victoris Capuani* (Marburg and Leipzig, 1868). Cf. also Carl Scherer, *Die Codices Bonifatiani in der Landesbibliothek zu Fulda* (*Fuldaer Geschichte-Verein, Vereinsgabe für das Jahr 1905*, ii; Fulda, 1905), pp. 6–12.

recently founded Benedictine Abbey of Fulda in Germany. The manuscript contains the entire New Testament, but in place of the separate Gospels it has a continuous narrative, arranged according to the plan of Tatian's Diatessaron, a copy of which, in Old Latin translation, had fallen into the bishop's hands. About 600 Old Latin readings remain in the text, which is predominantly that of Jerome's Latin Vulgate.

Two other Latin harmonies, which like Fuldensis contain pre-Vulgate readings, are the Munich MSS. 23,977 and 10,025 (34–123). According to Vogels,[1] who called attention to the two manuscripts, the Latin Diatessaron was the earliest form in which the Gospel narrative circulated in the West. Apart from such a supposition, however, the validity of which has been contested by others, it remains true that a Latin harmony lies behind a wide variety of medieval harmonies in western-European vernaculars, including harmonies in Old High German, Middle Dutch (Flemish), Old Italian, Old French, and Middle English. Likewise a few Tatianic readings have been detected in the Arabic translation made by Isaac Velasquez of Cordova (see p. 260 below), and in the Anglo-Saxon version (see p. 454 below).

(*g*) A large number of medieval German harmonies in various dialects have come to light, the oldest of which is an Old High German (East Frankish) bilingual manuscript dating from the second half of the ninth century,[2] the Latin text of which depends upon Bishop Victor's work in codex Fuldensis. The principal witnesses to the diatessaric tradition in German fall into three groups. One group, to which belong the Munich MS. Mon Cg 532 (A.D. 1367)[3] and the Zürich MS. C. 170 App. 56 (end of the thirteenth or beginning of the fourteenth century),[4] is closely

[1] H. J. Vogels, *Beiträge zur Geschichte des Diatessaron im Abendland* (*Neutestamentliche Abhandlungen*, viii, 1; Münster i. W., 1919).

[2] Edited by Eduard Sievers, *Tatian. Lateinisch und altdeutsch, mit ausführlichen Glossar*, 2te Aufl. (*Bibliothek der ältesten deutschen Literatur-Denkmäler*, v; Paderborn, 1874; 2nd edn., 1892).

[3] The manuscript was studied by Erich Ronneburger, *Untersuchungen über die deutsche Evangelienharmonie der Münchener Handschrift Cg 532 aus d. J. 1367* (Diss., Greifswald, 1903).

[4] Edited, with a collation of five other fourteenth- or fifteenth-century copies, as well as several fragments, by Christoph Gerhardt, *Diatessaron Theodiscum* (*Corpus sacrae scripturae neerlandicae medii aevi*, Series Minor, tom. 1 : *Harmoniae Evangeliorum*, vol. iv (Leiden, 1970); see also Gerhardt's dissertation, *Das Leben Jhesu. Eine mittelhochdeutsche Evangelienharmonie. Untersuchung* (Munich, 1969).

related to the Old Dutch tradition. Another group is made up of the so-called Schönbacher fragments from a fourteenth-century manuscript at Graz[1] derived from a Latin model more strongly influenced by the Vulgate than the harmonies in the first group, and which alone have preserved a textual tradition older than all other German and Dutch witnesses.[2] Finally, certain fragments from the bindings of books in the library of the Himmelgarten Monastery near Nordhausen represent, according to Baumstark,[3] a tradition independent of the two preceding groups.

Besides varying degrees of influence from Tatian's Diatessaron on medieval German harmonies, Tatianic readings have turned up also in individual Gospel manuscripts and in a variety of medieval accounts of the Life and Passion of Christ.[4] Connections have also been found between Tatian's Diatessaron and the Heliand (see pp. 459–60 below).

(*h*) Middle Dutch (Flemish) harmonies are among the more important Western witnesses to Tatian's Diatessaron.[5] Among nine such manuscripts,[6] dating from the thirteenth to the fifteenth centuries, the following are available in printed form.

---

¹ Edited by Anton E. Schönbach, *Miscellen aus Grazer Handschriften*. 10. *Bruchstücke einer altdeutschen Evangelienharmonie* (*Mittheilungen des historischen Vereins für Steiermark*, l; Graz, 1903), pp. 7–103.

² So A. Baumstark, 'Die Schönbach'schen Bruchstücke einer Evangelienharmonie in bayerisch-österreichischer Mundart des 14. Jahrhunderts', *OC*, 3rd ser., xii (1937), 103–18.

³ 'Die Himmelgartner Bruchstücke eines niederdeutschen 'Diatessaron'-Textes des 13. Jahrhunderts', *OC*, 3rd ser., xi (1936), 80–96.

⁴ For a list of such witnesses, see C. Peters, *Das Diatessaron Tatians*, pp. 187–8, to which may be added *Der Saelden Hort. Alemannisches Gedicht vom Leben Jesu, Johannes des Täufers und der Magdalena . . .*, ed. by Heinrich Adrian (*Deutsche Texte des Mittelalters*, xxvi; Berlin, 1927); W. Henss, 'Tatians Diatessaron im Saelden Hort. mit Beiträgen zur abendländischen Diatessaron-Tradition überhaupt' (Diss. Marburg, 1953); and R. van den Broek, 'A Latin Diatessaron in the "Vita Beate Virginis Marie et Salvatoris Rhythmica"', *NTS* xxi (1974–5), 109–32.

⁵ On medieval Dutch harmonies, see C. C. de Bruin, *Middelnederlandse Vertalingen van het Nieuwe Testament* (Groningen, 1935); F. C. Burkitt, 'Tatian's Diatessaron and the Dutch Harmonies', *JTS* xxv (1923–24), 113–30; W. B. Lockwood in the *Cambridge History of the Bible*, ii, *The West from the Fathers to the Reformation*, ed. by G. W. H. Lampe (Cambridge, 1969), pp. 415–36, especially 428–31; and Robert Murray, 'The Gospel in the Medieval Netherlands', *Heythrop Journal*, xiv (1973), 307–13.

⁶ For a list of the nine manuscripts, see Peters, ibid., pp. 140–2, and for a stemma showing the relationship of several Dutch Harmonies, see Th. Frings in *Literaturblatt für germanische und romanische Philologie*, xlvii (1926), cols. 150–5. (The Utrecht Harmony is lost, but, according to Baarda, 'elements of its text are found in the files of Baumstark present in Beurou' (letter dated 6 Jan. 1976).)

(1) The oldest and most markedly Tatianic of the Dutch harmonies is the Liège Diatessaron,[1] written about 1280 in the West Limburg dialect and close to, if not the same as, the version made by Willem van Afflighem, who from 1277 was prior of the Benedictine Abbey of St. Truiden (or Tryen) on the border between Belgian Brabant and Limburg.[2] Now in the Liège University Library (no. 437), it is a transcript of a copy that shared the same scribal error of *porter* for *potter* that occurs in van Maerlant's Rijmbijbel of 1271. 'Accordingly,' as Plooij remarks, 'it belongs to the great revival of Harmony-transcription and Harmony-comment of the XIth and XIIIth centuries.'[3]

(2) The Stuttgart Diatessaron is a Flemish Gospel harmony written in A.D. 1332 by Franse Scavijn, and based on a vulgatized version of the first Dutch Bible translation.[4] The latter was made probably in the abbey of Afflighem.

(3) The Haaren Diatessaron,[5] a small parchment codex preserved in the Library of the Great Seminary at Haaren in the

---

[1] Edited first by G. J. Meijer, *Het Leven van Jezus, een Nederlandsch handschrift uit de dertiende eeuw* (Groningen, 1835); re-edited, with evidence from other Middle Dutch Harmonies, by J. Bergsma, *De Levens van Jezus in het Middelnederlandsch* (*Bibliotheek van middelnederlandsche Letterkunde*, liv, lv, lxi; Groningen, 1895–8). The lack of an index in Bergsma's volume was supplied by C. A. Phillips, *Index to the Liège Diatessaron (Edition of Dr. J. Bergsma)*, privately printed for the members of the Bezan Club. A magnificent edition was begun in 1929 under the auspices of the Royal Netherlands Academy of Sciences, namely, *The Liège Diatessaron*, edited with a textual apparatus by Daniel Plooij, C. A. Phillips, and A. H. A. Bakker, Parts i–viii (*Verhandelingen der koninklijke nederlandsche Akademie van Wetenschappen*, afd. Letterkunde, Nieuwe Reeks, Deel xxix and xxxi; Amsterdam, 1929–70). An English translation of the Dutch text is provided by A. J. Barnouw. An index of Gospel passages in Plooij's edition of the Liège Diatessaron was compiled in 1973 by E. Kollmann under the supervision of Heinrich Greeven for the Evangelisch-theologisches Seminar at the University of Bochum. The most recent edition is by C. C. de Bruin, *Diatessaron Leodiense* (*Corpus sacrae scripturae neerlandicae medii aevi*, Series Minor, 1: *Harmoniae Evangeliorum*, vol. i (Leiden, 1970). Barnouw's English translation is printed on facing pages with the Dutch text. Unfortunately de Bruin provides no index of Scripture passages.

[2] For an analysis of the linguistic affinities of the dialect in which the Liège Harmony is written, with a translation into modern Dutch, see Geertruida Catharina van Kersbergen, *Het Luiksche Diatessaron in het Nieuw-Nederlandsch vertaald, met een inleiding over de herkomst van den Middelnederlandschen tekst* (Diss., Nijmegen, 1936). [3] Plooij, *The Liège Diatessaron*, p. vii.

[4] Edited by Bergsma (op. cit.) on facing pages with the Liège text.

[5] Edited by C. C. de Bruin, *Diatessaron Haarense* (*Corpus sacrae scripturae neerlandicae medii aevi*, Series Minor, 1: *Harmoniae Evangeliorum*, vol. ii (Leiden, 1970)); cf. also G. Quispel, 'Some Remarks on the Diatessaron Haarense', *VC* xxv (1971), 131–9.

province of North Brabant, was written about A.D. 1400 somewhere in Dutch Limburg in the local dialect. Its text, according to its editor, is almost identical with that of the Stuttgart Diatessaron.

(4) The Cambridge Diatessaron[1] is contained in a manuscript in the Library of Cambridge University (MS. Dd. 12.25), written by two scribes who lived in the first part of the fourteenth century. The dialect of one of the copyists was a mixture of Middle Dutch and the Lower Rhinish dialect; that of the other, Middle Dutch. Written, as it appears, at a monastery between Brabant and the Rhineland, the text is of interest as a specimen of the transition between the original text-type and a subsequent German redaction.[2]

(5) The Gravenhage Harmony (MS. Maastricht 421 in the Royal Library at The Hague) was written in the year 1473. Its readings are cited by Bergsma.[3]

(*i*) Two Old Italian harmonies of the Gospels survive from the thirteenth and fourteenth centuries, one in the Tuscan dialect preserved in twenty-four manuscripts, the other in the Venetian dialect preserved in one manuscript.[4] Although Vaccari[5] thought that the Tuscan text goes back to codex Fuldensis, Peters[6] argued that the most that can be said is that the Tuscan Harmony belongs to the orbit of that branch of the Western transmission of the Diatessaron to which Fuldensis also belongs. The Venetian Harmony, according to both Vaccari[7] and

---

[1] Edited by C. C. de Bruin, *Diatessaron Cantabrigiense* (*Corpus sacrae scripturae neerlandicae medii aevi*, Series Minor, 1 : *Harmoniae Evangeliorum*, iii (Leiden, 1970)).

[2] For a discussion of selected readings from this manuscript, see J. A. Robinson, *The Academy*, xlv (14 Mar. 1894), 249 f., and Anton Baumstark, 'Der Cambridger Text des mittelniederländischen Leven van Jezus', *OC*, 3rd ser., xiii (1938), 108–22. (Robinson was the first to draw attention to Diatessaric readings in Dutch harmonies.)

[3] Bergsma, op. cit. (see p. 23 n. 1 above).

[4] The two harmonies have been edited by Venanzio Todesco, Alberto Vaccari, and Marco Vattasso, *Il Diatessaron in volgare italiano, testi inediti dei secoli XIII–XIV* (*Studi e testi*, lxxxi; Vatican City, 1938). The editors provide indexes to passages from the Gospels included in the two harmonies.

[5] Ibid., p. iii; cf. also Vaccari, 'Propaganda del Diatessaron in Occidente', *Bib*, xxi (1931), 336–54.

[6] Curt Peters, 'Die Bedeutung der altitalienischen Evangelienharmonien im venezianischen und toskanischen Dialekt', *Romanische Forschungen*, lxi (1942) ,181–92, esp. 182.

[7] Vaccari in the Preface to *Il Diatessaron in volgare italiano*, p. iii.

Peters,[1] contains more remnants of an older form of text than does the Tuscan Harmony, and Peters found that it occasionally agrees even with Aphraates in singular readings.[2]

(*j*) A Middle English Harmony[3] is preserved in a manuscript (which once belonged to Samuel Pepys) in the Library of Magdalene College, Cambridge (MS. Pepys 2498, dating from about A.D. 1400). As is shown by the presence of French words and phraseology,[4] the text was translated from a French harmony, which in turn rested upon a Latin model.[5]

(*k*) The harmonized Gospel text on which Zacharias Chrysopolitanus (Zachary of Besançon, a Premonstratensian) wrote a commentary[6] during the first half of the twelfth century is the earliest Gospel harmony of the Middle Ages that has come down to us.

2. DIATESSARIC PROBLEMS AND RESEARCH

The investigation of Tatian's Diatessaron has led scholars into many byways of research. Although the Mechitarists' edition of the Armenian text of Ephraem's commentary on the Diatessaron

---

[1] Ibid., p. 187.

[2] For other studies of the text of the Italian harmonies, see A. Merk, 'Tatian im italienischen Gewande', *Bib*, xx (1939), 294–305, and A. Baumstark, 'Zwei italienische Diatessaron-Texte', *OC*, 3rd ser., xiv (1939–40), 225–42.

[3] Edited by Margery Goates, *The Pepysian Gospel Harmony* (*Early English Text Society*, Original Series, clvii; London, 1922; repr. New York, 1971).

[4] Examples are cited by Miss Goates, ibid., pp. xv ff.

[5] Other traces of the Diatessaron in Old French have emerged in the translation made by Guyart des Moulins at the close of the thirteenth century, known as the *Bible historiale* ('Story Bible'); so Arthur Vööbus, *Early Versions of the New Testament: Manuscript Studies* (*Papers of the Estonian Theological Society in Exile*, vi; Stockholm, 1954), p. 13; cf. also J. N. Birdsall, 'The Sources of the Pepysian Harmony', *NTS* xxii (1975–6), 215–23.

[6] The text of Zachary's *In unum ex quatuor, sive de concordia evangelistarum libri quatuor* is published in Migne, *PL* clxxvi, cols. 11–620. On the nature of the Gospel text, see J. P. P. Martin, 'Le Διὰ τεσσάρων de Tatien', *RQH* xliv (1888), 36–40; Otto Schmid, 'Zacharias Chrysopolitanus und sein Kommentar zur Evangelienharmonie', *TQ* lxviii (1886), 531–47; lxix (1887), 231–75; J. Rendel Harris, 'Some Notes on the Gospel-Harmony of Zacharias Chrysopolitanus', *JBL* xliii (1924), 32–45; D. Plooij, 'De Commentaar van Zacharias Chrysopolitanus op het Diatessaron', *Mededeelingen der koninklijke Akademie van Wetenschappen*, Afd. Letterkunde, Deel lix, Serie A., No. 5 (Amsterdam, 1925); and C. A. Phillips, 'The Winchester Codex of Zachary of Besançon', *BBC* ii (1926), 3–8 (this last presents selected readings from a manuscript of Zachary that contains a greater number of Old Latin readings than the text printed in Migne).

was published in 1836, it was not until nearly half a century later (1876) that Aucher's Latin rendering made it available to a wider public.[1] Even then, in some unaccountable way, several years elapsed before scholars became aware of its importance.[2] Since then, however, unrelenting efforts have been expended in order to reconstruct the original Diatessaron.[3]

A Gospel harmony has two independent characteristics; it has a text, and it has also a sequence. The Diatessaric witnesses enumerated above offer evidence bearing generally on either the text or the sequence of the original Diatessaron. Some of them, such as codex Fuldensis and the Arabic Diatessaron, represent more or less closely the framework of Tatian's Diatessaron,[4] but possess essentially a non-Tatianic form of text. In the case of codex Fuldensis, Victor accommodated almost perfectly the Old

[1] Curiously enough, during those very years it was debated whether Tatian had in fact composed a Diatessaron at all. In an erudite but wrong-headed anonymous work entitled *Supernatural Religion: an Inquiry into the Reality of Divine Revelation* (London, 1874; revised edn. 1879), the author (said to have been Walter Richard Cassels) soberly set forth arguments for disbelieving Eusebius, Theodoret, and other Fathers when they speak of Tatian's Diatessaron. Even J. B. Lightfoot, in his elaborate reply to Cassels in *The Contemporary Review* (1877), could point to no irrefutable proof of the existence of the Diatessaron—though ironically enough he had in his own library a copy of the Mechitarists' edition of Ephraem's Commentary on the Diatessaron! Twelve years later in a note appended to his *Essays on the Work entitled Supernatural Religion reprinted from the Contemporary Review* (London, 1889), Lightfoot confesses: 'I had for some years possessed a copy of this work in four volumes, and the thought had more than once crossed my mind that possibly it might throw light on Ephraem's mode of dealing with the Gospels, as I knew that it contained notes on St. Paul's Epistles or some portions of them. I did not, however, then possess sufficient knowledge of Armenian to sift its contents, but I hoped to investigate the matter when I had mastered enough of the language' (pp. 287 f.).

[2] Apparently the first public notice taken of Aucher's Latin translation was by Ezra Abbot in his book, *The Authorship of the Fourth Gospel; External Evidence* (Boston, 1880), p. 55. In the following year Theodor Zahn published his reconstruction of Tatian's Diatessaron from Ephraem's Commentary (*Tatians Diatessaron*, being vol. i of his *Forschungen zur Geschichte des neutestamentlichen Kanons* (Erlangen, 1881)).

[3] Among peripheral studies J. Rendel Harris's investigation of 'The Gospel Harmony of Clement of Llanthony' (*JBL* xliii (1924), 349–62) is valuable chiefly in showing how Tatian must have gone about the task of constructing his Harmony.

[4] For a convenient chart showing the sequence of sections in the Arabic and Latin harmonies, as well as of the Liège, the Venetian, and the Persian harmonies, see Louis Leloir, 'Le Diatessaron de Tatien', *OS* i (1956), 10–21. For the view that only the Dura fragment and Ephraem's Commentary represent with certainty Tatian's work, see O. C. Edwards, Jr., 'Diatessaron or Diatessara?' *Biblical Research*, xviii (1973), 44–56.

Latin form of text of the original to the current Vulgate. As regards the Arabic Diatessaron, the Syriac base on which it rests is largely the Peshitta, which has in most places supplanted the Old Syriac text of Tatian's harmony. The chief evidence, therefore, which these two witnesses provide is not textual but structural; the frequent agreements of the sequence of sections may be presumed to reflect accurately the framework of the original Diatessaron.

On the other hand, other witnesses, which have been constructed according to sequences having no connection with the framework of Tatian's work, may preserve Tatianic readings transmitted to these witnesses via the Old Syriac or Old Latin forms of text. This kind of Tatianic testimony is on a par with the type of text represented in Gospel quotations in, for example, Aphraates, the Syriac *Liber Graduum*, the Armenian and Georgian versions, and certain Manichaean literature—all of which appear to embody in varying degrees Diatessaric readings. In this connection it should be mentioned that the method of approving as genuinely Tatianic only those readings in the Arabic Diatessaron that differ from the Peshitta has been unwarrantably rigorous, for even when the Arabic Diatessaron agrees with the Peshitta, if the Old Syriac also agrees, such readings are proved to be more ancient than the Peshitta and may therefore be Tatianic. Such a possibility becomes a probability with overwhelming compulsion when Ephraem and other witnesses unrelated to the Peshitta add their support.[1]

One of the first problems that confronts the investigator of Tatian's Diatessaron has to do with its opening sentence. Tatian, on the explicit testimony of Dionysius bar Ṣalîbî,[2] began his harmony with John i. 1. Although bar Ṣalîbî's statement is confirmed by evidence from Ephraem's commentary, it is contradicted by the Arabic text (which begins with Mark, as does the Persian Harmony) and by codex Fuldensis (which begins with Luke i. 1 ff.). The force of the discrepancy, however, is mitigated when the introductory notices in the Arabic manuscripts are considered. A careful study of these suggests that the original text

---

[1] Cf. the sane and balanced statement of the correct methodology in Tatianic *Forschung*, which is drawn up with lapidary succinctness, in August Merk, *Novum Testamentum graece et latine*, ed. nona (Rome, 1964), pp. 17*–18*.

[2] Joseph S. Assemani, *Bibliotheca orientalis*, ii (Rome, 1721), 159–60.

of the Arabic Diatessaron did, in fact, begin with John i. 1.
Similarly, it is almost certain that the first four verses of Luke
were not in the text of the harmony which Victor copied, for they
are not mentioned in the table of contents, which begins with
John. It therefore appears that the present sequence of material
in both the Arabic Diatessaron and codex Fuldensis has been
modified in the course of its transmission.

During the past decades more than one scholar has given
renewed attention to problems concerning the over-all arrangement of Tatian's Diatessaron. Taking Ephraem's commentary on
the Diatessaron as a basis, Leloir compared the sequence of
material in the Arabic, Latin, Dutch, Italian (Venetian), and
Persian harmonies.[1] He also collected a considerable number of
Tatianisms preserved in the works of Ephraem and supported by
either the Armenian or the Georgian version.

In a study of the sequence and character of the Diatessaron,
Ortiz de Urbina[2] pointed out that, when one tabulates according to each Gospel the material quoted by Ephraem, the verses
cited appear in disorder so far as the sequence of each Gospel
is concerned. When, however, one considers the sequence of
material within the Diatessaron, it is obvious that Tatian grouped
passages from the four Gospels that pertain to the same context,
whether of episode, parable, dialogue, or preaching of Jesus.
The purpose of the Diatessaron, according to the same scholar,
was to supply a convenient text for liturgical usage as well as
catechetical instruction of the faithful.

One of the minor puzzles connected with the study of the
Diatessaron is the question why Victor of Capua referred to
Tatian's Diatessaron as *diapente*.[3] Some have thought that the
expression was chosen in order to indicate obliquely that, in
addition to the canonical Gospels, Tatian utilized a fifth source.
Frequently this fifth source has been supposed to have been the

---

[1] Louis Leloir, 'Le Diatessaron de Tatien', *OS* i (1956), 208–31 and 313–34.
See also Leloir's *L'Évangile d'Éphrem d'après les œuvres éditées. Recueil des textes* (*CSCO*
clxxx, *Subsidia*, xii; Louvain, 1958), and idem, *Témoignage d'Éphrem sur le Diatessaron*
(op. cit. ccxxvii, *Subsidia*, xix; Louvain, 1962).

[2] I. Ortiz de Urbina, 'Trama e carattere del Diatessaron di Taziano', *OCP* xxv
(1959), 326–57.

[3] In the Preface Bishop Victor states, 'Tatianus, vir eruditissimus et orator illius
temporis clari, unum ex quattuor compaginaverat evangelium, cui titulum *diapente*
composuit' (ed. E. Ranke).

Gospel according to the Hebrews (so, e.g., Grotius, Mill, and, more recently, Baumstark, Peters, and Quispel); occasionally it has been identified with the Protevangelium of James (Messina). Others have suggested that *diapente* is nothing more than a *lapsus calami* and therefore not to be taken seriously (Zahn).

Another suggestion, first proposed by Isaac Casaubon, that *diapente* should be understood as a musical term, was explored at length in a monograph by Bolgiani.[1] On the basis of information derived from Martianus Capella, Fulgentius, Macrobius, and other ancient authors, Bolgiani shows that διὰ τεσσάρων and διὰ πέντε are technical terms used in ancient musicology, one referring to three intervals of four notes, the other to four intervals of five notes. He therefore interprets Victor's comment to mean that Tatian's 'harmony' of the four Evangelists involves not merely four individual notes but four fundamental elements of symphonic harmony, the *diapente*. Thus both terms, *diatessaron* and Victor's metaphorical use of *diapente*, are appropriate descriptions of Tatian's Harmony of the Gospels.

Quite apart from the significance of Victor's use of *diapente* in referring to the Diatessaron, it is natural that, soon after the publication in 1956 of the Coptic Gospel of Thomas, an investigation should be made of the question whether the newly discovered text has any appreciable connection with Tatian's work. According to Quispel the Gospel of Thomas discloses influence from a Jewish–Christian source similar to the Gospel according to the Hebrews, which he considers to be a fifth source used by Tatian, portions of which are also embedded in the *Heliand*.[2]

---

[1] Franco Bolgiani, *Vittore di Capua e il 'Diatessaron'* (*Memorie dell'Accademia delle Scienze di Torino*, Classe di scienze morali, storiche e filologiche, ser. 4ᵃ, no. 2; Turin, 1962).

[2] Gillis Quispel, 'Some Remarks on the Gospel of Thomas', *New Testament Studies*, v (1958–9), 276–90; idem, 'L'Évangile selon Thomas et le Diatessaron', *VC* xiii (1959), 87–117. Quispel's investigations on the Heliand were severely attacked by the Germanist Willi Krogmann ('Heliand, Tatian und Thomas-evangelium', *ZNW* li (1960), 255–68), who tested passages adduced by Quispel from the *Heliand* and concluded that they are totally insufficient to support Quispel's thesis. In turn Quispel published a lengthy rebuttal of Krogmann's strictures, maintaining that though a Germanist may judge differently about the significance of this or that alleged parallel, yet the resemblances, he urged, are so numerous that they cannot be merely accidental ('Der Heliand und das Thomasevangelium', *VC* xvi (1962), 121–53). For the most recent stage in the debate, see Quispel, *Tatian and the Gospel of Thomas* (Leiden, 1975), which deals chiefly with the history of the diatessaron in the West.

The relationship of the text of the Gospel of Thomas to Tatianic witnesses was investigated independently by another Dutch scholar, Tjitze Baarda.[1] Setting forth in tabular form data of about 130 variant readings, Baarda showed that it is the Arabic Diatessaron that supplies the greatest number of agreements with Thomas (about sixty agreements) and that the Liège Diatessaron and the Persian Harmony have each about fifty agreements. The Venetian and Tuscan Harmonies agree about thirty times. Ephraem's commentary on the Diatessaron accounts for about twenty agreements.

The significance of such data has been disputed. Although Quispel has continued to maintain that 'the author of the Gospel of Thomas and the author of the Diatessaron used the same Jewish–Christian source',[2] other scholars[3] have been unable to see any influence on the *logia* in Thomas from an extra-canonical written source (as against oral sources). Furthermore, it is also possible that, when an agreement between Thomas and a Tatianic witness is not merely fortuitous, the agreement may have arisen from the dependence of both on a 'wild' text of the individual Gospels.[4]

Another much-debated question concerns the language in which the Diatessaron was first composed—a question that is closely connected with another equally debated problem, the place at which it was first published. Was it drawn up originally in Greek, and later translated into Syriac (so Harnack,[5] von Soden,[6] Preuschen,[7] Jülicher,[8] Lagrange,[9] Lake,[10] Kraeling[11]) ?

---

[1] See Baarda's contribution, 'Thomas en Tatianus', in R. Schippers, *Het Evangelie van Thomas* (Kampen, 1960), pp. 135–55.

[2] G. Quispel, 'The Latin Tatian or the Gospel of Thomas in Limburg', *JBL* lxxxviii (1969), 327 f.

[3] e.g. Haenchen, Grant, Michaelis, McArthur, Munck; for bibliography, see A. F. J. Klijn, *A Survey of the Researches into the Western Text of the Gospels and Acts*, Part Two, 1949–69 (Leiden, 1969), p. 23, no. 1.

[4] In view of the complexity of the kinds of Tatianic evidence, it would be desirable to create and maintain at one central repository a Tatianic file into which evidence could be added as new documents come to light. Baumstark's file of slips bearing Tatianic evidence, arranged according to Scripture passage, is on deposit in the library of the Vetus Latina Institute at Beuron. Unfortunately most of the slips, written with pencil, are blurred and most difficult to read.

[5] Adolf Harnack, *Geschichte der altchristlichen Literatur bis Eusebius*; ii, *Die Chronologie der altchristlichen Literatur-Geschichte*, i (Leipzig, 1897; repr. 1958), p. 289.

[6] Hermann von Soden, *Die Schriften des Neuen Testaments in ihrer ältesten erreichbaren Textgestalt*, I, *Untersuchungen*, iii (Berlin, 1910), 1536–9.

[*Footnotes 7–11 on opposite page*]

Or did Tatian compile it in his native tongue (so Zahn,[1] Hjelt,[2] Plooij,[3] Baumstark,[4] Peters,[5] Kahle,[6] Vööbus[7]) and, if so, did he work with the separate Old Syriac Gospels before him, or was it an original Syriac composition, made directly from the Greek texts, and designed to present in the easiest and most practical way the substance of the Greek Gospels to a Syriac-speaking Church? Or, as Burkitt[8] thought, was a Latin harmony put together by an unknown compiler at Rome as an epitome of the Gospels, a copy of which, in Greek, having come into Tatian's hands, he rearranged and improved, subsequently taking it with him to the East, where he translated it into Syriac?

In support of a Greek origin is (*a*) its Greek title, by which it was known even in Syriac;[9] (*b*) the silence of Eusebius, who,

[7] Erwin Preuschen, *Untersuchungen zum Diatessaron Tatians* (*SbHeid* 1918, Abh. 15), pp. 44–56; idem, *Tatian's Diatessaron aus dem Arabischen übersetzt*, ed. by August Pott (Heidelberg, 1926), p. 26.

[8] A. Jülicher, 'Der echte Tatiantext', *JBL* xliii (1924), 132–71, esp. p. 166.

[9] M.-J. Lagrange, *La Critique textuelle* (Paris, 1935), p. 191. Lagrange held this opinion long before the discovery of the Dura fragment (*RB* xxix (1920), 326).

[10] K. Lake, 'I believe that Tatian wrote Greek by preference, made the Diatessaron in that language, that we do not know who translated it into Syriac, and that the Arabic—tested by Ephrem's quotations—is so corrupt that it has very little value for reconstructing the original text of the Diatessaron', *JBL* lx (1941), 331.

[11] Kraeling, op. cit., p. 18.

[1] Theodor Zahn, *Geschichte des neutestamentlichen Kanons*, i (Erlangen, 1888), 414 f.

[2] A. Hjelt, *Die altsyrische Evangelienübersetzung und Tatians Diatessaron* (Leipzig, 1903), pp. 22 f.

[3] D. Plooij, 'A Fragment of Tatian's Diatessaron in Greek', *ExpT* xlvi (1934–5), 471–6.

[4] Baumstark, who thought earlier that Tatian composed the Diatessaron in Greek (see his *Geschichte der syrischen Literatur* (Bonn, 1922), pp. 19 f.), came to hold that it was composed in Syriac at Rome for a Syriac-speaking congregation ('Die Evangelienzitate Novatians und das Diatessaron', *OC*, 3rd ser., v (1930), 1–14, esp. 13). According to Roman tradition, even the bishop of Rome, Anicetus (*c.* 154–65), who was bishop while Tatian was there, was a Syrian from Emesa (*Liber pontificalis*, ed. by L. Duchesne, i (Paris, 1886), 134).

[5] Curt Peters, op. cit., pp. 206–10.

[6] Paul E. Kahle, *The Cairo Geniza* (London, 1947), p. 209; 2nd edn. (Oxford, 1959), p. 295.

[7] Arthur Vööbus, *Early Versions of the New Testament*, p. 6.

[8] *JTS* xxvi (1935), 255–8, and the *Cambridge Ancient History*, xii (1939), 493–95.

[9] See R. Payne Smith (*Thesaurus Syriacus*, i (1879), cols. 869 f.) s.v. ܡܚܰܠܛܳܐ؟ The force of this argument, however, is lessened not only by the use of the same word to describe the harmonies prepared by Ammonius and by Elias Salumensis, but also by the presence in Syriac of not a few Greek words taken over by transliteration.

though mentioning the Diatessaron, says nothing of its composition in Syriac; and (c) the circumstance of the very considerable influence that it exerted on the text of the Gospels in the
West. In support of its origin in Syriac is (a) the silence of many
Church Fathers (e.g. Irenaeus, Tertullian, Clement of Alexandria, Origen, and Jerome) who refer to Tatian or to his *Oration
to the Greeks*, but who never mention his Diatessaron; (b) the
widespread dissemination of the Diatessaron in Syria;[1] and
(c) the presence in the West, as well as in the East, of versions of
the Diatessaron that show themselves, directly or indirectly, to
rest upon a Syriac *Vorlage*.

Contrary to what might be expected, even the discovery at
Dura of a fragment of the Diatessaron in Greek does not settle the
matter, for diametrically opposite analyses have been made of its
significance. Burkitt,[2] on the one hand, pointed to differences
between its text of Luke xxiii. 51 and the Old Syriac Gospels (the
latter read 'the kingdom of Heaven' whereas the Dura fragment
reads $\beta[\alpha\sigma\iota\lambda\epsilon\iota\alpha\nu]$ $\tau o\hat{v}$ $\overline{\theta v}$, in agreement with the accepted Greek
text; the Old Syriac authorities paraphrase vs. 51a, whereas
the Dura fragment does not). Baumstark,[3] on the other hand,
identified several presumed Syriasms in the diction, as well as
accounted for the unusual spelling of Arimathea, $'E\rho\iota\mu\alpha\theta\alpha\iota\alpha$, in
terms of a Syriac origin (the ν can have arisen if ܪܡܬܐ had been
misread by the translator as ܪܝܡܬܐ, Syriac i and n being very
similar; likewise the initial e of the word can be easily explained
when one supposes a Syriac original).

Another area of Tatianic research to which not a little attention has been given has to do with analysing characteristic
features of the Diatessaron in the light of its compiler's theology.

---

[1] In the fourth century, for example, Theodoret, bishop of Cyrus, because of
Tatian's reputation as a heretic, ordered that some 200 copies of the Diatessaron
be destroyed, and that copies of the separate Gospels be put in their place (*Treatise
on Heresies*, i. 20). It is significant also that Eusebius' statement: $\acute{o}$ $T\alpha\tau\iota\alpha\nu\grave{o}s$ $\sigma\upsilon\nu\acute{a}$-
$\phi\epsilon\iota\acute{a}\nu$ $\tau\iota\nu\alpha$ $\kappa\alpha\grave{\iota}$ $\sigma\upsilon\nu\alpha\gamma\omega\gamma\grave{\eta}\nu$ $o\grave{\upsilon}\kappa$ $o\mathring{\iota}\delta$' $\acute{o}\pi\omega s$ $\tau\hat{\omega}\nu$ $\epsilon\mathring{\upsilon}\alpha\gamma\gamma\epsilon\lambda\acute{\iota}\omega\nu$ $\sigma\upsilon\nu\theta\epsilon\acute{\iota}s$, $T\grave{o}$ $\delta\iota\grave{a}$ $\tau\epsilon\sigma\sigma\acute{a}\rho\omega\nu$ $\tau o\hat{\upsilon}\tau o$
$\pi\rho o\sigma\omega\nu\acute{o}\mu\alpha\sigma\epsilon\nu$, $\acute{o}$ $\kappa\alpha\grave{\iota}$ $\pi\alpha\rho\acute{a}$ $\tau\iota\sigma\iota\nu$ $\epsilon\grave{\iota}s$ $\acute{\epsilon}\tau\iota$ $\nu\hat{\upsilon}\nu$ $\phi\acute{\epsilon}\rho\epsilon\tau\alpha\iota$ ('Tatian arranged a kind of joining
together and compilation of the Gospels, I know not how, to which he gave the
title The Diatessaron; and it is still to this day to be found in the hands of some',
Hist. eccl. IV. xxix, 6, trans. by Lawlor and Oulton) is modified in the fourth-
century Syriac translation of Eusebius' work by omitting the words $o\grave{\upsilon}\kappa$ $o\mathring{\iota}\delta$' $\acute{o}\pi\omega s$
and by reading 'it is still in widespread use today' (*The Ecclesiastical History of
Eusebius in Syriac*, ed. by W. Wright and N. McLean (Cambridge, 1898), p. 243).

[2] *JTS* xxxvi (1935), 258 f.

[3] *OC*, 3rd ser., x (1935), 244–52.

Was Tatian a heretic from the beginning? What kind of heresy or heresies did he adopt? How far are such tendencies disclosed in his Diatessaron?

Several scholars[1] portray Tatian as primarily a Valentinian Gnostic, although there is much in his *Oration to the Greeks* that runs counter to such an evaluation. Another scholar[2] explains Tatian chiefly in terms of Middle Platonism, but again there is much that does not fit such a philosophical framework. According to yet another, and somewhat more plausible, analysis of Tatian's heretical leanings, he is best explained as an eclectic radical Christian to whom an ascetic-encratite explanation of life appealed from the outset of his career as a Christian.[3] After he left Rome, possibly pausing for a time in Greece or at Alexandria where he may have taught Clement,[4] he returned to Mesopotamia where his tendency to extremes was to lead him outside the Church to become the founder of the Encratites,[5] a sect which rejected marriage as sinful and renounced the use of flesh or wine in any form, even to the extent of substituting water for wine in the Eucharistic service.

Readings that betray Encratite tendencies, preserved in one or more of the several Diatessaric witnesses, include the following selected examples.

[1] M. Zappalà, 'Taziano e lo gnosticismo', *Rivista trimestrade di studi filosofici e religiosi*, iii (1922), 307–38; A. Orbe, 'Variaciones gnósticas sobre las alas del Alma', *Greg*, xxxv (1954) 21–33; and Robert M. Grant, 'The Heresy of Tatian', *JTS*, n.s. v (1954), 62–8; idem, 'Tatian (*Or*. 30) and the Gnostics', ibid., n.s. xv (1964), 65–9.

[2] M. Elze, *Tatian und seine Theologie* (Göttingen, 1960). According to Elze, because Tatian was interested in truth as a whole, he thought that he should organize the four Gospels into one whole. Cf. also O. C. Edwards, Jr., 'Barbarian Philosophy, Tatian and the Greek Paideia' (unpublished Ph.D. dissertation, University of Chicago, 1971).

[3] Cf. Arthur Vööbus, *History of Asceticism and the Syrian Orient . . .*, i (*CSCO* clxxxiv; *Subsidia*, xiv; Louvain, 1958), pp. 31–45; L. W. Barnard, 'The Heresy of Tatian—Once Again', *Journal of Ecclesiastical History*, xix (1968), 1–10; and Edward A. Johnson, 'The First Harmony of the Gospels: Tatian's Diatessaron and its Theology', *Journal of the Evangelical Theological Society*, xiv (1971), 227–38.

[4] So *Strom*. i. 1 is usually interpreted.

[5] Irenaeus, *Haer*. I. xxviii. 1; cf. Origen, *Contra Celsum*, v. 65. The Hebrew text of the Samaritan Chronicle no. II describes Tatian's Diatessaron as 'the gospel [book] of the Encratites' (John Macdonald and A. J. B. Higgins, 'The Beginnings of Christianity According to the Samaritans', *NTS* xviii (1971–2), 67). On the passage in Irenaeus, cf. Franco Bolgiani, 'La tradizione eresiologica sull'encratismo; I, Le notizie di Ireneo', *Atti della Accademia delle Scienze di Torino*, Classe di scienze morali, storiche e filologiche, xci (1956–7), 343–419, especially 377–400.

(*a*) Instead of following the generally accepted Greek text of Matt. i. 19, Tatian avoided referring to Joseph as Mary's husband by omitting the definite article and possessive pronoun and by taking ἀνήρ in a general and not a marital sense: 'Joseph, because he was a just man' (so Ephraem's citation of the Diatessaron and the Persian and Venetian Harmonies).

(*b*) It is probable that Tatian reduced the connubial bliss of Anna the prophetess (Luke ii. 36, ζήσασα μετὰ ἀνδρὸς ἔτη ἑπτὰ ἀπὸ τῆς παρθενίας αὐτῆς) from seven years to seven days,[1] for so Ephraem refers to the passage in one of his Hymns[2] and so the Sinaitic Syriac transmits the passage (indeed, here the statement is even more emphatic by the presence of ܒܠܚܘܕ, 'seven days *only* she . . .'; Curetonian *hiat*). Though the Persian Harmony does not reduce the conjugal life enjoyed by Anna to such a short time, it fails to render ζήσασα, a word which suggests a normal married life, and transforms the married estate into a celibate life: 'She remained seven years a virgin with her husband' (*era rimasta sette anni vergine* [ܟܘ] *con suo marito*). With this one may compare the Stuttgart and Theodiscum Harmonies which, instead of reading ἀπὸ τῆς παρθενίας, have 'in her virginity'.[3]

(*c*) In several medieval Harmonies (Liège, Stuttgart, Gravenhage, and Theodiscum) the declaration, 'For this reason a man shall leave his father and mother and be joined to his wife' (Matt. xix. 5), is transferred from the voice of God to that of Adam. This completely changes the meaning of marriage: only a spiritual union between man and wife was intended by God, while the fleshly union is nothing more than an invention of Adam.[4]

(*d*) Instead of 'I am the true vine' (John xv. 1), the Persian Diatessaron (IV. 31) has Jesus declare, 'I am the tree of the fruit

---

[1] Adelbert Merx argued that 'seven days' is the original text; see his *Die vier kanonischen Evangelien nach ihrem ältesten bekannten Texte*; II. ii, *Die Evangelien des Markus und Lukas nach der syrischen im Sinaikloster gefundenen Palimpsesthandschrift* (Berlin, 1905), pp. 207–8.

[2] Edited by T. J. Lamy, *Sancti Ephraemi Syri hymni et sermones*, iii (Mechelen, 1889), col. 813, vs. 17.

[3] For a discussion of the evidence as far as it was known in 1913, see H. J. Vogels, 'Lk, 2, 36 im Diatessaron', *BZ* xi (1913), 168–71. Cf. also Messina, *Notizia su un Diatessaron Persiano tradotto dal Syriaco* (Rome, 1943), pp. 57–9.

[4] On the passage see D. Plooij, 'Eine enkratitische Glosse im Diatessaron', *ZNW* xxii (1923), 1–15, and, more briefly, *A Primitive Diatessaron* (Leyden, 1923), pp 54. f.

of truth' (من درخت ميوه راستى); cf. Aphraates (*Dem.* xiv. 24
(39)) 'He is the vineyard of truth.'[1]

(*e*) The allegation levelled against Jesus, 'Behold, a glutton
and a drunkard' (Matt. xi. 19), is absent from Ephraem's citations from the Diatessaron, as is also the statement in the account
of the marriage at Cana, 'when men have drunk freely' (John
ii. 10).

(*f*) At the crucifixion, instead of Jesus' being offered wine
mingled with gall (Matt. xxvii. 34), according to Ephraem's
quotation from the Diatessaron Jesus was given a mixture of
vinegar and gall.

In addition to readings that seem to have arisen as the result of
ascetical bias, Tatian has also been thought to disclose certain
anti-Judaic tendencies.[2] The examples that have been adduced
to prove such tendencies, however, are often either ambiguous or
open to the suspicion of being merely accidental variations.

Less disputed are several instances of the incorporation of
apocryphal additions into the Diatessaron.[3] For example, it
appears that Tatian supplemented the account of the baptism of
Jesus with a reference to the appearance of a great light or fire[4]
which rested upon the Jordan. This phenomenon, mentioned
by Tatian's teacher, Justin Martyr,[5] and included, according
to Epiphanius,[6] in the Gospel according to the Hebrews, is

[1] Cf. Robert Murray, *Symbols of Church and Kingdom* (Cambridge, 1975),
pp. 95 f., and Tjitze Baarda, 'An Archaic Element in the Arabic Diatessaron?
(T^A 46:18 = John xv. 2)', *NT* xvii (1975), 151–5.

[2] Cf. H. J. Vogels, *Handbuch der neutestamentlichen Textkritik* (Münster in W.,
1923), pp. 200 ff.; J. Rendel Harris, 'Was the Diatessaron Anti-Judaic?' *HTR*
xviii (1925), 103–9; Vööbus, *Early Versions*, pp. 18 f.; and C. Van Puyvelde,
Dictionnaire de la Bible, Supplément, vi (Paris, 1962), cols. 868 f.

[3] Cf. G. Messina, *Diatessaron Persiano*, pp. xxxv–lii; Juw fon Weringha, *Heliand
und Diatessaron* (Assen, 1965); Tj. Baarda, *Vier = Een; Enkele bladzijden uit de
geschiedenis van de harmonistiek der Evangeliën* (Kampen, *c.* 1969); and James H.
Charlesworth, 'Tatian's Dependence upon Apocryphal Traditions', *Heythrop
Journal*, xiv (1974), 5–17.

[4] The variation between light and fire may well have arisen, as Ernst Bammel
points out (*TU* xciii (1966), 57), through confusion in Syriac between ܢܘܗܪܐ
'light' and ܢܘܪܐ 'fire'. (Was the addition meant to suggest that after the heavens
opened the brilliance of the divine glory was reflected from the surface of the
Jordan?)

[5] *Dial. c. Try.* lxxxviii.

[6] *Panarion*, xxx. 13. 7 (K. Holl, pp. 350 f.), καὶ εὐθὺς περιέλαμψε τὸν τόπον
φῶς μέγα.

referred to by Ephraem in his Commentary[1] and is preserved in the Pepysian Harmony, as it is also in two Old Latin manuscripts at Matt. iii. 15, Vercellensis (MS. *a*: 'lumen ingens') and Sangermanensis (MS. *g*[1]: 'lumen magnum'). Messina has noticed that in the nativity story the Persian Diatessaron presents several readings that occur in the *Protevangelium Jacobi*.[2] On the whole, however, the amount of extra-canonical material that seems to have been present in Tatian's Diatessaron hardly justifies the opinion of some scholars[3] that Tatian made extensive use of a fifth, apocryphal Gospel when he compiled his Harmony.

III. THE OLD SYRIAC VERSION

1. WITNESSES TO THE OLD SYRIAC VERSION

Until the middle of the nineteenth century the Peshitta held the field as the earliest Syriac version of the New Testament.[4] In 1842, however, the British Museum acquired a large number of Syriac manuscripts from the monastery dedicated to St. Mary Deipara in the Nitrian Desert in Egypt. Among these was a heterogeneous codex put together from parts of several different manuscripts. The oldest section, comprising eighty or more leaves (now Add. MS. 14451), was discovered by William Cureton,[5] then assistant keeper in the department of manuscripts, to contain a hitherto unknown Syriac version of the Gospels, in the sequence Matthew, Mark, John, and Luke. As

---

[1] *Commentaire de l'Évangile concordant ou Diatessaron*, ed. by L. Leloir (*Sources chrétiennes*, no. 121: Paris, 1966), p. 95.

[2] G. Messina, 'Lezioni apocrife nel Diatessaron Persiano', *Bib*, xxx (1949), 10–27.   [3] See pp. 28–9 above.

[4] There were, however, occasional expressions of dissent, for as far back as the time of J. J. Griesbach (1745–1812) and J. L. Hug (1765–1846) it was suspected that the Peshitta was not the original form of the Syriac version; cf. C. H. Turner, 'Historical Introduction to the Textual Criticism of the New Testament; V. The Languages of the Early Church: (B) Syriac and the First Syriac Gospels', *JTS* xi (1910), 200.

[5] The text was printed and privately circulated in the volume *Quatuor Evangeliorum Syriace, recensionis antiquissimæ, atque in Occidente adhuc ignotæ quod superest: e codice vetustissimo Nitriensi eruit et vulgavit Guilielmus Cureton* (London, 1848). Ten years later the text, with an English translation as well as lengthy Preface containing Cureton's views concerning the origin of the version, was published in the volume *Remains of a Very Antient Recension of the Four Gospels in Syriac, hitherto unknown in Europe* (London, 1858).

soon as the text of the leaves was made available to scholars, it became obvious that the newly found version was a rival claimant to the priority of the Peshitta version. In fact, Cureton went so far as to suppose that in this version he had discovered the original of St. Matthew's Gospel![1]

Unfortunately the manuscript is very lacunose, and with fewer than half of the original 180 leaves surviving. These contain the text of Matt. i. 1–viii. 22; x. 32–xxiii. 25*a*; Mark xvi. 17*b*–20; John i. 1–42*a*; iii. 5*b*–vii. 37; xiv. 10*b*–12*a*, 15*b*–19*a*, 21*b*–24*a*, 26*b*–29*a*; Luke ii. 48*b*–iii. 16*a*; vii. 33*b*–xv. 21; xvii. 24–xxiv. 44*a*.

Further information was forthcoming when three additional folios of the same version, and probably of the same manuscript, were discovered to be bound as flyleaves of a Syriac manuscript in the Royal Library of Berlin (Orient Quad. 528). The leaves, which preserve Luke xv. 22–xvi. 12; xvii. 1–23; and John vii. 37–viii. 19, were edited first by Dr. Roediger[2] and subsequently by William Wright in a privately printed edition of one hundred copies,[3] in a format designed to range with Cureton's edition. Subsequently F. C. Burkitt produced what is now the standard edition of the Curetonian manuscript, along with the three stray leaves, and supplied a literal English translation as well as a volume of linguistic, historical, and text-critical comments.[4]

A second copy of the Old Syriac version came to light toward the close of the nineteenth century. While visiting the celebrated monastery of St. Catherine on Mount Sinai two Scottish ladies, Mrs. Agnes Smith Lewis and her twin sister Mrs. Margaret Dunlop Gibson,[5] discovered a palimpsest manuscript (MS. Sin. Syr. 30), the under-writing of which presents the text of the four Gospels. In its original form the codex contained 166 leaves, of

---

[1] 'This Syriac text of the Gospel of St. Matthew which I now publish has, to a great extent, retained the identical terms and expressions which the Apostle himself employed' (p. xciii of the 1858 edn.). The same had been advanced for the Peshitta by Widmanstadt in 1555 (see the preface in his edn., p. 52 n. 2 below).

[2] *Monatsbericht der königlich Preussischen Akademie der Wissenschaften zu Berlin* (July 1872), pp. 557–9.

[3] *Fragments of the Curetonian Gospels* (London, n.d.), 8 pages.

[4] *Evangelion da-Mepharreshe; the Curetonian Syriac Gospels, re-edited, together with the readings of the Sinatic palimpsest . . .* , 2 vols. (Cambridge, 1904).

[5] For an informative account of the lives of the Mesdames Lewis and Gibson, see A. Whigham Price, *The Ladies of Castlebrae* (Annual Lecture to the Presbyterian Historical Society [of England], Durham, 1964).

which 142 survive, preserving the text of Matt. i. 1–vi. 10a; vii.
3–xii. 4a, 6b–25a, 29–xvi. 15a; xvii. 11b–xx. 24; xxi. 20b–xxv.
15a, 17–20a, 25b–26, 32–xxviii. 7; Mark i. 12b–44a; ii. 21–iv. 17;
v. 1–26a; vi. 5b–xvi. 8; Luke i. 36b–v. 28a; vi. 12–xxiv. 52;
John i. 25b–47a; ii. 16–iv. 37; v. 6b–25a, 46b–xviii. 31a; xix.
40b–xxi. 25.

In view of the difficulty of deciphering the under-writing,
which was erased in the eighth century and the vellum reused for
the Syriac text of twelve Lives of Female Saints, it is understandable that here and there opinion differs as to the original
reading.[1] Unfortunately even a photographic facsimile of the
manuscript[2] fails to resolve all of the disputed readings.[3]

On the basis of palaeographical considerations the Curetonian
manuscript is thought to have been written about the middle of
the fifth century (Cureton) or during the second half of the fifth
century (Wright) or the early part of the fifth century (Burkitt).
The Gospel text of the Sinaitic manuscript is assigned either to
the beginning of the fifth or more probably to the close of the
fourth century.

Except for the Sinaitic and Curetonian manuscripts no other
copy of the Gospels in the Old Syriac version has been identified
with certainty.[4]

---

[1] The manuscript was edited first by R. L. Bensly, J. Rendel Harris, and F. C.
Burkitt, *The Four Gospels in Syriac transcribed from the Sinaitic Palimpsest* (Cambridge,
1894). Two years later Mrs. Lewis published *Some Pages of the Four Gospels retran-
scribed* (London, 1896). The standard edition is that of Mrs. Lewis, who visited the
monastery of St. Catherine six times in order to study the manuscript, *The Old
Syriac Gospels, or Evangelion da-Mepharreshe; being the text of the Sinai or Syro-Antiochian
Palimpsest, including the latest additions and emendations, with the variants of the Curetonian text . . .* (London, 1910).

[2] Prepared by Arthur Hjelt, *Syrus Syriacus* (Helsingfors, 1930).

[3] See W. D. McHardy, 'Disputed Readings in the Sinaitic Syriac Palimpsest',
JTS xlv (1944), 170–4, who points out several problems of representing in a critical
apparatus the evidence of the Sinaitic palimpsest where it is read differently by
different scholars.

[4] According to Atiya the 'Codex Arabicus' (Sinai Arab. MS. 514), which he
describes as a palimpsest of five layers of writing (though it appears that no
one folio presents all five layers), contains in its oldest layer portions of the Syriac
text of Matthew, John, and Mark, the latter of which presents a considerable
number of significant variants from the Peshitta text and is therefore conjectured to
represent a pre-Peshitta form of text (see A. S. Atiya, 'Codex Arabicus', *Homage
to a Bookman; Essays on Manuscripts, Books and Printing Written for Hans P. Kraus . . .*,
ed. by Hellmut Lehmann-Haupt (Berlin, 1967), pp. 25–85). Until, however, the
Syriac text is made available, nothing certain can be said other than to comment
that a non-Peshitta text is not necessarily a pre-Peshitta text.

Although no manuscript of an Old Syriac version of the Acts and Pauline Epistles is known, scholars have suspected from the form of quotations from these books in the writings of early Syriac and Armenian authors that an older form of the Syriac text of the Apostolos preceded that of the Peshitta (for a discussion, see pp. 164–8 below).

2. CHARACTERISTICS OF THE OLD SYRIAC VERSION

Although the Sinaitic and Curetonian manuscripts are far from containing identical texts,[1] they agree often enough to make it convenient to cite their readings over against the text of the later Syriac versions. This general unanimity of the two manuscripts has been interpreted in two ways. Most scholars have taken it to mean that the two manuscripts preserve two revisions of a common original, and therefore may be treated as representatives of a single version in different stages of development. Other scholars, however, impressed by the analogy of the divergences among the Old Latin witnesses—divergences which emerged because of a multiplicity of independent efforts to translate the Greek text into Latin—prefer to regard the two Syriac witnesses as the work of different translators living at different places and times.[2] In either case, however, it is instructive to consider characteristic readings shared by both the Sinaitic and Curetonian manuscripts. Among noteworthy agreements the following are typical examples.

Both manuscripts agree with ℵ and B in omitting 'first-born' in Matt. i. 25, and 'bless them that curse you, do good to them that hate you' and 'despitefully use you and' in v. 44. In x. 42 both read ἀπόληται ὁ μισθὸς αὐτοῦ, with D and the Old Latin. Both omit xii. 47 with ℵ* B L ('And someone told him, "Your mother and brothers are standing outside, asking to speak to you" '), as well as xvi. 2 and 3 ('When it is evening, you say, "It will be fair weather, for the sky is red." And in the morning "It will be

---

[1] For a collation of the two manuscripts with one another, the readings of the Peshitta being also added where they differ, for purposes of comparison, see Albert Bonus, *Collatio Codicis Lewisiani rescripti evangeliorum sacrorum Syriacorum cum Codice Curetoniano* (Oxford, 1896).

[2] e.g. Julius A. Bewer, 'The History of the New Testament Canon in the Syrian Church', *AJT* iv (1900), 64–98, 345–63; Charles C. Torrey, *Documents of the Primitive Church* (New York and London, 1942), p. 246; and Arthur Vööbus, *Early Versions of the New Testament*, pp. 80 f.

stormy today, for the sky is red and threatening." You know how to interpret the appearance of the sky, but you cannot interpret the signs of the times') and xvii. 21 ('But this kind never comes out except by prayer and fasting'), both times in company with ℵ and B. In xix. 16 both manuscripts add ἀγαθέ after διδάσκαλε, thus harmonizing the text with that of Mark. In xx. 22 and 23 both omit with ℵ B D L 'and to be baptized with the baptism that I am baptized with'.

In Luke both insert xxii. 17 and 18 in vs. 20, agreeing with no Greek manuscript. With 𝔓⁷⁵ ℵ B both omit 'in letters of Greek and Latin and Hebrew' in xxiii. 38, whereas in vs. 48 both add 'saying, Woe to us, what has befallen us! woe to us for our sins', agreeing partly with one Old Latin manuscript (g¹) and the Gospel of Peter (vii. 25). Both agree with D and the Old Latin in omitting xxiv. 40 ('And when he had said this, he showed them his hands and his feet').

In John i. 34 for 'the Son of God' both witnesses read (with ℵ*) 'the chosen of God'. In iii. 6 both insert after 'is spirit' the words 'because God is a living Spirit' (Curetonian omits 'living'). In vs. 8 both insert the words 'of water and' before 'the spirit', along with ℵ and the Old Latin. In company with the best authorities both manuscripts omit the *pericope de adultera* (vii. 53–viii. 11).

Among readings that are peculiar to either the Sinaitic or the Curetonian manuscript (sometimes because the other is defective at that place), the following deserve to be mentioned.

At Matt. i. 16 the Sinaitic Syriac stands alone among Greek and versional witnesses in reading ܝܘܣܦ ܝܘܣܦ ܐܘܠܕ ܝܥܩܘܒ ܕܡܟܝܪܐ ܗܘܬ ܠܗ ܡܪܝܡ ܒܬܘܠܬܐ ܐܘܠܕ ܠܝܫܘܥ ܕܡܬܩܪܐ ܡܫܝܚܐ ('Jacob begot Joseph; *Joseph, to whom was betrothed Mary the virgin, begot Jesus who is called the Christ'*). It is understandable that this reading should have attracted widespread attention, and indeed should be preferred by some as the original text.[1] Most textual critics, however, explain the origin of the reading either as a paraphrase of the reading preserved in the Curetonian Syriac ('Jacob begot Joseph, him to whom was betrothed Mary the

---

[1] Von Soden translated the Syriac text into Greek and printed Ἰακὼβ δὲ ἐγέννησεν τὸν Ἰωσήφ. Ἰωσὴφ δέ, ᾧ ἐμνηστεύθη παρθένος Μαριάμ, ἐγέννησεν Ἰησοῦν τὸν λεγόμενον Χριστόν, which James Moffatt rendered into English in his modern speech version (1913; revd. 1934).

virgin, she who bore Jesus the Christ') or as a purely mechanical imitation of the preceding pattern in the genealogy.[1] Matt. xviii. 11 ('For the Son of Man came to save the lost') is omitted by the Sinaitic Syriac with ℵ B D Θ and Origen, but retained by the Curetonian. In xxiv. 36 the Sinaitic omits the words 'neither the Son' against ℵ* B D Θ (Curetonian is defective here and for the rest of the Gospel). In xxvii. 16 and 17 Sinaitic has 'Jesus Barabbas' with Θ, several minuscules, and some manuscripts mentioned by Origen.

In Mark, for which Curetonian is defective except for four verses at the close of chap. xvi, the Sinaitic omits ix. 44 and 46 ('Where their worm does not die, and the fire is not quenched') with ℵ B C L W, and the latter half of vs. 49 ('and every sacrifice will be salted with salt') with ℵ B L (W); likewise xv. 28 ('And the scripture was fulfilled which says, "He was reckoned with the transgressors" ') with ℵ A B C D.

In Luke ii. 14 Sinaitic supports the common reading εὐδοκία, not εὐδοκίας found in ℵ* A B* D W and the Latin versions. In iv. 18 Sinaitic omits 'to heal the broken-hearted' with ℵ B D L W. In x. 41 Sinaitic (against Curetonian) omits 'you are anxious and troubled about many things' with partial support from Old Latin witnesses. Likewise Sinaitic (against Curetonian) omits xxii. 43 and 44 (the angel in the garden and the bloody sweat) with 𝔭⁷⁵ ℵ^a A B W, as well as xxiii. 34 ('Father, forgive them', etc.) with 𝔭⁷⁵ B D* W Θ. In xxiv. 51 Sinaitic reads 'he was lifted up from them', thus agreeing neither with ℵ* D, which do not expressly mention the Ascension ('he was parted from them'), nor with the other authorities.

As was mentioned above, in the Gospel of John Curetonian is very defective; in iii. 13 Sinaitic retains 'which is in heaven' against 𝔭⁶⁶,⁷⁵ ℵ B L, and in iv. 9 'for the Jews have no dealings with the Samaritans', against ℵ* D. In vi. 69 Sinaitic reads 'you are the Christ, the Son of God' against 𝔭⁷⁵ ℵ B C D L. In xi. 39 Sinaitic inserts in Martha's speech the words, 'Why are they

---

[1] Since every name in the genealogy up to Joseph is written twice in succession, it may be that the scribe of Syr[s] (or an ancestor of the manuscript), having followed carefully the stereotyped pattern of verses 2–15, in vs. 16 made the initial mistake of repeating the name 'Joseph', and then went on to produce the singular reading (see the discussion by the present writer, 'The Text of Matthew 1. 16', in *Studies in the New Testament and Early Christian Literature; Essays in Honor of Allen P. Wikgren*, ed. by David E. Aune (Leiden, 1972), pp. 16–24).

taking away the stone?' agreeing with no other authority. In xviii the sequence of the narrative is altered in Sinaitic, vs. 24 being inserted between verses 13 and 14, and verses 16–18 being placed after vs. 23, thus representing Caiaphas, not Annas, as the questioner of Jesus, and bringing together the whole narrative of Peter's denial.

Among the readings that are distinctive to the Curetonian manuscript in comparison with the Sinaitic manuscript, the following may be mentioned. The Curetonian inserts the names Ahaziah, Joash, and Amaziah in Matt. i. 8 with some support from D and five Ethiopic manuscripts, but the Sinaitic agrees with the mass of authorities in omitting them. In vi. 13 the Curetonian (against ℵ B D) retains the doxology to the Lord's Prayer, except the words 'and the power' (the Sinaitic is defective here). In Matt. xiii. 33 Curetonian is the only witness (along with Clement of Alexandria) that reads 'the kingdom of heaven is like leaven which a *wise* woman took and hid in meal, until it was all leavened'. On the other hand, Curetonian omits '*three measures of meal*'. Curetonian agrees with D in inserting a long additional passage after xx. 28, but Sinaitic is defective here.

As was mentioned earlier, Curetonian is defective in the whole of Mark, except one small fragment preserving xvi. 17–20, which is sufficient to show that it contained the last twelve verses of the Gospel, which Sinaitic, like ℵ and B, omits.

In Luke ix. 55 Curetonian has the words 'and he said, "You do not know what manner of spirit you are of"', with D (partially), the minor uncials, minuscules, and Latin versions, while Sinaitic omits them with 𝔭⁴⁵, ⁷⁵ ℵ B C L W. In xxiv. 42 Curetonian retains 'and of a honeycomb', whereas Sinaitic omits the words with 𝔭⁷⁵ ℵ A B D L W.

In John i. 35 Curetonian by an error reads 'Jesus' for Ἰωάννης of the Greek, and in vs. 36 inserts 'Lo, the Messiah!' before 'Lo, the Lamb of God!' In iii. 15 Curetonian omits 'should not perish but', with 𝔭⁷⁵ ℵ B W. In iv. 47 instead of 'and heal his son' Curetonian reads 'and see his son' (confusing, from similarity of sound, ܚܙܐ 'see' with ܐܣܝ 'heal'), and in vs. 52 the scribe reads 'ninth hour' for ὥραν ἑβδόμην, confusing ܬܫܥ with ܫܒܥ. In vi. 49 instead of 'manna' Curetonian reads 'bread'.

From the preceding examples it is obvious that the Old Syriac manuscripts preserve many noteworthy readings, some of which are not witnessed elsewhere.[1] In general the type of text represented in the two manuscripts belongs to the so-called Western type, though they also preserve many typically Alexandrian readings. Of the two witnesses Sinaitic differs from Curetonian in presenting, on the whole, a shorter text[2]—which is another way of saying that Curetonian incorporates a greater number of Western additions than does Sinaitic.

Linguistically the text of the Old Syriac Gospels, as Burkitt observed, 'is full of peculiarities of grammar and spelling which are hardly to be met elsewhere in Syriac literature, or are found only in the oldest and best preserved works'.[3] According to Torrey, the two manuscripts differ in that Sinaitic prefers words and idioms that are more typical of Palestinian Aramaic than of classical, Edessene Syriac.[4] Such a feature has been held to suggest an Antiochian origin of the form of text preserved in the Sinaitic manuscript.[5] Whether this was the work of one or of several translators was investigated by Hjelt, who, having made a comparison of parallel passages in the Gospels, concluded that the rendering represented in the Sinai palimpsest is not a unity, but that the individual Gospels were translated by three different persons, the oldest translation being the Gospel of Matthew, and the latest the Gospel of Luke.[6]

Although, as was mentioned earlier, no manuscript of the Old Syriac version of the Acts and Pauline Epistles has survived, more than one scholar has attempted to reconstruct fragments of such a version from citations of the Apostolos preserved in the writings

---

[1] For a discussion of the peculiarities of the text of the Curetonian manuscript, see Friedrich Baethgen, *Evangeliarfragmente. Der griechische Text des Cureton'schen Syrers wiederhergestellt* (Leipzig, 1885), pp. 32–54, and F. C. Burkitt, *Evangelion da-Mepharreshe*, ii (Cambridge, 1904), *passim*. The Sinaitic manuscript is the object of a learned and one-sided investigation by Adelbert Merx, *Die vier kanonischen Evangelien nach ihrem ältesten bekannten Texte. Übersetzung und Erläuterung der syrischen im Sinaikloster gefundenen Palimpsesthandschrift*, vol. i (Berlin, 1897), vol. ii in 3 parts (1902, 1905, 1911).

[2] For a list of important omissions in Syr[s], see A. S. Lewis, *The Old Syriac Gospels* (London, 1910), pp. xlvii–lxxviii.

[3] F. C. Burkitt, *Evangelion da-Mepharreshe*, ii (Cambridge, 1904), p. 39.

[4] Charles C. Torrey, *Documents of the Primitive Church*, pp. 250–69.

[5] So, e.g., Matthew Black, 'The Syriac Versional Tradition', in *Die alten Übersetzungen des Neuen Testaments, die Kirchenväterzitate und Lektionare*, ed. by K. Aland (Berlin and New York, 1972), p. 124.

[6] Arthur Hjelt, *Die altsyrische Evangelienübersetzung und Tatians Diatessaron, besonders in ihrem gegenseitigen Verhältnis* (Zahn's *Forschungen zur Geschichte des neutestamentlichen Kanons*, vii. 1; Leipzig, 1903), pp. 96–107, and 162 f.

of early Syrian Church Fathers. In the case of the Acts of the Apostles, the Armenian version of Ephraem's commentary[1] on that book discloses that 'the Syriac text used by Ephraem was distinctly, and doubtless thoroughly, Western'.[2] Zahn,[3] having made a detailed study of Aphraates' quotations from the Pauline Epistles, collected not a few passages that differ from the Peshitta. In still more systematic fashion, Molitor[4] combed the writings of Ephraem for citations from the Pauline Epistles; these show occasional agreements with Marcion and Tertullian, and often agree with G in opposition to a group of witnesses originating with D or supported by D.

The most extensive study of the Old Syriac text of Acts and the Pauline Epistles is that of Kerschensteiner. Although Acts was quoted much less frequently than Paul, sufficient evidence has survived to render it certain that Aphraates, Ephraem, and the author of the *Liber Graduum* used essentially the same 'Old Syriac' text of Acts.[5] In the case of the Pauline Epistles Kerschensteiner[6] collected and analysed nearly 700 citations and allusions from fifteen early Syriac authors. He found evidence to prove the existence of a unified Old Syriac text of fourteen Pauline Epistles[7] throughout the fourth century, and with no trace of an earlier, different text. The theological complexion of the text discloses no heretical traits, though there are not a few free and targumic-like renderings. Textually the version finds its nearest affinities with a mixed text-type comprising many Western and some Alexandrian readings, similar to that current in Asia Minor during the second century.[8]

The Catholic Epistles and the Apocalypse were not accepted as canonical by the early Syriac-speaking Church, and hence they do not form part of the Old Syriac version.

---

[1] F. C. Conybeare, 'The Commentary of Ephrem on Acts', in James H. Ropes, *The Text of Acts* (London, 1926), pp. 373–453.

[2] Ropes, op. cit., p. cxlviii.

[3] Theodor Zahn, *Geschichte des neutestamentlichen Kanons*, ii (Erlangen and Leipzig, 1890), pp. 556–64.

[4] Joseph Molitor, *Der Paulustext des hl. Ephraim aus seinem armenisch erhalten Paulinenkommentar untersucht und rekonstruiert* (Rome, 1938).

[5] Joseph Kerschensteiner, 'Beobachtungen zum altsyrischen Actatext', *Bib*, xlv (1964), 63–74.

[6] *Der altsyrische Paulustext* (*CSCO* cccxv, *Subsidia*, xxxvii; Louvain, 1970).

[7] Including 3 Corinthians (see pp. 161 and 163 below) and the Epistle to the Hebrews, but without Philemon.

[8] *Der altsyrische Paulustext*, p. 209.

3. PROBLEMS RELATING TO THE OLD SYRIAC VERSION

Despite the deal of research that has been expended upon the Old Syriac version, more than one vexing problem still remains unsolved. (*a*) What are the mutual relations between the Diatessaron and 'The Gospel of the Separated [Ones]', as the Sinaitic and Curetonian manuscripts were designated?[1] (*b*) What is the relation between the Old Syriac and the Peshitta? (*c*) How should we explain the rarity of extant manuscripts of the Old Syriac as compared with the numbers of Peshitta manuscripts?

The question of the mutual relations between the Diatessaron and the two extant witnesses to the Old Syriac version continues to be debated. Was Tatian's harmony the first form in which the evangelic narratives were known in Syria, and was the Syriac version of the separated Gospels made later, as is argued by Baethgen,[2] Wright,[3] Zahn,[4] Nestle,[5] Burkitt,[6] Turner,[7] Vogels,[8] Baumstark,[9] Dobschütz,[10] Lagrange,[11] Vööbus,[12] and Black?[13] Or, do the Sinaitic and Curetonian manuscripts

---

[1] At the beginning of the Curetonian manuscript stands the heading: 'Gospel of the *Mepharreshe*, Matthew'; the Sinaitic closes with a colophon: 'Here ends the Gospel of the *Mepharreshe*, four books.' The Syriac word *mepharreshe* ('separate ones [books]') is the passive participle of ܦܪܫ, and designates the individual Gospels as opposed to a harmony or diatessaron of the four Gospels (*Evangelion da-Meḥallete*, from ܚܠܛ, 'to mix or mingle').

[2] Friedrich Baethgen, *Evangelienfragmente*, pp. 95–6.

[3] William Wright, *A Short History of Syriac Literature* (London, 1895), p. 8.

[4] Theodor Zahn, *Theologische Litteraturblatt*, xvi (1895), pp. 17–21. Zahn had earlier favoured the priority of the separate Syriac Gospels; see his *Forschungen zur Geschichte des neutestamentlichen Kanons*, I. Theil (Erlangen, 1881), pp. 104–6.

[5] Eberhard Nestle in Hastings's *Dictionary of the Bible*, iv (1902), 457a.

[6] F. C. Burkitt, *Encyclopædia Biblica*, iv (1902), col. 4999, and *Evangelion da-Mepharreshe*, ii (Cambridge, 1904), 212.

[7] C. H. Turner, 'Historical Introduction to the New Testament', *JTS* xi (1910), 182 and 199.

[8] H. J. Vogels, *Die altsyrischen Evangelien in ihrem Verhältnis zur Tatians Diatessaron* (*Biblische Studien*, xvi. 5; Freiburg im Br., 1911), p. 144.

[9] Anton Baumstark, *Geschichte der syrischen Literatur mit Ausschluss der christlich-palästinensischer Texte* (Bonn, 1922), pp. 21–3.

[10] Ernst von Dobschütz, *Eberhard Nestle's Einführung in das griechische Neue Testament*, 4te Aufl. (Göttingen, 1923), p. 21.

[11] M.-J. Lagrange, *Critique textuelle*, ii. *La Critique rationnelle* (*Introduction à l'étude Ndu ouveau Testament*, ii; Paris, 1935), 204–13.

[12] Arthur Vööbus, *Studies in the History of the Gospel Text in Syriac* (*CSCO* cxxviii; Louvain, 1951), p. 168, and *Early Versions*, p. 78.

[13] Matthew Black, 'The Syriac Versional Tradition' (see p. 43 n. 5), pp. 126 ff. Earlier Black held to the priority of the separate Gospels (*An Aramaic Approach to the Gospels and Acts*, 3rd edn. (Oxford, 1967), pp. 265 ff.).

represent a pre-Tatianic form of the Syriac text, as Stenning,[1] Brockelmann,[2] Hjelt,[3] Lewis,[4] Harris,[5] Mingana,[6] and Torrey[7] have maintained?

On the one hand, it is argued that Tatian's harmony could not have been made from the Old Syriac version, in view of important differences in text and wording. For example, the Diatessaron apparently included the account of the great light on the Jordan at the Baptism of Jesus, as well as Matt. xvi. 2–3 and John v. 3–4, all of which are omitted by both Sinaitic and Curetonian, and the last twelve verses of Mark, Luke xxii. 43–4 and xxiii. 34, which are omitted in Sinaitic, but included by Curetonian.

On the other hand, those who think that the Old Syriac does not depend upon the Diatessaron pose the question: How should we conceive of the translator of the separated Gospels spending his time hunting through the Diatessaron to discover the rendering of this or that pericope, this or that verse? Furthermore, as Mingana phrases it, 'if this translator had considered the Diatessaron as an orthodox lucubration worthy of his attention, why did he omit all the apocryphal and mutilated verses that Tatian had accepted as authentic?'[8]

There is, of course, a third possibility, that Tatian and the Old Syriac represent more or less independent attempts to render the Greek. Burkitt championed this view, arguing that the Diatessaron reflects the type of Greek in use at Rome by the middle of the second century, while the Old Syriac is the work of someone who, while having some knowledge of the Diatessaron, was

---

[1] John F. Stenning ('Diatessaron', Hastings's *Dictionary of the Bible*, Extra Volume (New York, 1904), pp. 458–61), argues for the priority of the Old Syriac as represented by the Sinaitic manuscript.

[2] Carl Brockelmann, 'Die syrische und die christlich-arabische Litteratur', in Brockelmann, Finck, Leipoldt, and Littmann, *Geschichte der christlichen Litteraturen des Orients* (Leipzig, 1907), p. 8.

[3] Arthur Hjelt, op. cit. (p. 43 n. 6), pp. 162 f.

[4] Agnes Smith Lewis, 'Dr Vogels on the Old Syriac Gospels', *Exp*, 8th ser., v (1913), 52–62.

[5] J. R. Harris, 'An Important Reading in the Diatessaron', *ExpT* xxv (1913–14), 347–9.

[6] Alphonse Mingana, 'Lewisian and Curetonian Versions of the Gospels', *ExpT* xxxvi (1914–15), 47–8, 93–4, and 235–6.

[7] C. C. Torrey, *Documents of the Primitive Church*, p. 277.

[8] *ExpT* xxvi (1914–15), 235.

working from a Greek text in use at Antioch about the second half of the second century.[1]

Consideration of the relation between the Old Syriac and the Peshitta will be deferred until the following section, but the question of the rarity of extant manuscripts of the Old Syriac as compared with those of the later versions deserves a few comments here. The observation was made by Lake that

the various advocates of successive revisions [of the Syriac Scriptures] had apparently an almost unique aptitude for destroying all traces of rival predecessors. Theodoret, writing in the fifth century, mentions that he himself found over two hundred copies of Tatian in use in his province, and replaced them by the four Gospels. This vigorous line of action easily explains the disappearance of the Diatessaron, and the Old Syriac fared little better after the acceptance of the 'Vulgate', or Peshitta.[2]

There is also the possibility that instead of being, so to speak, an official Old Syriac version, the Old Syriac manuscripts may be merely the work of private individuals who wanted copies of the separated Gospels. When such activity began, according to Black, 'it is impossible to say, but the evidence we do possess points to the existence of such attempts in the middle of the fourth century'.[3] Most other scholars, however, would dispute so late a date, and, on the basis of the implications of evidence from earlier Syriac patristic quotations, argue for a much greater degree of antiquity of the Old Syriac version, holding that it goes back to the generation immediately following Tatian. In any case, few will dispute the judgement passed on the Curetonian manuscript by Hort a dozen years before the Sinai palimpsest was brought to light: 'The character of the fundamental text confirms the great antiquity of the version in its original form; while many readings suggest that, like the Latin version, it

---

[1] So Burkitt in *Evangelion da-Mepharreshe*, ii (1903), 207 ff. and 223 ff., summarized at the end of his life in *The Cambridge Ancient History*, xii (1939), 493 f. and 503. Lagrange, however, takes exception to classifying the Old Syriac as an Antiochian type of text (*La Critique textuelle*, p. 208).

[2] Kirsopp Lake, *The Text of the New Testament*, 6th edn., revd. by Silva New (London, 1928), p. 40.

[3] Black, 'The Syriac Versional Tradition', p. 130. Lagrange also saw no reason to date the Old Syriac texts earlier than the fourth century (*Critique textuelle*, pp. 208 and 212).

degenerated by transcription and perhaps also by irregular revision.'[1]

IV. THE PESHITTA SYRIAC VERSION

1. NOTEWORTHY MANUSCRIPTS OF THE PESHITTA NEW TESTAMENT

The word 'Peshitta'[2] is a passive participle of the verb ܦܫܛ ('stretched out') signifying, among other meanings, what is *simple* or *clear*. The word appears to have been employed for the first time in designating a version of the Scriptures by the Jacobite Moses bar Kepha (d. 903),[3] who applied it to the Syriac version of the Old Testament made from the Hebrew, in opposition to the version made by Paul of Tella from the Septuagint and supplied with complicated references drawn from Origen's Hexapla. In the case of the New Testament the same version would merit such an epithet in contrast to the Harclean version, which was furnished with a textual apparatus. Others interpret the word as meaning *widely diffused* or *current*. According to this interpretation the name 'Peshitta' is parallel to the Latin *Vulgata*.[4]

The Peshitta version antedates the division of Syrian Christianity into two rival communities, and hence it was accepted by the Nestorians as well as by the Jacobites. In its official form it includes twenty-two books of the New Testament, the four minor Catholic Epistles (2 Peter, 2 and 3 John, and Jude) and the Apocalypse being absent. It thus apparently reflects the canon according to the usage of the Church at Antioch in the fourth and fifth centuries. It does not include Luke xxii. 17–18 and the *pericope de adultera* (John vii. 53–viii. 11).

---

[1] *The New Testament in the Original Greek*; [ii] *Introduction [and] Appendix* (Cambridge, 1881), p. 84.

[2] The spelling 'Peshitto' represents the Jacobite pronunciation of the word. On the morphology of the word, see Eberhard Nestle, 'Zum Namen der syrischen Bibelübersetzung Peschiṭṭâ', *ZDMG* xlvii (1893), 157–9, and Ed. König, ibid., pp. 316–19.

[3] Syriac text in J. P. P. Martin, *Introduction à la critique textuelle du Nouveau Testament*, Partie théorique (Paris, 1883), p. 101 n. 1; French trans. of Syriac text in Rubens Duval, *Anciennes Littératures chrétiennes*; ii, *La Littérature syriaque*, 2nd edn. (Paris, 1900), pp. 31 f.

[4] Cf. M. Black in the *Bulletin* of the Studiorum Novi Testamenti Societas, i (1950), 51 f.

Syrian scribes devoted great care to the transcription of the
Peshitta version. A remarkable accord exists among the manuscripts of every age, there being on the average scarcely more
than one important variant per chapter.

At the beginning of the twentieth century Gregory[1] was able
to enumerate more than 300 Peshitta manuscripts of the New
Testament. Actually, however, the number is much larger, for
Gregory did not include all the manuscripts that are in the
libraries in the East. And since Gregory's time other manuscripts
have come to light, particularly in little-known collections in
the West.[2] Among manuscripts that have been catalogued the
following are noteworthy for one reason or another—usually by
reason of age.[3]

(1) What is considered[4] to be probably the oldest copy of a
portion of the New Testament in the Peshitta version is a fragment of a manuscript (Paris syr. MS. 296, 1°) containing Luke vi.
49–xxi. 37, written by what appears to be the same hand that

---

[1] See Caspar René Gregory, *Textkritik des Neuen Testamentes*, ii (Leipzig, 1902),
508–23; iii (1909), 1300–1 (it should be noted that in vol. ii Gregory provides
separate lists of manuscripts for the Gospels, the Acts and Catholic Epistles, and
the Pauline Epistles).

[2] See, e.g., Julius Assfalg's *Syrische Handschriften* (*Verzeichnis der orientalischen
Handschriften in Deutschland*, v; Wiesbaden, 1963); James T. Clemons, 'A Checklist
of Syriac Manuscripts in the United States and Canada', *OCP* xxxii (1966),
224–522; id., *An Index of Syriac Manuscripts containing the Epistles and the Apocalypse*
(*Studies and Documents*, xxxiii; Salt Lake City, 1968); and id., 'Some Additional
Information on Syriac Manuscripts in the United States', *Symposium Syriacum 1972*
(*Orientalia christiana analecta*, cxcvii; Rome, 1974), 505–8.

[3] On styles of Syriac writing, see W. H. P. Hatch, *An Album of Dated Syriac
Manuscripts* (Boston, 1946), pp. 24–40; on the dating of Syriac manuscripts, see
Ludger Bernhard, *Die Chronologie der syrischen Handschriften* (*Verzeichnis der orienta-
lischen Handschriften in Deutschland*, Suppl. xiv; Wiesbaden, 1971).

[4] So Anton Baumstark, *Geschichte der syrischen Literatur mit Ausschluss der christlich-
palästinenischen Texte* (Bonn, 1922), p. 73, Anm. 2. For a description of the manuscript, see J. B. Chabot in *JA*, ser. 9, viii (1896), 241.

The extravagant claims made by Norman M. Yonan for a seventh- or eighth-
century copy of the Peshitta New Testament known as the Yonan Codex, viz. that
it dates from about A.D. 350, that it is 'Christendom's most precious possession',
and that, being written in the language that Jesus used, it is more authentic than
any Greek manuscript of the New Testament, are altogether without foundation;
see the present writer's article, 'Is the Yonan Codex Unique?' *The Christian Century*, lxxiii (1956), 234–6, and Edward F. Siegman, 'The Yonan Codex of the New
Testament', *CBQ* xvii (1956), 151–7. A photographic facsimile of the manuscript,
which begins at Matt. ix. 35 and ends at Heb. xii. 9, is in the possession of the
Institute for Antiquity and Christianity, Claremont, California.

wrote British Museum MS. Add. 14425, which is dated A.D. 463/4.

(2) British Museum MS. Add. 14459 (fols. 1–66), written in a beautiful, Edessene Estrangela hand described by Wright (no. 90) as 'apparently of the vth century', contains the Gospels according to Matthew (beginning with vi. 20) and Mark.[1] It is bound with no. 8 below.

(3) The copy of the four Gospels known as codex Phillipps 1388, acquired in 1865 by the Royal Library in Berlin, was dated by Sachau[2] to the end of the fifth or the beginning of the sixth century. Certain features in its lectionary system have been thought to point to a date toward the close of the fifth century.[3] Its text seems to represent a stage between that of the Old Syriac and the fully developed Peshitta text (see p. 60 below).

(4) British Museum MS. Add. 17117, written in a good, regular Estrangela hand which is dated by Wright (no. 91) to the fifth century or the beginning of the sixth century (except fols. 1, 8, 23, 24, 63, and 64, which are perhaps three centuries later), contains the Gospels according to Matthew and Mark (i. 1–ix. 10).

(5) British Museum MS. Add. 14453, written in a large, regular Estrangela hand which is dated by Wright (no. 66) to the fifth or sixth century, contains the four Gospels (ending with John xx. 25).

(6) British Museum MS. 14470, written in an elegant Edessene hand which is dated by Wright (no. 63) to the fifth or sixth century (except fols. 96, 101, and 154–63, which seem to be of the ninth century), contains the four Gospels, the Pauline Epistles, Acts, James, 1 Peter, and 1 John.

(7) Morgan MS. 783, preserving 100 folios of a codex which is estimated to have had originally 216 folios, contains portions of

---

[1] Described by G. H. Gwilliam, 'An Account of a Syriac Biblical Manuscript of the Fifth Century', *Studia biblica* [*et ecclesiastica*, i] (Oxford, 1885), pp. 151–74.

[2] E. Sachau, *Verzeichnis der syrischen Handschriften der könig. Bibliothek zu Berlin*, i (Berlin, 1899), 10–15.

[3] Arthur Allgeier, 'Cod. syr. Phillipps 1388 und seine ältesten Perikopenvermerke', *OC*, N.S., vi (1916), 147–52; cf. also id., 'Cod. syr. Phillipps 1388 in Berlin und seine Bedeutung für die Geschichte der Pešitta', ibid., 3rd ser., vii (1932), 1–15.

three Gospels, beginning with Mark v. 23. According to Casey, 'the script is of the second half of the fifth or first half of the sixth century . . . not unlike that of British Museum Add. 14445, dated A.D. 532'.[1]

(8) The earliest-dated manuscript containing two of the Gospels in Syriac is British Museum MS. Add. 14459 (fols. 67–169), written, according to a partially legible colophon, between A.D. 528–9 and 537–8. It contains in a small, elegant Estrangela hand the Gospels according to Luke and John. It is bound with no. 2 above. For a specimen, see W. H. P. Hatch, *An Album of Dated Syriac Manuscripts* (Boston, 1946), plate xiii.

(9) The earliest-dated manuscript of the Peshitta Apostolos is British Museum MS. Add. 14479, written at Edessa in a small, elegant Estrangela hand in the year 533–4; it contains the Pauline Epistles. For a specimen, see Hatch's *Album*, plate xvi.

(10) The earliest-dated manuscript containing the four Gospels in Syriac is Vatican Cod. Sir. 12, written at Edessa in the year 548. For a specimen, see Hatch's *Album*, plate xx.

(11) The earliest-dated manuscript of the Syriac Gospels decorated with miniatures is the so-called 'Rabbula Gospels', written in the year 586 by a scribe named Rabbula in the Monophysite Monastery of Mar John, in Beth-Zagba. Today it is in the Laurentian Library of Florence (Plut. I, Cod. 56). For a specimen of the script, see Hatch's *Album*, plate xxxiv. A facsimile reproduction of all of the miniatures is available in *The Rabbula Gospels* . . . , ed. by Carlo Cecchelli, Giuseppi Furlani, and Mario Salmi (Olten and Lausanne, 1959).

Besides the manuscripts mentioned above which carry sixth-century dates in scribal colophons, on the basis of palaeographical considerations nearly fifty other Peshitta manuscripts have also been assigned to the sixth century.[2]

---

[1] R. P. Casey, 'New Testament Manuscripts in the Pierpont Morgan Library', *JTS*, n.s. ii (1951), 65.

[2] Of this number special attention may be drawn to Morgan MS. 784, a copy of the four Gospels, beginning at Matt. xix. 19, which is said by Casey (ibid., p. 65) to have a subscription at the close of the Gospel of Matthew identical with that in Phillipps MS. 1388. In view of this circumstance it would be of interest to determine to what extent variant readings characteristic of the Phillipps codex (no. 3 above) may be present also in the Morgan manuscript.

2. NOTEWORTHY PRINTED EDITIONS OF THE PESHITTA
NEW TESTAMENT[1]

The first printed edition of the Syriac New Testament[2] was prepared by the humanist Johann Albrecht Widmanstadt (or Widmanstetter), 1506–59, a senator and the Chancellor of Lower Austria. He had studied Syriac under Simeon, a Maronite bishop, and later collaborated with a Syrian Jacobite named Moses Mardinensis (i.e. from Mardin in Mesopotamia), who had been sent as legate to Pope Julius III. Moses brought with him a manuscript of the Syriac New Testament, which served as the basis of the printed volume. As regards the four Gospels Widmanstadt states that they were edited from two manuscripts. Besides the one belonging to Moses of Mardin, the other may have been a codex belonging to Teseo Ambrogio, whom Widmanstadt met at Reggio, but more probably was the Syriac tetraevangelion which he found in the Ptolemean Library at Sienna, and of which he made a transcript for himself.[3] Nothing further is known of these manuscripts, or of the manner in which Widmanstadt utilized them.

The Syriac type for the edition[4] was prepared from steel

---

[1] Toward the close of the nineteenth century Eberhard Nestle was able to list more than thirty editions of the Peshitta New Testament, several of them having been reprinted many times (*Syriac Grammar, with Bibliography, Chrestomathy and Glossary*, Eng. trans. from 2nd German edn., by R. S. Kennedy (Berlin, 1889)). Cf. also the anonymous article, 'The Printed Editions of the Syriac New Testament', *CQR* xxvi (1888), 257–9; I. H. Hall's Appendix, listing twenty-four editions of the Peshitta, in James Murdoch's English translation of the Peshitta New Testament, 6th edn. (Boston and London, 1893), pp. 496–98; and Alfred Durand, 'Les éditions imprimées du Nouveau Testament syriaque', *RSR* xi (1921), 385–409.

[2] ... *Liber Sacrosancti Evangelii de Iesu Christo Domino et Deo nostro. Reliqua hoc Codice comprehensa pagina proxima indicabit. Div. Ferdinandi rom. imperatoris designati iussu & liberalitate, characteribus & lingua Syra, Iesu Christo vernacula, Diuino ipsius ore cōsecrata, et à Ioh. Euāgelista Hebraica dicta, Scriptorio Prelo diligēter Expressa . . .* [Vienna, 1555].

Some copies are provided with about fifty additional pages (the colophon is dated February 1556), giving a primer of Syriac characters and syllables, as well as a reading-book arranged in four columns at each opening. The selections, which are given (right to left) in Syriac, in Hebrew characters, with transliteration of Syriac, and with Latin translation, include the Sanctus, the Lord's Prayer (with 'Forgive us our debts and our sins', i.e. a text made up from Matthew and Luke), the Athanasian Creed, the Magnificat, and a prayer for the dead. For a description of a copy printed in 1562, see F. C. Burkitt in *Proceedings of the Cambridge Antiquarian Society*, xi (1906), 265–8.

[3] See G. H. Gwilliam in *Studia biblica et ecclesiastica*, ii (Oxford, 1890), 267–9.

[4] The earliest Syriac type (Estrangela characters) was that used in Wilhelm

punches which a Swabian artist of Ellwagen, Caspar Crapht (Kraft), had engraved in imitation of the beautiful and distinctive handwriting of Moses of Mardin.[1] A thousand copies of the edition were printed at Venice in 1555 by Michael Cymbermann (Zimmermann) under the auspices and at the expense of Ferdinand I, King of Hungary and Bohemia, who three years later became Emperor of the Holy Roman Empire. In the Latin preface Widmanstadt expresses the hope that the edition might help promote the union of Christendom.

It is of interest that a reference to Widmanstadt's edition is included in the 1611 English Bible. In the preface, known as 'The Translators to the Reader', mention is made of versions of the Scriptures in various vernaculars; in this context it is stated, 'So the *Syrian* translation of the New Testament is in most learned mens Libraries, of *Widminstadius* his setting forth.'[2]

The second edition of the Syriac New Testament (Geneva, 1569) was prepared by Immanuel Tremellius, professor of Hebrew in the University of Heidelberg (1561–77). Although printed in Hebrew characters for lack of Syriac type, according to Darlow and Moule

it represents an advance on Widmanstadt's text, in that Tremellius attempted to give the vocalization fully, and especially collated for his text a Syriac MS. then preserved in the Elector Palatine's Library at Heidelberg. . . . The close Latin translation of the Syriac which he added was used as a basis for similar translations by later editors down to the time of Schaaf.[3]

At 1 John v. 7 Tremellius placed in the margin the *comma Johanneum*, translated by himself into Syriac.

Postel's *Linguarum duodecim characteribus differentium alphabetum* . . . and *Grammatica Arabica*, both published in 1538 at Paris. More than half a century earlier Bernhard von Breydenbach's *Peregrinatio in terram sanctam* . . . (Mainz, 1486) had utilized Syriac and other oriental alphabets in woodcut (see Eberhard Nestle, 'Geschichte des syrischen Drucks', in *Marksteine aus der Weltlitteratur in Originalschriften*, ed. by Johannes Baensch-Drugulin (Leipzig, 1902), pp. 35 ff. from end of volume, and Werner Strothmann, *Die Anfänge der syrischen Studien in Europa* (*Göttinger Orientforschungen*; I. Reihe: *Syriaca*, i; Wiesbaden, 1971).

[1] So Eberhard Nestle ('Zur Geschichte der syrischen Typen', *ZDMG* lxxv (1903), 16 f.), who thought he had identified the very manuscript used as a model.
[2] *The Translators to the Reader. Preface to the King James Version 1611*, ed. by Edgar J. Goodspeed (Chicago, 1935), p. 5 of facsimile.
[3] T. H. Darlow and H. F. Moule, *Historical Catalogue of the Printed Editions of Holy Scripture* . . . , ii (London, 1911), 1531.

The first edition of the Syriac New Testament to include the minor Catholic Epistles (2 Peter, 2 and 3 John, Jude) and the Apocalypse, though they formed no part of the original Peshitta, was that contained in volume v (issued in two parts, 1630, 1633) of Guy Michel Le Jay's Paris Polyglot Bible. Gabriel Sionita, a Maronite scholar from Syria who at that time was Regius Professor and Interpreter of Syriac and Arabic at Paris, was mainly responsible for editing the Syriac text and its Latin translation. The Syriac vowels are here fully printed for the first time.

Volume v of Brian Walton's London Polyglot Bible (1657) reproduces essentially the text of Sionita's edition, adding as well the *pericope de adultera* after John vii. 52. Aegidius Gutbier, whose edition (Hamburg, 1663, 1664) incorporates all of the above-mentioned additions, even went so far as to introduce 1 John v. 7 into the text.

The last of this series is the well-known edition of Johann Leudsen and Carl Schaaf (Leiden, 1708; 2nd edn., 1717), which inserts, with inferior manuscript authority, 'raise the dead' at Matt. x. 8 (see Tischendorf, ad loc., with the note of Pusey–Gwilliam). The sub-title of the edition proudly declares that the volume is furnished with a collation of the variant readings of all the previous editions ('Ad omnes editiones diligenter recensitum et variis lectionibus magno labore collectis adornatum').

According to Darlow and Moule,

the editors disagreed about the system of printing to be adopted. Accordingly up to Luke xviii. 26 they give the Chaldean system, used by Tremellius and others, which Leusden preferred. After xviii. 26 the printing follows the Syrian system, used in the Paris and London polyglots and approved by C. Schaaf. Leusden died in 1699, when the work had reached Luke xv. 20, and his colleague completed the task alone.[1]

The foundation for an edition of the Gospels based on the collation of many Syriac manuscripts was laid by Philip Edward Pusey (1830–80), the deaf and crippled son of Edward Bouverie Pusey, the Tractarian leader. After Pusey's death the work of collating was continued by George Henry Gwilliam, and in 1901 the Clarendon Press published at Oxford under both their names the edition entitled *Tetraeuangelium Sanctum juxta simplicem Syro-*

[1] T. H. Darlow and H. F. Moule, *Historical Catalogue of the Printed Editions of Holy Scripture* . . . , ii (London, 1911), 1537.

rum versionem. . . . The edition rests upon forty-two manuscripts, not all of which were collated fully,[1] and some of which
are fragmentary. The resultant text agrees, to a very remarkable
extent, with that of the *editio princeps* of 1555.[2] The edition
provides information from the Nestorian Massora, and the text
is divided into paragraphs in accordance with the evidence of
the most ancient manuscripts. A Latin translation is on facing
pages.

In 1905 the British and Foreign Bible Society published a
reprint of Pusey and Gwilliam's edition, modified in several
respects. The edition[3] is without the apparatus and other notes
of the 1901 edition; on the other hand, two passages, lacking in
all manuscripts of the Peshitta, are inserted, namely Luke xxii.
17–18 and John vii. 53–viii. 11. The passages, a note explains,
were taken from the Syriac New Testament prepared for the
Bible Society in 1816 by Dr. Samuel Lee, and 'for the sake of
completeness are inserted in this edition, but are placed within
special marks [heavy square brackets] to indicate the different
authority on which they rest'.

In 1920 the Bible Society issued the Syriac text of the entire
New Testament.[4] For the text of the Acts of the Apostles, the
three major Catholic Epistles (James, 1 Peter, 1 John), and the
Pauline Epistles (including Hebrews) permission was granted to
make use of the critical revision of the Peshitta prepared by
Gwilliam for the Clarendon Press along lines similar to his
earlier work on the Gospels. In the collation of manuscripts[5]

---

[1] e.g. the aberrant codex Phillipps 1388 (no. 3 in the list above) was only partially collated; see the note in Pusey and Gwilliam's edition, pp. 316 f.

[2] For the criticism that Gwilliam determined his text by a majority vote of his
manuscripts and therefore produced 'the latest not the earliest text of the Peshitta
Tetraeuangelium', see Matthew Black, 'The Text of the Peshitta Tetraeuangelium',
Studia Paulina in honorem Johannes de Zwaan (Haarlem, 1953), p. 26.

Besides codex Phillipps 1388 (which has no fewer than seventy Old Syriac
readings), two other Peshitta manuscripts mentioned in Gwilliam's apparatus contain an appreciable number of Old Syriac readings: a Vatican manuscript dated
A.D. 548 (no. 10 in the list above) and codex Dawkins III, of disputed date (Payne
Smith assigned it to the ninth century, but Burkitt and Gwilliam to a time prior
to the middle of the sixth century).

[3] *The Fourfold Gospel . . . Tetraeuangelium Sanctum. In the Peshitta Version* (London,
1905). Each Gospel is paginated separately, a feature which allowed the Bible
Society to issue the Gospels individually.

[4] *The New Testament in Syriac* (London, 1905–20; repr. 1950).

[5] For the identity of the several manuscripts, see R. Kilgour, *ExpT* xxxiii
(1921–2), 332, and A. Guillaume, ibid., pp. 519 f.

the editor received help from John Pinkerton, who carried on and completed this work after Gwilliam's death in 1913. The remainder of the New Testament is taken from John Gwynn's editions of the four minor Catholic Epistles (1909) and Revelation (1897); for these editions, see pp. 66 and 68 below.

The edition has a remarkable reading at Heb. ii. 16, apparently unknown to any other version or to any Greek manuscript: 'For not over angels has death authority [*or* dominion], but over the seed of Abraham it has authority [*or* dominion].' According to Albert Bonus,[1] this reading, which is not found in any other printed edition of the Peshitta, is supported by fourteen of twenty Syriac manuscripts which he inspected, including the two oldest.

3. PROBLEMS CONCERNING THE DATE AND TEXTUAL AFFINITIES OF THE PESHITTA NEW TESTAMENT

Until the beginning of the twentieth century it was commonly held that the Peshitta Syriac translation was one of the earliest versions, if not the earliest, of the New Testament to be made.[2] The constant tradition among Syrian Christians has been that it was the work of one or more of the original Apostles or Evangelists, some naming Mark and others Thaddeus as the translator. Among European scholars there was general agreement that the Peshitta was in existence by the end of the second century, and certainly by the beginning of the third. Several went so far as to suppose that it was made near the close of the first century or early in the second.[3]

---

[1] 'Heb. ii. 16 in the Peshitta Syriac Version', *ExpT*, xxxiii (1921–2), 234–6.

[2] See, e.g., Richard Simon, *Histoire critique des versions du Nouveau Testament* (Rotterdam, 1690), pp. 159–64; J. P. P. Martin, *Introduction à la critique textuelle du Nouveau Testament*, Partie théorique (Paris, 1883), pp. 98–135; S. P. Tregelles, vol. iv of Thomas H. Horne's *Introduction to the Critical Study and Knowledge of the Holy Scriptures*, 13th edn. (London, 1872), pp. 258–69; G. H. Gwilliam, 'The Materials for the Criticism of the Peshitta New Testament, with Specimens of the Syriac Massorah', *Studia biblica et ecclesiastica*, iii (Oxford, 1891), 47–103; and [id.] 'The Text of the Syriac Gospels', *CQR* xl (1895), 102–32.

[3] Those who assigned a first-century date include Brian Walton, Carpzov, Leusden, Bishop Lowth, and Kennicott. J. D. Michaelis ascribed the Syriac version of *both* Testaments to the close of the first or to the earlier part of the second century (*Introduction to the New Testament*, 4th edn., vol. ii, part 1 (London, 1823), 29–38).

In 1901 F. C. Burkitt published a slender monograph which altered scholarly opinion concerning the date of the Peshitta.[1] After separating the spurious writings of Ephraem from the genuine ones, Burkitt found that the numerous Gospel quotations made by that prominent Syrian ecclesiastic, who died about A.D. 373, afford no evidence that he was acquainted with the Peshitta text, but rather that he relied upon a different and presumably earlier rendering of the separated Gospels.

The same scholar also advanced the hypothesis that the Peshitta version of the New Testament was made by or for Rabbula, bishop of Edessa, probably in the early years of his episcopate, which extended from A.D. 411 to 435. Rabbula, according to a statement made by his biographer, an unknown cleric of Edessa writing about 450, 'translated by the wisdom of God that was in him the New Testament from Greek into Syriac, because of its variations, exactly as it was'.[2] This remark had indeed attracted the attention of scholars before Burkitt. Nestle thought that Rabbula's work involved a revision by way of further assimilation of the Peshitta to some Greek text.[3] Wright considered it more probable that Rabbula's revision was 'a first step in the direction of the Philoxenian version'.[4] Burkitt, however, connected the biographer's remark with the first publication of the Peshitta, arguing that 'from the time of Rabbula the Syriac Vulgate holds a position of absolute supremacy. Before Rabbula, no trace of the Peshitta: after Rabbula, hardly a trace of any other text.'[5]

The hypothesis of the Rabbulan authorship of the Peshitta New Testament soon came to be adopted by almost all scholars, being persuaded perhaps more by the confidence with which

---

[1] *S. Ephraim's Quotations from the Gospel* (*Texts and Studies*, vii; Cambridge, 1901; repr. Nendeln, Liechtenstein, 1967).

[2] J. J. Overbeck, *S. Ephraemi Syri Rabulae episcopi Edessani Balaei aliorumque opera selecta* (Oxford, 1865), p. 172, lines 18–20; the translation given here is that of Burkitt (op. cit., p. 57).

For what is known of Rabbula and his career as bishop of Edessa, see Georg G. Blum, *Rabbula von Edessa. Der Christ, der Bischof, der Theolog* (*CSCO* ccc, *Subsidia*, 34; Louvain, 1969). H. S. Pelser has promised the publication of his doctoral dissertation, *Rabbula, the Bishop of Edessa* (cf. Pelser in *De fructu oris sui, Essays in Honour of Adrianus von Selms*, ed. by I. H. Eybers *et al.* (Leiden, 1971), p. 162 n. 1).

[3] Eberhard Nestle, *Real-Encyklopädie für protestantische Theologie und Kirche*, 2te Aufl. xv (1885), 195.

[4] William Wright, *A Short History of Syriac Literature* (London, 1894), p. 11.

[5] *Evangelion da-Mepharreshe*, ii (1904), 161.

Burkitt propounded it than by any proof other than circumstantial evidence. Among the few dissenting voices,[1] Vööbus has
repeatedly attacked the validity of Burkitt's reconstruction of the
history of the Peshitta, pointing out that it rests solely on speculation and that, before one can confidently regard it as probable,
Rabbula's quotations from the New Testament must be examined
with a view to determining what version he himself commonly
used. In default of the existence of any extensive composition by
Rabbula himself, Vööbus analysed the New Testament quotations in Rabbula's Syriac translation of Cyril of Alexandria's
Περὶ τῆς ὀρθῆς πίστεως, written shortly after the beginning of the
Nestorian controversy in 430.[2] In this translation, instead of
rendering Cyril's quotations from Scripture, Rabbula inserted
the wording of the current Syriac version—a method which more
than one author followed in translating from Greek into Syriac.
Vööbus discovered that in this treatise, published by Rabbula
near the end of his life, only the shortest of the several citations
(totalling about thirty-five from the Gospels, and about forty
from the Epistles) agree with the Peshitta, and that many of the
others, in differing from the Peshitta, agree with either the Old
Syriac or the Diatessaron.[3]

Continuing his research into the history of the use made of the
Peshitta in the fifth century, Vööbus[4] analysed the nature of the
Gospel text used by Rabbula's contemporaries and successors, as
well as that included in the Syriac translation of the Acts of the
Synod of Ephesus. Here too there is little or no evidence of the
use of the Peshitta version among fifth-century Syriac sources.
Furthermore, contrary to Burkitt's dictum that after Rabbula
there is to be found hardly a trace of an Old Syriac text, Vööbus

---

[1] The most notable exceptions to the otherwise universal chorus of approval
of Burkitt's hypothesis were F. Nau in *Dictionnaire de la Bible*, v (Paris, 1912),
col. 1926; id., *RHR* ciii (1931), 115; J. R. Harris (tentatively), 'The Syriac New
Testament', *Exp*, 8th ser., vi (1913), 456–65; and Alphonse Mingana, 'The
Remaining Versions of the Gospels', *ExpT* xxvi (1915–16), 379; cf. id., 'A New
Doctrine of Christian Monachism', *Exp*, 8th ser., ix (1915), 378.

[2] The Syriac text is available in *Acta Martyrum et sanctorum*, ed. P. Bedjan, v
(Paris, 1895), 628 ff.; the Greek text is in Migne, *PG* lxxvi, cols. 1133 ff.

[3] Arthur Vööbus, *Investigations into the Text of the New Testament Used by Rabbula
of Edessa* (*Contributions of Baltic University*, no. 59; Pinneberg, 1947).

[4] *Researches on the Circulation of the Peshitta in the Middle of the Fifth Century*, and
Neue Ergebnisse in der Erforschung der Geschichte der Evangelientexte im Syrischen, being
Contributions of Baltic University, nos. 64 and 65 respectively (Pinneberg, 1948), and
'Das Alter der Peschitta', *OC*, 4th ser., ii (1954), 1–10.

collected not a few Old Syriac (or, at least, non-Peshitta) readings that continue to turn up in authors long after Rabbula.[1] In Vööbus's opinion, the Peshitta, though older than Rabbula's time,[2] met with considerable opposition, and was not introduced in Edessa as the official Gospel text until the end of the fifth or the beginning of the sixth century.[3]

Other scholars have joined Vööbus in challenging Burkitt's thesis, though they do not always see eye to eye with his reconstruction of the history of the Gospel text in Syriac. Matthew Black, for example, having analysed the quotations in Rabbula's translation of Cyril of Alexandria's treatise, concluded that Rabbula's quotations from the Gospels were made from a form of text that was 'a kind of half-way house between the Old Syriac represented by S and C and the final and definitive form of the Syriac Vulgate which has come down to us'.[4]

In analysing the nature of the Gospel text used in the biography of Rabbula, Baarda has found that the biographer's text of Matthew and Luke 'was less revised and contained more archaic elements than both S^P and S^{cs} have preserved. . . . The text of John used by the author of Rabbula's life was a more revised one than that of the extant Old Syriac manuscripts, although not yet the very same text that we have in the collated manuscripts of the Pešitta.'[5]

The question who it was that produced the Peshitta version of the New Testament will perhaps never be answered. That it was not Rabbula has been proved by Vööbus's researches. At the same time one is reluctant to believe that the statement by Rabbula's biographer is without any historical foundation. Baarda may well be correct in his supposition that Rabbula's work of revision was not a radical one: 'The purpose', he

---

[1] Arthur Vööbus, *Studies in the History of the Gospel Text in Syriac* (*CSCO* cxxviii, *Subsidia*, 3; Louvain, 1951), pp. 72–86.

[2] 'The Oldest Extant Traces of the Syriac Peshitta', *Mu*, lxiii (1950), 191–204.

[3] *Studies in the History of the Gospel Text in Syriac*, p. 175.

[4] 'Rabbula of Edessa and the Peshitta', *BJRL* xxxiii (1951), 209; cf. also id., 'The New Testament Peshitta and its Predecessors', *Bulletin of the Studiorum Novi Testamenti Societas*, i (1950), 51–62; 'Zur Geschichte des syrischen Evangelientextes', *TLZ* lxxvii (1952), cols. 705–10; and 'The Syriac New Testament in Early Patristic Tradition', *La Bible et les Pères, Colloque de Strasbourg (1er-3 octobre 1969)*, ed. by André Benoit and Pierre Prigent (Paris, 1971), pp. 263–78.

[5] Tj. Baarda, 'The Gospel Text in the Biography of Rabbula', *VC* xiv (1960), 124.

suggests, 'was to have a more accurate translation of passages that were important in the Christological discussions within the Edessenian clergy.'[1] Consequently, most of the changes Rabbula introduced involved passages in the Gospel according to John, a feature that, as was mentioned above, is reflected in the Gospel quotations included in the biography of Rabbula.

It appears that, besides Rabbula, other leaders in the Syrian Church also had a share in producing the Peshitta. The presence of a diversity of mannerisms and style in the Peshitta Gospels and Apostolos suggests that the revision of the Old Syriac was not homogeneous, but the work of several hands.[2] Whether, as Rendel Harris thought,[3] one of the translators was Mar Koumi, a well-known Syrian bishop of the fifth century, is problematic. In any case, however, in view of the adoption of the same version of the Scriptures by both the Eastern (Nestorian) and Western (Jacobite) branches of Syrian Christendom, we must conclude that it had attained a considerable degree of status before the division of the Syrian Church in A.D. 431. Despite the remarkable degree of unanimity of reading among most manuscripts of the Peshitta version, there are occasional copies, such as codex Phillipps 1388 (see p. 50 above), that preserve scores of Old Syriac *variae lectiones*, a feature that, as Black remarks, 'disposes of the textual myth of a fixed Peshitta New Testament text, with little or no internal evidence of variants to shed light on its development and history'.[4]

Finally, some attention must be given to problems involved in determining the textual affinities of the Peshitta version of the

---

[1] Tj. Baarda, 'The Gospel Text in the Biography of Rabbula', *VC* xiv (1960), 127.

[2] Cf. Arthur Vööbus, *Early Versions of the New Testament*, pp. 98 f., and T. C. Falla, 'Studies in the Peshitta Gospels; an Examination of Four Groups of Peshitta Gospel Words and their Contribution to the Study of the Peshitta as a Revision' (unpublished Ph.D. thesis, University of Melbourne, 1971), pp. 328–33, and id., 'Demons and Demoniacs in the Peshitta Gospels', *Abr-Nahrain*, ix (1969–70), 43–65, esp. 59.

In the Peshitta text of the Pauline Epistles evidence has been found of dependence upon an earlier West Aramaic version similar to that preserved in the Palestinian Syriac version (see L. Delekat, 'Die Syropalästinische Übersetzung der Paulusbriefe und die Peschitta', *NTS* iii (1956–7), 223–33).

[3] 'Some Notes on the History of the Syriac New Testament', *Exp*, 8th ser., vi (1913), 456–65.

[4] Matthew Black, 'The Text of the Peshitta Tetraeuangelium', *Studia Paulina in honorem Johannes de Zwaan* (Haarlem, 1953), p. 27.

New Testament. It has been frequently stated that the type of text represented by the Peshitta is what Hort designated the Syrian text and Ropes the Antiochian—a form of text which also appears in the writings of John Chrysostom and which eventually developed into the Byzantine Textus Receptus.[1] Nevertheless, in a considerable number of readings the Peshitta agrees with one or other of the pre-Syrian Greek texts, against the Antiochian Fathers and the late Greek text.[2] In a detailed examination of Matt. chaps. i–xiv, Gwilliam found that the Peshitta agrees with the Textus Receptus 108 times and with codex Vaticanus (B) sixty-five times, while in 137 instances it differs from both, usually with the support of the Old Syriac and/or the Old Latin, though in thirty-one instances (almost one-fourth of the whole number) it stands alone.[3] From these data he concluded that the unknown author of the Peshitta 'revised an ancient work by Greek MSS. which have no representatives now extant, and thus has transmitted to us an independent witness to the Greek Text of the New Testament'.[4]

In a similar examination of the Peshitta text of Mark,[5] Mrs. Downs collected all significant readings in that Gospel where the Sinaitic Syriac (the Curetonian manuscript fails almost completely for Mark) and the Peshitta are identical, but where all other witnesses disagree. Seventy unique agreements were found. She also drew up a list of agreements between the Sinai palimpsest and the Peshitta in Mark having some support in Greek manuscripts or in other versions or both. An analysis of the 135 readings of this list shows that

in no case is the Neutral, Caesarean, or Western the prime factor in the composition of the text which Rabbula and his assistants used in making the Peshitto. . . . The fact that the MSS and versions which share these readings with the Syriac are habitually allied to the

---

[1] So, e.g., Hermann von Soden, *Die Schriften des Neuen Testaments*; I. *Untersuchungen*, i (Berlin, 1902), 1459 f.

[2] So Westcott and Hort, *The New Testament in the Original Greek*, [ii] *Introduction [and] Appendix*, 2nd edn. (London, 1896), pp. 136 f.

[3] G. H. Gwilliam, 'The Place of the Peshitto Version in the Apparatus Criticus of the Greek New Testament', *Studia biblica et ecclesiastica*, v. (1903), 187–237.

[4] Ibid., p. 237.

[5] Hope Broome Downs, 'The Peshitto as a Revision: its Background in Syriac and Greek Texts in Mark', *JBL* lxiii (1944), 141–59. The article is a condensation of Mrs. Downs's unpublished Ph.D. dissertation (with the same title) at Bryn Mawr College (1943).

Evangelion da-Mepharreshe, not to the Peshitto, carries its own decisive evidence. . . . Obviously Rabbula used a copy of the Evangelion da-Mepharreshe as the basis of his translation.[1]

As for the textual affinities of the Greek manuscript or manuscripts used in revising an Old Syriac base, Mrs. Downs's research partly confirms and partly contradicts the generally accepted opinion of the textual complexion of the Peshitta. On the one hand, she found that of the 135 readings mentioned above the Peshitta agrees with the Ecclesiastical text in nearly half of the readings (48·9 per cent). On the other hand, of the several strands that account for the non-Ecclesiastical elements in the Peshitta, the Western type of text (D W[Mk i-v] Old Latin) provides an unexpectedly large proportion of agreement (29·1 per cent). Thus it appears that, contrary to the customary view which regards the Peshitta as an almost typical witness to the later form of text, a large number of its readings in Mark agree with the Old Syriac, and of the remainder only about one-half agree with the Koine or Ecclesiastical text.[2]

In the case of the Acts of the Apostles, Hatch found that the Peshitta 'contains many "Western" readings, but its text is mainly that of the Old Uncial family'.[3] According to the evaluation made by Ropes, the rendering is often very free, somewhat after the manner of the Western text; the translator has a habit of expressing one Greek word by two Syriac ones. With regard to its relation to the later type of text, Ropes declares: 'The readings which depart from the Old Uncial text and follow the Antiochian are usually also found in "Western" witnesses, and there seems no trace of the peculiar and distinctive selection of readings which is the chief recognizable characteristic of the Antiochian text.'[4]

For the rest of the New Testament in the Peshitta version very little research has been undertaken. In a hitherto unpublished dissertation James T. Clemons makes a study of the Syriac text of

---

[1] Hope Broome Downs, op. cit., p. 151.

[2] Ibid., p. 155.

[3] William H. P. Hatch (with James Hardy Ropes), 'The Vulgate, Peshitto, Sahidic, and Bohairic Versions of Acts and the Greek Manuscripts', *HTR* xxi (1928), 81.

[4] James Hardy Ropes, *The Text of Acts*, being vol. iii of *The Beginnings of Christianity*, Part I, *The Acts of the Apostles*, ed. by F. J. Foakes Jackson and Kirsopp Lake (London, 1926), p. cxlix.

the Epistle to the Galatians, based on the collation of eighteen manuscripts and five printed editions and illustrated by patristic citations preserved in about fifty Syriac treatises. As regards textual affinities, Clemons concludes that 'the Peshitta [of Galatians] contains several readings that cannot be traced entirely to a Greek original represented by the Textus Receptus'.[1]

In view of the abundance of manuscripts of the Peshitta, some of them of great antiquity, it is to be regretted that during the twentieth century so little scholarly effort has been directed to solving the many problems that clamour for attention. Among the most pressing *desiderata* is the publication of a concordance to the Peshitta New Testament.[2]

V. THE PHILOXENIAN AND/OR HARCLEAN VERSION(S)

1. THE NATURE OF THE PROBLEM

One of the most confused and confusing tangles connected with the Syriac versions involves the identification of the Philoxenian and/or Harclean version(s). The scanty evidence preserved in several colophons of Syriac manuscripts has usually been interpreted in one of two ways.[3] On the one hand, it has been held that the Syriac version produced in A.D. 508 for Philoxenus, bishop of Mabbûg (Hierapolis), by Polycarp his chorepiscopus

---

[1] 'Studies in the Syriac Text of Galatians', Ph.D. dissertation, Duke University, 1963; cf. *Dissertation Abstracts*, xxiv (Ann Arbor, 1964), pp. 4827 f. Clemons's article, 'Some Questions on the Syriac Support for Variant Greek Readings' (*NovT* x (1968), 26–30) draws upon his research concerning the rendering of Κηφᾶς, γάρ, and δέ in the Peshitta text of Galatians.

[2] In 1926 the Revd. Albert Bonus of Alphington, Exeter, finished making a handwritten copy (on about 600 sheets of foolscap) of a concordance of the Peshitta New Testament (an occasional section has been crossed out). Today Bonus's concordance is in the possession of the Department of Middle Eastern Studies, University of Melbourne. Dr. T. C. Falla is at work preparing a comprehensive index to the Peshitta Gospels, with indication of the corresponding Greek word for each Syriac word.

[3] The sceptical views of Gressmann and Lebon, that there is no certain trace of the Philoxenian version and that the Harclean has not yet been discovered, have found no approval among other scholars (Hugo Gressmann, 'Studien zum syrischen Tetraevangelium; I, Besitzen wir die Philoxeniana oder Harclensis?' *ZNW* v (1904), 248–52; Jules Lebon, 'La version philoxénienne de la Bible', *RHE* xii (1911), 413–36). Adequate rebuttals of these views are given in the criticism of Lebon (by Lagrange?) in *RB* ix (1912), 141–3, and the article by L.-J. Delaporte 'L'évangéliaire héracléen et la tradition karkaphienne', ibid. 391–402.

was reissued in 616 by Thomas of Harkel (Heraclea), bishop of Mabbûg, who merely added marginal notes derived from two or three Greek manuscripts (so White,[1] Tregelles,[2] Martin,[3] Clark,[4] New,[5] Lagrange,[6] Kümmel,[7] and McHardy[8]). On the other hand, it has been held that the Philoxenian version was thoroughly revised by Thomas, who also added in the margin certain readings which he considered to be important but not worthy of inclusion in the text (so Bernstein,[9] Gwynn,[10] Wright,[11] Burkitt,[12] Kenyon,[13] Ropes,[14] Lake,[15] Hatch,[16] Zuntz,[17] Vööbus,[18] and, tentatively, Black[19]).

[1] Joseph White, *Sacrorum evangeliorum versio Syriaca Philoxeniana ex codd. mss. Ridleianis in bibl. coll. Nov. Oxon. repositis nunc primum edita*, i (Oxford, 1778), pp. xviii–xxi.

[2] S. P. Tregelles, op. cit. (p. 56 n. 2 above), pp. 269–78.

[3] J. P. P. Martin, op. cit. (p. 48 n. 3 above), pp. 135–63.

[4] A. C. Clark states his view very briefly in *JTS* xxix (1927), 19, and subsequently at greater length in 'The Philoxenian Text' in his *The Acts of the Apostles* (Oxford, 1933), pp. 305–29.

[5] Silva New, 'The Harclean Version of the Gospels', *HTR* xxi (1928), 376–95.

[6] Lagrange, *Critique textuelle*, p. 229.

[7] W. G. Kümmel, 'Textkritik und Textgeschichte des Neuen Testaments, 1914–1937', *ThRu*, N.F., x (1938), 32.

[8] William Duff McHardy, 'James of Edessa's Citations from the Philoxenian Text of the Book of Acts', *JTS* xliii (1942), 168.

[9] G. H. Bernstein, *De Charklensi Novi Testamenti translatione Syriaca commentatio* (Breslau, 1937), p. 5.

[10] John Gwynn, articles 'Polycarpus Chorepiscopus' and 'Thomas Harklensis', in Smith and Wace's *Dictionary of Christian Biography*, iv (1887), 431–4 and 1014–21; *The Apocalypse of St. John in a Syriac Version hitherto unknown* . . . (Dublin, 1897); and *Remnants of the Later Syriac Versions of the Bible* (London, 1909; repr. Amsterdam, 1973).

[11] William Wright, *A Short History of Syriac Literature*, p. 16.

[12] F. C. Burkitt, *Encyclopædia Biblica*, iv, col. 5005.

[13] F. G. Kenyon, *Handbook to the Textual Criticism of the New Testament*, 2nd edn. (London, 1912), pp. 164–7. Kenyon refers to the two stages of the development of the Philoxenian and the Harclean version, and the considerable modification of the text which Thomas introduced.

[14] James H. Ropes, *The Text of Acts* (London, 1926), p. clx.

[15] K. Lake, *The Text of the New Testament*, 6th edn., p. 42.

[16] William H. P. Hatch, 'The Subscription in the Chester Beatty Manuscript of the Harclean Gospels', *HTR* xxx (1937), 143.

[17] G. Zuntz, *The Ancestry of the Harklean New Testament* (London, n.d.), p. 76.

[18] Arthur Vööbus, 'New Data for the Solution of the Problem Concerning the Philoxenian Version', *Spiritus et veritas. Festschrift Karl Kundzinš* (Eutin, 1953), pp. 169–86.

[19] Matthew Black, 'The Syriac Versional Tradition', op. cit. (p. 43 n. 5 above), pp. 139–41. According to Black, Thomas's revision of the Philoxenian 'hardly appears to have been a major operation. . . . At times Thomas does no more than "touch up" the Philoxenian version' (p. 141).

According to the former view, there is but one version which was republished with variant readings added in the margin; according to the latter view, there are two separate versions entirely, the later one being provided with marginalia. Furthermore, if the second reconstruction is the correct one, the Philoxenian version has disappeared except for certain manuscripts which contain the minor Catholic Epistles and the Book of Revelation. According to the former view, the Syriac version of these books was made by an unknown translator.

2. THE PHILOXENIAN VERSION

One of the most influential leaders of the Monophysite branch of the Church at the beginning of the sixth century was Philoxenus (Mar Aksenaya') of Mabbûg in eastern Syria, who, with his contemporary, Severus of Antioch, founded Jacobite Monophysitism. Despite acrimonious charges levelled against him by his theological opponents, his writings disclose him as an acute dialectician, a prolific author, a subtle theologian, and an uncompromising champion of the unity of the nature of Christ against what he regarded as the heresy of the two natures.[1]

The work of translating the New Testament was performed in 507–8, when the prestige of Philoxenus was at its height. Inasmuch as Philoxenus did not know Greek, he commissioned Polycarp, chorepiscopus in the diocese of Mabbûg, to revise the Peshitta version in accordance with Greek manuscripts.[2] Polycarp sometimes replaced Syriac words with synonyms, sometimes used different prepositions, and generally gave preference to the independent possessive pronoun over against the suffixes.[3] It appears that Polycarp sought to make a more theologically accurate rendering of the Greek than the current Peshitta rendering. In addition to the books included in the earlier

[1] See the comprehensive monograph by André de Halleux, *Philoxène de Mabbog, sa vie, ses écrits, sa théologie* (Louvain, 1963).

[2] This is the generally accepted view; Alphonse Mingana, however, thought that Philoxenus himself had prepared the version long before his episcopal ordination, in the monastery of Tel'eda, having possibly handed his work to Polycarp for the purpose of simple revision in 505–8 ('New Documents on Philoxenus of Hierapolis, and on the Philoxenian Version of the Bible', *Exp*, 8th ser., xix (1920), 159).

[3] For examples illustrating these and other modifications introduced by Polycarp, see Vööbus, loc. cit. (see p. 64 n. 18), pp. 180–3, and *Early Versions of the New Testament*, pp. 117 f.; cf. also de Halleux, op. cit., pp. 122 f.

translation, the Philoxenian included (seemingly for the first time in Syriac) 2 Peter, 2 and 3 John, Jude, and the Book of Revelation. Since the Philoxenian version was made and sponsored by Jacobite ecclesiastics, it was used only by the Mono-physite branch of Syriac-speaking Christendom.

Philoxenian manuscripts and editions

Apart from several manuscripts of the Gospels that have been thought by one or another scholar to preserve the Philoxenian version,[1] the only assuredly Philoxenian manuscripts are those that contain the four minor Catholic Epistles and the Apocalypse. The former were first published at Leiden in 1630 by Edward Pococke, from a late manuscript in the Bodleian (MS. Or. 119, written about A.D. 1610). In this edition the text is given in both Syriac and Hebrew characters, and at the foot of the page are a Greek text and a Latin rendering of the Syriac. After the edition of Pococke had appeared, it was not long before these Epistles were incorporated into printed editions of the Peshitta, a version with which they have really nothing to do.[2]

In 1909, on the basis of a collation of twenty manuscripts, the oldest of which is dated A.D. 823 (British Museum Add. 14623), John Gwynn produced a fully reliable edition of the four Epistles, with prolegomena, supplemental notes, and the reconstruction of the Greek text attested by the version.[3] Gwynn divided the manuscripts into two groups, an older (ninth–twelfth century), and a later (fifteenth–seventeenth century; from this the usual printed editions have been taken), besides several of inter-mediate character.[4]

---

[1] e.g. the three manuscripts in Florence, Rome, and Beirut, proposed succes-sively by Adler, Bernstein, and Hall; for bibliography see Anton Baumstark, *Geschichte der syrischen Literatur* (Bonn, 1922), pp. 144 f., and, for Hall, F. C. Burkitt, *JTS* xxxiii (1931–2), 255–62.

[2] This insertion was first made in the Paris Polyglot Bible (vol. v, part 1; 1630).

[3] *Remnants of the Later Syriac Versions of the Bible*; Part I: *New Testament. The Four Minor Catholic Epistles in the Original Philoxenian Version of the Sixth Century, and the History of the Woman Taken in Adultery* . . . (London and Oxford, 1909; repr. Amsterdam, 1974). See also Gwynn's earlier discussion, 'The Older Syriac Version of the Four Minor Catholic Epistles', *Hermathena*, vii (1890), 281–314.

[4] There is also an Arabic version of the Philoxenian text of the Catholic Epistles, contained in a ninth-century copy on Mount Sinai (see pp. 262–3 below), which agrees in many instances with the readings of the later copies as embodied in the ordinary printed text.

The textual affinities of the reconstructed Greek text of the Epistles seem to be more with the Alexandrian than with the Koine or Ecclesiastical text. Of 115 sets of variant readings, the Philoxenian agrees with ℵ sixty-five times; with A, sixty; with B, fifty-three; with C, forty-four; with K, fifty-one; with L, fifty-five; with P, fifty-one. Furthermore, the agreements of the Philoxenian with the Harclean, Gwynn reports, are more numerous than with any of the Greek texts, being seventy-six in all, about two-thirds of the 115 sets of readings.

In the case of the *pericope de adultera*, which is lacking in the Peshitta version,[1] Gwynn assembled evidence for the text of the passage from twelve manuscripts. The oldest copy is a note in a hand of probably the ninth century, appended to folio 1^v of British Museum Add. 14470, a Peshitta manuscript of the fifth or sixth century (no. 6 in the list above). Several copies, including the earliest, ascribe the translation of the *pericope* from Greek into Syriac to 'the Abbot Paul, who found it in Alexandria'. Gwynn identified the translator as presumably Paul of Tella of the early seventh century, to whom we owe the Syro-Hexaplar of the Old Testament. Brock, on the other hand, thinks it more probable that a contemporary Syrian scholar of the same name is meant, the Abbot Paul who was Monophysite bishop of Edessa until the Persian invasion, when he fled to Cyprus where he made in 623–4 a Syriac translation of the homilies of Gregory of Nazianzus.[2]

The Book of Revelation in Syriac exists in two forms, one of which, up to the twentieth century, has usually been printed in editions of the Syriac New Testament, beginning with the Paris Polyglot (volume v, part 2; 1633), edited by Gabriel Sionita. It was first published by Ludovicus de Dieu at Leiden in 1627 from a manuscript bequeathed by Scaliger to the library of the University of Leiden (cod. Scalig. 18 Syr.). At least ten other copies

---

[1] The *pericope* appeared for the first time in a printed book in L. de Dieu's *Animadversiones . . . in quatuor Evangelia* (Leiden, 1631), pp. 443–4. The text of the passage was taken from a manuscript (dated A.D. 1625) lent to him by James Ussher and now preserved in the Library of Trinity College, Dublin (see J. Gwynn, 'On a Syriac Manuscript belonging to the Collection of Archbishop Ussher', *Transactions of the Royal Irish Academy*, xxvii (1877–86), 269–316). The text contains an egregious scribal blunder—the omission of the negative in vs. 11, so as to read 'Go and sin more'! The ܠܐ accordingly appears in brackets in the text printed by de Dieu.

[2] Sebastian Brock, *The Syriac Version of the Pseudo-Nonnos Mythological Scholia* (Cambridge, 1971), p. 30.

of the same type of text have since become known, one of which identifies the text as a copy of the autograph of Thomas of Harkel.[1]

The other form of the book is preserved in a manuscript dating from the late twelfth or early thirteenth century[2]—a manuscript which is noteworthy as being the only one thus far known that contains the whole New Testament in Syriac.[3] Purchased by the Earl of Crawford and Balcarres from an unknown dealer in London about 1860, it is today in the John Rylands Library at Manchester. The text of the Book of Revelation in the manuscript was edited in 1897 by Gwynn,[4] who argued persuasively that the newly discovered version is nothing other than the unrevised Philoxenian version, and that the other form of the Apocalypse in Syriac is what is commonly called the Harclean version. The two forms differ in that the Philoxenian version is written in free and idiomatic Syriac, while the other Graecizes after the Harklensian fashion.

As for textual affinities of the text of Revelation in the Crawford manuscript, Gwynn concluded that it is a mixed text, the larger component of which is related to the uncials ℵ A C P (or a majority of them), while the smaller component agrees with B (Westcott and Hort's B₂) and the minuscules. Its special affinities are with ℵ and, among the Latin versions, with the Primasian, the earliest known form of the book in Old Latin.[5]

3. THE HARCLEAN VERSION

From the scattered pieces of information about Thomas of

---

[1] It is MS. 724 of the Library of the Dominican Convent of San Marco, Florence; see John Gwynn, 'On the Discovery of a Missing Syriac Manuscript of the Apocalypse', *Hermathena*, x (1899), 227–45. Clemons lists sixteen Syriac manuscripts of the Apocalypse, one of which is incomplete and another fragmentary; the type of text has not been analysed in all of them (James Clemons, *An Index of Syriac Manuscripts Containing the Epistles and the Apocalypse* (Salt Lake City, 1968)).

[2] For a discussion of the date of the manuscript, see John Gwynn, 'On a Syriac MS. of the New Testament in the Library of the Earl of Crawford, and an Inedited Version of the Apocalypse included in it', *Transactions of the Royal Irish Academy*, xxx (Dublin, 1893), 361–76.

[3] The order of the contents of the manuscript is Gospels, Harclean Passiontide Harmony, Revelation, Acts, Catholic Epistles, Pauline Epistles.

[4] John Gwynn, *The Apocalypse of St. John, in a Syriac Version hitherto unknown . . .* (Dublin, 1897). (This was the first book involving Syriac characters printed by the Dublin University Press.) For an appreciative review article, see T. K. Abbott in *Hermathena*, x (1899), 27–35.   [5] *The Apocalypse of St. John*, pp. lv–lxxvi.

Harkel it appears that he was born probably at Heracleia in Cyrrhestice, a short distance north-west of Mabbûg. After pursuing Greek studies at Qenneshê (i.e. the ancient Chalcis and the modern Qinneshrê), he became a monk in the Monastery of Tar'îl near Beroea. In the course of time he became bishop of Mabbûg. He was, however, expelled from his see by Domitian of Melitene, nephew of the Emperor Maurice, before A.D. 602, and went with other Syrian émigrés to the monastery of the Antonians, located at Enaton, the nine-mile relay station near Alexandria. Here, at the insistence of Athanasius I—the titular patriarch of Antioch—Paul of Tella, with assistance from others, translated the Old Testament from the Greek hexaplaric and tetraplaric text of a copy made by Eusebius and Pamphilus. According to a colophon a certain Thomas (doubtless Thomas of Harkel) was his chief assistant in translating the books of Kings. Other colophons state[1] that it was here at Enaton that Thomas produced his edition or revision of the Philoxenian New Testament (including all the twenty-seven books), which was completed in 616.

The chief characteristic of the Harclean version is its slavish adaptation to the Greek, to the extent that even clarity is sacrificed. For example, at Mark xiv. 58 διὰ τριῶν ἡμερῶν is translated in the Peshitta intelligibly, and in good Syriac, ܬܠܬܐ ܝܘ̈ܡܝܢ, but because διά is used in the Greek, the later version renders the passage in the following ridiculous and unintelligible manner, ܒܝܕ ܬܠܬܐ ܝܘ̈ܡܝܢ ܐܒܢܐ ܐܚܪܢܐ 'through [literally, 'through the hand'] three days, I build another'. As compared with the Peshitta, the Harclean not infrequently uses a Greek loan-word instead of a native Syriac one.[2] This preference for transliteration shows itself even in the case of Semitic proper names, when, instead of allowing them to display their Semitic etymology, the reviser represents the Greek orthography. For example, when Ἰάκωβος (Hebrew יעקב) occurs in the accusative, we find in this version the curious form ܠܐܝܩܘܒܘܢ. In short, the edition of the New Testament produced by Thomas appears to be

[1] Cf. Silva New, 'The Harclean Version of the Gospels', *HTR* xxi (1928), 376–95; W. H. P. Hatch, 'The Subscription in the Chester Beatty Manuscript of the Harclean Gospels', ibid. xxx (1937), 141–56; G. Zuntz, *The Ancestry of the Harklean New Testament* (London, [1945]); and id., 'Die Subscriptionen der Syra Harclensis', *ZDMG* ci (1951), 174–96.

[2] Cf. Joseph Molitor, 'Die syrische Übersetzung des 1. and 2. Thessalonicherbriefes', *OC*, 4th ser., xix (1971), 162.

a suitable counterpart to Paul of Tella's Syro-Hexaplar—a painfully exact imitation of Greek idiom, even in the order of words, often in violation of Syriac idiom. As a result the modern scholar is hardly ever in doubt as to the Greek text intended by the translator.[1]

It is otherwise as to the meaning of the obeli and asterisks with which Thomas identified readings in his complicated critical apparatus. The earliest assumption (held, e.g., by Wettstein), that the passages marked with obeli and asterisks had some relation to the Peshitta, was mistaken. Furthermore, though one might well suppose that the signs were used by Thomas in exactly the same way as by Origen in the Hexapla,[2] the data are not always susceptible of such an interpretation. Amid a variety of theories concerning their interpretation,[3] there is one point upon which everyone is agreed, namely that these signs were frequently confused in the course of transmission. As it happens, no obeli occur in the Catholic Epistles, and in the Gospels their distribution varies. Furthermore, not all Harclean manuscripts contain this critical apparatus, but its absence appears to be the result of later adaptation to liturgical use, not a more original form. The theory proposed by Black and others, that 'Thomas's Syriac *marginalia* are his rejected Philoxenus text',[4] prompts the query why they should have been kept at all if they were rejected as not primary. Moreover, Thomas occasionally provides a variant reading in Greek. How he wished the reader to take such a reading in relation to the Syriac text has not been resolved. Obviously a great deal of work remains to be done on problems raised by the Harclean marginalia.[5]

[1] See also the comments by Brock in section VII, pp. 83–98 below.

[2] Cf. C. T. Fritsch, 'The Treatment of the Hexaplaric Signs in the Syro-Hexapla of the Book of Proverbs', *JBL* lxxii (1953), 169–81.

[3] For somewhat different interpretations of the data in the Book of Acts, see A. C. Clark, *The Acts of the Apostles* (Oxford, 1933), pp. 308–29; James H. Ropes, *The Text of Acts* (London, 1934), pp. clxi–clxviii; and F. C. Burkitt, *JTS* xxxvi (1935), 192 f.

[4] Matthew Black, 'The Syriac Versional Tradition', op. cit. (p. 43 n. 5), p. 141 n. 85a.

[5] A start has been made by John D. Thomas in his unpublished Ph.D. dissertation at the University of St. Andrews, entitled 'The Harclean Margin: A Study of the Asterisks, Obeli, and Marginalia of the Harclean Syriac Version with Special Reference to the Gospel of Luke' (1973). It is Dr. Thomas's opinion that the obelized readings are originally from the hand of Polycarp, while the readings marked with asterisks are from Thomas's hand (p. 122).

Harclean manuscripts and editions

Among Harclean manuscripts, apart from lectionaries, passion-tide harmonies (see p. 74 n. 5 below), and certain copies of the Apocalypse (see p. 68 n. 1 above), about sixty have been catalogued by Gregory, Baumstark, and Mingana. Of this number the following are noteworthy for one or another reason:

(1) Moscow, Archaeological Society MS. 1, of the seventh century, contains on thirty-four folios portions of the four Gospels.[1]

(2) Selly Oak, Mingana MS. 124, of about A.D. 730, contains on 261 folios the four Gospels (with some lacunae, including John xviii. 3 to end). Some of the Greek marginal notes differ from those in White's edition.

(3) Florence, Laurentian MS. I. 40, A.D. 756/757, contains on 100 folios the four Gospels. Plate in Hatch's *Album of Dated Syriac Manuscripts*, no. liv.

(4) Rome, Vatican Syriac MS. 267, of the eighth century, contains on 163 folios the four Gospels.

(5) Selly Oak, Mingana MS. 42, dated A.D. 835, contains on 182 folios the four Gospels, Epistle of James, 2 Timothy, and a quotation from the Epistle to the Hebrews.

(6) London, British Museum, Add. 7163 Rich., of the eighth or ninth century, contains on thirty-six folios portions of the four Gospels.

(7) Rome, Vatican Syriac MS. 268, thought by Mai to have been written by Thomas of Harkel himself,[2] but attributed to A.D. 858–9 by Hatch, contains on 172 folios the four Gospels. Plate in Hatch's *Album*, no. lxix.

(8) The so-called Beirut codex, on loan to the Library of Union Theological Seminary, New York, attributed to the ninth century by Hall,[3] but to a date a little before 1200 by Burkitt,[4]

---

[1] Described and collated by R. Wagner, *ZNW* vi (1905), 286–90.

[2] Angelo Mai, *Scriptorum veterum nova collectio*, v (part 2) (Rome, 1831), pp. 4–5. Since the manuscript contains the Harclean Passiontide Harmony, the date when it was written will be known when the *floruit* of Rabban Mar Daniel, who drew up the Harmony, is known (see p. 75 n. 1 below). In any case, it cannot be Thomas's autograph!

[3] I. H. Hall, *JAOS*, Oct. 1877, pp. cxlvi–cxlix, and *JBL* (1883), pp. 142–52.

[4] F. C. Burkitt, 'Dr. I. Hall's "Philoxenian" Codex', *JTS* xxxiii (1931–2), 255–62.

contains on 203 folios the Gospels (with lacunae) in the Harclean version, and the rest of the Syriac canon in the Peshitta version.

(9) British Museum Add. 14469, A.D. 935–6, written by a priest named John in the Convent of St. Mary Deipara in Nitria for the abbot Moses of Nisibis, contains on 205 folios the four Gospels. Plate in Hatch's *Album*, no. lxxiii.

(10) Oxford, New College MS. 333, of the eleventh century, contains on 273 folios the entire New Testament according to the Syriac canon (lacking Heb. xi. 27–xiii. 25); used by White as the basis of his edition.

(11) Cambridge, Univ. Add. 1700, A.D. 1169–70, written by a scribe named Sâhdâ in the Convent of Mâr Ṣalîbâ in Edessa, contains on 216 folios the four Gospels, Acts, seven Catholic Epistles, and the Pauline Epistles (including Hebrews); and 1 and 2 Clement (which follow immediately after Jude). Plate in Hatch's *Album*, no. cxxix.

(12) Dublin, Chester Beatty MS. Syr. 3, A.D. 1177, written in the church of Mar Thomas the Apostle, contains on 229 folios the four Gospels.[1] Plate in Hatch's *Album*, no. lxxxiii.

The *editio princeps* of the [Philoxenian–]Harclean version of the New Testament was issued at the close of the eighteenth century by Joseph White, then Fellow of Wadham College and Professor of Arabic, afterwards Canon of Christ Church, Oxford.[2] He based his edition chiefly on one manuscript, Oxford, New College 333 (no. 10 in the list above). Where this manuscript is defective in the Gospels he employed two codices (Oxford, New College 334 and Bodleian Or. 361) which had been transcribed by Glocester (or Gloster) Ridley, Fellow of New College, Oxford.[3] Unfortu-

---

[1] On its colophon, see Hatch's article (p. 64 n. 16 above); on its text, see Paul E. Kahle, 'The Chester Beatty Manuscript of the Harklean Gospels', *Miscellanea Giovanni Mercati*, vi (*Studi e testi*, cxxvi; Vatican City, 1946), 208–13.

[2] *Sacrorum Evangeliorum versio Syriaca Philoxeniana ex codd. mss. Ridleianis in bibl. coll. Nov. Oxon. repositis nunc primum edita: cum interpretatione et annotationibus*, 2 vols. (Oxford, 1778); and *Actuum Apostolorum et epistolarum tam catholicarum quam Paulinarum, versio Syriaca Philoxeniana, ex codice ms. Ridleiano in bibl. coll. Novi Oxon. reposito, nunc primum edita: cum interpretatione et annotationibus*, 2 vols. (Oxford, 1799, 1803).

[3] For comments on the rather unsatisfactory manner in which White displayed the textual evidence, along with lists of errata in his volumes, see William Duff McHardy, 'The Text of Matthew and Mark in White's *Versio Syriaca Philoxeniana* and in the New College MS. 333', *JTS* xlix (1948), 175–8.

nately he had no manuscript to fill out the text of Hebrews, which breaks off at xi. 27.

A half-century later Bernstein published the text of the Gospel according to John from a Harclean manuscript in the Vatican.[1]

Finally, among the very few editions of Harclean materials[2] is Bensly's publication of the text of Heb. xi. 28 to the end of the Epistle, thus filling out the defective manuscript used for White's edition.[3]

In view of the general availability of a goodly number of Harclean manuscripts,[4] it is no credit to New Testament scholarship that there is still lacking an adequate edition of that version.

The textual affinities of the Harclean version have been described as belonging, on the whole, to the Antiochian[5] or Byzantine type of text.[6] But the apparatus which Thomas attached to the version has made it, at least for the Book of Acts, one of the most important witnesses to the Western text that have come down to us,[7] surpassed in this respect only by codex

---

[1] Georg Heinrich Bernstein, *Das heilige Evangelium des Iohannes. Syrisch in harklensischer Uebersetzung, mit Vocalen und den Puncten Kuschoi und Rucoch nach einer vaticanischen Handschrift, nebst kritischen Anmerkungen* (Leipzig, 1853). Bernstein utilized Vatican MS. Syr. 271, written A.D. 1483.

[2] The so-called Beirut Codex, supposed by some to contain the [Philoxenian–]-Harclean version (so E. J. Goodspeed, who edited part of the Gospel of Matthew, *JBL* xxv (1906), 58–81), is, in the judgement of F. C. Burkitt, a subsequent modification of the Harclean version (see p. 66 n. 1 above).

[3] Robert L. Bensly, *The Harklean Version of the Epistle to the Hebrews, Chapter XI, 28–XIII, 25, Now Edited for the First Time* . . . (Cambridge, 1889). Bensly utilized Cambridge MS. Add. 1700 (see no. 11 in the list above).

[4] From time to time previously uncatalogued manuscripts of the Harclean version come to light; e.g. in 1972 it was announced that two Harclean manuscripts had been photographed for the Institute for New Testament Textual Research at Münster (so the *Bericht der Stiftung zur Förderung der neutestamentliche Textforschung für die Jahre 1970 und 1971* (Münster/W., 1972), pp. 8 f.). A facsimile edition of a newly found Harclean manuscript of Revelation is being prepared by Vööbus.

It may be mentioned here that, according to a communication from C. F. Burney to the *Academy* (9 Feb. 1895, p. 131), the Library of St. John's College, Oxford, possesses the collations made by Henry Dean of several Harclean manuscripts of the Gospels, entered in an interleaved copy of White's edition (the copy which the Librarian showed to the present writer had the collations entered on the margins of the pages).

[5] So J. H. Ropes, *The Text of Acts* (London, 1926), p. clx.

[6] So K. Lake, *The Text of the New Testament*, 6th edn. (London, 1928), p. 42.

[7] For a discussion of the relation of the marginal readings in the Harclean Acts to an interesting group of Greek minuscules, see A. V. Valentine-Richards, *The Text of Acts in Codex 614 (Tisch. 137) and its Allies*, with an Introduction by J. M. Creed (Cambridge, 1934), pp. xvi–xix, and the comments of F. C. Burkitt, *JTS* xxxvi (1935), 191–4.

Bezae. In the case of the Gospels an analysis made by Mrs. New of the type of text represented in the marginal readings led her to conclude that for these books Thomas utilized a Greek manuscript with a predominantly Caesarean text and an Old Syriac copy akin to the Sinaitic Syriac.[1] On the basis chiefly of a detailed examination of the colophons in Harclean manuscripts, Zuntz[2] traced the Caesarean element in Acts and the Pauline Epistles back to a 'Euthalian' recension of these books, written in cola and commata, as constituted at Caesarea by Pamphilus and other grammarian theologians.[3]

4. HARCLEAN PASSIONTIDE HARMONIES

Not a few Harclean manuscripts contain the Syriac text of a harmony of the Passion narratives of the four Gospels.[4] A detailed study made by Morris A. Weigelt[5] of evidence from eight manuscripts reveals that the same basic harmony circulated in two somewhat different forms. One of them, which Weigelt designates Sequence A,[6] is characterized by relatively long citations of Gospel text and infrequent shifts from Gospel to Gospel. The other form, Sequence B,[7] involves about twice as

[1] So Silva New, *HTR* xxi (1928), 394.

[2] Günther Zuntz, *The Ancestry of the Harklean New Testament* (London, 1945), p. 121.

[3] For a critical assessment of Zuntz's research on the Harclean version, with evidence of not a few inaccuracies, see the review written by G. D. Kilpatrick and W. D. McHardy, *JTS* xlviii (1947), 92–9.

[4] The harmony is extant in more than two dozen manuscripts. For earlier descriptions of it, see J. P. P. Martin, *Introduction à la critique textuelle du Nouveau Testament*, Partie pratique, iii (Paris, 1885), pp. 121–44; id., 'Le Διὰ τεσσάρων de Tatien', *RQH* xxxiii (1883), 336–78; and the literature cited in the following footnote.

[5] In his unpublished dissertation, entitled 'Diatessaric Harmonies of the Passion Narrative in the Harclean Syriac Version' (Library of Princeton Theological Seminary, 1969), Weigelt provides collations of the harmony in six manuscripts, namely Vatican Syriac 268 (A.D. 859), British Museum Add. 18714 (A.D. 1214), Bibliothèque nationale Cod. Syr. 51 (A.D. 1138), Bibliothèque nationale Cod. Syr. 52 (A.D. 1165), Cambridge University Add. 1700 (A.D. 1169), and Bibliothèque nationale Cod. Syr. 31 (A.D. 1203). In addition he makes use of the evidence of two other witnesses, one published by H. H. Spoer ('Spuren eines syrischen Diatessaron', *ZDMG* lxi (1907), 850–9; George A. Barton and H. H. Spoer, 'Traces of the Diatessaron of Tatian in Harclean Syriac Harmonies', *JBL* xxiv (1905), 179–95) and the other by A.-S. Marmardji (*Diatessaron de Tatien* (Beirut, 1935), Appendix: 'Évangéliaire diatessarique syriaque', pp. 1*–75*).

[6] Contained in the first three manuscripts listed in the previous footnote.

[7] Contained in the last three manuscripts listed in n. 5 above, and in Spoer and Marmardji.

many separate citations, half as long as those in Sequence A. Furthermore, Sequence B begins at a later point in the Passion narrative than does Sequence A, and ends slightly earlier. At the same time, the two sequences share the same chronological scheme, show a preference for Matthean material, and contain certain duplicate accounts. Sequence B is thought by Weigelt to be probably an elaboration from Sequence A.

Information concerning the identity of the compiler of the Passion harmony is contained in a note at the close of the harmony in Mingana Syr. MS. 105 (fol. 215a). This reads: 'Here end the lessons for Good Friday, which are harmonized from the four Evangelists. . . . They were harmonized with great care by Rabban Mar Daniel, the man of many lights, from Beth Bātīn, a village which is near Ḥarran, and by the diligent Isaac, his disciple.'[1]

Textually the Harclean harmony agrees, as one would have expected, with the Harclean version; structurally it differs from Tatianic witnesses—both Eastern and Western.[2] Unlike them the compiler of the Harclean Passion harmony seldom rearranges the order of Gospel material and prefers, instead, to present several duplicate accounts, while omitting John, chaps. xiv–xvii. By way of summary Weigelt concludes that the Harclean Passiontide harmony is 'an independent harmony not influenced by Tatian's Diatessaron either in structure or text. Although less creatively and skilfully constructed than Tatian's Diatessaron, it represents an important stage in the process of constructing harmonies and provides an interesting glimpse into the history of the transmission of the Harclean Syriac version.'[3]

VI. THE PALESTINIAN SYRIAC VERSION

1. THE ORIGIN OF THE VERSION

What used to be called the Jerusalem Syriac version and has now come to be known as the Palestinian Syriac version might

---

[1] See Alphonse Mingana, *BJRL* xv (1931), p. 178. Baumstark refers to several liturgical treatises by a Jacobite ecclesiastic called Rabban Daniel (*Die Geschichte der syrischen Literatur* (Bonn, 1922), p. 283); J. de Zwaan, 'Harclean Gleanings from Mingana's Catalogue', *NovT* ii (1957–8), 176 f., who discusses the date of Mar Daniel's *floruit*.

[2] Contrary to Duncan Willey's opinion expressed in his discussion of the text of a page from a Harclean Passiontide Harmony ('A Fragment of Tatian's Diatessaron', *ExpT* xxv (1913–14), 31–5).   [3] Op. cit., p. 3 (of Abstract).

with still more propriety be designated the Christian–Palestinian–Aramaic version. The language of the version is the Aramaic dialect[1] used in Palestine during the early Christian centuries. The only claim to be called Syriac rests upon the script in which it is written, which resembles somewhat the Estrangela Syriac script, except that the characters are more square in their outline, and the *dolath* is usually without its diacritical point; there are two forms of the letter *pe*, representing the sounds 'ph' and 'p'. In both accidence and vocabulary the dialect is closer to Jewish Palestinian Aramaic than to the classical Syriac current at Edessa.

In addition to sepulchral inscriptions, the documents that preserve the written language are almost exclusively religious in content. Besides material from the Old and New Testaments (though no single book has been preserved in its entirety), there are twenty leaves of a homily of Chrysostom, fragments of the life of St. Anthony, an early creed, two stanzas of a hymn in honour of Peter and Paul, a Liturgy of the Nile, a Euchologium, and a fragment of an apostolic legend.

The language came to be used by Melchite Christians, as they were called, not only in Palestine, but in adjoining lands as well. By the sixth and seventh centuries a considerable number of Palestinian Christians had settled in Egypt, where they made use of a liturgy in their native Palestinian Aramaic for the blessing of the Nile.[2]

Although a few manuscripts are thought to date from the sixth century, almost all of them derive from the ninth and following centuries after the dialect had been replaced by Arabic as the speech of everyday life, though it continued to be used for some centuries longer as the liturgical language. Furthermore,

---

[1] In addition to discussions of the language in the standard grammatical treatises (e.g. Theodor Nöldeke, 'Über den christlich-palästinischen Dialekt', *ZDMG* xxii (1868), 443–527; Friedrich Schulthess, *Grammatik des christlichpalästinischen Aramäisch* (Tübingen, 1924)), see A. Dupont-Sommer, *La Doctrine gnostique de la lettre 'wâw' d'après une lamelle araméenne inédite* (Paris, 1946), pp. 78 ff.

[2] For this and other liturgical books in Palestinian Aramaic, see G. Margoliouth, 'The Liturgy of the Nile', *JRAS* (Oct. 1896), pp. 677–731; Matthew Black, *Rituale Melchitorum: A Palestinian Euchologion* (*Bonner orientalische Studien*, ed. by P. E. Kahle and W. Kirfel, Heft 22; Stuttgart, 1938); Hieronymus Engberding, 'Der Nil in der liturgischen Frömmigkeit des christlichen Ostens', *OC* xxxvii (1953), 56–88, esp. 79–83; and Black, *A Christian Palestinian Syriac Horologion* (*Texts and Studies*, N.S. i; Cambridge, 1954).

as Schulthess pointed out,[1] the manuscripts belonging to the eleventh, twelfth, and thirteenth centuries show that even the clergy did not have a sufficient knowledge of the language.

When the Palestinian Syriac version of the Bible was made is a moot question. Nöldeke[2] placed its origin sometime between A.D. 300 and 600, preferring an earlier rather than a later date within that period. Burkitt[3] assigned it to the sixth century. Lagrange[4] argued that sacred texts existed in oral tradition among Palestinian Christians during the fourth century, and that in the fifth century these took on written form. Sometime after the beginning of the fifth century seems to be required in the light of comments made by St. Egeria (Aetheria). During her pilgrimage to Palestine at the end of the fourth or beginning of the fifth century[5] she found:

In ea provincia pars populi et graece et siriste novit, pars etiam alia per se graece, aliqua etiam pars tantum siriste, itaque, quoniam episcopus, licet siriste noverit, tamen semper graece loquitur et nunquam siriste; itaque ergo stat semper presbyter, qui, episcopo graece dicente, siriste interpretatur, ut omnes audiant, quae exponuntur. Lectiones etiam, quaecumque in ecclesia leguntur, quia necesse est graece legi, semper stat, qui siriste interpretatur propter populum, ut semper discant.[6]

In other words, it appears that a Greek-speaking bishop was accompanied by a presbyter, who translated the Scripture lessons as well as his sermon into Syriac (i.e. Aramaic) so that all could understand. This suggests, as Vööbus points out,[7] that the Palestinian Syriac version did not exist at that time, but that the Church provided an official (*presbyter*) to translate the Greek Scriptures orally.

---

[1] Schulthess, op. cit., p. 1; cf. also id., *Lexicon syropalaestinum* (Berlin, 1903), pp. iv f. [2] Op. cit., p. 525.

[3] F. C. Burkitt, 'Christian Palestinian Literature', *JTS* ii (1901), 174–85, and *Encyclopædia Biblica*, iv (1903), cols. 5005 f.

[4] 'L'origine de la version syro-palestinienne des évangiles', *RB* xxxiv (1925), 481–504, esp. 497.

[5] The dates are those assigned by Berthold Altaner and Alfred Stuiber, *Patrologie* (Freiburg im Br., 1966), p. 245.

[6] S. Silvia, *Peregrinatio*, xlvii. 3 (*CSEL* xxxix. 99, lines 13–21). For a discussion of the problem presented by the use of Greek as the hieratic language of the liturgy in the East, cf. August Bludau, *Die Pilgerreise der Aetheria* (*Studien zur Geschichte und Kultur des Altertums*, xv; Paderborn, 1927), pp. 182 ff. Jerome (*Epist.* cviii. 30) mentions that at the funeral of Paula psalms were sung in Greek, Latin, and Syriac. [7] *Early Versions of the New Testament*, pp. 126 f.

2. NOTEWORTHY MANUSCRIPTS AND EDITIONS OF THE PALESTINIAN SYRIAC VERSION

The existence of an ancient parchment codex containing a Gospel lectionary in a dialect of Aramaic had been known to the scholarly world since about the middle of the eighteenth century when a full description of it was published by two Maronite scholars, the cousins Assemani.[1] During the next generation a Danish scholar, J. G. C. Adler, having examined the manuscript in the Vatican Library, published an extract from it of the Gospel of Matthew.[2]

It was not, however, until a century after the Assemanis had drawn attention to the manuscript that a full and, indeed, sumptuous edition of it, with a Latin translation, was published by Count Francesco Miniscalchi Erizzo.[3] On the eve of the discovery of two other manuscripts of the same lectionary, a posthumous edition was published of Paul de Lagarde's fresh collation of the Vatican manuscript, the text of which he had rearranged in scriptural sequence.[4]

In 1892 Mrs. Agnes Smith Lewis came upon another manuscript of the Palestinian Syriac lectionary in the library of the Monastery of St. Catherine on Mount Sinai, and the following year at the same place J. Rendel Harris found a third. In 1899 these were published, with the twice previously edited Vatican manuscript, by Mrs. Lewis and her twin sister, Mrs. Margaret Dunlop Gibson.[5]

The dates of the three manuscripts are known from colophons preserved in the documents. The Vatican codex was written in A.D. 1030, the other two in A.D. 1104 and 1118. Specimens of the three manuscripts, which are usually designated, respectively, codices A, B, and C, are included in Hatch's *Album*.[6] A colophon

---

[1] S. E. Assemani and J. S. Assemani, *Bibliothecae Apostolicae Vaticanae codicum manuscriptorum catalogus*, Pars I, Tom. ii (Rome, 1758), pp. 70–103.

[2] *Novi Testamenti versiones Syriacae simplex, Philoxeniana et Hierosolymitana* (Copenhagen, 1789), pp. 135–201.

[3] *Evangeliarium Hierosolymitanum ex codice Vaticano Palestino deprompsit, edidit, Latine vertit, prolegomenis ac glossario adornavit . . . ,* 2 vols. (Verona, 1861, 1864). The Latin rendering cannot always be trusted to represent accurately the original Palestinian Syriac, for the translator sometimes inadvertently adopted turns of expression familiar to him from the Latin Vulgate.

[4] *Bibliothecae Syriacae* (Göttingen, 1892), pp. 258–402.

[5] *The Palestinian Syriac Lectionary of the Gospels, re-edited from two Sinai MSS. and from P. de Lagarde's edition of the 'Evangeliarium Hierosolymitanum'* (London, 1899).

[6] *An Album of Dated Syriac Manuscripts* (Boston, 1946), pp. 248–51.

in codex A states that the scribe was a priest named Elias el-'Abûdî, and that the manuscript was written in the Monastery of Anbâ Mûsâ in Antioch of the Arabs,[1] in the district of ed-Dqûs. The scribe of codex B was a priest named Mafrîg ibn Abû 'l-Ḥair el-'Abûdî, and the scribe of codex C was a priest named Peter. The name of the place(s) at which codices B and C were written is not given.

The Palestinian Syriac lectionary is modelled directly upon a typical Greek lectionary, for not only is the sequence of pericopes like that of the usual type of Greek lectionaries,[2] but the choice and extent of the scriptural passages in the synaxarion are, with a few exceptions, identical with those appointed by the Byzantine Church. Even the incipits usually correspond with those commonly used in Greek lectionaries. Such a high degree of correspondence between Palestinian Syriac and Greek lectionaries is particularly noteworthy inasmuch as both the earlier and the later Syriac lectionary systems present very considerable divergences from this one.[3]

Besides the three primary witnesses to the Palestinian Syriac version, fragments of the text of the Gospels have survived in non-lectionary manuscripts, as well as portions of Acts, of all the Pauline Epistles (including Hebrews) except 2 Thessalonians and Philemon, and of James and 2 Peter, some passages in more than one witness.[4] The most recent acquisitions have come to light at

---

[1] The Assemanis, followed by Lagrange (*Critique textuelle*, p. 239), identified 'Antioch of the Arabs' with Gerasa, the modern Jerash, which was once known as Antiochia ad Chrysorrhoam. But Burkitt (*JTS* ii (1901–2), 179) and Hatch (*Album*, p. 249) think that the Antioch mentioned in the colophon must be Antioch in Syria, and that the phrase 'Antioch of the Arabs' may denote that part of the district which in the eleventh century was still under Mohammedan dominion.

[2] For a description of the arrangement of the several parts of the typical Greek lectionary, see the present writer's chapter, 'Greek Lectionaries and a Critical Edition of the Greek New Testament', in *Die alten Übersetzungen des Neuen Testaments, die Kirchenväterzitate und Lektionare*, ed. by K. Aland (Berlin and New York, 1972), pp. 479–97.

[3] For a discussion of similarities and differences see the present writer's contribution, 'A Comparison of the Palestinian Syriac Lectionary and the Greek Gospel Lectionary', in *Neotestamentica et semitica. Studies in Honour of Matthew Black*, ed. by E. Earle Ellis and Max Wilcox (Edinburgh, 1969), pp. 209–20.

[4] For a complete list of editions of Christian Palestinian texts, published before 1962, see Charles Perrot, 'Un fragment christo-palestinien découvert à Khirbet Mird', *RB* lxx (1963), 510 n. 5. For a list of scriptural passages preserved in texts of the Palestinian Syriac version edited before 1903, see Friedrich Schulthess, *Lexicon Syropalaestinum* (Berlin, 1903), pp. vii–xvi.

Khirbet Mird;[1] these include fragments from Luke (iii. 1, 3–4), Acts (x. 28–9, 32–41),[2] and Colossians (i. 16–18, 20 ff.).

3. CHARACTERISTICS OF THE PALESTINIAN SYRIAC VERSION

The vocabulary of the Palestinian Syriac version exhibits not a few Graecisms. Thus, while the earlier Syriac versions commonly represent ᾽Ιησοῦς by ܝܫܘܥ, the Palestinian Syriac almost always transliterates it ܝܣܘܣ. Even at Matt. xvi. 18 this version uses a transliteration of Πέτρος rather than the Semitic *Kêphā᾽* (as in the Curetonian [the Sinaitic Syriac is not extant here] and the Peshitta), destroying thereby the significance of the play on words in the context.[3]

Graecizing went so far even in common words that occasionally ordinary Syriac words are abandoned for Greek words in Syriac dress. A typical example is the forsaking of *kenšā᾽*, the customary word in the Peshitta for 'crowd', and the use in its stead of *᾽oklōs* (plural *᾽oklōsē᾽*). Schwally[4] lists about sixty words that are transliterated in the manner of ὄχλος.

Not only do individual words in Palestinian Syriac reveal their Greek origin, but the connected text displays instances of exceedingly mechanical translation, particularly where the Greek text preserves a Semitic word or phrase with an appended Greek translation. For example, in the Marcan narrative of the deaf and dumb man (vii. 34), the Greek text presents the Aramaic word used by Jesus, adding its meaning in Greek (᾽Εφφαθά [= אֶתְפְּתַח], ὅ ἐστιν, Διανοίχθητι). Here the Palestinian Syriac, oddly enough, renders the entire text: 'And he said to him, "Be thou opened," which is, "Be thou opened." '[5]

It was mentioned above that the Palestinian Syriac Lectionary makes use of the several varieties of incipit which are found in

[1] See R. de Vaux, 'Fouille au Khirbet Qumran', *RB* lx (1953), 85 f.

[2] Edited by Perrot, op. cit., pp. 506–55.

[3] For other examples of proper names rendered in a more or less Graecized form, see Metzger's contribution to Black's Festschrift (p. 79 n. 3 above), p. 213.

[4] Friedrich Schwally, *Idioticon des christlich palästinischen Aramaeisch* (Giessen, 1893), pp. 103–13. On Greek words in Syriac, see Anton Schall, *Studien über griechische Fremdwörter im Syrischen* (Darmstadt, 1960), and S. P. Brock, 'Greek Words in the Syriac Gospels (*vet* and *pe*)', *Mu*, lxxx (1967), 389–426.

[5] The Sinaitic Syriac (Curetonian *hiat*), Peshitta, and Arabic Diatessaron omit the explanatory phrase; the Harclean retains it. For other examples of pleonastic renderings, see p. 214 of the present writer's article mentioned above (p. 79 n. 3).

Greek lectionaries. There is, however, a difference in the manner in which the incipit is joined to the pericope. Greek lectionaries introduce minor modifications in whatever expressions of time happen to stand in the opening sentence of the lection. But in the Palestinian Syriac Lectionary the incipits are prefixed to the pericopes in an altogether mechanical way with no attempt at smoothing the sense. Naturally the result is sometimes unsatisfactory. For example, the very common Greek incipit τῷ καιρῷ ἐκείνῳ is represented in the Palestinian Syriac Lectionary with such *gaucheries* as: 'And at that time; moreover on the last day of the feast . . .'; 'And at that time; and on the next day he stood . . .'; 'At that time; and after this he walked . . .'.

The Palestinian Syriac version contains several unusual and noteworthy readings. Examples include the following:[1]

Matt. xii. 36: 'Men must give an account of every good word which they do not speak' (codex C).

Acts i. 12: 'Which is a journey *of the caravans* on a Sabbath.'

Rom. iii. 23: 'All have sinned and lack *the knowledge* of the glory of God.'

Rom. vi. 8: 'If we *are dying* with Christ we believe that we *are living* with him.'

Rom. x. 4: '*God's* end of the Law is Christ.'

Eph. iii. 20: 'According to the power *of him* that works in us.'

1 Thess. iv. 16: 'With the *sound of the* trumpet of God.'

2 Tim. ii. 10: 'That they may receive salvation in Jesus Christ with his glory *which is from heaven.*'

Tit. ii. 12: 'That in *fear* and righteousness and *the love of* God we may live in this world.'

Jas. i. 1: 'To the twelve tribes *of Israel.*'

Jas. i. 5: 'Let him ask of God who gives everything to him *little by little* and does not put to shame.'

The textual affinities of the Palestinian Syriac version have been variously described. The first analysis was made by Adler,

---

[1] For other examples see J. T. Marshall, 'Remarkable Readings in the Epistles found in the Palestinian Syriac Lectionary', *JTS* v (1903–4), 437–45. For a *caveat* concerning some of the conclusions drawn by Marshall, see F. C. Burkitt, ibid. vi (1904–5), 91–8.

who found that of 165 variations tabulated by him from codex A eleven agree with D alone; fourteen agree with D and another manuscript; and with D and many other manuscripts, fifty-four; making a total of seventy-nine. Manuscript B agrees with the same codex three times alone; and, with various other manuscripts, eighty-two times; making a total of eighty-five.[1]

Von Soden characterized the Palestinian Syriac version of the Synoptic Gospels as belonging to his *I* recension, with but very little influence from the *K* recension. The text of John, on the other hand, he found to exhibit considerably more *K* influence.[2] Hoskier noted points of contact between the text of this version and the twelfth-century Greek minuscule 157,[3] which has a curiously mixed type of text. More recently Lake, Blake, and New concluded that the Palestinian Syriac version is Caesarean in its textual affinities and thought that it derived its Caesarean colouring from a Syriac version of which no other trace remains.[4]

Finally, the Palestinian Syriac Gospels have been subjected to yet another kind of analysis. Black, prompted by occasional suggestions previously made that they contain several traces of the influence of the Diatessaron, undertook a more systematic induction of the evidence.[5] The result of his investigation confirms the earlier suspicions, for the text shows an unmistakable degree of Diatessaric influence.

It is obvious from the preceding characterizations that the text of the Palestinian Syriac version agrees with no one type of text, but embodies elements from quite disparate families and texts. At the same time it displays features that suggest a close relationship to its Greek antecedents. 'If one compares', Lagrange correctly observes, 'the Old Syriac, the Peshitta, and the Palestinian Syriac, one will easily recognize the first two as a single version revised, while in the third the vocabulary is so different and the contact with the Greek is so obvious that it gives the impression of an entirely new translation.'[6]

---

[1] Adler, op. cit., p. 201. [2] Von Soden, op. cit., pp. 1497–1506.
[3] H. C. Hoskier, 'Evan. 157 (Rome, Vat. Urb. 2)', *JTS* xiv (1913), 242 f.
[4] 'The Caesarean Text of the Gospel of Mark', *HTR* xxi (1928), 312–23. In the opinion, however, of Lagrange (*Critique textuelle*, p. 167, note 4) and Colwell (*JR* xvii (1937), 56) the hypothetical Syriac version has been postulated without adequate reason.
[5] Matthew Black, 'The Palestinian Syriac Gospels and the Diatessaron' [part i], *OC* xxxvi (1941), 101–11. (The continuation of this article appears never to have been published.)   [6] *Critique textuelle*, p. 239.

VII. LIMITATIONS OF SYRIAC IN REPRESENTING GREEK[1]

by Sebastian P. Brock

Because Syriac belongs to a completely different group of languages, translation into it from Greek imposed considerable problems, especially for the initial translators, who had little or no tradition of translation from Greek into Syriac on which to rely. As elsewhere in the sphere of biblical translation in antiquity, the combination of a steady increase in sheer experience and skill in translation (biblical and otherwise), and an ever greater reverence paid to the source-language and its contents, has meant that the latest translations into Syriac are the most literal, and the earliest the most free. Indeed, in the case of the seventh-century reviser, Thomas of Harkel, one can only admire the immense skill he displayed in the formal representation in Syriac of the niceties of the Greek original.

As a Semitic language Syriac is at a disadvantage in rendering a Greek original in the following main spheres:

Syriac, having no case endings, is unable to indulge in the great freedom of word order that is characteristic of Greek.

The Syriac and Greek tense systems differ very considerably.

Although Syriac technically has a postpositive article (the so-called 'emphatic state'), its use does not correspond at all to that of the Greek article.

Syriac prefers parataxis to hypotaxis, and this has led to the frequent restructuring of entire sentences (especially in the Old Syriac version).

Syriac is rarely able to denote the presence of prepositional

---

[1] Section VII, 'Limitations of Syriac in Representing Greek', makes use of the following sigla:

    ~ = 'is roughly equivalent to'
    C = Curetonian (Old Syriac)
  CPA = Christian Palestinian Aramaic (Palestinian Syriac)
    H = Harclean
    P = Peshitta
    S = Sinaitic (Old Syriac).

compound elements in verbs[1] and substantives, and compound words cannot be rendered literally, e.g.

Heb. vii. 16   ζωῆς ἀκαταλύτου

P   ܡܬܫܪܐ ܕܠܐ ܚܝܐܕ

(lit. 'life which is not dissolved')

1 Pet. i. 18   (ἀναστροφῆς) πατροπαραδότου

P   ܕܩܒܠܬܘܢ ... ܗܠܝܢ ܕܥܒ̈ܕܝܟܘܢ ܡܢ
ܐܒ̈ܗܝܟܘܢ

(lit. 'your works . . . which you have received
from your fathers')

Syriac is less rich in adjectives than is Greek, and, while H
normally provides (and even, if necessary, creates) suitable
adjectival forms, the other versions prefer a periphrasis, e.g.

Luke ii. 13   (στρατιᾶς) οὐρανίου

S C P   ܕܫܡܝܐ (lit. 'of heaven')

CPA   ܕܫܡܝܐ (id.)

H   ܫܡܝܢܝܬܐ (lit. 'heavenly')

Syriac has no comparative or superlative, e.g.

John v. 36   (μαρτυρίαν) μείζω τοῦ Ἰωάννου

C P H   ܪܒܐ ܡܢ ܕܝܘܚܢܢ

CPA   ܪܒܐ ܡܢ ܕܝܘܚܢܢ

(lit. 'great from (that) of John')

The conjunction *waw* has a far wider range of meaning than
καί, and the presence of *waw* (especially in S and C) by no
means implies that καί featured in their Greek *Vorlage*.

Syriac is comparatively poor in particles, and in the earlier
versions the Greek particles are not consistently rendered.

In the following pages it has been possible to deal with only
a selection of salient features, and for the most part attention has
been directed only to those that are of importance from the point

---

[1] Attempts to render compound verbs sometimes lead to the use of two separate
verbs, e.g. Luke x. 39 παρακαθεσθεῖσα ～ S C P 'she *came and* sat'.

of view of textual criticism. The vast majority of examples are taken from the Gospels, simply because here there are the most versions available for comparison. It may be assumed that what is said of the Peshitta Gospels applies *grosso modo* to the Peshitta in the Acts and Epistles, although there the revision of the lost Old Syriac[1] was perhaps rather less thorough than in the Gospels. The Pococke Epistles and Crawford Apocalypse[2] (which Gwynn considered to be the sole survivors of the Philoxenian version) represent a stage in translation technique somewhat between the Peshitta and Harclean, on the whole closer to the former than to the latter.

PROPER NAMES

The treatment of proper names in the New Testament (in particular in S, C, and P) has been discussed at some length by both Burkitt[3] and Schwen.[4]

Basically there are two ways open to the translator: the names may be transliterated, or they may be given their appropriate Semitic form (where applicable). In general it will be found that S, C, and P will provide the correct Semitic form for names of Semitic origin, whereas H and CPA are inconsistent (the latter providing many hybrids, as *Iuḥannis*, quoted above). Obviously, wherever a genuine Semitic form is found, one is left with no indication of the precise form of the translator's underlying Greek (e.g. *Urišlem* ∼ Ἰερουσαλήμ / Ἱεροσόλυμα; *b'lzbwb* (so 2 Kings i. 2 Peshitta) ∼ Βεελζεβούλ).

In the genealogies the tendency to assimilate the forms of the names to those found in the Peshitta Old Testament is particularly

---

[1] For the Epistles, cf. J. Kerschensteiner, *Der altsyrische Paulustext* (*CSCO* cccxv, *Subsidia* xxxvii; Louvain, 1970).

[2] Good descriptions of the character of their translation can be found in the introductions and supplementary notes in J. Gwynn's *Remnants of the Later Syriac Versions of the Bible* (London, 1909) and *The Apocalypse of St. John in a Syriac Version hitherto unknown* (Dublin, 1897).

[3] F. C. Burkitt, 'The Syriac forms of New Testament Proper Names', *Proceedings of the British Academy*, v (1911–12), 377–408. Burkitt pays special attention to problematical cases.

[4] P. Schwen, 'Die syrische Wiedergabe der neutestamentlichen Eigennamen', *ZAW* xxxi (1911), 267–303. Schwen gives a useful alphabetical list (his references to S and C need controlling, since he makes use only of the inadequate *editiones principes*); in it he notes the corresponding forms in the Peshitta Old Testament.

strong (above all in the earlier versions), even if this differs from the Greek form in Matthew and Luke, e.g.

			C S	P	H	CPA
Matt. i. 4–5	Luke iii. 32	Ruth iv. 20 Peshitta			Matt. and Luke	
Ναασσων	Ναασσων	nḥšwn	nḥšwn	nḥšwn	n''sswn[1]	nḥšwn
Σαλμων	Σαλα/Σαλμων	šl'	šl'	slmwn	slmwn	slmwn Matt. š'l'⎫ Luke sl' ⎭

The Old Syriac assimilates the two names wholly to the Syriac Old Testament, P and CPA only partly. Thus *šl'* in S and C cannot be claimed as evidence for Σαλα in Luke, while the spellings in P, CPA (*sl'*), and, of course, H are indicative of the reading in their underlying Greek text.

Elsewhere well-known names of Semitic origin, such as Elizabeth, Jesus, John, Mary, Simon, etc., are normally rendered in their correct Semitic form, and only H and CPA provide exceptions, although in neither version is usage very consistent. Less obvious Semitic names are not always correctly recognized: thus Μαναήν at Acts xiii. 1 is incorrectly semiticized as *mn'yl* (instead of *mnḥm*): in such places the Syriac cannot be quoted as a witness to a variant Greek reading. Occasionally Semitic names are not recognized at all, e.g. Ἀρέτας in 2 Cor. xi. 32 is simply transliterated *'rṭws* (the name should be *ḥrtt*).

Place-names are treated in much the same way as personal names: those with Semitic counterparts are usually given the normal Semitic form,[2] e.g. Ναζαρέθ:[3] *nṣrt*; Πτολεμαΐς: *'kw*; Τύρος: *ṣwr*; but Ἄζωτος is simply transliterated (Peshitta O.T. *'šdwd*).

In straight transliterations of proper names the following correspondences between Greek and Syriac consonants are regularly observed in all versions:

β	ܒ b	κ	ܩ q	π	ܦ p	φ	ܦ p
γ	ܓ g	λ	ܠ l	ρ	ܪ r	ψ	does not occur
δ	ܕ d	μ	ܡ m	σ	ܣ s		
ζ	ܙ z	ν	ܢ n	τ	ܛ ṭ		
θ	ܬ t	ξ	ܟܣ ks	χ	ܟ k		

---

[1] In Matthew *n''sswn* is followed by *nḥšwn*. This is characteristic of H (at least in the printed edition): the first occurrence of the name is very often given as a transliteration of the Greek, whereas later on the Semitic form is used; cf. Luke i. 5 *'lys'bht*, but i. 7 *'lyšb'*.

[2] This may not otherwise be attested, e.g. Κανα ∼ *qṭn'* in S C P and H.

[3] Also Ναζωραῖος etc., ∼ *naṣraya*, 'of Nazareth'.

The strictness with which this system is adhered to makes it certain, for example, that H's *'lys'bht* at Luke i. 35 represents -εθ, not -ετ.

Greek vowels, on the other hand, are very inconsistently represented by means of *matres lectionis* (supralinear vocalization does not antedate the late seventh century) : e.g. *alaph* represents α and ε ; *he* ε and η (mainly confined to H) ; *waw* ο ω ου οι υ ; and *yudh* ι. Very often an interconsonantal Greek vowel will not be represented at all in the Syriac transcription.

A whole variety of Greek nominal suffixes tend to be covered by *-ws* (as Ἀρέτας above ; Ἀθῆναι : *'tnws*). The different case endings are not usually expressed, although occasionally the vocative is reproduced (e.g. Τιμόθεε : *tymt''* in 1 Tim. vi. 20, but not i. 18 (*-t'ws*)). Owing to Syriac's dislike of certain consonantal clusters in an initial position a prosthetic *alaph* may be introduced, e.g. Σπανία *'spny'*.

In the case of proper names the older Syriac versions at times make use of local exegetical traditions : thus, while P renders Ματθίας in Acts i as *mty'*, and Ἄγαβος in Acts xi. 28 as *'gbws*, the Old Syriac (to judge from early quotations) substituted *tlmy* (Tolmay) and *'d'* (Adda) respectively. A similar sort of case is the removal of the anachronistic mention of the Elamites (Acts ii. 9) in P, which substitutes the more suitable *'lny'* (Alans), or the same version's rendering of Ζεύς in Acts xiv. 12 f. by *mare alahe* (Lord of the gods).[1]

Certain proper names are treated in a very free way in S, C, and, to a lesser extent, P and CPA, and require special attention.

(a) Ἰησοῦς / Κύριος

Burkitt pointed out[2] that S in particular was apt to render Ἰησοῦς by *maran*, 'our Lord', while the converse, *iso'* representing Κύριος where this refers to Jesus in the Greek, is common in S, C, and P. Throughout the Syriac versions there is a strong tendency to add the pronominal suffix 'my / our' to 'Lord'. A not dissimilar situation is found in CPA, where Ἰησοῦς is almost always rendered by *mare Isus*, 'the Lord Jesus'.

[1] Cf. H. J. W. Drijvers, *Old-Syriac (Edessean) Inscriptions* (Leiden, 1972), p. 13, for this deity.

[2] F. C. Burkitt, *Evangelion da-Mepharreshe*, ii (Cambridge, 1904), 97–9.

(*b*) Σίμων/Πέτρος/Κηφᾶς

The treatment of (Σίμων) Πέτρος in S, C, and P has been discussed by Burkitt,[1] Schwen,[2] and Clemons,[3] who found that, while Σίμων Πέτρος is almost always rendered by *šem'un kepa*, Πέτρος alone is treated in a very inconsistent way, and the evidence of S, C, and P needs handling with particular caution: since, for example, S, C, and P avoid the transcription *Pṭrws*, they cannot be used as evidence where the Greek manuscripts are divided between Κηφᾶς and Πέτρος.

(*c*) Διάβολος

The Syriac versions, with the exception of H, are far from consistent in their treatment of διάβολος. While S and C at times render this by *'akel qarṣa*, 'accuser', they more frequently substitute *saṭana* (Matt. iv. 1 (C), 8 (S); Luke iv. 2, 5, 13 (S); John vi. 70 (S C), xiii 2 (S)),[4] or *biša* (which represents ὁ Πονηρός at Matt. v. 37 etc.; so Matt. xiii. 39 (S C), John viii 44 (S)),[5] or, once, *b'eldbaba* 'enemy' (Luke viii. 12 (S C).[6] Only at Luke iv. 2 is a Greek variant attested, and in view of their usage elsewhere, it is impossible to say whether S and C really support the Greek variant Σατανᾶς there: certainly in all the other passages it is most unlikely that they represent an otherwise lost Greek variant, and their choice of rendering must be attributed to the lack of interest in the 'accusing' activity of the Devil that is observable in early Syriac writers. In this connection it may be noted that 'evil one' and 'enemy' are particularly common appellations of the Devil in Syriac literature.

P normally 'corrects' the Old Syriac, but *saṭana* has been left at Matt. xiii. 39 (S C, however, have *biša*), Luke iv. 5 (= S), John vi. 70 (= S C), xiii. 2 (= S), and 'enemy' at Luke viii. 12 (= S C). In no case can a Greek variant safely be posited. In Acts and the Epistles P has *saṭana* for ten out of the fifteen occurrences of διάβολος in the singular: *'akel qarṣa* occurs only at Acts xiii. 10,

---

[1] Op. cit., pp. 92–6, with useful tables.

[2] Art. cit.; table on pp. 296–7.

[3] J. T. Clemons, 'Some questions on the Syriac Support for Variant Greek Readings', *NovT* x (1968), 26–30.

[4] C is missing in Luke iv and John xiii.

[5] C is missing here. *biša* appears to be particularly favoured in the Syriac Diatessaron, where, for example, it is attested at Matthew xxv. 41, Luke iv. 13, John viii. 44.   [6] *Not* attributable to a harmonization.

Eph. iv. 27, and vi. 11, while at Acts x. 38 P has *biša*. Once again it is extremely doubtful whether P represents a Greek variant *Σατανᾶς*.[1]

The same feature is observable in CPA, where usage seems to be consistent: *διάβολος* is regularly rendered by *saṭana*. Again there is no question of any underlying Greek variant.

WORD ORDER

Of the Syriac versions only H adheres strictly to the word order of the original, in so far as this is possible in Syriac. At the other extreme the Old Syriac will on occasion completely restructure the sentence it is translating, and at times this has produced what can only be described as a free paraphrase.[2]

Certain general tendencies can be observed, which have their bearing on the evaluation of the older Syriac versions in individual passages. Thus there appears to be a strong inclination to provide the sequence: place + time, wherever the Greek has the reverse, e.g.

Luke iv. 25 *ἐν ταῖς ἡμέραις Ἠλίου | ἐν τῷ Ἰσραήλ* transpose S P.

No Greek variant is attested here, and it is not likely that the Syriac implies one.

Another instructive case is to be found a few verses later:

Luke iv. 28 *καὶ ἐπλήσθησαν πάντες θυμοῦ ἐν τῇ συναγωγῇ ἀκούοντες ταῦτα.*

Syriac prefers to give the verbs in their logical order, with the 'hearing' preceding the 'anger'; thus a literal translation of S would be: 'and when they heard—those who were in the synagogue—they were filled with wrath.' P leaves this word order, but inserts 'all of them' at the end of the sentence, to cover the Greek *πάντες*, inadequately represented in S (it is extremely unlikely that it was absent from S's Greek text). H and CPA, on the other hand, give the verbs in their Greek order.

---

[1] Renderings of *Σατανᾶς* are, as might be expected, much more regular. C, however, provides *'akel qarṣa* at Luke xiii. 16, where no Greek variant *διάβολος* is attested: since the whole tendency in S C is to *avoid* this term, it is possible that C may represent an otherwise lost variant. On the other hand it is conceivable that C represents a 'hypercorrection' (without reference to the Greek) of the kind that Burkitt envisaged in connection with *maran/išoʻ* (op. cit. ii. 99).

[2] Luke x. 25 is a striking example.

There are certain patterns of word order that Syriac is totally unable to represent. Thus the possessive pronoun can come only after the substantive (usually in the form of a suffix) : e.g. αὐτοῦ τὸ ὄνομα and τὸ ὄνομα αὐτοῦ can be rendered only by *šmeh/šma dileh* (lit. 'name-his', 'name of-him').

On specific points of word order, the over-all usage of the individual Syriac versions requires examination before they can safely be used as evidence for a Greek variant. The position of the demonstrative may serve as an illustration.

In Syriac, as in Greek, the demonstrative may be placed before or after the substantive. The Syriac versions (with the exception of CPA—see below) normally follow the word order of the original Greek exactly, but there is observable in S, C, and P a slight tendency to place the demonstrative *before* the substantive, where the Greek has it after. Thus in Luke S, C, and P (usually together) provide the order: demonstrative + substantive on fifteen occasions where the Greek has the reverse; only in seven of these passages is a variation in word order attested in the Greek tradition. It thus seems unlikely that S, C, and P can be quoted as supporting evidence for the variant order on those occasions where it *is* found in Greek manuscripts; they should certainly not be considered evidence for an otherwise unattested Greek variation in word order in the remaining eight passages.

In CPA the demonstrative regularly appears before the substantive, whatever the order of the Greek.[1]

TENSE

The differences between the Greek and Syriac tense systems posed certain difficulties for the translators, but various more or less standard ways of bridging these difficulties were evidently devised at an early date, for we find the following correspondences in fairly general use in all the Syriac versions:

> Greek present: Syriac participle (in the *peʿal* only distinguished from the perfect by the placing of a dot, which is often absent altogether in the two Old Syriac manuscripts).

---

[1] In Luke I have found only one exception in the Lectionaries (xii. 37); F. Schulthess, *Grammatik des christlich-palästinischen Aramäisch* (Tübingen, 1924), § 165, implies that both orders are equally common: this is certainly not true as far as the Gospel translations are concerned.

Greek imperfect: Syriac participle + auxiliary.
Greek future: Syriac imperfect, or (occasionally) participle.
Greek aorist and perfect: Syriac perfect.

Consistency in usage, however, can be expected only in H.

Subordinate clauses posed special problems, since Syriac has no subjunctive or optative: H is the only version to attempt some sort of formal representation, and this is confined to *εἰμι* and periphrases for *ἔχω* (which has no exact equivalent in Syriac), e.g.

Luke viii. 9	*τίς εἴη*
S C P	ܡܢܘ
H	ܡܢܐ ܬܗܘܐ ܐܝܬܝܗ̇
CPA	ܡܐ ܗܘ
John vi. 40	*ἵνα . . . ἔχῃ (ζωὴν αἰώνιον)*
S C	ܕ . . . ܐܝܬ ܠܗ
P	ܕ . . . ܢܗܘܘܢ ܠܗ
H	ܕ . . . ܢܗܘܐ ܐܝܬ ܠܗ
CPA	ܝܗܐ ܒܡܗ

PARTICIPLES

The frequent hypotactic use of the participle in Greek cannot be represented exactly in Syriac; S, C, and to a lesser extent P normally substitute the parataxis of two finite verbs, while the other versions (above all H) render the Greek participle by means of a subordinate clause consisting of a participle or perfect introduced by *kad*, 'when'. H regularly distinguishes between Greek present and aorist participles thus:

Greek present part.: *kad* + part. ± auxiliary verb.
Greek aorist part.: *kad* + perfect.

Examples of the different treatments of Greek participles in the various versions are:

Luke viii. 1	*διώδευεν . . . κηρύσσων καὶ εὐαγγελιζόμενος*
S C	ܡܬܟܪܟ ܗܘܐ . . . ܘܡܣܒܪ
P	ܡܬܟܪܟ ܗܘܐ . . . ܘܡܟܪܙ ܗܘܐ ܘܡܣܒܪ
H	ܡܬܟܪܟ ܗܘܐ . . . ܟܕ ܡܟܪܙ ܘܡܣܒܪ

Luke viii. 1 CPA ... ܡܟܪܙ ܘܡܣܒܪ ... ܫܒܠ ... ܗܘܐ

Luke xx. 27 προσελθόντες δὲ . . . ἐπηρώτησαν αὐτὸν λέγοντες

SC ܘܩܪܒܘ ... ܘܫܐܠܘܗܝ ܘܐܡܪܝܢ ܠܗ

P ܩܪܒܘ ܕܝܢ ... ܘܫܐܠܘܗܝ ܘܐܡܪܝܢ ܠܗ

H ܟܕ ܩܪܒܘ ܕܝܢ ... ܡܫܐܠܝܢ ܗܘܘ ܠܗ ܟܕ ܐܡܪܝܢ

Here H represents the variant ἐπηρώτων. (CPA is not extant at this point.)

Heb. xi. 30 (τὰ τείχη Ιερειχω) ἔπεσαν κυκλωθέντα

P ܢܦܠܘ ܡܢ ܕܐܬܟܪܟܘ

H ܢܦܠܘ ܟܕ ܐܬܟܪܟܘ

Apocalypse i. 1 καὶ ἐσήμανεν ἀποστείλας

Crawford Apoc. and H ܫܘܕܥ ܟܕ ܫܠܚ

DEMONSTRATIVES

The Syriac versions normally distinguish between ἐκεῖνος and οὗτος, although where the plural is involved there is apt to be slight inconsistency. There appears to be a slight tendency in S C P to substitute *halen*, 'these', in places where *hanon*, 'those', might be expected: thus *halen* renders κἀκεῖνα in Luke xi. 42 in S C P, and C has *halen* at Luke xiv. 24 to render ἐκείνων (S P *hanon*): in neither place is a Greek variant attested.

The converse, *hanon* in S C P for ταύταις etc., is actually rather more frequent, and in Luke it occurs at i. 39, vi. 12, xix. 15, xx. 16, xxiii. 7, and xxiv. 18 (*om.* S C). In each case, except xxiv. 18, a Greek variant ἐκείναις etc. is otherwise attested. Closer examination, however, shows that four of these passages concern the phrase ἐν ταῖς ἡμέραις ταύταις and it would appear that S C P regularly render this by 'in *those* days', for the same phenomenon is also found in Acts i. 15, vi. 1, and xi. 27, the only other New

Testament passages where it occurs. It is accordingly most unlikely that in these cases S C P can be quoted as representing the
variant ἐκείναις. In the remaining Lucan passages (xix. 15, xx.
16), however, there would appear to be no conditioning factor
behind the rendering in S C P, and, while certainty is impossible,
it would seem legitimate to quote them in support of the variant
ἐκεῖνος etc.

It should be noted that there are many places where *haw hanon*,
'that, those', simply represents the article in Greek, e.g.

> Mark iii. 5   λέγει τῷ ἀνθρώπῳ
>
> SCP   ܪܒܢܐ ܐܢܠ ܐܡܪ

PARTICLES[1]

To make up for the paucity of particles in Syriac many Greek
particles were taken over into the language, especially in the
later versions. The earlier versions (including P) are quite apt
to ignore particles altogether, and thus cannot be taken as ev
idence for their omission.

The great care needed in citing the evidence of the Syriac versions in this area will be obvious from the situation that is to be
found with the following three common particles.

(a) Γάρ

Γάρ is normally rendered by *ger*, even in the Old Syriac,
although occasionally *d-*, *meṭul*, or *w-* are employed (mostly
corrected to *ger* in P). Where γάρ is entirely unrepresented in
the Old Syriac, S and C can probably legitimately be cited as
evidence for the omission of the particle.

On the other hand, *ger* is found in a number of passages in
S, C, and to a lesser extent P, where γάρ is not to be found in the
Greek, even as a variant. This means that it is uncertain whether
the Syriac really represents the variant + γάρ in the cases where
that variant *is* otherwise attested.[2]

(b) Δέ

In S C P and CPA there is *no* exact equivalence in usage between δέ and *den*: δέ is represented in these versions not only by

[1] See further S. P. Brock, 'The Treatment of Greek Particles in the Old Syriac
Gospels, with Special Reference to Luke', *Studies in New Testament Language and
Text*, ed. by J. K. Elliott (Leiden, 1976), pp. 80–6.

[2] For the situation in Peshitta Galatians, see Clemons, art. cit.

den,[1] but also by *w*-, 'and', or nothing at all. Conversely *den* may represent καί, or have no equivalent at all in the Greek; while δέ is sometimes otherwise attested as a variant in such passages, there remain many places where it is not. It would thus seem clear that normally S C P and CPA cannot be quoted as evidence for the presence or absence of δέ in their underlying Greek texts.

(c) Οὖν

In the later Syriac versions οὖν is regularly represented by *hakil*, but in the Old Syriac the situation is complicated, for, whereas οὖν is fairly often rendered by *hakil*, there are many instances, as Burkitt pointed out,[2] where it is loosely rendered by *w*- or *den*; in such places P normally corrects to *hakil*, but there remain several instances (especially in John) where no such correction has been made. As a general criterion it may be said that, where *hakil* is present in S C P, it may be assumed that οὖν was to be found in their Greek *Vorlage*, but the absence of *hakil* does not necessarily mean that οὖν did not feature in their underlying Greek text either.

PREPOSITIONS

The Syriac system of prepositions differs considerably from the Greek, and Syriac is incapable of representing certain variations in Greek, such as ἀπό / ἐκ, ὑπέρ + g./περί + g., ἐπί + g./d./a.

To make up for the deficiency in prepositions, a number of prepositional phrases are employed to render particular Greek prepositions, e.g. διά + gen. ~ *byad*, 'by the hand of'. Here particular care is needed in assessing the evidence of the Syriac for certain variants in the Greek. Thus, for example, the older Syriac versions cannot safely be cited as evidence for the variation διά ± τοῦ στόματος (τοῦ προφήτου), for, while S C usually render διά in this sort of context by *b*- (P more frequently *byad*), C has *bpum* (lit. 'by the mouth of') three times (Matt. i. 22, viii. 17, xii. 17) and S once (Matt. ii. 15) where no Greek variant is otherwise known: in all likelihood this is an inner-Syriac stylistic feature, and the same will apply to P in Acts xxviii. 25, where διά is again rendered by *bpum*.

---

[1] In Luke δέ is represented by *den* in S and C in only about one-fifth of its total occurrences in that book. [2] Op. cit. ii. 89.

MISCELLANEOUS

(a) Ἐγένετο + articular infinitive

This Greek construction is almost always paraphrased in the Old Syriac, which provides no equivalent to ἐγένετο. In P this is only sometimes made good, e.g.

Luke xvii. 11   καὶ ἐγένετο ἐν τῷ πορεύεσθαι

S C   ܟܕ ܐܙܠܝܢ ܗܘܘ

P   ܘܗܘܐ ܕܟܕ ܐܙܠ

but Luke xvii. 14   καὶ ἐγένετο ἐν τῷ ὑπάγειν

S C = P   ܘܟܕ ܐܙܠܝܢ

H and CPA, on the other hand, regularly represent ἐγένετο.

(b) Indefinite τις

S C P and, *a fortiori*, the later versions are careful to render enclitic τις (by ḥad, (’)naš etc.), but there are also several instances where ḥad is present in S C P, but τις is not found in the Greek, even as a variant. Thus, while the absence of ḥad etc. in S C P can reasonably be taken as evidence for the absence of τις from their underlying Greek text, it is impossible to assume that the converse is true.

(c) Ὅτι recitativum

There is a tendency in all the Syriac versions (including H) to introduce quotations of direct speech by d-, even when ὅτι is absent from the Greek; no Greek variant can be assumed.

(d) Pronouns

One of the Semitic features of New Testament Greek is the over-use of the possessive pronoun αὐτοῦ (αὐτῶν). Syriac idiom in fact virtually demands the use of the suffix with, for example, words denoting parts of the body, and if there is variation ± αὐτοῦ in the Greek tradition, the Syriac (with the exception of H) cannot be cited as evidence for the presence of the pronoun in its Greek *Vorlage*. A single example will suffice to illustrate this: in Matthew χείρ occurs ten times without the possessive pronoun, and in four of these there is no Greek variant + αὐτοῦ attested, yet in all ten cases S C P and (where extant) CPA add the suffix.

H, on the other hand, goes against Semitic idiom by having no suffix in eight out of the ten places, and so it may legitimately be quoted as supporting the variant + αὐτοῦ in Matt. xv. 2 and xxvii. 24 where it *does* have the suffix.

(e) Verbs of saying

The older Syriac versions, in particular S and C, are very free in their handling of verbs of saying: the tense will be freely altered, an indirect object may be added, the construction altered by means of the addition or omission of the conjunction *waw*, the verb 'answered' may not infrequently be altogether dropped,[1] and if ἀποκρίνεσθαι occurs *alone* (i.e. without 'and said') in the original, the Old Syriac, and very often P too, render by the verb 'to say'.

Further, S C P and CPA do not distinguish between the constructions with dative and with πρός + accusative after verbs of saying, employing *l-* indiscriminately for both. H, on the other hand, uses *l-* to represent the dative, and *lwat* for πρός + acc.

OLD TESTAMENT QUOTATIONS[2]

Finally, it is important to consider the Syriac New Testament in the context of the Church which employed it, for the changing attitude of the Syriac-speaking Church over the course of time towards the Bible as a whole has left its mark on the various Syriac translations it has sponsored.

To the primitive Judaeo-Christian Church the authority of the Old Testament was greater than that of the (still emerging) New Testament, and particular importance was attached to Old Testament prophecies which were considered to have been fulfilled by Christ. Thus, in the earliest Syriac translations of the Gospels Old Testament quotations are very often found in a form that has been adapted to the wording of the Peshitta Old Testament, even when this may differ considerably from the form of the quotation in the Greek New Testament.

Later, however, the situation was reversed, and the wording of the Greek Gospels was regarded as the final authority: accordingly, in the later Syriac versions, Old Testament quotations

---

[1] As Burkitt pointed out (op. cit. ii. 91), all one can reasonably assume is that, where S and C have '*na*, 'answered', their Greek text contained the verb ἀποκρίνεσθαι. [2] Burkitt, op. cit. ii. 203–5.

are rendered strictly on the basis of their form in the Greek New Testament.

An interesting example of this whole process can be seen in the first half of Matt. xxi. 5 = Zech. ix. 9, one of the very few passages with Old Testament quotations for which we are fortunate enough to have the text of the Syriac Diatessaron, preserved here in Ephraem's *Commentary*. The fact that the Diatessaron turns out to stand closest to the Peshitta Old Testament,[1] and that C stands midway between it and P (S is not available), strongly suggests that the Diatessaron is both earlier than, and has exerted an influence on, the Old Syriac.[2]

Matt. xxi. 5   εἴπατε τῇ θυγατρὶ Σιων, ἰδοὺ ὁ βασιλεύς σου
ἔρχεταί σοι πραΰς (καὶ ἐπιβεβηκὼς ἐπὶ
ὄνον. . . .)

C P   ܐܬ̈ܪܝܢ ܐܘܪ̈ܒܬܐ ܕܝ̈ܐܬ ܗܡ̈ܝܢܘ . ܗܘ ܡܠܟܬܐ,ܐܡܪܬ܀
ܠܝ (+ ܕܝܘ̈ܢ ܘ C) ܒܟܡܝܢ

Diatessaron[3]   ܕܝܗ̈ܘ (sic) ܒܪ ܗܡ̈ܝܢܘ ܕ ܗܘܐ ܡܠܟܬܐ,
ܐܬ ܠܝ ܕܝ̈ܘܢ ܘ ܒܟܡ̈ܝܢܐ

Peshitta OT   ܕܝܗ̈ܘ, ܠܝ ܒܥ ܗܡ̈ܝܢܘ . . . ܗܘܐ ܡܠܟܬܐ,
ܐܬ ܠܝ ܕܝ̈ܘܢ ܘ ܩܒܘܠ ܘ ܒܟܡ̈ܝܢܐ

Assimilations to the Peshitta Old Testament are underlined. In numerous other passages too the Old Syriac (and to a much lesser extent P) has Old Testament quotations in a form strongly

---

[1] Contrast Burkitt, who considered that the Diatessaron was less influenced by the Peshitta Old Testament than was the Old Syriac (op. cit. ii. 205). An even more striking example is provided by a patristic quotation of Matt. xii. 18–20 (= Isa. xlii. 1–4), if the quotation genuinely represents the Syriac Diatessaron (text in I. Ortiz de Urbina, *Vetus Evangelium Syrorum, Diatessaron Tatiani* (Madrid, 1967), p. 234). Here the Diatessaron form of the quotation is almost entirely adapted to the Peshitta Old Testament (which differs considerably from the Greek New Testament form); much of this is still preserved in S and C, and even P has retained several traces.

[2] A conclusion many modern scholars would agree with on quite other grounds.

[3] Ephraem, *Comm. Diatessaron*, xviii. 1. While it is just possible that Ephraem is quoting the Peshitta Old Testament direct, the abbreviated form of the quotation suggests that it genuinely represents the Diatessaron reading at Matthew xxi. 5.

adapted to the Peshitta Old Testament text.[1] Obviously there is no question that in such passages the Syriac represents underlying Greek variant readings.

CONCLUSION

It will have been seen from the above examples that, while there are certain variations in Greek which cannot be represented in Syriac, the most problematical cases—from the text-critical point of view—are those where the Syriac at first sight appears formally to support a Greek variant; here a closer examination, taking into account *over-all usage* in a particular version and book, will often indicate that formal identity can by no means be used as evidence that the Syriac supports the Greek variant in question.[2] The citing of the Syriac-versional evidence in a Greek apparatus must accordingly go hand in hand with a study of the translation technique of each individual version in the book concerned.[3]

---

[1] A good example is provided by Luke iii. 4–6 (= Isa. xl. 3–5). Outside the Gospels P is again likely to be partly assimilated to the Peshitta Old Testament in quotations.

[2] Of the examples given above, the case of δέ ∼ *den* is perhaps the most striking.

[3] Although practically no work has been done on this, it would appear that in S C P there are certain differences in translation technique between different books or groups of books.

II

The Coptic Versions

I. THE INTRODUCTION OF CHRISTIANITY INTO EGYPT AND THE TRANSLATION OF THE NEW TESTAMENT

THE origins of the Church in Egypt are enveloped in deep obscurity. When it was that Christianity was first introduced into Egypt, and by whom, is totally unknown. According to Acts ii. 10 there were Jews from Egypt in Jerusalem at Pentecost, several of whom may have returned to their native land with some more or less clear knowledge concerning the new sect. By the middle of the first century, according to a Western reading in Acts xviii. 25, a certain form of Christianity had reached Alexandria. In this passage codex Bezae, supported by the Old Latin codex Gigas, adds ἐν τῇ πατρίδι after κατηχημένος, thereby asserting that Apollos, a Jewish Christian from Alexandria, 'had been instructed *in his own country* in the word (or way) of the Lord'. In their comment on the passage Lake and Cadbury make the observation, 'If this reading were right, or a correct inference (and this is not impossible), it would prove that Christianity had reached Alexandria, as it did Rome, not later than A.D. 50, and moreover that it was of the same type as the teaching of Apollos before he met Priscilla and Aquila.'[1]

According to a tradition reported by Eusebius on the basis of hearsay,[2] it was the Evangelist Mark who first established

[1] Ad loc. in vol. iv of *The Beginnings of Christianity*, Part I, ed. by F. J. Foakes Jackson and Kirsopp Lake (London, 1933), p. 233. Walter Bauer, who mistranslates the Western addition ('[Apollos] is said to have *preached* [*gepredigt*] already [in Alexandria]'), is inclined to discount the importance of the variant reading; see his *Orthodoxy and Heresy in Earliest Christianity*, Engl. trans. (Philadelphia, 1971), p. 46.

[2] *Hist. eccl.* II. xvi. 1: τοῦτον δὲ [Μάρκον] πρῶτόν φασιν ἐπὶ τῆς Αἰγύπτου στειλά-μενον, τὸ εὐαγγέλιον, ὃ δὴ καὶ συνεγράψατο, κηρῦξαι, ἐκκλησίας τε πρῶτον ἐπ' αὐτῆς Ἀλεξανδρείας συστήσασθαι. That Eusebius gained his information from oral tradition seems to be clear from his use of the formula 'they say' (φασίν). The tradition is repeated by Epiphanius (*Haer.* li. 6), Jerome (*de Vir. ill.* vii), and Nicephorus (*Hist. eccl.* ii. 43). For a brief account of the traditional view of Mark's part in founding the Church in Alexandria, drawn from the Arabic *History of the Patriarchs of the Coptic Church of Alexandria*, see Aziz S. Atiya, *History of Eastern Christianity* (London and Notre Dame, 1968), pp. 25–8.

Christian churches in Alexandria. Elsewhere Eusebius reports that Mark continued to be in charge of the diocese (παροικία, lit. colony or province) of Alexandria until the eighth year of the reign of Nero (i.e. A.D. 62), when Annianus succeeded him[1]—thus implying that the Evangelist died in that year.[2] This tradition, however, can scarcely be correct, for earlier and better-attested accounts report that Mark, having accompanied Peter as his interpreter,[3] composed his Gospel in Rome during the late sixties, either before Peter's death under Nero,[4] or (according to the better tradition) after Peter's death.[5] In the face of these irreconcilable dates,[6] most scholars regard the tradition of Mark's part in establishing churches in Alexandria as pure legend.

Apart from these two highly dubious pieces of information concerning Mark, Eusebius found nothing in his sources bearing on the introduction of Christianity into Egypt. In fact, for the period before the beginning of the lengthy episcopate of Bishop Demetrius of Alexandria (A.D. 188/9–231), about whom Eusebius provides not a little information, we look in vain for specific data concerning the dissemination of Christianity in Egypt. In such a situation the historian must rely on indirect hints and more or less cogent inferences based on those hints. He must canvass the early literature produced by and for Christians in Egypt, as well as collect the earliest papyrus fragments of the Scriptures preserved in the dry sands along the Nile. From these he can, perhaps, reconstruct the story of the planting and growth of the Church in Egypt during the first two centuries of the Christian era.

---

[1] *Hist. eccl.* II. xxiv. 1. Although Eusebius here avoids the word 'bishop', the *Apostolic Constitutions* (vii. 46) state that Mark ordained Annianus the first bishop of Alexandria.

[2] Jerome specifically states that Mark died in the eighth year of Nero and was buried in Alexandria (*de Vir. ill.* viii).

[3] So Papias, *ap.* Eusebius, *Hist. eccl.* III. xxxix. 15.

[4] So Clement of Alexandria, *ap.* Eusebius, *Hist. eccl.* VI. xiv. 5, followed by Jerome, *de Vir. ill.* viii.

[5] So Irenaeus, *Adv. haer.* III. i. 1–2, repeated by Eusebius, *Hist. eccl.* V. viii. 2.

[6] Despite the inconsistency of dating, Jerome combines the two traditions: 'Mark, the interpreter of the Apostle Peter, and the first bishop of the church in Alexandria . . . narrated those things which he had heard his master [viz. Peter] preaching . . .' (Prologue to the four Gospels from Jerome's *Com. in Matt.*, Wordsworth and White's *Nouum Testamentum Domini Nostri Jesu Christi Latine*, i (Oxford, 1889–1908), p. 12, lines 9–11).

Among Christian documents which during the second century either originated in Egypt or circulated there among both the orthodox and the Gnostics are numerous apocryphal gospels, acts, epistles, and apocalypses. Some of the more noteworthy are the Gospel according to the Egyptians, the Gospel of Truth, the Gospel of Thomas, the Gospel of Philip, the Kerygma of Peter, the Acts of John, the Epistle of Barnabas, the Epistle of the Apostles, and the Apocalypse of Peter. There are also fragments of exegetical and dogmatic works composed by Alexandrian Christians, chiefly Gnostics, during the second century. We know, for example, of such teachers as Basilides and his son Isidore, and of Valentinus, Ptolemaeus, Heracleon, and Pantaenus. All but the last-mentioned were unorthodox in one respect or another. In fact, to judge by the comments made by Clement of Alexandria, almost every deviant Christian sect was represented in Egypt during the second century; Clement mentions the Valentinians, the Basilidians, the Marcionites, the Peratae, the Encratites, the Docetists, the Haimetites, the Cainites, the Ophites, the Simonians, and the Eutychites. What proportion of Christians in Egypt during the second century were orthodox is not known.

In addition to the treatises, teachers, and sects just mentioned —for the knowledge of which we are dependent upon later writers and copies from subsequent centuries—a different kind of evidence has come to light proving the existence of Christians in various parts of Egypt during the second century; these are biblical texts which were copied in the second century by or for Christians living in Egypt. One of the earliest of these is the Rylands fragment of the Gospel of John ($\mathfrak{p}^{52}$), usually dated in the first half of the second century. Next come the fragments of an unknown gospel (Egerton Pap. 2), dated by its editors to about the middle of the second century.[1] From the close of the second century or the beginning of the third century come several papyri containing one or more books, or parts of books, of the Greek New Testament. These are $\mathfrak{p}^{46}$ (the Beatty codex of ten Pauline Epistles), $\mathfrak{p}^{64}$ and $\mathfrak{p}^{67}$ (parts of the same codex of Matthew,

---

[1] *Fragments of an Unknown Gospel and Other Early Christian Papyri*, ed. by H. Idris Bell and T. C. Skeat (London, 1935), p. 1. In his *Cults and Creeds in Graeco-Roman Egypt* (Liverpool, 1953), Bell states that 'the dates 125–165 probably give the approximate period within which this manuscript was written' (p. 80).

divided between Oxford and Barcelona),[1] 𝔭[66] (the Bodmer codex of John), and 𝔭[77], a fragment from Oxyrhynchus (no. 2683) containing the text of Matt. xxiii. 30–4, 35–9, a portion not otherwise represented among any of the eighty or so papyri of the New Testament. All of these are conservatively dated *c.* 200, while several have been assigned to dates well within the second century (Herbert Hunger,[2] for example, regards 𝔭[66] as coming from the middle, if not even from the first half, of the second century).

Besides copies of the New Testament transcribed in Egypt during the second century, several early fragments of the Greek Old Testament have also turned up in various parts of Egypt. Of course, a manuscript of the Old Testament might be of Jewish origin, but when that manuscript is in the form of a codex the presumption is that it was used by Christians—for Jews continued to prefer the roll for their sacred books. The earliest such Christian copy of the Septuagint appears to be a leaf from a codex of Genesis now at Yale University, dated by its editors to about A.D. 90.[3] Substantial portions of the books of Numbers and Deuteronomy survive in the Chester Beatty Papyrus VI, a codex which Kenyon dated to about the middle of the second century.[4] Since it contains examples of the *nomina sacra*, including Ἰησοῦς (= Joshua), it is almost certainly the work of a Christian scribe. One can also point to fragments of a second-century

---

[1] C. H. Roberts, 'An Early Papyrus of the First Gospel', *HTR* xlvi (1953), 233–7, and R. Roca-Puig, *Un papiro griego del Evangelio de san Mateo* (2nd edn.), con una note de Colin Roberts (Barcelona, 1962).

[2] 'Zur Datierung des Papyrus Bodmer II (P 66)', *Anzeiger der österreichischen Akademie der Wissenschaften*, phil.-hist. Kl., 1960, Nr. 4, pp. 12–33.

[3] *Yale Papyri*, ed. by John F. Oates, Alan E. Samuels, and C. Bradford Welles (*American Studies in Papyrology*, ii; New Haven and Toronto, 1967), 3. For a popular account, see Welles, 'The Yale Genesis Fragment', *Yale University Library Gazette*, xxxix (1964), 1–8, whose verdict is that 'the document . . . cannot have been written later than A.D. 100 and should be somewhat earlier' (p. 1). In his discussion of the fragment C. H. Roberts comments, 'Even if a somewhat later date be accepted, it remains one of the very earliest Christian MSS. extant' ('P. Yale 1 and the Early Christian Book', *Essays in Honor of C. Bradford Welles* (*American Studies in Papyrology*, i; New Haven, 1966), 25–8).

[4] Frederic G. Kenyon, *The Chester Beatty Biblical Papyri . . .*, fasc. 2, *Numbers and Deuteronomy* (London, 1935), p. ix, who says, 'It does not seem possible to date it later than the second century, or even, in my opinion, after the middle of that century. This is also the opinion of Mr. H. I. Bell and Professor Schubart, and is confirmed by Professor Wilcken (*Archiv für Papyrusforschung*, xi. 113), who speaks of the reign of Hadrian [A.D. 117–138].'

papyrus codex of Exodus and Deuteronomy at Heidelberg[1] and a leaf from a second-century papyrus codex of the Psalms from Antinoopolis.[2]

Still other indirect testimonies provide hints concerning the early dissemination and growth of Christianity not only in Alexandria but also in many villages along the Nile.[3] Enough has been cited here, however, to allow one to make certain deductions concerning the spread of Christianity in Egypt during the second century. It is scarcely necessary to point out that for every Christian manuscript fortuitously preserved over the centuries there were probably scores, perhaps hundreds, which perished or still lie hidden in the sand, and for every owner of such a manuscript there were probably many Christians, some of them illiterate, who had none. It is therefore altogether reasonable to conclude, as H. I. Bell does after making a careful survey of biblical and theological papyri in Egypt:

This evidence seems to justify the inference that even in the second century the number of Christians in Middle Egypt was by no means negligible and by the middle of the third was considerable. This papyrus evidence combines with *a priori* probability and the literary sources to make it likely that, although in the second century Christians formed only a small minority of the population and even till late in the third century were probably not a large one, yet the transition from an overwhelmingly pagan country to the predominately Christian one which we find in the fourth was by no means as sudden and cataclysmic as some writers have too hastily assumed.[4]

During the third century there is much more ample information concerning the external and internal expansion of Christianity throughout Egypt.[5] The earliest Christians used Greek,

---

[1] *Veröffentlichungen aus den badischen Papyrus-Sammlungen*, ed. by Friedrich Bilabel, iv (Heidelberg, 1924), 24–7, no. 56.

[2] *The Antinoopolis Papyri*, ed. by C. H. Roberts, i (London, 1950), no. 7. Roberts comments that the fragment, which preserves Ps. lxxxi. 1–8, 'may well have been written about the middle of the second century'.

[3] See Adolf von Harnack, *Die Mission und Ausbreitung des Christentums in den ersten drei Jahrhunderten*, 4te Aufl., ii (Leipzig, 1924), pp. 705–10 (Engl. trans. from 2nd Germ. edn., *The Mission and Expansion of Christianity in the First Three Centuries*, 2nd edn., ii (New York and London, 1908), 158–62).

[4] 'Evidences of Christianity in Egypt during the Roman Period', *HTR* xxxvii (1944), 185–204; quotation from p. 204. Cf. also C. H. Roberts, 'The Christian Book and the Greek Papyri', *JTS* l (1949), 155–68.

[5] See Harnack, op. cit. ii. 713–25 (Engl. trans., ii. 165–74), Mario Naldini, *Il Cristianesimo in Egitto. Lettere private nei papiri dei secoli ii–iv* (Florence, 1968); and

but soon the new faith found adherents outside the Hellenized
section of the population—which, it must be remembered, was
only a fraction in comparison with the number of native inhabitants who used only the Egyptian language. The present
state of our knowledge concerning the origin and early development of national Egyptian Christianity has been sketched by
Bardy.[1] It is sufficient here to mention that in a letter to Bishop
Fabius concerning the Decian persecution, Bishop Dionysius
distinguishes Greeks and Egyptians among the martyrs;[2] the
latter bear purely Coptic names, such as Bêsa and Amûn. Origen
(*Hom. in Luc.* xii) drops the remark that very many of the pros-
elytes among the Egyptians had accepted the Christian faith—
and by Egyptians he probably means the native-born peasants.
There is an interesting passage in Eusebius which mentions that
in A.D. 250 some 'country-folk' (χωρῖται), presumably native
Egyptians, near Alexandria took the part of the bishop and his
adherents against the soldiers of the governor.[3] The first native
Christian writer of whom it is reported that he wrote biblical studies in the Egyptian (Coptic) language was the ascetic
Hieracas,[4] who was born about A.D. 270 or a little earlier in
Leontopolis in the Delta and lived to be over ninety years of age.

Towards the end of the third century monasticism made its
appearance in Egypt, beginning, as it seems, with St. Antony
(*c.* A.D. 251–356). At about the age of twenty Antony decided
to give all he had to the poor and go as a hermit into the desert.
The decisive moment occurred, so Athanasius his biographer
states,[5] when one Sunday he heard the Scripture lesson of Matt.
xix. 21 ('If thou wouldest be perfect, go and sell that thou hast,

J. van Haelst's list of sixty-five Greek documentary papyri dating between *c.* A.D.
270 and 350 which were written by or about Christians ('Les sources papyrolo-
giques concernant l'Église en Égypte à l'époque de Constantin', *Proceedings of the
Twelfth International Congress of Papyrology*, ed. by Deborah H. Samuel (*American
Studies in Papyrology*, v; Toronto, 1970), pp. 497–503).

[1] Gustav Bardy, 'Les premiers temps du Christianisme de langue copte en
Égypte', *Mémorial Lagrange* (Paris, 1940), pp. 203–16. This is a far more balanced
discussion than that by Walter Bauer in his *Orthodoxy and Heresy in Earliest Christianity*, Eng. trans. (Philadelphia, 1971), pp. 44–60.
[2] Quoted by Eusebius, *Hist. eccl.* VI. xli.
[3] *Hist. eccl.* VI. xl. 5–9.
[4] Epiphanius, *Haer.* lxvii; cf. C. Schmidt 'Die Urschrift der Pistis Sophia',
ZNW xxiv (1925), 218–40, esp. 221–3, and Paul E. Kahle, *Bala'izah; Coptic Texts
from Deir el-Bala'izah in Upper Egypt*, i (London, 1954), 259 n. 1.
[5] Athanasius, *Vita Antonii*, ii (Migne, *PG* xxvi, col. 841).

and give to the poor . . .') read in a little village church in southern Egypt. If we take the story seriously—and there is no reason why we should not do so, for in his youth Athanasius had known Antony personally—we must suppose (in view of Antony's ignorance of Greek)[1] either that a copy of the Gospel of Matthew in Coptic was available to the preacher on that eventful Sunday, or that he provided an *ad hoc* translation of the Greek pericope into the local vernacular. In any case, it is probable that in the following few years the rapidly growing number of hermits and monks who imitated the example of Antony would have provided a strong impetus for the translation of the Scriptures into Coptic. We know that when Pachomius, the founder of coenobitic monasticism in Egypt, composed his rules *c.* A.D. 320, he required that all aspirants should be able to read twenty Psalms, or two Epistles, or a portion from another part of the Scriptures before being admitted to the monastic community— and anyone who could not read had to learn the passages by heart.[2] Such a rule implies the existence of most of the New Testament and the Psalter in the local vernacular. Before considering such Coptic versions themselves, however, it will be necessary to say something concerning the various dialectal forms which the native language had assumed throughout Egypt.

Coptic represents the last phase in the development of the ancient Egyptian language.[3] The words 'Copt' and 'Coptic' are

[1] Cf. Jerome, *De Vir. ill.* lxxxviii, 'Antonius monachus . . . misit aegyptiace ad diversa monasteria apostolici sensus sermonisque epistolas septem, quae in graecam linguam translatae sunt.'

[2] In the Coptic original we possess Pachomius' rules only in fragmentary form (edited by L. Th. Lefort in Amand Boon's *Pachomiana Latina* (Louvain, 1932)), but they were translated into Greek, and Jerome in turn provided a Latin rendering. For the requirement about reading portions of the Scriptures, see Boon, op. cit., pp. 49–50.

[3] Besides the grammars mentioned in the following footnote, cf. Georg Steindorff, 'Bemerkungen über die Anfänge der koptischen Sprache und Literatur', *Coptic Studies in Honor of Walter Ewing Crum* (Boston, 1950), pp. 189–214.

The question when it was that Coptic became a dead language (or at least passed out of common usage) has been answered variously. Usually it is said that by the close of the seventeenth century it ceased to be used as a living, spoken and written language. Cf. J. Simon, 'Wann starb das Koptische aus?' *ZDMG* xc (1936), 44* f.). There are, however, traces of its usage continuing still today. Besides Werner Vycichl's description of spoken Coptic in Zēnīya and other Coptic communities ('Pi-Solsel, ein Dorf mit koptischer Überlieferung', *Mitteilungen des deutschen Instituts für aegyptische Altertumskunde in Kairo*, vi (1936), 169–75; for a synopsis cf. W. H. Worrell in *AJSL* liv (1937), 1–11). See also the handbooks of Munīr Barsūm, one of which is a brief primer for self-instruction in Coptic along

derived from the Arabic Qobṭ (قبط), an incorrect pronunciation
of Qibṭ, which in turn is a shortened form of the Greek Αἰγύπτιος
('Egyptian', as the Arab conquerors called the Christian inhabitants of the land).

Just as in ancient Achaia, so also in the Nile valley topographi-
cal conditions were such as to foster the growth and differen-
tiation of similar but distinct dialects of the common parent
language. During the early Christian period the old Egyptian
language had assumed at least half a dozen dialectal forms, differing from one another chiefly in phonetics but also to some extent
in vocabulary and syntax.

Until the eighties of the last century only three Coptic dialects
were known: Sahidic in the southern part of the country (that is,
in Upper Egypt), Bohairic in the north around the Delta (that
is, Lower Egypt), and Fayyumic, which was spoken in the neighbourhood of the Oasis Fayyum.[1] Towards the end of the century
a variety of documents came to light written in still other Coptic
dialects, subsequently identified as Achmimic, sub-Achmimic,
and Middle Egyptian. Recent research has led to the recognition
that, long before the advent of Christianity, Sahidic was the
standard literary language over the whole of Egypt. Whether
Proto-Sahidic originated at Oxyrhynchus,[2] or in the Delta,[3] or
at Thebes,[4] it developed into a, so to speak, neutral dialect with
certain features found in, or drawn from, all the regional dialects. Until the eighth and ninth centuries Sahidic remained the

the lines of the idea of Basic English; cf. Ernst Hammerschmidt, 'Einige Beispiele
zu den Wiederbelebungsversuchen des Koptischen in heutigen Ägypten', *Probleme
der koptischen Literatur*, ed. by Peter Nagel (*II. Koptische Arbeitskonferenz des Instituts
für Byzantinistik, 1966* (Halle, 1968), pp. 225–31.

[1] The terminology is that of present-day Coptologists; previously somewhat different nomenclature was employed. For both systems see Georg Steindorff, *Koptische Grammatik*, Neudruck der zweiten Auflage mit Nachträge (Berlin, 1930), pp.
3–5; Walter Till, *Koptische Dialektgrammatik* (Munich, 1931), pp. 1–2; G. Steindorff,
Lehrbuch der koptischen Grammatik (Chicago, 1951); and especially Paul E. Kahle,
Bala'izah; Coptic Texts from Deir el-Bala'izah in Upper Egypt (London, 1954),
pp. 193–268 and 888 f., who also provides a discussion of the characteristics of
each dialect.

[2] So, e.g., William H. Worrell, *Coptic Sounds* (Ann Arbor, 1934), pp. 63–73.

[3] So, e.g., Kahle, *Bala'izah*, i. 233–52, esp. p. 247.

[4] So, e.g., H. J. Polotsky, 'Coptic', *Current Trends in Linguistics*, ed. by Thomas A.
Sebeok, vi (The Hague, 1970), 560–1; repr. in *Afroasiatic; a Survey*, ed. by Carleton
T. Hodge (*Janua linguarum*, Series Practica, clxiii; The Hague, 1971), pp. 68 f.
This had been the view of scholars (such as Chaîne and others) in an earlier
generation.

language used by the educated native classes throughout Egypt. Eventually it was superseded, first in the Delta and later in the rest of Egypt, by Bohairic. Of the surviving Coptic documents from the fifth century or earlier, those in Sahidic are more than twice as numerous as those in all the other dialects.

Instead of the ancient hieroglyphic writing, which continued to be employed until the third century A.D., and instead of the derivative hieratic and demotic scripts, a simplified alphabet was used in writing Coptic. This was an alphabet of thirty-one letters, of which twenty-four were borrowed from the contemporary uncial Greek script, while seven additional letters were taken from a more cursive variety of the native demotic script in order to express sounds that did not exist in spoken Greek. On the whole, Coptic was essentially the non-cultivated speech of chiefly rural folk, whereas the Egyptian 'aristocracy', being thoroughly hellenized, used Greek. Coptic, as compared with Greek, is much more wooden and lacking in suppleness and variety of expression.[1]

At first Coptic scribes were not quite certain how many, if any, additional demotic letters they should use. On the one hand, all the Old Coptic texts agree in using more demotic letters than Coptic was to do after it became standardized;[2] on the other

---

[1] Besides the discussion of limitations of Coptic in representing Greek found on pp. 141–52 below, reference may be made to similar lists in the following publications: [George Horner], *The Coptic Version of the New Testament in the Northern Dialect*, i (Oxford, 1898), xviii–xxxi; N. Peters, *Die sahidisch-koptische Übersetzung des Buches Ecclesiasticus (Biblische Studien*, iii. 3; Freiburg im Br., 1898), pp. 5–30; Joh. Leipoldt, in H. von Soden's *Die Schriften des Neuen Testaments in ihrer ältesten erreichbaren Textgestalt*, I. ii (Berlin, 1907), 1480 f.; Herbert Thompson, in J. H. Ropes's *The Text of Acts* (London, 1926), pp. 319–21 (Sahidic), and pp. 359–60 (Bohairic); M.-J. Lagrange, *Critique textuelle*; ii, *La critique rationnelle* (Paris, 1935), pp. 315–17; the lengthy introductory section of Rufus L. Moretz's 'The Textual Affinity of the Earliest Coptic Manuscripts of the Gospel of John [Bodmer II, sub-Achmimic John, and Fayyumic John]', Diss. Duke University, 1969 (see *Dissertation Abstracts International*, Section A, *The Humanities and Social Sciences*, xxx. 6 (Dec. 1969), 2608 f.); and Gerd Mink in *Die alten Übersetzungen des Neuen Testaments, die Kirchenväterzitate und Lektionare*, ed. by K. Aland (Berlin and New York, 1972), pp. 188–273.

[2] Cf. C. W. Goodwin, 'On an Egyptian Text in Greek Characters', *ZÄS* vi (1868), 18–24; F. Ll. Griffith, 'The Date of the Old Coptic Texts, and their Relation to Christian Coptic', ibid. xxxix (1901), 78–82; W. E. Crum, 'An Egyptian Text in Greek Characters', *JEA* xxviii (1942), 20–31; and idem, 'Coptic Documents in Greek Script', *Proceedings of the British Academy*, xxv (1939), 249–71. I have not seen R. Haardt, 'Versuch einer altkoptischen Grammatik' (typewritten, Vienna, 1948).

hand, the fifty or so Coptic glosses in the old Fayyumic dialect found in the margins of the Beatty Papyrus of Isaiah are written in Greek letters, without any supplementary letters borrowed from demotic.[1]

II. EARLY MANUSCRIPTS OF THE COPTIC VERSIONS

The Coptic versions of the Bible are for the most part preserved only in fragments which are scattered in collections all over the world.[2] Some of these have been published *in extenso* in books and articles; others are known merely from being listed in catalogues;[3] still others await discovery, or rediscovery, in archives and collections hitherto unnoticed. Earlier in the present century Vaschalde[4] performed the useful task of compiling lists of all published Coptic biblical texts in such a way that one can easily find any particular passage in the printed editions. More recently Till[5] compiled a supplementary index, listing those editions of

[1] Frederic G. Kenyon, *The Chester Beatty Biblical Papyri*, fasc. vi, supplemented by another leaf originally from the same codex published in *Papyri greci e latini* (PSI), xii (1951), no. 1273. Besides these Fayyumic glosses dating probably from the third century, we have other evidence that points to the presence of Christians in the neighbourhood of the Fayyum about A.D. 250. These are the *libelli* issued during the Decian persecution to those who offered sacrifices. Of the forty-one such certificates edited by J. R. Knipfing, two or three appear to have been issued to Christians ('The Libelli of the Decian Persecution', *HTR* xvi (1923), 345–90).

[2] The list of Jean Simon ('Répertoire des bibliothèques publiques et privées contenant des manuscrits coptes', *Mu*, xliv (1931), 137–51), while still valuable, needs to be revised and enlarged.

[3] It is regrettable that catalogues of several important collections of Coptic manuscripts have not yet been published. According to the late Theodore Petersen, 'A catalogue written by E. C. Amélineau of the Coptic manuscript collection in the Bibliothèque Nationale in Paris remains unprinted. The catalogue prepared by H. Hyvernat of the large collection of Coptic manuscripts in the Pierpont Morgan Library in New York can likewise be consulted at the Library only in type-script form. Of the 377 pages of this catalogue (exclusive of 17 pages of Introduction and 58 pages of Appendix) a section of 58 pages is given to the listing of the biblical texts owned by the Library and all of which remain unpublished to date except for the variants in a codex of the Epistles of Paul [MS. Morgan 570 included in Horner's Sahidic New Testament]' (*CBQ* xxiii (1961), 247).

[4] A. Vaschalde, 'Ce qui a été publié des versions coptes de la Bible', *RB* xxix (1920), 255–8; xxx (1921), 237–46; xxxi (1922), 81–8, 234–58 (Sahidic); idem, *Mu*, xlv (1932), 117–56 (Bohairic); xlvi (1933), 299–306 (Middle Egyptian); pp. 306–13 (Akhmimic).

[5] Walter C. Till, 'Coptic Biblical Texts Published after Vaschalde's Lists', *BJRL* xlii (1959), 220–40. The Institute for New Testament Textual Research at Münster has compiled an official listing of all known Coptic manuscripts of the New Testament, including lectionaries. A beginning has been made also of assembling a collection of microfilms of Coptic manuscripts of the New Testament.

Coptic biblical texts that appeared since Vaschalde's lists were made or that were overlooked by Vaschalde. Furthermore, Kahle has drawn up a very helpful list of early Coptic manuscripts (all prior to the sixth century), whether edited or still awaiting publication.[1] In what follows attention will be directed to New Testament manuscripts of each Coptic dialect that are noteworthy either because of age or for some other reason.

I. THE SAHIDIC VERSION

Until the twentieth century the Sahidic version of the New Testament was known only in relatively few and scattered fragments, some of which were edited by Woide[2] in 1799 and others by Amélineau[3] in 1884 and the following years. By the opening of the present century enough material had been acquired by the Borgian Museum to enable Balestri[4] to publish an edition of the Sahidic New Testament in tolerably complete form. Several years later, by piecing together widely scattered scraps of text, Horner[5] was able to produce an edition containing almost every verse of the entire New Testament. Monumental though Horner's work was in its time, today a new edition is called for not only because of the availability of earlier and more extensive manuscript sources but also because of certain defects that have appeared in Horner's work.[6]

---

[1] P. E. Kahle, *Bala'izah*, i. 269–78.

[2] C. W. Woide, *Appendix ad editionem Novi Testamenti graeci . . . in qua continentur fragmenta Novi Testamenti juxta interpretationem dialecti superioris Aegypti quae thebaica vel sahidica appellatur . . .* (Oxford, 1799).

[3] E. C. Amélineau, 'Fragments coptes du Nouveau Testament dans le dialecte thébain', *Recueil de travaux relatifs à la philologie*, v (1884), 105–39; he also edited other fragments in *ZÄS* xxiv (1886), 41–56, 103–14; xxv (1887), 42–57, 100–10, 125–35; xxvi (1888), 96–105.

[4] *Sacrorum Bibliorum fragmenta copto-sahidica Musei Borgiani*; iii, *Novum Testamentum*, ed. by Giuseppe Balestri (Rome, 1904; repr. Leipzig, 1970).

[5] [George W. Horner,] *The Coptic Version of the New Testament in the Southern Dialect, otherwise called Sahidic and Thebaic*, with Critical Apparatus, Literal English Translation, Register of Fragments, and Estimate of the Version, 7 vols. (Oxford, 1911–24; repr. Osnabrück, 1969). Because of the manner in which Horner's text had to be edited (from diverse texts of quite disparate dates and provenance), one must beware against attributing to the edition any measure of homogeneity.

[6] While acknowledging that Horner's work was a great achievement in its time, P. E. Kahle mentions a number of defects which became apparent to him as he worked on the manuscripts from Bala'izah. Nearly all of the New Testament manuscripts in the Bala'izah collection were used by Horner, 'but his citations of not only the variant readings but also the manuscripts themselves are so inaccurate and incomplete', Kahle declares, 'that it has been necessary to publish

In the spring of 1910 at Hamouli, on the site of the ruins of the monastery of the Archangel Michael near the southern border of the province of Fayyum, archaeologists came upon a large collection of ancient and complete manuscripts, almost all of them written in Sahidic. The collection, which comprises fifty-six biblical as well as patristic and hagiographic works, was acquired by the Pierpont Morgan Library in New York, and has been published in a magnificent facsimile edition.[1] Many of the manuscripts are dated from the first half of the ninth to the latter half of the tenth century. The collection is rich in biblical manuscripts. It contains six complete books of the Old Testament, namely, Leviticus, Numbers, Deuteronomy, 1 and 2 Samuel, and Isaiah. The New Testament is represented by three complete Gospels, Matthew, Mark, and John (Luke is unfortunately incomplete, lacking iv. 33–ix. 30, ix. 62–xiii. 18), the fourteen Epistles of Paul, 1 and 2 Peter, and 1, 2, and 3 John. Other famous collections which include Sahidic manuscripts of the Bible are the Chester Beatty collection in Dublin and the Martin Bodmer collection in Cologny–Geneva.

Among the longer and more noteworthy Sahidic manuscripts of the New Testament the following deserve to be mentioned.

Early Sahidic manuscripts

(1) The Crosby codex of the University of Mississippi, a single-quire papyrus manuscript of fifty-two leaves or 104 consecutive pages, contains a miscellaneous assortment of documents in Sahidic, among which is the complete text of 1 Peter.[2] According to William H. Willis, who is engaged in preparing a variorum

---

all the manuscripts in full. Also, in the case of fragmentary manuscripts Horner only attempted to read the more legible parts, and often very much more is extant than is indicated by him. I have found the same deficiencies in Horner's edition when collating manuscripts in the British Museum' (*Bala'izah*, i. 14).

[1] Henri Hyvernat, *Bybliothecae Pierpont Morgan codices coptici*, photographice expressi . . . , 56 vols. in 63 (Rome, 1922). For the contents of the volumes, see Hyvernat's *A Check List of Coptic Manuscripts in the Pierpont Morgan Library* (New York, 1919). The titles of the several volumes are cited in Winifred Kammerer's *A Coptic Bibliography* (Ann Arbor, 1950), pp. 33–4, item no. 726. The only Bohairic document in the series is a copy of the Gospel according to John (vol. vii).

[2] For a description of the codex, which contains, in addition to 1 Peter, a portion of 2 Maccabees, the book of Jonah, and Melito's Homily on the Pascha, see William H. Willis, 'The New Collections of Papyri at the University of Mississippi', *Proceedings of the IX International Congress of Papyrology* (Oslo, 1961), pp. 382–9.

edition of the Sahidic text of 1 Peter,[1] the manuscript is no later than the turn of the third and fourth centuries.

(2) British Museum MS. Or. 7594 comprises an unusual combination of books: Deuteronomy, Jonah, and Acts. The *editio princeps* by Budge[2] left something to be desired as regards accuracy, and in the following year Thompson[3] collated the edition against the manuscript and issued for private circulation a booklet of some forty pages of corrections and notes. The manuscript can be dated more closely and with greater certainty than most early texts. It was enclosed in a binding made of leather over a pasteboard made up of Greek papyrus fragments. These fragments, for the most part from documents, have been dated on palaeograpical grounds as well as from internal evidence to the late third or early fourth century. Furthermore, at the end of Acts a colophon has been added in a cursive Greek hand which Kenyon assigned with confidence to a date not later than the middle of the fourth century. All told, therefore, the evidence leads one, as Budge and Thompson point out, to fix upon A.D. 300–20 as the date when the manuscript was copied.

(3) Michigan MS. Inv. 3992 is a single-quire papyrus codex of rather small format, the pages being 14 to 15 cm. ($5\frac{1}{2}$ to 6 in.) in height and 9 to 10 cm. ($3\frac{1}{2}$ to 4 in.) in width. Fragments of forty-two folios have been identified, but a great number of fragments remain to be identified. So far as is known at present, the complete codex must have contained the Gospel according to John, an unknown text, 1 Corinthians, Titus, and the Book of Psalms, in this order, as well as Isaiah.[4] According to the editor, 'it was written perhaps as early as the third century A.D. and certainly not later than the fourth';[5] Kahle places it in the fourth century.[6]

---

[1] For a list of other Sahidic manuscripts of 1 Peter, see William H. Willis, 'An Unrecognized Fragment of First Peter in Coptic', *Classical, Mediaeval and Renaissance Studies in Honor of Berthold Louis Ullman*, ed. by Charles Henderson, Jr., i (*Storia e letteratura*, xciii; Rome, 1964), pp. 265–71.

[2] E. A. Wallis Budge, *Coptic Biblical Texts in the Dialect of Upper Egypt* (London, 1912).

[3] Herbert Thompson, *The New Biblical Papyrus; a Sahidic Version of Deuteronomy, Jonah, and Acts of the Apostles . . . Notes and a Collation* (Printed for Private Circulation, 1913).

[4] Elinor M. Husselman in *Coptic Texts in the University of Michigan Collection*, ed. by William H. Worrell (Ann Arbor and London, 1942), p. 6.

[5] Husselman, op. cit., p. 5.   [6] Kahle, *Bala'izah*, i. 270.

(4) Berlin MS. Or. 408 and British Museum Or. 3518 belong together, being parts of the same fourth-century codex containing the Book of Revelation, 1 John, and Philemon, in this order. The text of the Apocalypse was edited by Goussen[1] in 1895, and again by Delaport[2] in 1906. The latter also published the text of 1 John and Philemon from this manuscript.[3]

(5) Fragments of five parchment pages in the Bala'izah collection (Kahle's no. 22), judged by C. H. Roberts to be as early as the third or fourth century, are assigned by Kahle to the second half of the fourth century. The fragments contain the text of Eph. ii. 11 and 13; 1 Pet. ii. 15–iii. 1, 3, 4; 1 John ii. 4–15; and Jas. iii. 14, 15, 17, 18; iv. 3, 5, 6.

(6) Another parchment fragment in the Bala'izah collection (Kahle's no. 25) is thought to have been written by the same scribe who wrote the fragments described in no. 5 above. The leaf is from a Greek–Coptic lectionary (Horner's ζ'; Gregory–Dobschütz l1604); it preserves Matt. v. 17–19 in Coptic and vii. 28; viii. 3, 4, 7–9 in Greek (the latter shows some striking variant readings).

(7) With painstaking labours Fritz Hintze and Hans-Martin Schenke have identified and edited about seventy more or less fragmentary pages belonging to a papyrus codex of the Book of Acts (Berlin P. 15926). The text of the manuscript, which the editors assign to the fourth century, contains a significant number of Western readings as well as several 'wild' readings, two of which agree with the Middle Egyptian codex of Acts known as the Glazier manuscript (see pp. 117 and 119 below).[4]

(8) Two papyrus fragments, belonging to the private collection of Jules Garrido of Cairo, preserve the text of Matt. xiv. 20–2, 25–7, 30–1, 36, and xvi. 8, 12, 15–16, 20. They are dated by their owner to the fourth century.[5]

[1] Henri Goussen, *Studia theologica*, fasc. i (Leipzig, 1895).

[2] L. J. Delaport, *Fragments sahidiques du Nouveau Testament: Apocalypse* (Paris, 1906).

[3] *RB*, N.S. ii (1905), 377–97. According to Kahle (*Bala'izah*, i. 13), the text of 1 John represents a version independent of the normal Sahidic version.

[4] *Die Berliner Handschrift der sahidischen Apostelgeschichte* (P. 15 926) (*TU* cix; Berlin, 1970), pp. 21–31.

[5] 'Un nouveau papyrus de l'Évangile de saint Matthieu en copte sahidique', *Cahiers coptes*, xv (Cairo, 1957), 5–18, and 'Hallazgo de un papiro del Nuevo Testamento en copto sahídico', *EB*, seg. ép., xvii (1958), 107–8.

(9) Manuscript V of the Rainer Collection in Vienna[1] is a parchment codex of the Book of Acts in Sahidic dating from *c*. A.D. 400. Lacking the beginning and the ending of the book, its fragmentary leaves preserve only intermittent portions of the text from ii. 35 to xxvi. 24.

(10) A fourth- or fifth-century parchment codex in the Bodmer collection (no. XIX), containing the text of Matt. xiv. 28–xxxviii. 20 and Rom. i. 2–ii. 3, was published by Kasser in 1962.[2] The editor distinguishes the work of four scribes, one who wrote the text of Matthew, one who wrote the text of Romans, and two later correctors.

(11) A papyrus leaf in the Bala'izah collection (Kahle's no. 21), dating from the late fourth or early fifth century and containing the text of 1 Tim. iv. 12–v. 2, 4, 10, 11, 13–18, and Tit. i. 9–ii. 14, bears the page numbers ⲱⲗⲥ and ⲱⲗⲍ, i.e. 836, 837. These are very remarkable and presumably the manuscript originally contained the whole of the New Testament. Kahle declares, 'I know of no other Coptic manuscript earlier than the ninth century which was so extensive.'[3]

(12) The Seminario de Papirología de la Facultad Teológica at San Cugat del Vallés (Barcelona) has acquired a parchment codex containing the Sahidic version of the Gospels according to Luke and Mark.[4] The copying of the two gospels appears to have been done by two scribes, working at the same time in the same scriptorium during the first half of the fifth century. The text of Mark, which ends at xvi. 8, is divided into sections according to a pattern that differs markedly from the previously known divisions in Coptic versions.

(13 and 14) What seem to be two of the earliest copies of the complete text of the Book of Acts and of the Pauline corpus were acquired by Mr. A. Chester Beatty in 1924–5. They are carefully

---

[1] Carl Wessely, *Die Wiener Handschrift der sahidischen Acta Apostolorum* (*Sb Wien* clxxii, 2; Vienna, 1913).

[2] Rodolphe Kasser, *Papyrus Bodmer XIX, Évangile de Matthieu XIV, 28–XXVIII, 20, Épître aux Romains I. 1–II. 3 en sahidique* (Cologny–Geneva, 1962). The two books are paginated separately in the codex.

[3] *Bala'izah*, i. 382.

[4] Hans Quecke, *Das Markusevangelium saïdisch. Text der Handschrift PPalau Rib. Inv.-Nr. 182 mit den Varianten der Handschrift M 569* (Barcelona, 1972). The text of the Gospel of Luke, which precedes that of Mark, has not yet been published.

written, having been transcribed at the important monastery of Apa Jeremias at Saqqâra, and date from *c.* A.D. 600. One of them, designated codex A, contains the fourteen Epistles of Paul, with Hebrews next after 2 Corinthians and before Galatians (this is the order found in all Sahidic manuscripts containing the Epistles or so much of them as reveals their order). Codex B contains the Acts of the Apostles followed by the Gospel according to John. Each has a separate pagination. In view of the heterogeneous and not quite complete text of the Book of Acts and of the Pauline corpus in Horner's edition, it is good to have a complete and homogeneous text of these New Testament books,[1] dating from a period when the national Monophysite Church was in its full vigour.

2. THE ACHMIMIC VERSION

The Achmimic form of Coptic, which Kahle[2] thought originated at Thebes and then spread north to Akhmim, the ancient Panopolis, is preserved in a considerable number of texts[3] showing a more or less uniform dialect.[4] According to Kahle, 'already the earliest manuscript in this dialect, the Achmimic Proverbs, shows a high degree of standardization which must have been effected late in the third century.'[5]

What has survived of the New Testament in Achmimic is very little indeed, both in number of texts and in extent of text.

Early Achmimic manuscripts

(1) P. Osl. inv. 1661 is a pocket-sized codex, measuring 6·6 by 5·6 cm. (2½ by 2¼ in.) and dating from the early part of the fourth

---

[1] Manuscript A and the text of Acts in Manuscript B were edited by Sir Herbert Thompson, *The Coptic Version of the Acts of the Apostles and the Pauline Epistles in the Sahidic Dialect* (Cambridge, 1932).

[2] Kahle's opinion has been challenged by H. J. Polotsky ('Coptic', *Current Trends in Linguistics*, ed. by Thomas A. Sebeok, vi (The Hague, 1970), 560; repr. in *Afroasiatic; a Survey*, ed. by Carleton T. Hodge (*Janua linguarum*, Series Practica, clxiii (The Hague, 1971), p. 68).

[3] For a summary of Achmimic texts, see Jean Simon, 'Note sur le dossier des textes akhmimiques', *Mémorial Lagrange*, ed. by L.-H. Vincent (Paris, 1940), pp. 197–201).

[4] The dialect has been studied by Friedrich Rösch, *Vorbemerkungen zu einer Grammatik der achmimischen Mundart* (Diss., Strassburg, 1909), and by Walter Till, *Achmîmisch-koptische Grammatik, mit Chrestomathie und Wörterbuch* (Leipzig, 1928).

[5] Kahle, *Bala'izah*, i. 197.

century.[1] Fragments of thirteen leaves are extant, which once formed a single quire. After the text of Matt. xi. 25–30 in Greek the same passage follows in Coptic, but because of a lacuna the Coptic text breaks off at vs. 29. Following pages contain the Greek text of Dan. iii. 51–3, 55.

(2) A papyrus leaf of the fourth century, found in the Fayyum and now in Vienna,[2] preserves the Achmimic text of Jas. v. 17–18, 20.

(3) Three fragmentary leaves, one of which bears pagination numbers 177–8, indicating that it is part of a good-sized codex, preserve portions of Luke xii. 27–34, 37–44, 49–53, 58; xiii. 1–3; xvii. 27–37; xviii. 1–11. Lefort, who edited[3] the fragments, dates them to the fourth or fifth century, while Kahle prefers the fourth century.[4] Because the fragments are from what was once a single-quire codex, the editor is able to compute that this copy of the Gospels originally included Matthew, Luke, and John, but not Mark. The absence of Mark in a fourth-century Coptic codex of the Gospels is in harmony with the fact that neither the Life of Pachomius nor the Life of Shenoute contains any clear quotation from this Gospel. Among the interesting and unusual readings in this fragment (many of which are harmonizations with the text of Matthew) is the curious expression ϥⲛⲟⲩϩⲛ̄ⲧⲟⲩⲱⲟⲩ (from ⲧⲟⲩⲱ 'bosom') in Luke xii. 37, which corresponds here to ἀνακλινεῖ αὐτούς and the Sahidic ⲛϥ̄ⲧⲣⲉⲩⲛⲟϫⲟⲩ.

(4) Michigan MS. Inv. 3535a is two small contiguous fragments of a papyrus leaf, containing Gal. v. 11–14 on the recto and v. 22–vi. 1 (?) on the verso. Kahle dates it provisionally to the fourth or fifth century.[4]

3. THE SUB-ACHMIMIC VERSION

Sub-Achmimic stands between Achmimic and Middle Egyptian. According to Kahle, 'Unlike Achmimic we do not find a uniform dialect; [there are] two main groups, and apparently the new Gnostic find at Deir Chenoboskion provides yet a third

---

[1] Leiv Amundsen, 'Christian Papyri from the Oslo Collection', *SO* xxiv (1945), 121–40.

[2] Walter Till, 'Ein achmimisches Jakobusbrieffragment', *Mu*, li (1938), 69 ff.

[3] L. Th. Lefort, 'Fragments de S. Luc en akhmîmique', *Mu*, lxii (1949), 199–205; idem, 'Fragments bibliques en dialecte akhmîmique', ibid. lxvi (1953), 1–30.

[4] Kahle, *Bala'izah*, i. 273.

group.... But even within these main groups there are considerable dialectal variations ...'[1] The chief texts[2] of the first group are a copy of the Gospel according to John, the *Acta Pauli* (edited by C. Schmidt in 1904), and the remnants of a Gnostic (Ophitic) work (British Museum MS. Or. 4920(1), Crum's no. 522); the second group is formed by the Manichaean texts (edited by C. R. C. Allberry and by H. J. Polotsky); the Chenoboskion (Nag Hammadi) texts are in the course of publication.

One of the earliest manuscripts written in the sub-Achmimic dialect is an almost complete copy of the Gospel according to John (designated by the siglum Q), now in the library of the British and Foreign Bible Society.[3] Excavators at Qau el Kebir found the papyrus codex wrapped in a rag and tied with a thread, in a broken crock, buried some 18 inches under the surface in a cemetery near the village of Hamamieh. Comprising originally 100 numbered pages, the codex today has only forty-three leaves or fragments thereof; the text begins at ii. 12 on a page numbered 7 and ends at xx. 20 on page 96. Therefore it is clear that six numbered pages, i.e. three leaves of text, are missing at the beginning and at the end of the codex.

Each leaf measured originally about 25 cm. (10 in.) in height and about 12·5 cm. (5 in.) in width.[4] The handwriting bears a rather strong resemblance to that of codex Vaticanus, allowance being made for the circumstance that one is on papyrus and the other on vellum. In the opinion of Sir Frederic Kenyon, who studied photographs of the original, the manuscript was copied in the third quarter of the fourth century.

The manuscript is noteworthy not only because of its early date but also because its dialect indicates more or less exactly

[1] Kahle, *Bala'izah*, i. 206–7. For a study of the grammatical peculiarities of the dialect see Marius Chaîne, *Les Dialectes coptes assioutiques A²; Les Caractéristiques de leur phonétique, de leur morphologie, de leur syntaxe* (Paris, 1934). This was published at a time, however, when the Manichaean manuscripts had just recently become known, and only a few extracts had been published.

[2] For a summary of texts, large and small, that have survived in sub-Achmimic, see Jean Simon, 'Note sur le dossier des textes sub-akhmimiques', *Mu*, lix (1946), 497–509.

[3] *The Gospel of St. John according to the Earliest Coptic Manuscript*, edited with a translation by Sir Herbert Thompson (London, 1924).

[4] According to a suggestion made by Flinders Petrie, 'The height of the MS. indicates that it was for Church use, rather than a private copy. It appears that, when too defective for regular reading, it had been set aside, and buried reverently in the cemetery' (ibid., p. x).

where the codex was written. In fact, it is one of the very few early Gospel manuscripts of which we are sure of the provenance.[1]

4. THE MIDDLE EGYPTIAN VERSION

Very few documents are known in the Middle Egyptian dialect.[2] The earliest appears to be a Greek–Coptic glossary to Hosea and Amos, dating from the close of the third century and now in the British Museum.[3] Besides small fragments of Genesis, Job, and Romans which had been known previously, in May 1961 two parchment manuscripts in this dialect came into the possession of Hans P. Kraus, the well-known rare-book dealer in New York. One of them, which contains on 238 leaves, measuring 12·5 by 10·5 cm. (5 by 4⅛ in.), the complete text of the Gospel according to Matthew, has been acquired recently by William H. Scheide of Princeton, New Jersey. The other, containing—on 107 leaves of exactly the same dimensions as those of the Matthew codex—the text of Acts i. 1–xv. 3, was purchased by the late William S. Glazier, and is at present in the keeping of the Pierpont Morgan Library of New York City. The date of the two manuscripts is judged to be the end of the fourth century (Mrs. Husselman and Till), the very late fourth or the fifth century (Roberts), the fifth century (Skeat), or the fifth or sixth century (Haenchen and Weigandt).

Both manuscripts are written on good, but not first-rate parchment. Because both have holes (which the scribes avoided as they wrote) and because of the small size of the page, it is probable that they were not written for liturgical purposes, but for private

---

[1] Codex Washingtonianus (W) is the only Greek Gospel manuscript of early date (fifth century) of which we know the provenance. Though the exact spot in Egypt where it was found is not known, there are indications that it came from a monastery in the neighbourhood of the Pyramids.

[2] Kahle lists a dozen texts, half of them under the heading 'Middle Egyptian Proper' and the other half under 'Middle Egyptian with Fayyumic Influence', but in his Addenda he states that he has had second thoughts about the legitimacy of the second category, and prefers now to group them under the heading of Fayyumic texts (*Bala'izah*, i. 220–7; and ii. 888 f.). More recently several scholars have preferred to identify the dialect as the Oxyrhynchite dialect; cf. Jozef Vergote, *Grammaire copte*, 1a (Louvain, 1973), 4, and Tito Orlandi (see p. 119 n. 4 below).

[3] H. I. Bell and H. Thompson, 'A Greek–Coptic Glossary to Hosea and Amos', *JEA* xi (1925), 241–6. Bell and Thompson suggest that the glossary dates from a time when as yet no official version of the Minor Prophets was in existence.

use.[1] At the same time, according to the opinion of the late Theodore C. Petersen, 'it is clear from the appearance of the two manuscripts that they were produced by professional scribes trained in making *deluxe* copies of literary text for the book trade'.[2]

The Scheide manuscript,[3] which is in the original binding of wooden boards, is one of the very oldest complete copies of the Gospel of Matthew (only B and א of the fourth century, and W of about the same date as the Coptic manuscript, contain the entire text of Matthew; codices A and C preserve only small portions of Matthew; no Greek papyrus fragment preserves more than a relatively few verses of Matthew). The Coptic version of the present text appears to have been made directly from the Greek and is independent of all Coptic versions hitherto known.

The text of the Gospel is divided into 170 sections; these resemble the sections of codex Vaticanus, without, however, corresponding to those divisions. Textually the Coptic manuscript shows many affinities with B and א, supporting the shorter text, for example, at Matt. vi. 13; x. 12; xvi. 2 f.; xviii. 11; and xxiii. 14. At the same time, however, it abandons these witnesses by incorporating several notable Western readings, such as those at vi. 33; xi. 19; xii. 47; xvii. 21; xx. 16; and xxv. 41.

After the close of the Gospel of Matthew the manuscript contains, in a different hand, the Greek text of the Greater Doxology (*Gloria in excelsis Deo*), which is followed by the Greater Doxology in a Middle Egyptian translation. The oldest manuscript evidence hitherto known for the Greek text of the *Gloria* is found in the New Testament volume (fol. 569) of codex Alexandrinus, *c.* A.D. 400. The oldest manuscript evidence hitherto made known of the Coptic text of the *Gloria* is found in a tenth-century Sahidic leaf in the Berlin Library (P. 8099).

A curious feature of the Glazier codex of Acts is the circumstance that its text lacks a title and ends abruptly with xv. 3 on

[1] So Ernst Haenchen and Peter Weigandt, 'The Original Text of Acts?' *NTS* xiv (1968), 479. The authors are in error in designating the manuscript cop^G68; it is cop^G67 of the Glazier collection (see John Plummer, *The Glazier Collection of Illuminated Manuscripts* (New York, 1968), pp. 7 f.).

[2] 'An Early Coptic Manuscript of Acts: An Unrevised Version of the Ancient So-Called Western Text', *CBQ* xxvi (1964), 226 n. 4.

[3] For a fuller description of the Scheide codex, see the present writer's contribution to the Festschrift in honour of G. D. Kilpatrick, *Studies in New Testament Language and Text*, ed. by J. K. Elliott (Leiden, 1976), pp. 301–12.

fol. 155ʳ while the following verso has been left blank. This is followed by an additional leaf on the recto of which is painted a miniature to face the blank verso, giving the impression of a monumental diptych. The composition is dominated by a great *crux ansata* ('cross with handle'), known also as the *ankh-* or looped-cross, a motif appearing frequently in Coptic textiles and stone sculptures. The cross is constructed of interlace work, flanked by two peacocks. The artist used simple yellows, reds, and browns, so as to produce a warm and raw-earth-colour tonality.[1]

The text of the Glazier manuscript is a notable representative of the so-called Western type of text. How far it is valuable in ascertaining the primitive text of the Book of Acts depends largely on one's estimate of the character of the Western text: Epp[2] finds more than one original reading preserved in the manuscript, whereas Haenchen and Weigandt[3] regard the 'original' text of the manuscript to have been a revised Coptic form of the Western text produced between about A.D. 350 and 450.

Portions of ten Pauline Epistles in the Middle Egyptian dialect are preserved in a papyrus codex at the Instituto di Papirologia of the University of Milan (Pap. Mil. Cop. 1).[4] The manuscript, which the editor dates to about the first half of the fifth century, comprises fifty-four fragmentary folios of a single-quire codex which originally had about 150 folios. The surviving fragments contain portions of the following (in this order): Romans, 1 and 2 Corinthians, Hebrews, Galatians, Philippians, Ephesians, 1 and 2 Thessalonians, and Colossians. According to textual analyses made by Orlandi, the version agrees most frequently with the Sahidic, but it also contains singular and sub-singular readings, several of which coincide with readings that are preserved in minor Greek manuscripts.

---

[1] So Harry Bober, 'On the Illumination of the Glazier Codex; A contribution to Early Coptic Art and its Relation to Hiberno-Saxon Interlace', *Homage to a Bookman; Essays on Manuscripts, Books and Printing Written for Hans P. Kraus . . .* , ed. by Hellmut Lehmann-Haupt (Berlin, [1967]), pp. 31–49, with a coloured plate of the miniature.

[2] Eldon J. Epp, 'Coptic Manuscript G67 and the Role of Codex Bezae as a Western Witness in Acts', *JBL* lxxxv (1966), 197–212, and *The Theological Tendency of Codex Bezae Cantabrigiensis in Acts* (Cambridge, Mass., 1966), pp. ix, 10 f., 29 f., etc.   [3] Haenchen and Weigandt, op. cit., pp. 480 f.

[4] Tito Orlandi, *Lettere di san Paolo in copto-ossirinchita* (*Papiri della Università degli Studi di Milano*, v; Milan, 1974).

5. THE FAYYUMIC VERSION

In contrast with the Sahidic and Bohairic versions of the Coptic New Testament, both of which are available in their entirety, the Fayyumic version is only partially represented by a relatively few published documents, scattered widely in journals and monographs. It was Kahle's intention to publish detailed studies on the Fayyumic version, and before his death he had investigated all known fragments, both edited and unedited. According to a summary which he had drawn up,[1] for the Gospels there are twenty-two manuscripts from the sixth to the ninth century; for Acts there are two manuscripts, one of the fourth/fifth century (see no. 2 in the list below) and the other a late manuscript; for the Pauline Epistles there are fourteen manuscripts from the fourth/fifth century to the ninth century; and for the Catholic Epistles there are three manuscripts of the fifth to the seventh centuries.

Early Fayyumic manuscripts

(1) Michigan Inv. 3521 is a single-quire papyrus codex, containing portions of John vi. 11–xv. 10 on twenty-nine fragmentary folios.[2] Although Kahle had designated the dialect of the text as Middle Egyptian with Fayyumic influence,[3] the editor of the manuscript states that 'since the dialect of this codex is closer to the later standardized literary Fayumic than to either Sahidic or Bohairic, I should prefer to call it Fayumic, without attempting a closer classification'.[4] Palaeographically the script resembles that of British Museum Or. 7594 (see no. 2 in the list of Sahidic MSS. above), and is therefore dated by the editor to the early part of the fourth century.[5]

(2) British Museum MS. Or. 6948 (3–4) consists of two leaves written in a small uncial hand of the late fourth or early fifth century, containing Acts vii. 14–28 and ix. 28–39. The two pages are well preserved on the hair-side and present little difficulty,

---

[1] Kahle, *Bala'izah*, i. 282–5. For an earlier summary of Fayyumic texts, with important bibliographical notes, see Jean Simon, 'Note sur le dossier des textes fayoumiques', *ZNW* xxxvii (1939), 205–11.

[2] *The Gospel of John in Fayumic Coptic* (*P. Mich. Inv.* 3521), ed. by Elinor M. Husselman (Ann Arbor, 1962).

[3] Kahle, *Bala'izah*, i. 274; yet cf. ii. 888 f., where Kahle indicates that perhaps it would have been better to class the manuscript simply as Fayyumic.

[4] Husselman, op. cit., p. 11.

[5] Kahle considered it to be fourth or fifth century (*Bala'izah*, i. 274).

but the text on the flesh-side is extremely difficult to read. Because the two earlier editors[1] of the fragments differ considerably in their transcription of the flesh-side, Kahle collated the manuscript afresh, finding in the process that the text presents many agreements with the Bohairic version.[2]

(3) Several parchment leaves in the M. E. Saltykov-Shchedrin State Public Library in Leningrad (Copt. MS. 53, new series) contain, with lacunae, Mark xiv. 35–xvi. 20. They were edited first by Oscar von Lemm,[3] who was unable to identify the verso of his fragments II and III. Upon rearrangement of the fragments in their proper order Kahle found that the manuscript contains both the shorter and the longer ending of the Gospel of Mark.[4] The text of the fragments has lately been re-edited by A. I. Elanskaja,[5] who makes several corrections in von Lemm's transcription.

6. THE BOHAIRIC VERSION

Of the several Coptic dialects, Bohairic is the only one that continues to be used today as the liturgical language of the Coptic Orthodox Church.[6] During the eleventh century the seat of the Coptic Patriarch was moved from Alexandria, where Bohairic was widely used, to Cairo, where the use of Sahidic was common. Here it eventually superseded Sahidic, while Arabic, the official language of Egypt, drove out the other Coptic dialects.

The two most notable features in which Bohairic differs from all other Coptic dialects are its use of the letter ϭ and ⲟⲩⲟϩ for ⲁⲩⲱ. In a few points it agrees with all or most of the sub-dialects against Sahidic, notably in the use of ⲣ- with Greek verbs.

---

[1] Edited in 1910 by Sir Stephen Gaselee in *JTS* xi (1909–10), 514–17, and a few years later by L. Th. Lefort and H. Copptiers in *Mu*, n.s. xv (1914), 49–60.

[2] Kahle, *Bala'izah*, i. 286–90.

[3] 'Mittelägyptische Bibelfragmente', *Études archéologiques, linguistiques et historiques dédiées à M. le Dr. C. Leemans* (Leiden, 1885), pp. 95–102. Cf. also W. Till, 'Faijumische Bruchstücke des Neuen Testamentes', *Mu*, li (1938), 232–5.

[4] P. E. Kahle, 'The End of St. Mark's Gospel. The Witness of the Coptic Versions', *JTS* n.s. ii (1951), 49–57.

[5] *PS* xx (83) (Leningrad, 1969), 96–117; cf. G. M. Browne, *BASP* xiii (1976), 41–3.

[6] See J. D. Prince, 'The Modern Pronunciation of Coptic in the Mass', *JAOS* xxiii (1902), 289–306; G. P. Sobhy, 'The Pronunciation of Coptic in the Church of Egypt', *JEA* ii (1915), 15–19; idem, 'The Traditional Pronunciation of Coptic in the Church of Egypt', *Bulletin de la Société d'archéologie copte*, vi (1940), 109–17; and especially William H. Worrell, *Coptic Sounds* (Ann Arbor, 1934).

From what has been said earlier, it is no surprise that of the several Coptic versions of the New Testament the Bohairic has been known much longer and studied more fully than any of the others. Already in the seventeenth century Thomas Marshall, Rector of Lincoln College, made collations of its text for the apparatus in Bishop John Fell's edition of the Greek New Testament (Oxford, 1675). The *editio princeps* of the complete text of the Bohairic New Testament was published at Oxford in 1716 by David Wilkins, a Prussian by birth but an Oxonian by adoption· Unfortunately his knowledge of the language was not thoroughly accurate, and his Latin translation cannot be trusted. Likewise the text itself was not constructed on any consistent or trustworthy principles, the editor following capriciously now one and now another source with no information given concerning the manuscript authority for the printed text in any particular passage.

The standard edition today is that of George W. Horner,[1] who made use of forty-six manuscripts for the Gospels, twenty-four for the Epistles and the Acts of the Apostles, and eleven for the Apocalypse. In the apparatus Horner cites all important variant readings of the manuscripts that he collated against the printed text, which is that of the oldest manuscript available for each section of the New Testament. In the Introduction, which contains a Coptic Grammar *in nuce*, the editor provides precise palaeographical descriptions of the manuscripts which he investigated. The descriptions of the manuscripts, in fact, range far beyond merely palaeographical interests; Horner includes, for example, the prayers that scribes appended as colophons to their manuscripts, sometimes in Bohairic, sometimes in Arabic.[2]

In 1934 the Coptic Orthodox Society 'Abnaa el-Kanisa' at Cairo published a handsome one-volume edition of the Bohairic

---

[1] *The Coptic Version of the New Testament in the Northern Dialect, otherwise called Memphitic and Bohairic*, with Introduction, critical Apparatus, and literal English Translation, 4 vols. (London, 1898–1905; repr. Osnabrück, 1969).

[2] Much valuable information relating broadly to the history of culture is preserved in colophons and other notes by scribes of manuscripts; cf. Henri Hyvernat, 'Les notes de copistes dans les manuscrits orientaux comme instrument de recherche et de critique historique', *Miscellanea di storia ecclesiastica e studii ausiliarii*, i, no. 3 (1902–3), 93–5. For colophons in Coptic manuscripts, see Arnold van Lantschoot's *Recueil des colophons des manuscrits chrétiens d'Égypte*; Tome i, *Les Colophons coptes des manuscrits sahidiques* (Louvain, 1929). Tome ii (*Les Colophons monolingues des manuscrits bohairiques*) seems never to have been published. For colophons in Armenian manuscripts, see below, p. 169.

New Testament. The text chosen for this edition is that of Henry Tattam's edition of the Coptic New Testament (2 vols., London, 1847–52). Tattam's text, which had been published by the S.P.C.K. for ecclesiastical use, is revised, and its errors and omissions are rectified. For this purpose, in addition to Horner's edition, two manuscripts in Old Cairo were consulted, one of A.D. 1331 and the other of A.D. 1250.[1] In the light of its origin it will be appreciated that this edition is not intended for those who wish to use the Bohairic version for critical studies, but is for Copts and such students of Coptic as may desire merely a correct text of the New Testament in the Bohairic dialect.[2]

The sequence of the groups of books within the Apostolos of Bohairic manuscripts is regularly: Pauline Epistles, Catholic Epistles, Acts of the Apostles. The Book of Revelation is preserved in relatively few manuscripts. It is very seldom included in the same manuscript with other New Testament books; when it is included, the book is distinguished in some marked manner from the rest of the contents of the manuscript, suggesting the copyist's doubt regarding its canonical status.

Early Bohairic manuscripts

(1) Until about a century ago the oldest Bohairic biblical manuscripts (and indeed the oldest Bohairic manuscripts) known to scholars were no earlier than the ninth century.[3] Then in 1922 the University of Michigan acquired a most interesting school exercise book written in Bohairic,[4] which competent palaeographers date to the beginning of the fourth century (so Bell, Youtie, Roberts, and, eventually, Kahle). The exercise book (which has been given the inventory no. 926) consists of a single quire of eight folios, with a bit of thread fastening four of the

[1] These two manuscripts seem to be nos. 675 and 151, respectively, of Georg Graf's *Catalogue de manuscrits arabes chrétiens conservés au Caire* (Vatican City, 1934); the latter is the ancestor of MS A₁ of Horner's edition (cf. vol. iii, pp. x–xiii).

[2] It may be mentioned here that Paul Boetticher's *Epistulae Novi Testamenti copticae* (Halle, 1852) was reprinted photo-mechanically in 1967 at Osnabrück under the name he adopted in 1854, Paul de Lagarde (the name of a great-aunt). The edition rests upon four Bohairic manuscripts, the collations of which leave much to be desired in the way of accuracy and completeness (see the devastating review by Heinrich Brugsch in *ZDMG* vii (1853), 115–21).

[3] See L. Th. Lefort, 'Littérature bohairique', *Mu*, xliv (1931), 115–35.

[4] Elinor M. Husselman, 'A Bohairic School Text on Papyrus', *JNES* vi (1947), 129–51.

folios together. The source of the manuscript was given by the dealer as Harît, the site of ancient Theadelphia in the Fayyum. The booklet contains a syllabary (in which each of the Greek consonants is combined with each of the seven vowels in order, concluded by either a Greek or a Coptic consonant), a list of biblical names, and the Bohairic text of Rom. i. 1–8, 13–15 and Job i. 1. The editor of the papyrus suggests that perhaps the two passages were written as an exercise in memory rather than in dictation or copying, for though they agree generally with the published texts, variants occur which are, for the most part, unique, not only in Coptic but in the other versions as well.[1]

(2) Among the large collection of Coptic manuscripts found in 1907 at Deir el-Bala'izah, situated on the west bank of the Nile some twelve miles south of Assiut, there is a parchment fragment containing Phil. iii. 19–iv. 9, dated by Kahle to the fourth/fifth century. He describes the dialect as 'Bohairic with a number of Sahidicisms'.[2]

(3) The most extensive early Bohairic manuscript that has so far come to light is a copy of the Gospel according to John which M. Bodmer of Geneva acquired with other documents that had been found, it was said, in Upper Egypt. On palaeographical grounds the editor has assigned the codex to the fourth century.[3] Originally the codex contained 239 numbered pages, but the first twenty-two are badly damaged and only small fragments have survived; beginning at about the middle of the fourth chapter of John the text is much better preserved. The Gospel of John is followed by the text of Genesis with page numbers beginning with ⲁ in a new series. The text breaks off unaccountably at Gen. iv. 2 with most of the final page left blank. Written on papyrus of mediocre quality, the number of letters per line varies within rather wide limits; 54 per cent of the lines have twenty to twenty-two letters, but the number goes up to thirty

---

[1] Elinor M. Husselman, 'A Bohairic School Text on Papyrus', *JNES* vi (1947), 132 f.

[2] 'A Biblical Fragment of the IVth–V^th Century in Semi-Bohairic', *Mu*, lxiii (1950), 147–53. Kahle re-edited the fragment, making a few minor corrections, in *Bala'izah*, i. 377–80.

[3] Rodolphe Kasser, *Papyrus Bodmer III. Évangile de Jean et Genèse I–IV, 2 en bohairique* (*CSCO* clxxvii, *Scriptores coptici*, xxv; Louvain, 1958). Kasser has also supplied a French translation of the Coptic text (*CSCO* clxxviii, *Scriptores coptici*, xxvi; 1958).

and not a few lines are shorter than the average. On the verso of folio 28 (page ͞ι͞π) the script changes markedly, being smaller and more compressed, resembling, so the editor states, the style typical of Coptic manuscripts of the Middle Ages.[1] The codex contains numerous corrections made by the original scribe.

Among the many perplexing aspects of this manuscript are certain features which have been interpreted by the editor and others[2] as signs that the copyist may have been a Gnostic. On the other hand, none of the features is absolutely unique to Gnosticism, and K. H. Kuhn concludes that 'though it is possible that it [the Bodmer Papyrus III] may have been included in a library belonging to a Gnostic sect, the text itself reveals no clear Gnostic affinities'.[3]

III. THE DATE AND MUTUAL RELATIONSHIP OF THE COPTIC VERSIONS

When it was that the Coptic versions of the New Testament were made and what their relationship is to one another are questions to which scholars have given very diverse answers. Toward the close of the last century it was customary to date the Bohairic version in the second century (so, for example, Lightfoot,[4] Westcott and Hort,[5] Headlam,[6] and Hyvernat.[7] But in 1889 Guidi challenged the generally accepted opinion and sifted afresh the evidence upon which an early dating had been based.[8] As a result, many scholars[9] were inclined to push the date of the

---

[1] Curiously enough, this page contains the text of John vii. 51–2; viii. 12–16. The editor confesses his inability to find a satisfactory explanation of the questions when and by whom the page was written.

[2] e.g. Éd. Massaux, 'Quelques variantes importantes de P. Bodmer III et leur accointance avec la gnose', *NTS* v (1959), 210–12.

[3] In a review of Kasser's edition of P. Bod. III in *JTS*, n.s. x (1959), 368.

[4] J. B. Lightfoot in F. H. A. Scrivener, *A Plain Introduction to the Criticism of the New Testament*, 3rd edn. (Cambridge, 1883), p. 371.

[5] *The New Testament in the Original Greek*; [vol. ii,] *Introduction [and] Appendix*, 2nd edn. (Cambridge, 1896), pp. 85 f.

[6] A. C. Headlam in Scrivener–Miller, *A Plain Introduction* ..., 4th edn., ii (London, 1894), 126 ff.

[7] Henri Hyvernat, *RB* vi (1897), 67–8.

[8] Ignazio Guidi, 'Le traduzioni dal copto', *Nachrichten von der königlichen Gesellschaft der Wissenschaften zu Göttingen*, 6 Feb. 1889, no. 3, pp. 49–52

[9] But not all; H. C. Hoskier, for example, dated its origin in A.D. 250 or even 200 (*Concerning the Date of the Bohairic Version* (London, 1911), p. 1). Hoskier tried to prove that the scribe of codex Sinaiticus had the Bohairic version before him and

Bohairic version forward to the seventh or even the eighth century (as, for example, Forbes Robinson,[1] Burkitt,[2] Leipoldt,[3] Baumstark,[4] and Hatch[5]).

After the discovery, however, of the fifth-century manuscript of the Gospel of John in the sub-Achmimic dialect, the text of which agrees with the Bohairic version in a third of all the cases where it differs from the Sahidic,[6] scholars found it difficult to be satisfied with such a late date for the Bohairic. Hedley, while maintaining still the customary seventh-century date for the Synoptic Gospels in Bohairic, declared that he was 'emboldened by the evidence of the sub-Achmimic codex . . . [to date the Bohairic] a couple of centuries earlier in writing of the Fourth Gospel'.[7]

With the discovery of the Bala'izah fragment of Philippians in semi-Bohairic and the Bodmer papyrus of John, the picture became entirely changed. According to Kahle, 'There can be no question that the Bohairic version of the New Testament was made not later than the fourth century, since it appears not only in the semi-Bohairic text of the present collection [i.e. Bala'izah], but also in a number of early Fayyumic manuscripts of the late fourth or early fifth century.'[8]

The Bodmer papyrus of John, while written in Bohairic, presents a form of text that differs somewhat from the Coptic

was influenced by it. But his examples prove only that in the Apocalypse there is a relationship between the Greek text on which the Bohairic version was based and ℵ, a circumstance which is not surprising, since Hoskier himself considered that ℵ was written in an Egyptian scriptorium.

[1] 'The Egyptian Versions', Hastings's *Dictionary of the Bible*, i (1898), 670–3.

[2] *Encyclopædia Biblica*, iv (1903), cols. 5008 f., and *Encyclopaedia Britannica*, 14th edn., iii (1928), 517.

[3] Johannes Leipoldt, *CQR* lxii (1906), 292–322, and 'Geschichte der koptischen Litteratur', in Brockelmann, Finck, Leipoldt, and Littmann, *Geschichte der christlichen Litteraturen des Orients* (Leipzig, 1907), p. 179.

[4] Anton Baumstark, *Die christlichen Litteraturen des Orients*, i (Leipzig, 1911), 111.

[5] William H. P. Hatch, in James H. Ropes and Hatch, 'The Vulgate, Peshitto, Sahidic, and Bohairic Versions of Acts and the Greek Manuscripts', *HTR* xxi (1928), 88.

[6] Sir Herbert Thompson, *The Gospel of John according to the Earliest Coptic Manuscript* (London, 1924), p. xxv.

[7] P. L. Hedley, 'The Egyptian Texts of the Gospels', *CQR* cxviii (1934), 207.

[8] *Bala'izah*, i. 250; cf. also idem, *Mu*, lxiii (1950), 152, and *Bala'izah*, i. 279–90; the latter deals with the parallels between the Bohairic version and the British Museum fragment of Acts (no. 2 on p. 124 above).

versions previously known. According to Garitte[1] and Kasser,[2] this version is independent of both the Bohairic and the Sahidic and may be regarded as an early precursor (but not a direct ancestor) of what became the classic Bohairic version.

The question of the date of the Sahidic version has found more widespread agreement among scholars than that of the Bohairic version. Most have assigned it to the third or fourth century (e.g. Forbes Robinson,[3] Steindorff,[4] Burkitt,[5] Hatch,[6] and Lagrange[7] favoured the third century; Guidi,[8] Leipoldt,[9] and Baumstark[10] favoured the fourth century). Horner[11] and Thompson,[12] however, were inclined to carry the version back to the second half of the second century.

In view of the steadily increasing number of early Coptic texts coming to light, by the middle of the twentieth century the desideratum became more and more pressing that a systematic survey and comprehensive integration should be made of the available data, set forth in terms of the mutual relationship among the several Coptic versions. One such investigation was undertaken by Kasser, whose knowledge of the texts is both broad and intimate, and the results are set forth in an imaginatively written article published in *Biblica*.[13] The following is a précis of Kasser's essay, often expressed in his own words (the footnotes have been supplied by the present writer).

Before attempting to define the Coptic dialects already known, it is necessary to state precisely the terminology we shall utilize. What should one call—indeed, what *can* one call exactly a 'dialect'? Should one give this term a rather broad sense, or a rather narrow one? What criteria are at our disposal today to differentiate the diverse dialectal forms of Coptic in

[1] Gérard Garitte, in a review of Kasser's edition of P. Bod. III, *Mu*, lxxiii (1960), 437–9.

[2] Rodolphe Kasser, 'Le Papyrus Bodmer III et les versions bibliques coptes', *Mu*, lxxiv (1961), 423–33.

[3] Op. cit.   [4] *Koptische Grammatik*, 2te Aufl. (Berlin, 1930), p. 2.

[5] Op. cit.   [6] Op. cit., p. 86.

[7] *Critique textuelle* (Paris, 1935), p. 325.   [8] Op. cit., p. 50.

[9] 'Geschichte der koptischen Litteratur', in Brockelmann, Finck, Leipoldt, and Littmann, *Geschichte der christlichen Litteraturen des Orients* (Leipzig, 1907), p. 139.

[10] Op. cit., p. 110.

[11] *The New Testament . . . Sahidic*, iii (Oxford, 1911), 398–9.

[12] Op. cit., p. xxix.

[13] Rodolphe Kasser, 'Les dialectes coptes et les versions coptes bibliques', *Bib*, xlvi (1965), 287–310, reproduced in slightly condensed form as the prefatory section in Kasser's *L'Évangile selon saint Jean et les versions coptes* (Neuchâtel, 1966), pp. 7–27.

antiquity? *Theoretically* the Coptic dialects were distinguished, one from another, by their pronunciation, but *practically*, for the scholar today, they are identified by their orthography, in accord with what we find in the manuscripts that are available to us. It would be unwise to affirm categorically that the different Coptic orthographies always represent exactly the differences in the pronunciation of the various Coptic dialects. Certainly in a country as vast as Egypt, it is possible that writing in Coptic began almost simultaneously in different parts of Egypt, and that each one of these attempts opened the way for the initiative of different schools of scribes.

It is not difficult to suppose that a variety of different orthographic conventions developed, distinguished from one another by the different usage they made of the same letters. On the other hand, the multiplicity of orthographic forms of the word ⲉⲃⲟⲗ *S B* (*A* and *A*² archaic MSS.), or ⲁⲃⲁⲗ *A A*² (and some ancient or popular *S* texts), ⲉⲃⲁⲗ *M F* (*S* and *A*² popular texts), ⲁⲃⲟⲗ *P* (and popular *S*), ⲛⲃⲟⲗ, ⲉⲃⲱⲗ, ⲉϧⲟⲗ (popular *S*), ⲉⲡⲟⲗ *G* (Bashmuric texts?), and even ⲉⲃⲟⲩⲣ (popular *F*) leads us to think that none of these spellings corresponded exactly to a specific locality. Of course, the pronunciation of this word varied a little from one region of Egypt to another, but one can believe that these variations were much less important than the orthography might lead us to suppose.

At the same time, however, such considerations do not carry us very far, and practically we are forced to suppress our scruples and to deal with the abstraction that we have just now been condemning. For us, then, a 'Coptic dialect' is identical with an 'orthographic system' or a 'system of writing', by means of which the dialectal nuances are expressed. We must not forget, however, that these premises are more or less arbitrary, and that they weaken our conclusions quite considerably.

If we refer to the purely orthographic testimony in ancient sources, we discover the existence of eight or nine Coptic dialects (without counting the various sub-dialects or mixed dialects).[1] To those who are surprised at the

---

[1] Besides the six dialects generally recognized, Kasser has identified also an Achmuninic dialect (discussed at greater length in his article, 'Dialectes, sous-dialectes, et 'dialecticules' dans l'Égypte copte', *ZÄS* xcii (1965), 112 f.), the dialect *P* (preserved in a copy of the book of Proverbs, *P. Bodmer VI*, ed. by Kasser (Louvain, 1960)), characterized, *inter alia*, by the use of the so-called Old Coptic letters (cf. Kasser in *JEA* xlix (1963), 157–60, and J. Vergote, 'Le dialecte copte P (P. Bod. VI: Proverbes). Essai d'identification', *Revue d'égyptologie*, xx (1973), 50–7), and the Bashmuric dialect, for which we have no identifiable text but only the testimony of Athanasius of Kus that the dialect still existed in the eleventh century in the region of Bashmūr (Mansura), east of the Delta. For an attempt to subdivide still further various Coptic dialects, see Kasser's comments in his *Compléments au Dictionnaire copte de Crum* (Cairo, 1964), pp. xi–xvii. For a critique of Kasser's tendency to multiply dialects and sub-dialects, see Peter Nagel, 'Der frühkoptische Dialekt von Theben' [deals, *inter alia*, with Kasser's identification of the 'P' dialect], *Koptologische Studien in der DDR*, ed. by Institut für Byzantinistik der Martin-Luther-Universität (Halle–Wittenberg, 1965), pp. 30–49, and idem, 'Der Bedeutung der Nag Hammadi-Texte für die koptische Dialektgeschichte', *Von Nag Hammadi bis Zypern, Eine Aufsatzsammlung*, ed. by Peter Nagel (*Berliner byzantinistische Arbeiten*, xliii; Berlin, 1972), pp. 16–27.

multiplicity it must be said at once that only two of these dialects, the Sahidic and the Bohairic, continued long enough to become standardized, that is, to eliminate the greatest part of their internal orthographic variations, and to create, in the domain of orthography, more or less stable rules. The other dialects can be described as minor or embryonic. Each of the manuscripts that represents them is strongly individualized with reference to other witnesses of the same dialect, and one cannot explain these differences solely by having recourse constantly to the very convenient hypothesis of reciprocal influences among the dialects. We think that many of the resemblances between aberrant dialectal forms and forms of other dialects are the result of fortuitous coincidence rather than reciprocal influences. These minor dialects never passed beyond the stage of orthographic tentativeness, and however narrowly some of them may have been localized in space and in time, they appear to lack that minimum regularity that would allow them to be considered as veritable dialects and not as individual attempts (such as, perhaps, the dialect *P*).

One can observe a striking difference between the dialects of the north and those of the south; the former have manifested a vitality and a resistance much superior to the latter. Whatever the reasons may have been historically for such a situation (and we may suggest that Hellenistic influences stimulated a nationalistic reaction that found a literary outlet), it appears, as Kahle has argued, that Sahidic emerged first in the north and then made its way southward throughout all Egypt. Thereupon Sahidic entered into contact with most of the other Coptic dialects spoken in Egypt (as Attic among the Greek dialects), and little by little destroyed their most distinctive characteristics.

The history of the development and the decline of Coptic dialects is linked closely to the history of the Coptic versions of the Bible. We may identify the following seven stages[1] of their development.

(1) Preliminary Stage (A.D. 150–200). During this period *ad hoc* oral translations of individual passages were made for liturgical use. We can imagine that some person in the congregation would have been emboldened to make rapid notes of these first, improvised translations, for his private use or for the benefit of his friends. Though improvised and, naturally, uncorrected, they probably had considerable literary freshness and great spontaneity of expression. Such translations would have been made almost anywhere in local dialects, though the Sahidic had, no doubt, the preference, because this dialect was the most widespread.

(2) The Pre-Classical Sahidic Stage (A.D. 200–50). As the number of native Coptic Christians increased appreciably, the need was felt in various local communities to make available good translations of this or that

---

[1] Kasser makes it clear that the seven stages are merely convenient categories which he has chosen for the purpose of tracing the course of the evolution of the Coptic texts, and that between these fixed points there are intermediate stages in which one can observe reminiscences of the preceding stage as well as symptoms of preparation for the following stage.

biblical book. Though most of these translations were in Sahidic, from this period dates also the proto-Bohairic version of the Gospel of John. Some translations were made by those ill equipped to do a careful piece of work. Such, for example, is the pre-classical Sahidic version of Joshua;[1] it teems with errors, and was, without doubt, abandoned by the Church during the following period.

Not all books of the Bible were translated at this stage,[2] and some books (those most frequently read, such as the Fourth Gospel) were rendered into Coptic several times, in different styles, by local translators, who ignored others that were working at the same task. Other books of the Bible remained entirely neglected, as they did not seem to correspond to the real needs of the churches. In any case, for these translators only the Greek text was regarded as the sacred text, the Coptic rendering being received only as an auxiliary means for evangelization.

(3) The Classical Sahidic Stage (A.D. 250–c. 300). During this period the Coptic Church of Egypt seems to have bounded ahead; one sees, at any rate, that it was passing from a stage somewhat disordered to a stage characterized by organization and centralization. At a time when it was seeking to preserve a certain unity in its doctrines against Gnosticism and Manichaeism, it sought also to unify the diverse biblical texts utilized in its congregations. It should not be surprising, therefore, to find that, along with the fragments of the diverse pre-classical Sahidic versions mentioned above, an official Coptic Bible had come into being. This was in the Sahidic dialect, which for some time had been the only neutral dialect that could be understood throughout most of the country. The new version was more literal than the preceding renderings, and the translators (or revisers) were guided by rather precise criteria. In some passages they were content to choose the best of the pre-classical Sahidic versions, emending it a little here and there. For other passages, having judged the earlier versions to be too imperfect, they made a totally new rendering.

Even though this first Coptic version rested upon the Greek text, it was far from being a robe without seams. On the contrary it was a hetero-

---

[1] The text survives in a manuscript divided between the Bodmer and the Beatty collections; cf. Rodolphe Kasser, *Papyrus Bodmer XXI. Josué VI, 16–25, VII, 6–XI, 23, XXII, 1–2, 19–XXIII, 7, 15–XXIV, 23, en sahidique* (Cologny-Geneva, 1963), and A. F. Shore, *Joshua I–VI and Other Passages in Coptic* (*Chester Beatty Monographs*, ix; Dublin, 1963). Kasser dates the manuscript to the fourth century; Shore to the first half of that century.

[2] In the absence of any Coptic biblical texts that can be dated with assurance earlier than the latter part of the third century, Kasser's argument concerning Stages 1 and 2 of his reconstruction must remain totally hypothetical. Even the fragments of the Sahidic version of Gen. xxxii. 5–21 and xlii. 27–30, 35–8, recently retrieved from the binding of codex VII of the Nag Hammadi gnostic texts— a binding which appears to date from about 345–50—supply no firm evidence of any third-century Coptic biblical text still extant (see Rodolphe Kasser, 'Fragments du livre biblique de la Genèse cachés dans la reliure d'un codex gnostique', *Mu*, lxxxv (1972), 65–89). Who can say how much time must elapse before a manuscript becomes so dilapidated as to be fit only for reinforcing the binding of another volume?

geneous work composed of disparate pieces, as one can prove by analysing its vocabulary. It is not the work of a single translator or of a group of translators working together. It reveals, rather, the labours of extremely diverse authors, separated by time (or space), whose productions were put together finally because they found favour in the eyes of a commission of experts who made a more or less thorough revision. This classical Sahidic version is attested by most of the manuscripts from antiquity and the Middle Ages. At the same time the official version did not drive out the earlier, independent renderings, some of which, even though they had not been utilized in the official version, were no less excellent. One finds good copies of these independent translations in manuscripts of the sixth century. In fact, they were perpetuated for a much longer time, while degenerating textually, outside the control of the Church. These are the so-called 'wild' texts.

(4) The Pre-Classical Bohairic Stage (c. A.D. 300–500). During this period the Coptic Church, having entered the Constantinian era, played a role it had not known before. Benefiting from the power of the State, it undertook to evangelize the countryside systematically. Since the Sahidic dialect was not sufficiently understood there, it was necessary to translate the classical Sahidic version into the principal minor dialects, thereby promoting them to the status of literary dialects. From this period come fragments of the official Sahidic version retranslated into Achmimic and sub-Achmimic, into Middle Egyptian and the *P* dialect, and perhaps also into Fayyumic. The literary flowering of local dialects, however, was extremely ephemeral, for these dialects were quickly suffocated by the Sahidic, and these secondary versions, without originality, disappeared as soon as their ecclesiastical usage no longer seemed indispensable.

(5) The Classical Bohairic Stage (A.D. 500–650). During this period, the last stage before the Arab conquest, Christianity penetrated deeply into all regions of Egypt. The Sahidic version continued to exercise a preponderant influence in all of Christian Egypt except perhaps in the Bohairic region and its immediate vicinity. The *P*, *A*, *A*², and *M* dialects were still extant, but were in the process of disappearing. With their disappearance the Coptic versions made in those dialects also disappeared, having no more real usefulness. The only texts still surviving were the Fayyumic, certain of which were in the sphere of Bohairic influence and participated in the resistance that this northern dialect offered to Sahidic penetration. At this time, besides, the Bohairic was not content merely to survive; it proved its vitality and independence through a revision of its ancient pre-classical versions and through the creation, in turn, of a classical version. The criteria of translation utilized in the editing of the classical Bohairic version display the same attention given to literalism which we earlier observed in the creation of the classical Sahidic version, but this time literalism was pushed much further, producing a rendering that in places is excessively rigid.

(6) The Final Sahidic Stage (A.D. 650–c. 1000). During this period Coptic civilization, smothered under the feet of Islam, began to die.

Egyptian Christianity in the Sahidic orbit declined slowly, and the classical Sahidic version gave way finally, throughout all Egypt, to the classical Bohairic version. It was perhaps in the seventh century that the classical Bohairic version adopted certain disputed passages, such as John vii. 53–viii. 11; such passages were certainly translated much later than the rest of the official Bohairic text. Finally, in this declining stage of the Sahidic dialect the remaining minor dialects began to disappear as well.

(7) The Final Bohairic Stage (after *c.* A.D. 1000). During this period the classical Bohairic version became the official text of the whole Christian Church in Egypt. But the Coptic language itself had no real vigour; even during the long centuries of its existence, it was incapable of producing any original literature. Sahidic was finally extinguished around the fourteenth century in the countryside of southern Egypt, where it had succeeded in maintaining itself until this time. As for Bohairic, one could say that it was still spoken, though artificially enough, in certain Coptic families until the twentieth century. Today Coptic should be considered a dead language, though still being utilized in the liturgy of the Coptic Church services.

The preceding summary of Kasser's reconstruction of the development of the Coptic dialects and the Coptic versions of the Bible will be assessed differently by different persons, but most will admire its comprehensive scope and plausible depiction of the *Sitz im Leben* in which it appears that the several Coptic versions emerged. Although one or another of Kasser's opinions concerning aspects of dialect or version will undoubtedly require modification or correction[1] in the light of further investigation[2]— and he has acknowledged[3] the existence of certain weaknesses in his methodology—his broad and imaginative delineation of the evolution of the major Coptic dialects as the matrix of the several versions of the Scriptures is a welcome contribution to the ongoing research of philologist and textual critic alike.

[1] Kasser's opinion that the versions in the chief minor dialects were translated from the Sahidic version (see his section 4, 'The Pre-Classical Bohairic Stage') is not shared by other scholars; Peter Weigandt, e.g., argues that they are independent witnesses to the New Testament text ('Zur Geschichte der koptischen Bibelübersetzungen', *Bib*, l (1969), 80–95. (Most of this review article is a detailed and relentless critique of the main sections of Kasser's book mentioned in p. 127 n. 13 above.)

[2] Kasser's synthesis is presented without exhibiting the supporting evidence; we are told only that his data come from an investigation of seven biblical books, but even their identity is undisclosed!

[3] 'Réflexions sur quelques méthodes d'étude des versions coptes néotestamentaires', *Bib*, lv (1974), 233–56. Cf. also Kasser's article, 'Les dialectes coptes', *Bulletin de l'institut français d'archéologie orientale*, lxxiii (1973), 71–99.

IV. TEXTUAL AFFINITIES OF THE COPTIC VERSIONS

As might be expected from the manner in which the several Coptic versions appear to have been made, the earlier manuscripts present a wide spectrum of variant readings, a few of which are preserved in the later standardized texts. The textual affinities of the Sahidic and Bohairic versions have been the subject of not a few analyses, some more refined than others. On the basis of collations prepared by Johannes Leipoldt, von Soden[1] found that both the major Coptic versions belong predominantly to the Hesychian recension, though during their transmission they suffered contamination in different degrees from the Koine recension. More detailed analyses of the several Coptic versions reveal textual profiles characteristic of the several sections of the New Testament.

1. THE SAHIDIC VERSION

According to earlier textual analyses undertaken by Horner[2] for the Gospels and by Hatch[3] for the Acts of the Apostles, the Sahidic version discloses a complex character, combining elements found in the Alexandrian and the Western texts. Inasmuch as the Sahidic version of Acts lacks almost all of the major Western readings, whereas it reads a large number of minor Western variants, the likelihood is that the Greek text of Acts on which the Sahidic was based was in origin a Western text which had been corrected in accordance with another of the Alexandrian type.[4] In the Pauline and Catholic Epistles, and in the Apocalypse, Lagrange confirmed von Soden's opinion that the Sahidic version belongs to the Alexandrian recension.[5] A more detailed picture of the textual affinities of the Sahidic New Testament is revealed by the following recent studies.

[1] Hermann von Soden, *Die Schriften des Neuen Testaments in ihrer ältesten erreichbaren Textgestalt*, I. Teil, *Untersuchungen*, ii (Berlin, 1902), 1478–92; iii (1910), 1674–81, 1863–7, and 2072–3.

[2] *The Coptic Version of the New Testament . . .*, iii (1911), 386–90.

[3] William H. P. Hatch in J. H. Ropes and Hatch, 'The Vulgate, Peshitto, Sahidic, and Bohairic Versions of Acts and the Greek Manuscripts', *HTR* xxi (1928), 86–8.

[4] So J. H. Ropes, *The Text of Acts* (London, 1926), p. cxliii. Otherwise we should need to suppose that a corrector inserted into an Alexandrian type of text the smaller and unimportant Western readings, while passing by the more interesting and important ones.

[5] Lagrange, op. cit., pp. 522, 569–70, and 618–19.

In the Gospels, according to an analysis made by Adams of the evidence provided in the apparatus of the United Bible Societies' edition of the Greek New Testament (1966),[1] 'the Sahidic agrees with ℵ B against D in 195 instances, and with D against ℵ B in 69; to these may be added: agreements with ℵ against B D 41, with B against ℵ D 80, with ℵ D against B 44, and with B D against ℵ 45'.[2] The over-all figures are:

	With Sahidic	*Against Sahidic*
ℵ	360	252
B	401	212
D	225	347
Old Latin	282	317

From the table it is clear that the Sahidic is in the main Alexandrian, and closer to B than to ℵ. The proportions, however, vary in the different Gospels, the influence of D being, according to Adams, greatest in John and least in Luke.

Although the Sahidic Gospels preserve a certain proportion of Western readings, there is a notable absence of the longer additions characteristic of codex Bezae (in contrast, Adams remarks, to the Bohairic). Furthermore, as concerns the major omissions of codex Bezae the Sahidic regularly joins the Alexandrian and other authorities in including such passages; for example, Matt. ix. 34 (exorcism), xxi. 44 (the stone that crushes), Luke v. 39 (old and new wine), xii. 21 (treasure with God), xix. 25 (they said, Lord, he has ten pounds), xxii. 19*b*–20 (Last Supper—second cup), xxiv. 6*a*, 12, 36*b*, 40 (the Resurrection), John xii. 8 (the poor always with you).[3]

The most recent detailed research on the Coptic versions of the book of Acts, that of Anton Joussen,[4] reinforces and refines the conclusions of earlier investigators, namely that the Sahidic and the Bohairic versions of Acts are independent translations from the Greek, while the Fayyumic is dependent on the Bohairic. The Greek text presupposed by the Sahidic and the Bohairic (Fayyumic) belongs to the Alexandrian type represented by ℵ

---

[1] In the Gospels this edition supplies evidence for more than 600 sets of variant readings.

[2] A. W. Adams's revision of Frederic G. Kenyon's *The Text of the Greek Bible* (London, 1975), p. 138.

[3] Ibid., p. 139.

[4] *Die koptischen Versionen der Apostelgeschichte* (*Kritik und Wertung*) (*Bonner biblische Beiträge*, xxxiv; Bonn, 1969), pp. 198–200.

and B but contains many Western textual elements. The fact, observed earlier in the century by Theodor Zahn,[1] that the Sahidic and the Bohairic exhibit a considerable number of readings which occur elsewhere only in Latin and Syriac witnesses, is to be accounted for by the supposition that all three versions have incorporated elements from the same type of Greek *Vorlage*.[2]

According to Adams's analysis of readings in Acts, selected on the same basis as in the Gospels (see above), the Sahidic is seen to agree with ℵ B against D fifty-seven times, and with D against ℵ B thirty-one times. The over-all figures are:

	With Sahidic	*Against Sahidic*
ℵ	101	83
B	101	83
D	56	91
Old Latin	79	73

'It is clear', continues Adams, 'that, although Alexandrian readings predominate, there is a strong Western element, as can easily be seen by inspection of an *apparatus criticus*. On the other hand, of the major additions and variants characteristic of D and its allies it has very few.'[3]

For the Sahidic version of the Catholic Epistles the most comprehensive collection of evidence is included in a lengthy dissertation (858 pages) by Karlheinz Schüssler.[4] Instead of piecing together fragments from various manuscripts (as Horner was compelled to do), Schüssler has collated papyrus, parchment, and paper manuscripts (including lectionaries) of the Epistles against MS. M572 of the Pierpont Morgan Library and part of the same manuscript in the Coptic Museum of Cairo (no. 3813).

Among noteworthy readings of the Sahidic New Testament the following deserve to be mentioned. The doxology of the Matthean form of the Lord's Prayer is binary in form: 'For thine is the power and the glory for ever' (vi. 13, with which agree also the Fayyumic version and the doxology of the Lord's Prayer in the Didache (viii. 2)). In the Matthean account of the rich man (xix. 16 f.) the Sahidic (with a manuscript of the Bohairic) makes the

---

[1] *Die Urausgabe der Apostelgeschichte des Lucas* (Leipzig, 1916), p. 225.
[2] So Janssen, op. cit., p. 200.   [3] Op. cit., p. 140.
[4] *Epistularum catholicarum versio Sahidica*, 2 vols. (Inaug.-Diss., Münster, 1969).

youth ask, 'Good master, what is that which I shall do, that I should obtain the eternal life?' And Jesus replies, 'Why callest thou to me, Good? There is not good except one, God.' Since this is scarcely the original reading of Matthew, one must assume that the Marcan and Lucan accounts have influenced the Sahidic of the first Gospel. A notable reading, as far as the extant witnesses are concerned, is represented by the Sahidic at Luke xvi. 19. Here the version reads, 'There was a rich man, with the name Nineuê, who clothed himself', etc. This reading perhaps was formerly more widespread than we are able to ascertain today; at any rate, besides a scholium of uncertain date contained in the Greek manuscripts 36 and 37 ($\epsilon\hat{\upsilon}\rho\sigma\nu$ $\delta\acute{\epsilon}$ $\tau\iota\nu\epsilon\varsigma$ $\kappa\alpha\grave{\iota}$ $\tau\sigma\hat{\upsilon}$ $\pi\lambda\sigma\upsilon\sigma\acute{\iota}\sigma\upsilon$ $\acute{\epsilon}\nu$ $\tau\iota\sigma\iota\nu$ $\mathring{\alpha}\nu\tau\iota\gamma\rho\acute{\alpha}\phi\sigma\iota\varsigma$ $\tau\sigma\mathring{\upsilon}\nu\sigma\mu\alpha$ $N\iota\nu\epsilon\acute{\upsilon}\eta\varsigma$ $\lambda\epsilon\gamma\acute{\sigma}\mu\epsilon\nu\sigma\nu$), the Bodmer Luke–John ($\mathfrak{p}^{75}$) of about A.D. 200 reads $\pi\lambda\sigma\acute{\upsilon}\sigma\iota\sigma\varsigma$ $\mathring{\sigma}\nu\acute{\sigma}\mu\alpha\tau\iota$ $N\epsilon\nu\eta\varsigma$ (the spelling is the result of a scribal error arising from the accidental omission of two letters of the exemplar, $ONOMAT\langle IN\rangle INEYH\Sigma$).[1]

The mixed character of the Sahidic text, mentioned above, combining elements of the Alexandrian and Western types of text, is illustrated most plainly in the reading of the so-called Apostolic Decree (Acts xv. 19 f. and 28 f.). As is well known, the decree has been transmitted in two main forms: the Alexandrian text, as well as most other witnesses, has four items of prohibition, whereas the Western has three prohibitions followed by the negative Golden Rule. The Sahidic version, however, not only has the four prohibitions but they are also followed by the negative Golden Rule. Such a conflate text, which presupposes and draws upon the Eastern as well as the Western tradition, must be the product of one or more early Coptic scholars who compared manuscripts and took from each what seemed best to them.

In Rom. v. 12 the Sahidic has an addition peculiar to itself, with no support in any Greek or Latin manuscript. The four known manuscripts of the Sahidic version of this passage add after $\mathring{\eta}\mu\alpha\rho\tau\sigma\nu$ (with slight variations), 'so also through one man life came forth'. It is remarkable that the addition should be found in all the known Sahidic texts, which are derived from

---

[1] For other names that were given to the anonymous rich man, see the present writer's article, 'Names for the Nameless in the New Testament; a Study in the Growth of Christian Tradition', in *Kyriakon: Festschrift Johannes Quasten*, ed. by Patrick Granfield and Josef A. Jungmann, i (Münster/W., 1970), pp. 89 ff.

different parts of the country and span a period of six centuries (third to ninth).[1]

2. THE BOHAIRIC VERSION

In the opinion of most investigators the Bohairic version is closer to the Alexandrian type of text than is the Sahidic.[2] The basic Greek text lying behind the Bohairic is best represented, according to Burkitt[3] and Nestle,[4] by the Greek codex L, and among the Fathers by Cyril of Alexandria. (For examples of the special characteristics of the Bodmer Bohairic Papyrus III, see the section below on Minor Coptic Versions.)

In the Gospels Adams found that the Bohairic version, as represented by the evidence presented in the apparatus of the United Bible Societies' edition of the Greek New Testament, agrees and disagrees with ℵ, B, D, and the Old Latin in the following proportions:

	With Bohairic	Against Bohairic
ℵ	390	223
B	388	227
D	218	354
Old Latin	282	317

These statistics indicate, as Adams points out, that 'whereas the Sahidic is somewhat closer to B than to ℵ, in the Bohairic the balance is slightly the other way; in fact, this leaning towards ℵ is more marked in the Synoptic Gospels, particularly in Luke, whereas in the fourth Gospel where ℵ has a not inconsiderable Western element, both Bohairic and Sahidic are closer to B'.[5] Further analysis of passages in which the Bohairic witnesses are divided between an Alexandrian and a Western reading, and

---

[1] For the Coptic text of the four manuscripts, see Sir Herbert Thompson, *The Coptic Version of the Acts of the Apostles and the Pauline Epistles in the Sahidic Dialect* (Cambridge, 1932), p. 97 in loc. Thompson aptly remarks that the origin of the reading 'is evidently to be sought in the desire to complete the well-known anacoluthon here'.

[2] For example, von Soden, op. cit. I. iii (1910), 1955 and 2072–3; J. H. Ropes, *The Text of Acts* (London, 1926), p. cxlv and pp. 357–8; M.-J. Lagrange, *Critique textuelle* (Paris, 1935), pp. 320, 452 f., 522, and 618.

[3] *Encyclopædia Biblica*, iv, col. 5010.

[4] 'Egyptian Coptic Versions', *The New Schaff–Herzog Encyclopedia of Religious Knowledge*, ii (1908), 133.

[5] A. W. Adams's revision of Frederic G. Kenyon's *The Text of the Greek Bible* (London, 1975), p. 142.

the Western reading has been assimilated into the Byzantine text, indicates that 'the earlier forms of the Bohairic Gospels were closely associated with the ℵ B type, but that they had, as we see in the later forms, undergone revision not on the basis of Western Greek MSS but on those of Byzantine type'.[1]

For the Book of Acts, Adams found that in about 180 sets of variant readings representative witnesses agree and disagree with the Bohairic version in the following proportions:

	With Bohairic	Against Bohairic
ℵ	127	57
B	132	50
D	36	107
Old Latin	73	76

'These figures', Adams concludes, 'show that the Bohairic is very close to the ℵ B text, containing far fewer readings of the D type than the Sahidic.'[2] Furthermore, according to Koole, in the Acts the Bohairic never agrees with codex Vaticanus when that manuscript disagrees with the other Alexandrian witnesses.[3]

In the Pauline Epistles the Bohairic version, according to Koole's research, presents a greater number of Western readings than does the Sahidic.[4] Moreover, when Western readings occur, the Sahidic witnesses are usually divided, leading one to conclude (as is true also concerning the Sahidic Gospels) that originally that version stood closer to the type of text in B, and that only at a later time was its character altered by Western influences. Western tendencies in the Bohairic are seldom pure, but generally have other attestation, chiefly Byzantine or Koine.[5]

3. MINOR COPTIC VERSIONS

Little is known concerning the textual affinities of the fragmentary remains of the New Testament in the other Coptic dialects. The Qau papyrus codex of the Gospel of John in the sub-Achmimic dialect, like the Sahidic version with which it is

---

[1] A. W. Adams's revision of Frederic G. Kenyon's *The Text of the Greek Bible* (London, 1975), p. 142. [2] Ibid., p. 143.

[3] J. L. Koole, 'Die koptische Übersetzung der Apostelgeschichte', *BBC* xii (1937), 69–70.

[4] *Studien zum koptischen Bibeltext; Kollationen und Untersuchungen zum Text der Paulusbriefe in der unter- und oberägyptischen Überlieferung* (Berlin, 1936), p. 89.

[5] Ibid., p. 67.

related, appears to be allied to the group of Greek manuscripts headed by the uncials ℵ B L W.[1] In the 459 readings in John where B and ℵ differ, Q supports B against ℵ in 263 and ℵ against B in 137. And in the same set of readings Q and W go together in 262, of which 202 are in company with B and sixty with ℵ. That is, Q follows B and W about twice as often as it follows ℵ.

Among noteworthy readings of Q perhaps the most curious is its agreement with early Greek and Latin witnesses (ℵ* W it[b] (*l*)) in omitting John ix. 38–39*a* (ὁ δὲ ἔφη, Πιστεύω, κύριε· καὶ προσεκύνησεν αὐτῷ. καὶ εἶπεν ὁ Ἰησοῦς). Whether this omission is to be regarded as strong evidence for the existence of an early Greek–Latin–Coptic trilingual manuscript, as Thompson thought,[2] it is difficult to make up one's mind. Another unusual reading which Q shares only with the Bohairic Bodmer Papyrus III is that of John vi. 63, '. . . the words that I have spoken to you are spirits and are life', on which Thompson comments: 'OL a c f Vg and Tert [*Resurr. carn.* 37], since the subject *verba* is plural, have *spiritus sunt et vita* (with varr.), which suggests an origin for this queer corruption. It may not be necessary to jump at once to a Latin–Coptic bilingual, as it may have come in as a gloss originally from a Gr.–Lat. bilingual.'[3]

The editor of the Fayyumic Gospel of John (P. Mich. Inv. 3521) has assessed its textual affinities with the text of John in other Coptic dialects, with the following results.[4] The text exhibits twenty-five readings peculiar to it alone; it agrees with the Sahidic against the Bohairic sixty-eight times; and it agrees with the Bohairic against the Sahidic thirty times. Of particular interest are three passages where omissions from the text show a close relationship between the sub-Achmimic Q and Mich. 3521. Both manuscripts omit ⲙⲙⲟⲛ ⲁⲗⲗⲁ in ix. 9, and both (with Bodmer Bohairic Papyrus III) omit ⲉϣϫⲉ ⲁⲡⲛⲟⲩⲧⲉ ϫⲓ ⲉⲟⲟⲩ ϩⲣⲁⲓ at the beginning of xiii. 32. Perhaps even more significant is the omission in these two manuscripts of the whole of ix. 38 and the first four words of vs. 39.

---

[1] So Sir Herbert Thompson, op. cit., p. xxvi.

[2] Ibid., p. xvi.

[3] Ibid., p. xxii.

[4] E. M. Husselman, *The Gospel of John in Fayumic Coptic* (Ann Arbor, 1962), pp. 14–17. The statistics cited here differ from those provided in Mrs. Husselman's summaries, for she counts as only one instance a given grammatical or lexical variant even though it may occur in more than one passage.

The special nature of the Bodmer Bohairic Papyrus III has been alluded to more than once in the preceding paragraphs.[1] Another of its idiosyncratic readings, which it shares with only one other known witness ($\mathfrak{p}^{66}$), is at John xiii. 5. Here the other witnesses read 'he poured water into the basin (εἰς τὸν νιπτῆρα)', but $\mathfrak{p}^{66}$ and the Bodmer Bohairic have the reading ποδονιπτῆρα 'foot-basin'. The origin of the reading is uncertain, but in any case we have another example of close contact between the Coptic versions and the Bodmer Greek texts.

Yet another noteworthy example of agreement between an early Greek papyrus manuscript and the Coptic versions is the reading 'I am the shepherd of the sheep' (John x. 7), supported by $\mathfrak{p}^{75}$, three Coptic witnesses, the Sahidic version, the fourth-century Fayyumic John at Michigan, and the fifth-century Achmimic bilingual papyrus 380 at Strasbourg.[2] Such early and presumably independent evidence has led Weigandt[3] to regard ὁ ποιμήν as deserving of at least equal consideration to that accorded the traditional reading ἡ θύρα.

As was mentioned earlier, the text of the Glazier codex of Acts in the Middle Egyptian dialect belongs to a Western type of text. More specifically, many typically Western readings, hitherto known from codex Bezae, the Fleury Old Latin manuscript (*h*), and the margin of the Harclean Syriac version, are now found to have been current also in Egypt. Examples include the following:[4]

i. 1 chosen] + to preach the gospel

ii. 37 what shall we do?] + Show us!

v. 36 claiming to be *a great* somebody

vi. 15 an angel] + standing in their midst

---

[1] A recent study by Rufus L. Moretz of the text of John in the Bodmer Boh. III, the sub-Achmimic Q, and the Michigan Fayyumic MS. 3521 finds the three of them to be closest to $\mathfrak{p}^{75}$ and B and most distant from D ('The Textual Affinity of the Earliest Coptic Manuscripts of the Gospel of John', Diss. Duke University, 1969; cf. *Dissertation Abstracts*, xxx (1969), 2608A).

[2] The Greek and Achmimic text of John was edited by Friedrich Rösch, *Bruchstücke des ersten Clemensbriefes nach dem achmimischen Papyrus . . . mit biblischen Texten* (Strassburg, 1910), p. 123. Because of a lacuna in the papyrus the Greek of this part of John x is not available.

[3] Peter Weigandt, 'Zum Text von Joh. x, 7. Ein Beitrag zum Problem der koptischen Bibelübersetzung', *NovT* ix (1967), 43–51.

[4] The examples are cited from Petersen's preliminary article (*CBQ* xxvi (1964), 225–41).

xii. 21 began to address them] + and he came to an agreement with
the Tyrians

xiii. 43 + The Word however spread through the whole city

xiv. 25 Attalia] + and they preached to them.

There are also many other readings which remind one of
typically Western accretions but which are not found in any
other known witness. Examples include the following:[1]

ii. 25 David says] + in the Psalms

vi. 1 The Hebrew deacons were neglecting the Greek widows

vii. 31–4 (The text is amplified by several extensive accretions from
the Pentateuch.)

vii. 42 the book of the prophets] + Amos the prophet

vii. 48 prophet] + Isaiah

viii. 35 Then Philip *took his* beginning from the Scripture, *and now
he was in the spirit,* [and] *he began to explain to him from the Scripture,*
[and] preached *the Lord* Jesus *Christ* to him

viii. 39 When they came up out of the water *the Holy Spirit came upon
the eunuch. But* the *Angel* of the Lord took Philip away *from him*

xi. 30 to the presbyters *who are in Jerusalem*

xii. 8–9 . . . and follow me. *But he seized him and drew him along before
him and came out with him,* and *Peter* followed

V. LIMITATIONS OF COPTIC (SAHIDIC) IN REPRESENTING GREEK[2]

by J. Martin Plumley

It might be expected that in Egypt, which possessed at Alexandria a world-famous school of Greek grammar, the translation
of a Greek work into the native language of the country would
have been well done; and the resultant translation might also be
expected to indicate how the Greek original could be recovered
with some degree of exactness. Although in many respects the
Coptic[3] version of the New Testament realizes this expectation,

[1] For other examples of Western readings in the Glazier manuscript, see the
investigations of Epp and of Haenchen and Weigandt mentioned in p. 119 nn. 2
and 3 above.

[2] For bibliography of other statements concerning limitations of Coptic in
representing Greek, see p. 107 n. 1 above.

[3] Throughout section v, 'Coptic' is to be taken to refer to the Sahidic dialect.

there are many instances where it cannot afford help, or, at the best, where its testimony is ambiguous. For, apart from the natural limitations of one language in relation to another, it is always to be borne in mind that a translator will on occasion— sometimes for reasons best known only to himself—force his native tongue to abnormal constructions which he would not use in a purely original composition. While there are limitations to the use which can be made of the Coptic version as an aid to the recovery of the original Greek text of the New Testament, and while it is the purpose of the present discussion to point out some of those limitations, it should also be recognized that by and large the Coptic version can be a valuable aid to the scholar engaged in textual criticism, and because in certain passages it preserves very ancient traditions of interpretation, it ought to be of considerable interest to the scholar working on the history and development of Christian doctrine.

When Christianity came to Egypt a long-established system of writing was still in use, but the propagators of the new faith decided that a new form of writing should be used for the purposes of evangelism. The old system of writing, though capable of expressing the new truth, was both far too intricate and too gravely contaminated by its content of many symbolic forms redolent of an ancient and discredited paganism. A new system of writing was therefore devised based on the uncial form of the Greek alphabet, supplemented by seven extra signs taken from demotic to express sounds which were unknown to the Greeks. This modified alphabet was able to represent the phonetics of any of the several dialects of Coptic that were currently spoken in the Nile Valley.

The New Testament writings are fully represented in the two main dialects of Coptic: Sahidic and Bohairic, but much less fully in Achmimic, Sub-Achmimic, and Fayyumic, early dialects which eventually gave way to Sahidic and Bohairic. There are scanty remains of yet other dialects, witnesses to early penetrations of Christianity into the various districts of Egypt.

By the sixth century it would seem that a standard text of the Coptic version of the New Testament had been fixed in Egypt, and variants after that century are the exception rather than the rule. It is possible that a careful comparison of the extant Coptic translations of the Greek New Testament prior to the sixth century would be a rewarding study, especially in respect of the 'Western' readings.

While the Coptic version may rightly be used in attempting to recover the original Greek text of the New Testament, one important and overriding fact about the Coptic language must always be borne in mind. Coptic, like the ancient Egyptian language from which it is the direct descendant, is a language of strict word order. This is so since there are no case endings. Word order is paramount. In the earliest written forms of the language of the Nile Valley the normal word order of a sentence was: VERB—SUBJECT—OBJECT—INDIRECT OBJECT—ADVERB (or ADVERB EQUIVALENT). During the course of many centuries various changes took place in the language, especially in the use of auxiliaries for expressing the various aspects of the verb. But the main features of the sentence remained unchanged: AUXILIARY—SUBJECT—VERBAL ROOT—OBJECT—INDIRECT OBJECT—ADVERB (or ADVERBIAL EQUIVALENT). It would seem that to the ancient Egyptians and to their descendants, the Copts, verbal action was the primary interest in a sentence, and therefore was to be placed at the beginning of a sentence, the normal place of emphasis. Thus in translating a simple sentence such as, 'Moses wrote the Law for our fathers', Coptic would read, 'Did [the auxiliary of the perfect]—Moses—write—the Law—for our fathers.'

Cf. Luke ii. 9: καὶ ἄγγελος κυρίου ἐπέστη αὐτοῖς καὶ δόξα κυρίου περιέλαμψεν αὐτούς, where the Coptic has ⲁ-ⲡⲁⲅⲅⲉⲗⲟⲥ ⲙ̄ⲡⲭⲟⲉⲓⲥ ⲟⲩⲱⲛϩ̄ ⲛⲁⲩ ⲉⲃⲟⲗ ⲁⲩⲱ ⲁ-ⲡⲉⲟⲟⲩ ⲙ̄ⲡⲭⲟⲉⲓⲥ ⲣ̄ⲟⲩⲟⲉⲓⲛ ⲉⲣⲟⲟⲩ, lit. 'Did the angel of the Lord appear to them forth and did the glory of the Lord become light for them.'

However, for the purpose of emphasis and sometimes no doubt to imitate as closely as possible the order of the Greek, Coptic is able to place the subject or the object at the beginning of the sentence, and at the same time to indicate its normal place in the sentence by means of a resumptive pronoun.

E.g. Matt. xix. 23: Ὁ δὲ Ἰησοῦς εἶπεν τοῖς μαθηταῖς αὐτοῦ, where the Coptic has ⲓ̄ⲥ̄ ⲇⲉ ⲡⲉϫⲁϥ ⲛ̄ⲛⲉϥⲙⲁⲑⲏⲧⲏⲥ, lit. 'Jesus (δέ) he said to his disciples'; likewise Matt. xix. 17: ὁ δὲ εἶπεν αὐτῷ, where the Coptic has ⲛ̄ⲧⲟϥ ⲇⲉ ⲡⲉϫⲁϥ ⲛⲁϥ, lit.

'He (δέ) he said to him.' Note too John x. 27 τὰ πρόβατα τὰ ἐμὰ
τῆς φωνῆς μου ἀκούουσιν, where the Coptic has ⲛⲁⲉⲥⲟⲟⲩ
ⲁⲛⲟⲕ ϣⲁⲩⲥⲱⲧⲙ̅ ⲉⲧⲁⲥⲙⲏ, lit. 'My sheep of mine they are
accustomed to hear my voice.'

In the same way it is possible to lay emphasis on the object.

E.g. Luke xviii. 21 : ταῦτα πάντα ἐφύλαξα ἐκ νεότητος, Coptic
ⲛⲁⲓ ⲧⲏⲣⲟⲩ ⲁⲓⲁⲣⲉϩ ⲉⲣⲟⲟⲩ ϫⲓⲛⲧⲁⲙⲛⲧⲕⲟⲩⲓ, lit. 'These
all I have kept them since my youth'; and John ix. 25 : ἓν οἶδα,
Coptic ⲟⲩⲁ ⲁⲛⲟⲕ ⲡⲉϯⲥⲟⲟⲩⲛ ⲙ̅ⲙⲟϥ, lit. 'One [thing] I it is
who know it.'

In a number of instances where no special emphasis was laid
upon the subject, but where there seems to have been some
desire on the part of the translator to preserve in Coptic as far as
possible the order of the original Greek, use could be made of the
particle ⲛ̅ϭⲓ, placed before the subject.

E.g. John xi. 12 : εἶπαν οὖν αὐτῷ οἱ μαθηταί, Coptic ⲡⲉϫⲁⲩ
ϭⲉ ⲛⲁϥ ⲛ̅ϭⲓ ⲙ̅ⲙⲁⲑⲏⲧⲏⲥ, lit. 'Said they therefore to him,
i.e. the disciples.' Also John xi. 17 Ἐλθὼν οὖν ὁ Ἰησοῦς, Coptic
ⲛ̅ⲧⲉⲣⲉϥⲉⲓ ϭⲉ ⲛ̅ϭⲓ ⲓ̅ⲥ̅, lit. 'When he had come therefore, i.e.
Jesus.'

In a number of instances both the subject and the object could
stand first in the Coptic sentence, their normal positions in
the sentence being indicated by resumptive pronouns. Striking
examples of this appear in 1 Cor. i. 22 and 23.

ἐπειδὴ καὶ Ἰουδαῖοι σημεῖα αἰτοῦσιν καὶ Ἕλληνες σοφίαν
ζητοῦσιν . . . Ἰουδαίοις μὲν σκάνδαλον, ἔθνεσιν δὲ μωρίαν, Coptic
ⲉⲡⲉⲓⲇⲏ ⲅⲁⲣ ⲛ̅ⲓⲟⲩⲇⲁⲓ ϩⲉⲛⲙⲁⲉⲓⲛ ⲛⲉⲩⲁⲓⲧⲉⲓ ⲙ̅ⲙⲟⲟⲩ
ⲛ̅ⲣⲉⲗⲗⲏⲛ ⲇⲉ ⲉⲩϣⲓⲛⲉ ⲛ̅ⲥⲁ ⲟⲩⲥⲟⲫⲓⲁ . . . ⲛ̅ⲓⲟⲩⲇⲁⲓ ⲙⲉⲛ
ⲟⲩⲥⲕⲁⲛⲇⲁⲗⲟⲛ ⲛⲁⲩ ⲡⲉ ⲟⲩⲙ̅ⲛⲧⲥⲟϭ ⲇⲉ ⲡⲉ ⲛ̅ⲛϩⲉⲑⲛⲟⲥ,
lit. 'For since the Jews signs they were seeking them, the
Greeks (δέ) they are inquiring after (a) wisdom . . . The Jews
(μέν) a stumbling-block it is to them, (a) foolishness (δέ) it is
to the nations.'

Here it would seem that the Coptic was attempting to reproduce as closely as possible the original Greek.

It is to be noted that since to the Coptic mind it seemed
entirely logical that the employment of a transitive verb implied

the use of an object, an object, usually a pronoun, appears more often than not in the Coptic text. Thus the translation ⲙ̄ⲡⲉⲧⲛ̄ϩⲁⲣⲉϩ ⲉⲣⲟϥ, lit. 'You did not keep it', for the original οὐκ ἐφυλάξατε (Acts vii. 53) does not necessarily imply an original αὐτόν. In Coptic an object is so regularly used with certain verbs, especially ⲟⲩⲱϩ 'to follow' and ϫⲱ 'to say', that it would be rash to imply from its presence a like representation in the Greek original.

Generally speaking, in Coptic, as in ancient Egyptian, the adverb or its equivalent could not stand at the beginning of a sentence. The only regular exception to this general rule is when the adverb or its equivalent indicates some notion of time.

E.g. John i. 1 : Ἐν ἀρχῇ ἦν ὁ λόγος, Coptic ϩⲛ̄ⲧⲉϩⲟⲩⲉⲓⲧⲉ ⲛⲉϥϣⲟⲟⲡ ⲛ̄ϭⲓ ⲡϣⲁϫⲉ, lit. 'In the beginning he was existing, i.e. the Word.' Luke x. 21 : Ἐν αὐτῇ τῇ ὥρᾳ ἠγαλλιάσατο, Coptic ϩⲛ̄ⲧⲉⲩⲛⲟⲩ ⲇⲉ ⲉⲧⲙ̄ⲙⲁⲩ ⲁϥⲧⲉⲗⲏⲗ, lit. 'In the hour (δέ) that he rejoiced.'

Since the normal position of the adverb or its equivalent was at the end of the sentence, Coptic had to indicate emphasis on the adverb or its equivalent, wherever it occurred, by means of special forms of the auxiliary verb, the second tenses.

E.g. Luke xiii. 28 : ἐκεῖ ἔσται ὁ κλαυθμὸς καὶ ὁ βρυγμὸς τῶν ὀδόντων is represented in Coptic by ⲉⲣⲉⲡⲣⲓⲙⲉ ⲛⲁϣⲱⲡⲉ ⲙ̄ⲙⲁⲩ ⲙⲛ̄ ⲡⲥⲁϭⲣ̄ ⲛ̄ⲛⲟⲃϩⲉ, lit. 'It is there the weeping will happen with the gnashing of teeth.' Also Luke vii. 14 : νεανίσκε, σοὶ λέγω, ἐγέρθητι, Coptic ⲡϩⲣ̄ϣⲓⲣⲉ ⲉⲓϫⲱ ⲙ̄ⲙⲟⲥ ⲛⲁⲕ ⲧⲱⲟⲩⲛⲧ̄, lit. 'Young man, it is to thee that I say, Arise.'

Because this is the normal way in which Coptic achieves emphasis on the adverb or its equivalent, the rendering of Luke xx. 2 as ⲉⲕⲉⲓⲣⲉ ⲛ̄ⲛⲁⲓ ϩⲛ̄ ⲁϣ ⲛ̄ⲉⲝⲟⲩⲥⲓⲁ, where ⲉⲕⲉⲓⲣⲉ is the second tense of the present auxiliary, quite properly represents the Greek ἐν ποίᾳ ἐξουσίᾳ ταῦτα ποιεῖς and cannot be held to imply the order ποιεῖς ταῦτα ἐν ποίᾳ ἐξουσίᾳ.

It should be noted that this precise indication of stress upon the adverb or its equivalent in Coptic is a valuable witness to the interpretation of certain passages of the New Testament in early times. It is particularly valuable where the original Greek might not seem to indicate any special emphasis on the adverb or its equivalent.

E.g. Matt. i. 22 : Τοῦτο δὲ ὅλον γέγονεν ἵνα πληρωθῇ τὸ ῥηθὲν ὑπὸ κυρίου διὰ τοῦ προφήτου where the Coptic has ⲡⲁⲓ ⲇⲉ ⲧⲏⲣϥ̄ ⲛ̄ⲧⲁϥϣⲱⲡⲉ ϫⲉⲕⲁⲥ ⲉϥⲉϫⲱⲕ ⲉⲃⲟⲗ ⲛ̄ϭⲓ ⲡⲉⲛⲧⲁ ⲡϫⲟⲉⲓⲥ ϫⲟⲟϥ ϩⲓⲧⲙ̄ ⲡⲉⲡⲣⲟⲫⲏⲧⲏⲥ. The form ⲛ̄ⲧⲁϥϣⲱⲡⲉ is the second perfect and implies that in the sentence the emphasis falls upon the fulfilment of what was spoken by the Lord rather than on the fact of the happening. Thus the Coptic is to be translated literally, 'In order that fulfilled should be what the Lord spoke by the prophet, all this happened.'

Although as a rule an adverb or its equivalent could not stand at the beginning of a sentence, a number of exceptions can be found in the Coptic version of the New Testament, more especially in the Epistles. No doubt in such cases the translator felt that there were special reasons for retaining as far as possible the word order of the original Greek.

E.g. Heb. i. 1 : Πολυμερῶς καὶ πολυτρόπως πάλαι ὁ θεὸς λαλήσας τοῖς πατράσιν ἐν τοῖς προφήταις, Coptic ϩⲛ̄ϩⲁϩ ⲙ̄ⲙⲉⲣⲟⲥ ⲁⲩⲱ ϩⲛ̄ϩⲁϩ ⲛ̄ⲥⲙⲟⲧ ⲉⲁⲡⲛⲟⲩⲧⲉ ϣⲁϫⲉ ⲙⲛ̄ⲛⲉⲛⲉⲓⲟⲧⲉ ⲛ̄ϣⲟⲣⲡ̄ ϩⲛ̄ⲛⲉⲡⲣⲟⲫⲏⲧⲏⲥ, lit. 'In many ways and in many guises did God speak with our fathers at first by the prophets.' Ibid. xi. 4 : πίστει πλείονα θυσίαν Ἄβελ παρὰ Κάϊν προσήνεγκεν τῷ θεῷ, Coptic ϩⲛ̄ⲟⲩⲡⲓⲥⲧⲓⲥ ⲁⲁⲃⲉⲗ ⲧⲁⲗⲉϩⲟⲩⲉⲑⲩⲥⲓⲁ ⲉϩⲣⲁⲓ ⲡⲁⲣⲁⲕⲁⲉⲓⲛ ⲙ̄ⲡⲛⲟⲩⲧⲉ, lit. 'In a faith did Abel offer a sacrifice up more than Cain to God.' Ibid. xi. 8 : πίστει καλούμενος Ἀβραὰμ ὑπήκουσεν, Coptic ϩⲛ̄ⲟⲩⲡⲓⲥⲧⲓⲥ ⲉⲁⲩⲙⲟⲩⲧⲉ ⲉⲁⲃⲣⲁϩⲁⲙ ⲁϥⲥⲱⲧⲙ̄, lit. 'In a faith, when they called Abraham, he heard.'

The employment of Greek loan-words is a feature of the earlier Coptic versions. Later, and more especially during the period when the final redaction of the Bohairic version was made, there was a deliberate replacement of many of these loan-words by purely native Egyptian words. This replacing of many once acceptable Greek loan-words was symptomatic of the rise of nationalistic feeling in the Coptic Church during the centuries which followed the Arab invasion of Egypt in A.D. 641 when

Greek influence began to wane and Arabic was increasingly supplanting the old language of the Nile Valley.

The use of so many Greek loan-words in the earliest period of Christianity in Egypt was due to the need to supply certain technical terms which could not be easily or satisfactorily represented by purely native words, e.g. μετανοεῖν, παρρησία, χρεία, etc. In some instances there were perfectly adequate native words, but they were thought to be contaminated by their use in pagan contexts, and therefore were considered quite unsuitable for use in a Christian setting and were replaced by Greek words; e.g. σῶμα, ψυχή. In other cases the Greek words of the original were repugnant to the Coptic translators because, though current in Egypt, they possessed pagan connotations. Thus ἱερεύς tended to be used only of a pagan priest and was normally replaced by the Greek πρεσβύτερος.

Certain Greek words found in the New Testament seem to have been unfamiliar in Egypt. These are replaced in the Coptic text by better-known Greek words; e.g. Matt. xxiii. 25 ⲡⲓⲛⲁϫ for ⲡⲁⲣⲟⲯⲓⲥ, Acts viii. 27 ⲭⲣⲏⲙⲁ for ⲅⲁⲍⲁ, ibid. xi. 8 ⲥⲱⲙⲁ for ⲡⲧⲱⲙⲁ, ibid. xi. 9 ⲧⲁⲫⲟⲥ for ⲙⲛⲏⲙⲁ.

In transcribing Greek loan-words Coptic regularly represents substantives and proper names in their nominative singular form without modification for the plural or any of the oblique cases. Thus it is impossible to say if the Coptic transcription ⲕⲁⲧⲁ ⲡⲟⲗⲓⲥ (Acts viii. 4) represents πόλιν or πόλεις.

Since Coptic has only two genders, the Greek neuter is generally, but not invariably, treated as if it were masculine. Nevertheless, transcriptions of neuter nominative endings are not uncommon; e.g. ⲁⲅⲁⲑⲟⲥ and ⲁⲅⲁⲑⲟⲛ; ⲡⲟⲛⲏⲣⲟⲥ and ⲡⲟⲛⲏⲣⲟⲛ. Greek verbs appear in their imperative singular active form, and to all intents and purposes are treated grammatically as if they were substantives.

In the transcription of loan-words variations in spelling, especially in the vowels, are frequent. Some of these spellings are probably due to mistakes made by scribes writing from dictation, but others had undoubtedly been corrupted by long use in Egypt before the advent of Christianity.

Since Coptic does not distinguish between *d* and *t*, the Greek δ was generally confined to the transcription of loan-words. Even so, there was always a tendency in such words to replace ⲇ by ⲧ.

Thus ⲥⲕⲁⲛⲧⲁⲗⲟⲛ for σκάνδαλον, and ⲉⲛⲧⲏⲙⲁ for ἔνδυμα. For this reason it is not possible to decide if the Coptic ⲇⲉ represents δέ or τέ (or, indeed, if ⲧⲉ represents τέ or δέ). Similarly, the writing of ⲟⲩⲧⲉ may point to either an original οὔτε or οὐδέ.

Although Coptic possesses both a definite and an indefinite article, their presence or absence in a sentence or phrase must not be taken to imply that the same was the case in the original Greek text. For example, Coptic does not admit of the definite article before a personal name. On the other hand, the Coptic definite article is always used before Χριστός and κύριος since these are regarded as titles. Where a personal name afterwards became the name of a people, the article could be used; e.g. ⲡⲓⲥⲣⲁⲏⲗ. Names of peoples, especially when used in the plural, often have the plural definite article where the original Greek has none (cf. Acts ii. 9–11). Similarly, Acts ii. 7 shows the indefinite plural article ϩⲉⲛⲅⲁⲗⲓⲗⲁⲓⲟⲥ. As a general rule, the definite article is used with the names of countries. The Coptic name for 'Egypt', ⲕⲏⲙⲉ, never seems to have the article. Most cities do not take the article, but a number beginning with a vowel frequently do.

The definite article is rarely used before a feminine substantive or personal name beginning with the letter theta, since it was wrongly assumed by the Copts that a word such as ⲑⲁⲗⲁⲥⲥⲁ was a writing of ⲧϩⲁⲗⲁⲥⲥⲁ; that is to say, the feminine definite article ⲧ prefixed to an assumed aspirated Greek word ἄλασσα. The usual Coptic transcription of Ἱεροσόλυμα as ⲑⲓⲉⲣⲟⲥⲟⲗⲩⲙⲁ, or more commonly in its abbreviated form ⲑⲓⲗⲏⲙ, indicates that the use of the article with this name is regular.

Sometimes the Coptic indefinite article is equivalent to enclitic τις.

Although Coptic possesses a considerable number of simple and compound prepositions, it is rarely possible to establish with absolute certainty what Greek prepositions are represented in the original Greek texts. Thus, while the more commonly used prepositions ἀπό, εἰς, ἐκ, ἐν, ἐπί, κατά, μετά, πρό, πρός, σύν, etc., can each be represented by prepositional forms in Coptic, it is not possible to demonstrate that such and such a Coptic prepositional form always represents one and the same Greek counterpart. For example, ἀντί, ἀπό, διά, ἐκ, παρά, πρό, πρός are each represented in different Coptic texts by compound prepositions, all of which include the element ⲃⲟⲗ with a basic meaning of 'loosing'. Again, it is very difficult in many instances to demonstrate from the Coptic any real distinction between ἐπί and πρό, or πρός and σύν, etc.

Certainly it is impossible from the Coptic evidence to find support for the restoration of the special distinction which can be indicated in Greek when a preposition stands before a word or, as often happens, when no preposition is written and its function is preserved by the case-ending of the word. It is therefore quite impossible to infer from the Coptic of Acts iii. 16 if the Greek had τῇ πίστει or ἐπὶ τῇ πίστει.

Coptic possesses an ample number of conjunctions which could be used to translate their Greek counterparts. Nevertheless, a small number of Greek conjunctions were accepted into the Coptic literary language. Both ἀλλά and δέ are common. Very frequently ⲇⲉ equals καί, and it cannot be assumed with any certainty which conjunction originally stood in the Greek text.

There is no Coptic equivalent for μέν. Occasionally it is transcribed into Coptic as ⲙⲉⲛ, but is often represented by ⲇⲉ.

Although Coptic does possess a number of conjunctions and borrows a small number from the Greek, the pervading practice of asyndeton makes it unlikely in many cases that the omission of a conjunction in Coptic implies any Greek variant.

In questions where the Greek differentiates between the introductory particles οὐ or μή, Coptic, if it transcribes the Greek negative particle, always uses the form ⲙⲏ. No inference can therefore be drawn from the Coptic, where ⲙⲏ occurs, that the original Greek also showed μή.

The well-developed system of auxiliary verbs in Coptic, while capable of dealing with the main temporal aspects of the Greek verb, are less able to represent the more subtle distinctions of mood, especially the subjunctive. Thus, where Coptic uses a future tense containing the element -ⲛⲁ-, it is not possible to decide whether the Greek text showed the future indicative or the aorist subjunctive.

Nor can Coptic truly represent the Greek passive since it possesses only the active voice. The passive, in use in the earlier periods of the ancient Egyptian language, had already begun to show signs of disuse during the third millennium, being eventually replaced by the impersonal use of the third person plural of the active verb.

Thus Rom. viii. 36: ἕνεκεν σοῦ θανατούμεθα ὅλην τὴν ἡμέραν, ἐλογίσθημεν ὡς πρόβατα σφαγῆς, Coptic ⲉⲧⲃⲏⲏⲧⲕ̅ ⲥⲉⲙⲟⲩⲟⲩⲧ ⲙ̅ⲙⲟⲛ ⲙ̅ⲡⲉϩⲟⲟⲩ ⲧⲏⲣϥ̅ ⲁⲩⲟⲡⲛ̅ ⲛ̅ⲑⲉ ⲛ̅ⲛⲓⲉⲥⲟⲟⲩ ⲉⲕⲟⲛⲥⲟⲩ, lit. 'Because of thee they are killing us in every day; they have reckoned us in the manner of the sheep to slay them.' Some peculiar literal translations of the Greek text result from this periphrastic use, as may be seen in Matt. i. 16: Ἰακὼβ δὲ ἐγέννησεν τὸν Ἰωσὴφ τὸν ἄνδρα Μαρίας, ἐξ ἧς ἐγεννήθη Ἰησοῦς ὁ λεγόμενος Χριστός, Coptic ⲓⲁⲕⲱⲃ ⲇⲉ ⲁϥϫⲡⲟ ⲛ̅ⲓⲱⲥⲏⲫ ⲡϩⲁⲓ ⲙ̅ⲙⲁⲣⲓⲁ ⲧⲁⲓ ⲉⲛⲧⲁⲩϫⲡⲉ ⲓ̅ⲥ̅ ⲉⲃⲟⲗ ⲛ̅ϩⲏⲧⲥ̅ ⲡⲁⲓ ⲉϣⲁⲩⲙⲟⲩⲧⲉ ⲉⲣⲟϥ ϫⲉ ⲡⲉⲭ̅ⲥ̅, lit. 'Jacob (δέ) he begat Joseph the husband of Mary, this one (fem.) they begat Jesus through her, this one (masc.) whom they are wont to call him, the Christ.'

As has already been observed, Coptic by means of its system of auxiliary verbs could represent reasonably adequately the main temporal aspects of the Greek finite verb. Nevertheless, it must be recognized that the Coptic translator was not always able to appreciate the more delicate shades of meaning presented by such and such a Greek verb form. For example, where the Greek uses the imperfect tense, the Coptic will frequently employ the perfect auxiliary, an auxiliary which could be equally used by the translator to represent the Greek aorist. For this reason it is impossible to decide whether the Coptic perfect represents the imperfect or the aorist in the Greek text. Coptic did, however, possess an auxiliary which is termed the imperfect. The fundamental idea of this auxiliary is that there formerly existed a time when an action continued, but that the period of time containing the action no longer exists. It is perhaps because of this conception that in Coptic the use of the imperfect is comparatively rare. In the translation of Greek originals it may be accepted that where Coptic uses the imperfect auxiliary the presence of the Greek imperfect is implied.

The earlier forms of the Egyptian language had possessed a number of verbal forms comparable to Greek participles, but in the last stage of the language, i.e. Coptic, these forms had been superseded largely by a verbal auxiliary, distinguishable in most of its forms from the present and perfect auxiliaries only by the presence of a prefixed ⲉ-. These forms, known as the circumstantial and the less-frequent past circumstantial, can and often do represent a Greek participle followed by a finite form of the verb.

Matt. xxii. 41: Συνηγμένων δὲ τῶν Φαρισαίων ἐπηρώτησεν αὐτοὺς ὁ Ἰησοῦς λέγων, Coptic ⲉⲩⲥⲟⲟⲩϩ ⲇⲉ ⲉϩⲟⲩⲛ ⲛϭⲓ ⲫⲁⲣⲓⲥⲁⲓⲟⲥ ⲁϥϫⲛⲟⲩⲟⲩ ⲛϭⲓ ⲓⲥ ⲉϥϫⲱ ⲙⲙⲟⲥ, lit. 'They-being-gathered [circumstantial] (δέ) in i.e. the Pharisees, he-asked-them [perfect] i.e. Jesus, (he-) saying [circumstantial] it.'

In many instances the reversing of the participle and the finite verb of the Greek into the finite verb and the circumstantial of the Coptic is in accordance with the idiom of the language and does not necessarily imply any variant in the Greek.

Matt. xxvi. 49: καὶ εὐθέως προσελθὼν τῷ Ἰησοῦ εἶπεν, Χαῖρε, ῥαββί, Coptic ⲁⲩⲱ ⲛⲧⲉⲩⲛⲟⲩ ⲁϥϯⲡⲉϥⲟⲩⲟⲉⲓ ⲉⲓⲥ ⲉϥϫⲱ ⲙⲙⲟⲥ ⲇⲉ ⲭⲁⲓⲣⲉ ϩⲣⲁⲃⲃⲉⲓ, lit. 'And immediately he-made-his-way [perfect] to Jesus, (he-) saying [circumstantial] it, "Greetings, Master!"'

In the translation of the next verse of this chapter the participle and finite verb of the Greek are rendered in the Coptic, as is frequently the case, by two finite verbal forms without connecting conjunctions.

Matt. xxvi. 50: τότε προσελθόντες ἐπέβαλον τὰς χεῖρας ἐπὶ τὸν Ἰησοῦν καὶ ἐκράτησαν αὐτόν, Coptic ⲧⲟⲧⲉ ⲁⲩϯⲡⲉⲩⲟⲩⲟⲉⲓ ⲁⲩⲉⲓⲛⲉ ⲛⲛⲉⲩϭⲓϫ ⲉϩⲣⲁⲓ ⲉϫⲛ ⲓⲥ ⲁⲩⲁⲙⲁϩⲧⲉ ⲙⲙⲟϥ, lit. 'Then they-made-their-way [perfect], they-bore [perfect] their hands down upon Jesus, they-seized [perfect] him.'

It may therefore be assumed that the Coptic version is not helpful in determining whether the original Greek text had a participle or a finite form of the verb.

Coptic does not possess any grammatical construction comparable with *oratio obliqua*; consequently, recourse is made to direct speech.

Cf. Acts v. 36 where the Greek ἀνέστη Θευδᾶς, λέγων εἶναί τινα ἑαυτόν is rendered in Coptic by ⲁϥⲧⲱⲟⲩⲛ ⲛϭⲓ ⲑⲉⲩⲇⲁⲥ ⲉϥϫⲱ ⲙ̄ⲙⲟⲥ ⲉⲣⲟϥ ϫⲉ ⲁⲛⲟⲕ ⲡⲉ, lit. 'He arose, i.e. Theudas, (he) saying it of himself, "I am he." '

In concluding this short survey it should perhaps be stated that it would be possible to add to the list of limitations the Coptic version presents when used as a means to the recovery of the original Greek text. Nevertheless, while the list given above does not claim to be exhaustive, it is hoped that the most important limitations have been indicated, and in such a way that the survey will be useful both to those whose knowledge of Coptic is minimal and to those who are totally unacquainted with that language.

III

The Armenian Version

I. THE INTRODUCTION OF CHRISTIANITY INTO ARMENIA AND THE TRANSLATION OF THE NEW TESTAMENT

ARMENIA claims the honour of being the first kingdom to accept Christianity as its official religion. According to unsubstantiated ecclesiastical tradition, the apostles Thaddaeus and Bartholomew laboured among the Armenians.[1] Although we cannot determine exactly when the Gospel was first preached in Armenia, according to Eusebius the Church was already established there by the middle of the third century, for Dionysius, the venerable bishop of Alexandria (died c. 264), wrote an epistle on the theme of repentance 'to the brethren in Armenia, whose bishop is Meruzanes'.[2]

On the testimony of Agathangelos, who was secretary to Tiridates III, king of Armenia (c. 284–314), the founder of Armenian Christianity was Gregory the Illuminator (c. 257–331).[3] The latter, an Armenian of royal lineage who had received Christian training at Caesarea in Cappadocia, toward the end of the third century returned as a missionary to his native land.

[1] Cf. 'The Acts and Martyrdom of the Holy Apostle Thaddaeus' and 'The Acts and Martyrdom of the Holy Apostle Bartholomew', translated by S. C. Malan in his *Life and Times of S. Gregory the Illuminator; the Founder and Patron Saint of the Armenian Church* (London, 1868), pp. 66–103.

[2] Eusebius, *Hist. eccl.* VI. xlvi. 3. Harnack points out that the name is Armenian (an Armenian satrap is so called in Faustus of Byzantium), but where Meruzanes' see was located, he is unable to say (see *Die Mission und Ausbreitung des Christentums in den ersten drei Jahrhunderten*, 4te Aufl. ii (Leipzig, 1924), 747; Engl. trans. from 2te Aufl., *The Mission and Expansion of Christianity in the First Three Centuries*, 2nd edn. ii (New York and London, 1908), 197.

The variant reading in Acts ii. 9 (where Tertullian and Augustine substituted *Armenia* for 'Ιουδαίαν) is curious but probably unrelated to the historical question of the Christianization of Armenia. Concerning the textual problems in Acts ii. 9, see the contribution by the present writer to *Apostolic History and the Gospel; Biblical and Historical Essays presented to F. F. Bruce*, ed. by W. W. Gasque and R. P. Martin (Exeter, 1970), p. 133.

[3] Cf. Gérard Garitte, *Documents pour l'étude du livre d'Agathange* (Studi e testi, cxxvii; Vatican City, 1956), and David M. Lang, *Armenia, Cradle of Civilization* (London, 1970), pp. 155–74.

Just after the beginning of the fourth century Tiridates, who previously had been a persecutor of the Church, was converted, as well as large numbers of nobles. Thereupon Christianity was made by royal edict[1] the established religion of Armenia, and was embraced by the populace through wholesale baptisms.

About 302 Gregory was consecrated bishop for Armenia by Leontius, bishop of Caesarea in Cappadocia. Subsequently he travelled east and at Ashtishat in the province of Taron destroyed the most celebrated pagan sanctuary of the country; in its place a splendid Christian sanctuary, 'the mother of all Armenian churches', was erected. From Taron Gregory went to the province of Ararat, where also a famous pagan sanctuary was turned into a Christian church. Gregory's cathedral was in the city of Valarshabad on the spot which he had named Etchmiadzin. In 325 Gregory was summoned to take part in the Council of Nicaea, but being unable to go himself sent his son Aristakes, who, with another delegate named Akritis,[2] brought back the Nicaean decrees for the Armenian Church.

In his programme of evangelization Gregory was assisted by co-workers from various backgrounds; by Armenians who had been trained in Hellenistic culture, as well as by Armenians who had been under Syrian influence. During this period, before the invention of an Armenian alphabet, books and documents existed only in Greek and Syriac and their translation was left to oral interpretation. Consequently it was through such cultural bridges that the Armenians received both Greek and Syrian Christianity, as well as the literature of both these peoples. Accordingly there came into the Armenian vocabulary a considerable number of Greek and Syriac terms that were connected with the Christian cultus. For example, of Greek derivation are the Armenian words meaning 'martyr', 'bishop', 'Christian', 'Sunday', 'church', etc., and of Syriac derivation the Armenian words meaning 'ascetic' or 'monk', 'priest', 'fasting', 'preacher', 'Satan', etc.[3]

---

[1] According to Sozomen (*Hist. eccl.* II. viii), Tiridates 'issued commands to all his subjects, by a herald, to adopt Christianity'.

[2] Cf. Henricus Gelzer, Henricus Hilgenfeld, Otto Cuntz, *Patrum Nicaenorum nomina* (*Scriptores sacri et profani*, ii; Leipzig, 1898), pp. lxii and 192.

[3] Henrich Hübschmann, *Armenische Grammatik* (Leipzig, 1897; repr. Darmstadt, 1962), pp. 299 ff. and 337 ff.

Toward the latter part of the fourth century (between 384 and 390) Armenia was partitioned between the Byzantine and the Persian Empires. The latter acquired about four-fifths of the country, including Taron and the headquarters of the Armenian Church. Thereafter Greek books were banned and burnt, and ecclesiastical literature circulated only in Syriac. In the following centuries, however, Greek influence was permitted once again to make itself felt in many ways. In fact, judging from extant Armenian manuscripts, Armenian scribes learned their codicological and palaeographic techniques—such as the general format of the page (as regards size and use of two columns), the uncial appearance of Armenian script, and the use of enlarged initials—from Greek rather than Syriac models.[1]

The foundation of Armenian national literature, including the translation of the Bible, dates from the early part of the fifth century. The chief promoters of this cultural development were the catholicos of the Armenian Church, Sahak (Isaac, born *c.* 350, died 7 Sept. 439), a son of Nerses the Great and a descendant of Gregory the Illuminator, and Sahak's friend and helper, Mesrop (Mesrob or Mashtotz or Maštoç, born *c.* 361, died 17 Feb. 439), who had changed a military career for the life of a monk, missionary, and teacher.

The earliest attempt to construct an Armenian alphabet was made by a certain Bishop Daniel. Since he was a Syrian, he probably took the Aramaic alphabet as a pattern. According to the historian Koriun,[2] the alphabet was found to be unsuited to represent the sounds of the Armenian language. At length and with the encouragement of King Vramshapuh (*c.* 395–*c.* 415), Mesrop succeeded, with the help of a Greek hermit and calligrapher, Rufanos of Samosata,[3] in producing about A.D. 406 an Armenian alphabet of thirty-six letters.[4] The question of the model or models of script on which Mesrop based his creation has

---

[1] Cf. August Merk, 'Armenische und griechische Palaeographie', *Miscellanea Francesco Ehrle; Scritti di storia e paleografia . . .* , iv (Rome, 1924), 1–21.

[2] Koriun, *Beschreibung des Lebens und Strebens des hl. Lehrers Mesrop*, translated by Simon Weber in *Bibliothek der Kirchenväter*, lvii (Munich, 1927), 205–7.

[3] Koriun, op. cit., pp. 207 ff.

[4] Cf. E. G. Ter-Minassian, 'De la date de l'invention de l'alphabet arménien et autres questions s'y rapportant' [in Armenian, with Russian and French résumés], *Banber Matenadarani*, vii (1964), 25–48. In the twelfth century two more letters were added at the end of the Armenian alphabet, viz. *ō* and *fē*.

received considerable attention.[1] Among the various theories that have been suggested two deserve to be mentioned here. According to the view advanced by Junker,[2] both the Armenian and the Georgian alphabets are based on the Pahlavic script with the addition of some letters from the Avestan alphabet, while Greek influence was felt in the creation of vowels, the direction of writing, and the upright and regular position of the characters. What may be called the traditional view, which is held by most scholars, is that Mesrop depended chiefly upon the Greek alphabet, twenty letters coming directly from this source, twelve others being formed after a Greek model, and four being taken from Syriac.[3]

After creating the Armenian alphabet Mesrop gathered about him a band of keen scholars. Sending some of them to Edessa, to Constantinople, and as far as Rome in search of manuscripts of the Scriptures and of ecclesiastical and secular writers, he inaugurated a programme of translation which enriched and consolidated Armenian culture.[4] The first book of the Bible

---

[1] See Heinrich Hübschmann, 'Über Aussprache und Umschreibung des Altarmenischen', *ZDMG* xxx (1876), 53–73; Viktor Gardthausen, 'Über den Ursprung der armenischen Schrift', ibid. 74–80; J. Marquart, *Über den Ursprung des armenischen Alphabets in Verbindung mit der Biographie des hl. Mašt'oc'* (Vienna, 1917); and H. Adjarian, 'The Varieties and Developments of Armenian Uncial Writing' [in Armenian], *HA* xxxviii (1924), cols. 507–21; cf. idem, xxix (1915), cols. 135–72; xxxv (1921), cols. 298–315; and lii (1938), cols. 289–318; P. Peeters, 'Pour l'histoire des origines de l'alphabet arménien', *RÉA* ix (1929), 203–37; F. Feydit, 'Considérations sur l'alphabet de saint Mesrop', *HA* lxxvi (1962), cols. 183–200, 361–84; lxxvii (1963), cols. 37–58, 225–36, 359–72, and 515–30; and Jens J. Jensen, 'Die Reihenfolge der Buchstaben des altarmenischen Alphabets', *HA* lxxxi (1967), cols. 433–8.

[2] Heinrich F. J. Junker, 'Das Awesta Alphabet und der Ursprung der armenischen und georgischen Schrift', *Caucasica*, ii (1925), 1–91, and iii (1926), 82–139.

[3] Cf. Louis Leloir in *Dictionnaire de la Bible, Supplément*, vi (Paris, 1960), col. 811, and Achot Hovhannissian, 'L'alphabet arménien et son action historique', *RÉA*, n.s. ii (1965), 361–73, and iii (1966), 359–67.

[4] Something of the broad scope of this burst of literary activity can be judged from the fact that Karékin Zarbhanalian's *Catalogue des anciennes traductions arméniennes (siècles iv–xiii)* (Venice, 1889) fills a volume of nearly 800 pages. In not a few instances we are dependent upon the Armenian translation for our knowledge of earlier books and treatises no longer extant in Greek and Syriac; e.g. certain treatises of Philo Judaeus; the chronicle of Eusebius; the apology of Aristides; homilies of Severianus of Gabala; the commentaries of Ephraem on the Bible; and various writings of Basil the Great, Chrysostom, Cyril of Jerusalem, Athanasius, Epiphanius, Euthalius, Gregory Thaumaturgus, and others.

that Mesrop translated was the Book of Proverbs;[1] this was followed by the New Testament. With the help of Sahak and perhaps other translators, the rest of the Old Testament was translated into Armenian, the work being finished about 410–14.

II. EARLY MANUSCRIPTS OF THE ARMENIAN VERSION

It is not generally realized how abundant are the manuscripts of the Armenian version of the New Testament. Contrary to a rather widespread impression of their rarity,[2] more manuscripts of this version are extant than of any other ancient version, with the exception only of the Latin Vulgate.

A tool which is of great assistance to scholars in the study of the Armenian version is Rhodes's annotated list of Armenian New Testament manuscripts.[3] After consulting scores of printed and handwritten catalogues of Armenian manuscripts and culling out those that contain all or part of the New Testament (except lectionaries and commentaries on the New Testament text), Rhodes compiled a list of 1,244 manuscripts, for most of which he supplies information concerning their location, contents, physical description, scribes, place and date of writing, as well as references to previous lists and monographs in which the manuscripts have been cited.

Catalogues of collections of Armenian manuscripts published since Rhodes's volume include those edited by Sirarpie Der

---

[1] According to A. T. Kanalanian, Mesrob considered the Book of Proverbs, with its practical advice concerning ethical and social problems, not less important for his people, in the given circumstances, than the more purely religious parts of the Scriptures ('Pourquoi Machtotz traduisit les Proverbes de Salomon' [in Armenian, with Russian and French résumés], *Banber Matenadarani*, vii [1964], 113–24).

[2] See, e.g., F. G. Kenyon's *Our Bible and the Ancient Manuscripts*, 5th edn., revised by A. W. Adams (London, 1958), p. 237.

[3] Erroll F. Rhodes, *An Annotated List of Armenian New Testament Manuscripts* (Ikebukuro, Tokyo, 1959). Several years ago the Academy of the Armenian Soviet Socialist Republic began moving manuscripts from outlying districts to its central repository at Erevan, which now has more than 1,500 Gospel manuscripts and 100 complete Bible manuscripts, not to mention incomplete and fragmentary manuscripts. Inasmuch as Rhodes lists 267 manuscripts in the Erevan collection, it will be seen that there is room for a revised and enlarged edition of his useful catalogue.

Nersessian,[1] K. Roszko,[2] J. Assfalg and J. Molitor,[3] B. Sargissian and G. Sargissian,[4] Bogharian,[5] and Mouradian and Mardirossian,[6] as well as by a number of contributors to the Armenian journal *Handes Amsorya*.[7]

The largest collection of Armenian manuscripts of the New Testament in the United States is in the possession of Mr. Harry Kurdian of Wichita, Kansas. At the beginning of 1975 the collection numbered fifty-nine manuscripts of the complete New Testament, and forty-one of part of the New Testament.

The most ancient Armenian manuscripts of the Gospels, all dating from the ninth and tenth centuries, are the following.

(1) The oldest dated manuscript (Rhodes's *Annotated List*, no. 991) is a tetraevangelium copied in A.D. 887. It is written on 229 folios of parchment in majuscules (*erkat'agir*) of twenty-two

---

[1] *Armenian Manuscripts in the Freer Gallery of Art* (Washington, 1963).

[2] Roszko's catalogue of Armenian (and Georgian) manuscripts deposited in Polish libraries is vol. iii of *Katalog rękopisów orientalnych ze zbiorów polskich*, ed. by S. Strelcyn (1959). A brief account of the work of assembling the catalogue is given in *Przegląd orientalistyczny*, iii (24) (1957), 307–12.

[3] *Armenische Handschriften* (*Verzeichnis der orientalischen Handschriften in Deutschland*, iv; Wiesbaden, 1962).

[4] B. Sargissian, *Grand Catalogue des manuscrits arméniens de la bibliothèque des PP. Mékhitharistes de St.-Lazare*, i (Venice, 1914); ii (1924); with G. Sargissian, iii (1966) (in Armenian).

[5] N. Bogharian, *Le Grand Catalogue des manuscrits de S. Jacques*, 6 vols. (Jerusalem, 1966–72) (in Armenian).

[6] S. A. Mouradian [Muratean] and N. B. Mardirossian [Martirosean], *Catalogue of Armenian Manuscripts of St. Arakelotz-Tarkmanchatz Monastery* (*Moush*) *and the Environs*, ed. by A. Kalaydjian [Galayčean] (Jerusalem, 1967) (in Armenian).

[7] N. Akinian lists and describes the Armenian manuscripts in Cyprus (at present in Antilias, Lebanon), *HA* lxix (1955), cols. 170 ff.; the Armenian manuscripts in the Armenian Hospital of St. Blasius in Rome, ibid., lxxi (1957), cols. 282–91, 420–39, 537–58; and in the Pont. Leoniano Collegio in Rome, ibid. lxxii (1958), cols. 49–82; T. Balian, the Armenian manuscripts at the Monastery of St. Karapet in Caesarea, ibid. lxxiii (1959), cols. 253–74, 421–43, 540–51; lxxiv (1960), cols. 537–50; J. Kossian, the Armenian manuscripts in the Arznian School in Erzerum, ibid. lxxvii (1963), cols. 23–38, 207–20, 371–91, 505–15; lxxviii (1964), cols. 29–37, 153–60, 323–32; H. Oskian, the Armenian manuscripts of the Capuchin monastery in Beirut, ibid. lxxiv (1960), cols. 550–67; in the University Library at Graz, ibid. lxxviii (1964), cols. 479–85; in the Austrian National Library in Vienna, ibid. lxxiv (1965), cols. 361–72, 479–99; in the Armenian Patriarchate at Istanbul, ibid. lxxx (1966), cols. 425–87; lxxxi (1967), cols. 439–48; in the Church of the Holy Cross at Gart'al, ibid. lxxx (1966), cols. 321–38; in the Library of the Sultan Ahmed III of Constantinople, ibid. lxxxi (1967), cols. 183–96; and G. Kalemkiarian, the Armenian manuscripts in the Czartoryski Library at Cracow, ibid. lxxx (1966), cols. 67–78, 185–94 (all in Armenian).

lines per page. A photographic reproduction was published at Moscow in 1899.[1]

(2) A manuscript at Erevan (number unknown; Rhodes no. 974) is described as a ninth-century tetraevangelium with miniatures.

(3) MS. 68 in the Mekhitarist Monastery of St. Lazarus in Venice (Rhodes no. 301) is a mutilated tetraevangelium, lacking many folios of Mark. It dates from the ninth or tenth century.

(4) MS. 190 in the Mekhitarist Monastery of St. Lazarus in Venice (Rhodes no. 312) is a mutilated tetraevangelium, lacking several folios of John. It dates from the ninth or tenth century.

(5) MS. 25 in the Kurdian collection at Wichita, Kansas (Rhodes no. 1072), contains Matthew i. 10–28: 20 and John i. 15–ix. 24 (John iii. 6–22; vii. 38–viii. 33 lacking). It dates from the ninth or tenth century.

(6) MS. 1144 of the Mekhitarist Monastery of St. Lazarus in Venice (Rhodes no. 369) is a handsome copy of the Gospels with many miniatures, presented by Queen Mlk'e to the Varag Monastery.[2] It was written in A.D. 901–2.

(7) MS. 6202 in the Matenadaran at Erevan (Rhodes no. 966) is a tetraevangelium written in A.D. 909.

(8) A tetraevangelium written in A.D. 965, whose present location is unknown, was formerly at the Sevan Monastery (Rhodes no. 1019).

(9) MS. 537 of the Walters Art Gallery in Baltimore (Rhodes no. 1113), a tetraevangelium written in A.D. 966, 'is probably one of the oldest examples of the penetration of ornaments and miniatures into the Gospel text'.[3]

---

[1] G. Khalatheants, *Évangile traduit en langue arménienne ancienne et écrit en l'an 887. Édition phototypique du Ms. de l'Institut Lazareff des langues orientales* (Moscow, 1899).

[2] Cf. Frédéric Macler, 'Raboula-Mlqe', *Mélanges Charles Diehl. Études sur l'histoire et sur l'art de Byzance* (Paris, 1930), pp. 81–97, and A. Baumstark, 'Abendländischer Einfluss in armenischen Buchmalerei des 10. Jahrhunderts?' *OC*, 3rd ser., xi (1936), 26–53.

[3] Sirarpie Der Nersessian, 'Armenian Gospel Illustration as seen in Manuscripts in American Collections', *New Testament Manuscript Studies*, ed. by M. M. Parvis and A. P. Wikgren (Chicago, 1950), p. 139. On the basis of extensive textual analyses of the manuscript, Casimir Roszko concludes that it agrees frequently with the Armenian text of the Diatessaron used by Armenians up to the eighth century, and differs greatly from the text of Zohrab's printed edition of 1805 ('Traces of the First Armenian Version of the Gospels in an Early Manuscript', *Studii Biblici Franciscani Liber Annuus*, xxiii (1973), 15–66).

(10) MS. 580 of the National Library at Sofia, Bulgaria (Rhodes no. 48), is a tetraevangelium written in A.D. 966.

(11) A tetraevangelium dated A.D. 974, whose present location is unknown, was formerly in Axalçxay, Georgia (Rhodes no. 1168).

(12) MS. 7445 in the Matenadaran at Erevan (Rhodes no. 928) is a tetraevangelium written in A.D. 986.

(13) A tetraevangelium formerly at Holy Saviour's Church, Leninakan, and now at Erevan (Rhodes no. 982), was written in A.D. 988.

(14) MS. 2374 in the Matenadaran at Erevan (formerly Etchmiadzin 229; Rhodes no. 724) is a tetraevangelium written, according to a colophon, in A.D. 989 'from ancient and exact exemplars'. In 1920 the manuscript was published by Macler in photographic facsimile.[1] For the much discussed gloss at Mark xvi. 8 ('of the presbyter Ariston'), see p. 163 below.

(15) MS. 2555 of the Armenian Patriarchate in Jerusalem (Rhodes no. 496), though dated A.D. 602, is generally assigned to the tenth century.[2]

(16) MS. 899 of the University of Chicago Library (Rhodes no. 1037), preserving portions of Matthew and Mark, dates from the tenth century.

Except for a tetraevangelium of disputed age,[3] as well as several stray leaves of ancient manuscripts used in the binding and

---

[1] Frédéric Macler, *L'Évangile arménien, édition phototypique du Manuscrit no. 229 de la Bibliothèque d'Etchmiadzin*, publié sous les auspices de M. Léon Mantacheff (Paris, 1920). For a critique of the text of manuscript 229, see Louis Mariès, 'Le texte arménien de l'Évangile d'après Matthieu et Marc', *RSR* x (1920), 26–54, and 'Le meilleur exemplaire de la version arménienne des évangiles', ibid. xii (1922), 69–72.

[2] So Rhodes, Weitzmann, Nordenfalk; on the other hand Mlle Der Nersessian assigns it to the ninth century and Clark to the eleventh century (for bibliographic references, see Rhodes, p. 71).

[3] Following Conybeare's opinion, Rhodes in his catalogue (no. 110) assigned a ninth-century date to Armenian MS. 1 in the John Rylands Library, Manchester. After having inspected the manuscript, however, he now indicates (letter dated 26 Apr. 1973) that he has 'grave doubts that it could possibly be 9th century' and prefers to assign it to the eleventh century. For an analysis of certain Western readings in its text of Mark, see A. F. J. Klijn, 'An Old Witness of the Armenian Text', *JTS* N.S. ii (1951), 168–70.

repair of later codices,[1] all other copies of the Armenian Gospels mentioned in Rhodes's catalogue are assigned to dates after the twelfth century.

The earliest Armenian manuscript of Acts, the Catholic and the Pauline Epistles, and the book of Revelation is a bilingual Greek–Armenian codex at the Bibliothèque Nationale in Paris (Arm. MS. 27, *olim* Arm. MS. 9; Gregory–Aland no. 301; Rhodes no. 151). The Greek portion of the manuscript is dated by Gregory and Aland to the eleventh century; the Armenian portion is dated by Conybeare and Macler to the twelfth century.

III. NOTEWORTHY FEATURES OF THE ARMENIAN VERSION

Among noteworthy features of the Armenian version of the Bible was the inclusion of certain books that elsewhere came to be regarded as apocryphal. The Old Testament included the History of Joseph and Asenath and the Testaments of the Twelve Patriarchs, and the New Testament included the Epistle of the Corinthians to Paul and a Third Epistle of Paul to the Corinthians.[2]

---

[1] These fugitive fragments have been sought out and collected by Vööbus, *Early Versions of the New Testament* (Stockholm, 1954), pp. 156–9; cf. also R. P. Casey ('An Early Armenian Fragment of Luke xvi. 3–25', *JTS* xxxvi (1935), 70–3), who edited the text of a fragment from the ninth century incorporated into a fifteenth-century codex.

[2] As late as the thirteenth century 3 Corinthians was read at the Mass; cf. Augustin Szekula, *Die Reihenfolge der Bücher des Neuen Testamentes bei den Armeniern* (Vienna, 1949), p. 95.

The existence of 3 Corinthians was first made known to European scholars through an Armenian manuscript from Smyrna to which Archbishop James Ussher called attention (*In Polycarpianam epistolarum Ignatianarum Syllogen Annotationes* ... (Oxford, 1644), p. 29). From this manuscript, which is incomplete, David Wilkins published the Armenian text with a Latin translation (Amsterdam, 1715). A complete text from a less accurate manuscript from Aleppo was published with a Latin translation by La Croze (Milan, 1719). William and George Whiston, sons of William Whiston the translator of Josephus, included the Armenian text, with a Latin and a Greek translation, in an Appendix to their *History of Moses of Chorene* (London, 1736), pp. 369–84. Lord Byron made an English translation of the Epistle and published it with the original text in his Armenian grammar and chrestomathy (Venice, 1819). The first more or less critical edition of the text was prepared by Zohrab for his edition of the Armenian Bible (Venice, 1805). For other information on 3 Corinthians, see Bernard Pick, *International Journal of the Apocrypha*, ser. ix, no. 32 (Jan. 1913), 9–13; Karl Pink, 'Die pseudo-paulinischen Briefe', *Bib*, vi (1925), 73–91; and A. F. J. Klijn, 'The Apocryphal Correspondence Between Paul and the Corinthians', *VC* xvii (1963), 2–23.

Another characteristic feature of the Armenian version involves what N. Marr called 'Targum translations'.[1] These are readings that are not to be considered as derivative from a Greek *Vorlage*, but, as Vööbus points out, 'must be put into a special category and be understood in the light of idiomatic Armenian'.[2] Examples of this feature of the translation include the following.[3] The Greek text of Mark vii. 25 speaks of a little daughter who 'had' (εἶχεν) an unclean spirit, but the Armenian replaces this simple verb with * նեղեալ էր*, meaning 'was pressed' or 'was squeezed'. The paralytic at the Pool of Bethesda (John v. 7) says, 'but while I go thither' (ἐν ᾧ δὲ ἔρχομαι ἐγώ), which seemed not sufficient and was replaced in Armenian by the paraphrase *քանզքաշիմ*, 'while I drag myself' or 'while I walk slowly'. In John vii. 49, instead of ὁ ὄχλος οὗτος, the Armenian text offers *այս խառնամբոխ ամբոխս*, 'this riotous crowd'. In rendering οὐκ ἔγνωκάς με, Φίλιππε (John xiv. 9) the Armenian makes use of a verb that means 'to take knowledge of', so that the passage comes to signify: 'Have I been with you so long, and yet you have not come to know me, Philip?' Here and there, instead of writing merely 'Egypt' or 'Galilee' or 'Jordan' the Armenian translators expand to 'the land of the Egyptians', 'the regions of the Galileans', 'the river Jordan'.[4] Despite such paraphrastic turns—or perhaps because of them—the Armenian version has been called the Queen of the

---

[1] 'Echmiadzinskij fragment drevne-gruzinskoj versii Vetkhago Zaveta', *KhV* ii (1913), 387.

[2] Arthur Vööbus, *Early Versions of the New Testament* (Stockholm, 1954), p. 163. Cf. also Giancarlo Bolognesi, 'La traduzione armena del Vangelo; problemi di critica testuale', *Studi sull'Oriente e la Biblia offerti al P. Giovanni Rinaldi nel 60⁰ compleanno* . . . (Genoa, 1967), pp. 123–40, who considers passages (mentioned by Vlad Bănăţeanu, *La Traduction arménienne des tours participiaux grecs* (Bucharest, 1937), and by Hans Jensen, *Altarmenische Grammatik* (Heidelberg, 1959)), where the Armenian version may reflect a different Greek text from that generally received.

[3] The first three examples are cited by Vööbus, *Early Versions of the New Testament*, p. 163.

[4] Such turns of expression occur more frequently in the older form of the version as quoted by early Armenian Church Fathers, though some still remain in the printed editions of the version today (Joseph Molitor, *Der Paulustext des hl. Ephräm, aus seinem Armenisch erhalten Paulinenkommentar* (Rome, 1938), pp. 10*–11*). Cf. also Georges Cuendet, 'Exactitude et adresse dans la version arménienne de la Bible', *HA* xlix (1935), cols. 563–70, and Pier Giuseppe Scardigli, 'Per una valutazione linguistica della versione armena dei Vangeli', *Atti della Accademia Nazionale dei Lincei*, viii ser., *Rendiconti*, Classe di scienze morali, storiche e filologiche, xiv, fasc. 7–12 (Rome, 1959), 370–87.

Versions.[1] In any case, the version, by introducing in some degree the work of commentator as well as that of translator, provides the reader with a generally faithful and idiomatic rendering praised for its clarity and dignity of expression.

Among significant, and indeed unique, readings in Armenian manuscripts mention must be made of the following. In 1891 Conybeare found in the Patriarchal Library at Etchmiadzin an Armenian manuscript of the Gospels written in A.D. 989 (no. 14 in the list above) in which the last twelve verses of the Gospel according to Mark are introduced by a rubric, *Of the presbyter Ariston*.[2] Some scholars, following Conybeare's suggestion, have thought that the words are intended to identify the long ending of Mark as the work of the Aristion who is mentioned by Papias[3] as one of the disciples of the Lord. On the other hand, the identification has been contested by, for example, B. W. Bacon[4] and Clarence R. Williams,[5] who took the Ariston to be Aristo(n) of Pella, who, according to one interpretation of a statement of Moses of Chorene, was the secretary of the Evangelist Mark.[6] The historical worth of the gloss is, moreover, reduced to almost nil if, as has been argued, it was not written by the original scribe of the manuscript, but was added in the fourteenth or fifteenth century by an unknown scribe.[7] In any case, Colwell has made it abundantly plain that the last twelve verses of Mark were not part of the original Armenian version.[8] Of 220 Armenian manuscripts which

---

[1] The first to describe the Armenian version thus was La Croze, who, according to Bredenkamp, allowed his love for the Armenian people to make such a 'purely partisan judgement' (Eichhorn's *Allgemeine Bibliothek der biblischen Litteratur*, iv. 4 (Leipzig, 1793), 633 f.).

[2] F. C. Conybeare, 'Aristion, the Author of the Last Twelve Verses of Mark', *Exp*, 4th ser., viii (1893), 241–54; and 'On the Last Twelve Verses of St. Mark's Gospel', ibid., 5th ser., ii (1895), 401–21.

[3] *Apud* Euseb., *Hist. eccl.* III. xxxix.4.

[4] Cf. Bacon's article 'Aristion (Aristo)', Hastings's *Dictionary of Christ and the Gospels*, i (1908), 118.

[5] *The Appendices to the Gospel According to Mark: A Study in Textual Transmission* (*Transactions of the Connecticut Academy of Arts and Sciences*, xviii; New Haven, 1915), 383 f.

[6] For bibliography on the debate that ensued after Conybeare's confident interpretation of the gloss in Etchmiadzin MS. 229, see Louis Mariès in *RÉA* vi (1926), 221–3, and E. C. Colwell in *JBL* lvi (1937), 382–6.

[7] So Joseph Schäfers in *BZ* xiii (1915), 24–5.

[8] Ernest C. Colwell, 'Mark 16: 9–20 in the Armenian Version', *JBL* lvi (1937), 369–86. For corrections in the tables of manuscripts on pp. 371 and 373, see ibid. lix (1940), 53, note. Cf. also P. P. Férhatian, 'Mark 16: 9–20 among the Armenians'

he studied, only eighty-eight include Mark xiv. 9–20 without comment; ninety-nine end the Gospel at xiv. 8; and in the others there is evidence which shows that the scribes had doubts whether the passage was authentic.

It may also be mentioned that the so-called shorter ending of Mark's Gospel (i.e. the one that begins, 'But they reported briefly to Peter . . .') occurs in several Armenian texts[1]—including a manuscript of the twelfth century (Etchmiadzin MS. 303; Rhodes, no. 798), which places the words of this ending at the close of Luke's Gospel.[2]

IV. THE BASE OF THE ARMENIAN VERSION

In view of the influence of both Greek and Syrian Christianity upon the primitive Armenian Church, it is not surprising that diverse opinions have been held concerning the primary base of the Armenian version.[3] Already among early Armenian authors we find opposing statements. According to Koriun and Lazar of P'arp, who wrote during the fifth and sixth centuries respectively, their vernacular version was Mesrop's faithful rendering made from the Greek, but according to the testimony of Moses of Chorene of the fifth century, Sahak made the version from the Syriac.

At first Conybeare was inclined to accept both accounts and held that the Bible was translated into Armenian twice before the end of the fourth century.[4] But after the publication of an essay on the Armenian version by J. Armitage Robinson, in which were pointed out certain slight affinities between the Armenian and

---

(in Armenian), *Huscharzan, Festschrift . . . der Mechitharisten Congregation in Wien* (Vienna, 1911), pp. 372–8, and Albert J. Edmunds, 'The Six Endings of Mark in Later Manuscripts and Catholic and Protestant Imprints of the Old Armenian Version', *Monist*, xxix (1919), pp. 520–5.

[1] See Augustin Szekula, 'The "Short" Ending of Mark in the Armenian Version' [in Armenian], *HA* lxiv (1950), cols. 448–52.

[2] Cf. Lyonnet in M.-J. Lagrange, *Critique textuelle* (Paris, 1935), pp. 345 and 372, and Colwell, *JBL* lvi (1937), 379–80.

[3] For a conspectus of opinions of scores of scholars, extending from Richard Simon (1684) to World War I, reference may be made to Frédéric Macler, *Le Texte arménien de l'évangile d'après Matthieu et Marc* (*Annales du Musée Guimet*, xxviii; Paris, 1919), pp. xxiv–lxxiv.

[4] F. C. Conybeare in Scrivener–Miller, *A Plain Introduction to the Criticism of the New Testament*, 4th edn., ii (London, 1894), 151.

various Syriac versions,[1] Conybeare adopted the opinion, which he held to the end of his life, that the Armenian version was made from the Syriac.[2] Merk,[3] Blake,[4] Baumstark,[5] and Williams[6] shared this view. On the other hand, scholars of no less stature (such as Macler,[7] Lyonnet,[8] and Colwell[9]) have been impressed by several types of evidence pointing to a close affinity between the Armenian and the Greek text.

Although the question cannot be regarded as settled, Colwell has argued with some degree of persuasion for the view that regards the Armenian as based directly upon the Greek and explains the Syriacisms as due partly to unconscious influence of the Syriac upon the translator, and partly to the translator's direct use of the Syriac version where the Greek was obscure or especially difficult. Syrian influence can also be seen in the circumstance that the early Armenian New Testament included the apocryphal Third Epistle to the Corinthians,[10] as did the early Syriac canon.

V. TEXTUAL AFFINITIES OF THE ARMENIAN VERSION

What are the textual affinities of the Armenian version? According to Blake it belonged to the Caesarean family, deriving its characteristic readings from a postulated intermediary

---

[1] *Euthaliana* (*Texts and Studies*, iii. 3; Cambridge, 1895), pp. 72–98.

[2] 'The Growth of the Peshittâ Version of the New Testament, Illustrated from the Old Armenian and Georgian Versions', *AJT* i (1897), 883–912; 'The Armenian Version of the New Testament', Hastings's *Dictionary of the Bible*, i (1898), 153–4; and 'An Armenian Diatessaron?' *JTS* xxv (1924), 232–45.

[3] August Merk, 'Die Armenischen Evanglien und ihre Vorlage', *Bib*, vii (1926), 40–70. Merk assembles a table of about 200 readings in the four Gospels where the Armenian version agrees with the Syriac against the Greek.

[4] R. P. Blake, 'The Caesarean Text of Mark', *HTR* xxi (1928), 307 ff.

[5] Anton Baumstark, 'Zum georgischen Evangelientext', *OC* 3rd ser., iii/iv (1930), 117–24.

[6] C. S. C. Williams, 'Syriasms in the Armenian Text of the Gospels', *JTS* xliii (1942), 161–7. Williams finds, however, only one of the ten examples on which Robinson based his case to be convincing.

[7] Op. cit., pp. 403 ff.

[8] Stanislas Lyonnet, 'La version arménienne des évangiles et son modèle grec; l'évangile selon saint Matthieu', *RB* xliii (1934), 69–87; 'Les versions arménienne et géorgienne', in Lagrange, *Critique textuelle* (Paris, 1935), pp. 353 ff.; 'Aux origines de l'église arménienne, la traduction de la Bible, et le témoignage des historiens arméniens', *RSR* xxv (1935), 170–87.

[9] 'The Caesarean Readings of Armenian Gospel Manuscripts', *ATR* xvi (1924), 113–32, and 'Slandered or Ignored: the Armenian Gospels', *JR* xvii (1937), 48–61.

[10] See p. 161 n. 2 above.

Syriac version no longer extant. Later, some time before the middle of the fifth century, it was thoroughly revised to the Byzantine standard and only faint traces of its Caesarean ancestor remain.[1]

Part or all of this reconstruction has been vigorously challenged by Baumstark, Colwell, Lyonnet, Peradse, and Williams. Simultaneously Colwell[2] and Lyonnet[3] published studies which show that many Armenian manuscripts and even Zorab's printed edition contain a text of Matthew and Mark which, far from being predominantly Byzantine, is strongly Caesarean in character. More recently Williams, who likewise found Caesarean influence in the Armenian, denied the need of postulating an intermediate Syriac version between the Greek and the Armenian.[4] The Caesarean complexion was derived, he suggested, from Greek manuscripts which Mesrop's disciples brought back with them from Cappadocia, where, at an earlier period, Origen had stayed with Bishop Firmilian for at least two years during the persecution under Maximinus.

Striking out in a different direction, Baumstark[5] and Peradse[6] criticized the results of the Lake–Blake–New study of the Caesarean text and interpreted the presence of several harmonistic readings in the Armenian as proof of dependence upon Tatian's Diatessaron. Although these two scholars provide insufficient evidence in support of their theory, Essabalean[7] and Lyonnet,[8] following a suggestion thrown out by Conybeare in the last article to come from his pen,[9] argued on the basis of readings

---

[1] *HTR* xxi (1928), 307–10; see also K. Lake, *The Text of the New Testament*, 6th edn. (London, 1928), p. 44.　　　　[2] *ATR* xxvi (1934), 113–32.

[3] *RB* xliii (1934), 69–87; see also idem, 'Un important témoin du texte césaréen de saint Marc; la version arménienne', *Mélanges de l'université saint-Joseph* (Beyrouth), xix. 2 (1935), 1–66.

[4] C. S. C. Williams, 'The Armenian Text of Mark *I* in the Bodleian MS. Arm. d. 5', *JTS* xlviii (1947), 196–200.　　　　[5] *OC* 3rd ser., iii/iv (1930), 117–24.

[6] Gregor Peradse, 'Die Probleme der georgischen Evangelienübersetzung', *ZNW* xxix (1930), 308–9.

[7] Paul Essabalean, *The Diatessaron of Tatian and the First Translation of the Armenian Gospels, A Critical Study* (Vienna, 1937) (in Armenian, with a French résumé). The present writer has been unable to find a copy of this work and has depended upon reviews of it by R. P. Casey in *JBL* lvii (1938), 95–101, Lyonnet in *Bib*, xix (1938) 214–16, and Hengstenberg in *ByzZ* xxxvii (1937), 520.

[8] 'Vestiges d'un Diatessaron arménien', *Bib*, xix (1938), 121–50.

[9] 'An Armenian Diatessaron?' *JTS* xxv (1924), 232–45. Cf. also Conybeare's private comments on the subject, published by G. Krüger in *ZNW* xxiii (1924), 4–5.

preserved in the Armenian Breviary and Ritual that behind the present Armenian text of the Gospels there was an early Armenian Diatessaron which rested upon the Syriac Diatessaron of Tatian.

A new stage was reached in 1950 with the publication of a thorough and painstaking investigation of the origins of the Armenian version.[1] In this monograph Lyonnet, working along lines previously argued on the basis of far less evidence, has marshalled extensive and compelling data showing that an Armenian version of the Gospels (= Arm[1]) existed before the emergence of the vulgate type of text represented by the edition of Zohrab (= Arm[2]). Its existence is attested by the usage of ancient authors and translators[2] who, in their quotations from the Gospels, often agree with readings preserved in the text of Ephraem's commentary on the Diatessaron and against the text of Zohrab. The conclusions which Lyonnet reached (with greater assurance in some cases than others) are as follows: (1) The basis of the earliest Armenian version was certainly a Syriac text. (2) This Syriac text differs widely from the Peshitta and agrees with the type of text represented by the Old Syriac. (3) This form of Old Syriac text comes closer to what we think Tatian read than it does to either the Sinaitic or the Curetonian Syriac manuscripts. (4) Without making a categorical statement, Lyonnet concluded that the earliest form of the Armenian text of the Gospels was probably a harmony of the Gospels.

With respect to the last-mentioned opinion, Vööbus has entered a demurrer. On the one hand he acknowledges that the Diatessaron of Tatian had its partisans among the Armenians, but on the other hand he cannot find evidence that it was officially countenanced by ecclesiastical authorities, such as Mesrop and Sahak. He concludes, therefore, that the Armenian text of the Gospels in *official* use was based upon Old Syriac texts of the separated Gospels.[3]

---

[1] S[tanislas] Lyonnet, *Les Origines de la version arménienne et le diatessaron* (*Biblica et orientalia*, xiii; Rome, 1950).

[2] There is also an extensive collection of quotations from Matthew made by ancient authors; see L. Leloir, *Citations du Nouveau Testament dans l'ancienne tradition arménienne*; I, A, *L'Évangile de Matthieu, i–xii*; and I, B, *Matthieu, xiii–xxviii* (*CSCO* cclxxxiii–iv, *Subsidia*, xxxi–xxxii; Louvain, 1967).

[3] Arthur Vööbus, 'La première traduction arménienne des évangiles,' *RSR* xxxvii (1950), 581–6; and idem, *Early Versions of the New Testament* (Stockholm, 1954), pp. 152–4.

As for the textual character of the rest of the Armenian New Testament, there is very little to report. Preliminary analyses made by Lyonnet[1] reveal that in Acts and the Pauline Epistles the version represents a mixture of the Alexandrian and Western texts in the proportion which is characteristic of the Caesarean text. In an analysis of the textual complexion of the Armenian version of the Epistle to the Ephesians,[2] Molitor found that the text rests upon an Old Syriac version, traces of which have been transmitted in the Peshitta version. These Syriacisms are often represented in the variant readings which Zohrab cites under the siglum 'many [manuscripts]' in the apparatus of his edition.

The seven Catholic Epistles in Armenian manuscripts are always (so Lyonnet states)[3] found placed immediately after the Book of Acts in the following order: James, 1 and 2 Peter, 1, 2, and 3 John, Jude. According to the same scholar, the textual affinities of these Epistles in the Armenian text are with the Greek codex Vaticanus.[4]

Thanks to the labours of Conybeare and others, our knowledge of the Armenian text of the Book of Revelation is relatively full. Translated in the fifth century, the text underwent a remarkable series of revisions, of which Conybeare thought he could identify five.[5] The extant manuscripts fall into two groups depending on whether or not they reflect the work of Nerses of Lambron, who was bishop of Tarsus in the twelfth century. Although it would be natural to infer that the Armenian version of Revelation was made from the Greek, Conybeare was impressed by certain features which suggested to him that an Old Latin original was rendered into Armenian in the early fifth century, if not even the fourth century, and a short time later reworked from Greek manuscripts. Whether or not this reconstruction of its genealogy

---

[1] In Lagrange, *Critique textuelle* (Paris, 1935), pp. 459 and 527–8.

[2] 'Der armenische Epheserbrief und die syrische Textüberlieferung', *HA* lxxviii (1964), cols. 301–10.

[3] In Lagrange, *Critique textuelle*, p. 575.

[4] Ibid., p. 578.

[5] *The Armenian Versions of Revelation . . . Edited from the Oldest MSS. and Englished* (London, 1907). Another edition of the same book, based on only two manuscripts (one of A.D. 1198–1202; the other of A.D. 1535) is Fr. Murad's *Die Offenbarung Johannis in einer alten armenischen Übersetzung, nach zwei Handschriften zum erstenmal herausgegeben, mit dem griechischen Texte verglichen, und mit einer Einleitung und mit Anmerkungen* (in Armenian); Teil ii, *Text* (Jerusalem, 1905), Teil iii, *Anmerkungen* (1906), Teil i, *Einleitung* (1911).

is correct,[1] the Armenian version of the Apocalypse is a valuable text and in some cases it alone may preserve the original reading of a book whose textual history is notoriously obscure and difficult.

As was mentioned earlier, a very great number of manuscripts of the Armenian version of the New Testament have been preserved. Most of their scribes were careful and obviously made an effort to transmit the Scriptures with relatively few modifications. As with the Peshitta Syriac version, once the Armenian text was standardized, scribes carefully maintained its purity, introducing relatively few variations.[2]

A noteworthy feature of Armenian manuscripts in general is the presence in many of them of lengthy colophons which supply information on a broad range of topics. Frequently these comments provide eyewitness or contemporary accounts of historical events that transpired during the production of the manuscripts.[3] Among collections of colophons the most ambitious is that of the late Catholicos Garegin I Yovsēpʻean, who projected the publication, in four volumes, of thousands of colophons from manuscripts extending from A.D. 887 (i.e. MS. no. 1 in the list above) to the eighteenth century. Unfortunately only volume i,[4] extending to the year 1250, was published before his death, but the work was carried on by L. S. Khatchikian, director of the Matenadaran (Library of Manuscripts) at Erevan, who collected and published three volumes of colophons from manuscripts copied in the years 1301 to 1480.[5]

---

[1] On the basis of a collation of the Armenian text of Revelation in the editions of Zohrab, Murad, and Conybeare, Molitor became convinced that the text of this book was translated directly from the Greek ('Zum Textcharakter der armenischen Apokalypse', *OC* lv (1971), 90–148; lvi (1972), 1–48; see esp. 45–6).

[2] Cf. August Merk, 'Die Einheitlichkeit der armenischen Evangelien-Übersetzung', *Bib*, iv (1923), 356–74; P. A. Vardanian, 'The Unity of the Armenian Translation of the Gospels' [in Armenian], *HA* xlii (1928), cols. 481–90; and Erroll F. W. Rhodes, 'Mark I; The Internal Consistency and External Relations of the Armenian Version' (unpublished dissertation, University of Chicago, 1948).

[3] Cf. L. S. Khatchikian, 'Colophons of Armenian Manuscripts as a Historical Source', *XXV International Congress of Orientalists; Papers presented by the USSR Delegation* (Moscow, 1960).

[4] Garegin I Katʻolikos, *Yišatakarankʻ Jeṙagracʻ*, i (Antilias, Lebanon, 1951).

[5] *XIV Dari Hayeren Jeṙagʻeri Hišatakaranner* (Erevan, 1950), and *XV Dari Hayeren Jeṙagreri Hišatakaranner*, Part 1 covering 1401 to 1450 (Erevan, 1955), Part 2 covering 1451 to 1480 (Erevan, 1958). For an English translation of selected colophons see Avedis K. Sanjian, *Colophons of Armenian Manuscripts, 1301–1480; A Source for Middle Eastern History* (Cambridge, Mass., 1969). About seventy of these contain brief quotations from the Bible cf.; the list in Appendix E, pp. 441 f.

The first printed edition of the Armenian Bible was published in 1666[1] at Amsterdam by an Armenian cleric named A. D. Oskan (or Usgan). It is based on a manuscript copied for King Haitho (Hethum) in 1295.[2] Here and there Oskan adjusted the text to the Latin Vulgate.[3] A later edition, issued in 1733 at Venice by Mekhitar, the founder of the monastery of San Lazzaro, is mainly a reprint of the edition of 1666. The only so-called critical edition of the Armenian Bible is that of Yovhan Zohrabian (John Zohrab); the New Testament was published at Venice in 1789, the entire Bible in 1805.[4] The text of this edition reproduces, in the main, manuscript 1508 of the Mechitarist Monastery at Venice, containing the complete Bible and dating from A.D. 1319.[5] In the apparatus Zohrab cites variant readings from eight other manuscripts of the Bible, thirty of the Gospels, fourteen of the Apostolos, and four lectionaries. Unfortunately, however, none of these is identified in the apparatus, and variant readings are introduced by such vague designations as 'one manuscript reads', 'some', 'several', and 'many'. It is obvious

[1] The date is not infrequently given (erroneously) as 1668 (or even 1669). The copy in the Library of the American Bible Society has eight unnumbered pages of front matter, plus 1–628 pages from Genesis to the end of Esther, plus 1–834 pages from Job to the end of the Book of Revelation. For bibliography on Oskan's Bible, see *Studia orientalia christiana, Collectanea*, no. 12 (Cairo, 1967), pp. 618–21.

[2] This manuscript is preserved today at Erevan (Rhodes no. 671), with corrections which are undoubtedly those of Oskan.

[3] Passages where Oskan's text agrees with the Latin Vulgate against all known Armenian manuscripts include Matt. xvi. 2–3; xxiii. 14; John viii. 1–11; Acts xv. 34; xxiii. 24; xxviii. 25; and most significant of all, 1 John v. 7. For a discussion, see S. P. Tregelles, 'Armenian Version', in William Smith's *Dictionary of the Bible*, revised and edited by H. B. Hackett, iv (New York, 1870; repr. Grand Rapids, 1971), p. 3374. For an account of the difficulties that were put in the path of Oskan, but which he finally surmounted, see Albert C. de Veer, 'Rome et la Bible arménienne d'Uscan d'après la correspondance de J.-B. van Neercassel' [Apostolic Vicar of the United Provinces, 1662–86], *Revue des études byzantines*, xvi (= *Mélanges Séverien Salaville*, Paris, 1958), 172–82; translated into Armenian, *HA* lxxx (1966), cols. 337–52.

[4] The title is *Astowacašownç matean hin ew nor katakaranc* (God-inspired Scriptures of the Old and New Covenants) (Venice, 1805). According to a suggestion made by Rhodes (letter dated 26 Apr. 1973), since Zohrab's notes distinguish between *yōrinakin* ('the exemplar') and *ōrinak mi* ('an exemplar'), 'the former term may indicate the Venice Mekhitarist Ms. 1508, but I am not aware that a check on this possibility has ever been made.'

[5] A list of the principal editions of the Armenian Bible is given by A. Ghazikian, *Nouvelle bibliographie arménienne et encyclopédie de la vie arménienne 1512–1905* (Venice, 1912), cols. 206–18, 265–77: cf. also the list (compiled by Rhodes) in *Book of a Thousand Tongues*, ed. by E. A. Nida (New York, 1972), pp. 20–1.

that a good critical edition of the Armenian New Testament is an urgent *desideratum*.

VI. LIMITATIONS OF ARMENIAN IN REPRESENTING GREEK

by Erroll F. Rhodes

In the discussion that follows attention is concentrated on the contribution of the Armenian version to a critical apparatus of the Greek New Testament. The flexibility and sensitivity of the version permit it to reflect at times even the fine nuances of the Greek text in astonishing detail. Yet there are also instances where it is utterly useless for distinguishing between different Greek readings. We shall review in turn several phonetic, morphological, syntactical, and other characteristics of the Armenian version, observing briefly the nature of certain limitations which the textual critic should consider in evaluating its relevance for his work. The text of the Armenian New Testament used is that of Zohrab, 1805.

1. PHONETICS

The translator(s) of the Armenian New Testament found that a few proper nouns could be rendered by traditional Armenian forms (e.g. "Ἕλλην / *Yoyn* or *het'anos*, ᾽Ιουδαῖος / *hreay*, Καππαδοκία / *Gamirs*), while others were more effectively translated than transliterated (e.g. καλοὶ λιμένες / *gełec̣ik nawahangist* Acts xxvii. 8, or Βαριωνᾶ / *ordi Yovnanow* 'son of Jonah' Matt. xvi. 17). In some instances the tradition is divided over the wisdom of transliteration as against translation (e.g. λεγιών / *gownds* Matt. xxvi. 53, but *Lēgēovn* Mark v. 9). But most frequently the proper nouns of the New Testament are patently transliterated from a Greek base. An examination of these yields the following observations.

Greek consonants are quite consistently represented by their corresponding Armenian letters, though with certain qualifications. While θ is always *t'*, and τ is usually *t*, such forms as *Ant'ipas* would suggest that τ is not invariably *t*. The double consonants ξ and ψ are represented by *k's* and *p's* (not *ks* and *ps*). Double β δ κ μ ν σ and τ are frequently represented by double consonants in Armenian, but sometimes by a single consonant (e.g. Ἀδδί / *Addi*, but Θαδδαῖος / *Tʿadēos*, Ἀττάλεια / *Atalia*). The liquids λ and ρ may each be represented by two different letters : *l* and *ł*, *r* and *ṙ*. The second of each pair frequently represents an initial or double liquid, but this distinction is not consistently observed (e.g. Παῦλος / *Pawłos*, Ἀπολλῶς / *Apołos*, ῥαββί / *ṙabbi*), and an initial ῥ may also frequently become *hṙ* (e.g. Ῥαχήλ / *Hṙakʿēl*).

Greek vowels tend to be adapted more freely. *A* is most frequently represented by *a*, but it may also become *e* by dissimilation (Matt. i. 5 Ῥαχάβ / *Hṙekʿab*text, *Hṙakʿeb*mss, *Hṙakʿab*mss), or be elided (John i. 28 *Betʿabra*). *E* is usually *e*, but it may become *ē* (Συχέμ / *Siwkēm*), or *a* by dissimilation (*Betʿłahem*). *H* is usually *ē*, but it frequently becomes *e* (Ἡρῴδης / *Herovdēs*), and sometimes *a* (*Getʿsamani* Matt. xxvi. 36text, Mark xiv. 32mss), or *i* (Ἡσαῦ / *Isaw* Heb. xi. 20, but *Esaw* Heb. xii. 16; cf. Μιτυλήνη / *Mitilinē*). *I* is usually *i*, but it may also be *iw* (Κιλίκια / *Kiwlikia*), *w* (Νίγερ / *Nwgēr*), *y* (Ἰάϊρος / *Yayros*), *ē* (λεγιών / *Lēgēovn*), or elided (Ἰσαάκ / *Isahak* Matt. i. 2, or *Sahak* Matt. viii. 11, Ἰσκαριώθ / *Iskariovtaçi* Luke xxii. 3, or *Skariovtaçi* Matt. x. 4). *O* is usually *o*, but it is also found as *aw* (Ἀπολλῶς / *Apawłos*), or *a* by dissimilation (Ζοροβαβέλ / *Zorababēl* Matt. i. 12text, but also *Zawrobabēl*mss). *Y* is usually *i* or *iw* (Ἐλύμας / *Elimas*, Ἀκύλας / *Akiwlas*), but it may also be *a* (Βιθύνια / *Biwtʿania*), or *e* (Σύχαρ / *Sekʿar* John iv. 5text, but also *Sikʿar*mss, and *Siwkʿar*mss). *Ω* is usually *ov*, but it is requently shortened to *o* (Ἀαρών / *Aharon* Heb. v. 4, but also *Aharovn* Heb. vii. 11).

Diphthongs are treated with less variety, e.g. αι may be *e* (Αἴγυπτος / *Egiptos*), or *ē* (Θαδδαῖος / *Tʿadēos*) ; αυ is regularly *aw* (Ἡσαῦ / *Isaw*), as ευ is *ew* (Εὐοδία / *Ewodia*), and ου is *ow* (Ἀβιούδ / *Abiowd*, but cf. Αὔγουστος / *Awgostos*) ; οι is either *i* (Φοίβη / *Pʿibē*), or *iw* (Φοινίκη / *Pʿiwnikē*). Juxtaposed vowels which are not diphthongs are sometimes separated by *h* (Ἀαρών / *Aharon*), *y* (Ναῖν / *Nayin*), or *x* (Ῥαάβ / *Raxab* Heb. xi. 31).

Breathings are largely ignored in transcription, but there are exceptions (Ἄβελ / *Abeł* Matt. xxiii. 35, *Habeł* Heb. xi. 4 ; Ἡρῴδης / *Herovdēs* regularly). Sometimes Syriac influence may be suspected, as in John v. 2 *Betʿ Hezda* ܒܶܝܬ ܚܶܣܕܳܐ. Greek forms which are similar are not always differentiated in Armenian, e.g. Ἄννα Luke ii. 36 and Ἄννας Acts iv. 6 are both *Anna* (with the variant *Ana* for Ἄννας Luke iii. 2, John xviii. 13), and in Rom. xvi. 14

both ʿΕρμᾶς and ʿΕρμῆς are *Ermeay* (but cf. *Hermēs* Acts xiv. 12). But again, the version also introduces some distinctions which are not present in the Greek text, e.g. ᾿Ιησοῦς is generally *Yisows*, but for Barabbas it is *Yesow*, and for Joshua (Heb. iv. 8) it is *Yesovay*.

2. MORPHOLOGY

The Armenian noun is characterized by two numbers and seven cases. Like the Koine Greek noun it does not have a dual number, but it differs in lacking the vocative case and grammatical gender.

The plural form is usually found where a noun has a plural meaning (the characteristic suffix of the nominative plural is *-kʿ*). There are many words, however, that are found only in the plural, e.g. *pʿaṙkʿ* / δόξα, *aławtʿkʿ* / προσευχή, *štemarankʿ* / ἀποθήκη, *ereskʿ* / πρόσωπον, *kamkʿ* / θέλημα, etc. *Mełkʿ* translates ἁμαρτία and ἁμάρτημα as well as ἁμαρτίαι. Some nouns are used in both the singular and plural forms with no difference in meaning, e.g. μισθός is usually translated *varjkʿ*, but *varj* is also found (Luke x. 7). *Baniw* (Matt. viii. 8, sg. instr.) translates ἐν λόγῳ, but so does *baniwkʿ* (Matt. xxii. 15, pl. instr.). A more vividly concrete or specific meaning may attach to the plural of some nouns than to the singular, e.g. *jowr* 'water', but *jowrkʿ* 'river' (Mark i. 10) or 'sea' (Luke viii. 25). Also, the plural of an adjective may be used as an abstract noun, e.g. *bari* / ἀγαθός, *barikʿ* / τὸ ἀγαθόν (Rom. xii. 9).

Although seven cases are distinguished for syntactical analysis, it is rare for a noun to have more than four different forms in either the singular or the plural. The coincidence of cases with forms is shown in Table 1 (p. 180), with variations given in parentheses. Note that the accusative and locative forms may be distinguished in the singular but not in the plural. The Greek distinction between ἐν with the dative for 'position in' and εἰς with the accusative for 'motion toward' is represented in the singular by the preposition *i* with the locative and accusative cases respectively, but in the plural this distinction vanishes. The vocative is represented by the nominative with the enclitic pronoun (γύναι / *kin dow* John ii. 4), or with a preposed vocative particle (ὦ ἄνθρωπε / *ov mard* Rom. ii. 1), but also frequently by the simple nominative form.

The personal pronoun has the same form whether used emphatically or as an enclitic. The distinction is expressed syntactically, with the emphatic pronoun preceding its verb. The emphatic pronoun may require a transposition of words, as in Matt. xviii. 6 τῶν πιστευόντων εἰς ἐμέ / *yis hawataçeloç*, just as it is necessary to transpose the unemphatic pronoun in Matt. xv. 8 με τιμᾷ / *patowē zis*. The relative pronoun has two plural forms in the nominative case, one of which is identical with the nominative singular form: when the latter is used there is no clue to the underlying Greek form (cf. John xi. 45).

Instead of a single definite article in Armenian, there are suffixes -*s*, -*d*, and -*n* (corresponding to the Latin *hic, iste,* and *ille*) derived from the demonstrative pronominal stems. While these are commonly identified as equivalent to the definite article, they are also roughly associated with the first, second, and third persons (e.g. Luke i. 44 τὸ βρέφος / *manowks* '(my) child', Matt. ii. 13 τὸ παιδίον / *manowkd* '(your) child', Matt. ii. 14 τὸ παιδίον / *manowkn* '(his) child'). Although these suffixes usually reflect a definite article in the Greek text (there are exceptions; e.g. Mark viii. 20 anarthrous σπυρίδων / *zkotoroçn*), their absence does not necessarily imply the lack of an article in Greek (e.g. οἱ ἄγγελοι is regularly translated with the suffix in Luke, but not in Matthew and Mark; in Mark vii. 37 neither *xliç* nor *hamerç* / κωφοὺς . . . ἀλάλους has a suffix). There is also no indefinite article in Armenian, but *mi* / εἷς and *omn* / τὶς occur much more frequently with nouns than in Greek (e.g. Matt. ix. 9 ἄνθρωπον / *ayr mi*, Luke xviii. 1 παραβολήν / *aṙak mi*, Luke ii. 44 ἡμέρας / *awowr mioy*, Luke iv. 13 ἄχρι καιροῦ / *aṙ žamanak mi*, etc.).

The Armenian verb is characterized by number and person, by two tense systems (or stems), and by three moods, the indicative, imperative, and conjunctive. The outline in Table 2 (pp. 180 f.) indicates the Greek forms commonly translated by the Armenian forms. Some of the implications of Table 2 should be noted explicitly. There is no perfect stem in Armenian: the perfect tense is translated periphrastically. Although the present and aorist stems appear in the indicative, the imperative, and the conjunctive moods, there is neither an aorist infinitive nor a present participle. The present imperative is not used for positive commands, nor is the aorist imperative used for negative commands. There is no future tense: the conjunctive mood, which is used to express action as unreal, whether as possible, conditional, or desirable, serves to express future and imperative action as well.[1] The aorist conjunctive form *pahesǰikʻ* in John xiv. 15 can stand equally well for any of the variants τηρήσετε, τηρήσητε, τηρήσατε. No distinction is drawn between Matt. viii. 2 ἐὰν θέλῃς and Matt. xvii. 4 εἰ θέλεις: both are interpreted as real conditions, and are translated by the indicative *etʻē kamis*.

The Armenian infinitive (characteristic ending: -*el*) is versatile, translating not only the Greek infinitive but participial expressions as well, and on occasion summarizing a temporal clause (e.g. Luke xvii. 22 ὅτε ἐπιθυμήσετε / *çankanaloy jez*, literally τοῦ ἐπιθυμῆσαι ὑμᾶς). The Greek infinitive, however, is also rendered by several other Armenian constructions, such as an adverbial clause (Luke xi. 27 ἐν τῷ λέγειν αὐτὸν ταῦτα / *minçderʿ xōsēr zays* 'while he was saying this'), or even a noun (Matt. xxiii. 5 πρὸς τὸ θεαθῆναι / *i çoyç* 'for a show').

The Armenian participle (characteristic ending: -*eal*), however, contrasts strikingly with its Greek counterpart: it does not decline, and it is usually intransitive or passive in meaning.[2] It is used attributively and predicatively, and with auxiliary verbs to form periphrastic tenses (e.g. the perfect γέγραπται / *greal ē*). While the participle generally translates a Greek participle (e.g. Luke i. 9 εἰσελθών / *mteal*), it is instructive to observe some of the alternative forms used by the Armenian translators. (1) Prepositional clauses: Matt. ii. 3 ἀκούσας / *ibrew lowaw* 'when he heard', Mark i. 19 καταρτίζοντας / *minç kazmēin* 'while they were mending'. (2) The indicative with *ew* / καί: Matt. ii. 7 καλέσας . . . ἠκρίβωσεν / *koçeaç . . . ew stowgeaç* 'he summoned and inquired', Matt. iv. 23 περιῆγεν . . . διδάσκων . . . καὶ κηρύσσων / *šrǰēr . . . owsowçanēr . . . ew kʻarozēr* 'he was going about . . . teaching . . . and preaching'. (3) Relative clauses: Luke ii. 13 αἰνούντων / *or ōrhnēin* 'who were praising'. (4) Noun clauses: Matt. xiv. 26 περιπατοῦντα / *zi gnayr* 'that he was walking'. (5) Infinitives, interpreting the participle as purposive: Matt. iii. 1–2 παραγίνεται . . . κηρύσσων . . . καὶ λέγων / *gay . . . kʻarozel . . . ew asel* 'he comes . . . to preach . . . and to say'. The genitive absolute is

---

[1] See further C. Hannick, 'Der Gebrauch des Konjunctivs in der altarmenischen Evangelienübersetzung', *ZVS* lxxxix (1975), 152–73.

[2] Transitive active examples may also be found, cf. Luke iv. 20 πτύξας τὸ βιβλίον / *xpʻeal zgirsn*.

usually translated by a temporal prepositional clause, a simple participle, or a prepositional infinitive clause.

Voice is not fully developed in the Armenian verb system. The passive voice has a separate form in the aorist stem (except for the participle), and to a limited extent in the present stem, where verbs in *-em* may have a passive *-im* form in the present indicative and in the imperative and conjunctive moods (but not in the imperfect indicative or the infinitive). A difference in Greek voice, however, may be represented by a change of verb, as ἀνακλιθῆναι / *bazmel* 'to sit down' (Mark vi. 39) and ἀνακλῖναι / *bazmeçowçanel* 'to cause to sit down' (Luke xii. 37).[1] The middle voice does not have an independent form in Armenian: it is generally expressed by the passive form (e.g. John ix. 15 ἐνιψάμην / *lowaçay*), although at times it is not distinguished from the active (e.g. the active form *spasēin* translates Mark iii. 2 παρετήρουν, Luke vi. 7 παρετηροῦντο, and Luke xiv. 1 ἦσαν παρατηρούμενοι).

3. SYNTAX

Word order in the Armenian sentence is generally quite unrestricted, depending upon the intended emphasis of the sentence, and with stress or importance given to the words coming first in the sentence. The subject (S), object (O), and verb (V) may stand in almost any order (SVO, OVS, VOS, SOV, VSO are common). Not infrequently the precise word order of a Greek sentence is preserved in the Armenian version. Within the units comprising a sentence, however, there is less freedom of word order than in Greek. The following comments suggest certain characteristic limitations.

Phrases and related word groups tend to preserve their unity, resisting the intrusion of foreign elements, e.g. Luke i. 10 πλῆθος ἦν τοῦ λαοῦ προσευχόμενον / *bazmowt'iwn žoƚovrdeann kayin yaƚot's* (transposing the Greek word order 13425), Luke ii. 19 πάντα συνετήρει τὰ ῥήματα ταῦτα / *zamenayn zbans zaysosik pahēr* (transposing 13452). Similarly, adjectival phrases in the attributive position require rephrasing, frequently as relative clauses, e.g. Luke i. 1 περὶ τῶν πεπληροφορημένων ἐν ἡμῖν πραγμάτων / *vasn iraçn hastateloç i mez* (transposing 126345), Luke i. 4 περὶ ὧν

---

[1] Matt. xiv. 19 is only an apparent exception: the translator understood τοὺς ὄχλους to be the object rather than the subject of the infinitive.

κατηχήθης λόγων / *zbaniçn oroç ašakerteçar* (transposing 1423, cf. John vi. 14).

Unstressed or supplementary words follow immediately the words with which they are construed, e.g. Luke ii. 12 τοῦτο ὑμῖν σημεῖον / *ays nšanak jez* (transposing 132), John xiv. 3 ἑτοιμάσω τόπον ὑμῖν / *patrastem jez tełi* (transposing 132), Luke xviii. 2 ἔν τινι πόλει / *i kʻałakʻi owremn* (transposing 132). There are also certain expressions in which the Greek word order may vary, but not the Armenian, e.g. ταῦτα πάντα and πάντα ταῦτα are both *ays amenayn*, while *hogi sowrb* is constant for ἅγιον πνεῦμα, πνεῦμα ἅγιον, and τὸ πνεῦμα τὸ ἅγιον.[1] In nominal sentences the verb tends to follow the predicate, e.g. in Matt. vi. 22 the Armenian places the verb last in all three clauses. In subordinate clauses also the verb tends to be placed last, e.g. Mark ix. 38 ἐκβάλλοντα δαιμόνια / *zi dews hanēr*, literally ὅτι δαιμόνια ἐξέβαλλεν.

There is a tendency to avoid the absolute use of the verb. This is done in two ways: by supplying an object or some other modification to the verb, or by a paraphrastic construction. Examples of the former are Luke ii. 36 ἦν / *and ēr* (literally, ἐκεῖ ἦν), Luke vi. 9 ἐπερωτῶ ὑμᾶς / *harçiç inçʻ jez* (literally, ἐπερωτῶ τι ὑμᾶς), Mark vii. 3 οὐκ ἐσθίουσιν / *haç oçʻ owten* (literally, ἄρτον οὐκ ἐσθίουσιν).[2] The paraphrastic alternative may be illustrated by the translation of προσεύχεσθαι: the verb *ałōtʻel* 'to pray' is avoided in favour of such expressions as *ałotʻs aṙnel* 'to make prayers' (Matt. xxvi. 41), *yałotʻs kal* 'to stand at prayers' (Matt. vi. 9), or *ałotʻs matowçanel* 'to offer prayers' (Luke xviii. 11). Similarly, the verb ἐπιτάσσειν is translated *hramayel* 'to command' (Mark vi. 27), and also *hraman tal* 'to give a command' (Mark ix. 25).

Asyndeton is also a common characteristic of idiomatic usage, especially when a Greek participle is followed immediately by a verb, e.g. Matt. ii. 8 πορευθέντες ἐξετάσατε / *gnaçēkʻ stowgeçēkʻ* (literally, πορεύθητε ἐξετάσατε), Matt. ii. 16 ἀποστείλας ἀνεῖλεν / *aṙakʻeaç kotoreaç* (literally, ἀπέστειλεν ἀνεῖλεν). Asyndeton may also occur in the idiomatic translation of a single verb, e.g. Luke viii. 54 ἔγειρε / *ari kaç* (literally, 'get up! stand!').

Conjunctions, prepositions, and other relational particles are

---

[1] On the other hand, *bazowm* / πολύς follows the word order of the Greek text quite freely.

[2] Note, however, that the object 'bread' is lacking in Armenian in Mark vi. 44 and Luke vii. 33.

particularly elusive for the textual critic. Armenian has no postpositive conjunctions. Both καί and δέ are translated *ew*; *ard*
translates not only οὖν Matt. i. 17, but also νῦν Matt. xxvi. 65, νῦν
οὖν Acts 10. 33, ἄρα Matt. xix. 17, ἰδού Luke xxiii. 15, and even
ἄρτι John ix. 25; *zi* translates both γάρ and ὅτι, while (*e*)*t'ē* translates ὅτι and εἰ; *bayç* may represent not only δέ, but ἀλλά and εἰ
μή as well. Greek particles are certainly not translated with
literal consistency, but in a variety of ways as their contexts
require: ὥστε may be translated by *minč* or *minčew* with the
infinitive 'so much so that' (Matt. viii. 24; xiii. 2), by *apa owremn*
'so then, therefore' (Matt. xii. 12), or by the simple infinitive 'in
order to' (Matt. x. 1). Nor are prepositional expressions any more
closely identifiable in translation: *i veray* 'upon' may represent
ἐπί with the genitive (Matt. vi. 10, 19 ἐπὶ [τῆς] γῆς), with the
accusative (Matt. vii. 24 ἐπὶ τὴν πέτραν), or with the dative (Matt.
xvi. 18 ἐπὶ . . . τῇ πέτρᾳ), while in the space of four verses ἐπὶ
πίνακι is translated *i veray skteł* (Matt. xiv. 8) and also by the
simple instrumental *sktełb* (Matt. xiv. 11). Further, as the instrumental case is sufficient without the aid of a preposition to
indicate agency or means, there is no way to confirm whether
the translator read the presence or the absence of the preposition in Mark i. 8 (ἐν) ὕδατι . . . (ἐν) πνεύματι ἁγίῳ. On the
other hand, there are certain parallels of usage which are rather
closely observed. Παρά with the dative 'with' and with the
genitive 'from' correspond closely to *aṙ* with the genitive and *i*
with the ablative respectively (John viii. 38, cf. Luke i. 37; for εἰς
and ἐν, cf. p. 173 above). In the Gospels πιστεύειν with εἰς and
with the dative are consistently translated by *hawatal* with *i* (and
accusative) and with the simple dative, although in Acts πιστεύειν with εἰς, with ἐπί, and with the dative are all translated by
hawatal i and the accusative.

4. OTHER CONSIDERATIONS

Beside the phonetic, morphological, and syntactical limitations
mentioned above, there should also be recognized certain limitations of a lexical and idiomatic nature. It is true that there
is a remarkable consistency in the translation of many common
words, such as λαλεῖν / *xōsel*, λέγειν / *asel*, etc. In the Gospels

οὐράνιος (and in the Epistles ἐπουράνιος) is consistently *erknawor*, distinguished from ὁ ἐν τοῖς οὐρανοῖς / or *yerkins(n)* *ē*. But variety in translating is not lacking. Ἄρτος is *haç* 'bread', but it is also *nkanak* 'loaf'; ἐρωτᾶν is *harçanel* 'to question', and also *ałaçel* or *xndrel* 'to request'. Also typical is the example of χώρα, which becomes *ašxarh* 'territory' (Luke viii. 26), *gawaṙ* 'country(side)' (Luke xxi. 21), *tełi* 'place' (Luke ii. 8), *and* 'land (field)' (Luke xii. 16), *geawł* 'village' (Acts viii. 1), *artorayk'* 'fields' (John iv. 35), or *kołmank'* 'region' (Acts xvi. 6). The same is also true in reverse: *ašxarh* may translate χώρα, but it is also used for κόσμος (in John always), αἰών (Matt. xii. 32), οἰκουμένη (Luke iv. 5), περίχωρος (Luke vii. 17), and βίος (Luke viii. 14). Greek words which are synonymous are often not distinguished, but translated by the same word, e.g. *ayl* translates both ἄλλος and ἕτερος (Gal. i. 6, 7); *ĕnd mimeans* may be πρὸς ἀλλήλους, πρὸς ἑαυτούς, or ἐν ἑαυτοῖς; *çaragorc* is both κακοποιός and κακοῦργος; *datawor* may be κριτής or δικαστής; *hiwand* translates ἀσθενής, ἀσθενῶν, and κακῶς ἔχειν as well. *Satanay* is used consistently for both σατάν (and σατανᾶς) and διάβολος, except in a few instances where διάβολος is rendered literally by *çaraxos* (twice) or *bansarkow* (twice), and at Rev. xii. 9, where it is paired with ὁ Σατανᾶς and translated *Bēelzebowł*.

Variation in translation may be due at times to stylistic considerations. The technical term ἐφημερία is translated *dasakarg* 'rank' in Luke i. 5, but in Luke i. 8 it becomes *(karg) awowrcn hasaneloy* 'service schedule' (literally 'days of appearance'), yet hardly with any implication of a different translation base. A distinction has been proposed between εὐθύς / *vałvałaki* and εὐθέως / *noynžamayn* in Mark i, but a survey of the six different translations (besides omissions) that are found in the forty-two relevant passages in the Gospel of Mark suggests stylistic freedom rather than literalism as the determinative factor.

Nor should other factors be forgotten. At Matt. v. 32 and xix. 9 the Armenian text reads *ew or zarjakealn aṙnē šnay* / καὶ ὁ (τὴν) ἀπολελυμένην γαμῶν μοιχᾶται (or, μοιχεύει). Although this is close to the reading of codex B (which lacks the article and reads γαμήσας), it is identical with the parallel Armenian text of Luke xvi. 18. Its significance, then, may be rather as an example of intraversional parallelism than as relevant to a translation base.

5. CONCLUSION

It is not simply because of its fidelity as a literal translation that the Armenian version has been called the Queen of the versions, but rather because of its quality, its idiomatic ease and graceful authority. A review of the limitations of the language in reproducing a Greek text helps the textual critic to appreciate the elements of warning as well as of promise in the words of Fr. Lyonnet:

The Armenian translators . . . were able to give their work two qualities which are usually lacking: an elegance which has made it a model of the classical language no less than such original works as Eznik's *Treatise on God*, while remaining scrupulously faithful. . . . The differences are quite minimal and very definite. If they are kept in mind the model followed by the translator can be reconstructed: for the same care which he took in rendering precisely the nuances of an expression prevented him from ignoring details, and also led him to model his sentence structure on that of his exemplar whenever possible. This is what makes the Armenian version so valuable for the exegete, and what makes it possible to identify clearly the nature of his exemplar.[1]

TABLE I. *Cases and forms in declensions*

Singular	Plural
Nom., Acc. (Loc.)	Nom.
Gen., Dat. (Loc., Abl., Instr.)	Acc., Loc.
Abl.	Gen., Dat., Abl.
Instr.	Instr.

TABLE 2. *Verb forms and Greek parallels*[2]

Armenian	Greek
Indic. present	Indic. present (subj. present)
imperfect	Indic. imperfect, present participle, optative
aorist	Indic. aorist, aorist participle

[1] S. Lyonnet in M.-J. Lagrange, *Critique textuelle* (Paris, 1935), pp. 348, 351.

[2] These equivalents are only rough and are not to be pressed; e.g. the Greek present tense is sometimes translated by an imperfect (Matt. ii. 18 ὅτι οὐκ εἰσίν / *zi oč̣ ēin*), or by an aorist (Matt. ii. 22 βασιλεύει / *t'agaworeac̣*); the Greek imperfect may also be translated by a present (Matt. iii. 14 διεκώλυεν / *argelow*), or by an aorist (Matt. ii. 9 προῆγεν / *aṙaǰnordeac̣*). The narrative aorist εἶπε(ν) is most frequently translated by the present tense *asē*.

Armenian	*Greek*
Imperative present	Imper. present or aorist (negative)
aorist	Imper. present or aorist (positive)
Conj. present	Subj. present (or aorist), imper., indic. future
aorist	Subj. aorist (or present), imper., indic. future, optative
Infinitive (present stem)	Infinitive, prepositional phrases
Participle (aorist stem)	Participle

IV

The Georgian Version

I. THE INTRODUCTION OF CHRISTIANITY INTO GEORGIA AND THE TRANSLATION OF THE NEW TESTAMENT

AT the opening of this century, C. R. Gregory began his discussion of the Georgian version with the sentence, 'We know little concerning this version.'[1] In fact, so little information was available that Gregory's comments on this translation are briefer than those on any other ancient version treated in his comprehensive *Textkritik des Neuen Testamentes*. Happily, however, during the past half-century research has made commendable progress[2] despite the limited number of Western savants who are acquainted with Georgian, a Caucasian language.[3]

Now within the Union of Soviet Socialist Republics and called by the Russians Gruziya, the country of Georgia was anciently known as Iberia, whence is derived the name of the illustrious monastery of Iveron on Mount Athos. The earliest tradition regarding the introduction of Christianity among the Iberians tells of the missionary work of a Christian slave woman named Nino, who, during the reign of the Emperor Constantine, was taken captive by Bakur, the pagan king of Georgia.[4] Apart from legendary details concerning miracles performed by Nino,[5]

---

[1] *Textkritik des Neuen Testamentes*, ii (Leipzig, 1902), 573.

[2] For an account of the history of 'Georgian Studies at Oxford', see David M. Lang's chapter bearing that title in vol. vi of *Oxford Slavonic Papers*, edited by S. Konovalov (Oxford, 1955), pp. 115–43.

[3] The relation of the Georgian language to other languages has been greatly disputed. Some have sought connections with Basque (see René Lafon, 'Pour la comparaison du basque et des langues caucasiques', *BedK* xxv (1968), 13–26, and xxvi (1969), 13–17, xxvii (1970), 7–23; xxviii (1971), 9–23, xxi–xxx (1972), 8–31), or even with Sumerian (so, e.g., M. Tsereteli, 'Sumerian and Georgian; a Study in Comparative Philology', *JRAS* xlv (1913), 783–821; xlvi (1914), 1–36; xlvii (1915), 255–88; and xlviii (1916), 1–58).

[4] As reported by Rufinus, *Hist. eccl.* i. 10, and repeated by Socrates, i. 20, Sozomen, ii. 7, and Theodoret, i. 23.

[5] See 'Life of St. Nino', translated from the Georgian by Margery Wardrop and J. O. Wardrop, *Studia biblica et ecclesiastica*, v (1903), 1–88.

historians are inclined to accept the date of about the middle of the fourth century for the introduction of Christianity among the Georgians.[1]

Of the two forms of the *Life of St. Nino* that have been handed down, traditions preserved in the shorter and apparently incomplete account, which bears internal characteristics of very great antiquity, suggest that the Christian message was brought to Georgia at least in part by Jewish Christians. For example, according to this account, after 'St. Nino left the city of Mtzkheta, and went to the mountaineers, to carry the gospel to men in the form of wild beasts . . . Abiathar, the Jewish priest, was left here— he who was a second Paul, who ceaselessly, day and night, preached Christ and his glory.'[2] How far such a tradition preserves historical reminiscences of Jewish-Christian origins in the evangelization of Georgia, it is difficult to say. Assuming that such may have been the case, Vööbus speculates that perhaps 'the Aramaic Gospel according to the Hebrews satisfied the needs of these circles, the question concerning the translation of the Gospel text [into Georgian] being not raised'.[3] The slender basis for such speculation is the evidence that came to light in 1940, when Georgian archaeologists, excavating a tomb dating from the second century A.D. in the region of ancient Mtzkheta, discovered several inscriptions in Greek and in an Aramaic dialect.[4]

---

[1] So, e.g., Kornelios Kekelidze, *Die Bekehrung Georgiens zum Christentum* (*Morgenland, Darstellungen aus Geschichte und Kultur des Ostens*, Heft 18; Leipzig, 1928), who fixed upon the year 355–6; Josef Markwart, 'Die Bekehrung Iberiens und die beiden ältesten Dokumente der iberischen Kirche', *Caucasica, Zeitschrift für die Erforschung der Sprachen und Kulturen des Kaukasus und Armeniens*, fasc. 7 (Leipzig, 1931), pp. 111–67, who dates the beginnings of Christianity in Iberia in the decade 350–60; W. E. D. Allen, *A History of the Georgian People* (London, 1932), p. 267; and Gregor Peradze, 'Die Probleme der ältesten Kirchengeschichte Georgiens', *OC*, 3rd ser., vii (1932), 153–74, both of whom are content with a more general dating during the course of the fourth century. For earlier literature on the subject, see Peradze in *ZKG* xlix (1930), 96.

[2] The Georgian text, *Akhali Varianti Tsm. Ninos Tzkhovrebisa*, ed. by E. S. Takaishvili, is translated by the Wardrops, op. cit., p. 48 n. 1. For discussions of the variant traditions, see P. Peeters, 'Les débuts du christianisme en Géorgie d'après les sources hagiographiques', *AB* i (1932), 5–58; G. Peradze, *OC*, 3rd ser., vii (1932), 169; M. Tarchnisvili, 'Die Legende der heiligen Nino und die Geschichte des georgischen Nationalbewusstseins', *ByzZ* xl (1940), 48–75; and Nino Salia, 'Notice sur la conversion de la Géorgia par sainte Nino', *BedK* xxi–xxii (1966), 52–64.

[3] Arthur Vööbus, *Early Versions of the New Testament* (Stockholm, 1954), p. 174.

[4] For a discussion see the chapter entitled, 'A Greek and Aramaic Inscription

Without deciding now the cogency of such speculation, what concerns us here is the question of the early translation of the Scriptures into Georgian.

Before a translation could be made, however, the Georgians needed an alphabet of their own. According to Armenian traditions (see p. 156 above), after St. Mesrop had drawn up an alphabet for his fellow countrymen, he became concerned also about the lack of an alphabet among the Georgian people. When he had invented an alphabet that represented the sounds which occur in that language, King Bakur of Georgia arranged that it should be taught to boys of the lower social classes in various districts and provinces.[1] How far such traditions may need modification in the light of the discovery of ancient inscriptions bearing Georgian characters, it is perhaps premature to say. At any rate, according to the philologist Salia, 'The existence of a Georgian script before the fifth century seems at present altogether possible.'[2]

How soon after the earliest evangelization of Georgia a translation of the Scriptures was made in the native language is not known exactly, but a careful induction of many strands of evidence has led most scholars to suppose that at least the Gospels and other parts of the New Testament were translated before the middle of the fifth century.[3] During subsequent centuries this version was revised, perhaps more than once, and traces of such revision are discernible in terms of both philology and textual criticism.

From the standpoint of philology, an idiosyncrasy of Georgian morphology serves in some measure to date the several stages of the development of the Georgian language. During the earliest phase the velar fricative *ḫ* (= *ḫan*) was used as a prefix in the

---

Discovered at Armazi in Georgia', in the present writer's *Historical and Literary Studies; Pagan, Jewish, and Greek* (Leiden and Grand Rapids, 1968), pp. 34–47.

[1] Koriun's 'Life and Death of St. Mesrop', translated into German by Simon Weber in *Bibliothek der Kirchenväter*, 2te Aufl., lvii (Munich, 1927), 214.

[2] e.g., K. Salia, 'Note sur l'origine et âge de l'alphabet géorgien', *BedK* xv–xvi (1963), 5–18; quotation from p. 18. For other discussions concerning the age of Georgian writing, see M. Tarchnisvili, 'Les récentes découvertes épigraphiques et littéraires en géorgien', *Mu*, liii (1950), 249 ff.; Gerhard Deeters, 'Das Alter der georgischen Schrift', *OC* xxxix (1955), 56–65; and George Tseret'eli, 'The Most Ancient Georgian Inscriptions in Palestine', *BedK* xi–xii (1961), 111–30.

[3] So, e.g., R. P. Blake, *HTR* xxi (1928), 358–75, especially 360, and Arthur Vööbus, *Early Versions of the New Testament* (Stockholm, 1954), p. 178.

second and third persons of the verb and also in the comparative degree of the adjective. Later the use of this prefix was considered superfluous (*meti* = 'superfluous'), and therefore those texts which use the prefix are called the *ḥan-meti* texts. Since it appears, according to Džavakhishvili, that the prefix *ḥ* began to disappear in the first half of the seventh century, it is necessary to date the *ḥan-meti* texts in the sixth century.[1] The second phase started, according to the same scholar, with the eighth century, and this is characterized by the aspirate *h* (= *hae*), which replaced *ḥ* as prefix, and which later was abandoned as old-fashioned, too. The texts that show this distinctive characteristic of the second phase are called *hae-meti* texts.[2]

A feature of Georgian palaeography that bears in some measure upon questions of the dating of manuscripts is the style of script. The Georgians have employed three alphabets: (*a*) The *asomtʻavruli* script, or ecclesiastical majuscule characters (sometimes called *mrglovani* script), was in general use until the end of the tenth century, and sporadically thereafter in manuscripts (it was used until a much later time in inscriptions). (*b*) The *ḥutsuri* script, or ecclesiastical minuscules, was regularly used in theological manuscripts of the eleventh to the nineteenth century. (*c*) The *mḥedruli*, literally the 'warrior' or 'knightly' hand, is the ancestor of the modern Georgian script. The oldest dated manuscript using this alphabet, according to R. P. Blake, was written A.D. 1245, but there seem to be sporadic instances of its use in earlier undated documents.[3] With these explanations by way of preface, it will be appropriate now to list several of the earliest and most important of the extant manuscripts preserving the Georgian version.[4]

---

[1] I. Džavakhishvili and A. Shanidze in *Bulletin de l'Université de Tiflis*, ii (1922–3), 371 ff.; iii (1923–4), 366 ff.; vii (1926), 125 ff.; ix (1929), 329 ff., as reported by A. Vööbus, *Early Versions of the New Testament* (Stockholm, 1954), pp. 183 f. Other scholars (e.g. Blake, *HTR* xxi (1928), 370 f.) date the change about A.D. 700.
According to Dr. J. Neville Birdsall (letter dated 7 May 1974) the change was not carried out everywhere in the chronological sequence *ḥan*, *hae*, zero, for '*ḥan* and *hae* forms have survived in Georgian dialects, and the textual affiliations show that a *ḥanmeti* document can have a text which is probably later than a non-*ḥanmeti*.' Cf. also Birdsall, 'Some recently discovered Georgian Palimpsest Fragments of the Gospels', *Studia evangelica*, vi, ed. by E. A. Livingston (*TU* cxii, Berlin, 1973), 11 f.
[2] Cf. Joseph Molitor, 'Die altgeorgische Chanmeti- und Haemeti-Bibelfragmente', *Lexis*, iv (1954), 79–84.   [3] *Byzantion*, xvi (1943–3), 228 n. 6.
[4] For libraries and collections that contain Georgian manuscripts, see Jean

II. EARLY MANUSCRIPTS OF THE GEORGIAN VERSION

(1) Eighteen *ḫan-meti* fragments of the four Gospels, Romans, and Galatians, and twenty-three *hae-meti* fragments of the four Gospels, all of them published previously, were collected and re-edited in 1956 by Molitor, who also published a series of studies bearing on textual and linguistic features of the *ḫan-meti* fragments.[1] More recently still other *ḫan-meti* fragments of the Synoptic Gospels have been edited, and furnished with a Latin translation, by Birdsall[2] and by Outtier.[3]

(2) The Adysh manuscript, so named because it was found in the village of Adysh (or Hadisi) in upper Swanetia, comes from

Simon, 'Répertoire des bibliothèques publiques et privées d'Europe contenant des manuscrits géorgiens', *Orientalia*, iii (1934), 98–103 (lists the titles of catalogues and libraries in twenty European cities), supplemented by Gregor Peradze, 'Georgian MSS. in England', *Georgica*, i (1935), 80–8; and Julius Assfalg, *Georgische Handschriften* (*Verzeichnis der orientalischen Handschriften in Deutschland*, iii; Wiesbaden, 1963), list on pp. 75–7.

The most extensive collections of Georgian manuscripts are, as would be expected, in the Ḥelnaçerta Instituti (Institute of Manuscripts) at Tiflis, the catalogues of which now run to seven volumes (vol. vii, 1973). Other extensive collections of Georgian manuscripts are described in the following: 'Professor Tsagareli's Catalogue of the Georgian Manuscripts in the Monastery of the Holy Cross at Jerusalem', translated by Oliver Wardrop, *JBL* xii (1893), 168–79; Robert P. Blake, 'Catalogue des manuscrits géorgiens de la bibliothèque Patriarcale grecque à Jérusalem', *Revue de l'Orient chrétien*, xxiii (1922–3), 345–413; xxiv (1924), 190–210, and 387–424; idem, 'Catalogue des manuscrits géorgiens de la bibliothèque de la Laure d'Iviron au Mont Athos', *ROC* xxviii (1931–2), 289–361; xxix (1933–4), 114–59, and 225–71; and Gérard Garitte, *Catalogue des manuscrits géorgiens littéraires du Mont Sinai* (Louvain, 1956).

Theodor Kluge's description of two Apostolos manuscripts, dated by him to the seventh or eighth century, leaves something to be desired ('Über zwei altgeorgische neutestamentliche Handschriften', *NovT* i (1956), 304–21).

[1] Joseph Molitor, *Monumenta Iberica Antiquiora. Textus Chanmeti et Haemeti ex Inscriptionibus, S. Bibliis et Patribus* (*CSCO* clxvi, *Subsidia*, x; Louvain, 1956); id., 'Chanmetifragmente. Ein Beitrag zur Textgeschichte der altgeorgischen Bibelübersetzung'; 1. Die Matthaustexte', *OC* xli (1957), 22–34; '2. Die Markustexte', xliii (1959), 17–23; '3. Die Lukastexte', xliv (1960), 17–24; xlv (1961), 115–26; xlvi (1962), 19–24; '4. Die Johannestexte', xlix (1965), 38–56. Two other valuable tools for the study of the Georgian text are Molitor's *Glossarium Ibericum in quattuor Evangelia et Actus Apostolorum antiquioris versionis etiam textus Chanmeti et Haemeti complectens* (*CSCO* ccxxviii and ccxxxvii; *Subsidia*, xx and xxi; Louvain, 1962; xxiii (1964), and *Glossarium Latinum–Ibericum–Graecum . . .* , (op. cit. cclxxx, *Subsidia*, xxix [= xxx], 1967).

[2] J. Neville Birdsall, 'Khanmeti Fragments of the Synoptic Gospels from ms. Vind. Georg. 2', *OC* lv (1971), 62–89; cf. idem, *TU* cxii (1973), 11–13.

[3] B. Outtier, 'Un feuillet du lectionnaire géorgien hanmeti à Paris', *Mu*, lxxxv (1972), 399–402.

the Shatberd monastery in Tao-Klardžet'i of south-west Georgia, which was founded by Gregory of Ḥandzt'a at the beginning of the ninth century. The manuscript, which contains the four Gospels in the *asomt'avruli* characters, was written in A.D. 897. According to Shanidze[1] the text of Luke iii. 9–xv. 7 and xvii. 25–xxiii. 2 differs as regards terminology and grammar from the text of Matthew, Mark, and John. It appears, therefore, that the original from which the Adysh manuscript was copied, or, at any rate, one of its prototypes, was an imperfect manuscript. The character of the text in the two sections of Luke resembles that of the Džruč and Parḥal manuscripts (nos. 4 and 6 below). The Adysh manuscript, which is now at Tiflis, was published in photographic facsimile by A. S. Khakhanov and E. S. Takaishvili (*Materialy po arxeologii Kavkaza*, xiv (Moscow, 1916)).

(3) The Opiza manuscript of the four Gospels comes from the Opiza monastery in Tao-Klardžet'i and is now preserved in the Iveron monastery on Mount Athos. Written by a scribe named Grigol in rather small *asomt'avruli* characters, it dates from A.D. 913.[2]

(4) The Džruč manuscript derives its name from the circumstance that it had been kept at the Džruči monastery in upper Imereti before being transferred to the Institute of Manuscripts at Tiflis. The manuscript, which contains the four Gospels in *asomt'avruli* characters, came originally from the Shatberd monastery, where it was written in A.D. 936.

(5) What appears to be the oldest dated Georgian manuscript containing the Epistles of Paul, the Book of Acts, and the Catholic Epistles is MS. Athos Iviron georg. no. 42. It was written by a priest named Mik'ael at the monastery of SS. Cosmas and Damien on Mount Olympus in Bithynia during the reign of Nicephorus Phocos (between 959 and 969). A dozen of

---

[1] Akaki Shanidze, *Two Old Recensions of the Georgian Gospels according to Three Shatberd Manuscripts (A.D. 897, 936, and 973)* [in Georgian], (*Monuments of the Old Georgian Language*, ii; Tiflis: Academy of Sciences, 1945), p. 062.

[2] For a plate showing the end of the Gospel according to Mark (at xvi. 8) in the Opiza manuscript, see H. Goussen, 'Die georgische Bibelübersetzung', *OC* vi (1906), between pp. 300 and 301. The text of Matthew and of Mark in the Opiza and Tbet' manuscripts was edited by Vladimir Beneševič, *Quattuor Evangeliorum versio Georgiana vetus. E duobus codicibus (aa. p. Chr. n. 913 et 995)* (St. Petersburg, 1909; and 1911); his edition of Luke and John never appeared.

its pages were edited by F. C. Conybeare,[1] who retranslated the Georgian into Greek.

(6) The Parḫal manuscript owes its name to the circumstance that it was prepared for presentation to the monastery of Parḫal in Tao-Klardžet'i. For some unknown reason, however, it was kept as early as the eighteenth century at Zemo-Č'ala, near Khasuri (ancient Mikhailov), and from there has been taken to the Institute of Manuscripts at Tiflis. Written in *asomt'avruli* characters in A.D. 973, it contains the Gospels.

(7) MS. Sinai georg. 39, dated A.D. 974, comprises today 132 leaves of parchment, being mutilated at the beginning (it lacks the first four leaves of the first signature). Written in *asomt'avruli* characters, with occasional lines here and there in *ḫutsuri*, it contains the text of Acts (except i. 1–ii. 17) and the Pauline Epistles. A microfilm of the manuscript is at the Library of Congress in Washington.

(8) Another manuscript containing the Epistles of Paul and Acts, written in *asomt'avruli* characters and dating from A.D. 977, is also at St. Catherine's Monastery, Mount Sinai. Divided into three sections, it is identified as MSS. Sin. georg. 58 (comprising forty-five leaves), 31 (121 leaves containing Acts), and 60 (twelve leaves). A microfilm of the three sections is at the Library of Congress in Washington.

(9) The oldest Georgian manuscript of the Book of Revelation, written by a monk named Saba at the monastery of Kranim in Bithynia, dates from A.D. 978. Formerly in the monastery of Shio-Mghwimé, the manuscript today is in the Institute of Manuscripts at Tiflis. Photographs of the manuscript are in the J. P. Morgan collection of manuscript photographs at Harvard.

(10) MS. Sinai georg. 38, described as having 144 folios, two of which bear illumination (Mark standing and Matthew standing), dates from A.D. 979. A microfilm of the manuscript is at the Library of Congress in Washington.

(11) The Tbet' manuscript of the four Gospels, previously deposited in the Public Library at Leningrad (no. 212), has now been transferred to the Caucasian Museum at Tiflis. It derives its name from the monastery of the Holy Apostles at Tbet' in

---

[1] 'The Old Georgian Version of Acts,' *ZNW* xii (1911), 131–40.

Šavšet'ia, where it was written in *asomt'avruli* characters in A.D. 995.[1] Photographs of the manuscript made by Kirsopp Lake are at Harvard University Library.

(12) The Gospels of Bert'ay, a monastery situated north-west by north from Artanuj, is written in *asomt'avruli* characters dating from the tenth century. It is now in the museum of the Andover–Newton Theological School, Newton Center, Massachusetts.[2]

(13) MS. Athos Iviron georg. 62, written in *ḥutsuri* characters, contains the four Gospels in the revision of St. George the Athonite. It is thought that this manuscript was produced at Mount Athos about the middle of the eleventh century.

The Adysh manuscript of the Gospels (no. 2 in the list above) forms the basis of an edition published by Blake and Brière in *Patrologia Orientalis*,[3] against which are collated the Opiza and Tbet' manuscripts (nos. 3 and 11 above). The Georgian text and variants are supplied with a Latin translation. In view, however, of the latitude which Blake allowed himself in the use of synonyms in order to avoid monotony, the rendering is not altogether satisfactory for text-critical work. A more literally exact translation has been published by Molitor, who attempted to ensure that every Georgian word should be rendered by one and the same Latin equivalent. His translation of the Adysh manuscript is supplied with an apparatus of variant readings from parallel texts.[4]

The Adysh manuscript, along with the Džruč and Parḥal manuscripts (nos. 4 and 6 in the list above), has also been edited by A. Shanidze.[5]

Two manuscripts of the Acts of the Apostles from the monastery of St. Catherine on Mount Sinai (nos. 7 and 8 in the list above)

---

[1] See p. 187 n. 2 above.

[2] Cf. R. P. Blake and Sirarpie Der Nersessian, 'The Gospels of Bert'ay; an Old Georgian MS of the Tenth Century', *Byz*, xvi (1943–4), 226–85.

[3] Robert P. Blake, *The Old Georgian Version of the Gospel of Mark* (*PO* xx (Paris, 1929), 435–574); *Matthew* (ibid. xxiv (1933), 1–168); *John*, edited by Blake and Maurice Brière (ibid. xxvi (1950), 454–599); and *Luke*, edited by Brière (ibid. xxvii (1955), 276–448; includes corrigenda for the editions of Matthew, Mark, and John, pp. 449–57).

[4] Joseph Molitor, 'Das Adysh-Tetraevangelium, neu übersetzt und mit altgeorgischen Parallel-texten verglichen', *OC* xxxvii (1953), 30–5; xxxviii (1954), 11–40; xxxi (1955), 1–32; xl (1956), 1–15; xli (1957), 1–21; xlii (1958), 1–18; xliii (1959), 1–16. [5] See p. 187 n. 1 above.

have been edited, with a Latin translation, by Gérard Garitte.[1] Unknown to Garitte,[2] five years earlier eight other manuscripts of the book of Acts from the tenth to the fourteenth centuries had been edited by Ilia Abuladze.[3]

In addition to his many other studies and investigations, Joseph Molitor has made a literal Latin rendering of the Georgian version of the Catholic Epistles[4] and of the Book of Revelation.[5] The textual basis of the former is the edition prepared by Mme K'et'evan I. Lort'k'ip'anidze;[6] it rests upon four manuscripts dating from the tenth to the fourteenth century, including the notable tenth-century Kala-Lectionary,[7] which Kornelius Kekelidze discovered in 1911 at the monastery of SS. Cyriacus and Julitta in Kala. The textual basis of Molitor's translation of the Apocalypse is the edition prepared by Ilia V. Imnaišvili[8] and rests upon the oldest known Georgian manuscript of that book (see no. 9 in the list above), with variant readings from two other manuscripts.

III. THE BASE OF THE GEORGIAN VERSION

Opinion differs as to the question of the language from which the Georgian version was made. Conybeare[9] at first thought that it was made from the Greek, but later altered his opinion to the view that it was translated from a Syriac text.[10] Following his

---

[1] *L'Ancienne Version géorgienne des Actes des Apôtres* (*Bibliothèque du Muséon*, vol. xxxviii; Louvain, 1955). [2] Ibid., p. 7 n. 11.

[3] *The Acts of the Apostles according to the Old Manuscripts* [in Georgian], (*Monuments of the Old Georgian Language*, vii; Tiflis, 1950).

[4] 'Die altgeorgische Version der katholischen Briefe ins Lateinische übertragen', *OC* xlix (1965), 1–17; l (1966), 37–45.

[5] 'Die georgische Version der Apokalypse (von 978) ins Lateinische übertragen und untersucht,' *OC* l (1966), 1–12; li (1967), 1–28; lii (1968), 1–21.

[6] *The Version of the Catholic Epistles according to Manuscripts of the 10th–14th Centuries* [in Georgian] (*Monuments of the Old Georgian Language*, ix; Tiflis, 1956).

[7] Cf. Michel Tarchnischvili, *Le Grand Lectionnaire de l'Église de Jérusalem*, i (Louvain, 1959), pp. x–xi.

[8] *The Apocalypse of John and its Commentary* [in Georgian] (Tiflis, 1961). The commentary is that of Andrew of Caesarea (d. 637), which is current also in many Greek manuscripts.

[9] In Scrivener–Miller, *A Plain Introduction to the Criticism of the New Testament*, 4th edn., ii (London, 1894), 156; Conybeare's opinion was adopted by Ll. J. M. Bebb, 'The Georgian Version', Hastings's *Dictionary of the Bible*, iv (1902), 861.

[10] *The Academy*, 1 Feb. 1896, p. 99, and more fully in 'The Growth of the Peshitta Version of the New Testament illustrated from the Old Armenian and Georgian Versions', *AJT* i (1897), 909; see also p. 903.

lead, Vööbus[1] and Molitor[2] have pointed out a not inconsiderable number of Syriacisms which are preserved in the Georgian version of the Gospels. Most scholars have been impressed by similarities between the Georgian and the Armenian versions, and Goussen,[3] Baumstark,[4] and Peradse[5] refer to the two versions as 'twin sisters', a term which Karst[6] also evidently approved, though he preferred to speak of the 'Armenian–Syriac' basis of the Georgian. Other investigators, however, such as Kluge,[7] Burkitt,[8] Blake,[9] and Lyonnet,[10] regard the relationship between the Armenian and the Georgian as that of parent and daughter. On the other hand, Zorell[11] and Shanidze[12] have adopted Conybeare's original view, that the Georgian version was made directly from the Greek.

The question has been raised concerning the earliest form of the Gospel traditions that circulated in Georgia: was only the tetraevangelium translated into Georgian, or did Tatian's Diatessaron find its way into Georgian Christianity too? Considering the wide popularity of the latter in Syria, and possibly also in Armenia, one would not be surprised to find that its influence extended as far as Georgia. Some slight trace of the

---

[1] Arthur Vööbus, *Zur Geschichte des altgeorgischen Evangelientextes* (Stockholm, 1953), pp. 26 f.

[2] Joseph Molitor, 'Syrische Lesarten im altgeorgischen Tetraevangelium', *BedK* xix–xx (1965), 112–18; 'Altgeorgische Evangelienübersetzung als Hüterin syrischer Tradition', ibid. xxii–xxiv (1967), 136–42; xxv (1968), 185–93; xxvi (1969), 162–9.

[3] Henri Goussen, 'Die georgische Bibelübersetzung', *OC* vi (1906), 299–318, especially 309.

[4] *Die christlichen Litteraturen des Orients*, ii (Leipzig, 1911), 103.

[5] 'Die altgeorgische Literatur und ihre Probleme', *OC*, 3rd ser., ii (1927), 207–8.

[6] J. Karst, *Littérature géorgienne chrétienne* (Paris, 1934), pp. 40–1.

[7] Theodor Kluge, 'Über das Alter des georgischen Übersetzung des Neuen Testaments', *ZNW* xi (1910), 161–6.

[8] *Encyclopaedia Britannica*, 14th edn., iii (1928), 517. Earlier, however, Burkitt thought that the Georgian was made from the Old Syriac; cf. *Encyclopædia Biblica*, iv (1903), col. 5012.

[9] *HTR* xxi (1928), 294; *PO* xx (1929), 445–6; and *Quantulacumque, Studies Presented to Kirsopp Lake*, ed. by Robert P. Casey *et al.* (London, 1937), pp. 355–63.

[10] In M.-J. Lagrange, *Critique textuelle* (Paris, 1935), p. 381.

[11] Franz Zorell, 'Ursprung und Eigenart des georgischen Bibelübersetzung', *HA* xli (1927), cols. 669–80: 'The Georgian translation of the Bible was made from a Greek model, but it has many variant readings from the Armenian and Syriac' (col. 680).

[12] A. Shanidze, *Two Old Recensions of the Georgian Gospels According to Three Shatberd Manuscripts* (Tiflis, 1945), pp. 07–08, and 6–7.

Diatessaron has been thought to be reflected in the Acts of Martyrdom of St. Eustathius of Mzkheta,[1] dating from the second half of the sixth century. As long ago as 1901 von Harnack published in the *Proceedings of the Berlin Academy* a German rendering of the text, with a detailed commentary.[2] In this document it is recorded that before his martyrdom in A.D. 545 Eustathius the Cobbler gave an account of his Christian belief before the Persian governor of Tiflis. Part of this apologia reports sections of the Old Testament and a narrative of the life and sufferings of Christ. The latter is recounted in a cento of incidents drawn from all four Gospels, reminiscent of Tatian's Diatessaron. Here and there the pericopes as well as the words are combined with elements taken from parallel passages. As Vööbus points out, 'This harmonistic combination does not seem to be accidental but seems to belong to the structure of the narrative with which the author was familiar.'[3] More recently the question was opened by Birdsall,[4] who shows conclusively that, though the collocation of incidents appears to depend upon some kind of harmony, there is no evidence that the harmony had any connection with Tatian's Diatessaron. Furthermore, from textual considerations it appears that the harmonized account, whatever its origin, must be dated later than the translation of the separate Gospels in Georgian.

Besides the harmonizing fusion of evangelic materials recounted in the Martyrdom of St. Eustathius, traces of harmonistic influence have been detected in the text of the separate Gospels. In their analyses of the Georgian text of Mark i,

[1] Translated into English by D. M. Lang, *Lives and Legends of the Georgian Saints* (London and New York, 1956), pp. 95–114.

[2] Dschawachoff [Dzavachishvili], 'Das Martyrium des heiligen Eustatius von Mzchetta', vorgelegt und bearbeitet von A. von Harnack, *SbBer*, xxxvii (1901), 897 ff.

[3] Arthur Vööbus, *Early Versions of the New Testament* (Stockholm, 1954), p. 181.

[4] J. Neville Birdsall, ' "The Martyrdom of St. Eustathius of Mzketha" and the Diatessaron: an Investigation', *NTS* xviii (1971–2), 452–6.

The narrative of the Martyrdom, it may be pointed out, contains not a few targumic-like expansions, several of which occur elsewhere as variant readings. For example, Jesus took the widow of Nain's son *by the hand* and restored him alive to his mother; the woman with an issue of blood came *with stealth* behind Jesus and touched the hem of his garment and was healed; Lazarus came *joyfully* out of the tomb; at the trial of Jesus some hit him on the head *with their fists*; at the crucifixion Jesus was made to drink vinegar *mingled with gall*. Such features remind one of similar targumic renderings in the Armenian version (see p. 162 above).

Baumstark[1] and Molitor[2] concluded that the translation was not made from the Greek text but from the Armenian version in the form of a harmony.[3] Furthermore, in an examination of the New Testament quotations in a *ḫan-meti* fragment of patristic citations (chiefly from Chrysostom), Molitor detected traces of influence from both Greek and Armenian sources; he also discovered one Tatianism, namely, the presence of οὐκ in Matt. xxi. 16a.[4] In this connection it should be mentioned that several scholars have argued that the Georgian expression *ot'ḫt'avi* (i.e. 'four-chapters' [of the same work, of the same Gospel]), used with reference to the primitive Georgian tetraevangelium, seems to suggest a reminiscence of a Gospel harmony that preceded the separate Gospels in Georgia.[5]

Whatever the origin of the Georgian version may have been,[6] during subsequent centuries its text underwent various revisions. According to the research of Vööbus,[7] the evolution of the style and language of the Georgian Gospels passed through the following stages. In the rendering preserved in the Adysh manuscript

---

[1] Anton Baumstark, 'Zum georgischen Evangelientext', *OC*, 3rd ser. iii/iv (1930), 117–24. According to Baumstark, the Georgian exhibits a relationship with the Middle Netherlandish recension of the Diatessaron.

[2] Joseph Molitor, 'Zur Harmonistik des altgeorgischen Evangelientextes', *BZ*, N.F. i (1957), 289–96.

[3] Though he provides no examples of readings, Gregor Peradze declares that he had come to the same conclusion on the basis of an examination of the entire text of Mark in Georgian; see his 'Die Probleme der georgischen Evangelienübersetzung', *ZNW* xxix (1930), 304–9.

[4] 'Evangelienzitate in einen altgeorgischen Väterfragment', *OC* xl (1956), 16–21. Cf. idem, 'Synoptische Evangelienzitate in Sinai-Mravelthavi von 864', ibid. xlviii (1964), 180–96.

[5] So Molitor, 'Zur Harmonistik . . .' (see n. 2 above), and A. Strobel, 'Der Bergriff des 'vierkapiteligen Evangeliums' in Pseudo-Ephraem C', *ZKG* lxx (1959), 112–20. Molitor has also compared the Syriac text in Ortiz de Urbina's edition of Tatian's Diatessaron (see p. 19 n. 4 above) with the Old Georgian Gospel tradition ('Tatian's Diatessaron und sein Verhältnis zur altsyrischen und altgeorgischen Überlieferung', *OC* liii (1969), 1–88; liv (1970), 1–75; lv (1971), 1–61).

[6] Lang, though seemingly balanced and cautious, opens the door to pure speculation: 'It would be going too far to postulate that a translation of the *Diatessaron* necessarily preceded the rendering of the complete Gospels into Georgian, for although the Adysh text is represented only in a manuscript of the late ninth century, its language retains features characteristic of the fifth. There is, of course, nothing to prevent us from supposing that the four Gospels existed in early Christian Georgia alongside with some form of Gospel harmony, very possibly deriving from the *Diatessaron*' ('Recent Work on the Georgian New Testament', *BSOAS* xix (1957), 82 f.).

[7] Arthur Vööbus, *Early Versions of the New Testament* (Stockholm, 1954), pp. 193–7.

one finds traces of asyndeton similar to that present in early
Armenian texts where one Greek verb is rendered by two
Armenian ones. This feature was subsequently eliminated from
the Georgian Gospels. The simplicity of construction in the
Adysh text, which avoids complicated syntax and prefers simple
parataxis, is in time modified by the introduction of hypotaxis
characteristic of Greek models. Since the *ḫan-meti* and *hae-meti*
Gospel fragments already show signs of revision by reference to
the Greek, they represent an intermediate stage of development
between the prototype reflected in the Adysh Gospels and the
text that is found in such codices as the Opiza and the Tbetʿ.
Along with the two latter codices, which Lang,[1] following
Shanidze, calls the 'proto-Vulgate' family of Georgian manuscripts, there is to be added the Gospels of Bertʾay (no. 12 in
the list above).

IV. TEXTUAL AFFINITIES OF THE GEORGIAN VERSION

As was mentioned earlier in connection with the style and
language of the Georgian Gospels, the Adysh, Opiza, and Tbetʿ
manuscripts preserve two strains of Georgian text. The text of the
Adysh manuscript, which appears to be archaic and lacks all
trace of direct Greek influence, Blake designated Georgian 1;
while the Opiza and Tbetʿ manuscripts, which reveal in different
amounts the influence of Greek upon style and syntax, he called
A and B of Georgian 2. All three manuscripts, Blake thought,
exhibit Caesarean tendencies; the Adysh manuscript he ranged
with the group Θ, 565, and 700. The other two manifest special
affinities to Family 1 and Family 13. The methodology that Blake
followed is indicated by the sentence, 'If one rejects the different
K variants found in the three manuscripts of Mark, the residuum
of readings, when combined, affords a very pure Caesarean
text.'[2] The text of Matthew is much the same as that of Mark,
but according to Blake, it 'has suffered more admixture of, and
undergone more correction from, extraneous sources of various
types'.[3]

Blake's research, however, has not met with the approval of all
textual critics. Colwell, for example, pointed out that Georgian 2

---

[1] D. M. Lang, 'Recent Work on the Georgian New Testament', pp. 84 f.
[2] *PO* xx. 3 (1929), 447.   [3] *PO* xxiv. 1 (1933), 7.

exhibits greater affinity to the Caesarean text than does Georgian 1.[1] Furthermore, Colwell has shown that the Georgian text, contrary to Blake's opinion (an opinion shared by Lake as well),[2] is not so good a representative of the primitive stage of the Armenian text as are certain extant Armenian manuscripts themselves.

The textual character of the *ḫan-meti* fragments is not unified; some of the fragments are closer to Georgian 1, and others are closer to Georgian 2.[3] An analysis of a *hae-meti* fragment from the eighth or ninth century discloses a much closer affinity with Georgian 2 than with Georgian 1 (readings from twenty-three pericopes from all four Gospels show 298 agreements with Georgian 2 as against twenty-four agreements with Georgian 1).[4]

Conybeare's analysis of the text of the Acts, limited to a study of about four chapters of the book in a manuscript which he attributed to the twelfth or thirteenth century,[5] but which was actually written before 969,[6] led him to conclude that its type of text resembles that of the bilingual Greek and Latin codices D and E, abounding in early Western readings. Although Conybeare confessed that he expected to find evidence of Syriacisms, he was unsuccessful in his search for them.

More recently Garitte's publication of an edition of the Book of Acts in Old Georgian has enabled him to provide a broad assessment of its textual affinities. He comes to the following conclusions:[7] (1) It was translated from the Armenian. (2) The Armenian that served as a model of the Georgian version was not the vulgate Armenian extant today (the manuscripts of which do not come from earlier than the thirteenth century). (3) The Old Armenian, now lost, which was the origin of the primitive Georgian version, appears to have depended upon an Old Syriac

---

[1] *ATR* xvi (1934), 127.

[2] K. Lake, *The Text of the New Testament*, 6th edn., revd. by Silva New (London, 1928), p. 44.

[3] Joseph Molitor, 'Neuere Ergebnisse zur Textgeschichte des georgischen Neuen Testamentes', *BedK* xxi–xxii (1966), 111–20, especially 115–17.

[4] Joseph Molitor, 'Das Haemeti-Palimpsestfragment Tiflis 1329 und sein Verhältnis zum altgeorgischen Evangelientext', *Neutestamentliche Aufsätze; Festschrift für Prof. Josef Schmid* (Regensburg, 1963), pp. 175–84.

[5] 'The Old Georgian Version of Acts', *ZNW* xii (1911), 131–40.

[6] See manuscript no. 5 in the list above (pp. 187 f.).

[7] Gérard Garitte, *L'Ancienne Version géorgienne des Actes des Apôtres* (Louvain, 1955), pp. 19–20. Cf. also Michel Tarchnišvili, 'A propos de la plus ancienne version géorgienne des Actes des Apôtres', *Mu*, lxix (1956), 347–68.

version (different from the Peshitta). (4) The Georgian version, translated from the Armenian, has undergone revisions tending to conform it to a Greek text. It will be seen that this reconstructed history of the Georgian version of Acts resembles that which many scholars hold concerning the Georgian version of the Gospels.

Some of the more noteworthy readings of the Georgian text of Acts include the following (the Latin rendering is that of Garitte) :

i. 26 *connumeratus-est undecim apostolis ut-duodecimus.*

viii. 27 *indus* (for Aἰθίοψ) and *Indiae* (for Aἰθιόπων).

ix. 11 *in templis* (= *aedibus*) *Iudae* (for ἐν οἰκίᾳ 'Ιούδα).

xv. 26 *se ipsos tradiderunt* (for παραδεδωκόσι τὰς ψυχὰς αὐτῶν).

The textual complexion of the Epistle of James in the Georgian version, as in the case of other New Testament books, is characteristically variegated. Molitor[1] finds fifty-three examples of what he calls 'pure Syriac readings' and fifty-one instances of 'pure Armenian readings'. He also finds fifty-nine instances of 'Syriac–Armenian coloration', fifty-nine instances of otherwise unattested free renderings, and seven readings that can be explained only on the basis of the Greek text. Thus there are for the Epistle of James 163 non-Greek readings and sixty-six non-oriental readings. From these statistics Molitor concludes, 'Therefore it is clearly proved that the Old Georgian text of the Epistle of James goes back essentially to a Syriac–Armenian translation.'[2]

V. THE REVISED GEORGIAN VERSION

A new stage in the history of the spiritual, literary, and cultural life of Georgia began at the close of the tenth century. Inaugurated by the Athonite school,[3] which took over the principal role under the leadership of the Georgian monastery on Mount

---

[1] Joseph Molitor, 'Zum Textcharacter der altgeorgischen katholischen Briefe: 1, Der altgeorgische Jakobusbrief', *OC* li (1967), 51–66; cf. also idem, 'Die Bedeutung der georgischen Version des Neuen Testaments für die Novi Testamenti Graeci editio maior critica aufgezeigt am Textcharacter des altgeorgischen Jakobusbriefes', *BedK* xxviii (1971), 249–52. Since it is not evident how thoroughly Molitor has searched for parallel readings in other witnesses, one should, perhaps, be cautious about accepting in every case his evaluation of the 'purity' of a reading.

[2] *OC* li (1967), 66.

[3] Cf. the chapter 'The Georgian Athonites' in David M. Lang's *Lives and Legends of the Georgian Saints* (London and New York, 1956), pp. 154–68.

Athos, there was a noticeable reorientation toward Greek culture. The Iviron monks, sensitive to any accusation of doctrinal deviation that might be levelled against them by their
Greek confrères, set to work to revise their Church books in
accordance with Byzantine models. One of the most vigorous
of the Georgian Athonites was St. Euthymius (d. 1028), who,
according to his biographer, did much of this work at night by
candlelight after a full day spent in administering the laura and
in religious exercises.

The blessed Euthymius [he tells us] went on translating without
respite and gave himself no repose; day and night he distilled the
sweet honey of the books of God, with which he adorned our language
and our Church. He translated so many divine works that nobody
could enumerate them, since he worked at his translations not only on
Mount Olympus and Mount Athos (which works we can list in detail),
but also in Constantinople, and while travelling, and in all kinds of
other places.[1]

In addition to translating hagiographical and homiletic works,
St. Euthymius early turned his attention to revising and completing the Georgian New Testament. The Book of Revelation,
which for centuries was not regarded as canonical by the
Georgian Church,[2] was first translated into Georgian by St.
Euthymius. His work must have been completed sometime
before A.D. 978, which is the date of the earliest known Georgian
manuscript of the Apocalypse (no. 9 in the list above). The base
for his version appears to have been a copy of Andreas' Greek
text of the book. Euthymius' translation must have been rather
free, for, according to Molitor, the Georgian rendering shows
traces of influence from the Philoxenian Syriac version and the
Armenian version of that book.[3] Such reminiscences are particularly noticeable in the spelling of proper names.[4]

---

[1] Quoted by D. M. Lang, *Landmarks in Georgian Literature; An Inaugural Lecture*,
School of Oriental and African Studies, University of London (1966), p. 12. For
further details about the literary and ecclesiastical work of St. Euthymius, see
Michael Tarchnišvili, *Geschichte der kirchlichen georgischen Literatur* (Vatican City,
1955), pp. 126–54.

[2] According to R. P. Blake, the Apocalypse, 'strictly speaking, never became
canonical among the Georgians' (*HTR* xxi (1928), 287).

[3] Joseph Molitor, 'Die georgische Version der Apokalypse (von 978) ins
Lateinische übertragen und untersucht', *OC* lii (1968), 21.

[4] Joseph Molitor, 'Die Eigennamen in der Johannesapokalypse des Euthymius',
BedK xvii–xviii (1964), 127–31.

The terminus of the labours on the Athonite revision came in the eleventh century with the work of St. George the Hagiorite (d. 1065), who, like Euthymius, was abbot of the Iberian monastery on Mount Athos. St. George's work, as Blake points out,

may be considered as a continuation, and to some extent a rectification, of that of Euthymius. He translated some things which had not previously existed in Georgian, revised some others, and improved the translations of Euthymius. Among the latter he revised the Gospels, the Apostolic writings, and the Psalter—i.e. those sections which were used in the liturgy, and his versions displaced all others in common use.[1]

Most of the modifications introduced by St. George were relatively minor and seem to have been based on Greek manuscripts of von Soden's *K*-type. Typical of his work is the comment on Matt. xxiv. 66 found in some copies of his recension, to the effect that 'since the words οὐδὲ ὁ υἱός [of vs. 36] did not occur in the three Greek Gospels, neither have I written them, says [George] the Hagiorite'.[2] One of the chief points of difference between his revision and that of St. Euthymius, according to Blake, is the inclusion of the *pericope de adultera* (John vii. 53–viii. 11) in St. George's text, a passage that is absent from all earlier forms of the Gospel of John in Georgian.[3]

As might have been expected, it is the work of the Athonite school of translators that is represented in the great majority of Georgian manuscripts, including virtually all of those written in *ḫutsuri* characters. This revision became the vulgate of the Georgian Church and forms the basis of printed editions, beginning with that of 1709 (the Gospels) published at Tiflis by King Vakhtang VI on the printing press newly established by him, and (according to Brière) reproduced without change in at least twelve editions of the Gospels and six editions of the whole New Testament.[4]

---

[1] R. P. Blake, 'Georgian Theological Literature', *JTS* xxvi (1925), 57 f.

[2] Cited by A. Shanidze, *Two Old Recensions . . .* , p. 063.

[3] *HTR* xxi (1928), 293, n. 36. Blake's statement, however, needs modification in the light of information kindly provided by Dr. Birdsall, namely that in Sinai MS. georg. 16, written at the Monastery of the Holy Cross at Jerusalem and dated (according to Tsagareli) A.D. 992, as well as in Vatican MS. iber. 1 (of about the same date), the *pericope de adultera* stands after John vii. 44.

[4] So Brière in *PO* xxvii (1955), 291 f. The *editio princeps* of the entire Georgian

VI. LIMITATIONS OF GEORGIAN IN REPRESENTING GREEK

by the late Canon Maurice Brière[1]

For convenience of reference we have classified the examples of the limitations of the Georgian language in representing Greek under the headings of phonetics, morphology, and syntax.[2] All the Scripture references are to chapter and verse in the Gospel according to St. Luke. The Georgian evidence is drawn from six manuscripts, five of which are commonly designated by the names Adysh, Opiza, Džruč, Parḫal, Tbetʻ, and a sixth which is at Mount Athos. We shall designate the first manuscript 'G₁', and the four other named manuscripts, respectively, 'G₂₁', 'G₂₂', 'G₂₃', 'G₂₄', their combination 'G₂' (when all four agree in giving the same text), and the Mount Athos manuscript 'g'.[3]

The Adysh manuscript contains the Georgian text of the four Gospels which represents a version preserved in fragmentary texts called 'ḫanmeti' and 'haemeti'. The Opiza, Džruč, Parḫal, and Tbetʻ manuscripts, which rest upon the text of the Adysh manuscript and correct it, form a 'proto-Vulgate' of the Georgian Gospels, to use Professor A. Shanidze's expression. The Mount

Bible was published in 1743; see the description in T. H. Darlow and H. F. Moule, *Historical Catalogue of Printed Editions of Holy Scripture . . .* , ii (London, 1911), 429. At this time the Tetraevangelium and the Apostolos were brought together in one corpus for the first time; cf. Theodor Kluge, 'Über das Alter des georgischen Übersetzung des Neuen Testaments', *ZNW* xi (1910), 344.

[1] [The material in section VI, 'Limitations of Georgian in Representing Greek', was drawn up (in French) by the late Canon Maurice Brière, Honorary Professor of l'Institut catholique de Paris, to accompany his collation of the Old Georgian version of Luke against the Greek Textus Receptus (Oxford, 1871) for the International Greek New Testament Project. The reader will therefore find, in addition to information concerning limitations of Georgian in representing Greek, the citation of variant readings in manuscripts of the version as well as occasional comments on the form of Brière's Latin rendering of the Old Georgian text of Luke published in *PO* xxvii (1955), 302–448. For other, briefer accounts of the characteristics of Georgian in comparison with Greek, see Franz Zorell, *Grammatik zur altgeorgischen Bibelübersetzung, mit Textproben und Wörterverzeichnis* (Rome, 1930), pp. 6–8, and Joseph Molitor in *Die alte Übersetzungen des Neuen Testaments, die Kirchenväterzitaten und Lektionare*, ed. by K. Aland (Berlin and New York, 1972), pp. 318–25. B. M. M.]

[2] For further details the reader is referred to *La Langue géorgienne* by N. Marr and M. Brière (Paris, 1931). [The deficiencies of this grammar, as Dr. Birdsall has pointed out to me, are set forth in Hans Vogt's critical review of it in *JA* ccxxiii (juillet–décembre 1933; fascicule annexe), 142–5. B. M. M.]

[3] [For brief descriptions of the six manuscripts see nos. 2, 3, 4, 6, 11, and 13 in the list on pp. 186–9 above. B. M. M.]

Athos manuscript,[1] which is the result of several revisions on the basis of the Greek text,[2] comprises the 'Vulgate' of the Georgian Gospels, which was transmitted unchanged from the *editio principis* of 1709 to the present day.[3] In the following discussion we shall make use of our edition of the Georgian version of Luke's Gospel[4] for the Adysh, Opiza, and Tbet' manuscripts, Professor A. Shanidze's edition of the four Gospels[5] for the Džruč and Parḫal manuscripts, and a microfilm for manuscript no. 62 from Mount Athos, which has not yet been edited.

I. PHONETICS[6]

Under this heading we shall deal with the orthography of proper names, limiting ourselves to only one reference (in Luke) by way of illustrating each item.

A. *Consonants*

(1) Change of one consonant to another

(*a*) Dentals

(i) Very frequent change of voiceless τ to voiceless aspirated θ.

'Ελισάβετ] *Elisabet'* $G_{21-22-24}$; cf. *Elisabed* G_1G_{23}g (i. 5)
Ναζαρέτ] *Nazaret'* G_1G_2g (i. 26)
σάββατον] *šabat'* G_2g; cf. *šabad* G_1 (iv. 31)
Γεννησαρέτ] *Genesaret'* G_1G_2g (v. 1)
Λώτ] *Lot'* $G_1G_{21-22-23}$g; cf. *Lot* G_{24} (xvii. 28)

---

[1] For a description of this manuscript see Robert P. Blake's account under no. 62 in his 'Catalogue des manuscrits géorgiens de la bibliothèque de la Laure d'Iviron au Mont Athos', *ROC* xxix (1933–4), 251.

[2] Blake considered this manuscript, which presents a large number of corrections, to be the copy which St. George the Athonite corrected in making his revision of the text already corrected by St. Euthymius. For information concerning these two tenth- and eleventh-century scribes, see *Geschichte der kirchlichen georgischen Literatur, auf Grund des ersten Bandes der georgischen Literaturgeschichte von K. Kekelidze*, by Michael Tarchnišvili with the assistance of Julius Assfalg (Città del Vaticano, 1955), pp. 126–74.

[3] *PO* xxvii (1955), 291 f.

[4] Ibid. 275–457.

[5] *Two Old Recensions . . .* , pp. 179–293.

[6] [It will be observed that here and there variations of spelling among the Georgian manuscripts complicate the attempt to present tidy categories of the limitations of Georgian in representing Greek. B. M. M.]

(ii) Change of voiced δ to voiceless aspirated θ.

Δαβίδ] *Davit'* G_1G_2g (i. 27)

(iii) Change of voiceless τ to voiced δ.

'Ελισάβετ] *Elisabed* $G_1G_2$$_3$g; cf. *Elisabet'* $G_{21-22-24}$ (i. 5)
σάββατον] *šabad* G_1; cf. *šabat'* G_2g (iv. 31)

(*b*) Gutturals

(i) Change of voiceless κ to voiceless aspirated χ and to voiced γ.

Φαλεκ] *P'alek'* G_1; *P'aleg* G_2g (iii. 35)

(*c*) Labials

(i) Change of voiceless π to voiceless aspirated φ.

Καπερναούμ] *Kap'arnaom* G_1G_{23}; *Kap'arnaum* $G_{21-22-24}$; cf. *Kapernaum* g (iv. 23).

(ii) Change of voiceless aspirated φ to voiced β.

'Ιωσήφ] *Ioseb* $G_{21-22-23}$g; cf. *Iosep'* G_1G_{24} (i. 27)
Βηθφαγή] *Bet'bage* $G_1G_{21-22-23}$g; cf. *Bet'p'age* G_{24} (xix. 29)

(*d*) Sibilants

(i) Change of voiceless s to voiced ζ.

Φάρες] *P'arez* G_1G_2g (iii. 33)
Ματθαῖος] *Mat'eoz* $G_1G_{21-22-23}$; cf. *Mat'eos* G_{21}; *Matt'eos* g (vi. 15)
'Εμμαοῦς] *Emmaoz* g; cf. *Emmaüs* G_1G_{22}; *Evmaüs* G_{21}; *Evmaos* G_{23-24} (xxiv. 13)

(ii) Change of voiced ζ to voiceless s.

Βόοζ] *Boos* $G_1G_{21-22-23}$g; cf. *Bovoz* G_{24} (iii. 32)

(2) Dissimilation of consonants

Georgian does not favour the repetition of *l* or *r* in the same word and replaces one of the occurrences with the other letter.[1]

Βεελζεβούλ] *Berzebul* G_{23}; cf. *Belzebul* G_1G_{22}g; *Beelzebul* G_{21-24} (xi. 15)

---

[1] Cf. *La Langue géorgienne*, § 28.

(3) Epenthesis of a consonant.

> In order to avoid hiatus, the consonant *v* is inserted between two vowels, especially when one of them is *o*.[1] The consonant *h*, which is found in the same position, seems to have been taken from the Hebrew.

Ἰωάννης] *Iovane* $G_1G_{21-22-23}$g; *Iohane* G_{24} (i. 13)
Ἀβραάμ] *Abraham* G_2g; cf. *Abraam* G_1 (i. 73)
Βόοζ] *Bovoz* G_{24}; cf. *Boos* $G_1G_{21-22-23}$g (iii. 32)
Νῶε] *Nove* $G_{21-22-23}$; cf. *Noe* G_1G_{24}g (iii. 36)
Ἰωάννα] *Iohana* G_1G_2; cf. *Ioanna* g (viii. 3)
γέεννα] *gehenia* G_1G_2g (xii. 5)
Σιλωάμ] *Silovam* G_{23}; cf. *Siloam* $G_1G_{21-22-24}$g (xiii. 4)

(4) Reduction of two consonants

(a) The same consonant doubled

Ἰωάννης] *Iovane* $G_1G_{21-22-23}$g; *Iohane*$_{24}$ (i. 13)
Ἄννα] *Ana* $G_{21-22-23}$; cf. *Anna* G_1G_{24}g (ii. 36)
Φίλιππος] *P'ilipe* G_2G_1g (iii. 1)
Ἄννα] *Ana* G_1G_{22-23}; cf. *Anna* G_{21-24}g (iii. 2)
Ἰαννά] *Iane* G_1g; cf. *Ionne* $G_{21-22-23}$; *Ianne* G_{24} (iii. 24)
Ματταθίας] *Matat'* G_1G_2g (iii. 25)
Ναγγαί] *Nage* G_1G_2g (iii. 25)
Ματταθίας] *Matat'* G_1g; *Matit'* G_2 (iii. 26)
Ἰωαννᾶ] *Ioanan* g; cf. *Oanna* $G_1G_{21-22-24}$; *Onna* G_{23} (iii. 27)
Ματταθά] *Matat'an* $G_{21-23-24}$g; *Maat'an* G_{22}; cf. *Matt'an* G_1 (iii. 31)
Ἰεσσαί] *Iese* $G_1G_{21-22-23}$g; *Ieyse* G_{24} (iii. 32)
Ναασσών] *Naason* G_1G_2g (iii. 32)
σάββατον] *šapat'* G_1; *šabat'* G_2g (iv. 16)
Ἐλισσαῖος] *Elise* G_1G_2g (iv. 27)
Γεννησαρέτ] *Genesaret'* G_1G_2g (v. 1)
Ἰωάννα] *Iohana* G_1G_2; cf. *Ioanna* g (viii. 3)
Σουσάννα] *Susana* $G_1G_{22-23-24}$; *Susani* (or: *Susan*) G_{21}; cf. *Susanna* g (viii. 3)
γέεννα] *gehenia* G_1G_2g (xii. 5)
Βαραββᾶς] *Baraba* G_1G_2g (xxiii. 18)

[1] *La Langue géorgienne*, § 25, no. 1.

(*b*) Two different consonants belonging to the class of mutes

  (i) The dentals τθ reduce to θθ, ττ, or θ.

Ματθάτ] *Mat't'an* G$_{21-24}$; cf. *Matt'an* G$_1$G$_{22}$; *Matat'an* G$_{23}$g (iii. 24)

Ματθάτ] *Mattat'* g; cf. *Matat'* G$_1$G$_2$ (iii. 29)

Ματθαῖος] *Mat'eoz* G$_1$G$_{21-22-23}$; *Mat'eos* G$_{24}$; cf. *Matt'eos* g (vi. 15)

  (ii) The gutturals κχ reduce to χ.

Ζακχαῖος] *Zak'e* G$_1$G$_{21-22-23}$g; *Zak'ee* G$_{24}$ (xix. 2)

B. *Vowels*

  (1) Reduction of two vowels

    (*a*) The same vowel doubled

Βηθλεέμ] *Bet'lem* G$_1$G$_2$g (ii. 15)

'Ισαάκ] *Isak* G$_1$G$_{21-23}$g; cf. *Isaak* G$_{22-24}$ (iii. 34)

Νεεμάν] *Neman* G$_1$G$_{21-22-23}$g; cf. *Neeman* G$_{24}$ (iv. 27)

Βεελζεβούλ] *Belzebul* G$_1$G$_{22}$g; *Berzebul* G$_{23}$; cf. *Beelzebul* G$_{21-24}$ (xi. 15)

Note: Ἀαρών] *Ahron* G$_1$G$_2$g (i. 5), where the influence of Hebrew can be recognized.

    (*b*) Two different vowels forming a diphthong

'Ιτουραία] *Iturea* G$_2$; *Itwrea* g; cf. *Tyrii* G$_1$ (iii. 1)

Ναγγαί] *Nage* G$_1$G$_2$g (iii. 25)

Σεμεΐ] *Semi* g; cf. *Semei* G$_1$G$_{22-23-24}$; *Semii* G$_{21}$ (iii. 26)

'Ελιακείμ] *Eliakim* G$_1$G$_2$g (iii. 30)

Μαϊνάν] *Menan* G$_1$G$_2$; cf. *Maynan* g (iii. 31)

'Ιεσσαί] *Iese* G$_1$G$_{21-22-23}$g; *Ieyse* G$_{24}$ (iii. 32)

'Ελισσαῖος] *Elise* (instead of *Elisee*) G$_1$G$_2$g (iv. 27)

Βαρθολομαῖος] *Bart'lome* (instead of *Bart'lomee*) G$_1$G$_{21-22-23}$g; *Bart'olome* (instead of *Bart'olomee*) G$_{21}$ (vi. 14)

Ματθαῖος] *Mat'eoz* G$_1$G$_{21-22-23}$; *Mat'eos* G$_{24}$; *Matt'eos* g (vi. 15)

Ἀλφαῖος] *Alp'e* (instead of *Alp'ee*) G$_1$G$_2$g (vi. 15)

Γαλιλαία] *Galilea* G$_1$G$_2$; *Galile* (instead of *Galilee*) g (viii. 26)

'Ιάειρος] *Iairos* g; cf. *Iaros* G$_1$G$_2$ (viii. 41)

Ζακχαῖος] *Ẑak'e* (instead of *Ẑak'ee*) $G_1G_{21-22-23}g$; *Ẑak'ee* G_{21} (xix. 2)

Note: Καῖσαρ] *Keisar* $G_1G_{21-22-23}g$; *Keysar* G_{22} (xx. 24)

(2) Change of vowel η to diphthong *ey* (pronounced 'ê')

'Ισραήλ] *Israeyl* G_1G_2g (ii. 34)

Ἀσήρ] *Aseyr* G_1; cf. *Aser* G_2g (ii. 36)

'Ιερουσαλήμ] *Ierusaleym* (written in contracted form: *I‾eylm*) G_1G_2g (ii. 41). This orthography is preferable to the spelling *Ieyrusalem*.[1]

Ἀβιληνή] *Abileyna* $G_{21-22-23}$; cf. *Abileni* G_1; *Abilena* $G_{24}g$ (iii. 1)

'Ηρωδιάς] *Eyrodia* G_{24}; cf. *Herodia* $G_1G_{21-22-23}g$ (iii. 19)

'Ηλί] *Eyli* G_{21-23}; cf. *Eli* $G_1G_{22-24}g$ (iii. 23)

'Ιωσήφ] *Ioseyp'* G_{24}; cf. *Iosep'* G_1; *Ioseb* $G_{21-22-23}g$ (iii. 26)

'Ρησά] *Reysa* G_1; cf. *Resa* G_2g (iii. 27)

Νηρί] *Neyri* $G_{21-23-24}$; cf. *Neri* $G_1G_{22}g$ (iii. 27)

Ἤρ] *Eyr* G_1G_{21-23}; cf. *Er* $G_{22-24}g$ (iii. 28)

Σήμ] *Seym* G_{21}; cf. *Sem* $G_1G_{22-23-24}g$ (iii. 36)

Μαλελεήλ] *Maleleyl* G_{23-24}; cf. *Malilel* G_1; *Malel* G_{21-22}; *Maleleil* g (iii. 37)

Σήθ] *Seyt'* G_1G_{21-24}; cf. *Set'* G_{22-23}; *Seit'* g (iii. 38)

'Ηλίας] *Eyelia* G_1; cf. *Elia* G_2g (iv. 25)

'Ηρώδης] *Heyrode* G_{22}; cf. *Erode* G_1; *Herode* $G_{21-23-24}g$ (viii. 3)

Μωσῆς] *Moseys* G_{21}; cf. *Mose* $G_1G_{21-22-23}g$ (xx. 37)

2. MORPHOLOGY

A. *Declension*

(1) Nouns or substantives

Proper names generally end in a vowel.

(a) Change of *a* to *e*

'Ιαννά] *Iane* G_1g; *Ionne* $G_{21-22-23}$; *Ianne* G_{24} (iii. 24)

Γαλιλαία] *Galile* (instead of *Galilee*) g; cf. *Galilea* G_1G_2 (viii. 26)

---

[1] Cf. A. Shanidze, *Caucasus Polyglottus*, i. 99.

(*b*) Change of αs to *a* and of ιαs to *ia* or *e*

Ζαχαρίας] *Zak'aria* $G_1G_{21-23-24}g$; cf. *Zak'arian* G_{22} (i. 5)
Ἡλίας] *Elia* G_1G_2g (i. 17)
Λυσανίας] *Lusania* G_1; *Lwsane* G_2g (iii. 1)
Καϊάφας] *Kayapa* G_1G_{22}; *Kaiapa* $G_{21-23-24}g$ (iii. 2)
Ἡσαΐας] *Esaya* G_1; *Esaia* G_2g (iii. 4)
Ἡρωδιάς] *Herodia* $G_1G_{21-22-23}g$; *Eyrodia* G_{24} (iii. 19)
Ἀνδρέας] *Andria* G_1G_{22}; *Andrea* $G_{21-23-24}g$ (vi. 14)
Θωμᾶς] *T'oma* G_1G_2g (vi. 15)
Ἰούδας] *Iuda* G_1G_2g (vi. 16)
Χουζᾶς] *K'oza* $G_1G_{21-22-23}g$; *K'uza* G_{24} (viii. 3)
Ἰωνᾶς] *Iona* G_1G_2g (xi. 29)
μαμωνᾶς] *mamona* G_1G_2g (xvi. 11)
Βαραββᾶς] *Baraba* G_1G_2g (xxiii. 18)
Κλεόπας] *Kleopa* G_1G_2g (xxiv. 18)

(*c*) Change of ης to *e*

Ἰωάννης] *Iovane* $G_1G_{21-22-23}g$; *Iohane* G_{24} (i. 13)
Ἰορδάνης] *Iordane* G_1G_2g (iii. 3)
Ἡρώδης] *Erode* G_1; *Herode* $G_{21-23-24}g$; *Heyrode* G_{22}
   (viii. 3)
Μωσῆς] *Mose* $G_1G_{21-22-23}g$; cf. *Moseys* G_{24} (xx. 37)

(*d*) Change of ος to *e* (or dropped) and of ιος to *ia* (or
dropped)

Αὐγοῦστος] *Avguste* G_{24}; cf. *Agustos* G_1; *Agwstos* G_{21-22-}
   $_{23}g$ (ii. 1)
Κυρήνιος] *Kwrine* G_1G_2g (ii. 2)
Τιβέριος] *Tiberia* G_1; *Tiber* G_2g (iii. 1)
Πιλᾶτος] *Pilate* G_1G_2g (iii. 1)
Φίλιππος] *P'ilipe* G_1G_2g (iii. 1)
Χριστός] *K'riste* G_1G_2g (iii. 15)
Πέτρος] *Petre* G_1G_2g (v. 8)
Ἰάκωβος] *Iakob* G_1G_2g (v. 10)
Ζεβεδαῖος] *Zebede* (instead of *Zebedee*) G_1G_2g (v. 10)
Βαρθολομαῖος] *Bart'lome* (instead of *Bart'lomee*) G_1G_{21-}
   $_{22-23}g$; *Bart'olome* (instead of *Bart'olomee*) G_{21} (vi. 14)
Ἀλφαῖος] *Alp'e* (instead of *Alp'ee*) G_1G_2g (vi. 15)
Λάζαρος] *Lazare* G_1G_2g (xvi. 20)

Ζακχαῖος] * Zak'e* (instead of *Zak'ee*) $G_1G_{21-22-23}g$; *Zak'ee* G_{24} (xix. 2)

(e) Expansion of *a* to *an*

Ζαχαρίας] *Zak'arian* G_{22}; cf. *Zak'aria* $G_1G_{21-23-24}g$ (i. 5)

'Ιωαννᾶ] *Ioanan* g; cf. *Oanna* $G_1G_{21-22-24}$; *Onna* G_{23} (iii. 27)

Ματταθά] *Matt'an* G_1; *Matat'an* $G_{21-23-24}g$; *Maat'an* G_{22} (iii. 31)

Note: Ματθάτ] *Matt'an* G_1G_{22}; *Mat't'an* G_{21-24}; *Matat'-an* $G_{23}g$ (iii. 24)

(2) Reflexive pronoun.

The reflexive pronouns, 'myself', 'yourself', 'himself', etc., are expressed in Georgian by the noun 'the head' (or by another substantive having an analogous sense), generally accompanied by the possessive adjective ('my head', 'your head', 'his head', etc.).

βάλε σεαυτόν] 'praecipita temetipsum' (*litt.* 'caput tuum') G_2g; cf. 'cade' G_1 (iv. 9)

ἐμαυτὸν ἠξίωσα] 'egometipse' (*litt.* 'caput meum') 'dignus videbar' G_1G_2; 'a memetipso' (*litt.* 'capite meo') 'dignus videbar' g (vii. 7)

καὶ τὴν ἑαυτοῦ ψυχήν] 'semetipsum quoque' (*litt.* 'caput quoque suum') G_1G_2; cf. 'animam quoque suam' g (xiv. 26)

εἰς ἑαυτὸν δὲ ἐλθών] 'cogitavit *in* semetipso (*litt.* 'capite suo') G_2; 'cum venisset ad semetipsum' (*litt.* 'caput suum') g; cf. 'rediit ad mentem suam' G_1 (xv. 17)

ἐπιδείξετε ἑαυτούς] 'ostendite vos' (*litt.* 'capita') G_1; 'ostendite vosmetipsos' (*litt.* 'capita vestra') G_2g (xvii. 14)

B. *Conjugation*

(1) Objective pronominal particles

Objects of the verb (direct or indirect), which may be nouns or pronouns, are indicated in the verbal formation by pronominal particles called objectives.

When the objects are expressed before or after the verb, we omit these pronominal particles in the translation to avoid useless repetition. But when they are not expressed explicitly, we have translated these pronominal particles by putting them in italics and without brackets.

ἀποκριθείς] 'respondit *ei*' G₁G₂g (i. 19)

εἶπεν αὐτῷ] 'et dixit *ei*' G₁G₂g (i. 19)

ἀπολύεις] 'dimitte *me*' G₂₁₋₂₂₋₂₃; cf. 'dimittes' G₁; 'dimitte' G₂₄g (ii. 29)

ἀπὸ τοῦ αἴροντος τὰ σά] 'qui auferet *tibi*' G₁; 'qui auferet tibi' G₂g (vi. 30)

κατέδησε τὰ τραύματα αὐτοῦ] 'et alligavit *ei* vulnus illud' G₁G₂₁₋₂₂₋₂₃; cf. 'et alligavit ei vulnus illud' G₂₄; '*cum* alligasset *ei* vulnus illud' g (x. 34)

ἔλεγε δέ] 'et dicebat *eis*' G₂₁₋₂₂₋₂₃; cf. 'et dicebat eis' G₁g; 'et dicebat' G₂₄ (xiii. 6)

(2) Indication of the plural

When a transitive verb in the future or aorist of the active voice has a direct object in the plural, this is indicated in the verb form. But when the direct object is expressed neither before nor after the verb, we add it in the translation under either the nominal form (in italics and with brackets) or the pronominal form (in italics and without brackets).

ἐπέβλεψεν] 'coniecit ⟨*oculos*⟩' G₁g; cf. 'respexit' G₂ (i. 48)

ἀπολύετε] 'dimittite ⟨*debita*⟩' G₁; cf. 'dimittite' G₂g (vi. 37)

ἐξέμαξε] 'extersit *eos mihi*' G₁G₂₁₋₂₂₋₂₄: 'extersit *eos*' G₂₃g (vii. 44)

περιζωσάμενος] 'praecinge ⟨*lumbos tuos*⟩' G₂g; cf. 'cingulum cinge' G₁ (xvii. 8)

ἀνάβλεψον] 'recipe *eos*' G₁G₂g (xviii. 42)

ἀνέβλεψε] 'recepit *eos*' G₁G₂g (xviii. 43)

C. *Invariable words. Negatives.*

The two negatives *ara* and *ver* differ in that the former expresses the reality of the fact and the latter its possibility. In order to note this difference in our translation, when a verb is accompanied by the negative *ver*, we customarily precede its infinitive form with the verb 'possum,' placing it in italics and without brackets.

μὴ εὑρόντες] 'non *potuerunt* invenire' G₂; cf. 'cum non invenissent' G₁; 'non invenerunt' g (ii. 45)

οὐ συνῆκαν τὸ ῥῆμα] 'non *potuerunt* intelligere verbum illud' G₂g; cf. 'non cognoverunt verbum eius' G₁ (ii. 50)

οὐκ ἤκουσαν] 'non *potuerunt* audire' g; cf. 'non audierunt' G₁G₂ (x. 24)

οὐκ ὄψεσθε] 'non *poteritis* videre' G₁; cf. 'non videbitis' G₂g (xvii. 22)

3. SYNTAX

A. *Order of words*

In our Latin translation we retain the order of words in the Georgian text except for the following three cases:

(1) Postpositives corresponding to Greek prepositions

ἐν τῷ ναῷ] 'in templo illo' (*litt.* 'templo illo in') G₁G₂g (i. 21)

ἐπὶ γῆς εἰρήνη] 'in terra (*litt.* 'terra super') pax' G₁G₂g (ii. 14)

(2) The conditional conjunction *t'u* with the sense of 'if'

ὅταν κληθῇς] 'si vocaverit (*litt.* 'vocaverit si') *te* aliquis' G₁; 'cum vocaverit *te* aliquis' G₂g (xiv. 10)

(3) The adversative conjunction *holo*, signifying 'but'

ἡ δέ] 'illa autem' (*litt.* 'autem illa') G₂g; cf. 'et illa' G₁ (i. 29)

B. *Function of words*

(1) Determination of the noun by means of the definite article

Georgian makes up for its lack of the article by placing after the noun the adjective or demonstrative pronoun in one of the three persons (usually the third).[1]

---

[1] Cf. *La Langue géorgienne*, § 310.

ἐν ταῖς ἡμέραις] '*in* diebus illis' G₁G₂g (i. 5)

τοῦ βασιλέως] 'regis illius' G₁; cf. 'regis' G₂g (i. 5)

τῆς 'Ιουδαίας] 'Iudaeae' G₁G₂g (i. 5)

On the one hand proper nouns (as in the last citation), and on the other hand common nouns modified by a qualifying adjective or by another noun playing the role of complement, are not usually followed by a demonstrative pronoun in the third person.

τὸ ὄνομα τῆς παρθένου] 'nomen virginis illius' G₁G₂g (i. 27)

τὸν θρόνον τοῦ πατρὸς αὐτοῦ] 'thronum patris eius (*litt.* 'sui')' G₁G₂g (i. 32)

ἡ μήτηρ τοῦ Κυρίου] 'mater Domini' G₁G₂g (i. 43)

τῶν ἐχθρῶν ἡμῶν] 'inimicorum nostrorum' G₂g; cf. 'inimicorum' G₁ (i. 74)

ὁ πατήρ σου κἀγώ] 'pater tuus et ego' G₁; 'ego et pater tuus' G₂g (ii. 48)

Notes

(*a*) Placed after the noun, 'ille' corresponds to the definite article; placed before the noun, 'ille' corresponds to the demonstrative adjective.

ταύτας τὰς ἡμέρας] 'dies illos' (τάς) G₁g; 'dies hos' (ταύτας) G₂ (i. 24)

ἐν ταῖς ἡμέραις ταύταις] '*in* diebus illis' (ταῖς) G₁: *om.* G₂₁; 'in his (ταύταις) diebus' G₂₂₋₂₃₋₂₄; 'in illis (ταύταις) diebus' g (i. 39)

(*b*) Is it not necessary to relate this usage of 'ille' to the adverb 'inde' (derived from the same adjective or third person demonstrative pronoun) in the following construction?

ἀπὸ τῆς πόλεως] 'inde de civitate' (= 'de civitate illa') G₁G₂g (ix. 5)

ἀπὸ τοῦ ὄρους] 'inde de monte' (= 'de monte illo') G₁G₂g (ix. 37)

'inde de mundo' (= 'de mundo illo') G₂; 'inde' g (xvi. 9)

ἀπὸ τῆς προσευχῆς] 'inde ab oratione' (= 'ab oratione illa') G₁G₂g (xxii. 45)

(2) Possessive adjective of the third person

While good usage in Latin employs 'eius' or 'suus' according as the possessor is or is not the same as the subject of the phrase, Georgian, on the other hand, can make use of the adjective or demonstrative pronoun of one of the three persons in the first case, or of the reflexive pronoun 'the head' (see above) in the second case, placing one or the other in the genitive. Although Georgian is far from rigorously observing this rule, our translation conforms to the Latin syntax.

ἐν ταῖς ἡμέραις αὐτῶν] '*in* diebus suis' (*litt.* 'eorum' G₂g) G₁G₂g (i. 7)

ἐπὶ τῷ ὀνόματι τοῦ πατρὸς αὐτοῦ] 'ad nomen patris eius' (*litt.* 'sui' G₂) G₁G₂g (i. 59)

εἰς τὴν πόλιν αὐτῶν] *in* civitatem suam' (*litt.* 'eorum' G₁) G₁G₂g (ii. 39)

εἰς τὴν χεῖρα αὐτοῦ] '*in* manum istius' G₁; '*in* manum eius' G₂g (xv. 22)

δέκα δούλους ἑαυτοῦ] 'decem servos suos' (*litt.* 'eius' G₂₁) G₁G₂g (xix. 23)

(3) Interrogative adjective and pronoun

When two interrogative words closely follow each other in a single question, we place one of them within square brackets (especially the superfluous word).

ποταπός] 'quomodo [quid]' G₁; 'quomodo' G₂g (i. 29)

τί ἄρα] 'quidnam [quid]' G₁; 'quidnam' G₂g (i. 66)

πόσον] 'quantum [quid]' G₁; 'quantum' G₂g (xvi. 5, 7)

τίς] '[quomodo] quisnam' G₁; 'quisnam' G₂g (xix. 3)

(4) Infinitive

It sometimes happens that the infinitive in Georgian does not differ in function from a noun.

ἐθαύμαζον ἐν τῷ χρονίζειν αὐτόν] 'mirabantur quod moraretur ille' (*litt.* '*in* mora illa eius') G₁; 'mirabantur moram illam eius' G₂g (i. 21)

ἀπογράφεσθαι πᾶσαν τὴν οἰκουμένην] 'censio totius mundi' G₁; 'ut censeretur totus mundus' G₂g (ii. 1) ἐν αἷς δεῖ ἐργάζεσθαι] 'in quibus oportet operari' (*litt.* 'opus') G₁G₂g (xiii. 14)

(5) Prepositions and postpositives

(*a*) Because in Georgian, as in other languages, a preposition or postpositive has several meanings, it is not always a question of using the same word when translating into Latin. Conversely, a Latin preposition does not necessarily correspond to the same Georgian preposition or postpositive.

(*b*) The two prepositions that correspond to ἐν or εἰς and ἐπί in Greek and to 'in' and 'super' in Latin are often understood in Georgian, the dative/accusative which they govern having a locative or a temporal sense. Therefore in our translation we place 'in' and 'super' in italics and without brackets.

ἐν τῷ ναῷ] '*in* templo illo' G₁; 'in templo illo' G₂g (i. 22)
εἰς τὸν οἶκον] '*in* domum illam' G₁; '*in* domum' G₂g (i. 40)
ἐν ταῖς ἡμέραις ἐκείναις] '*in* diebus illis' (ταῖς) G₁; 'in illis (ἐκείναις) diebus' G₂g (ii. 1)
ἐπὶ τὸν τράχηλον αὐτοῦ] '*super* collum eius' G₁; 'super collum eius' G₂g (xv. 20)
Note: εἰσελθὼν εἰς τὸν ναόν] '*cum* ingressus esset templum illud' G₁; 'et ingressus est templum' G₂g, where the verb 'ingredior' governs the accusative without a preposition.

(*c*) In Georgian the instrumental (which has the varied meanings of the Latin ablative) is sometimes used for ἐν followed by the dative. In translating we employ various prepositions, such as 'in' and 'cum' printed in roman type and without brackets.

ἐν πνεύματι καὶ δυνάμει] 'in spiritu (*instr.*) et virtute (*instr.*)' G₁G₂g (i. 17)
ἐν ἀφέσει ἁμαρτιῶν αὐτῶν] 'cum remissione (*instr.*) peccatorum nostrorum' ('eorum' g) G₂g; cf. 'ad remittendum peccata eorum' G₁ (i. 77)
ἐν εἰρήνῃ] 'in pace (*instr.*)' G₁G₂g (ii. 29)

(*d*) Sometimes εἰς followed by the accusative is translated in Georgian by the final clause (motion toward); we render it by means of the prepositions 'in' or 'ad' printed in roman type and without brackets.

εἰς τὸν οἶκον] 'in domum (*fin.*)' G₁G₂g (i. 56)

εἰς τὸν οὐρανόν] 'ad caelum (*fin.*)' G₁G₂g (ii. 15)

(6) Temporal conjunction 'cum'

In order to render the Greek participle (which is very frequently used in the Gospels), the Georgian translator often employs a temporal preposition introduced by the subordinate conjunction 'cum', which is either expressed or understood; in the latter case we print 'cum' in italics and without brackets.[1]

πορευόμενοι] '*cum* ambularent' G₁; cf. 'et ambulabant' G₂g (i. 6)

ἀγραυλοῦντες] '*cum* in agris starent' G₂g; cf. 'foris stantes' G₁ (ii. 8)

ἐπιγνοὺς δέ] '*cum* intellexissent' G₁g; '*cum* intellexisset' G₂ (v. 22)

κηρύσσων καὶ εὐαγγελιζόμενος] '*cum* praedicaret et evangelizaret' G₁G₂g (viii. 1)

δεξάμενος ποτήριον] '*cum* accepisset calicem' G₁G₂₁₋₂₂₋₂₃; cf. 'accepit calicem' G₂₄g (xxii. 17)

(7) Enclitics

(*a*) The particle *ve* sometimes indicates identity ('the same'), sometimes generality.[2]

(i) Joined to the adverb of place 'eo', it corresponds to the adverb 'eodem'.

ὑπέστρεψαν] 'reversi sunt eodem' G₁; cf. 'reversi sunt et abierunt' G₂g (ii. 39)

ἀνέπεμψεν αὐτόν] 'et misit eodem' G₁; cf. 'et miserunt eum' (*om.* g) G₂₁₋₂₄g; 'et misit eum' G₂₂₋₂₃ (xxiii. 11)

(ii) Joined to a personal pronoun in the plural or to a noun indicating number, it adds the sense of 'omnes', which we place in italics and without brackets.

---

[1] *La Langue géorgienne*, § 424, no. 1 *in fine*, and *PO* xxvii (1955), 288–90.
[2] Ibid., § 426, no. 3.

αὐτοί] 'illi *omnes*' G₁G₂g (xi. 19)

οἱ δέκα] 'decem *omnes*' G₂g; cf. 'hi decem' G₁ (xvii. 17)

οἱ γὰρ ἕπτα] 'etenim septem *omnes*' G₁; 'etenim septem *omnes* illi' G₂g (xx. 33)

(b) The particle *ca*, which renders the conjunction καί in the sense of 'quoque', is added to the relative pronoun and adverb and to the interrogative pronoun and adverb, as is ordinarily the case in medieval and modern Georgian.

οὗ] 'ubi quoque' G₁G₂g (iv. 16)

ὁ καλέσας] 'qui quoque vocavit' G₁G₂g (vii. 39)

ᾧ τὸ πλεῖον ἐχαρίσατο] 'cui quoque plus dimisit' G₁G₂g (vii. 43)

οὗ] 'quo quoque' G₂₃g; cf. 'in quem' G₁G₂₁; 'quo' G₂₂₋₂₄ (xxiv. 28)

The foregoing account of various particularities of the Georgian language is designed to draw attention to certain features germane to the language itself. As we have previously stated, these variants did not originate in the particular readings of the original text from which the Georgian version of the Gospel of Luke derives.

Still other variants have arisen—purely accidentally—from confusion of similar words in Georgian which resemble each other either in pronunciation or in spelling.

κόφινοι] 'turres' (*godoli*) G₁; cf. 'cophinos' (*godori*) G₂g (ix. 17)

ἐν αὐτῇ] 'tunc' (*mašin*) G₁; 'in illa' (*mas šina*, or abbreviated *m˜s š˜a*) G₂g (xxiv. 18)

The following two variants, which arose through confusion, are found in almost all the manuscripts and in all the editions—yet are overlooked in all revisions.

συγκύπτουσα] 'tristis' (*dagonebul*) G₁G₂₁₋₂₂₋₂₃g; cf. 'incurvata' (*dagunebul* or *dagownebul*) G₂₄ (xiii. 11)

ἐξεκρέματο] 'subiectus erat' (*damorčilebul*) G₁G₂g, where 'suspensus erat' (*damokidebul*) is expected (xix. 48)

In addition to what was said about traces of influence of the Greek text in the Georgian version, the following three passages may be noted.

ἥψατό μού τις] 'aliquis (τις) tetigit me' $G_1G_{21-22-24}g$; 'quis (τίς) tetigit me?' G_{23} (viii. 46).

ὁ ἰσχυρότερος αὐτοῦ] 'fortior eo' G_1; 'fortior eius' G_2g, where αὐτοῦ, which is the complement of the comparative, is taken as the possessive genitive (xi. 22).

ὅτι αὐτὸς ἐγώ εἰμι] 'quia ego idem sum' G_1; 'quia ipse ego sum' G_2g, αὐτός having these two meanings in Greek (xxiv. 39).

V

The Ethiopic Version

I. THE INTRODUCTION OF CHRISTIANITY INTO ETHIOPIA
AND THE TRANSLATION OF THE NEW TESTAMENT

THE early history of Ethiopia, or Abyssinia,[1] is shrouded in legend. Native tradition ascribes the name of the country and the foundation of the state to Ethiops, the son of Cush, the son of Ham. The queen of Sheba who visited Solomon is identified with an Ethiopian queen, Makeda, who bore to Solomon a son, Menelik. The tradition continues that Menelik, after being educated in Jerusalem by his father, returned to the old capital Aksum (modern Axum), bringing with him Jewish priests and the ark of the covenant. The latter, which had been taken by stealth from the temple in Jerusalem, was deposited in the cathedral at Aksum. The official version of this legend, much elaborated, is contained in a voluminous work, greatly treasured, known as the *Kebra-Nagast*, or 'Glory of Kings', the current recension of which dates from the fourteenth century of the Christian era.[2]

---

[1] A distinction between the terms 'Ethiopia' and 'Abyssinia' is sometimes made on the basis that the former has a historical and the latter a geographical reference (so Enno Littmann, *Abessinien* (Hamburg, 1935), p. 13). The two terms have entirely different origins. The name 'Abyssinians' is of Semitic derivation (though whether, as many have thought, it is from the south Arabian 'Ḥabashat' is now made doubtful by A. K. Irvine, 'On the Identity of Ḥabashat in the South Arabian Inscriptions', *JSS*, x (1965), 178–96) and refers to the ethnic and political entity which flourished during the old Aksumite kingdom. The word 'Ethiopians', on the other hand, as a personal name goes back to Mycenaean Greek of the second millennium B.C., and comes later to designate 'People with burnt faces' or 'People with burning, radiant faces' (cf. A. Dihle, *Umstrittene Daten. Untersuchungen zum Auftreten der Griechen am Roten Meer* (Köln–Opladen, 1965), pp. 65–79, and Ernst Hammerschmidt, *Äthiopien. Christliches Reich zwischen Gestern und Morgen* (Wiesbaden, 1967), pp. 150 f.). In the Septuagint Αἰθίοψ and Αἰθιοπία are the standard renderings of 'Cush' (כּוּשׁ), except in Gen. x. 7, where the transliteration Χούς is used.

For bibliography on Ethiopica, ancient and modern, an indispensable tool is George F. Black's 'Ethiopica and Amharica; A List of Works in the New York Public Library', *Bulletin of the New York Public Library*, xxxii (1928), 443–81, 528–62.

[2] First edited by Carl Bezold in *AbhMu*, xxiii, 1 (Munich, 1905); edited sub-

Chary of relying upon such legendary sources, modern scholars are content to sketch only in the broadest outline the several waves of Hamitic (Cushite) and Semitic invaders that subjugated the indigenous Negroid population. Between 1000 B.C. and 400 B.C. Semitic intruders from south-west Arabia (Yemen) brought with them a more highly developed social organization, architecture, and art, as well as a system of writing. Although the origin of the Ethiopic alphabet has been disputed, most linguists today regard it as a development from the South Semitic alphabet known as Sabaean.[1] From the evidence of inscriptions it appears that in the first half of the fourth century A.D. Sabaean speech and script were replaced by the early Ethiopic language and writing. While it is probable that the script as a whole was a gradual development of the South Semitic alphabet, the introduction of vocalization was no doubt effected by a single individual. The vowel following each Ethiopic consonant is expressed by adding small appendages to the right or the left of each of the basic characters, or at the top or the bottom, by shortening or lengthening one of its main strokes, and by other differentiations. There are thus seven forms of each of twenty-six letters. Unlike other Semitic scripts Ethiopic is read from left to right.

Of the various settlements formed by the invaders the most important was that centred at Aksum, whose port was Adulis on the Gulf of Zula, a sheltered inlet of the Red Sea. Through this port a whiff of Greek culture reached Aksum, as can be deduced from the discovery of a number of Greek inscriptions, some of which date from about the first century A.D.[2] The epigraphical evidence is supported also by literary evidence. The *Periplus*

sequently by E. A. Wallis Budge under the title, *The Queen of Sheba and her Only Son, Menyelek . . .* (London, 1922).

[1] Earlier scholars sought the source of the Ethiopic alphabet in such widely diverse alphabets as Greek, Syriac, Coptic, Samaritan, and Indian scripts, or even the runes (cf. David Diringer, *The Alphabet, a Key to the History of Mankind*, 3rd edn., i (New York, 1948), 179). More recently Jacques Ryckmans (*Bibliotheca orientalis*, xii (1955), 2–8) and A. J. Drewes (*Annales d'Éthiopie*, i (1955), 121–6), have argued that the Ethiopic alphabet had its origin in a Thamūdic (north Arabian) form of writing; but see the objections to this theory raised by W. Leslau (*AJA* lxii (1958), 112) and Edward Ullendorff (*The Ethiopians, an Introduction to Country and People*, 2nd edn. (London, 1965), p. 133 n. 1).

[2] Enno Littmann, *Sabaische, griechische und altabessinische Inschriften* (*Deutsche Aksum-Expedition*, iv; Berlin, 1913), pp. 2–5, and idem, 'Äthiopische Inschriften', *Miscellanea Academica Berolinensia*, ii. 2 (Berlin, 1950), 97–127. Cf. also Sergew Hable-Selassie, *Beziehungen äthiopiens zur griechische-romischen Welt* (Bonn, 1964).

Maris Erythraei, an anonymous account of travel and trade on the
Red Sea and the Indian Ocean written in the latter half of the
first century A.D., describes the port of Adulis and states that
eight days' journey inland lay the metropolis of the Aksumites,
ruled by Zoscales, 'who is miserly in his ways and always striving
for more, but otherwise upright and acquainted with Greek
literature (γραμμάτων Ἑλληνικῶν ἔμπειρος)'.[1]

The time and circumstances of the planting of the Church in
Ethiopia are difficult to ascertain. The account in Acts viii. 26–39
of the conversion by Philip of an Ethiopian who was chamberlain
of the Candace (or queen) of the Ethiopians is often assumed to
have a bearing on the introduction of Christianity into Ethiopia.[2]
Apart from other considerations, however, it is fatal to this interpretation that evidence is lacking that Ethiopia was governed at
that time by a woman, whereas it is known that Candace was the
title of the queens who ruled for some centuries over the kingdom
of Meroë, which, lying to the north of the kingdom of Aksum,
was often confused with it.[3] Conflicting traditions in the early
Church assign the evangelization of Ethiopia to different apostles.
Thus Rufinus[4] and Socrates[5] report that Matthew preached in
Ethiopia;[6] Gelasios of Cyzicus[7] links the name of Bartholomew
with that country; and the confused account concerning the
preaching of the apostles which is attributed to Epiphanius of

---

[1] Wilfred H. Schoff, *The Periplus of the Erythraean Sea* (New York, 1912), p. 23;
cf. also A. H. M. Jones and E. Monroe, *A History of Abyssinia* (Oxford, 1935),
repr. as *A History of Ethiopia* (1955), p. 22, and Albrecht Dihle, *Umstrittene Daten*,
pp. 9 ff. It is worth noting that coins of Axum bore Greek characters down to the
eighth century; see Arturo Anzani, 'Numismatica Axumita', *Rivista Italiana di
numismatica e scienze affini*, xxxix (1926), 5–110.

[2] The assumption was made as early as Irenaeus (*Adv. Haer.* IV. xxiii. 2) and
Eusebius (*Hist. eccl.* II. i. 13).

[3] See, e.g., K. Lake and H. J. Cadbury in vol. iv of *The Beginnings of Christianity*
(London, 1933), pp. 95 f.; Dale H. Moore, 'Christianity in Ethiopia', *Church
History*, v (1936), 271; and Albrecht Dihle, op. cit., pp. 42 f.

[4] *Hist. eccl.* x. 9.

[5] *Hist. eccl.* i. 19.

[6] The tradition that Matthew preached in Ethiopia is expanded with many
details in the *Martyrium Matthaei*, composed in Ethiopia after 524 and preserved
in translation in the so-called Abdias Collection (J. A. Fabricius, *Codex apocryphus
Novi Testamenti*, ed. sec. ii (Hamburg, 1719), 636–68; on the Abdias Collection see
R. A. Lipsius, *Die apokryphen Apostelgeschichten und Apostellegenden*, i (Braunschweig,
1883), 124, 168, and 223; ii. 2 (1884), 124–41.

[7] *Hist. eccl.* iii. 9; cf. Anton Glas, *Die Kirchengeschichte des Gelasios von Kaisareia.
Die Vorlage für die beiden letzten Bücher der Kirchengeschichte Rufins* (Leipzig, 1914),
pp. 48 f.

Cyprus[1] mentions Ethiopia in connection with the work of Andrew in evangelizing the Scythians, the Sogdianoi and Gorsinians (?), and those who lived in Sebastopolis the Great.

Except for a brief comment by Origen ('The Gospel is not said to have been preached to *all* the Ethiopians, especially to such as live beyond the River'),[2] the first more or less firm literary evidence we have for the presence of Christianity in Ethiopia comes from the end of the fourth century. According to Rufinus,[3] it was during the time of Constantine the Great (about 330) that two young men, Frumentius and Ædesius, accompanied their uncle, a philosopher from Tyre named Meropius, on a voyage on the Red Sea. The ship having stopped at a port on the Ethiopian coast for provisions, the natives attacked and murdered the crew and Meropius; only Frumentius and Ædesius survived. The two youths were taken captive to Aksum, where they won confidence and honour, and eventually were allowed to preach Christianity. Some time later Ædesius returned to Tyre; Frumentius, after converting the royal family to the new faith, went to Alexandria, where he obtained missi-wonary coorkers from Athanasius, and was himself consecrated bishop and head of the Ethiopian Church, with the title *Abba Salama*, 'Father of Peace', which is still in use along with the later *Abuna*, 'Our Father'. Although there are doubtless many unhistorical elements in this romantic story, it may well preserve an essentially authentic core, particularly in view of Rufinus' claim that he had learned the facts 'from the mouth of Ædesius himself . . . who was later made a priest in Tyre'.

---

[1] *Prophetarum vitae fabulosae, indices apostolorum discipulorumque Domini . . . vindicata*, ed. by Theodor Schermann (Leipzig, 1907), pp. 108 f. The manuscripts present variant readings for Sogdianoi and Gorsinians (= Georgians?). Cf. also Francis Dvornik, *The Idea of Apostolicity in Byzantium and the Legend of the Apostle Andrew* (Cambridge, Mass., 1958), p. 174 n. 111, and pp. 208 f.

[2] *In Matth. Comm.*, ser. 39 (Lommatzsch, iv, p. 269 f.). On the other hand, however, Origen's comment that Ps. lxxii. 9 (ἐνώπιον αὐτοῦ προσπεσοῦνται Αἰθίοπες καὶ οἱ ἐχθροὶ αὐτοῦ χοῦν λείξουσιν) and Zeph. iii. 10 (ἐκ περάτων ποταμῶν Αἰθιοπίας οἴσουσιν θυσίας μοι) are to be fulfilled at the second coming of Christ suggests that he regarded the Ethiopians as pagan (*Hom.* xvi. 3 *in lib. Jesu Nave*, p. 148).

[3] *Hist. eccl.* i. 9. The story is repeated, with some variations, in the ecclesiastical histories of Socrates (i. 19), Sozomen (ii. 24), and Theodoret (i. 23). For additional information about Frumentius from Ethiopic sources, see Carlo Conti Rossini, 'A propos des textes éthiopiens concernant Salāmā (Frumentius)', *Æthiops: Bulletin Ge'ez*, i (1922), 2–4, 17–18.

In any case, apart from the credibility of certain details in Rufinus' account, one can point to epigraphical and numismatic evidence that confirms his central point concerning the arrival of Christianity in Ethiopia during the fourth century. Among the numerous stelae found at Aksum several record in Greek, Sabaean, and Ethiopic the military exploits of King Ezana, whose reign is dated by most scholars to the second and third quarters of the fourth century.[1] Besides mentioning Ezana's efforts to defend his kingdom and to safeguard the routes which meant everything to its prosperity, the inscriptions also provide evidence bearing upon the king's conversion to Christianity. In the last of a series of several inscriptions found at Aksum, Ezana no longer attributes his military victories to the tutelary god Maḥrem (i.e. Ares), but to 'the Lord of the heavens who has power over all beings in heaven and earth'.[2] Still more explicit is a recently discovered stele on which Ezana makes confession of his faith in the triune God, Father, Son, and Holy Spirit, through whose support and guidance the king was enabled to overcome his enemies.[3] Likewise numismatic evidence supplies confirmatory data bearing on Ezana's conversion to Christianity. His early coins bear the astral symbols of the crescent and the disc, whereas his later coins bear the cross.[4]

How rapidly the new faith spread among the populace we have no information. There is no indication that the conversion of the king was followed by any royal decree for the enforcement of the

[1] So, e.g., Alfred Rahlfs, 'Zur den altabessinischen Königsinschriften', *OC*, N.S. ii (1916), 282–305; A. Kammerer, *Essai sur l'histoire antique d'Abyssinie* (Paris, 1926), pp. 85–97; E. Littmann, *Miscellanea Academica Berolinensia*, ii. 2 (Berlin, 1950), 97; J. Doresse, *Ethiopia* (London, 1959), pp. 30 f.; E. Ullendorff, *The Ethiopians* (London, 1960), pp. 54 f.; and E. Hammerschmidt, *Äthiopien* (Wiesbaden, 1967), pp. 39–42. On the other hand, Franz Altheim and Ruth Stiehl place the rule of Ezana about a century later ('Die Datierung des Königs Ēzānā von Aksum', *Klio*, xxxix (1961), 234–48, and *Christentum am Roten Meer*, i (Berlin, 1971), 393–431 and 467–71).

[2] Enno Littmann, *Deutsche Aksum-Expedition*, iv (Berlin, 1913), 32 f.

[3] Francis Anfray, André Caquot, and Pierre Nautin, 'Une nouvelle inscription grecque d'Ézana, roi d'Axoum', *Journal des savants* (1970), pp. 260–73; cf. Sergew Hable Sellassie [*sic*], *Ancient and Medieval Ethopian History to 1270* (Addis Ababa, 1972), pp. 102 f.

[4] For coins minted by Ezana, see, besides the monograph by Anzani (p. 217 n. 1 above), Francis Anfray, 'Les rois d'Axoum d'après la numismatique', *JES* vi, no. 2 (1968), 1–5, and R. Pankhurst, 'The Greek Coins of Aksum', *Abba Salama*, vi (1975), 70–83, esp. 79. Ezana's coins were among the earliest coins of any country to carry the Christian symbol of the cross.

faith on his people. Yet within a short time after its introduction into the country the Church had developed so significantly that the Emperor Constantius, who had adopted Arianism, thought of drawing it to his side. In 356 he wrote a letter[1] to 'his most honoured brothers' Ezana and Saizana (the latter is mentioned also on one of Ezana's inscriptions) alleging that Athanasius was 'guilty of ten thousand crimes' and that therefore the canonical appointment of Frumentius by Athanasius was doubtful. Frumentius, the letter urged, must be examined on doctrinal matters and instructed by the 'most venerable George', the Arian bishop imposed upon Alexandria. The advice and threats of Constantius, however, appear not to have moved the rulers at Aksum, and Frumentius continued to preside as bishop of the Ethiopian Church.

One of the problems concerning the earliest evangelization of Ethiopia is the conflict between Rufinus' account, on the one hand, and the account of his slightly later contemporary Philostorgius,[2] who speaks as if a certain Theophilus was responsible for the conversion of the Auxoumites in A.D. 356. It may well be, however, as Winstedt[3] supposes, that Theophilus, who is called ὁ Ἰνδός (i.e. the 'Ethiopian'), was Frumentius' successor. Another conflict occurs between Rufinus' account and the (later) traditional Ethiopian version of the story. The latter knows nothing of Ezana, but makes two twin brothers, Ashbeha and Abreha, the first Christian kings of Ethiopia. In seeking for a reconciliation between the two accounts, scholars have pointed to the tendency often observed in popular history to attach famous events to famous names. During the sixth century two champions of the Christian faith ruled, one at Aksum named Ella Asheba and the other at Himyar in Yemen named Abraham.[4] Although the two rulers were not related to each other, eventually legends gathered about both in Abyssinian and Arabic tradition, and they came to be celebrated as the twin brothers who introduced Christianity

---

[1] The letter is preserved in Athanasius' *Apologia ad Constantium Imperatorem*, 31 (Migne, *PG* xxv, cols. 635 ff.), Eng. trans. by J[ohn] H[enry] N[ewman] in Athanasius' *Historic Tracts* (*A Library of the Fathers* (Oxford, 1843)), pp. 182 f.

[2] *Hist. eccl.* iii. 6, ed. Joseph Bidez (*Die griechischen christlichen Schriftsteller*, xxi; Leipzig, 1913), p. 35.

[3] E. O. Winstedt, *The Christian Topography of Cosmas Indicopleustes* (Cambridge, 1909), p. 346.

[4] For an account of the two rulers, see Jones and Monroe, op. cit., pp. 29–31.

into Ethiopia. Their names have symbolic significance, Asbeha meaning 'He who has brought about dawn', and Abreha, 'He who has made light'.

Concerning the following century and a half little specific information about the status of the Church in Ethiopia has come down to us. Early in the sixth century, Cosmas Indicopleustes visited the country and reported that he found it thoroughly Christianized.[1] The stimulus to growth seems to have come partly because of support given by Christian rulers and partly from encouragement provided by the immigration of Christian believers from other lands. The latter were chiefly Monophysites who, having been condemned at the Council of Chalcedon in 451, were persecuted by Byzantine rulers and found refuge in Ethiopia, which, because of its remote geographical location, remained unaffected by the religious controversies that were raging elsewhere. Noteworthy among the immigrants who helped to evangelize the remaining pagan areas in the northern part of the Aksumite kingdom were not a few monks, nuns, priests, and hermits from Egypt and Syria. Among these newcomers were nine celebrated monks who, because of their vigorous missionary activity and reputation for piety in Ethiopia, were accorded the status of sainthood.[2] They founded monasteries, made translations of sacred books into the native language, developed the liturgy, and propagated Monophysite theology.[3] According to the Chronicle of the Kings and the Ethiopic Synaxarion the names of the Nine Saints are as follows: Za-Mîkâ'êl (called 'Aregâwî), Panṭeléôn, Isaak (called Gerîmâ), 'Afṣê, Gûbâ, Alêf (called ʿOs), Matâʿ or Yemʿatâ, Liqânôs, and Ṣeḥmâ. This list of names is highly interesting because, as Vööbus points out, 'it offers Aramaic names and reveals to us that these monks were Syrians', a judgement which Vööbus finds confirmed by a variety of details bearing on their religio-ascetic ideas and habits.[4]

[1] *Topographia Christiana*, iii (Migne, *PG* lxxxviii, col. 169), Eng. trans. by J. W. McCrindle (London, 1897), p. 120. Cf. also the article by the Ethiopian student Bairu Tafla, 'The Establishment of the Ethiopian Church', *Tarikh*, ii. 1 (Ibadan, 1967), 32 f., and W. H. C. Frend, *The Rise of the Monophysite Movement; Chapters in History of the Church in the Fifth and Sixth Centuries* (Cambridge, 1972), pp. 304 ff.

[2] Cf. J.-B. Coulbeaux, *Histoire politique et religieuse d'Abyssinie*, i (Paris, *c.* 1928), 167–74, and G. Bardy and L. Bréhier in *Histoire de l'Église depuis les origines jusqu'à' nos jours*, ed. by Augustine Fliche and Victor Martin, iv (Paris, 1937), 524 f.

[3] Cf. A. Kammerer, op. cit., pp. 103 f.

[4] Arthur Vööbus, *Early Versions of the New Testament; Manuscript Studies* (Stock-

The question when the Bible, or at least the New Testament, was translated into Ethiopic (or Ge'ez, as the Ethiopians called their language) has been given the most widely divergent answers, extending at one extreme from the apostolic age to a time after the fourteenth century at the other. The learned Bishop Brian Walton, editor of the London Polyglot Bible, assumed that the Ethiopian eunuch whom Philip converted (Acts viii. 26–39) was successful in winning many of his fellow countrymen to the Christian faith and, on the basis of the dictum that the Church cannot exist without the Scriptures, concluded that there is every probability that the Ethiopic version was made 'ab exemplaribus Graecis antiquis, a proximis Apostolorum temporibus'.[1] Just as improbable, on the other hand, was de Lagarde's opinion that the version (at least of the Old Testament) was made from the Arabic or Coptic version after the fourteenth century.[2] Native Ethiopian traditions make the claim that the version was executed in the time of Frumentius,[3] a view which is followed by Méchineau[4] and Coulbeaux.[5] Since, however, the nucleus of the Ethiopian Church was formed by Roman merchants resident in the country, the liturgical language may well have been Greek, and

holm, 1954), p. 246, and idem, *Die Spuren eines älteren äthiopischen Evangelientextes im Lichte der literarischen Monumente* (Stockholm, 1951), pp. 13 f. For the role of the Nine Saints as well as of other Aramaic-speaking (Jewish) Christians in the creation and shaping of Ethiopian Christianity, see Sergew Hable Sellassie [*sic*], *Ancient and Medieval Ethiopian History to 1270* (Addis Ababa, 1972), pp. 115–21, and Ephraim Isaac, 'An Obscure Component in Ethiopian Church History', *Mu*, lxxxv (1972), 238 f., and idem, *A New Text-Critical Introduction to Maṣhafa Behrān* (Leiden, 1974), pp. 51–73.

[1] *Prolegomena* to the London Polyglot Bible, xv, § 12 (Wrangham's edn., ii (Cambridge, 1828), 600).

[2] Paul de Lagarde, *Gesammelte Abhandlungen* (Leipzig, 1866), pp. 61, 113, and his *Ankündigung einer neuen Ausgabe der griechischen Übersetzung des Alten Testaments* (Göttingen, 1882), p. 28. Concerning an Arabic *Vorlage*, cf. Gesenius's comment: 'According to native accounts the translation of the New Testament was made from the Arabic; but this refers without doubt only to the apocryphal part of the New Testament, the Synodus, and has been quite erroneously transferred to the entire New Testament' (*Allgemeine Encyclopädie der Wissenschaften und Künste*, ed. by J. S. Ersch and J. G. Gruber, ii (Leipzig, 1819), p. 113).

[3] According to one group of Ethiopic chronicles the propagation of the Gospels in Ethiopic was the work of certain individual monks, such as Abba Yohannes, who founded the monastery of Debra-Sina, or Abba Libanos, also known as Mata'e, of Byzantine origin, who was sent to Ethiopia at the instigation of St. Pachomius (cf. Jean Doresse, *Ethiopia* (London 1959), p. 64).

[4] 'Version éthiopienne de la Bible', in Vigouroux's *Dictionnaire de la Bible*, ii (Paris, 1899), col. 2031.   [5] *Op. cit.* i. 172.

need for an Ethiopic version would have arisen only at a later time, when Christianity became diffused among the indigenous population. Consequently many modern scholars date the origin of the Ethiopic version during the fifth and/or sixth century, in connection with the missionary activity of the Nine Saints.[1]

II. EARLY MANUSCRIPTS OF THE ETHIOPIC VERSION

Of the several thousand Ethiopic manuscripts in European and American collections,[2] about three hundred contain the text of one or more books of the New Testament. Unfortunately most of these manuscripts are relatively late, dating from the sixteenth to the nineteenth century. Until recently the oldest known Ethiopic manuscript of the Bible was a copy of the four Gospels in the Bibliothèque Nationale, thought by Zotenberg to have been copied in the thirteenth century[3] and by Grébaut[4] at the end of the fourteenth century (see no. 6 in the list below). Within the last decade information has become available

---

[1] Ignazio Guidi, *Storia della letteratura etiopica* (Rome, 1932), p. 13; Luca dei Sabelli, *Storia di Abissinia*, i (Rome, 1936), 158 ff.; Vööbus, *Early Versions*, p. 248; B. Botti, *Supplément au Dictionnaire de la Bible*, vi (Paris, 1960), col. 827; and Eduard Ullendorff, *Ethiopia and the Bible* (London, 1968), pp. 38 ff. Cf. also W. H. C. Frend, *The Rise of the Monophysite Movement* (Cambridge, 1972), pp. 305 f. Bardy and Bréhier (op. cit., p. 525 n. 1), who agree with this view, draw attention to a statement in the *Syriac Book of Mysteries*, a vast collection of ecclesiastical traditions put together at the beginning of the fifteenth century by a monk named George of Sagla: 'As for the New Testament which we have in Ethiopia, it was translated entirely from Greek into Ethiopic before the doctrine of Nestorius appeared, before the confession of Leo was formed, before the Council of the Arians had been called, that is, of the bishops of Chalcedon.'

[2] The largest collections of Ethiopic manuscripts outside Ethiopia are those in the Bibliothèque Nationale of Paris (688 manuscripts in 1952), the British Museum (500 manuscripts), the Vatican Library (287 manuscripts in 1935), and the Bodleian Library at Oxford (just over 100 manuscripts in 1958). For an alphabetic list (arranged by author and title of work) of Ethiopic manuscripts in fourteen European collections, see Carlo Conti Rossini, 'Manuscritti ed opere abissine in Europa', *Rendiconti della Reale Accademia dei Lincei*, Classe di scienze morali, storiche e filologiche, 5th ser., viii (Rome, 1899), 606–36. For a bibliography of catalogues and collections of Ethiopic manuscripts, see Silvio Zanutto, *Bibliografia etiopica* (Rome, 1932), supplemented by the bibliography in I. Yu. Krachkovskii, *Vvdenie v efiopskuyu filologiyu* (Leningrad, 1955), pp. 177–209.

[3] [H. Zotenberg,] *Catalogue des manuscrits éthiopiens (gheez et amharique) de la Bibliothèque Nationale* (Paris, 1877), p. 29.

[4] Sylvain Grébaut, 'L'Âge du ms. Éth. n° 32 de Paris (Bibliothèque Nationale)', *Æthiops: Bulletin Ge'ez*, iv (1931), 9–11.

concerning the existence of several older Ethiopic manuscripts. While visiting various monasteries in Ethiopia, Donald M. Davies, professor emeritus of Lincoln University, Pennsylvania, took photographs of not a few manuscripts, several of which, on the basis of evidence provided by colophons and palaeographic analysis, he regards as older than the Paris manuscript (see nos. 1 to 5 in the list below).[1]

The oldest known copy of Acts and the Epistles in Ethiopic is included in a polyglot manuscript which is assigned to the end of the fourteenth or the beginning of the fifteenth century (no. 7 below). The oldest Ethiopic manuscripts of the Apocalypse date from the fifteenth century (nos. 11, 22, and 24 below). One of the most remarkable Ethiopic manuscripts from the point of view of iconography is the Pierpont Morgan MS. 828 of the four Gospels (no. 11 below), which, according to the judgement of Patrick W. Skehan, 'is noteworthy in all of its parts; and in respect of the illuminations it is to a considerable extent unique, and in general intensely interesting'.[2] Doubtless still other important manuscripts will come to light as the result of a project for the systematic microfilming of manuscripts in monasteries and libraries in Ethiopia, sponsored by the Monastic Manuscript Library of Saint John's University, Collegeville, Minnesota. A descriptive catalogue of the manuscripts is being produced by William J. Macomber (vol. i, 1975).

LIST OF EARLY ETHIOPIC MANUSCRIPTS[3]

(1) Abba Garima, MS. 1; tenth century;[4] 185 folios; contains

---

[1] The present writer is grateful to Dr. Davies for his kindness in providing information concerning these five manuscripts as well as nos. 12, 14, 15, and 16.

[2] 'An Illuminated Gospel Book in Ethiopic', *Studies in Art and Literature for Belle da Costa Greene*, ed. by Dorothy Miner (Princeton, 1954), p. 350. On other illuminated Ethiopic manuscripts, see Otto A. Jäger and Lisolotte Deininger-Engehart, 'Some Notes on Illuminations of Manuscripts in Ethiopia', *Rassegna di studi etiopici*, xvii (1961), 45–60, and *Ethiopia. Illuminated Manuscripts*. (UNESCO World Art Series.) Introduction by Jules Leroy, Text by Stephen Wright and Otto A. Jäger (New York, 1961).

[3] For further information concerning the manuscripts included in this list, reference may be made to the following catalogues:

For nos. 6, 8, 9, 17, and 18, see Herman Zotenberg (p. 223 n. 3 above).

For no. 7, see Grébaut (p. 226 n. 1 below).

For no. 10, see Murad Kamil, 'Die abessinischen Handschriften der Sammlung Littmann in Tübingen', *Abhandlungen für die Kunde des Morgenlandes*, xxi, 8 (Leipzig, 1936; reprinted, Nendeln, 1966), pp. 11 f.

For no. 11, see Skehan (n. 2 above).

[*Footnotes 3 and 4 continue on opposite page*]

the four Gospels (with fugitive folios from the next two manuscripts) ; bound in boards overlaid with silver.

(2) Abba Garima, MS. 2 ; eleventh century; 263 folios; contains the four Gospels (many folios out of order, and the end of John lacking) ; bound with the following manuscript.

(3) Abba Garima, MS. 3 ; eleventh century; 170 folios; contains the four Gospels, each preceded by a portrait of the Evangelist; bound with the preceding manuscript.

(4) Lalibela–Medhani Alem; fourteenth century; 208 folios; contains the four Gospels; at the close of John a colophon states, 'Given by King Lalibela, and my regnal name is Gubre Mascal' (A.D. 1314–44).

(5) Addis Ababa, National Library; A.D. 1349–50; 327 folios; contains the four Gospels, portraits of the Evangelists, fifteen miniatures of the life of Christ, the Epistle of Eusebius to Carpianus, and the Eusebian canons.[1]

(6) Paris, Bibliothèque Nationale, Éth. MS. 22 (Zotenberg 32) ; thirteenth century (Zotenberg), end of xiv cent. (Grébaut), before A.D. 1420 (Davies) ; 207 folios; contains the four Gospels, divided into sections nearly corresponding to the ancient τίτλοι, with the Letter of Eusebius to Carpianus, the Eusebian canons, and a treatise on the harmony of the four Gospels.

For no. 13, see Berhard Dorn, 'Über die Aethiopischen Handschriften der öffenlichen Kaiserlichen Bibliothek zu St.-Petersburg', *Bulletin scientifique publié par l'Académie impériale des sciences de Saint-Pétersbourg*, iii (1838), 145–51.

For no. 15, see Thomas Pell Platt, *A Catalogue of the Ethiopic Manuscripts in the Royal Library of Paris, and in the Library of the British and Foreign Bible Society* . . . (London, 1822).

For nos. 19 and 26, see Edward Ullendorff, *Catalogue of Ethiopian Manuscripts in the Bodleian Library*, ii (Oxford, 1951).

For nos. 20, 21, 22, 23, and 24, see Sylvain Grébaut and Eugène Tisserant, *Codices Aethiopici Vaticani et Borgiani* . . . , i (in Bybliotheca Vaticana, 1935).

For no. 25, see William Wright, *Catalogue of the Ethiopic Manuscripts in the British Museum Acquired since the Year 1847* (London, 1877).

[4] Cf. the discussion of the iconography of this manuscript by Jules Leroy, who, after having argued that the codex should be assigned to the ninth or tenth century, indicates in a postscript that a fresh examination of similar Byzantine and Armenian monuments has led him to think that the manuscript should be assigned to the x–xi century ('L'Évangéliaire éthiopien du couvent d'Abba Garima et ses attaches avec l'ancien art chrétien de Syrie', *Cahiers archéologiques*, xi (1960), 131–43).

[1] On this manuscript see Pawlos Ṣādwā, 'Un manoscritto etiopico degli Evangeli', *RSE* xi (1952 (1953)), 9–28.

(7) Milan, Biblioteca Ambrosiana, MS. B. 20 inf. (parts 1 and 2); end of fourteenth or beginning of fifteenth century (Grébaut).[1] Part 1 has 275 folios and contains the (fourteen) Epistles of Paul in five languages. On the recto the order of the columns (left to right) is Ethiopic, Syriac, Coptic (Bohairic), Arabic, and (to the end of fol. 175^v, Eph. chap. vi) Armenian; on the verso the order of the languages is reversed. Part 2 has 186 folios and contains the Catholic Epistles and the Acts of the Apostles in four languages (the column for the Armenian is vacant).

(8) Paris, Bibliothèque Nationale, Éth. MS. 27 (Zotenberg 45); A.D. 1378; 162 folios; contains the Epistles of Paul (including Hebrews after 2 Thess.).

(9) Paris, Bibliothèque Nationale, Éth. MS. 143 (Zotenberg 40); fourteenth century; 27 folios; contains fragments of the Gospel of Luke ix. 23–xx. 25 (lacks xi. 2b–18a, xiii. 14–28). According to Zotenberg the text does not accord entirely with that in other manuscripts.

(10) Tübingen, Littmann Collection, 2; fourteenth–fifteenth century; two pages from a lectionary; contains Matt. xx. 20 ff. and Mark x. 35 ff.

(11) New York, Pierpont Morgan Library, MS. 828; A.D. 1400–1; 206 folios; contains the four Gospels, twenty-six full-page miniatures, eight ornamented canon tables, four ornamental incipit folios.

(12) Kebran, Lake Tana; A.D. 1413; 241 folios; contains the four Gospels, portraits of the Evangelists, nineteen miniatures of

---

[1] S. Grébaut, 'Catalogue des manuscrits éthiopiens de la Bibliothèque Ambrosienne', *ROC*, 3rd ser., ix (1933–4), 27–32. For a description of the Coptic, cf. [G. Horner,] *The Coptic New Testament in the Northern Dialect*, iii (Oxford, 1905), pp. xvii–xx. (Horner finds that the Coptic is in two hands, one of which he dates to the twelfth century and the other to the fourteenth century.) For other descriptions of the manuscript, see C. R. Gregory, *Textkritik des Neuen Testamentes*, iii (Leipzig, 1909), 1310, and Enrico Galbiati, 'I manoscritti etiopici dell'Ambrosiana (Breve inventario)', *Studi in onore di Mons. Carlo Castiglione (Fontes Ambrosiani*, xxxii; Milan 1957), pp. 339–40. According to Dr. Helge Mæhlum, who kindly provided information about the manuscript (letter dated 23 Jan. 1974), the Ethiopic text of Colossians represents an old form of text.

For what appears to be a companion volume (the page dimensions are the same as the Ambrosian manuscript), see the Vatican Pentaglot Psalter (Barberini or. 2), acquired in 1635 by the Monastery of St. Macarius in the Scetis desert; dated by Tisserant to the fourteenth century (Eugène Tisserant, *Specimina codicum orientalium* (Bonn, 1914), plate 80).

the life of Christ, Epistle of Eusebius to Carpianus, the Eusebian canons.

(13) Leningrad, M. E. Saltykov-Shchedrin State Public Library, Efiop. 612 (Dorn 3); A.D. 1426; 153 folios; contains the four Gospels.

(14) Lalibela–Ashetin Maryam; fifteenth century (dated by a colophon to the reign of Zara Yaqob, A.D. 1434–68); 144 folios; contains the four Gospels.

(15) London, British and Foreign Bible Society, MS. 3; early fifteenth century (Davies); 52 folios; contains fragments of Matt. (38 folios) and Luke (14 folios).

(16) Lake Haik, Monastery of St. Stephen; xv cent. (dated by a colophon to A.D. 1478–1494); 201 folios; contains the four Gospels, with portraits of the Evangelists.

(17) Paris, Bibliothèque Nationale, Éth. MS. 21 (Zotenberg 35); A.D. 1483; 202 folios; contains the four Gospels; each Gospel is followed by a table of the chapters.

(18) Paris, Bibliothèque Nationale, Éth. MS. 26 (Zotenberg 42); fifteenth century; 102 folios; contains the Catholic Epistles (in the order 1 and 2 Peter, 1, 2, 3 John, James, Jude) and the Acts of the Apostles (lacks iv. 5–18; ix. 5b–18; xiii. 11b–24; xvi. 17b–29).

(19) Oxford, Bodleian Library, MS. Aeth. c. 2 (Ullendorff 41); fifteenth century; ninety-eight folios; contains substantial portions of the Gospel of Matthew, Mark in its entirety, most of Luke, part of John chap. i; portraits of Mark, Luke, John; rubricated chapter headings added without much consistency.

(20) Vatican, Eth. MS. 25; fifteenth century; 266 folios; contains the four Gospels, Ammonian section numbers, and Eusebian canon numbers. This manuscript was used by Tasfā-Ṣĕyōn in preparing the *editio princeps* of the Ethiopic Gospels (Rome, 1548); see pp. 228–30 below.

(21) Vatican, Eth. MS. 68; fifteenth century; 129 folios; contains the Gospel of John without divisions or titles; the Apocalypse of John (used by Tasfā-Ṣĕyōn for his edition of the New Testament).

(22) Vatican, Eth. MS. 47; fifteenth century; 217 folios; contains the Gospel of John; the Apocalypse of John; a hymn; a prayer; the creed.

(23) Vatican, Eth. MS. 11; fifteenth century; 144 folios; contains the Catholic Epistles (in the order 1 and 2 Peter, 1, 2, and 3 John, James, Jude); a prayer for offering incense; litanies; anaphoras; lessons from the New Testament (1 John i. 1–7; Acts xiii. 27–39).

(24) Vatican, Eth. MS. 49; fifteenth century; 134 folios; contains the Apocalypse of John; prayers; a magical incantation.

(25) London, British Museum, Orient. MS. 507 (Wright 33); fifteenth century; 149 folios; containing the four Gospels, with portraits of the Evangelists.

(26) Oxford, Bodleian Library, MS. Aeth. c. 1 (Ullendorff 40); probably end of fifteenth century; 207 folios; contains the four Gospels, Epistle of Eusebius to Carpianus, Eusebian canons.

III. PRINTED EDITIONS OF THE ETHIOPIC NEW TESTAMENT

The first printed edition of the Ethiopic New Testament was published in 1548–9 at Rome in two quarto volumes. The first volume contains, in this order, the Gospels, Apocalypse, Catholic Epistles (in the order of 1, 2, and 3 John, 1 and 2 Peter, James, Jude), Hebrews, Acts, the Anaphora of Our Lord and that of Our Lady Mary; the second volume, which is foliated consecutively with the first, contains the Pauline Epistles. The Latin title of the first volume contains the following information; *Testamentum Novum cum Epistola Pauli ad Hebreos tantum, cum concordantijs Euangelistarum Eusebij & numeratione omnium verborum eorundem.* Missale cum benedictione incensi ceræ et c. Alphabetum in lingua ግእዝ፡ gheez, id est libera quia a nulla alia originem duxit, & vulgo dicitur Chaldea, Quae omnia Fr. Petrus Ethyops . . . curavit. Anno Salutis M.D.XLVIII.

The work was edited by three Abyssinian monks of the monastery of Dabra Libanos who had fled their country during the Muslim devastations then raging, bringing with them sacred manuscripts. Their names were Tasfā-Ṣĕyōn ('Hope-of-Sion'),

Tanse'a-Wald ('Resurrection-of-the-Son'), and Za-Šellāsē ('He-of-the Trinity'). Finding refuge at the monastery of St. Stefano in Rome they assumed the Latin names, respectively, Petrus, Paulus, and Bernardus. Petrus, who had been born (according to the inscription on his monument at Rome)[1] 'beyond the tropic of Capricorn' of noble parents, was well versed in many languages and appears to have been the leader of the three, for his name alone is mentioned on the title-page of the edition.

The printers[2] of the edition, the brothers Valerius Doricus and Ludovicus, were ignorant of the Ethiopic language and therefore had to work constantly under the supervision of the editor,[3] who in several colophons requests the indulgence of the readers. After the Pauline Epistles, for example, there stands the following note in Ethiopic and Latin: 'Fathers and Brethren, be pleas'd not to interpret amiss the faults of this edition; for they who compos'd it could not read [viz. Ethiopic]; and for ourselves we know not how to compose. So then we help'd them, and they assisted us, as the blind leads the blind; and therefore we desire you to pardon us and them.'[4]

The edition leaves not a little to be desired so far as a scientific edition is concerned. Besides being disfigured by countless typographical errors, which, in view of the ignorance of the Ethiopic language on the part of the printers, is not surprising, the text of the Book of Acts is a hodge-podge. The colophon to

---

[1] The tomb of Petrus, who died on 28 Aug. 1552, in his forty-second year, is in the Church of S. Stefano dei Mori in Rome; see S. Euringer, 'Das Epitaphium des Tasfâ Ṣejon', *OC*, 3rd ser., i (1926–7), 49–66.

[2] For an account of early printers of Ethiopic, see Hendrik F. Wijnman, *An Outline of the Development of Ethiopian Typography in Europe* (Leiden, 1960) (repr. from *Books on the Orient*).

[3] See Ignazio Guidi, 'La prima stampa del Nuovo Testamento in etiopico, fatta in Roma nel 1548–1549', *Archivio della R. Società Romana di Storia Patria*, ix (1886), 273–8. For other information concerning Petrus and his edition, see Job Ludolf, *ad suam Historiam . . . Commentarius* (Frankfurt a.M., 1691), Bk. III, chap. iv; James Townley, *Illustrations of Biblical Literature*, ii (London, 1821), 148, and iii. 60 f.; George F. Black, op. cit. (see p. 215 n. 1 above), pp. 534 f.; R. Lefevre, 'Documenti e notizie su Tasfā Ṣeyon e la sua attività romana nel sec. XVI', *RSE* xxiv (1969–70), 74–133; and Oscar Löfgren, 'San Stefano dei Mori och de första etiopiska Bibeltrycken', *Corona amicorum; Studier tillögnade Tönnes Kleberg* (Uppsala, 1968), pp. 153–80.

[4] Other similar laments appear in colophons to the Gospels and Acts. The quaint English rendering of the colophon cited above is that of the translator of Ludolf's work, who identifies himself simply as J. P., Gent. (*A New History of Ethiopia* (London, 1682), p. 263).

that book acknowledges that 'these Acts of the Apostles, for the most part, were translated [by the editor] from the Latin and the Greek by reason of the imperfection of the [Ethiopic] archetype; for what we have added or omitted, we beg your pardon, and request you to amend what is amiss'. The manuscripts which Petrus used for his edition included the two fifteenth-century copies mentioned above (nos. 20 and 21) and a sixteenth-century copy of the Catholic Epistles and Hebrews (Vatican, Eth. MS. 5).

The text of Tasfā-Ṣĕyōn's New Testament was republished by Brian Walton in the New Testament volume (1657) of the London Polyglot Bible. The Ethiopic is accompanied by a Latin translation, prepared by Dudley Loftus of Dublin and revised by Edmund Castell. Unfortunately the new printing of the text incorporated additional corruptions, and its Latin rendering has more than once been excoriated as being far from accurate. In the middle of the eighteenth century Christoph August Bode devoted himself to a carefully executed Latin translation and critical study of Walton's text of the Ethiopic New Testament.[1]

Another edition of the Ethiopic New Testament was published in 1826 (the Gospels) and 1830 (the rest of the New Testament) by the British and Foreign Bible Society. This edition, printed by Richard Watts from type cast from matrices made a century and a half earlier by Job Ludolf and preserved in the Public Library at Frankfurt a.M., was prepared by Thomas Pell Platt, formerly Fellow of Trinity College, Cambridge. According to a statement in the volume containing the Gospels,

the text of this edition is a recension based on a collation of Ethiopic mss. in the Royal Library at Paris; of certain mss. lent to, or purchased by, the B[ritish and] F[oreign] B[ible] S[ociety]; and of others containing between them the whole New Testament, purchased at Jerusalem by J. Jowett, and presented by the C[hurch] M[issionary] S[ociety] in 1824; the whole being compared with the Ethiopic text given in the London Polyglot.[2]

---

[1] *Novum Domini nostri Iesu Christi Testamentum ex versione Æthiopici interpretis in Bibliis Polyglottis Anglicanis editum ex Æthiopica lingua in Latinam transtulit* C. A. Bodius, 2 vols. (Brunswick, 1753, 1755).

[2] For the Acts and Epistles Platt had access to only one manuscript and Walton's text.

Unfortunately Platt preserved only the most desultory account of the several manuscripts that he had consulted,[1] and, in view of the missionary purpose of the edition, the editor proceeded in an eclectic manner and provided no variant readings.[2]

Platt's text was reprinted three times, with inconsequential emendations: in 1874–8 a diglot edition with an Amharic version on facing pages was prepared by J. Ludwig Krapf, a missionary to Abyssinia, and published at Basel under the auspices of the British and Foreign Bible Society; in 1899 an edition, revised by Franz Praetorius at the request of the Mission of the Swedish Evangelical National Society in Eritrea, was issued at Leipzig; and in 1968 the Platt–Praetorius text was reissued at Addis Ababa by the American Bible Society.

The most recent edition of the Ethiopic New Testament was prepared by Francesco da Bassano, with the assistance of Edoardo Gruson, and published in 1920 at Asmara by the Dominican Mission in Abyssinia.[3] According to Oscar Löfgren[4] the text is 'in the main that of Platt, corrected and revised'. A second edition, which was published in 1934, carries the information in a preface signed by the publishers to the effect that some expressions, more conformed to the Latin Vulgate than to the Greek text, which appeared in the first edition, were allowed to remain in the second edition.

It is not difficult to see that one of the most pressing *desiderata* is the preparation of a critical edition of the Ethiopic New Testament. In view of the relatively important place which the Ethiopic version holds in textual studies of the Old Testament,[5] it is certainly not to the credit of New Testament scholars that so

[1] For a list of the manuscripts, with several more or less inconclusive guesses as to their identity, see Samuel P. Tregelles in vol. iv of Thomas H. Horne's *An Introduction to the Critical Study and Knowledge of the Holy Scriptures*, 13th edn. (London, 1872), p. 318, n. 2.

[2] According to Tregelles (op. cit., p. 318), L. A. Prevost of the British Museum collated Platt's text with that of Walton, and gave a literal translation of the variations between the two.

[3] *Hadīs kīdān. Wangēl qedūs za'egzi'ena wamadhānina 'Iyasūs Krestōs* . . . (Asmara, 1912). The date 1912 of the imprint is an error; the correct date is 1921. The imprimatur is dated, '8 Dicembris, 1920'.

[4] See his review of the edition in *Le Monde oriental*, xxiii (1929), 180.

[5] For a survey of critical work on the Ethiopic Old Testament see Edward Ullendorff, *Ethiopia and the Bible* (London, 1968), pp. 33 f. and Ernst Hammerschmidt, *Ethiopian Studies at German Universities* (Wiesbaden, 1970), pp. 38–44.

little has been accomplished toward filling this lacuna in New Testament studies.[1]

IV. TEXTUAL AFFINITIES OF THE ETHIOPIC VERSION

With only a few exceptions all textual analyses of the Ethiopic New Testament have been based on the quite uncritical printed editions of the text or on Latin renderings of these editions. In view of this circumstance, the textual analyses of John Mill and H. C. Hoskier are the more surprising. In 1707 Mill[2] pointed out not a few Ethiopic readings in which the London Polyglot text (or, rather, the Latin translation of the Ethiopic) is in agreement with codex Alexandrinus. Indeed, there are several readings supported by the Ethiopic alone, or with very few other witnesses, which he adjudged to preserve the original text.[3] More recently Hoskier[4] identified more than fifty readings in the Pauline Epistles (without taking account of Hebrews) where the Ethiopic is practically alone in support of the Chester Beatty Papyrus II ($\mathfrak{p}^{46}$).

I. THE GOSPELS

Scientific examination of the transmission of the Ethiopic text of the Gospels began with Zotenberg's analysis of the form of text preserved in what was at that time the oldest known copy of the Ethiopic Bible (Ethiopic MS. 22 in the Bibliothèque Nationale; no. 6 in the list above). In his descriptive account of the manuscript, Zotenberg pointed out that its text, which differs from that in the printed editions, displays primitive features which indicate an origin from an original Greek *Vorlage* of the Alexandrian recension.[5] These include (1) proper names that preserve

---

[1] Cf. Oscar Löfgren, 'The Necessity of a Critical Edition of the Ethiopian Bible', *Proceedings of the Third International Conference of Ethiopian Studies*, Addis Ababa, 1966 (Institute of Ethiopian Studies, Haile Sellassie I University; Addis Ababa, 1970), pp. 167–61.

[2] *Novum Testamentum Graecum*, 2nd edn. by Ludolf Küster (Leipzig, 1723), Prolegomena, §§ 1190–1212. For Mill's acknowledgement that he depended upon the Latin rendering, see § 1472.

[3] Ibid., §§ 1213–18.

[4] *Appendix to an Article on the Chester Beatty Papyrus of the Pauline Epistles known as* $\mathfrak{p}^{46}$ ... (Oxford, 1937), p. 5.

[5] [Zotenberg,] *Catalogue des manuscrits éthiopiens*, p. 25.

the Greek spelling; (2) instances of Greek words that have been transliterated rather than translated; and (3) a certain number of mistranslations that can be explained only on the assumption that one Greek word or expression was erroneously taken for another. According to Zotenberg all other known Ethiopic manuscripts (and printed editions) present a revised form of text.[1] The investigation of the origin of the secondary features of the revised form of the Ethiopic version was left by Zotenberg for others to pursue.

One such investigation was undertaken by Dillmann, who suggested that the numerous variations in the more widely read books of the New Testament, such as the Gospels, were due to the influence of the Coptic and Arabic versions.[2] The basis for such an assumption he found in the following facts: (1) Prolegomena translated from the Arabic were prefixed to the Ethiopic New Testament; (2) names of New Testament books derived from the Arabic displaced occasionally in later times the native nomenclature (e.g. the Acts were called *Abraxis* (= Πράξεις), and Revelation *Abukalamis* (= Ἀποκάλυψις); and (3) the Arabic–Coptic *Sinôdôs* was naturalized early in the Ethiopic Church. Dillmann's preliminary studies were developed further by Guidi, who, in a study devoted principally to the translation of the Gospels into Arabic, pointed out that the Alexandrian 'vulgate' of the Arabic contaminated in varying degrees all manuscripts that present the revised form of the Ethiopic.[3]

The next stage of the investigation was undertaken several years later by Hackspill on the basis of a meticulous examination of the text of Matthew i–x in several Ethiopic manuscripts.[4] While confirming the opinion that the Ethiopic text of the Gospels was translated from a Greek base, Hackspill disagreed with Zotenberg's view that that base was an Alexandrian type of text; it was, Hackspill concluded, a Syrian or Syro-Western type of text, such as that represented by the Greek manuscripts (C) D E F G K

---

[1] Ibid., p. 30.

[2] A. Dillmann, 'Äthiopische Bibelübersetzung', Herzog's *Protestantische Real-Enzyclopädie*, ii (Leipzig, 1877), 203–6.

[3] Ignazio Guidi, 'La traduzioni degli Evangelii in arabo e in etiopico', *Memorie della Reale Accademia dei Lincei*, Classe di scienze morali, storiche e filologiche, 4th ser., vol. iv, part 1ᵃ (Rome, 1888), 33–7.

[4] L. Hackspill, 'Die äthiopische Evangelienübersetzung (Math. I–X)', *Zeitschrift für Assyriologie*, xi (1896), 117–96 and 367–88.

and the Latin Vulgate. At the same time he acknowledged that the version does present a number of typically Alexandrian readings, agreeing with manuscripts א B (C).[1]

Beyond these textual analyses, however, Hackspill also investigated the kinds of alterations that were introduced into Ethiopic manuscripts after the Arabizing strain entered Abyssinia at the close of the fourteenth century. After that date Ethiopic manuscripts generally fall into two classes: in some the new, Arabized readings appear side by side with the original text (Hackspill calls this the 'Kompilationsmethode'), while in others the new reading has displaced the older text (the 'Substitutionsmethode').[2]

An example that illustrates Hackspill's 'compilation-method' can be found at the close of the Gospel according to Mark. The present writer, having examined the ending of Mark in sixty-five Ethiopic manuscripts, discovered that none, contrary to statements made by previous investigators, closes the Gospel at xvi. 8, but that most (forty-seven manuscripts) present the so-called shorter ending directly after vs. 8, followed immediately by the longer ending (verses 9–20).[3]

In short, the chief characteristic of the Ethiopic version of the Gospels is heterogeneity. In some passages it presents a slavish rendering, so that even the word order of the Greek has been preserved. In other passages—and these constitute the great majority—one finds a surprising freedom, involving transposition of parts of clauses, simplification of more complicated phrases, abbreviations for the sake of simplicity, and many peculiar readings and additions.

2. THE ACTS OF THE APOSTLES

At the request of James Hardy Ropes, whose wide-ranging monograph on the text of Acts could present no analysis of the

---

[1] L. Hackspill, 'Die äthiopische Evangelienübersetzung (Math. I–X)', *Zeitschrift für Assyriologie*, xi (1896), p. 142.   [2] Ibid., p. 192.

[3] 'The Ending of the Gospel according to Mark in Ethiopic Manuscripts', *Understanding the Sacred Text; Essays in Honor of Morton S. Enslin on the Hebrew Bible and Christian Beginnings*, ed. by John Reumann (Valley Forge, 1972), pp. 165–80. The shorter ending, which is transmitted with a number of variant readings in individual Ethiopic manuscripts, is as follows: 'And all things which he [Jesus] commanded Peter and those who were his, they finished telling, and after this Jesus manifested himself to them; and from the rising of the sun as far as the west he sent them to preach eternal salvation by the holy Gospel, which is incorruptible.'

Ethiopic text of Acts for lack of reliable critical material, James A. Montgomery undertook to make a study of what seemed to be the oldest known copy of the Book of Acts in that version.[1] This is a fifteenth-century parchment codex which contains the Catholic Epistles and the Acts of the Apostles (see no. 18 in the list above). The scribe, according to Zotenberg, 'presents a great number of variations, of errors and small lacunae, sometimes of a word, sometimes of a phrase'.[2] Montgomery, who is more severe in his judgement on the ability of the scribe, describes him as 'most careless as copyist, committing all kinds of stupid omissions and duplications; he appears to have had little understanding of what he was copying, as is evident from his constant failure to distinguish among the several sets of very similar letters in the Ethiopic alphabet. . . . He appears unskilled in his native lexicography and grammar.'[3]

The most marked characteristic of the Ethiopic text of Acts in this rather imperfect copy is its brevity. Indeed, the overwhelming urge to abbreviate is quite unlike anything in the numerous Old Testament Ethiopic texts that have been critically established. Montgomery concludes that the Greek exemplar used by the translator approached the Antiochian, or Syrian, form but did not possess the polish of the latter, being, in fact, a fair example of the Oriental Textus Receptus of the day. At the same time, there are a number of coincidences with the Greek codex Vaticanus (B) and other early texts.[4] In fact, four times it agrees with B alone against all other witnesses, vii. 21 ἑαυτῇ υἱόν; xi. 8 the order of B; xiv. 26 omission of κἀκεῖθεν; xxii. 11 οὐδέν; and twice in association with the Sahidic, xx. 21 Ἰησοῦν; xxvii. 37 the number '76' instead of '276'.

By way of general summary, Montgomery ends his analysis with the sentence:

In fine, we possess in the three texts studied [the Paris manuscript, the London Polyglot text, and the Bible Society's text] as many different strata of translation and revision: in P a mutilated form of primitive text; in L one that is still free from Arabism, but which has been revised at a late day from the Latin; and in B an Arabizing text, belonging to the category of most Ethiopic Biblical manuscripts.[5]

[1] 'The Ethiopic Text of Acts of the Apostles', *HTR* xxvii (1934), 169–205.
[2] Ibid., p. 40. [3] Ibid., pp. 172 f. [4] Ibid., p. 193.
[5] Ibid., p. 205.

3. THE PAULINE EPISTLES

Except for Hoskier's surprising statistics concerning agreements of the Ethiopic version with readings of $\mathfrak{P}^{46}$ (see p. 232 above), no other significant research on the Pauline Epistles has appeared in published form. It may be mentioned, however, that a Norwegian scholar, Helge Mæhlum of the Norsk Lærerakademi in Bergen, is preparing a critical edition and textual analysis of the Ethiopic text of the Captivity Epistles (Eph., Phil., Col., and Philem.).

4. THE CATHOLIC EPISTLES

Of the Catholic Epistles only the Epistle of James has been investigated. On the basis of nine Ethiopic manuscripts (one a fragment of six verses), all of which present basically the same text as that of the printed editions, Josef Hofmann[1] concludes that the version was made from a Greek *Vorlage*, for the Ethiopic occasionally reproduces the Greek word order. It is difficult to determine to which textual family this *Vorlage* belonged, for in many cases the same Ethiopic text can represent one or another of the Greek variants. Furthermore, the Ethiopic shows only immaterial agreements with other versions (Sahidic, Bohairic, Peshitta), and these are probably accidental. As to possible influence from Arabic texts, Hofmann is unable to say any more than that he regards it as not impossible that those Arabic texts which were translated from Greek or Syriac have influenced the Ethiopic, but that those which were translated from Bohairic did not.

5. THE BOOK OF REVELATION

Of all the books of the New Testament in Ethiopic, the Apocalypse has received the most thorough study. On the basis of a collation of twenty-six manuscripts,[2] ranging in date from the

---

[1] 'Das Neue Testament in äthiopischen Sprache; Probleme der Übersetzung und Stand der Forschung', *Die alten Übersetzungen des Neuen Testaments, die Kirchenväterzitate und Lektionare*, ed. by K. Aland (Berlin and New York, 1972), pp. 345–73, especially pp. 364–7.

[2] In four of the manuscripts which Hofmann (see the next footnote) utilized the Apocalypse follows the Gospel of John; in one it follows Acts and precedes the Catholic Epistles; in another it follows Paul (Romans–1 Thess. iii. 12); in eight it follows Philemon, Hebrews, Acts, and the Catholic Epistles; the other twelve manuscripts contain only the Apocalypse.

fifteenth to the nineteenth century, Hofmann edited the text and provided a literal rendering into Latin.[1] All the manuscripts appear to go back to one common text-type. That this rests upon a Greek *Vorlage* can be deduced from various considerations; for example, the personal names that occur only in the Apocalypse and the names of the twelve precious stones (xxi. 18 ff.) are transliterated from Greek. In Hofmann's opinion the *Vorlage* represented a very good Greek text, which, in terms of Schmid's analysis of the Greek manuscripts of the Apocalypse,[2] presents the following profile: (*a*) *Av* and *K* have had no influence upon the Ethiopic; (*b*) the Ethiopic agrees with the Greek manuscripts A C at places which are or appear to be original; (*c*) there is no relation with 𝔭⁴⁷; and (*d*) the Ethiopic has something in common with the ℵ text-type.[3]

According to Hofmann, the translator of the Apocalypse, who did his work between A.D. 550 and 650, was not the same as the one who rendered the Gospels into Ethiopic. He was a most competent workman, whose version is an important witness for the textual criticism of the Apocalypse. It is to be regretted, therefore, that we no longer have his rendering in its original form, for what the manuscripts offer is a text that has been greatly contaminated by various influences over the centuries, including *Schlimmverbesserungen*, revisions, and alterations made on the basis of other versions.[4]

The most noteworthy of the latter are the changes that were introduced from the Coptic and the Arabic versions. According to Hofmann, two different revisions were made on the basis of the current Arabic versions.[5] The first revision has affected manuscripts dating from the fourteenth or fifteenth century; it could thus have taken place in the fourteenth or at the beginning of the fifteenth century. The influence of the second revision shows

---

[1] Josef Hofmann, *Die äthiopische Übersetzung der Johannes-Apokalypse* (textus aethiopicus: *CSCO* cclxxxi, tom. 55; versio latina: cclxxxii, tom. 56; Louvain, 1967).

[2] Joseph Schmid, *Studien zur Geschichte des griechischen Apokalypse-Textes*; ii. *Die alten Stämme* (Munich, 1955), pp. 24 and 146–51.

[3] Hofmann, *Die äthiopische Johannes-Apokalypse kritisch untersucht* (*CSCO* ccxcvii, *Subsidia*, 33; Louvain, 1969), p. 65.

[4] Ibid., p. 66.

[5] 'Der arabische Einfluss in der äthiopischen Übersetzung der Johannes-Apokalypse; textkritische Untersuchung auf Grund von Handschriften,' *OC* xliii (1959), pp. 24–53; xliv (1960), pp. 25–39.

itself in manuscripts of the seventeenth century, and thus apparently was made in the sixteenth century. Less easy to identify are the influences from the Coptic, particularly those of the Bohairic version, since the latter version lies also behind the Arabic. There are, however, traces of direct influence from the Sahidic,[1] though these are not so strong as to suggest that the Ethiopic version was made directly from the Sahidic, as Goussen thought.[2] Despite such extensive contamination, however, the considerable value of the Ethiopic version of the Apocalypse, Hofmann concludes,[3] rests upon (*a*) its being a direct translation from the Greek, (*b*) its being based on a good Greek *Vorlage*, and (*c*) its having been made by a competent translator.

6. THE QUESTION OF SYRIAC INFLUENCE

Besides influence from Coptic and Arabic on the text of the Ethiopic version, a certain amount of Syriac coloration has also been detected, though the degree and nature of such influence is debated. In 1882 Gildemeister[4] pointed out several Aramaic (Syriac) features in the vocabulary of the version. He argued that the formation of ecclesiastical Ethiopic and the translation of the Bible belong to different periods, and that those who made the version from the Greek employed words and expressions that had been brought to Abyssinia by Monophysite Syrian monks. Burkitt[5] was impressed by Gildemeister's observations and proposed the theory that behind the existing Ethiopic version of the Gospels, made from the Greek, there was a yet older version, made from the Syriac. Traces of this version survive, he thought, in occasional readings where the Ethiopic agrees with the Old Syriac against almost all other authorities (e.g. at Mark x. 50 it reads ἐπιβαλών for ἀποβαλών, supported only by 565 and Syrˢ).

---

[1] Joseph Hofmann, 'Beziehungen der sa'idischen zur äthiopischen Übersetzung der Johannes-Apokalypse', *Neutestamentliche Aufsätze, Festschrift für Prof. Josef Schmid zum 70. Geburtstag*, ed. by J. Blinzler *et al.* (Regensberg, 1963), pp. 115–24.

[2] Henri Goussen, *Apocalypsis S. Johannis Apostoli, versio sahidica* (Leipzig, 1895), p. vii. In this opinion Goussen revived the judgement of Stephen Evodius Assemani.

[3] Hofmann, op. cit. (p. 237 n. 3 above), p. 169.

[4] Reported in Caspar René Gregory, *Prolegomena*, being vol. iii of Tischendorf's *Novum Testamentum Graece*, 8th edn. (Leipzig, 1884), pp. 895 f., and in Gregory's *Textkritik des Neuen Testamentes*, ii (Leipzig, 1902), 554 f.

[5] F. C. Burkitt, 'Texts and Versions', *Encyclopædia Biblica*, iv (London and New York, 1903), col. 5012.

The debate was carried on by Vööbus, who argued that it is *a priori* unlikely that Syrian monks would have carried with them Greek manuscripts of the New Testament.[1] Furthermore, while combing through hagiographic texts in Ethiopic, Vööbus found scriptural quotations that have parallels in Old Syriac manuscripts and patristic texts.[2] Such data, Vööbus holds, make it probable that the Ethiopic text of the Gospels was translated from an Old Syriac *Vorlage*.

It is no doubt premature to attempt to reach a firm conclusion in a domain where the relevant patristic and hagiographic material has not yet been fully sifted and assessed and where the existing manuscripts of the version are relatively so late. At the same time, the investigation concerning Aramaic and/or Syriac terminology in Ethiopian Christianity has been carried forward in an eminently sane and sensible discussion contributed by Polotsky. In the light of his researches, it appears that the Aramaic loan-words which Gildemeister thought were introduced by Christian monks into ecclesiastical Ethiopic are in fact part of the Judaic leaven within Christianity. None of them is characteristically and exclusively Syriac, and none is distinctively Christian in meaning.[3] There still remain to be taken into account, however, occasional variant readings in the Ethiopic Gospels that find support only in Syriac witnesses, as well as several proper names that are transliterated from Syriac, to which a Greek ending has been attached (such as the names for John and Jeremiah). In the face of such data side by side with equally clear evidence of a Greek *Vorlage*, Boismard, in a study of Ethiopic manuscripts of the Gospel of John, has ventured to suggest the theory that there once existed 'two primitive, independent texts, one derived from the Syriac, the other from the Greek'.[4] Confronted by such diversity of opinions, one can

---

[1] Arthur Vööbus, *Early Versions*, pp. 253 ff.

[2] Vööbus, *Die Spuren*, pp. 25 ff., and 'Ta'āmera Iyasūs. Zeuge eines älteren äthiopischen Evangelientypus', *OCP* xvii (1951), 462–7.

[3] H. J. Polotsky, 'Aramaic, Syriac, and Gəʿəz', *JSS* ix (1964), 1–10; repr. in Polotsky's *Collected Papers* (Jerusalem, 1971), pp. 8–17.

[4] M.-E. Boismard, *RB* lxiii (1956), 454. Independently of Boismard, Ullendorff reached a similar assessment of the conflicting data: 'I fail to understand the position of those who claim either an exclusively Greek or an exclusively Syriac *Vorlage*. . . . Some respectable pieces of evidence can be adduced in favour of each of several hypotheses, but it seems that reality was a good deal more complex and eclectic than is sometimes conceded, and the linguistic facts refuse to fall into neat

appreciate Hofmann's cautious—and altogether realistic—evaluation: 'The question of the *Vorlage* of the Ethiopic Gospels is open and doubtless will remain so for a long time.'[1]

In conclusion, it is clear that the several parts of the Ethiopic New Testament must be examined separately. Whereas the text of the Gospels is far from homogeneous and its base, or bases, quite uncertain, for the Acts of the Apostles, the Catholic Epistles, and the Apocalypse the version was made from a Greek *Vorlage*, and therefore, despite subsequent accommodation here and there to an Arabic text of the so-called Egyptian Vulgate, is still of significance for the New Testament textual critic.

VI. LIMITATIONS OF ETHIOPIC IN REPRESENTING GREEK

by *Josef Hofmann*

Whoever translates the Greek New Testament into Ethiopic must take certain limitations into account, for Ethiopic is so totally different from Greek that it can only to a certain degree represent the fine distinctions and nuances of the latter.

1. PHONETICS

The difficulties already begin with the transcription of foreign words and proper names, for not every Greek sound can be represented by means of an exactly corresponding Ethiopic

patterns. . . . On the face of it, work on one single linguistic *Vorlage* was, perhaps, the exception rather than the rule in the peculiar circumstances that obtained in the Aksumite kingdom of the fourth–sixth centuries' (*Ethiopia and the Bible* (London, 1968), p. 56).

Ullendorff's earlier investigation of the possibility that an Aramaic text of the book of Enoch underlay the Ethiopic version of that book has no necessary bearing on the problem of the *Vorlage* of the Ethiopic version of the New Testament; cf. his contribution 'An Aramaic "Vorlage" of the Ethiopic Text of Enoch?' in *Atti del Convegno internazionale di Studi Etiopici*, Roma 2–4 Apr. 1959 (*Problemi attuali di scienza e di cultura*, quad. N. 48; Accademia nazionale dei Lincei, anno ccclvii (Rome, 1960), pp. 259–67).

[1] 'Das Neue Testament in äthiopischer Sprache', op. cit. (p. 236 n. 1), p. 359.

sound. The transliteration[1] of consonants can be represented by the following scheme:

β	γ	δ	ζ	θ	κ	λ	μ	ν	ξ	π	ρ	σ	τ	φ	χ	ψ
b	g	d	z	t	q	l	m	n	ks	p, f, p̣	r	s	ṭ	f	k	s

Double consonants are pronounced twice but written only once. The rendering of the vowels and diphthongs can be illustrated by the following basic scheme:

βα	βᾱ	βε	βη	βι	βο	βυ	βου	βω	βαι
ba, bā	bā	be, bē	bē, bī	bī, be, bē	bō	be, bī, bū	bū	bō	bē

βαυ	βει	βευ	βοι
bāw	bī, be	bēw	bī, bē

The representation of vowels in Ethiopic reflects the itacistic pronunciation of later Greek. The accent is not marked. When an 'i' or an 'e' is followed by a second vowel, a 'y' or a 'w' (respectively) is inserted as a hiatus-filler. If the first vowel is an 'i', the combination 'iy' is usually dissimilated to 'ey'. From the manner of writing one cannot discern whether an Ethiopic letter is to be read without a vowel or with an 'e', and thus whether or not a vowel should follow the Greek letter which it represents.

> Ἰάϊρος] ᾽iyā᾽īrōs, Μαθθαῖος] māttēwōs, σπόγγοι] sefeng, Λυκαονία] līqā᾽ōneyā, Συροφοινίκισσα] sīrōfīnīqīs, (Rev. xxi. 20) χρυσόλι-θος] kerīsōlītōbē (3 MSS.), kereselītōbē (4 MSS.), kerīseletōbē (1 MSS.), kerīsōlōtōbē (1 MS.), kerīsōlētōbē (2 MSS.)

2. MORPHOLOGY

Inasmuch as Ethiopic has not developed the same grammatical categories as those in Greek, there is no exact correspondence between the two as concerns the forms of individual sentence-units.

A. *Substantives*

Ethiopic has no compound substantives; Greek compounds,

---

[1] The transliteration of the Ethiopic alphabet adopted here is as follows: **U**, ha; **ለ**, la; **ሐ**, ḥa; **መ**, ma; **ሠ**, ša; **ረ**, ra; **ሰ**, sa; **ቀ**, qa; **በ**, ba; **ተ**, ta; **ኀ**, ḫa; **ነ**, na; **አ**, ᾽a; **ከ**, ka; **ወ**, wa; **ዐ**, ᾽a; **ዘ**, za; **የ**, ya; **ደ**, da; **ገ**, ga; **ጠ**, ṭa; **ጰ**, p̣a; **ጸ**, ṣa; **ፀ**, ṣa; **ፈ**, fa; **ፐ**, pa; **ኈ**, kwa; **ጐ**, gwa; **ቈ**, qwa; **ኈ**, ḫwa.

therefore, are usually expressed by the construct state, and even by the infinitive or by relative sentences.

1 Tim. i. 10: ἀνδραποδισταῖς] *saraqta sabe'* 'fures hominum'

Rom. xii. 13: φιλοξενία] *'afqarō nagd* 'diligere hospitem' 'dilectio hospitis' (objective gen.)

1 Tim. i. 10: ἀρσενοκοίταις] *wa-'ella yaḥawerū dība be'esī* 'et-qui vadunt ad virum'

(1) *Gender*

Ethiopic lacks the neuter gender, a fact which is especially apparent in rendering the substantive use of an adjective. In such cases Ethiopic employs the masculine (less frequently the feminine) form of the adjective to represent the missing neuter.

Rom. ix. 11: τι ἀγαθὸν ἢ φαῦλον] *šannāya wa-'ekūya* (masculine accusative) 'bonum et-malum'

Matt. vii. 6: τὸ ἅγιον] *qeddesta* (feminine accusative) 'sanctum'

(2) *Number*

Ethiopic clearly distinguishes between singular and plural.

(3) *Case*

One can hardly speak of a declension in Ethiopic.

Genitive: expressed primarily by the construct state or by periphrasis.

Dative: expressed by the preposition *la-* ('to', 'towards'); instrumental dative by the preposition *ba-* ('with').

Accusative: expressed by changing the ending or by periphrasis.

Vocative: expressed by prefixing or suffixing of *-ō-*; sometimes by prefixing and suffixing at the same time.

Rev. xiii. 15: τῇ εἰκόνι τοῦ θηρίου] *la-'amsāla* (dative; construct state) *zektū 'arwē* 'imagini illius bestiae'

Rev. xiii. 15: ἡ εἰκὼν τοῦ θηρίου] *meslū la-we'etū 'arwē* (periphrasis) 'imago (-eius sc.) eius bestiae'

Matt. ii. 21: τὸ παιδίον καὶ τὴν μητέρα αὐτοῦ] *ḥesāna wa-'emō* (by the ending) 'infantem et-matrem-eius'

Matt. i. 3: ἐγέννησεν τὸν Φάρες] *walada ferēs-hā* (acc. by virtue of affix)

Matt. i. 2 : ἐγέννησεν τὸν ᾽Ιακώβ] *waladō la-yāʿeqōb* (periphrasis) 'genuit-eum (sc.) Iacobum'

John ii. 4: γύναι] *'ō-be'esītō* (Luke xxii. 57 : *be'esītō*)

(4) *Determination*

Ethiopic possesses neither a definite nor an indefinite article. Ordinarily determination is expressed only when it is not self-evident; thus it is lacking with proper names and with substantives accompanied by a demonstrative or possessive pronoun. Should it be desired, however, to represent a substantive as unconditionally determined, then either the demonstrative pronoun (usually forms of *we'etū* 'is') or a possessive suffix compensates for the article in Ethiopic. The indeterminate, indicated in Greek by τις or εἷς, can be indicated by the numeral *'aḥadū* ('unus').

Rev. viii. 5 : ὁ ἄγγελος] *we'etū mal'ak* 'is angelus'

Luke xxiii. 6 : εἰ ὁ ἄνθρωπος Γαλιλαῖός ἐστιν] *la'emma galīlāwī be'esīhū* 'si Galilaeus vir(-eius)'

Luke xvi. 19: ἄνθρωπος δέ τις] *'aḥadū be'esī* 'unus vir'

Matt. viii. 19: εἷς γραμματεύς] *'aḥadū ṣaḥāfī* 'unus scriba'

B. *Adjectives*

The primary deficiency consists in the fact that the Ethiopic adjective has no heightened form. Only the following preposition *'em-* indicates that the comparative or the superlative is meant. In most cases the heightened adjective is expressed verbally.

Acts xxviii. 23 : ἦλθον . . . πλείονες] *wa-maṣ'ū . . . bezūḥān* 'et-venerunt . . . multi'

Matt. xi. 11 : ὁ δὲ μικρότερος . . . μείζων αὐτοῦ ἐστιν] *za-yene'es yaʿabī 'emennēhū* 'qui-parvus- (-minor-, -minimus-) est, maior-est quam is'

C. *Pronouns*

Ethiopic possesses a fully developed system of personal, demonstrative, interrogative, possessive, and indefinite pronouns. Since reflexive pronouns are, however, lacking, the Greek reflexive possessive is expressed in Ethiopic by the usual possessive pronoun, and the reflexive personal pronoun by either the verb form (III-stem) or by a substitute substantive such as *re'es* ('caput'), *nafs* ('anima'), *šegā* ('caro'), or *lebb* ('cor').

Rev. vi. 15 : ἔκρυψαν ἑαυτούς] *taḥab'ū* (III-stem) 'se absconde-runt' (also : 'absconditi sunt')

Luke iv. 23 : θεράπευσον σεαυτόν] *faẉẉes re'esaka* 'sana caput-tuum'

Luke xii. 17 : καὶ διελογίζετο ἐν ἑαυτῷ] *wa-ḥallaya ba-lebbū* 'et-cogitavit in-corde-suo'

Mark v. 5 : καὶ κατακόπτων ἑαυτόν λίθοις] *wa-yegēmed šegāhū ba-'eban* 'et-concidit carnem-suam (in-) lapidibus'

Rom. xiii. 9 : ἀγαπήσεις τὸν πλησίον σου ὡς σεαυτόν] *'afqer bīṣaka kama nafseka* 'dilige socium-tuum ut animam-tuam'

D. *Numerals*

Words expressing numerals are, comparatively speaking, adequately translated. A minor difficulty is involved in the circumstance that Ethiopic has no special word for 'one thousand'. The word *'elf*, whose etymological equivalents in other Semitic languages mean 'one thousand', has in Ethiopic the value of 'ten thousand'. Thousands are counted as ten times the hundreds.

Rev. vii. 5 : δώδεκα χιλιάδες] *'elf wa-'ešrā me'et* 'myrias et-viginti centum'

Ordinals are missing from the number eleven onwards. To represent them, appropriate numbers are used with a relative pronoun.

Rev. xxi. 20 : ὁ ἑνδέκατος] *wa-'enta 'ešrū wa-'aḥatī* 'et-quod decem et-unum'

E. *Verbs*

The Ethiopic verb, like the Greek, has a conjugation; i.e. it indicates through particular forms the person and number. In terms of time, gender, and mood, however, there are consider-able differences, so that Ethiopic is capable of expressing only a very limited measure of the information that is contained in a Greek verb-form.

(1) *Time*

The Ethiopic verb has no reference to time. It indicates only whether an action is regarded as complete (Perfect) or incomplete (Imperfect). In the New Testament the Greek tenses are represented according to the following scheme:

Present, Future, Present Perfect = Ethiopic Imperfect
Aorist, Perfect = Ethiopic Perfect
Imperfect, Pluperfect = Ethiopic Imperfect or Perfect, according to the interpretation

Mark i. 37: ζητοῦσίν σε] *yaḥaśeśūka* (impf.) 'quaerunt-te'

Mark i. 8: βαπτίσει ὑμᾶς] *yāṭameqakemmū* (impf.) 'baptizabit-vos'

1 Cor. xv. 27: ὑποτέτακται] *yegarer* (impf.) 'subagitur'

Acts i. 5: ἐβάπτισεν] *'aṭmaqa* (perf.) 'baptizavit'

John i. 15: κέκραγεν] *kalleḥa* (perf.) 'clamavit'

Mark i. 32: ἔφερον] *'amṣe'ū* (perf.) 'attulerunt'

Luke vi. 19: ἐζήτουν] *yefaqedū* (impf.) 'volunt'

Luke viii. 29: συνηρπάκει αὐτόν] *yā'abedō* (impf.) 'amentem-facit-eum'

Luke viii. 2: ἐξεληλύθει] *waṣ'ū* (perf.) 'exierunt'

(2) *Mood*

Of the four Greek moods, only the indicative and the second person imperative have an exact correspondence in Ethiopic. The Greek subjunctive, optative, third person imperative, and negative imperative (prohibition) are expressed either by the Ethiopic subjunctive—which has also assumed the function of a jussive and can be reinforced by the particle *la*—or simply by the indicative. In this way many modal nuances in Greek (the number of which is increased even more by the presence of ἄν) remain disregarded in Ethiopic.

Luke iii. 10: τί οὖν ποιήσωμεν] *menta negbar* (subj.) 'quid faciamus'

Matt. v. 20: οὐ μὴ εἰσέλθητε] *'ī-tebawe'ū* (ind.) 'non-intratis'

Acts viii. 20: σοὶ εἴη] *la-yekūnka* (subj.) '(ut-) fiat-tibi'

Acts xvii. 18: τί ἂν θέλοι] *menta yefaqed* (ind.) 'quid vult'

Mark iv. 3: ἀκούετε] *seme'ū* (imperat.) 'audite'

Matt. xi. 15: ἀκουέτω] *la-yesmāʿ* (subj.) '(ut-) audiat'

John vi. 20: μὴ φοβεῖσθε] *ʾī-tefreḥū* (subj.) 'ne-timeatis'

Mark xv. 36: ἴδωμεν] *nerʾay* (subj.) 'videamus'

(3) *Voice of the Verb*

The Ethiopic verb has no special formal ending which can give it an active, passive, or middle sense. In this respect it can operate only within its own system of stems:

I Stem = transitive, active; intransitive
II Stem = causative, transitive, active
III Stem = reflexive; passive
IV Stem = causative and reflexive

Thus, for the active voice Ethiopic has available the I and also the II Stem; for the passive and middle it has the III stem, and also in some cases the IV Stem.

Luke xxiv. 20: ἐσταύρωσαν αὐτόν] *wa-saqalewō* (transitive, I Stem) 'et-crucifixerunt-eum'

1 Cor. i. 13: ἐσταυρώθη] *tasaqla* (passive, III Stem) 'crucifixus-est'

Matt. xxvii. 5: ἀπήγξατο] *wa-taḥanqa* (reflexive, III Stem) 'et-se-suspendit' (but also: 'et-suspensus-est')

2 Cor. ii. 2: ἐγὼ λυπῶ ὑμᾶς] *ʾana ʾatēkezakemmū* (transitive, II Stem) 'ego contristo-vos'

2 Cor. ii. 4: ἵνα λυπηθῆτε] *kama tetakkezū* (passive, III Stem) 'ut contristemini'

Rev. xii. 1, 3: ὤφθη] *ʾastarʾaya* (reflexive and causative, IV Stem) 'apparuit' (= 'ließ sich sehen')

The active is frequently preferred to the unpopular passive.

Matt. xxvii. 22: σταυρωθήτω] *seqelō* 'crucifige-eum'

Rev. viii. 7: ἐβλήθη] *warada* 'descendit' (Rev. xii. 9 *wadqa* 'cecidit')

(4) εἶναι

Ethiopic lacks a precise equivalent for εἶναι used as a copula. If the meaning of the sentence is clear, the copula is simply passed over; otherwise it is expressed by means of the pronoun *weʾetū*

('is'). Occasionally functioning as a copula are *haḷḷawa* ('adest')
and *kōna* ('factus est'), despite their more literal meanings.

Matt. v. 11 : μακάριοί ἐστε] *beṣūʿ ān ʾanteṃṃū* 'beati vos'

Matt. v. 13 : ὑμεῖς ἐστε τὸ ἅλας] *ʾanteṃṃū we'-ētū ṣēw* 'vos id
(= estis) sal'

Matt. xiv. 23 : μόνος ἦν ἐκεῖ] *bāḥetītū haḷḷō heya* 'solus adest ibi'

Matt. xv. 26 : οὐκ ἔστιν καλὸν λαβεῖν] *ʾī-kōna šannāya našiʾa* 'non-
fuit (= factum-est) bonum sumere'

(5) ἔχειν

Ethiopic possesses no special word for 'to have'. Instead it
employs *beya* ('with me'), *beka* ('with you'), *ʾalbeya* ('not with
me'), or *ʾalbeka* ('not with you'), which are construed sometimes
with the nominative (corresponding to the original meaning)
and sometimes with the accusative (= 'I have'). But one also
finds circumlocutions with the preposition *mesla* ('cum') or with
verbs like *ṣōra* ('portavit'), *ʾasneʿa* ('tenuit'), *rakaba* ('invenit'),
or *haḷḷō+ḥaba* ('adest apud').

Rev. ii. 7 : ὁ ἔχων οὖς] *za-bō ʾezna* (acc.) 'qui-habet aurem' or:
za-bō ʾezn (nom.) 'cui-adest auris'

Rev. iv. 8 : καὶ ἀνάπαυσιν οὐκ ἔχουσιν] *wa-ʾalbōmū ʿerafta* (acc.)
'et-non-habent requiem'

Rev. vi. 2 : ἔχων τόξον] *qasta yāṣaneʿ* 'arcum tenet'

Rev. xii. 12 : ἔχων θυμὸν μέγαν] *mesla ʿabīy ḥemzū* 'cum magno
furore-suo'

(6) *Participles*

The most frequently used participial form si the *qetūl*-form,
which corresponds exactly to the perfect passive participle as well
as being employed almost exclusively for the rendering of this
form. As regards the forming of other participial forms, the
Ethiopic language is limited in its possibilities. Similarly all
the Greek participles, whether used substantively or adjectivally,
can be rendered into Ethiopic only by means of helping constructions: either by complete clauses, whether paratactic or
hypotactic (the latter by means of relative clauses as well as even
by causal or temporal clauses), or by the gerund.

Matt. ix. 36: ἐσκυλμένοι καὶ ἐρριμμένοι] *serūḥān 'emūntū wa-gedūfān* 'vexati ii et-perditi'

Luke iii. 3: καὶ ἦλθεν . . . κηρύσσων] *wa-ʿōda wa-sabaka* 'et-circumiit et-praedicavit'

Mark xiii. 14: ἑστηκότα] *za-yeqawem* 'qui-stat'

Luke v. 12: ἰδὼν . . . πεσών] *wa-sōba re'eya . . . sagada* 'et-quando vidit . . . adoravit'

Rev. xii. 12: εἰδώς] *'esma yā'amer* 'quia scit'

Rev. xiii. 5: στόμα λαλοῦν] *'af kama yenbab* 'os ut loquatur'

Ethiopic frequently employs the adverbial accusative of the infinitive with the suffix (gerund) as a pregnant rendering of Greek participial expressions (particularly the genitive absolute) and even of complete clauses (as a rule temporal clauses).

Matt. ii. 22: ἀκούσας δέ] *wa-samīʿō* 'und bei seinem Hören'

Matt. ii. 19: τελευτήσαντος δὲ τοῦ ʿΗρώδου] *wa-mawītō hērōdes* 'und bei seinem Sterben Herodes'

John iv. 45: ὅτε οὖν ἦλθεν] *wa-bawīʾō* 'und bei seinem Kommen'

John iv. 1: ὡς οὖν ἔγνω] *wa-'a'emīrō* 'und bei seinem Wissen'

Because of the lack of a copula and the poverty of participial forms in Ethiopic, it is virtually impossible to imitate exactly the frequent New Testament periphrastic verbal forms (εἶναι+participle). Generally in these cases the simple verb is used.

Mark xiii. 25: ἔσονται . . . πίπτοντες] *yewadequ* 'cadent'

2 Cor. ii. 17: οὐ γάρ ἐσμεν . . . καπηλεύοντες] *'esma 'ī-kōnna . . . 'ella yetmēyanewō* 'quia non-fuimus (facti-sumus) . . . qui falsant'

(7) *Infinitive*

Both languages have a full range of infinitives. Whereas the Greek infinitive incorporates a temporal aspect, the Ethiopic infinitive is completely indifferent as regards time. In spite of this, however, the area of application of the infinitive in both languages is not greatly different. At the same time, Ethiopic also often uses the subjunctive (with or without the conjunction *kama* 'ut') instead of the infinitive. Where the Greek infinitive is dependent upon a preposition, usually a complete clause is employed in Ethiopic.

Luke ii. 6: αἱ ἡμέραι τοῦ τεκεῖν αὐτήν] 'elata walidōtā 'Tag ihres Gebärens'

Luke ii. 21: ἡμέραι ὀκτὼ τοῦ περιτομεῖν αὐτόν] samūn 'elat kama yegzerewō 'octavus dies ut circumciderent-eum'

Luke iii. 8: δύναται . . . ἐγεῖραι] yekel 'anše'ō 'potest suscitare'

Luke iv. 21: ἤρξατο δὲ λέγειν] wa-'aḥaza yebalōmū 'et-coepit (ut) diceret-eis'

Matt. xxvi. 32: μετὰ δὲ τὸ ἐγερθῆναί με] wa-'emkama tanšā'ekū 'et-ut surrexi'

Matt. xiii. 4: καὶ ἐν τῷ σπείρειν αὐτόν] wa-'enza yezare' 'et-dum seminat'

F. *Indeclinables*

(1) *Adverbs*

Ethiopic has a sufficient range of temporal, local, and modal adverbs to render the corresponding Greek expressions almost exactly. Moreover, adjectives and substantives can be made to express an adverbial sense by placing them in the adverbial (= accusative) case. Several Greek adverbs are rendered by means of a verbal construction.

Matt. ii. 8: ἀκριβῶς] ṭeyūqa (acc.) 'accurate'

Luke xviii. 7: ἡμέρας καὶ νυκτός] ma'alta wa-lēlīta (acc.) 'die et-nocte'

Luke ix. 59: ἐπίτρεψόν μοι πρῶτον ἀπελθόντι θάψαι] 'abeḥanī 'eḥūr 'eqdem 'eqberō 'permitte-mihi (ut) vadam (ut) praeveniam (ut) sepeliam-eum'

Matt. iii. 10: ἤδη ἡ ἀξίνη . . . κεῖται] wadde'a māḥesē . . . yenaber 'perfecit securis . . . iacet'

Greek has three negatives: ἀ privative (which negates a substantive or an adjective), οὐ, and μή. The two latter words negate a complete sentence; as a rule οὐ precedes the indicative, whereas μή precedes the other moods, infinitives, and participles. In Ethiopic the relationships are somewhat different. There the most frequently used negative is the prefixed particle 'ī-, which can negate both a single word and a complete sentence. If the negation is intensively expressed, one uses the particle 'akkō. By

this means the clause which is to be negated is stressed; the train
of thought can then be carried on by means of a relative clause.

Matt. xvii. 17: ὦ γενεὰ ἄπιστος] '*ō-tewled 'ī-'amānīt* 'o genus
infidele'

Matt. v. 17: οὐκ ἦλθον καταλῦσαι] '*ī-maṣā'ekū 'es'arōmū* 'non-
veni (ut) dissolvam'

Matt. vii. 1: μὴ κρίνετε] '*ī-tekwannenū* 'ne-iudicetis'

Matt. vi. 13: καὶ μὴ εἰσενέγκῃς ἡμᾶς εἰς πειρασμόν] *wa-'ī-tābe'ana
westa mansūt* 'et-ne-inducas-nos in tentationem'

Matt. ix. 13: ἔλεος θέλω καὶ οὐ θυσίαν] *meḥrata 'efaqed wa-'akkō
maśwā'eta* 'misericordiam volo et-non sacrificium'

Matt. ix. 24: οὐ γὰρ ἀπέθανεν τὸ κοράσιον] '*esma 'akkō za-mōtat
ḥeṣān* 'quia non (est) quod-mortua-est infans'

(2) *Conjunctions*

The quantity and significance of conjunctions available in
Ethiopic are adequate, even though here and there a corresponding precision with the Greek is lacking. For example, an equivalent to ἄν is absent in Ethiopic; consequently the specific nuances
indicated by this important particle must remain unexpressed in
Ethiopic.

Mark x. 43 ὃς ἂν θέλῃ] *za-yefaqed* 'qui-vult'

1 Tim. ii. 4 ὃς . . . θέλει] *we'etū yefaqed* 'is vult'

(3) *Prepositions*

Ethiopic has a sufficient quantity of prepositions and of
adverbs with a prepositional function; so here there are no
limitations in representing Greek.

(4) *Interjections*

Genuine interjections seldom occur in the New Testament; one
of them is οὐαί (= '*allē*)+the dative (or+a suffix). Some Greek
imperatives are interjections in Ethiopic: Χαῖρε *bāḥa*, ἰδού *nāhū*,
ἔρχου *na'ā*.

3. SYNTAX

Translating a sentence from Greek into Ethiopic involves
various kinds of limitations which have their basis in Ethiopic

syntax. But their number is smaller than might have been imagined in view of the dissimilarity of the two languages.

A. *Word Order*

In Ethiopic there is great freedom in terms of word order, and generally it can follow the word order of the Greek. Thus the qualifier may stand either before or after that which is qualified; the verb need not necessarily be placed at the beginning of a sentence. The only really strict rule demands that, in the case of the construct relation, that which is possessed must stand immediately before that which possesses. But if any attribute is placed between them, another genitive construction must be used.

Luke ix. 26: καὶ τῶν ἁγίων ἀγγέλων] *wa-za-qeddūsān malā'ektīhū* 'et-sanctorum angelorum-suorum'

Mark viii. 38: μετὰ τῶν ἀγγέλων τῶν ἁγίων] *mesla malā'ektīhū qedūsān* 'cum angelis-suis sanctis'

John xvii. 3: καὶ ὃν ἀπέστειλας Ἰησοῦν] *wa-za-fannawkō 'īyasūs* 'et-quem-misisti Iesum'

B. *Sentences*

Ethiopic, like Greek, makes use of both parataxis and hypotaxis.

(1) *Principal Clauses*

In the construction of principal clauses—whether declarative, imperative, optative, or interrogative—Ethiopic differs very little from Greek.

(a) *Declarative sentences*

In both languages a special meaning can be given declarative sentences by means of specific particles; e.g. γάρ = 'esma gives a causal meaning, and ἀλλά = 'allā an adversative meaning.

John xvi. 13: οὐ γὰρ λαλήσει ἀφ' ἑαυτοῦ, ἀλλ' ὅσα ἀκούσει λαλήσει] *'esma 'ī-yenager za-'emhabēhū wa-za-sam'a dā'emū yenager* 'nam non-loquetur quod-ex-eo, et-quod-audivit autem loquetur'

(b) *Imperative sentences*

In Greek the form of the verb is either the imperative or the negative subjunctive, whereas Ethiopic employs either the imperative or subjunctive (= jussive). The future with an imperative sense is handled much like a normal imperative.

John xix. 15: ἆρον, σταύρωσον αὐτόν] *'a'etetō wa-seqelō* 'tolle-eum et-crucifige-eum'

John iii. 7: μὴ θαυμάσῃς] *'ī-tānker* 'ne-mireris'

Matt. v. 21: οὐ φονεύσεις] *'ī-teqtel nafsa* 'ne-occidas animam'

(c) Sentences involving wishes

Here the Ethiopic subjunctive corresponds to the Greek subjunctive.

Rev. iii. 15: ὄφελον ψυχρὸς ἦς] *wa-retū'-sa tekūn qwarīra* 'utinam esses frigidus'

(d) Interrogative sentences

(1) Dependent interrogations are recognizable in both languages in terms of the question posed by the introductory pronoun or adjective.

(2) Independent interrogations have in Greek no special mark (apart from the written sign of the interrogative). They are made recognizable in Ethiopic by means of the enclitic *-nū* or *-hū*.

John i. 38: ῥαββὶ ποῦ μένεις;] *rabbi 'aytē taḥader* 'Rabbi, ubi habitas?'

John xi. 26: πιστεύεις τοῦτο;] *ta'amenī-nū zanta* 'credis-ne hoc?'

(2) Subordinate Clauses

Even in rendering subordinate clauses Ethiopic is not at all limited.

(a) Subject clauses

In the New Testament subject clauses are usually introduced by ἵνα+the subjunctive. In Ethiopic the corresponding clause has *kama*+the subjunctive (or *kama* may be omitted).

John xvi. 7: συμφέρει ὑμῖν ἵνα ἐγὼ ἀπέλθω] *yeḫēyesakemmū* [*kama*] *'eḥūr 'ana* 'melius-est-vobis (ut) vadam ego'

(b) Object clauses

Whereas the normal Greek collocation is ὅτι+the indicative, Ethiopic employs *kama*+the perfect or imperfect indicative.

After verbs of wishing or knowing, Greek normally uses the infinitive, whereas Ethiopic employs the subjunctive with (or sometimes without) *kama*, but the infinitive is also possible.

John ix. 29 : οἴδαμεν ὅτι Μωϋσεῖ λελάληκεν ὁ θεός] *nā'amer kama la-mūsē tanāgarō 'egzi'abeḥēr* 'scimus quod Moysi collocutus-est-ei Deus'

John iv. 47 : ἠρώτα ἵνα καταβῇ] *wa-sa' alō kama yerad* 'et-rogavit-eum ut descenderet'

Matt. xxvi. 37 : ἤρξατο λυπεῖσθαι] *wa-'aḥaza yetakkez* 'et-coepit (ut) contristaretur'

John iii. 2 : οὐδεὶς . . . δύναται ταῦτα τὰ σημεῖα ποιεῖν] *'albō za-yekel yegbar zanta ta'āmera* 'non-est qui-potest (ut) faciat haec signa'

Matt. ix. 28 : δύναμαι τοῦτο ποιῆσαι] *'ekel zanta gabīra* 'possum hoc facere'

(c) *Attributive clauses*

Attributive relative clauses in Ethiopic do not differ essentially in construction from those in Greek. When the relative pronoun is not in the nominative, Ethiopic must frequently clarify the logical connection by means of a suffix. Neither the annexation nor the attraction of relative clauses is imitated in Ethiopic.

Acts ii. 36 : Ἰησοῦν ὃν ὑμεῖς ἐσταυρώσατε] *'īyasūs za-'antemmū saqalkemmewō* 'Iesum quem-vos crucifixistis'

Acts vii. 45 : ἦν (relative clause connective) καὶ εἰσήγαγον] *wa-'abe'ewā* 'et-duxerunt-eam'

Acts vii. 45 : τῶν ἐθνῶν ὧν ἐξῶσεν ὁ θεός] *'aḥzāb 'ella 'awṣe'ōmū 'egzī 'abeḥēr* 'gentium quas expulit Deus'

(d) *Interrogative clauses*

Indirect interrogative clauses are uncongenial to Ethiopic; a direct form is preferably used for questions. This applies especially to disjunctive questions. Indirect deliberative questions are introduced by εἰ in Greek, but Ethiopic either employs (*la-*)*'emma* or alters the sentence to the direct form.

Luke xii. 5 : ὑποδείξω δὲ ὑμῖν τίνα φοβηθῆτε] *wa-'ar'eyakemmū manna tefareḥū* 'et-monstrabo-vobis quem timeatis' (indic.)

Luke ix. 46: Εἰσῆλθεν δὲ διαλογισμὸς . . . τὸ τίς ἂν εἴη μείζων
αὐτῶν] *wa-ḫallayū* . . . *mannū yaʿabī ʾemennēhōmū* 'et-meditati-
sunt quis maior-sit (indic.) ex-iis'

Mark xv. 44: ἐπηρώτησεν αὐτὸν εἰ πάλαι ἀπέθανεν] *wa-yebēlō*
waddeʾa-nū mōta 'et-dixit-ei: perfecit-ne mortuus est?'

Luke xiv. 31: βουλεύσεται εἰ δυνατός ἐστιν] *wa-yemaker la-ʾemma*
yekel 'et-deliberabit si possit' (indic.)

(e) Temporal clauses

Ethiopic lacks the fine distinctions which Greek makes between a temporal sentence with the indicative and one such as
ἄν+the subjunctive. In both cases Ethiopic employs either the
perfect or the indicative of the imperfect, depending upon the
tense of the Greek.

John ii. 22: ὅτε οὖν ἠγέρθη] *wa-ʾama tanŝeʾa* 'et-quando surrexit'

John iv. 25: ὅταν ἔλθῃ ἐκεῖνος] *wa-ʾama maṣʾa weʾetū* 'et-quando
venit is'

2 Cor. iii. 15: ἡνίκα ἂν ἀναγινώσκηται] *sōba yānabebū* 'cum
legunt'

(f) Final clauses

The manner of expression of final clauses in Ethiopic corresponds to the Greek: ἵνα, ὅπως, ὡς are translated by *kama*+the
subjunctive.

John xvii. 4: ἵνα ποιήσω] *kama ʾegbar* 'ut faciam'

Matt. vii. 1: ἵνα μὴ κριθῆτε] *kama ʾī-tetkwannanū* 'ut non-
iudicemini'

Matt. vi. 5: ὅπως φανῶσιν] *kama yāstarʾeyū* 'ut appareant'

(g) Causal clauses

In Ethiopic there is no difference between a principal clause
having causal meaning and a subordinate causal clause; both
have *ʾesma* (= γάρ and ὅτι) as the characteristic conjunction.

John xx. 29: ὅτι ἑώρακάς με πεπίστευκας] *ʾesma reʾīkanī-hū*
ʾamankanī 'quia vidisti-me credidisti-mihi?'

Matt. i. 21: αὐτὸς γὰρ σώσει] *ʾesma weʾetū yādeḫen* 'nam is
salvabit'

(h) Consecutive clauses

Greek prefers the infinitive following ὥστε. Ethiopic, on the other hand, employs '*eska* (*sōba*) only with the finite verb.

John iii. 16: ὥστε τὸν υἱόν . . . ἔδωκεν] '*eska waldō* . . . *wahaba* 'usque filium-suum . . . dedit'

Matt. viii. 28: ὥστε μὴ ἰσχύειν] '*eska sōba* '*ī-yekel* 'usque quando non-potest' (indic. imperf.)

(i) Conditional clauses

Ethiopic has difficulties with the precise rendering of Greek conditions. Greek, unlike Ethiopic, can express all possible shades of condition by means of tense, mood, and the insertion of ἄν. In general the following rules apply:

(α) Real conditions: The conditional particle is εἰ (ἐάν) = '*emma*, and the Ethiopic verb form corresponds to the time expressed in the Greek clause. Whereas the Greek form of the apodosis is in the future (Ethiopic = imperfect), the Ethiopic protasis prefers the perfect (= precise future).

(β) Unreal conditions: The conditional particle is ἐάν = *sōba* with the perfect. In the apodosis Ethiopic places the particle '*em*- before the verb in the perfect tense.

John iv. 48: ἐὰν μὴ . . . ἴδητε, οὐ μὴ πιστεύσετε] '*emma* . . . '*ī-re'īkemmū* '*ī-ta'amenū* 'si . . . non videritis, non-credetis'

Matt. vi. 14: ἐὰν γὰρ ἀφῆτε . . . ἀφήσει] '*esma* '*emma ḥadaggemū* . . . *yaḥadeq* 'nam si remiseritis . . . remittet'

Luke xi. 20: εἰ δὲ . . . ἐκβάλλω . . . ἄρα ἔφθασεν] *wa-'emma-sa* '*ana 'awa-ṣe'ōmū* . . . *yōgīkē baṣḥat* 'et-si-autem ego expello . . . utique pervenit'

John iv. 10: εἰ ᾔδεις . . . σὺ ἂν ᾔτησας αὐτόν] *sōba-sa tā'amerī* . . . '*antīnī 'ādī 'em-sa'alkīyō* 'si autem scires (perf.) . . . tu-etiam amplius rogares-eum' (perf.)

Ethiopic frequently transforms a conditional clause into a relative clause, especially sentences beginning with εἴ τις. Such clauses, however, are constructed with the verb-form which a pure conditional clause might also have.

John vi. 51: ἐάν τις φάγῃ . . . ζήσει] *za-bal'a* . . . *yaḥayū* 'qui-manducaverit . . . vivet'

(j) *Concessive clauses*

Concessive clauses, which are similar to conditional sentences in both languages, are introduced by εἰ καί = 'e͟m͟ma-nī, 'e͟m͟ma-hī, or by la-'m͟mea-nī, la-'e͟m͟ma-hī, or simply by 'e͟m͟ma.

> 2 Cor. vii. 8: εἰ καὶ ἐλύπησα ὑμᾶς . . . οὐ μεταμέλομαι] wa-'emma-nī 'atak͟kazkūke͟m͟mū . . . 'ī-yānēseḥanī 'etsi contristavi-vos . . . non-poenitet-me'

As the comparison of both languages indicates, Ethiopic, along with all other Semitic languages, exhibits many limitations *vis-à-vis* Greek. In spite of this, however, its grammar permits certain freedoms and concessions which enable it to represent the text of the Greek New Testament better than many other related languages.

VI

Minor Eastern Versions

THE minor Eastern versions that are considered in the present chapter are the Arabic, Nubian, Persian, Sogdian, and Caucasian Albanian versions.[1]

I. THE ARABIC VERSIONS

1. THE ORIGIN OF THE ARABIC VERSIONS

In antiquity Arabia as a geographical term comprised the territory west of Mesopotamia, east and south of Syria and Palestine, extending to the isthmus of Suez. This area, about one-fourth that of Europe and one-third that of the United States, was divided by the geographer Ptolemy into three regions: Arabia Felix, the Happy or Fertile; Arabia Petraea, the Stony; and Arabia Deserta, the Desert. When and how and by whom the Gospel was brought to these diverse areas is not known, for the data are scattered and inconclusive. According to Harnack, by the middle of the third century there were numerous bishoprics

---

[1] Whether there was a version in the Hunnic language is problematic. According to information included in the *Chronicle* of Zacharias Rhetor (d. before 553), about the middle of the sixth century Ḳardūṣaṭ, bishop of Arrān, sent three (or seven) priests beyond the Caspian Gates to minister to those taken captive by the Huns from the land of the Romans. As a result of the work of the missionaries not only were many of the captives baptized, but converts were made also among the Huns. The account closes with the statement that the priests 'were there for a week of years, and there they translated books into the Hunnic tongue' (Bk. XII, chap. vii of the Syriac text ed. by E. W. Brooks in *CSCO*, Scriptores Syri, III ser., vi (Paris, 1921), 216; Eng. trans. by F. J. Hamilton and E. W. Brooks, *The Syriac Chronicle known as that of Zachariah of Mitylene* (London, 1899), p. 330). Although the identity of these books is not disclosed, it is altogether probable that they included one or more books of the Bible.

As early as 635 a group of Nestorian missionaries arrived at Ch'ang-an, the capital of the newly founded T'ang Dynasty, where they prepared a Chinese translation of their sacred books, including, it would seem, the Gospels (see John Foster, *The Church of the T'ang Dynasty* (London, 1939)). The monument at Si-nang-fu (see p. 275 n. 5 below) speaks of 'the twenty-seven standard works of His [Christ's] Sûtras' (Saeki's trans.). It is disputed whether this refers to the New Testament or to other Christian documents (see Sten Bugge, 'Den syriske kirkes nyt. kanon i China', *Norsk teologisk tidsskrift*, xli (1940), 97–118).

in towns lying south of the Hauran and the Dead Sea, all of which were grouped together in a single synod.[1] On at least two occasions Origen was invited to Arabia in order to participate in doctrinal discussions that were convened because of certain heretical tendencies on the part of Beryllus[2] and of Heraclides.[3] At a later date efforts were made to introduce Christianity among the nomad tribes. According to Socrates, during the fourth century Mavia the queen of the Ishmaelites (the Saracens) arranged that Moses, a pious monk, should be consecrated bishop over her nation.[4] It also appears that during the same century Christian missions penetrated the southern part of the Arabian peninsula from Ethiopia. According to Philostorgius, through the efforts of one Theophilus, an Abyssinian of Arian faith, churches were built in Zafar, the capital of Ḥimyaric Arabia, in Aden, and along the Persian Gulf.[5]

Who it was that made the first translation of the Scriptures into Arabic is not known. Various traditions have assigned the honour to different persons. According to a story reported by Michael the Syrian (died 1199) in his *Chronicle*,[6] in the seventh century 'Amr bar Sa'd bar abī Waqqās, the emir of the Arabs, requested John, the Jacobite Patriarch at Antioch (631–48), to make a translation of the Gospels from Syriac into Arabic, but to eliminate all references to the divinity of Jesus as well as mention of the Cross and baptism. After the Patriarch had vigorously remonstrated against the restrictions, he proceeded to gather a group of bishops who prepared the translation, but without

---

[1] Adolf von Harnack, *Die Mission und Ausbreitung des Christentums in den ersten drei Jahrhunderten*, 4te Aufl., ii (Leipzig, 1924), 699 ff. (*The Mission and Expansion of Christianity in the First Three Centuries*, 2nd edn., ii (London, 1908), 153 ff.). For a list of the chief churchmen in the several bishoprics, see R. Devreesse, 'Le christianisme dans la province d'Arabie', *Vivre et Penser*, ii (= *RB* li) (1942), 110–46; for a rich bibliography on 'Christentum im vorislamischen Arabien', see Joseph Henninger in *NZMRW* iv (1948), 222–4.

[2] See Eusebius, *Hist. eccl.* VI. xxxiii, and cf. Georg Kretschmer, 'Origines und die Araber', *ZTK* l (1953), 258–79.

[3] Ibid. VI. xxxvii, and cf. the papyrus codex discovered in 1941 at Tura near Cairo containing the Greek text of Origen's *Discussion with Heraclides* (ed. by J. Scherer; Cairo, 1949).

[4] *Hist. eccl.* iv. 36; cf. Theodoret, *Hist. eccl.* iv. 20. See also L. Duchesne, 'Les missions chrétiennes au sud de l'empire romain', *Mélanges d'archéologie et d'histoire*, xvi (1896), 112–18.

[5] *Hist. eccl.* iii. 6 (ed. J. Bidez, pp. 33 f.).

[6] *Chronique de Michel le Syrien*, edited by J.-B. Chabot, ii (Paris, 1901; repr. Brussels, 1963), 431 f.

making the specified deletions. Although Baumstark[1] thought there might be some kernel of truth in the account, Graf,[2] with more caution, raised serious questions concerning the general plausibility of the story. In any case, nothing further is known of such a translation, nor have any traces of it been discovered in extant manuscripts.

Another tradition concerning the translator of the Arabic version of the Bible is preserved in the encyclopedic work known as *al-Fihrist*. The author of this tenth-century survey of Muslim culture states that during the califate of Ma'mūn (813–33) a Muslim by the name of Aḥmad ibn-'Abdullāh ibn-Salām made a translation, from the Hebrew and Greek, of 'the Torah, the Gospels, and the books of the prophets and disciples'.[3] The passage has been studied by Kračkovskij, who suggests the possibility that the Encylopedist confused the translator with a Jew who had been converted to Islam named 'Abd Allāh ibn Salām (died 663).[4] Still another tradition, which for several centuries gained widespread currency,[5] has it that during the early part of the eighth century a Spanish bishop, John of Seville, translated the Gospels from the Latin Vulgate into Arabic. The story, however, was shown by Lagarde[6] to rest upon a misunderstanding; though manuscripts are known to contain an Arabic rendering made from the Latin, they have nothing to do with John of Seville.

---

[1] 'Eine frühislamische und eine vorislamische arabische Evangelienübersetzung aus dem Syrischen', *Atti del XIX Congresso internationale degli orientalisti . . . Roma 1935* (Rome, 1938), p. 382.

[2] Georg Graf, *Geschichte der christlichen arabischen Literatur*, i (*Studi e testi*, vol. cxviii; Vatican City, 1944), 35.

[3] Translated by Bayard Dodge, *The Fihrist of al-Nadīm*, i (New York, 1970), p. 42.

[4] Ignaz Kračkovskij, 'O perevode biblii na arabskij yazyk pri Khalife al-Ma'mūne', *Khristianskij Vostok*, vi (1918), 189–96. For an Arabic manuscript of the Pentateuch dated A.D. 820, which was translated for a certain 'Abdallāh al-Ma'mūn, see Graf, op. cit., pp. 88 f., n. 2.

[5] The tradition is mentioned in the Preface to the 1611 version of the English Bible on the authority of a certain Vas[s]eus, who dates the translation A.D. 717; see Edgar J. Goodspeed, *The Translators to the Reader; Preface to the King James Version 1611* (Chicago, 1935), p. 24. In the nineteenth century J. L. Hug still repeated the same tradition (*Introduction to the New Testament*, translated by David Fosdick, Jr. (Andover, 1836), § 100).

[6] Paul de Lagarde, *Die vier Evangelien arabisch* (Leipzig, 1864; repr. Osnabrück, 1972), pp. xi–xvi; cf. also Peter Le Page Renouf, 'On the Supposed Latin Origin of the Arabic Version of the Gospels', *The Atlantis; or Register of Literature and Science of the Catholic University of Ireland*, iv (1863) 241–59.

2. THE VARIETY OF ARABIC VERSIONS

The variety of Arabic versions of the New Testament is almost bewildering. Lagarde, with characteristic piquancy, commented that there are more Arabic versions of the Gospels than can be welcome to theologians, pressed as they are with other urgent tasks.[1] According to the pioneering survey of more than seventy-five Arabic manuscripts made by Ignazio Guidi,[2] the Arabic versions of the Gospels existing in manuscripts fall into five main groups: (1) those made directly from the Greek; (2) those made directly from or corrected from the Syriac Peshitta; (3) those made directly from or corrected from the Coptic; (4) manuscripts of two distinct eclectic recensions produced by the Alexandrian Patriarchate during the thirteenth century; and (5) miscellaneous manuscripts, some of which are characterized by being cast into the form of rhymed prose made classic by the Koran. Furthermore, more than one Arabic version has been corrected from others derived from a different *Vorlage*. The situation is complicated still further, for example, in a fifteenth-century manuscript containing the Pauline epistles, some of which were translated from Syriac, others from Sahidic, and still others from Bohairic.[3]

In addition to the classes of Arabic versions enumerated above, translations were also made from Latin into Arabic. The first to do so, it seems, was Isḥāq ibn Balašk (or Isaac, son of Velasquez), a Spanish Christian of Cordova, who in 946 prepared a rather free translation of the Gospels. His *Vorlage* was a manuscript with an Old Latin text (preserving several Tatianisms), strongly influenced by the Vulgate.[4] Whether Isaac also translated other parts of the New Testament is not known. In any case, a fragment of an Arabic–Latin manuscript of Galatians has been discovered which, on palaeographical grounds, is dated to the ninth or tenth century (see MS. no. 5 below).

---

[1] Op. cit., p. iii.

[2] 'Le traduzioni degli Evangelii in arabo e in etiopico', *Atti della R. Accademia dei Lincei, Memorie* anno CCLXXV, serie quarta, classe di scienze morali, storiche e filologiche, iv, Partie 1ª (Rome, 1888), pp. 5–76.

[3] Anton Baumstark, *Die christliche Literatur des Orients*, ii (Leipzig, 1911), 15.

[4] So Anton Baumstark, 'Markus, Kap. 2 in der arabischen Übersetzung des Isaak Valasquez', *OC*, 3rd ser., ix (1934), 226–39; idem, 'Neue orientalistische Problems biblisches Textgeschichte', *ZDMG* lxxxix (1935), 107–9; cf. also Curt Peters, *Das Diatessaron Tatians* (*Orientalia christiana analecta*, cxxiii; Rome, 1939), pp. 175–7.

Subsequent to Guidi's preliminary survey two other monographs were published that provide the researcher in this field
with an exceptionally broad range of codicological, textual, and
bibliographical information: they are Graf's extensive research[1]
based on Guidi's categories, and Henninger's briefer account of
Arabic translations made for Melchites, Maronites, Nestorians,
Jacobites, and Copts.[2]

3. EARLY MANUSCRIPTS OF THE ARABIC VERSIONS

Among the earliest known Arabic manuscripts of the Gospels
and Praxapostolos, the following may be mentioned as particularly noteworthy.

(1) What Burkitt considered to be 'perhaps the oldest monument of Arabic Christianity'[3] is a manuscript formerly belonging
to the Monastery of Mār Sābā near Jerusalem, now cod. Vaticanus arabicus 13, called by Tischendorf ar^{vat} (Greg. cod. 101),
and assigned by Cardinal Mai and Guidi to the eighth century,
but by Graf and Vööbus to the ninth century. Written in Kufic
letters, originally it contained the Psalter, the Gospels, Acts, and
all the Epistles; of these only the Pauline Epistles, along with
limited portions of the Synoptic Gospels, have survived on 178
folios. The Arabic text, which was translated freely from the
Syriac, occasionally preserves Old Syriac readings.[4]

(2) What appears to be the oldest dated copy of the Arabic
Acts of the Apostles, and the Catholic Epistles, is cod. Sinai arab.
151. Written in A.D. 867 in what Atiya describes as a 'rubricate
transitional hand between Naskh and Kufic',[5] the codex contains
many annotations in the margin which provide exegetical comments on the Scripture text. The text of Romans, 1 and 2
Corinthians, and Philippians, along with the annotations, has
been edited, with an English translation, by Harvey Staal.[6]

(3) MS. Borg. arab. 95 of the ninth century (according to
Vööbus it was copied before about A.D. 885) contains on 173

---

[1] Op. cit., pp. 138–85.

[2] Joseph Henninger, 'Arabische Bibelübersetzungen vom Frühmittelalter bis
zum 19. Jahrhundert', *NZMRW* xvii (1961), 210–23.

[3] 'Arabic Versions', Hastings's *Dictionary of the Bible*, i (Edinburgh and New
York, 1898), 136.   [4] So Curt Peters, *Das Diatessaron Tatians*, pp. 56 ff.

[5] Aziz S. Atiya, *The Arabic Manuscripts of Mount Sinai* (Baltimore, 1955), p. 6.

[6] *Codex Sinai Arabic* 151, *Pauline Epistles*; Part I (*Rom., I & II Cor., Phil.*) (*Studies
and Documents*, vol. xl; Salt Lake City, 1969).

folios the four Gospels; the translation, made from the Greek, was presumably done at the Monastery of Mār Sābā. For a specimen of the script, see Eugenius Tisserant, *Specimina codicum orientalium* (Bonn, 1914), plate 55.

(4) A codex of 226 folios and dated A.D. 892, brought by Tischendorf to the Imperial Library at St. Petersburg, contains the Pauline Epistles in a version that appears to have been made from a Nestorian copy of the Peshitta.[1] Its text, which Tischendorf quotes as ar[pet], was studied by Stenij.[2]

(5) The library of the Chapter of Següenza has a parchment leaf, containing some portions of Galatians in Latin and Arabic, which is dated by its editors[3] on palaeographical grounds to the close of the ninth or the beginning of the tenth century.

(6) MS. Sinai arab. 155, dating from the ninth or tenth century, contains on 216 folios the Arabic version of the Wisdom of Sirach and several of the Pauline Epistles. The text of the latter was published by Margaret Dunlop Gibson.[4]

(7) MS. Sinai arab. 154, dating from the ninth century, contains a translation, made from Syriac, of Acts (beginning with vii. 37) and all seven Catholic Epistles (in the Greek order).[5] The

---

[1] One of the extraordinary readings of the manuscript is in Heb. ii. 9, 'And so he without God, who had united Himself with him as a temple, tasted death for all men.' According to Burkitt, who called attention to the reading (op. cit., p. 137, n. §), the variant χωρὶς θεοῦ is not found in the Syriac Vulgate except in Nestorian copies. For other noteworthy readings in the manuscript, see F. Delitzsch, *Commentar zum Briefe an die Hebräer* (Leipzig, 1857), pp. 764–9.

[2] Edv. Stenij, *Die altarabische Übersetzung der Briefe an die Hebräer, an die Römer und an die Korinther, aus einem in St. Petersburg befindlichen Codex Tischendorfs vom Jahre 892 n. Chr.* (Helsinki, 1901). I am grateful to Professor Harald Riesenfeld for obtaining for me a copy of this rare monograph.

[3] Donatien De Bruyne and Eugène Tisserant, 'Une feuille arabo-latine de l'Épître aux Galates', *RB*, n.s. vii (1910), 321–43. With a plate.

[4] *An Arabic Version of the Epistles of St. Paul to the Romans, Corinthians, Galatians, with Part of the Epistle to the Ephesians* (*Studia Sinaitica*, No. ii; London 1894). The text of 1 Corinthians in this manuscript was made the subject of a Ph.D. dissertation by Robert H. Boyd ('The Arabic Text of I Corinthians in *Studia Sinaitica*, No. II; a Comparative, Linguistic and Critical Study', Princeton University Library, 1942).

[5] *An Arabic Version of the Acts of the Apostles and the Seven Catholic Epistles* . . . , ed. by Margaret Dunlop Gibson (*Studia Sinaitica*, No. vii; London, 1899). Another transcription of the text of the disputed Catholic Epistles, made by Mrs. A. Persis Burkitt, was edited by Adelbert Merx, 'Die in der Peschito fehlenden Briefe des Neuen Testamentes in arabischer der Philoxeniana entstammender Übersetzung', *Zeitschrift für Assyriologie*, xii (1897), 240–52, 348–81; xiii (1898), 1–28.

disputed Catholic Epistles (2 Peter, 2 and 3 John, and Jude) appear to have been rendered from the Philoxenian Syriac version; Acts and the rest of the Epistles, from the Syriac Peshitta.

(8) Two fragmentary leaves, one at Sinai and the other at Leningrad, of a bilingual manuscript of the Gospels in Greek and Arabic, dating from the ninth century, preserve portions of Matt. xiii, xiv, and xxv–xxvi. The two leaves are identified today as Gregory-Aland 0136 and 0137; the Arabic text of the latter was edited by Agnes Smith Lewis in her *Catalogue of the Syriac MSS. in the Convent of S. Catherine on Mount Sinai (Studia Sinaitica*, No. I; London, 1894), pp. 105 f.

Other early Arabic manuscripts at Sinai, which, like those already mentioned, are available in microfilm copies at the Library of Congress in Washington, are the following (the comments are those provided by Atiya in his catalogue).

(9) MS. Sinai arab. 70, the four Gospels, about the ninth century, 'in excellent simple Kufic divided according to the readings of the Greek calendar'.

(10) MS. Sinai arab. 72, the four Gospels, dated A.D. 897, 'complete and excellent dated copy in neat Kufic, divided according to the readings of the Greek calendar'.

(11) MS. Sinai arab. 73, Epistles of Paul (including Hebrews after 2 Thess.), dating from about the ninth century; incomplete text, beginning Rom. vi. 20, ending 2 Tim. iii. 8; 'divided according to the Greek calendar'.[1]

(12) MS. Sinai arab. 74, the four Gospels, about the ninth century, written in 'old Kufic; divided according to readings of the Greek calendar'.

When the several Arabic versions that are represented in the extant manuscripts originated is not known. Most scholars have thought it improbable that any of them antedate Muhammad.[2]

---

[1] The beginning and ending of the manuscript (containing Rom. i. 1–vi. 19 and 2 Tim. iii. 9–iv. 22, Titus, and Philemon) have been identified as parts of Paris Bib. Nat. MS. arab. 6725 (see Gérard Troupeau, 'Une ancienne version arabe de l'épître à Philémon', *Mélanges de l'Université Saint-Joseph*, xlvi (1970), 343–51, who provides a transcription of the Arabic text of Philemon).

[2] e.g. M. J. de Goeje, 'Quotations from the Bible in the Qorān and the Tradition', in *Semitic Studies in Memory of Alexander Kohut* (Berlin, 1897), pp. 179–85; Martin Schreiner, 'Beiträge zur Geschichte der Bibel in der arabischen Literatur', ibid., pp. 495–513; Burkitt, op. cit., p. 136; Georg Graf, *Die christlich-arabische*

On the other hand, Baumstark[1] and Peters[2] contended for a pre-Islamic date (of as much as a century), basing their argument partly on certain liturgical data but chiefly on the consideration that missions to Arabia would require vernacular renderings of the Scriptures for the work of evangelization.

By the beginning of the thirteenth century, amid the multiplicity of independent translations, a need was felt for a more fixed type, and one which took account of all the three great national Vulgates of the East—the Greek, the Syriac, and the Coptic. Consequently, about A.D. 1250 a scholar at Alexandria named Hibat Allāh ibn al-'Assāl prepared a revised text of the Gospels with variant readings from the Greek, the Syriac, and the Coptic.[3] The edition, however, was found to be too complicated for popular use, and towards the end of the thirteenth century it was superseded by a less cumbersome recension. According to Guidi, this appears to have been translated from a Coptic (Bohairic) text very like that preserved in cod. Vatican Coptic 9, dated A.D. 1204/5, filled out by inserting from the Syriac or the Greek various passages present in the later forms of those texts but absent from the ancient Coptic version.[4] In many manuscripts these additions are indicated by marginal notes.

During the succeeding centuries this recension, called the 'Alexandrian Vulgate', became widely influential. Its text was

Literatur bis zur fränkischen Zeit (Freiburg im Br., 1905), p. 60; Vööbus, *Early Versions of the New Testament*, p. 293; Joseph Henninger, art. cit., *NZMW* xvii (1961), 206–10; and, on the basis of linguistic considerations, Joshua Blau, 'Sind uns Reste arabischer Bibelübersetzungen aus vorislamischer Zeit erhalten geblieben?' *Mu*, lxxxvi (1973), 67–72.

[1] Anton Baumstark, 'Das Problem eines vorislamischen christlichen-kirchlichen Schrifttums in arabischer Sprache', *Islamica*, iv (1931), 562–75; 'Arabische Übersetzung eines altsyrischen Evangelientextes', *OC*, 3rd ser., ix (1934), 165–88 (with an addendum, ibid., pp. 278 f.); and 'Eine frühislamische und eine vorislamische arabische Evangelium-übersetzung aus dem Syrischen', *Atti del XIX congresso internazionale degli orientalisti, Roma, 23–29 Settembre 1935* (Rome, 1938), pp. 682–4.

[2] Curt Peters, *Das Diatessaron Tatians* (Rome, 1939), pp. 48–62; 'Von arabischen Evangelientexten in Handschriften der Universitäts-Bibliothek Leiden', *AO* xviii (1939–40), 124–37; and 'Grundsätzliche Bemerkungen zur Frage der arabischen Bibeltexte', *RSO* xx (1942–3), 129–43.

[3] For details of Ibn al-'Assāl's work, see Guidi, op. cit., pp. 18–22, and D. B. Macdonald, 'The Gospels in Arabic', *Hartford Seminary Record*, iii (1893), 163–76, and 252.

[4] Guidi, op. cit., pp. 22–4. According to Vööbus (*Early Versions*, p. 289), the same type of text is found also in a codex at the University of Beirut, dated A.D. 1048.

not only the source of corruptions in other classes of Arabic versions, as well as most manuscripts of the Ethiopic version, but it also formed the basis of all printed editions of the Arabic Gospels from the *editio princeps* of 1591[1] down to the twentieth century. It should also be mentioned that all of the four Arabic versions of the Book of Revelation, which was not regarded as canonical in the East, are of Coptic origin.[2]

For the Arabic Diatessaron, see pp. 14–17 above.

4. EARLY PRINTED EDITIONS OF THE ARABIC VERSIONS

As was mentioned above, all printed editions of the Arabic Gospels down to the present century represent varieties of the eclectic 'Alexandrian Vulgate', prepared at the close of the thirteenth century. They have, therefore, very little value for critical purposes.

(1) The *editio princeps* of the Gospels in Arabic (*al-Inǧīl al-muqaddas. Evangelium sanctum . . .*) was printed at Rome in the Medicean printing-house; 1590 stands on the title-page, 1591 in the subscription. It was edited by Giovanni Battista Raimundi (Raymund), superintendent of the printing-office established by Cardinal Fernando de' Medici. A second printing in 1591 has an interlinear Latin translation made by Antonius Sionita. The edition was reissued with a new title-page in 1619 and again in 1774. The manuscript base of the edition is unknown.

(2) The *editio princeps* of the New Testament in Arabic was prepared by Thomas Erpenius (Erpe; 1584–1624) and published at Leiden in 1616. The text of the Gospels was based on a manuscript bequeathed to the Leiden Library by Joseph Scaliger (MS. or. 2369), said to have been written in the monastery of St. John in the Thebaid, in the year of the Martyrs 1059 (A.D. 1342–3). Two other manuscripts also employed by Erpenius for the Gospels are now in the Cambridge University Library (G. 5. 33 and G. 5. 27, written in A.D. 1285). The Acts, Pauline Epistles, James, 1 Peter, and 1 John in this edition are translated from the Peshitta; in the remaining Catholic Epistles the version seems to have been made directly from the Greek. In the Book of

---

[1] So Burkitt, op. cit., p. 137, and T. H. Darlow and H. F. Moule, *Historical Catalogue of the Printed Editions of Holy Scripture*, ii (London, 1911), 63.

[2] Georg Graf, 'Arabische Übersetzungen der Apokalypse', *Bib*, x (1929), 170–94.

Revelation the text, according to Burkitt,[1] is perhaps a combination of translations from the Greek and the Coptic.

In 1752 a Latin rendering of Erpenius's Arabic text of the Gospel of Mark was published at Lemgo by C. A. Bode.

(3) The Arabic version of the entire New Testament is included in the Paris Polyglot Bible (vol. v, in two parts, 1630 and 1633). The editor, Guy Michel Le Jay, put two Maronite scholars from Lebanon, Johannes Hesronita and Gabriel Sionita, in charge of editing the Arabic text and its vocalization, as well as preparing the Latin translation.[2] The recension of the Gospels, contrary to de Lagarde's opinion,[3] was not an interpolated reprint of Raimundi's Roman edition, but appears to be based on a manuscript from Aleppo similar to Paris Anc. f. 27 (of A.D. 1619) and Coisl. 239 (new Suppl. Ar. 27).[4]

(4) The Arabic version of the Paris Polyglot was reprinted, with minor alterations in text and Latin translation, in Walton's London Polyglot (1657). In the work on the Arabic text the editor was assisted by Edward Pococke, who also revised the Latin translation of the Arabic.

(5) The *editio princeps* of the complete Bible in Arabic, apart from the text given in the Paris and London Polyglots, was prepared, under the direction of the Congregatio de Propaganda Fide, by Sergius Risius (Sarkīs ar-Ruzzī), the Maronite Archbishop of Damascus, who had come to Rome in 1624, bringing with him manuscripts of the Arabic Scriptures. After Risius's death in 1638 the work was carried on by others; the completed work, with the Arabic text and the Latin Vulgate printed side by side, was finally published at Rome in three volumes in 1671. Inasmuch as the Arabic has been brought into conformity with the Vulgate, the version possesses no independent critical value.

(6) In 1703 Faustus Naironus edited at Rome the Arabic New Testament in Karshunic characters for the use of Maronites, from a manuscript brought from Cyprus. It was reprinted at

---

[1] Op. cit. (p. 261 n. 3), p. 137.

[2] For information about the basic texts and quality of translation of the Arabic version of the Paris and London Polyglots, see John A. Thompson, 'The Major Arabic Bibles', *BibT* vi (1955), 1–12, 51–5, 98–106, and 146–50; repr. in pamphlet form (New York, 1956).   [3] Op. cit. (p. 259 n. 6), p. xi.

[4] So J. Gildemeister, *De evangeliis in Arabicum e simplici Syriaco translatis* (Bonn, 1865).

Paris in 1827. The Acts, Epistles, and Apocalypse represent the same version as that of Erpenius, but in a different recension.

(7) In 1708 the Gospels in Arabic were published at Aleppo by the Melchite Patriarch Athanasius IV of Antioch, with the financial assistance of a Russian Cossack hetman, Ivan Masepa.[1]

5. TEXTUAL AFFINITIES OF EARLY ARABIC MANUSCRIPTS

Many problems remain unsolved in the study of the earliest Arabic translations of the New Testament. For example, no more than a beginning has been made in analysing the textual affinities of individual Arabic manuscripts.[2] Curt Peters, who tested sample passages from all four Gospels in a group which Guidi found to be translated from Greek, concluded that not a few Tatianisms have found their way into this Arabic version.[3] In a thorough analysis of the entire text of Matthew and Mark in two Arabic manuscripts which were translated from the Greek, Bernhard Levin found that in addition to Tatianisms many readings characteristic of the Caesarean text are also present.[4] The version preserves an interesting agraphon as an expansion of Matt. vi. 34: 'Sufficient unto the day is the evil thereof, and unto the hour the pain thereof (والساعة شدتها).'[5]

On the basis of a detailed analysis of sixty-three variant readings in the text of 1 Corinthians contained in codex Sinai arab. 155 (MS. no. 6 in the list above), Robert Boyd concluded that the underlying Greek text 'was of a predominantly Neutral or Alexandrian type which shows little effect of the assimilation toward the late Byzantine type of text'.[6] In view of the relative freedom from influence by the Byzantine recension, Boyd thought that the Arabic translation was made before the seventh century —a conclusion, however, that is not required if the translator

---

[1] For a description of the edition, see *ZDMG* viii (1854), 386–9.

[2] Besides Guidi, op. cit., see the debate regarding two alleged 'sister' manuscripts now in the Vatican, Alberto Vaccari, 'Una Bibbia araba per il primo Gesuita venuto al Libano', *Mélanges de l'Université Saint-Joseph* (Beirut), x (1925), 79–104, and Sebastian Euringer, 'Zum Stammbaum der arabischen Bibelhandschriften Vat. ar. 468 and 467', *ZSG* vii (1929), 259–73.

[3] 'Proben eines bedeutsamen arabischen Evangelientextes', *OC*, 3rd ser., xi (1936), 188–211; also, idem, *Das Diatessaron Tatians*, pp. 54–62.

[4] *Die griechisch-arabische Evangelien-Übersetzung, Vat. Borg. ar. 95 und Ber. orient. oct. 1108* (Diss., Uppsala, 1938), pp. 67–9.

[5] The same reading occurs in MSS. B and C of the Palestinian Syriac Lectionary (MS. A deest).   [6] Op. cit (p. 262 n. 4), p. 153.

had utilized a relatively old copy of the Greek text, antedating the emergence of the Byzantine recension.

Following a lead partly pursued by Baumstark, Vööbus has discovered abundant traces of an Old Syriac type of text reflected in the Scripture quotations made by Christian Arabic writers.[1] It is also significant that the Muslim Ibn Isḥāq, who about A.D. 725 wrote at Medina the treatise *Sīrat Rasūl Allāh* (the earliest prose work in the Arabic language to come down to us), seems to have derived his knowledge of the Gospels from the Palestinian Syriac version, with which some of his quotations and allusions agree.[2]

The limitations of Arabic version(s) in representing the underlying Greek text involve the following categories of testimony:

(*a*) Variations in the number of the noun;

(*b*) Variations in the aspect, mood, or voice of the verb;

(*c*) Addition or omission, and variation in the use of conjunctions;

(*d*) Addition or omission of possessive pronouns and objective pronouns, indicating the specific person of reference;

(*e*) Unique variations in the use of certain personal pronouns; and

(*f*) Addition or omission of demonstrative pronouns.[3]

II. THE NUBIAN VERSION[4]

During the early centuries of the Christian era Nubia, which lay between Egypt on the north and Ethiopia on the south, comprised three distinct and independent kingdoms, each with its own king or chieftain. They were Nobatia (Arabic Nūbā) in the

---

[1] Vööbus, *Early Versions*, pp. 276 ff.

[2] Cf. A. Baumstark, 'Eine altarabische Evangelienübersetzung aus dem Christlich-Palästinenischen', *ZSG* viii (1930–2), 201–9; Alfred Guillaume, 'The Version of the Gospels Used in Medina circa A.D. 700', *Al-Andalus*, xv (1950), 289–96; and J. Schlacht, 'Une citation de l'Évangile de St. Jean dans la *Sira* d'Ibn Isḥāq', ibid. xvi (1951), 489–90.

[3] For examples from the Arabic version of 1 Corinthians illustrating each of these categories, see Boyd, op. cit. (p. 262 n. 4 above), pp. 138–42.

[4] For a more detailed account of the Christianization of Nubia and the Nubian version, with fuller bibliography than is given here, reference may be made to the chapter on this subject in the present writer's volume, *Historical and Literary Studies, Pagan, Jewish, and Christian* (*New Testament Tools and Studies*, vol. viii; Leiden and Grand Rapids, 1968), pp. 111–22. Cf. also the Christian inscriptions in Greek discovered at Faras in Jadwiga Kubińska, *Inscriptions grecques chrétiennes* (Warsaw, 1974). Announcement has been made of the publication by the National Museum at Warsaw of a volume to be entitled *Studia Nubiana*, comprising the papers presented at a colloquium held at Warsaw, 19–22 June 1972.

north, between the First and Second Cataracts, with its capital at Pachoras (now Faras); Alodia (Arabic 'Alwah) in the south, with its capital at Sōbā near the modern city of Khartoum; and between the two, Makuria (Arabic Makurrah), with its capital at (Old) Dongola. When the Romans, during the reign of Diocletian (A.D. 284–305), withdrew from the Nile valley above Philae (just north of Nobatia near Aswan), they placed in it and in the stations up the river colonies of Nobadae, who acted as a buffer between them and marauding tribes of the fierce Blemmyes from the eastern deserts. After a series of disturbances the power of the Blemmyes was broken by a powerful chieftain of the Nobadae named Silkō, whose exploits are recounted at length in a Greek inscription which he caused to be cut about A.D. 500 on a wall in the temple of Talmis (modern Kalabsha).

When it was that Christianity first reached Nubia is not known. Probably Christian influences began to penetrate Nubia from the time that the Church became firmly established in Upper Egypt during the third and fourth centuries. Before 373 there must have been a number of Christians living at Philae, for Athanasius (who died in 373) says that he consecrated a certain Marcus as bishop of Philae.[1] During the fourth century the vast stretches south of Philae would have given shelter to more than one Christian driven from Egypt by the persecutions ordered by Diocletian. The first formally designated missionaries arrived in Nubia about the middle of the sixth century. According to the account of a contemporary writer, John of Ephesus,[2] about 545 a Monophysite priest named Julian, feeling deeply concerned for the spiritual condition of the Nobadae, sought the advice and assistance of his patroness, the Empress Theodora. Being an ardent champion of Monophysitism the Empress promised to do everything in her power for the conversion of the Nubian tribes from

---

[1] Athanasius, *Letter to the Antiochians*, 10 (Migne, *PG* xxvi, col. 808). In addition to the bibliography mentioned on pp. 112 ff. of the chapter referred to in the preceding footnote, see L. P. Kirwan, 'Prelude to Nubian Christianity', *Mélanges offerts à Kazimierz Michałowski* (Warsaw, 1966), pp. 121–8, and Margarite Rassart, 'La Nubie chrétienne, terre de rencontre de l'Égypte copte et de l'Éthiopie chrétienne', *Annuaire de l'Institut de Philologie et d'Histoire orientales et slaves*, xx (1968–72; published 1973), 363–77.

[2] *The Third Part of the Ecclesiastical History of John, Bishop of Ephesus* . . . , trans. by R. Payne Smith (Oxford, 1860), iv. 6–9 and 49–53; the Syriac text is more conveniently available in the edition of E. W. Brooks in *CSCO* cv (Louvain, 1936; repr. 1952).

paganism. Rather injudiciously, however, she informed the Emperor Justinian of her plans. When her husband learned that the person she intended to send was opposed to the Council of Chalcedon, he decided to send a rival mission of his own so that the heathen might be saved from the errors of heresy. With picturesque detail, much of which is doubtless legendary, the historian relates how, despite many difficulties, Julian was successful in converting the king and nobles of Nobatia. A few years later (about 569) another Monophysite priest, named Longinus, baptized the king and nobles of Alodia.

This story, told with charming *naïveté* by John of Ephesus, himself an ardent Monophysite, arouses scepticism in view of the difficulty of reconciling it with the reported conversion of the more remote kingdom of Makuria to the orthodox faith.[1] Moreover, he is contradicted by the later historian Eutychius,[2] who asserts in his *Annals* that all Nubia was originally Melkite (i.e. Orthodox), but transferred its allegiance in 719 to the Coptic faith after the Arab conquest of Egypt led to the suppression of the Melkites and the removal of their patriarch.

In any case, at the beginning of the introduction of Christianity in Nubia there appears to have been active competition between the advocates of the Monophysite and the Melkite persuasions. Questions as to how far each group prospered, what language or languages were used in the liturgies, and whether it is possible to determine from the surviving ruins of churches which form of Christianity prevailed at a given place, need not detain us here.[3] It is enough to mention that during the succeeding centuries the

---

[1] According to a statement made by a contemporary chronicler in Spain, John of Biclarum, among the events that occurred in the third year of Justin II (i.e. about 569), 'Maccuritarum gens his temporibus Christi fidem recepit'—and by *Christi fidem* John means, of course, the orthodox Catholic faith.

[2] Migne, *PG* cxi, cols. 1122 f. Eutychius was the Dyophysite Patriarch of Alexandria from A.D. 933 to 940.

[3] For recent discussions of these and related questions concerning early Nubian Christianity, see, besides the literature cited in the chapter mentioned above (p. 268 n. 4), Martin Krause, 'Zur Kirchen- und Theologiegeschichte Nubiens', *Kunst und Geschichte Nubiens in christlicher Zeit*, ed. by Eric Dinkler (Rechlinghausen, 1970), pp. 71–86; idem, 'Neue Quellen und Probleme zur Kirchengeschichte Nubiens', in Franz Altheim and Ruth Stiehl, *Christentum am Roten Meer*, i (Berlin, 1971), 509–31; Kazimierz Michałowski, 'Open Problems of Nubian Art and Culture in the Light of the Discoveries at Faras', *Kunst und Geschichte Nubiens*, ed. by Eric Dinkler, pp. 11–20; and W. H. C. Frend, 'Coptic, Greek, and Nubian at Q'asr Ibrin', *Byslav*, xxviii (1972), 224–9.

number of churches in Nubia multiplied and were counted, we are told, by the hundreds.[1] For about five centuries Christianity flourished,[2] providing the chief cohesive element in Nubian society.

The decline of the Church coincided with the inroads made by Arab invaders pressing southward from Muslim Egypt. According to a recent account that makes use of archaeological as well as literary resources,

excavations have shown that there was still a bishop at Qasr Ibrîm in 1372, but the fact that his see had been combined with that of Faras is a measure of the diminished size of his flock. Probably Christianity had already vanished from a large part of Nubia by this time, and we know that the 'royal' church at Dongola had been transformed into a mosque fifty years earlier.[3]

By the end of the fourteenth century, having been cut off for centuries from the rest of the Christian world, the weakened Nubian Church was ready to expire. The growing power of the Arabs hemmed in the Nubian Christians on the north, east, and west, and finally the whole population apostatized and embraced Islam.

No one knows when the Scriptures were translated into Nubian. If, however, the pattern of evangelization was similar to that in other lands, it is probable that, soon after the introduction of Christianity on a wide scale in the sixth century, a vernacular version would have been called for by the new converts. Before the twentieth century, however, nothing was known of the Nubian version. Our knowledge of it today rests upon only a most meagre basis.

In 1906 Dr. Carl Schmidt purchased in Cairo some Nubian fragments which had come from Upper Egypt. At first he and

[1] A. J. Butler in B. T. A. Evetts's edition of the early thirteenth-century treatise by Abû Ṣâliḥ, *The Churches and Monasteries of Egypt and Some Neighbouring Countries* (Oxford, 1895), pp. 263 f. For a recent archaeological study see William Y. Adams, 'Architectural Evolution of the Nubian Church, 500–1400 A.D.', *Journal of the American Research Center in Egypt*, iv (1965), 87–139.

[2] For information from medieval Ethiopic records on Christian Nubia, see Yu. M. Kobishchanov, 'Soobščenija srednevekovyx efiopiskix istochnikovo xristianskoj Nubii', *PS* vii (70, 1962), 35–43; for anthropological aspects, see Bruce G. Trigger, *History and Settlement in Lower Nubia* (*Yale University Publications in Anthropology*, 69; New Haven, 1965), pp. 145–50.

[3] William Y. Adams, 'Post-Pharaonic Nubia in the Light of Archaeology' *JEA* li (1965), 177.

Heinrich Schäfer were inclined to date the fragments in the eighth century,[1] but on further study they assigned them to the tenth or eleventh century.[2] The document consists of a quire of sixteen mutilated pages from a parchment codex, containing a portion of a lectionary for Christmastide. The appointed lessons extend from the 24th of Choiak to the 30th of Choiak, corresponding to 20 to 26 December. For each day a pericope is supplied from the Apostolos and the Gospel. The identity of the Gospel passage is marked by the name of the Evangelist and by the Ammonian number of the first section. The contents of the fragment are as follows:

[24 Choiak Epistle . . .]
 Gospel, Matt. i. 22–5 (cf. 28th of Choiak)
[25 Choiak] Epistle, Phil. ii. 12–18
 Gospel, Matt. v. 13–19
[26 Choiak] Epistle, Rom. xi. 25–9
 [Gospel]
27 Choiak Epistle, Heb. v. 4–10
 Gospel, John xvi. 33–xvii. 25
28 Choiak Epistle, Heb. ix. 1–5
 Gospel, Matt. i. 18–25 (by reference; cf. 24th of Choiak)
29 Choiak Epistle, Gal. iv. 4–7
 Gospel, Matt. ii. 1–12
[30 Choiak] Epistle, Rom. viii. 3–7 (or more)
 [Gospel . . .]

Except for two instances, the sequence and choice of the lessons find no parallel in the Greek or Coptic lectionaries hitherto examined. The exceptions involve the two passages appointed for 25 December (Gal. iv. 4–7 and Matt. ii. 1–12), which coincide with those of Greek menologia. Since the extant folios of the lectionary are numbered 100 to 115 and contain (as was mentioned above) daily lessons for the period corresponding to 20 to 26 December, it appears that the lectionary began with 1 September (as do also the Greek menologia). The presence of the Ammonian section numbers makes it probable that the lectionary was constructed from a non-lectionary text, at least so far as the Gospel pericopes are concerned.

---

[1] Heinrich Schäfer and Carl Schmidt, 'Die ersten Bruckstücke christlicher Literatur in altnubischen Sprache', *SbBer* (1906), pp. 774–85.
[2] 'Die altnubischen Handschriften der königlichen Bibliothek zu Berlin', ibid. (1907), pp. 602–13.

Like other texts of Nubian, the lectionary is written in an alphabet that is essentially Coptic, reinforced by several additional
letters needed to represent sounds peculiar to the language. Unlike later Nubian dialects, which include many words borrowed
from the Arabic, the language of the lectionary is characterized
by the presence of Graecized forms of peculiarly biblical words.
It is perhaps significant that in a related Nubian text recounting
the miracles of St. Mena,[1] the proper names Alexandria and
Mareotis appear under their Greek forms, and not the Coptic
equivalents ⲣⲁⲕⲟⲧⲉ and ⲡⲁⲛⲓϥⲁⲓⲁⲧ. As Griffith[2] points out,
these features indicate that Nubians translated their religious
literature from Greek, not Coptic. In accordance with this conclusion is the statement made by Abû Ṣâliḥ that the liturgy and
prayers in the Nubian churches were in Greek.[3]

The textual affiliations of the Nubian version are difficult to
ascertain with precision. The chief reason for this is the paucity
of text that has been preserved; only about seventy verses are
extant, and some of these are very imperfectly represented.
Furthermore, one must bear in mind the distinction between
renderings and readings, of which only the latter are of primary
assistance in determining the textual analysis of a version. In spite
of these circumstances, however, it is possible to draw tentative
conclusions regarding the broad classification of the version.

An examination of the variants disclosed by a collation of
Griffith's reconstructed Greek text against the Textus Receptus
and against the text of Westcott and Hort[4] reveals that the Nubian
version agrees with the Textus Receptus against the Westcott–
Hort text in six of the twelve variants, but it never agrees with
Westcott–Hort against the Textus Receptus. In six variants the
Nubian goes against both the Textus Receptus and Westcott–
Hort; two of these instances are unique readings.

If the variants are examined from the standpoint of the textual
characteristics of supporting witnesses, one finds that several
have Western and/or Caesarean affinities. Although occasionally
the Sahidic version (or some of the Sahidic manuscripts) supports

---

[1] See *Texts Relating to Saint Mêna of Egypt and Canons of Nicaea in a Nubian Dialect*,
ed. by E. A. Wallis Budge (London, 1909).

[2] F. Ll. Griffith, *The Nubian Texts of the Christian Period* (*AbhBer* (1913), No. 8),
p. 71.　　　　　　　　　　　　　[3] Op. cit. (see p. 271 n. 1), p. 272.

[4] A list of the variant readings, with supporting evidence from Greek manuscripts and versions, is given in the chapter mentioned in p. 268 n. 4 above.

the Nubian, in most cases it does not. In one instance codex Vaticanus and MS. 1739 agree with the Nubian in an omission.

If one may generalize on the basis of such a limited amount of textual data, it appears that the Nubian version as represented in the fragments of the lectionary was made from a Greek text which was predominantly Byzantine in character, but which preserved a mixture of other readings as well.[1]

During the past decade several other biblical fragments in Nubian have come to the attention of scholars. One is a leaf, found in a church on the Nile island of Sunnarti, containing portions of ten lines of script on each side. According to C. Detlef G. Müller, the fragment is apparently from a lectionary.[2] In 1964 during the excavations of Qasr Ibrim a number of parchment leaves were found on the floor of the cathedral. According to J. Martin Plumley (letter dated 19 August 1974) they contain the Nubian text of John xi. 22–31a, 32–41, and Rev. vii. 15–17; viii. 1–8; and xiv. 6–14. In addition there is a page from an Epistolary containing readings for the first three Sundays in the month of Mesore. Two of the readings appear to be 1 Cor. ii. 6–10 and xiv. 35–40; the third reading has not yet been identified.

III. THE PERSIAN VERSION

How and when the Gospel reached Persia is not known, but by the third and fourth centuries we find a relatively wide dissemination of Christianity in that country. Of course neither the reference to 'Parthians and Medes and Elamites' (Acts ii. 9) at Jerusalem on the day of Pentecost nor the tradition that the Apostle Thomas took Parthia as his missionary sphere[3] provides any specific information, and the latter should be given little credence. Likewise the statistics provided by Mari, the disciple of Addai,[4] that by the second century there were 360 churches in Assyria and Persia does not really tell us how far Christianity had

---

[1] The preceding ten paragraphs are reproduced, with minor alterations, from the present writer's study referred to above, p. 268 n. 4.

[2] 'Deutsche Textfunden in Nubien', *Kunst und Geschichte Nubiens*, ed. by Eric Dinkler, pp. 245–56.

[3] The tradition regarding Thomas is reported by Eusebius, *Hist. eccl.* iii. 1; and is repeated in the Clementine *Recognitions* (ix. 29) and by Socrates, *Hist. eccl.* i. 19.

[4] Reported by Assemani, *Bibliotheca Orientalis*, iii. 1, p. 611.

been extended in the latter country. But the statement made by Philip, a pupil of Bardesanes, at the close of his *Book of the Laws of the Countries*, to the effect that Christianity made great social and moral changes wherever it had gone ('. . . the Parthian Christians are not polygamists, nor do Christians in Media expose their dead to dogs, nor do Persian Christians marry their own daughters, nor are those in Bactria and among the Gelae debauched . . .')[1] presupposes, by the beginning of the third century, a considerable extension of Christianity, even as far as the eastern districts of Persia. According to traditions incorporated in the Chronicle of Arbela,[2] by A.D. 224 there were two bishoprics in Susiana—at Bait-Lapaṭ and Hormizd-Ardašîr. Furthermore, as Harnack observed, the great Persian persecution during the fourth century points to a notable spread of Christianity in the course of the third century.[3] Under the guidance of Papa (247–326), bishop of Seleucia–Ctesiphon, the hierarchic organization of the Church under a catholicos was finally completed, to be followed by a period of consolidation under Shemʿon bar Ṣabbaʿe (326–344/5).[4] Despite the fierce persecution of Christians begun in 340 under Shapur II, the Church in Persia managed to survive. In the following century, at the Synod of Bait-Lapaṭ (Jundi Shapur) in A.D. 484, a majority of the delegates embraced Nestorianism; it was this form of Christianity that Persian missionaries carried to countries still farther east.[5]

---

[1] Euseb. *Praep. evang.* vi. 10 (Migne, *Patrologia Graeca*, xxi, col. 476).

[2] Eduard Sachau, *Die Chronik von Arbela. Ein Beitrag zur Kenntnis der ältesten Christentums im Orient* (*AbhBer*, 1915, No. 6), p. 61. (On the legendary character of the early parts of the Chronicle, see p. 7 n. 5 above.) Cf. also Sachau, 'Vom Christentum in der Persis', *SbBer* (1916), pp. 958–60.

[3] Adolf von Harnack, *Die Mission und Ausbreitung des Christentums in den ersten drei Jahrhunderten*, 4te Aufl., ii (Leipzig, 1924), pp. 694–8. (Engl. trans., *The Mission and Expansion of Christianity in the First Three Centuries*, ii (London, 1908), 147).

[4] Shemʿon's death in the Great Massacre occurred between Sept. 344 and Jan. 345; see M. J. Higgins, 'Aphraates' Dates for Persian Persecutions', *ByzZ* xliv (1951), 265–71. For a general discussion of the work of Papa and Shemʿon, see J. Labourt, *Le Christianisme dans l'empire perse sous la dynastie Sassanide (224–632)* (Paris, 1904).

[5] In the seventh century Nestorian missionaries reached China, and in the following century erected the celebrated monument at Si-ngan-fu, with an extensive inscription in Chinese and Syriac characters (A.D. 781). Persian names have been found on Nestorian grave monuments in Siberia (cf. Otakar Klíma in Jan Rypka, *Iranische Literaturgeschichte* (Leipzig, 1959), p. 59). For further information cf. Alphonse Mingana, 'The Early Spread of Christianity in Central Asia and the Far East: A New Document', *BJRL* ix (1925), 297–371, and P. Y. Saeki, *The Nestorian Documents and Relics in China* (Tokyo, 1937; repr. 1951).

During the earlier centuries of the Church in Persia it appears that Christians were accustomed to read the Scriptures in Syriac. When it was that one or more parts of the Bible were first translated into Middle Persian we do not know. To be sure, at the close of the fourth century John Chrysostom[1] declared that the doctrines of Christ had been translated into the languages of the Syrians, the Egyptians, the Indians, the Persians, and the Ethiopians—but when he added 'and ten thousand other nations (καὶ μύρια ἕτερα ἔθνη)', he weakened his own evidence in regard to the Persian or any one version in particular. In the following century Theodoret wrote that the Persians 'venerate the writings of Peter, of Paul, of John, of Matthew, of Luke, and of Mark, as having come down from heaven'[2]—a statement which some have interpreted to imply that these had been translated into the vernacular. Inasmuch as during the second half of the fifth century an eminent teacher, Ma'nā of Shīrāz,[3] made translations of the works of Diodorus, Theodore of Mopsuestia, and other ecclesiastical writers, from Syriac into his native Persian dialect, we may be confident that the Scriptures had already been translated.

It is, however, much to be lamented that of all these early Christian literary monuments in Middle Persian next to nothing has survived.[4] Of the Scriptures, not a page of the New Testament is known today, and of the Old Testament only a dozen fragmentary leaves of the Psalter written in archaic Pahlavi script were discovered earlier this century at Bulayiq near Turfan.[5] After the first verse of each Psalm is a canon or response,

---

[1] *Hom. in Joh.* (written about A.D. 391), ii, on John i. 1 (Migne, *PG* lix, col. 32).

[2] *Graecarum affectionum curatio*, ix. 936 (Migne, *PG* lxxxiii, col. 1045C).

[3] See Eduard Sachau, 'Vom Christentum in der Persis', pp. 971 and 979. It is generally assumed that this Ma'nā was bishop of Rêvârdashîr (so Addai Scher, *ROC*, 2nd ser., i (1906), 7, and Sachau), but Vööbus has more recently suggested that he was another Persian churchman with the same name (*History of the School of Nisibis* (Louvain, 1965), pp. 18 and 38 n. 21).

[4] There exists only part of a leaf preserving in extremely fragmentary form a logion of Jesus that is introduced by the formula, 'Thus Jesus says . . .'. For a description see Mary Boyce, *A Catalogue of Iranian Manuscripts in Manichean Script in the German Turfan Collection* (Berlin, 1960), p. 78, no. 1738; for a transcription and translation, see Werner Sundermann, 'Christliche Evangelientexte in der Überlieferung der iranisch-manichäischen Literatur', *Mitteilungen des Instituts für Orientforschung*, xiv (Berlin, 1968), 404.

[5] F. C. Andreas, 'Bruchstücke einer Pehlewi-Übersetzung der Psalmen aus der Sassanidzeit', *Sitzungsberichte der königlich Preussischen Akademie der Wissenschaften* (Berlin, 1910), pp. 869–72, and Kaj Barr's edition of F. C. Andreas's 'Bruchstücke

written in red ink. The presence of such canons, which were appointed in the Syrian Church about the middle of the sixth century, shows that the fragments originated after that time. Since the translation, which was made from the Syriac, lacks several of the corruptions that are present in the oldest extant copies of the Peshitta Psalter dating from the end of the sixth century, Andreas is inclined to assign the translation to the first quarter of the fifth century.[1]

The beginning of the period of Modern or New Persian is generally placed about the year 1000, and during the following centuries more than one translation of parts of the Bible was made.[2] Although these do not belong, strictly speaking, to the category of 'early' versions, it may be appropriate to include information concerning two Persian versions of the Gospels which have sometimes been quoted in *apparatus critici* to the New Testament.

(1) Volume v of Walton's Polyglot Bible contains the Persian version of the Gospels derived from an Oxford manuscript written in A.D. 1341, which belonged to Edward Pococke. The version, which was obviously made from the Peshitta Syriac, is 'often so periphrastic as to claim a character of its own'.[3] Of several noteworthy readings mention may be made of Matt. xvi. 23, where Jesus addresses Peter as 'faithless one' rather than 'Satan'.[4] The Persian text in the London Polyglot is provided with a Latin translation made by Samuel Clarke, and notes (printed in section vii of the Appendix, op. cit., vol. vi, pp. 57–98) supplied by Thomas Graves (or Greaves). A century later

einer Pehlevi-Übersetzung der Psalmen', *SbBer* (1933), pp. 91–152, containing Psalms xciv–xcix and cxix–cxxxvi.

[1] Ibid., p. 870.

[2] For the Old Testament cf. F. W. K. Müller, 'Ein syrisch-neupersisches Psalmenstück aus Chinesisch-Turkistan', *Festschrift Eduard Sachau* (Berlin, 1915), pp. 215–24, and Walter J. Fischel, 'The Bible in Persian Translation', *HTR* xlv (1952), 3–45. On the New Persian Renaissance, see Richard N. Frye, *The Heritage of Persia* (Cleveland and New York, 1963), pp. 241–3.

[3] S. C. Malan, *St. John's Gospel, translated from the Eleven Oldest Versions except the Latin* . . . (London, 1872), p. xi. Richard Simon complained that he could not see the utility of the Persian version in the London Polyglot, for, among other reasons, the translator from the Syriac had not always been very intelligent (*Histoire critique des versions du Nouveau Testament* (Rotterdam, 1690), p. 205).

[4] In the parallel passage in Mark viii. 23, however, the Persian reads 'O Satan'. For other noteworthy readings see Francis Wrangham's edition of Walton's *Prolegomena* to the London Polyglot Bible, ii (Cambridge, 1828), 619–21.

Clarke's work was revised by C. A. Bode,[1] from whose edition Tischendorf derived his references to the version, identified as pers[P].

(2) An edition of the Gospels in Persian[2] was prepared by Abraham Wheelocke (Wheloc), professor of Arabic and Anglo-Saxon and University Librarian at Cambridge. The basis of the text, according to Darlow and Moule, was 'an Oxford MS of a version (14th century?) apparently made from the Greek, which the editor in his elaborate notes at the end of each chapter compared with a MS (apparently made from the Syriac and dated 1341) in the possession of E. Pococke, at Oxford, and another MS (dated 1607) at Cambridge'.[3] Shortly after the first 108 pages (to Matt. xviii. 6) had been printed, Wheelocke died (1653); but his whole text and Latin rendering, being found ready for the press, were carried forward by an anonymous editor, said by Edmund Castell (*Lexicon Heptaglotton, praef.*) to be a certain Pierson, otherwise unknown. In 1657 the book was published with a second title-page and a short Preface by the editor, who in lieu of Wheelocke's notes appended a collation of the Pococke manuscript from Matt. xviii. 7 onward to the end. The edition thus represents a mixed text, resting as it does upon manuscripts of versions made in one case from Greek and in the other from Syriac. Tischendorf identifies readings from the edition by the siglum pers[w].

At the beginning of the twentieth century Gregory catalogued thirty-seven Persian manuscripts of the Gospels, dating from the fourteenth to the nineteenth century.[4] No other part of the New Testament seems to be available in Persian, except in editions prepared in recent centuries for missionary purposes.

[1] *Evangelium ex versione Persici interpretis in bibliis polyglottis Anglicis editum . . .* (Helmstedt, 1750 and 1751).

[2] *Quatuor evangeliorum . . . versio Persica, Syriacam et Arabicam suavissime redolens, ad verba et mentem Graeci textus fideliter et venuste concinnata codd. tribus perlatis, operose invicem diligenterque collatis per* A. W. (London, 1657).

[3] T. H. Darlow and H. F. Moule, *Historical Catalogue of the Printed Editions of Holy Scripture . . .* , ii (London, 1911), 1201. On the difficulty of ascertaining the identity of the Oxford manuscript used by Wheelocke, see Herbert Marsh's notes on J. D. Michaelis's *Introduction to the New Testament*, 4th edn., ii (London, 1823), 618.

[4] C. R. Gregory, *Textkritik des Neuen Testamentes*, ii (Leipzig, 1902), 577 f., and iii (1909), 1322 f. For a seventeenth-century manuscript of the four Gospels in Persian (written in Georgian characters), with specimen passages, see N. Marr, 'Opisanie persidskago rykopisnago četveroevangelija', *Zapiski vostočnago otdelenija imperatorskago russkogo arxologičeskago obščestva*, iii (1888, published 1889), 377–81.

As for the textual affinities of the Persian version(s), Kirsopp Lake and Silva New mention that 'the suggestion has been made that the Persian shows traces of Caesarean readings'.[1] For the Persian Diatessaron, see pp. 17–19 above.

IV. THE SOGDIAN VERSION

The Sogdian language, a Middle Iranian tongue, was an eastern member of the Indo-European family of languages. During the second half of the first millennium of the Christian era it was widely used in East Turkestan and adjacent areas of Central Asia. According to Diringer,[2] 'Sogdian was actually for a long time the *lingua franca* of Central Asia.' Because of the Sogdians' energetic pursuit of colonization and trading activity, documents in their language were carried far and wide. 'In this respect', as Frye observes, 'the Sogdians played in Central Asia the same role as the Greeks in the ancient world, but on a much smaller scale.'[3]

In contrast to what is now known to have been the widespread dissemination of Sogdian, before the beginning of the twentieth century modern scholars knew next to nothing about the language. Then in 1903 Professor Albert Grünwedel, director of the Indian Department of the Museum für Völkerkunde at Berlin-Dahlem, acquired a variety of Sogdian manuscripts, either by purchase or by actual exploration, from a place near Turfan. After the language had been deciphered it was found that, in addition to extensive remains of Manichaean and Buddhist texts, there were several Christian documents,[4] written in a purely consonantal script resembling Estrangela Syriac. These proved to be several hagiographical treatises[5] and a section of Hermas'

---

[1] *The Text of the New Testament*, 6th edn. (London, 1928), p. 48.

[2] David Diringer, *The Alphabet: A Key to the History of Mankind*, 3rd edn., i (New York and London, 1968), 244.

[3] Richard N. Frye, 'Sughd and the Sogdians; A Comparison of Archaeological Discoveries with Arabic Sources', *JAOS* lxiii (1943), 16.

[4] For a brief survey of Christian Sogdian literature, see Olaf Hansen, 'Die christliche Literatur der Soghdier. Eine Übersicht', *Jahrbuch der Akademie der Wissenschaften und der Literatur in Mainz*, 1951, pp. 296–302. For popular accounts of the Sogdian material, see J. Rendel Harris, *Side-Lights on New Testament Research* (London, 1908), pp. 115–24, and Louis H. Gray, 'New Testament Fragments from Turkestan', *ExpT* xxv (1913–14), 59–61.

[5] Olaf Hansen, *Berliner soghdische Texte*, I. *Bruchstücke einer soghdischen Version der Georgspassion (C1) (AbhBer* (1941), Nr. 10), and *Berliner soghdische Texte*, II. *Bruch-*

Shepherd,[1] as well as fragments preserving a considerable number of passages of Matthew, Luke, and John (in the form of a lectionary), and a few small scraps of 1 Corinthians and Galatians. There is also the Sogdian text of most of the Nestorian Confession of Faith, written in Uighur script (an offshoot of the Sogdian script) and in Syriac.[2]

The preceding documents, which have been assigned to the period from the ninth to the eleventh century, testify to the existence of a vigorous Nestorian mission in Sogdiana, and the translation of the New Testament into the native language. The nature of the translation appears to be rather literal. There are occasional instances of a Syriac word embedded in the Sogdian rendering, probably where no corresponding Sogdian word was as yet available. Most of these words are distinctively 'Christian' terms, such as the words for altar, bishop, deacon, cross, canon, Christ, Psalm, Eucharist, and Church.[3] It may be concluded that the translation was made at the beginning of the Christian mission in Sogdiana, perhaps in the seventh century.

The extant New Testament fragments in Sogdian are the following.[4]

(1) Portions of a Gospel lectionary, which, in Burkitt's opinion,[5] is at least as early as the tenth century, are preserved on forty-nine fragments which belong to twenty-three leaves. Most (but not all) of the lessons agree with the Nestorian Syriac Gospel lectionary, known to us from manuscripts of the eleventh

---

stücke der grossen Sammelhandschrift C2 (AbhMainz (1954), Nr. 15). The latter contains fragments of the accounts of the Martyrdom of Sts. Anahita, Adurhormizd, Pethion, Yazdin, Tharbo, Sǎhdost, Eustathius, and Theodosius; and fragments from the Apophthegmata Patrum, the Apostolic Canons, and several miscellaneous pieces. Cf. also E. Benveniste, 'Études sur quelques textes sogdiens chrétiens', *JA* ccxliii (1955), 297–335, and D. N. MacKenzie, 'Christian Sogdian Notes', *BSOAS* xxxiii (1970), 116–24.

[1] F. W. K. Müller, 'Eine Hermas-Stelle in manichäischer Version', *SbBer* (1905), pp. 1077–83. The passage is *Sim.* ix. 12–25.

[2] Edited by F. W. K. Müller in *Soghdische Texte*, i (see n. 4, below), pp. 84–8.

[3] For examples of these and other terms, see Olaf Hansen, 'Über die verschiedenen Quellen der christlichen Literatur der Sogder', *Iranian Studies Presented to Kaj Barr* . . . , ed. by Jes Peter Asmussen and Jørgen Læssøe (Copenhagen, 1966), pp. 95 ff.

[4] Edited by F. W. K. Müller, 'Neutestamentliche Bruchstücke in soghdischer Sprache', *SbBer*, 1907, pp. 260–70 (Luke i. 63–80 and Gal. iii. 25–iv. 6); and *Soghdische Texte*, i (*AbhBer*, 1912, Nr. 2) (portions of Matthew, Luke, and John).

[5] F. C. Burkitt, *The Religion of the Manichees* (Cambridge, 1925), pp. 119–25.

and succeeding centuries.[1] The section that survives begins with the first Sunday in December. This fragment, which is the first written leaf of the codex, contains Luke i. 1–4 in bilingual format, with interlinear Syriac and Sogdian text. After Easter and again after the third Sunday of Summer are lessons commemorating the Confessors S. Barsabbas (?) and SS. Sergius and Baccus.

(2) A fragment, preserving parts of lines, some of which are very faint,[2] contains Luke xii. 24, the wording of which has been influenced by vs. 31.[3]

(3) Two fragments containing the Syriac and Sogdian text of 1 Cor. v. 7 and xi. 24 in alternate lines.[4]

(4) A fragment thought by Müller to be from a homily, containing the quotation of 1 Cor. xi. 23–5 in Sogdian.[5]

(5) A single leaf containing the Syriac and Sogdian text of Gal. iii. 25–iv. 6 in alternate lines.[6]

The textual affinities of the Sogdian version are, as would be expected, closely related to the Syriac Peshitta. After analysing the Gospel fragments Peters concluded that the type of Peshitta text lying behind the Sogdian was one in which there were embedded not a few Old Syriac[7] and Tatianic readings.[8] This circumstance led Peters to make two observations: (a) the Peshitta was not a stiff uniform entity, for the boundary between the Old Syriac and the Peshitta was more fluctuating than has generally been thought; and (b) the variant readings from the Sogdian texts ought to be entered into future critical editions of the Peshitta.[9]

---

[1] See the table of lessons in Burkitt, ibid., pp. 121–3, and the discussion by Baumstark in *OC*, n.s. iv (1914), 123–6.

[2] For a description of the fragment see Mary Boyce, *A Catalogue of the Iranian Manuscripts in Manichean Script in the German Turfan Collection* (Berlin, 1960), p. 26, no. 399.

[3] For a transcription and translation see Werner Sundermann, 'Christliche Evangelientexte in der Überlieferung der iranisch-manichäischen Literatur', *Mitteilungen des Instituts für Orientforschung*, xiv (1968), 403 f.

[4] Müller, *Soghdische Texte*, i (see p. 280 n. 4 above), pp. 80–2.

[5] Idem, pp. 80 f.

[6] Idem, 'Neutestamentliche Bruchstücke . . .' (see p. 280 n. 4 above), pp. 263–6, and *Soghdische Texte*, i. 82–4.

[7] 'Der Text der soghdischen Evangelienbruckstücke und das Problem der Peshitta', *OC*, 3rd ser. xi, (1936), 153–62.

[8] Peters, *Das Diatessaron Tatians* (*Orientalia christiana analecta*, cxxiii; Rome, 1939), pp. 46–8.   [9] *OC*, 3rd ser., xi (1936), 161.

V. THE CAUCASIAN ALBANIAN VERSION

Between the fifth and eleventh centuries of the Christian era the Albans or Alvans, a people of uncertain ethnic origin who lived in the part of the Caucasus that today is included within the Soviet Republic of Azerbaijan, developed a rich literature. Inasmuch as virtually all literary texts in their language have perished, present knowledge of the language depends mostly on inscriptions on stones and pottery sherds.[1] According to Armenian traditions, St. Mesrop, besides inventing the Armenian and Georgian alphabets, created yet another for the Albanians,[2] who had been evangelized through the labours of two of his disciples, Enoch and Dana. Sometime later, according to the same traditions, a certain Bishop Jeremiah set his hand to translating the Scriptures into the language of the Albanians.

How much of the Bible was rendered into Albanian we do not know; in any case, nothing of the version has survived. Eventually the Church of the Albanians was submerged in the Islamic conquests, and the people themselves who had escaped annihilation were assimilated by the Seljuk Turks.[3] It is thought probable that Caucasian Albanian still survives in the Udi dialect, spoken in the villages of Vartashen and Nish in the district of Nukha to the north of the river Kur or Kura.[4]

[1] For a list of the fifty-two letters of the Caucasian Albanian alphabet, found in a manuscript written before 1446, see the articles by A. Shanidze, 'The Newly Discovered Alphabet of the Caucasian Albanians and its Significance for Science', and I. Abuladze, 'On the Discovery of the Alphabet of the Caucasian Albanians', both in Georgian in the *Bulletin of the Marr Institute* (Tiflis), iv (1938), summarized by H. W. Bailey, *JRAS* (1943), p. 4. For another copy of the alphabet, made about 1580, see Harry Kurdian, 'The Newly Discovered Alphabet of the Caucasian Albanians', *JRAS* (1956), pp. 81–3. For discussions of the alphabet and literature written in that alphabet, see Robert H. Howsen, 'On the Alphabet of the Caucasian Albanians', *RÉA* n.s. i (1964), 427–32, and H. S. Anassian, 'Un mise au point relative à l'lAbanie caucasienne', ibid. vi (1969), 298–330. Cf. also Kamilla V. Trever, 'The Culture of Caucasian Albania', *XXV International Congress of Orientalists; Papers presented by the USSR Delegation* (Moscow, 1960), pp. 6–11.

[2] Koriun's *Life of St. Mesrop*, 15, trans. by Simon Weber in *Bibliothek der Kirchenväter*, lvii (Munich, 1927), 217–19; and Moses Kałankatuaçi's *History of the Caucasian Albanians*, i. 27, trans. by C. J. F. Dowsett (London, 1961), pp. 54 f. The latter work was written in the tenth century. The Armenian scholar Akinian interprets Koriun's reference to mean an alphabet for the Goths (*OC*, 4th ser., iii (1955), 110 f.).

[3] See Georges Dumézil, 'Une chrétienté disparue: les Albaniens du Caucase', *Mélanges asiatiques* (*JA* ccxxxii (1940)), pp. 125–32.

[4] D. Diringer, *The Alphabet, a Key to the History of Mankind*, 3rd edn., i (New York and London, 1968), 255.

PART TWO

The Early Western Versions of the New Testament

VII

The Latin Versions

IT would be difficult to over-estimate the importance of the influence exerted by the Latin versions of the Bible, and particularly by Jerome's Latin Vulgate. Whether one considers the Vulgate from a purely secular point of view, with its pervasive influence upon the development of Latin into the Romance languages,[1] or whether one has in view only the specifically religious influence, the extent of penetration into all areas of Western culture is well-nigh beyond calculation. The theology and the devotional language typical of the Roman Catholic Church were either created or transmitted by the Vulgate. Both Protestants and Roman Catholics are heirs of terminology that Jerome either coined anew or rebaptized with fresh significance—words such as salvation, regeneration, justification, sanctification, propitiation, reconciliation, inspiration, scripture, sacrament, and many others.

The history of the Latin versions of the New Testament bristles with difficult and disputed problems, not least of which are the questions when, where, and by whom the earliest Latin rendering was made.

I. THE OLD LATIN VERSIONS

1. THE ORIGIN OF THE OLD LATIN VERSIONS

Our information concerning the Old Latin translation of the New Testament is very defective, but it is certain that it was not

---

[1] One example from many of the influence of the Vulgate on the development of vernacular languages among the Romance peoples is the suppression of all derivatives from the Latin word *verbum*. The forms do indeed occur in the religious, technical sense (meaning 'the Word'), but in the popular speech of the people they are replaced by representatives of the Latin word *parabola*, a word originally far less common than *verbum* (e.g. French, *parole*; Spanish, *palabra*; Portuguese, *palavra*; Italian, *parola*); see, *inter alia*, Fritz Abel, *L'Adjectif démonstratif dans la langue de la Bible latine. Étude sur la formation des systèmes déictiques et de l'article défini des langues romanes* (*Beiheft zur Zeitschrift für Romanische Philologie*, cxxv; Tübingen, 1971), who gives a wide-ranging bibliography on the influence of the Latin Bible on the Romance languages.

one uniform work; the books were translated a number of times and no single translator did all twenty-seven books. The exact date of the first Latin version of the Bible, or indeed of any part of the Bible, is uncertain. It is a remarkable fact that the Latin churches do not seem to have retained any memory of this great event in their history. Latin patristic writers report no legend or tradition bearing on the subject, and so we are reduced to building up a theory from scattered and sometimes ambiguous indications.

The roots of the Old Latin version(s) are doubtless to be found in the practice of the double reading of holy Scripture during divine services, first in the Greek text (the Septuagint for the Old Testament), then in the vernacular tongue. The reading would probably be done in more or less brief sections, one after another, just as the Jews were accustomed to provide an Aramaic Targum at the reading of the Hebrew Scriptures. At first the Latin translation would have been oral, without book, but as part or all of it came to be written down and stereotyped, it was easier to take an existing text and to modify it to suit local requirements than to make an entirely new translation. For convenience the translation would at times have been interlinear; later on, manuscripts with two columns of text, sometimes arranged in cola and commata for ease of phrasing during the public reading of the lessons, were prepared. In some instances the Latin rendering, which may have been made earlier from a different Greek *Vorlage*, was accommodated to the Greek text to which it was now attached. The final stage came when the custom of reading the lesson in Greek died out, and thereafter copies would be made of the Latin texts alone.

Although one might have supposed that the Latin Bible had its origin at Rome, the matter is complicated and far from certain. When the Church was founded in Rome, probably during the fourth or fifth decade of the first century, a major part of the population was of Greek-oriental origin,[1] using Greek rather than Latin. Juvenal speaks with indignation concerning the extent to which Rome was being converted to 'a Greek city',[2] and

---

[1] Cf. what Seneca says concerning the mixed character of the Roman population, the greater part of which had left their original places of residence and flocked to Rome for a wide variety of reasons (*De consolatione ad Helviam*, vi. 2–3).

[2] *Sat.* iii. 60 f.; cf. vi. 187 ff.

Martial regards ignorance of Greek as a mark of rusticity.[1] Among Jewish inscriptions found at Rome, the overwhelming proportion are in Greek, with only a minority in Latin.[2] As for the earliest Christians at Rome, it must be remembered that in the sixth decade the Apostle Paul wrote his letter to the congregations there in Greek, and at the close of the first century through Clement the Roman Church addressed a letter of admonition in Greek to the Church at Corinth. In the first decade of the second century Ignatius used the same language in writing to the Christians at Rome. Early Christian authors in Rome—such as Hermas, Justin Martyr, and Hippolytus, whose literary activity continued as late as 230—all wrote in Greek. The names of the earliest bishops of Rome are predominantly non-Latin.[3] As late as 250 Bishop Cornelius of Rome sent letters written in Greek to Bishop Fabian at Antioch.

But Latin was slowly making its way. Pope Victor (*c.* 190) is mentioned by Jerome as the first author to write theological treatises in Latin.[4] Among Christian authors in Rome whose writings have survived, Novatian is the first who made use of Latin rather than Greek—and this was at the middle of the third century. By this time sepulchral epitaphs of Christians begin to be written in Latin,[5] and soon thereafter the liturgy and the creed exchange a Greek dress for a Latin one.[6]

How these data are to be interpreted so far as they bear on the question when Christians at Rome would have called for a Latin translation of the Bible is not altogether clear. To many scholars

[1] *Epigr.* xiv. 58.

[2] J.-B. Frey, *Corpus inscriptionum Iudaicarum*, i (Vatican City, 1936; repr., with Prolegomenon by Baruch Lifshitz, New York, 1975).

[3] Of the twelve bishops of Rome from Linus to Eleutherius (*c.* A.D. 174–89), not more than three (Clement, Sixtus I (= Xystus), and Pius) bear Latin names. And of these three, Clement wrote in Greek, as did Pius' brother, Hermas.

[4] Jerome, *De vir. illustr.* 34 and 53. According to G. La Piana ('The Roman Church at the End of the Second Century', *HTR* xviii (1925), 201–77, esp. 231), with the advent of Victor, a North African by birth, as bishop of Rome, Latin presumably became the official language of the Church.

[5] Josef Wilpert, *Die Papstgräber und die Cäciliengruft in der Katakombe des hl. Kallistus* (Freiburg im Br., 1909), and C. M. Kaufmann, *Handbuch der altchristlichen Epigraphik* (Freiburg im Br., 1917), pp. 234 ff.

[6] C. P. Caspari, *Quellen zu Geschichte des Taufsymbols und der Glaubensregel*, iii (Christiania, 1875), 286–8, 303–34. Theodor Klauser dates the transition of the Roman anaphora to Latin as during the pontificate of Damasus (366–84) ('Der Übergang der römischen Kirche von der griechischen zu lateinischen Liturgiesprache', *Miscellanea Giovanni Mercati*, i (Vatican City, 1946), 467–82).

it appears probable that no later than the beginning of the third century, if not indeed during the second part of the second century, Christians at Rome are likely to have produced a Latin version of the New Testament Scriptures.[1]

But the question rises whether, in fact, the need for a Latin version of the New Testament made itself felt elsewhere before one was provided for Christians at Rome. At the close of the nineteenth century several scholars suggested that Antioch in Syria was the place where the Old Latin version(s) originated.[2] The strongest arguments in support of a Syrian origin are the knowledge of Hebrew and Aramaic which is revealed by the translators[3] and the unmistakable relations with the Old Syriac version.[4] Since, however, Jewish-Christian translators may have left their mark on the Old Latin version wherever it was produced, and since agreements between the Old Latin and the Old Syriac may just possibly find their explanation in Tatian's bringing Western readings from Rome to the East, there remains no solid reason for regarding Antioch as the birthplace of the Latin Scriptures, and scholars today are inclined to look to North Africa as the home of the first Latin version of the New Testament. The following considerations seem to point in that direction.

In North Africa at the opening of the Christian era, Punic, Berber, Greek, and Latin were used by various segments of the population. Soldiers and colonists spoke Latin, which was also used by officials of every level, as well as by merchants from Italy. It would have been necessary for the indigenous population to know Latin in order to enter into relations with their masters. While it may well be that the preaching of the Gospel in North Africa was first addressed to Greeks (in the *Passion of SS. Perpetua and Felicitas, c.* A.D. 202–3, we read that Perpetua conversed in

---

[1] Cf. Matti A. Sainio, *Semasiologische Untersuchungen über die Entstehung der christlichen Latinität* (Helsinki, 1940); Gustave Bardy, *La Question des langues dans l'église ancienne,* i (Paris, 1948), 100 ff.; cf. also Christine Mohrmann, 'Les origines de la latinité chrétienne', *VC* iii (1949), 67–106, 163–83; id., 'Die Rolle des Lateins in der Kirche des Westens', *ThRu,* lii (1956), 1–18.

[2] e.g. William Sanday in the *Guardian,* 25 May 1892, p. 787, and H. A. A. Kennedy, 'The Old Latin Versions', in Hastings's *Dictionary of the Bible,* iii (1900) 54f.

[3] Cf. D. S. Blondheim, *Les Parlers judéo-romains et la Vetus Latina* (Paris, 1925), pp. xcviii f.

[4] Cf. F. H. Chase, *The Old Syriac Element in the Text of Codex Bezae* (London, 1893) and *The Syro-Latin Text of the Gospels* (London, 1895).

Greek with the bishop Optatus), at an early date Latin would have become the official language of the Church of Africa.[1]

In A.D. 180 there was an outbreak of persecution in parts of the African province of Numidia (modern Tunisia). A record of the trial of Christians in a town named Scillium is the most ancient document that survives of African Christianity. This account, the *Acts of the Scillitan Martyrs* which was drawn up in Latin, identifies those who met their death by decapitation. It is significant that most of the martyrs bear Latin names: Speratus, Nartgalus, Cittinus, Donata, Secunda, Vestia. Still more significant is the information that, when one of them, Speratus, was asked by the proconsul what he had in the box or receptacle (*capsa*) which he carried, he replied: 'Books and letters of a just man, one Paul.' Since it is not likely that the Scillitan Christians, so obviously plebeian and without culture, were able to read Greek, we are driven to conclude that they possessed at least the Epistles of Paul in a Latin version. And if the Pauline Epistles were circulating in a Latin version by A.D. 180, there is no doubt that the Gospels were likewise available in Latin.[2]

While the earliest evidence for the existence of part of the New Testament in Latin comes to us from North Africa, the question has been raised whether the birthplace of the Latin New Testament might not have been at Rome after all.[3] More than a century ago Zahn pointed out many Latinisms in the Greek of the *Shepherd* of Hermas.[4] One of these Latinisms, as Mlle Mohrmann has argued,[5] provides evidence bearing on the existence at Rome of Latin technical terms relating to the Christian life. For example, Hermas uses the expression στατίωνα ἔχω and explains the phrase by the Greek word νηστεύω, 'I am fasting'. Now *statio* as a technical term for *ieiunium* is known from Tertullian; it

---

[1] It is noteworthy that almost all the persons who figure in the *Passion of SS. Perpetua and Felicitas* have Latin names: besides Perpetua and Felicitas there are Revocatus Saturninus, Secundulus, Optatus, Tertius, Pomponius, Saturus, Jucundus, Artaxius, Rusticus; only Dinocrates bears a true Greek name.

[2] So, e.g., Arthur Vööbus, *Early Versions of the New Testament* (Stockholm, 1954), pp. 35–7.

[3] See B. M. Peebles, 'Bible: Latin Versions', *New Catholic Encyclopedia*, ii (New York, 1967), 437.

[4] Theodor Zahn, *Der Hirt des Hermas* (Gotha, 1868), pp. 485 ff. The subject has been investigated more recently by R. G. Tanner, 'Latinisms in the Text of Hermas', *Colloquium*, iv (1972), 12–23.

[5] Christine Mohrmann in *VC* iii (1949), 76 f.

designates a particular type of fast on Wednesdays and Fridays. Thus Hermas attests the existence of a highly technical term in Latin relating to the organization of Christian life fifty years before Tertullian and perhaps thirty years before the composition of the *Acts of the Scillitan Martyrs*. That he wrote in Greek is no less significant—a Christian Latin idiom was emerging even while the official language of the Church remained Greek. It is possible, therefore—but no more than possible—that, as Vööbus phrases it, parallel with such 'a national awakening in the Christian community in Rome . . . the need for a translation [of the New Testament] among the uneducated masses may have been held to be pressing'.[1]

When one turns from the meagre evidence preserved in second-century Christian literature bearing on the use of Latin to examine statements made by later writers about the Latin versions of the Scriptures, much more specific comments are available. According to a well-known passage in Augustine's *De doctrina Christiana*, in the early centuries of the Church a very great number of Latin translations were in circulation:

> Those who translated the Scriptures from Hebrew into Greek can be counted, but the Latin translators are out of all number. For in the early days of the faith, every man who happened to gain possession of a Greek manuscript [of the New Testament] and who imagined he had any facility in both languages, however slight that might have been, dared to make a translation.[2]

Elsewhere Augustine refers to the infinite variety of the Latin translators, and Jerome complains that there are almost as many different Latin versions of the Scriptures as there are manuscript copies (see p. 334 below).

A problem arises concerning the nature of one of these versions, called the *Itala* by Augustine in a much-debated statement. The passage, with its immediate context, is as follows:

> Those who are anxious to know the Scriptures ought in the first place to use their skill in the correction of the texts, so that the uncorrected ones should give way to the corrected, at least when they are copies of the same translation. Now among the translations them-

---

[1] Ibid., p. 36.
[2] II. 16: 'Qui enim Scripturas ex hebraea lingua in graecam verterunt, numerari possunt, Latini autem interpretes nullo modo. Ut enim cuique primis fidei temporibus in manus venit codex graecus, et aliquantulum facultatis sibi utriusque linguae habere videbatur, ausus est interpretari.'

selves the Italian (*Itala*) is to be preferred to the others, for it keeps closer to the words without prejudice to clarity of expression.[1]

Among the many divergent interpretations that have been placed on Augustine's words,[2] the following deserve to be mentioned.

(1) The traditional interpretation[3] is that Augustine refers to a biblical version, or a revision of such a version, which was used in the political diocese of Italy, which at that time comprehended Verona, Aquileia, Brescia, Ravenna, and Milan. Although the words seem, on the surface, to bear such a meaning, many difficulties stand in the way of accepting it as what Augustine really meant. For example, if he thought that, among the early Latin renderings, the *Itala* was to be preferred because of its fidelity and clarity, one would expect that he would have referred to it repeatedly in his writings. But his works contain no other reference to it.

(2) In 1896 F. C. Burkitt published his famous monograph on the subject[4] in which he rejected the prima-facie meaning of Augustine's words as referring to an Old Latin version and argued that by *Itala* Augustine meant Jerome's Vulgate. This interpretation was, in fact, not new, but was a revival of the opinion of Isidore of Seville,[5] which was in turn restated in 1824 by C. A. Breyther.[6] Burkitt's main argument is that the Gospel quotations in Augustine's *De consensu evangelistarum* and a passage in his *Contra Felicem* stand in closest agreement with the Vulgate. But even supposing that Augustine did use the Vulgate in one or more

---

[1] Ibid., II. 21–2: 'nam codicibus emendandis primitus debet invigilare solertia eorum qui Scripturas divinas nosse desiderant, ut emendatis non emendati cedant, ex uno dumtaxat interpretationis genere venientes. (22) In ipsis autem interpretationibus Itala ceteris praeferatur, nam est verborum tenacior cum perspicuitate sententiae . . .'

[2] For surveys of the several interpretations given to the passage, see B. Botte, 'Itala', *Dictionnaire de la Bible, Supplément*, iv (1949), cols. 777–82, and Johannes Schildenberger, 'Die Itala des hl. Augustinus', *Colligere fragmenta. Festschrift Alban Dold*, ed. by B. Fischer and V. Fiala (Beuron, 1952), pp. 84–102.

[3] It received the approval, e.g., of Samuel Berger, *Histoire de la Vulgate pendant les premiers siècles du Moyen Âge* (Paris, 1893; repr. New York, 1958), p. 6.

[4] *The Old Latin and the Itala* (*Texts and Studies*, iv. 3; Cambridge, 1896). For Burkitt's reply to certain criticisms of the theory, see 'Saint Augustine's Bible and the Itala', *JTS* xi (1910), 258–68, 447–58.

[5] *Etymologiae*, vi. 4 (Migne, *PL* lxxxii, col. 236).

[6] *De vi quam antiquissimae versiones quae extant Latinae in crisin Evangeliorum iv habeant* (Diss., Merseburg, 1824).

of his treatises (and there is no reason why he may not have done so), it is difficult to see how this proves that he designated it by the name *Itala* in the celebrated passage quoted above. The form in which Burkitt set forth his supporting argumentation convinced such scholars as Zahn,[1] Berger,[2] Corssen,[3] Ropes,[4] and Lake and New;[5] it was rejected, however, by others equally eminent, such as Wordsworth and White,[6] Mercati,[7] Kennedy,[8] Denk,[9] Eb. Nestle,[10] Vogels,[11] and Lagrange.[12]

(3) Several theories involving emendation of the passage in *De doctrina Christiana* have been proposed. In 1915 Vaccari conjectured that instead of *Itala* we should read *Aquila*.[13] This emendation, however, does violence to the syntax of the phrase, for if it had been Augustine's intention to refer to Aquila's work he would have used the genitive *Aquilae [interpretatio]*.

(4) D'Alès, who pointed out the inconcinnity involved in Vaccari's conjecture, supposed that *Itala* is a copyist's blunder for *illa*.[14]

(5) Still another conjectural emendation supporting the hypothesis that Augustine had referred to Aquila's version was pro-

---

[1] *Theologisches Literaturblatt*, xvii (1896), cols. 374 f.

[2] *Bulletin critique*, 2nd ser., ii (5 Sept. 1896), 25.

[3] Peter Corssen, *Göttingische gelehrte Anzeigen*, clix (1897), 416–24, and his 'Bericht über die lateinischen Bibelübersetzungen', in Bursian's *Jahresberichte über die Fortschritte der klassischen Altertumswissenschaft*, ci (1899), 1–83. Corssen refined Burkitt's view by pointing out that in the context of the passage in *De doctrina Christiana* Augustine refers particularly to the Old Testament, and one ought consequently to apply the term *Itala*, not to the Vulgate Bible as a whole or the Vulgate New Testament (as Burkitt tended to do), but only to the Vulgate Old Testament.

[4] James H. Ropes, *The Text of Acts* (London, 1926), p. cxxii.

[5] K. Lake, *The Text of the New Testament*, 6th edn., revd. by S. New (London, 1928), p. 29.

[6] *Novum Testamentum . . . Latine*, i (Oxford, 1889–98), 656 n. 1.

[7] *RB* vi (1897), 474 ff.   [8] Hastings's *Dictionary of the Bible*, iii (1900), 57.

[9] Jos. Denk, *BZ* vi (1908), 225–44.

[10] *The New Schaff-Herzog Encyclopedia of Religious Knowledge*, ii (1908), 121.

[11] *BZ* iv (1906), 267–95, and repeated in *Biblische Studien*, xiii. 5 (1908), 477–506.

[12] *Critique textuelle* (Paris, 1935), p. 257 f.

[13] Alberto Vaccari, 'Alle origini della Volgata', *CC* lxvi. 4 (1915), 21–37; and 'L'Itala di S. Agostino', ibid. lxvii, 1 (1916), 77–84.

[14] Adhémar d'Alès, *RSR* xi (1921), 219; and id., *Novatien; étude sur la théologie romaine au milieu du IIIe siècle* (Paris, 1925), pp. 38 f. D'Alès was not the first to propose this emendation; Bentley had suggested it in 1734, changing also *nam* to *quae* (see Scrivener–Miller, *A Plain Introduction to the Criticism of the New Testament*, 4th edn., ii (1894), 42, note).

posed by Quentin,[1] who supposed that the textual transmission of the portion of Augustine's treatise at one stage involved a lacuna in the text between *ita* and *la*. Instead of the generally received text Quentin conjectured that the original read *In ipsis autem interpretationibus ita* [. . . *unde fit ut a Iudaeis Aqui*]*la ceteris preferatur*, etc. This restoration is assuredly ingenious, but whether it is persuasive, opinions will differ. If, in fact, Augustine was re-ferring to Aquila's Greek version of the Old Testament, the Itala vanishes, having, as Vaccari comments, 'no more real existence than the phoenix—one is only in the pen of the copyist, the other in the imagination of the poet'.[2] Degering's subsequent refine-ment (*In ipsis autem interpretationibus ita* [*lata est a Iudaeis sententia ut eam quam fecit Aqui*]*la ceteris* . . .)[3] is no better, for one cannot see any reason for Augustine's mentioning Aquila in this context.

In view of the lack of certainty concerning the meaning of Augustine's reference to the Itala—although Schildenberger[4] has made it probable that Augustine meant one European form of the Old Latin—it is to be regretted that Jülicher gave this name to his edition of the Old Latin as a whole. Present-day scholars prefer to speak of the Old Latin Bible or the pre-Vulgate, though to be strictly accurate they ought to speak of the Old Latin versions.

2. MANUSCRIPTS OF THE OLD LATIN VERSIONS

As compared with the more than 10,000 manuscripts—some of them *de luxe* copies—of Jerome's Latin Vulgate, the manuscripts of the Old Latin versions are relatively few in a number and un-pretentious in format.

No one manuscript contains the entire New Testament in the Old Latin version. Most of the copies are fragmentary and/or palimpsest.[5] In some cases a copy of the complete New Testament

---

[1] Henri Quentin, 'La prétendue *Itala* de saint Augustin', *RB* xxxvi (1927) 216–25.

[2] 'Una "Itala" fenice negli scritti di S. Agostino', *CC* lxxx. 4 (1929), 108–17.

[3] Hermann Degering and Albert Boekler, *Die Quedlinburger Italafragmenta* (Berlin, 1932), p. 23.   [4] Op. cit. (p. 291 n. 1 above).

[5] In an instructive study entitled 'Codices rescripti: a List of the Oldest Latin Palimpsests with Stray Observation on their Origin' (*Mélanges Eugène Tisserant*, v (*Studi e testi*, ccxxxv; Vatican City, 1964), 67–113, with six plates), E. A. Lowe points out that 'of palimpsested lower texts the largest group seems to have been condemned on the grounds of obsolescence; next come cases of duplication. Thus

in Latin may present Jerome's Vulgate text in most of the books, and the Old Latin in only one or two books. In other cases the number of Old Latin readings in a given book or books may be relatively few, making it problematic whether the text should not be classified as mixed Vulgate rather than Old Latin.

It is customary to list Old Latin manuscripts according to their contents, in the categories of Gospels, Acts, Pauline Epistles, Catholic Epistles, and the Book of Revelation (in some cases the same manuscript falls into two or more categories). The following check-list enumerates forty-six witnesses for the Gospels, nineteen for Acts, twenty for Paul (including Hebrews), twelve for the Catholic Epistles, and seven for the Book of Revelation.[1] It should be noted that these figures include all manuscripts that have been considered, for one reason or another, to present an Old Latin text. Only a few (e.g. *k e a j* for the Gospels) are pure Old Latin; most are more or less mixed with the Vulgate text.

Each Old Latin manuscript is designated by a lower-case italic letter (a custom begun by Karl Lachmann in his 1842–50 edition of the Greek and Latin New Testament), followed by the arabic numeral (enclosed within parentheses) which has been assigned to the manuscript by the Vetus Latina Institute at Beuron. Inasmuch as the total number of Old Latin manuscripts now exceeds the capabilities of the letters of the alphabet, more recently discovered witnesses can be cited only by numerals.

The following check-list provides information concerning each manuscript as to (*a*) its date, given by century in roman numerals (followed by abbreviations of the names of those who have assigned it to such a date); (*b*) its present location; (*c*) the contents of the manuscript; and (*d*) bibliographical details concerning editions, including a reference to a facsimile specimen of its script (when such is available) in E. A. Lowe's *Codices Latini Antiquiores*. For full bibliographical information concerning the editions of Sabatier, Bianchini, Jülicher, cited in the check-list merely by the editor's name, see pp. 319–22 below.

It should be noted that, in view of the varying degrees of mixture of Vulgate readings in several of the Old Latin manuscripts,

---

pre-Jerome translations of the Bible were superseded by the Vulgate, and the Vulgate is found as the lower text [of manuscripts that antedate the ninth century] much more often than as the upper.'

[1] But see the Appendix, p. 461 below.

scholars may differ in their opinion concerning the legitimacy of classifying a given witness as Old Latin. In general the tendency among modern scholars has been to classify doubtful cases as 'mixed texts' rather than continuing to identify them as Old Latin witnesses. For the sake of historical interest and convenience in referring to the older literature, the check-list includes witnesses that no longer are generally regarded as Old Latin (e.g. δ, *dem*, *m*, x_1, x_2).

CHECK-LIST OF OLD LATIN MANUSCRIPTS OF THE NEW TESTAMENT[1]

Ay = Teófilo Ayuso Marazuela, *La Vetus Latina Hispana*; i. *Prolegómenos* (Madrid, 1953).

Beu = Erzabtei Beuron, *Vetus Latina: Die Reste der altlateinischen Bibel*; i, *Verzeichnis der Sigel* (Freiburg, 1949); xxiv/1, *Epistula ad Ephesios* (1962–64); xxiv/2, *Epistulae ad Philippenses et ad Colossenses* (1966–71); xxvi/1, *Epistulae Catholicae* (1956–69).

B = José M. Bover, *Novi Testamenti biblia Graece et Latine*, 3rd edn. (Madrid, 1953).

J = A. Jülicher, *Itala: Das Neue Testament in altlateinischer Überlieferung*; i, *Matthäus-Evangelium* (Berlin, 1938; 2nd edn. 1972); ii, *Marcus-Evangelium* (1940; 2nd edn. 1970); iii, *Lucas-Evangelium* (1954; 2nd edn. 1976); iv, *Johannes-Evangelium* (1963).

K = G. D. Kilpatrick, *H KAINH ΔIAΘHKH*, 2nd edn. (London, 1958).

L = S. C. E. Legg, *Novum Testamentum Graece . . . Euangelium secundum Marcum* (Oxford, 1935); *Euangelium secundum Matthaeum* (Oxford, 1940).

Lo = E. A. Lowe, *Codices Latini Antiquiores: A Palaeographical Guide to Latin Manuscripts Prior to the Ninth Century*, Parts i–xi (Oxford, 1934–66), *Supplement* (1971); Part ii, 2nd edn. (1972).

M = Augustinus Merk, *Novum Testamentum Graece et Latine*, 9th edn. (Rome, 1964).

N = E. Nestle and K. Aland, *Novum Testamentum Graece*, 25th edn. (Stuttgart, 1963).

R = J. H. Ropes, *The Text of Acts* (*The Beginnings of Christianity*, Part I, ed. by by F. J. Foakes Jackson and K. Lake, iii; London, 1926).

S = A. Souter, *Novum Testamentum Graece*, 2nd edn. (Oxford, 1947).

T = C. von Tischendorf, *Novum Testamentum Graece*; vol. iii, *Prolegomena*, by C. R. Gregory (Leipzig, 1884–94).

[1] The check-list was compiled by Dr. Robert P. Markham, Co-ordinator of Reference Services at the James A. Michener Library, University of Northern Colorado, and is used here with his kind permission. The present writer has reorganized the sequence within each description and has made small additions, chiefly by completing the citation of references to specimens in E. A. Lowe's *Codices Latini Antiquiores*. See also the Appendix, p. 461 below.

V = H. J. Vogels, *Novum Testamentum Graece et Latine*, 4th edn. (Freiburg, 1955).
W = J. Wordsworth and H. J. White, *Novum Testamentum Domini Nostri Iesu Christi Latine*, 3 vols. (Oxford, 1889–1954).

THE GOSPELS

a (3). Codex Vercellensis, saec. iv (Ay B Beu K M S T), iv–v (J N V W), iv² (Lo), at Vercelli, Biblioteca Capitolare, contains the four Gospels (in the sequence Matt., John, Luke, Mark), with many lacunae; ed. by J. A. Irico, *Codex Vercellensis* (Milan, 1748), Bianchini (repr. in Migne, *PL* xii, cols. 141–538); J. Belsheim, *Codex Vercellensis* (Christiania, 1897); A. Gasquet, *Codex Vercellensis* (*Collectanea biblica Latina*, iii; Rome, 1914), for corrections see H. J. Vogels, *BZ* xv (1918–19), 301–18; Jülicher; Lowe, iv, no. 467.

a² (16), see also *n*, *o*. Codex Curiensis, saec. v (Beu J Lo T W), v–vi (M V), at Chur, Rhätisches Museum, contains Luke xi. 11–29; xiii. 16–34; ed. by J. Wordsworth, W. Sanday, H. J. White, *Portions of the Gospels According to St. Mark and St. Matthew* (*Old Latin Biblical Texts*, ii; Oxford, 1886); Jülicher; for specimen of script, see Lowe, vii, no. 978a.

aur (15), so B J V; is designated *z* by K M N. Codex Aureus Holmiensis, saec. vi–vii (V), vii (Ay Beu J), vii–viii (B), viii (K M), vi–viii (N), at Stockholm, Kungl. Biblioteket, contains the four Gospels; ed. by J. Belsheim, *Codex Aureus* (Christiania, 1878); Jülicher; for specimen of script, see Lowe, xi, no. 1642.

b (4). Codex Veronensis, saec. iv–v (B W), v (Ay J K N T), v ex (Beu Lo), v–vi (S), at Verona, Bibioteca Capitolare, Cod. VI, contains the four Gospels (in the sequence Matt., John, Luke, Mark), with several lacunae; ed. by Bianchini; J. Belsheim, *Codex Veronensis. Quattuor Evangelia . . .* (Prague, 1904); E. S. Buchanan, *The Four Gospels from the Codex Veronensis* b (*Old Latin Biblical Texts*, vi; Oxford, 1911), pp. 1–197 (but see H. A. Sanders, 'Buchanans Publikationen altlateinischer Texte. Eine Warnung', *ZNW* xxi (1922) 291–9; and G. Mercati, 'Un paio di appunti sopre il codice purpureo Veronese dei vangeli', *RB* xxxiv (1925), 396–400); Jülicher; for specimen of script, see Lowe, iv, no. 481.

β (26). Codex Carinthianus, saec. vi–vii (Lo), vii (Beu J), at St. Paul in Carinthia (Austria), Stiftsbibliothek, 25.3.19 (XXV a. 1), two folios, serving as front fly-leaves of a fifth-century manuscript, contains Luke i. 64–ii. 50; ed. by D. De Bruyne, *RBén*, xxxv (1923), 62–80; Jülicher; for specimen of script, see Lowe, x, no. 1449.

c (6). Codex Colbertinus, saec. xi (W), xii (Ay B J K M N S T V), xii–xiii (Beu), at Paris, Bibliothèque Nationale, Lat. 254 (Colbertinus 4051), contains the four Gospels and Acts in Old Latin, with the rest of the New Testament in the Vulgate; ed. by J. Belsheim, *Codex Colbertinus Parisiensis . . . 4051* (Christiania, 1888); H. J. Vogels, *Evangelium Colbertinum*, 2 vols. (*Bonner biblische Beiträge*, iv and v; Bonn, 1953); Jülicher.

d (5). Codex Cantabrigiensis, Codex Bezae (D), saec. v (Beu S), v–vi (K), vi (Ay B J M N T V W), v in. (Lo²), at Cambridge, University Library, Nn. 2.41, contains the four Gospels (in the sequence Matt., John, Luke, Mark), Acts, 3 John, with lacunae, Greek and Latin on facing pages; ed. by Sabatier; Thomas Kipling, *Codex Theodori Bezae Cantabrigiensis*, 2 vols. (Cambridge, 1793); F. H. Scrivener, *Bezae Codex Cantabrigiensis* (Cambridge, 1864); *Codex Bezae Cantabrigiensis* (photographic facsimile edition) 2 vols. (Cambridge, 1899); Jülicher; Lowe, ii², no. 140. An index verborum of *d* is included by Robert C. Stone in his monograph, *The Language of the Latin Text of Codex Bezae (Illinois Studies in Language and Literature*, xxx, nos. 2–3; Urbana, 1946).

δ (27). Codex Sangallensis, saec. ix (Ay B Beu K T W), at St. Gallen, Stiftsbibliothek, MS. 48, contains the four Gospels; ed. by H. C. M. Rettig, *Antiquissimus quatuor evangeliorum canonicorum Codex Sangallensis, Graeco-Latinus interlinearis* (Zürich, 1836), facsimile edition.

e (2). Codex Palatinus, saec. iv–v (B K M N W), v (Ay Beu J Lo S T V), at Trent, Museo Nazionale (Castel del Buon Consiglio) (formerly Hofbiblio-thek, Vienna, Lat. 1185); one leaf at Dublin, Trinity College 1709 (N.4.18 = Matt. xiii. 12–23) and one at London, British Museum, Add. 40107 (= Matt. xiv. 11–22), contains the four Gospels (in the sequence Matt., John, Luke, Mark), with many lacunae; ed. by C. von Tischendorf, *Evangelium Palatinum ineditum* (Leipzig, 1847); J. Belsheim, *Codex Palatinus* (Christiania, 1896); T. K. Abbott, *Par palimpsestorum Dublinensium* (Dublin, 1880); A. Souter, 'A Lost Leaf of Codex Palatinus (e) of the Old Latin Gospels Recovered', *JTS* xxiii (1921–2), 284–6; Jülicher; for specimen of script, see Lowe, iv, no. 437.

f (10). Codex Brixianus, saec. vi (Ay B J K M N S T V W), vi¹ (Beu Lo), at Brescia, Biblioteca civica Queriniana (deposited in Museo d'Arte Cristiana), contains the four Gospels with several lacunae; ed. by Bianchini; Words-worth and White, *Novum Testamentum Latine secundum editionem S. Hieronymi*, i (Oxford, 1889–98); Jülicher; for specimen of script, see Lowe, iii, no. 281.

ff, *ff*¹ (9). Codex Corbeiensis I (Sangermanensis 21), later Petropolitanus, saec. viii (W), x (Beu S T), x–xi (Ay V), xi (B K M N), at Leningrad, Public Library, O.v.I,3 (Corb. 21), contains Matthew, predominantly Vulgate text; ed. by J. Martianay, *Vulgata antiqua Latina et versio Evangelii secundum Matthaeum* ... (Paris, 1695); Sabatier; Bianchini; J. Belsheim, *Das Evangelium des Matthäus nach dem lateinischen Codex ff*¹ *Corbeiensis* . . . (Christiania, 1881); Jülicher; for specimen of script, see Lowe, xi, no. 1624.

*ff*² (8). Codex Corbeiensis II (195), saec. v (B Beu K Lo M N S V), v–vi (Ay J W), vii (T), at Paris, Bibliothèque Nationale, fond. lat. 17225 (Corb. 195), contains the four Gospels (in the sequence Matt., Luke, John, Mark), with lacunae; ed. by Sabatier; J. Belsheim, *Codex Corbeiensis 195* (*ff*²) (Christiania, 1887); E. S. Buchanan, *The Four Gospels from the Codex Corbeiensis ff*² (*Old Latin Biblical Texts*, v; Oxford, 1907), pp. 1–96 (cf. H. A. Sanders, 'Bucha-nans Publikationen altlateinischer Texte. Eine Warnung', *ZNW* xxi (1922), 291–9); Jülicher; for specimen of script, see Lowe, v, no. 666.

g, *g*¹ (7). Codex Sangermanensis I, saec. vii (B), viii (J T V), ix (Ay Beu K N W), x (B M S), at Paris, Bibliothèque Nationale, fond lat. 11553 (Sangermanensis 15), contains the Vulgate Bible, of which, in the New Testament, the Gospels contain Old Latin readings (Beu); ed. by Sabatier; J. Wordsworth, *The Gospel According to St. Matthew from St. Germain* MS *g*¹ . . . (*Old Latin Biblical Texts*, i; Oxford, 1883), pp. 5–46; Jülicher.

*g*² (29). Codex Sangermanensis II, saec. x (Ay B Beu K M N T V W), at Paris, Bibliothèque Nationale, fond lat. 13169, contains the four Gospels; ed. by Sabatier.

gat (30). Codex Gatianum, saec. vii (S), viii (Beu K), at Paris, Bibliothèque Nationale, nouv. acquis. lat. 1587, contains the four Gospels; ed. by Sabatier; J. M. Heer, *Euangelium Gatianum* (Freiburg, 1910); for specimen of script, see Lowe, v, no. 684.

h (12). Codex Claromontanus, saec. iv–v (W), v (B K M N S T V), v–vi (Ay J), v ex. (Beu Lo), at Rome, Biblioteca Apostolica Vaticana, Lat. 7223, fols. 1–66, contains the four Gospels, of which only Matthew (lacks i. 1–iii. 15; xiv. 33–xviii. 12) is Old Latin; ed. by Sabatier; Angelo Mai, *Scriptorum veterum nova collectio*, iii. 2 (Rome, 1828), pp. 257–88; J. Belsheim, *Evangelium secundum Matthaeum . . . e codice olim Claromontano nunc Vaticano* (*Christiania Videnskabs-Selskabs Forhanlinger*, 1892, no. 5; Christiania, 1892); Jülicher; for specimen of script, see Lowe, i, no. 53.

i (17). Codex Vindobonensis, saec. v (K N), v ex. (Beu Lo), v–vi (Ay J S T V), vii (B M W), at Naples, Biblioteca Nazionale, Lat. 3 (formerly at Vienna, Hofbibliothek, lat. 1235), contains fragments of Luke (x. 36–xxiii. 10) and Mark (ii. 17–iii. 29; iv. 4–x. 1; x. 33–xiv. 36; xv. 33–40); ed. by J. Belsheim, *Codex Vindobonensis membranaceus purpureus . . .* (Leipzig, 1885); Jülicher; for specimen of script, see Lowe, iii, no. 399.

j (J K M) = *z* (T) (22). Codex Saretianus or Sarzanensis, saec. v (T W), v–vi (Ay K N), vi (J M), vi in. (Beu Lo), in the church at Sarezzano near Tortona (Prov. Alessandria), contains Luke xxiv and John (with many lacunae); John xviii. 36–xx. 14 is by another hand; ed. by G. Godu, *Codex Sarzanensis, Fragments d'ancienne version latine du quatrième Évangile* (*Spicilegium Casinense*, ii; Montecassino, 1936); Jülicher; for specimen of script, see Lowe, iv, no. 436a (and no. 436b).

k (1). Codex Bobiensis, saec. iv (S), iv–v (Ay B Beu K Lo M N V W), v (T), v–vi (J), at Turin, Biblioteca Universitaria Nazionale, G VII 15, contains Mark (viii. 8–11, 14–16; viii. 19–xvi. 9) and Matthew (i. 1–iii. 10; iv. 2–xiv. 17; xv. 20–36); ed. by J. Wordsworth, W. Sanday, H. J. White, *Portions of the Gospels According to St. Mark and St. Matthew* (*Old Latin Biblical Texts*, ii; Oxford, 1886), pp. 1–54, 95–122; C. H. Turner, F. C. Burkitt, 'A Re-Collation of Codex *k* of the Old Latin Gospels', *JTS* v (1903–4), 88–107; C. Cipolla, *Il codice evangelico k della Biblioteca Universitaria nazionale di Torino* (Torino, 1913; facsimile edition); Jülicher; for specimen of script, see Lowe, iv, no. 465.

l (11). Codex Rehdigeranus, saec. vii (S T), vii–viii (Ay Beu J V), viii (B K M N), viii[1] (Lo), at Breslau, Stadtbibliothek, Rehd. 169, contains the four Gospels contaminated by the Vulgate (Ay); John lacks xvi. 13–xxi. 25; ed. by H. J. Vogels, *Codex Rehdigeranus* (*Collectanea Biblica Latina*, ii; Rome, 1913); Jülicher; for specimen of script, see Lowe, viii, no. 1073.

m (PS–AU spe). Speculum (M T), Speculum Ps-Augustine (K S V) or Sessorianus (B), a florilegium, saec. v, contains passages from all the books of the New Testament except 3 John, Hebrews, and Philemon. The superscript numbers used by Tischendorf indicate the page in the Mai edition; ed. by A. Mai, *Spicilegium romanum*, IX. 2 (Rome, 1843), 61–86; A. Mai, *Nova Patrum Bibliotheca*, I. 2 (Rome, 1852), 1–117; F. Weihrich, *S. Augustini liber qui appellatur Speculum et Liber de Divinis Scripturis sive Speculum quod fertur S. Augustini* (*CSEL* xii; Vienna, 1887), pp. 287–700; J. Belsheim, *Fragmenta Novi Testamenti in libro 'Speculum'* (Christiania, 1899).

μ (35). Book of Mulling or Codex Mull. Dublinensis, saec. vii (Ay K), vii ex. (Beu Lo), viii ex. (Lo Suppl), at Dublin, Trinity College 60 (A.1.15), contains the four Gospels; ed. by H. J. Lawlor, *Chapters on the Book of Mulling* (Edinburgh, 1897); for specimen of script, see Lowe, ii, no. 276.

n (16), see also *a*[2], *o*. Codex Sangallensis, saec. iv–v (S), v (Beu, J[Jn] Lo T W), v–vi (B K M N V), vi (J[Mt Mk]), vi–vii (Ay), at St. Gall, Stiftsbibliothek 1394, II. 51–88; Stiftsbibliothek 172, p. 256; and Vadiana 70, contains fragments of the four Gospels; ed. by J. Wordsworth, W. Sanday, H. J. White, *Portions of the Gospels According to St. Mark and St. Matthew* (*Old Latin Biblical Texts*, ii; Oxford, 1886), pp. 55–7; Bernhard Bischoff, 'Neue Materialen zum Bestand und zur Geschichte der altlateinischen Bibelübersetzungen', *Miscellanea Giovanni Mercati*, i (*Studi e testi*, cxxi; Vatican City, 1946), 420–4; Jülicher; for specimen of script, see Lowe, vii, no. 978a.

o (16), see also *a*[2], *n*. Codex Sangallensis, saec. vii (Beu T V), vii–viii (J W), at St. Gallen, Stiftsbibliothek, 1394, III. 91–2, contains Mark xvi. 14–20; ed. by J. Wordsworth, W. Sanday, H. J. White, *Portions of the Gospels According to St. Mark and St. Matthew* (*Old Latin Biblical Texts*, ii; Oxford, 1886); Jülicher; for specimen of script, see Lowe, vii, no. 978b.

p (20). Codex Sangallensis, saec. vii–viii (B M W), viii (Ay Beu J Lo T), at St. Gallen, Stiftsbibliothek, 1395, VII. 430–3, contains John ix. 14–44; ed. by J. Wordsworth, W. Sanday, H. J. White, *Portions of the Gospels According to St. Mark and St. Matthew* (*Old Latin Biblical Texts*, ii; Oxford, 1886); pp. 75–7; Bernhard Bischoff, *Miscellanea Giovanni Mercati*, i (*Studi e testi*, cxxi; Vatican City, 1946), 425–7; Jülicher; Lowe, vii, no. 989.

π (J) = *w* (Ay) (18). Fragmenta Stuttgartensia, Weingartensia, Constantiensia, saec. vii (Ay Beu J), at Stuttgart, Landesbibliothek, H.B. VII. 29; Darmstadt, Landesbibliothek, 895; Donaueschingen, Fürstenbergische Hofbibliothek, 192, 193, contains palimpsest fragments of Luke xiv. 8–12; John vii. 24–32, 37–8; iv. 22–32; xi. 19–21, 26, 38–48; xx. 25, 28, 29, 30; ed. by A. Dold, *Konstanzer altlateinische Propheten- und Evangelien-*

Bruchstücke mit Glossen (*Texte und Arbeiten*, i, 7–9; Beuron, 1923), pp. 194–224; Jülicher; for specimen of script, see Lowe, viii, no. 1176.

q (13). Codex Monacensis, saec. vi (T), vi–vii (Ay J Lo V), vii (B Beu K M N S W), at Munich, Bayerische Staatsbibliothek, Clm. 6224 (Frising. 24), contains the four Gospels (in the sequence Matt., John, Luke, Mark), with lacunae; ed. by H. J. White, *The Four Gospels from the Munich MS.* (*q*) (*Old Latin Biblical Texts*, iii; Oxford, 1888), pp. 1–137; cf. D. De Bruyne, *RBén,* xxviii (1911), 75–80; Jülicher; for specimen of script, see Lowe, ix, no. 1249.

r, r¹ (14). Codex Usserianus I, saec. vi (S T), vi–vii (Ay B K M N V), vii in. (Beu J Lo), at Dublin, Trinity College, 55, formerly A. 4. 15; contains the four Gospels (in the sequence Matt., John, Luke, Mark), with lacunae; ed. by T. K. Abbott, *Evangeliorum Versio antehieronymiana ex codice Usseriano* (Dublin, 1884); Jülicher; for specimen of script, see Lowe, ii, no. 271.

r² (28), Codex Usserianus II, saec. viii (K), viii–ix (Beu Lo), ix (Ay B M N V) at Dublin, Trinity College 56 (A.4.6), contains the four Gospels in a mixed text; ed. by T. K. Abbott, *Evangeliorum Versio antehieronymiana ex codice Usseriano,* vol. ii, Appendix (Dublin, 1884), pp. 819–63; H. J. Lawlor, *Chapters on the Book of Mulling* (Edinburgh, 1897), pp. 186–201; H. C. Hoskier, *The Text of Codex Usserianus 2.* *r₂* ('*Garland of Howth*'), *with critical notes to supplement and correct the collation of the late T. K. Abbott* (*Old Latin Biblical Texts;* London, 1919) (so the title page; the paper cover reads: *r₂.* *New and Complete Edition of the Irish Latin Gospel Codex Usser. 2 or r₂, otherwise known as* '*The Garland of Howth,*' *in Trinity College Library, Dublin* (*Old Latin Biblical Texts;* London, 1919)); for specimen of script, see Lowe, ii, no. 272.

ρ (24). Codex Ambrosianus, saec. vii–viii (Beu J Lo), at Milan, Biblioteca Ambrosiana M. 12 sup., palimpsest, contains John xiii. 3–17 as a pericope in a liturgical book; ed. by A. Wilmart, *RB* xxxi (1922), 182–202; for specimen of script, see Lowe, iii, no. 354.

s (21). Codex Ambrosianus, saec. v ex. (Beu Lo), vi (T V W), v–vi (Ay), vi–vii (J), vii (B), vii–viii (M), at Milan, Biblioteca Ambrosiana O.210 sup. (formerly C.73 inf., fol. 73–6), contains fragments of Luke xvii–xxi; ed. by A. M. Ceriani, *Monumenta sacra et profana e codicibus praesertim Bibliotecae Ambrosianae,* I. 1 (Milan, 1861), 1–8; J. Wordsworth, W. Sanday, H. J. White, *Portions of the Gospels According to St. Mark and St. Matthew* (*Old Latin Biblical Texts,* ii; Oxford, 1886), pp. 83–8; Jülicher; for specimen of script, see Lowe, iii, no. 360.

t (19). Fragmenta Bernensia, saec. v–vi (Ay J M V), v² (Lo), vi (Beu W), at Bern, Universitätsbibliothek 611, fols. 143 and 144, contain Mark i. 2–23; ii. 22–7; iii. 11–18, palimpsest; ed. by H. Hagen, 'Ein Italafragment aus einem Berner Palimpsest des VI Jahrhunderts', *Zeitschrift für wissenschaftliche Theologie,* xxvii (1884), 470–84; J. Wordsworth, W. Sanday, H. J. White, *Portions of the Gospels According to St. Mark and St. Matthew* (*Old Latin Biblical Texts,* ii; Oxford, 1886), pp. 89–94; Jülicher; for specimen of script, see Lowe, vii, no. 867.

v (25). Codex Vindobonensis, saec. vi–vii (Lo), vii (Ay B Beu J T), at Vienna, Nationalbibliothek, cod. lat. 502 end-paper, contains John xix. 27–xx. 11; ed. by H. J. White, *The Four Gospels from the Munich MS. q (Old Latin Biblical Texts,* iii; Oxford, 1888), pp. 161–3; Jülicher; for specimen of script, see Lowe, x, no. 1481.

w (Ay) = *π* (J)

z (K M N) = *aur* (B J V)

z (T) = *j* (J K M)

23. Fragmentum Aberdonense, saec. v (Ay Beu J Lo), at Aberdeen, University Library, Papyrus 2ᵃ, contains John vii. 27–8, 30–1; ed. by E. O. Winstedt, *The Classical Quarterly,* i (1907), p. 266; E. G. Turner, *Catalogue of Greek and Latin Papyri and Ostraca in the Possession of the University of Aberdeen* (Aberdeen, 1939), pp. 1–2; for specimen of script, see Lowe, ii, no. 118.

31. Ordo Scrutiniorum, saec. vi (Ay), xi (Beu), at Milan, Biblioteca Ambrosiana, T. 27 sup., contains O.T. and N.T. lessons and musical texts; ed. by C. Lambot, *North Italian Services of the XIth Century (Henry Bradshaw Society,* lxvii; 1931), pp. 7–35.

32. Codex Weiss. Guelferbitanus (Wolfenbüttel), *c.* 500 (Beu), saec. v–vi ¡Ay) vi in. (Lo), at Wolfenbüttel, Herzog-August-Bibliothek Weissenb. 76, palimpsest, contains lections from Old and New Testament; ed. by A. Dold, *Das älteste Liturgiebuch der lateinischen Kirche. Ein altgallikanisches Lektionar des 5/6. Jahr. aus dem Wolfenbütteler Palimpsest Codex Weissenburg (Texte und Arbeiten,* xxvi–xxviii; Beuron, 1936); for specimen of script, see Lowe, ix, no. 1392.

33. Codex Parisiensis saec. v ex. (Beu), v–vi (Ay Lo), at Paris, Bibliothèque Nationale, fond. 10439, contains the Gospel of John; chaps. i–vi are Old Latin, the rest is Vulgate; cf. S. Berger, *Histoire de la Vulgate* (Paris, 1893), pp. 89–90; for specimen of script, see Lowe, v, no. 600.

34. Codex Cryptoferratensis, saec. ? (Ay, Beu), at Grottaferrata, Badia cod. *Γ.β.*VI, contains John i. 1–17; ed. by J. Cozza, *Sacrorum Bibliorum vetustissima fragmenta Graeca et Latina ex palimpsestis codicibus Bibliothecae cryptoferratensis,* ii (Rome, 1867), 336.

36. Fragmentum Got. Giessenense, saec. v (Ay Beu), vi (Lo), at Giessen, Universitätsbibliothek cod. 651/20, contained Luke xxiii. 3–6; xxiv. 5–9 (see p. 381 below); ed. by P. Glaue, *ZNW* xi (1910), 1–17 (with facsimile); cf. Franz Rühl, ibid. xii (1911), 85–6; for specimen of script, see Lowe, viii, no. 1200.

37. Hieronymus in Matthaeum, saec. viii (Ay Beu) viii., ex (Lo), at Boulogne-sur-Mer, Bibliothèque Municipale (42) 47, contains portions of Matthew; ed. by A. Souter, in *Quantulacumque: Studies presented to Kirsopp*

Lake . . . , ed. by Robert P. Casey *et al.* (London, 1937), pp. 349–54; for specimen of script, see Lowe, vi, no. 736.

38. Hieronymus in Matthaeum, saec. ix (Ay Beu), at Rome, Biblioteca Apostolica Vaticana cod. Palat. lat. 177, contains portions of Matthew; ed. by A. Souter, in *Quantulacumque: Studies presented to Kirsopp Lake* . . . , ed. by Robert P. Casey *et al.* (London, 1937), pp. 349–54.

39. Codex Pictaviensis, saec. ix (Ay Beu), viii ex. (Lo), at Poitiers, Bibliothèque Municipale, MS. 17 (65), fols. 3–14, contains citations of the Gospels in Eusebian Canon Tables; ed. by P. Minard, 'Témoins inédits de la vieille version latine des Évangiles. Les canons à *initia* évangéliaires de Sainte-Croix de Poitiers et la Trinité de Vendôme', *RBén*, lvi (1945–6), 58–92; for specimen of script, see Lowe, vi, no. 821.

40. Codex Vennessenus, saec. x (Ay Beu), at Vendôme, Bibliothèque Municipale 2, contains citations of the Gospels in Eusebian Canon Tables; ed. by P. Minard, 'Témoins inédits de la vieille version latine des Évangiles. Les canons à *initia* des évangéliaires de Sainte-Croix de Poitiers et la Trinité de Vendôme', *RBén*, lvi (1945–6), 58–92.

41. Lectionarium Veronense, saec. viii (Ay), viii[1] (Beu Lo), at Verona, Biblioteca Capitolare vii (7), contains lessons from Matt. i–ix; for specimen of script, see Lowe, iv, no. 482.

42. Codex Juv. Cantabrigiensis, saec. ix (Ay Beu), at Cambridge, University Library Ff.4.32, contains marginal glosses from the Gospels in a manuscript of Juvencus; ed. by A. W. Haddan and W. Stubbs, *Councils and Ecclesiastical Documents relating to Great Britain and Ireland*, i (Oxford, 1869), 198; W. A. Lindsay, *Early Welsh Script* (Oxford, 1912), pp. 16–18.

43. Codex Dim. Dublinensis, Book of Dimma, saec. viii (Ay Beu Lo), at Dublin, Trinity College 59 (A.4.23), contains the four Gospels; R. I. Best, 'On the Subscriptions in the Book of Dimma', *Hermathena*, xx (1930), 84–100 and two plates; H. C. Hoskier, *On the Genesis of the Versions of the New Testament*, i (London, 1910), *passim*, and ii (1911), 95 ff.

THE ACTS OF THE APOSTLES

c (6). See *c* in list of Gospels manuscripts.

ct (56). See manuscript *t* below.

d (5). See *d* in list of Gospels manuscripts.

dem (59). Codex Demidovianus, saec. xii–xiii (R), xiii (Beu K W), (in the eighteenth century belonged to a certain Paul Demidov Gregorovitch, but its present location is unknown), contained the Vulgate Bible, with Old Latin readings in Acts, Catholic Epistles, Pauline Epistles; ed. by C. F. Matthaei, *Novum Testamentum*, 12 vols. (Riga, 1782–8), see esp. vol. ix, pp. xxx–xxxiii.

e (50). Codex Bodleianus Laudianus (E), Latin–Greek, saec. vi (Ay Beu Lo M S T V W), vi–vii (R), at Oxford, Bodleian Library, Laudianus Gr. 35 (1119), (formerly F.82), contains Acts (lacks xxvi. 29–xxviii. 26); ed. by Sabatier; C. von Tischendorf, *Monumenta sacra inedita, Nova collectio*, ix (Leipzig, 1870); J. Belsheim, *Acta Apostolorum ante Hieronymum latine translata ex codice latino-graeco Laudiano Oxoniensi* (Christiania, 1893); for specimen of script, see Lowe, ii, no. 251.

g, gig (51). Codex Gigas, saec. xiii (Ay Beu K M N R T V W), at Stockholm, Kungl. Biblioteket, contains the Vulgate Bible, but Acts and Revelation are Old Latin; ed. by J. Belsheim, *Die Apostelgeschichte und die Offenbarung Johannis in einer alten lateinischen Übersetzung aus dem 'Gigas librorum' auf der königlichen Bibliothek zu Stockholm* (Christiania, 1879); J. Wordsworth, H. J. White, *Novum Testamentum Latine secundum editionem S. Hieronymi*, ii (Oxford, 1905); iii (1954); H. J. Vogels, *Untersuchungen zur Geschichte der lateinischen Apokalypse-Übersetzung* (Düsseldorf, 1920), pp. 165–75.

*g*² (52). Fragmentum Mediolanense, saec. viii (Ay), viii² (Beu Lo), x–xi (R S T W), at Milan, Biblioteca Ambrosiana B. 168 sup., contains Acts vi. 8–vii. 2; vii. 51–viii. 4 as a pericope in a lectionary of the Ambrosian rite; ed. by A. M. Ceriani, *Monumenta sacra et profana e codicibus praesertim Bibliotecae Ambrosianae*, I. 2 (Milan, 1866), 127–8; for specimen of script, see Lowe, ii, no. 310.

h (B K M R S V) = *reg* (T) (55). Codex Floriacensis, saec. v (Beu Lo N R S), vi–vii (Ay B K M), vii (T V W), formerly at Fleury, now at Paris, Bibliothèque Nationale, fond. lat. 6400G, fols. 113–30, palimpsest, contains fragments of Acts, Catholic Epistles, and Revelation; ed. by Sabatier; S. Berger, *Le palimpseste de Fleury. Fragments du Nouveau Testament en latin* (Paris, 1889); E. S. Buchanan, *The Four Gospels from the Codex Corbeiensis . . . (Old Latin Biblical Texts*, v; Oxford, 1907), pp. 99–120; for specimen of script, see Lowe, v, no. 565.

l (67). Codex Pal. Legionensis or León palimpsest, saec. vii (Ay Beu Lo), at León, Archivo Catedralicio MS. 15, is a Vulgate manuscript containing an Old Latin text of Acts viii. 27–xi. 13, xiv. 21–xvii. 25; Jas. iv. 4–1 Pet. iii. 14; 1 John i. 5–3 John 10; cf. R. Beer, in *Boletín de la Real Academia de la Historia*, xi (Madrid, 1887), 345–9.

m. See *m* in list of Gospels manuscripts.

p (54). Codex Perpinianus or Perpinianensis, saec. xiii (Ay B Beu K N R S V W), at Paris, Bibliothèque Nationale, fond. lat. 321, contains the Vulgate New Testament; Old Latin in Acts i. 1–xiii. 6; xxviii. 16–31, and Catholic Epistles; ed. by S. Berger, 'Un ancient texte latin des Actes des Apôtres retrouvé dans un manuscrit provenant de Perpignan', *Notices et extraits des manuscrits de la Bibliothèque Nationale*, xxxv. 1 (1895 [1896]), 169–208; F. Blass, *Theologische Studien und Kritiken*, lxix (1896), 436–71; E. S. Buchanan, 'An Old Latin Text of the Catholic Epistles', *JTS* xii (1910–11), 497–534.

r (Ay) (62). Codex Rodensis or Bible de Rosas, saec. x (Beu), at Paris, Bibliothèque Nationale, fond. lat. 6, a four-volume Vulgate Bible containing Old Latin readings in Acts, both text and margin; ed. by J. Wordsworth, H. J. White, *Novum Testamentum Latine secundum editionem S. Hieronymi*, pars II. 1, Oxford, 1905; see T. Ayuso in *EB*, segunda ép., ii (1943), 23 ff., 33 ff.; iv (1945), 35 ff., 259 ff.; v (1946), 5 ff., 429 ff.; vi (1947), 187 ff., 347 ff.; vii (1948), 147 ff.

r (K M R) = *scel* (57). Codex Schlettstadtensis, saec. vii–viii (Ay Beu K M R), viii (Lo), at Selestat, Bibliothèque Municipale 1093, a lectionary containing Old Latin readings in lessons from Acts; ed. by G. Morin, *Études, textes, découvertes* (*Anecdota Maredsolana*, 2nd ser. i; Maredsous, 1913), pp. 440–56; for specimen of script, see Lowe, vi, no. 829.

reg (T) = *h* (B K M R S V).

s (53). Codex Bobiensis, saec. v (T), v–vi (Ay B K M), vi (Beu Lo N S V W), Naples, Biblioteca Nazionale, cod. Lat. 2 formerly at Vienna, Pal. (16), foll. 42*, 43–56, 71–5, palimpsest, contains fragments of Acts and Catholic Epistles; ed. by J. Belsheim, *Fragmenta Vindobonensia* (Christiania, 1886); H. J. White, *Portions of the Acts of the Apostles, of the Epistle of St. James, and of the First Epistle of St. Peter, from the Bobbio Palimpsest* (*s*) (*Old Latin Biblical Texts*, iv; Oxford, 1897), pp. 5–50; J. Bick, 'Wiener Palimpseste', *SbWien*, clix. 7 (Vienna, 1908), 50–89; for specimen of script, see Lowe, iii, no. 395.

scel = *r* (K M R).

t (56) Liber Comicus, Lectionarius Toletanus (V), or Liber Comicus Toletanus (B M), saec. xi (B Beu K M N R S V W), at Paris, Bibliothèque Nationale, nouv. acquis. Lat. 2171, contains Old Latin readings in lessons from Acts, Catholic and Pauline Epistles, Revelation; ed. by G. Morin, *Liber Comicus sive Lectionarius Missae, quo Toletana Ecclesia ante annos mille et ducentos utebatur* (*Anecdota Maredsolana*, i; Maredsous, 1893); J. Pérez de Urbel, A. González y Ruiz-Zorrilla, *Liber Commicus*, 2 vols. (Madrid, 1950–5).

w (58). Codex Wernigerodensis *or* Stolbergensis, saec. xv (B Beu K M N R S V), at Prague, Comenius Evangelical Theol. Fac., formerly at Wernigerode am Harz, contains the Vulgate New Testament with Old Latin readings in Acts and Catholic Epistles; cf. F. Blass, *TSK* lxix (1896), 436–71; H. J. Frede, *Vetus Latina*, xxiv/2, p. 265.

x₁. saec. vii–viii (T), viii¹ (Lo), at Oxford, Bodleianus 3418 (Selden, 30), contains Acts (lacking xiv. 26–xv. 32); described by Westcott in William Smith's *Dictionary of the Bible*, iv, American edn. (New York, 1870; repr. Grand Rapids, 1971), 3458b; ed. by Wordsworth/White (ms. O); for specimen of script, see Lowe, ii, no. 257.

60. Codex Boverianus, saec. xiii (Beu), at Sarriá (Barcelona), Colegio Máximo S.J., s.n. (fol. 112ᵛ–113ᵛ); contains Acts i. 15–26; ed. by J. M. Bover, 'Un fragmento de la Vetus Latina (Ac 1 : 15–26) en un Epistolario del Siglo XIII', *Estudios eclesiásticos*, vi (1927), 331–4.

61. Codex Armachanus, or Book of Armagh, saec. ix (Beu), *c.* 807 (Lo), at Dublin, Trinity College 52, contains the Vulgate New Testament, but many Old Latin readings in Acts and an Old Latin text of the Pauline Epistles; ed. by J. Wordsworth, H. J. White, *Novum Testamentum Latine* (Oxford, 1905); J. Gwynn, *Liber Ardmachanus. The Book of Armagh* (Dublin, 1913); for specimen of script, see Lowe, ii, no. 270.

63. Michigan MS. 146, saec. xii (Beu), at Ann Arbor, University of Michigan Library, contains the Book of Acts and other material; ed. by H. A. Sanders and J. Ogden, 'The Text of Acts in MS. 146 of the University of Michigan', *Proceedings of the American Philosophical Society*, lxxvii. 1 (Philadelphia, 1937), 1–97.

THE PAULINE EPISTLES

c (6). See *c* in list of Gospels manuscripts.

d (75). Codex Claromontanus (D), Graeco-Latin, saec. v (Lo), v–vi (Beu), vi (Ay B K M N S T V W), at Paris, Bibliothèque Nationale grec 107 (*olim* Reg. 2245), contains the Pauline Epistles (Rom. i. 1–7, 24–7 supplied by a later hand); ed. by Sabatier; C. von Tischendorf, *Codex Claromontanus* (Leipzig, 1852); for specimen of script, see Lowe, v, no. 521.

dem (59). See *dem* in list of Acts manuscripts.

e (76). Codex Sangermanensis (E), formerly Petropolitanus Caesareus Maralti xx, Graeco-Latin, saec. ix (Ay B Beu K M N T W), at Leningrad, Public Library, F.v.20, contains the Pauline Epistles (lacks Rom. viii. 21–33; xi. 15–25; 1 Tim. i. 1–vi. 15; Heb. xii. 8–xiii. 25; ed. by Sabatier; J. Belsheim, *Epistulae Paulinae ante Hieronymum Latine translatae ex codice Sangermanensi Gr.-Lat.* (Christiania, 1885).

f (78). Codex Augiensis (F), Graeco-Latin, saec. ix (Ay B Beu K M N T V W), at Cambridge, Trinity College, B.17.1, contains the Pauline Epistles (lacks Rom. i. 1–iii. 19); ed. by F. H. Scrivener, *An Exact Transcript of the Codex Augiensis* (Cambridge, 1859).

g (77). Codex Boernerianus (G), Graeco-Latin, saec. ix (Ay B Beu K N S T V W), at Dresden, Landesbibliothek MS. A. 145^{b}, contains the Pauline Epistles (lacks Rom. i. 1–5; ii. 16–25; 1 Cor. iii. 8–16; vi. 7–14; Col. ii. 1–8; Philem. 21–5; all of Hebrews); ed. by A. Reichardt, *Der Codex Boernerianus der Briefe des Ap. Paulus in Lichtdruck nachgebildet* (Leipzig, 1909).

gue (T) = *w* (B M).

l (67). See *l* in list of Acts manuscripts.

m (PS–AU spe). See *m* in list of Gospels manuscripts.

p (W) = *r*⁴ (Ay).

r, *r*¹, *r*², *r*³ (64). Frisingensia Fragmenta, saec. v–vi (V W), vi (N S T), vi and vii (Beu·Lo), vii (M), vii–viii (B K), at Munich, Bayerische Staatsbibliothek, Clm 6436 (Fris. 236), and Clm 6220, 6230, 6277, 6317, 28135; Munich, Universitätsbibliothek, 4°. 928; Gottweig, Stiftsbibliothek MS. 1 (9), fol. 23–4, contain portions of the Pauline and Catholic Epistles; ed. by D. De Bruyne, *Les Fragments de Freising* (*Collectanea biblica latina*, v; Rome, 1921); for specimens of script, see Lowe, ix, nos. 1286a and 1286b.

r^4 (Ay) = p (W) (80). Fragmenta Heidelbergensia, saec. vi (Ay Beu W), vii (Lo), at Heidelberg, Universitätsbibliothek 1334 (369/256), contain portions of Romans v and vi; ed. by R. Sillib, *ZNW* vii (1906), 82–6; for specimen of script, see Lowe, viii, no. 1223.

t (56). See t in list of Acts manuscripts.

v (81). Fragmentum Veronense, *c.* 800 (Beu), saec. vii–viii (N W), viii–ix (Lo), at Paris, Bibliothèque Nationale lat. 653, contains fragments of the Epistle to the Hebrews; ed. by A. Souter, 'A Fragment of an Unpublished Latin Text of the Epistle to the Hebrews', *Miscellanea Francesco Ehrle*, i (*Studi e testi*, xxxvii; Rome, 1924), 39–46; for specimen of script, see Lowe, v, no. 527.

w (B M) = *gue* (T) (79). Codex Guelferbytanus, Gothic and Latin, saec. vi (Ay B Beu M W), at Wolfenbüttel, Herzog-August-Bibliothek 4148, palimpsest, contains Rom. xi. 33–xii. 5; xii. 17–xiii. 1; xiv. 9–20; ed. by W. Streitberg, *Die gotische Bibel*; i, *Der gotische Text und seine griechische Vorlage*, 6th edn. (Heidelberg, 1971), pp. 239–49.

x_2 (T). Codex Bodleianus Laudianus, saec. viii–ix (B), ix (T), at Oxford, Bodleian Library, Laud. lat. 108, contains the Pauline Epistles (lacking Heb. xi. 34–xiii. 25); described by Westcott in Wiliam Smith's *Dictionary of the Bible*, iv, American edn. (New York, 1870; repr. Grand Rapids, 1971), 3458b.

z (65). Codex Harleianus, saec. vii (B), viii (Ay Beu), viii–ix (V), at London, British Museum, Harley 1772, contains the Pauline and Catholic Epistles and Revelation (to xiv. 16) in the Vulgate text; but Heb. x–xiii; 1 Pet. ii. 9–iv. 15; 1 John 1. 1–iii. 15 are Old Latin; ed. by E. S. Buchanan, *The Epistles and Apocalypse from the Codex Harleianus* (London, 1912); for specimen of script, see Lowe, ii, no. 197.

82. Fragmenta Monacensia, saec. ix (Beu), at Munich, Bayerische Staatsbibliothek, Clm 29055a, contain Heb. vii. 8–26; x. 23–39; ed. by Bernhard Bischoff, 'Neue Materialen zum Bestand und zur Geschichte der altlateinischen Bibelübersetzungen', *Miscellanea Giovanni Mercati*, i (*Studi e testi*, cxxi; Rome, 1946), 427–36.

84. Fragments of a list of Pauline pericopes, saec. viii (Beu Lo), at Rome, Biblioteca Apostolica Vaticana, cod. Regin. lat. 9, fols. 2–3, contains passages from the Pauline Epistles; ed. by A. Dold, *Die im Codex Vat. Reg. lat. 9 vorgeheftete Liste paulinischer Lesungen für die Messfeier* (*Texte und Arbeiten*, xxxv; Beuron, 1944).

85. Fragmentum Florentinum, saec. iv–v (Ay Beu Lo), at Florence, Biblioteca Mediceo-Laurenziana, P.S.I. 1306, Greek–Latin parchment leaf, contains Eph. vi. 5–6 (Greek Eph. vi. 11–12); ed. by G. Mercati, *Papiri della Società Italiana*, xiii (1949), 87–102; for specimen of script, see Lowe, *Supplement*, no. 1694.

86. Fragmentary manuscript, saec. x (Beu²⁴), ix ex. (Beu²⁵), at Monza, Biblioteca Capitolare, $\frac{i-2}{9}$, contains portions of Pauline Epistles; ed. by H. J. Frede, *Altlateinische Paulus-Handschriften* (*Vetus Latina. Aus der Geschichte der lateinischen Bibel*, iv; Freiburg, 1964), pp. 121–286.

87. Fragments of a lectionary, saec. vii–viii (Beu²⁴ Lo), viii² (Beu²⁵), at Sélestat, Bibliothèque Municipale MS. 1b, contains pericopes from Rom., 1 and 2 Cor., Gal., Eph., Phil., Col., 1 and 2 Thess.; for specimen of script, see Lowe, v, no. 831.

THE CATHOLIC EPISTLES

c (6). See *c* in list of Gospels manuscripts.

d (5). See *d* in list of Gospels manuscripts.

dem (59). See *dem* in list of Acts manuscripts.

ff (66). Codex Corbeiensis (*olim* Sangermanensis 625), saec. vi (K), ix (Beu (*Vetus Latina* 26/1, p. 16*) N), ix–x (S), x (Ay B M T V W), x–xi (Beu Verzeichnis)), at Leningrad, Public Library, Q.v.I.39, contains the Epistle of James; ed. by Sabatier; J. Belsheim, *Die Brief des Jakobus im alter lateinischer Übersetzung aus der Zeit vor Hieronymus . . .* (Christiania, 1883); J. Wordsworth *et al.*, *Studia biblica* [*et ecclesiastica*], i (Oxford, 1885), 113–50; W. Sanday, ibid. 233–63; J. B. Mayor, *The Epistle of St. James*, 2nd edn. (London, 1897), pp. 3–27; J. Belser, *Die Epistel des heil. Jakobus* (Freiburg, 1909), pp. 206–10; cf. A. Staerk, *Les Manuscrits latins du Vᵉ au XIIIᵉ siècle conservés à la Bibliothèque Imperiale de Saint Petersbourg*, i (St. Petersburg, 1910), 132–4.

h (55). See *h* in list of Acts manuscripts.

l (67). See *l* in list of Acts manuscripts.

m (PS–AU spe). See *m* in list of Gospels manuscripts.

p (54). See *p* in list of Acts manuscripts.

q (64). See *r* in list of Pauline manuscripts.

r (Ay K M N) = *q* (B M S T V).

s (53). See *s* in list of Acts manuscripts.

t (56). See *t* in list of Acts manuscripts.

z (65). See *z* in list of Pauline manuscripts.

THE BOOK OF REVELATION

c (6). See *c* in list of Gospels manuscripts.

dem (59). See *dem* in list of Acts manuscripts.

g (51). See *g* in list of Acts manuscripts.

h (55). See *h* in list of Acts manuscripts.

m (PS–AU spe). See *m* in list of Gospels manuscripts.

reg (T) = *h* (B K S).

t (56). See *t* in list of Acts manuscripts.

z (65). See *z* in list of Pauline manuscripts.

CONVERSION TABLES OF OLD LATIN MANUSCRIPTS

I. Traditional sigla to Beuron numbers

The abbreviations in the column marked 'Content' are as follows: e = Gospels; a = Acts; p = Pauline Epistles; c = Catholic Epistles; r = Revelation.

Traditional sigla	Content	Beuron
a	e	3
*a*², *n, o*	e	16
aur, z	e	15
b	e	4
β	e	26
c	eapcr	6
d	eac	5
d	p	75
δ	e	27
dem	apcr	59
e	e	2
e	a	50
e	p	76
f	e	10
f	p	78
*ff, ff*¹	e	9
ff	c	66
*ff*²	e	8
*g, g*¹	e	7
g, gig	ar	51
g	p	77
*g*²	e	29

Traditional sigla	Content	Beuron
g^2	a	52
gat	e	30
gue, w	p	79
h	e	12
h	acr	55
i	e	17
j, z	e	22
k	e	1
l	e	11
l	ac	67
m	eapcr	PS-AU spe
μ	e	35
n, o, a^2	e	16
o, n, a^2	e	16
p	e	20
p	ac	54
p, r^4	p	80
π, w	e	18
q	e	13
q	p	64
q, r	c	64
r, r^1	e	14
r, scel	a	57
r	a	62
r	p	64
r, q	c	64
r^2	e	28
r^2	p	64
r^3	p	64
r^4	p	80
ρ	e	24
s	e	21
s	ac	53
scel, r	a	57
t	apcr	56
t	e	19
v	e	25
v	p	81
w, π	e	18
w	a	58
w, gue	p	79
x_1	a	—
x_2	p	—
z, aur	e	15
z, j	e	22
z	pcr	65

II. Beuron numbers to traditional sigla

Beuron numbers	Content	Traditional sigla
1	e	k
2	e	e
3	e	a
4	e	b
5	eac	d
6	eapcr	c
7	e	g^1
8	e	ff^2
9	e	ff^1
10	e	f
11	e	l
12	e	h
13	e	g
14	e	r^1
15	e	aur, z
16	e	a^2, n, o
17	e	i
18	e	w, π
19	e	t
20	e	p
21	e	s
22	e	j, z
23	e	—
24	e	ρ
25	e	v
26	e	β
27	e	δ
28	e	r^2
29	e	g^2
30	e	gat
31	e	—
32	eapc	—
33	e	—
34	e	—
35	e	μ
36	e	—
37	e	—
38	e	—
39	e	—
40	e	—
41	e	—
42	e	—
43	e	—
50	a	ϵ
51	ar	g, gig

Beuron numbers	Content	Traditional sigla
52	a	g^2
53	ac	s
54	ac	p
55	acr	h
56	apcr	t
57	a	$r, scel$
58	a	w
59	apcr	dem
60	a	—
61	ap	—
62	a	r^2
63	a	—
64	pc	r^1, r^2, r^3, q
65	pcr	z
66	c	ff
67	ac	l
75	p	d
76	p	e
77	p	g
78	p	f
79	p	gue, w
80	p	p, r^4
81	p	v
82	p	—
83	p	—
84	p	—
85	p	—
86	p	—
87	p	—

Among the more noteworthy[1] Old Latin manuscripts several

[1] One of the *curiosa* in the study of Latin manuscripts concerns the so-called Huntington or Tarragona codex, a medieval Latin Missal formerly in the possession of the Cathedral at Tarragona and subsequently acquired by Mr. Archer M. Huntington for the Museum of the Hispanic Society of America, New York City. According to E. S. Buchanan the manuscript is a palimpsest, the under-writing of which presents the text of the Gospels and Acts in a form hitherto unknown, but which he regarded as more authentic than the traditional text. The outstanding characteristic of the new text is the frequent use of the word 'spirit'; God is called 'the Father of spirits', Jesus is 'the Saviour of spirits', men are designated 'the spirits of men'. There is no reference to hades or Gehenna, no day of judgement, no reference to the end of the age, and no mention of baptism.

Buchanan's edition of the text was never published, for the firm of G. P. Putnam's Sons, which had set up type for the volume, was advised that such eminent palaeographers as K. Lake, C. C. Edmunds, and E. A. Lowe could detect in the codex no trace of under-writing whatever! (A complete set of the proofs of the book is in the British Museum.) In several shorter publications Buchanan provided specimen passages of what he thought he saw as the under-writing of the manu-

deserve more extended comment than can be given in the check-list above. They are codex Vercellensis (*a*), codex Colbertinus (*c*), codex Palatinus (*e*), codex Brixianus (*f*), codex Gigas (*g*), the Fleury palimpsest (*h*), codex Bobiensis (*k*), the bilingual[1] codices Bezae (D, *d*), Laudianus (E, *e*), Augiensis (F, *f*), and Boernerianus (G, *g*), as well as two or three more recently edited manuscripts.

Codex Vercellensis (*a*), according to a tradition recorded in a document of the eighth century, was written by St. Eusebius, bishop of Vercelli, who died in the year 370 or 371. Inasmuch as its production is attributed to the hand of a saint, the manuscript has been highly venerated by the faithful, whose kisses over the centuries have damaged the writing on many pages, so that a con-siderable portion of text is no longer legible. The manuscript is written in gold and silver letters on purple vellum, as are also codices *b e f i j*. The Gospels are in the usual Western order, Matthew, John, Luke, Mark (so also *b d e ff*[2] *q r*). The last four leaves of the codex (after Mark xv. 15) have been cut out, and then follows a single leaf containing Mark xvi. 7 (from the word *galileam*) to 20 in a later hand and in the Vulgate text. According to calculations of space made by C. H. Turner, the four excised

---

script: 'The Codex Huntingtonianus Palimpsestus', *Bibliotheca Sacra*, lxxiv (1917), 114–47; *Gospel of St. Luke (Unjudaized Version) from the Huntington Palimpsest . . .* (London, 1918); *Evangelium sec. Lucam (sine Judaizantium emendationibus) e codice rescripto Tarragonensi . . .* (New York, 1919); *Euangelium sec. Iohannem . . .* (New York, 1919); *Actus discipulorum . . .* (New York, 1919); *An Unique Gospel Text (31 Selections) from a Latin Palimpsest in the Collection of the Hispanic Society of America* (London, 1919). A more or less sympathetic account of Buchanan's claims was written by P. A. Gordon Clark, 'The Huntington Palimpsest', *Expository Times*, xxxi (1919–20), 567–8. Six articles in two French newspapers, written by Camille Pitollet and Mgr. Pierre Batiffol for and against Buchanan, were reprinted, with an English translation, in *The Oldest Text of the Gospels . . .*, with an Introduction by E. S. Buchanan (New York, 1924). Cf. also H. A. Sanders, 'Buchanans Publika-tionen altlateinischer Texte. Eine Warnung', *Zeitschrift für die neutestamentliche Wissenschaft*, xxi (1922), 291–9, especially 297 ff., and comments by K. Lake, C. C. Edmunds, and E. A. Lowe in the *New York Times*, 30 Apr. 1923, p. 5; 4 May 1923, p. 10 (Lowe suggests that here and there in the manuscript one finds traces of an off-set of ink from the facing page).

[1] On the part played by early bilingual (and perhaps trilingual) manuscripts in the transmission of the text of the New Testament, reference may be made to data and theories set forth by H. C. Hoskier, *Concerning the Genesis of the Versions of the New Testament*, 2 vols. (London, 1910, 1911); H. A. Sanders, 'Hoskier's Genesis of the Versions', *AJP* xxxiii (1912), 30–42; Kirsopp Lake, *The Text of the New Testament*, 6th edn. (London, 1928), p. 76; and A. C. Clark, *The Acts of the Apostles* (Oxford, 1933), pp. lviii–lxiii.

leaves probably did not contain the long ending of Mark, 'unless both very drastic methods of compression were employed in the text itself, and also there was a complete absence of colophon or subscription. . . . [The manuscript] must have had either the shorter ending or none at all.'[1]

Codex Colbertinus (*c*), a twelfth-century copy of the New Testament,[2] preserves the Old Latin text of the Gospels, and the Vulgate in the rest of the New Testament. The manuscript was written in Languedoc, where the use of the Old Latin version, prepared a thousand years earlier, lingered on long after other parts of France had adopted Jerome's Vulgate. Matthew and John are much less purely Old Latin than Mark and Luke, which are strongly influenced by the African type of Old Latin text.[3] Here and there the manuscript offers noteworthy ancient readings, some of which cannot be found in the much older codices.

Codex Palatinus (*e*), a fifth-century copy of the Gospels, was found about 1730 in the Castle of the Bishop of Trent. Subsequently it was housed in the imperial library of Vienna (Bibliotheca Palatina MS 1185), but after World War I it was moved back to Trent. It is written with silver and gold ink on purple vellum. The text contains the Gospels, which stand in the Western order (Matthew, John, Luke, Mark), with lacunae. The manuscript presents an African type of text, though less pure than that of *k*.

Codex Brixianus (*f*), written in silver letters on purple vellum, and dating from the sixth century, contains the text of the four Gospels, nearly complete. In their edition of the Vulgate Wordsworth and White printed the text of this manuscript underneath that of Jerome for comparison's sake as probably containing the text most nearly resembling that on which Jerome based his recension. Subsequent research, however, has disclosed that *f* is closely related to the famous Gothic codex Argenteus (see

---

[1] 'Did Codex Vercellensis (*a*) contain the Last Twelve Verses of St. Mark?' *JTS* xxix (1927–8), 16–18.

[2] According to H. J. Vogels, it was written in the second half of the twelfth century (*Evangelium Colbertinum*, ii (*Bonner biblische Beiträge*, iv; Bonn, 1953) 6). For a facsimile of a typical folio, see Vogels, *Codicum Novi Testamenti specimina* (Bonn, 1929), plate xxxiii.

[3] Hans von Soden, *Das lateinische Neue Testament in Africa zur zeit Cyprians* (*Texte und Untersuchungen*, xxxiii; Leipzig, 1909), and J. Mizzi, 'A Comparative Study of Some Portions of Cod. Palatinus and Cod. Bobiensis', *RBén* lxxv (1965), 7–39.

pp. 385–6 below). F. C. Burkitt held that the text of Brixianus was corrected from the Vulgate, and afterwards altered in conformity with the Gothic.[1] The Germanic philologist F. Kauffmann independently corroborated Burkitt's view, differing only in believing that the text of Brixianus was derived from an earlier Latin manuscript which had been altered in conformity with the Gothic, and that it was *afterwards* assimilated to the Vulgate.[2]

Codex Gigas (*g* or *gig*), formerly in Prague but in 1648 taken to Stockholm by the Swedish army as war booty, is deservedly called the *gigas* ('giant') codex, for it is one of the very largest manuscripts in the world, requiring (it is said) two men to lift it. It contains the entire Latin Bible, Isidore of Seville's *Etymologiae* (a general encyclopedia in twenty books), a Latin translation of Josephus' *Antiquities of the Jews*, Cosmas of Prague's *Chronicle of Bohemia*, as well as other works. Only in Acts and the Book of Revelation does Gigas present an Old Latin text. Since its textual affinities are with the text of Acts as used by Lucifer of Cagliari in Sardinia—who cites more than an eighth of Acts verbatim in his treatises written between A.D. 355 and 362—Gigas attests a Latin version of Acts that was made before the middle of the fourth century. According to Ropes, 'Lucifer shows no trace of the use of any Greek text with different readings from those of gig. Both he and gig are very rarely affected by the Vulgate.'[3] In the Book of Revelation its text is not, on the whole, as ancient as that in Acts.

The Fleury palimpsest (*h*), of the fifth century, formerly belonging to the Abbey of Fleury on the Loire and now at the Bibliothèque Nationale in Paris, preserves fragments of the Apocalypse, Acts, 1 and 2 Peter, and 1 John, probably in this order. The script contains many errors, and the rendering into Latin is often

---

[1] *JTS* i (1899–1900), 129–34.

[2] *ZDP* xxxii (1899), 305–35. According to Kauffmann codex Argenteus and codex Brixianus are in the same script, and were written at the same place in northern Italy in the sixth century. For a discussion of the import of the Preface in codex Brixianus and the problem of Gothic–Latin bilingual manuscripts of the Bible, see Walter Henss, *Leitbilder der Bibelübersetzung im 5. Jahrhundert. Die Praefatio im Evangelienkodex Brixianus (f) und das Problem der gotisch-lateinischen Bibelbilinguen* (*AbhHeid*, 1973, 1. Abh).

[3] J. H. Ropes, *The Text of Acts*, being vol. iii of *The Beginnings of Christianity*, ed. by F. J. Foakes Jackson and Kirsopp Lake (London, 1926), p. cx.

very free, although the Greek text followed can usually be discerned. Of about 203 verses of Acts that are extant in *h*, there are only ten differences from the text of Acts quoted in the *Testimonia* of Cyprian.[1]

Codex Bobiensis (*k*), of which only ninety-six pages survive (fairly large portions of Mark; smaller parts of Matthew), is said, according to creditable tradition, to have belonged to St. Columban, who died in 615 at the monastery he founded at Bobbio in northern Italy. It is the most important, as regards text, of all the Old Latin copies, being undoubtedly the oldest existing representative of the African type. Dated by Burkitt and Souter to the fourth century, it was thought by Hoogterp to be 'a direct copy of an archetype of the end of the third century',[2] and Lowe considered it, on palaeographical grounds, to have been copied from a second-century papyrus.[3] The scribe, though committing many blunders in writing, was not uneducated, for he writes with a firm and practised hand. Burkitt supposed that he was a professional copier of books, perhaps a pagan or only a recent convert. At any rate, 'he seems to have been quite unfamiliar with Christian phraseology: a scribe who writes *ueni ad regnum tuum* in the Lord's Prayer (Matt. vi. 10) could not have known his Paternoster very well'.[4] He stumbles over the names of Peter and Mary, writing *cum puero* for *cum Petro* (Mark xvi. 8 *ad fin.*) and *Maxriam*[5] for *Mariam* (Matt. i. 20). On the other hand he twice brings in pagan deities: 'he calls Elias' appears as *Helion*[6] *vocat* (Mark xv. 34), and 'How much does a man differ from a sheep' is made into *Quanto ergo differt homo Ioui* (Matt. xii.

---

[1] Hans von Soden, *Das lateinische Neue Testament in Afrika zur Zeit Cyprians* (*TU* xxxiii; Berlin, 1909), pp. 221–42; 323–63; 550–67.

[2] P. W. Hoogterp, *Étude sur le latin du Codex Bobiensis (k) des Évangiles* (Wageningen, 1930), p. 17. Whether the manuscript was written in Ireland, as Mme Bakker thought (cf. A. H. A. Bakker, *A Study of Codex Evang. Bobbiensis (k)* (Amsterdam, 1933), pp. 9 ff. and 79 ff.), is less certain; see *per contra*, F. C. Burkitt, *JTS* xxxv (1934), 330.

[3] Reported by D. Plooij in *BBC* xi (1936), 11.

[4] *JTS* v (1903–4), 106. Cf. also Burkitt in the *Cambridge University Reporter*, xxxi (5 Mar. 1901), 603. According to J. Mizzi, 'The text of *k* seems to be free from European and Italian influence [and it] betrays a tendency toward literal translation' ('A Comparative Study of Some Portions of Cod. Palatinus and Cod. Bobiensis', *RBén*, lxxv (1965), 39).

[5] According to the editors (*Old Latin Biblical Texts*, ii), the letter 'x' in *maxriam* was expunged by the first hand (with a dot placed over the letter), and was deleted by the second hand (with a line drawn through the letter).

[6] *Helion* (i.e. Phoebus) instead of *Heliam* (or *Helian*).

12)! Thus the name of Jupiter was still on the tip of the tongue when *k* was being written.

The manuscript contains a type of New Testament text akin to that used by Cyprian. The Greek text underlying it has a large element in common with D, as well as one almost equally large in common with B ℵ. It stands alone among witnesses in presenting only the shorter ending of Mark, an ending which is read also by L Ψ 274 *al.* in addition to the long ending. In Mark xv. 34 *k* reads (as ascertained by Burkitt[1]) *maledixisti*, agreeing with ὠνείδισάς με (i.e. 'My God, my God, why *hast thou taunted me?*') which is attested by D^gr and the pagan philosopher cited by Macarius Magnes (ii. 12, ed. C. Blondel, p. 21), as well as by the Latin manuscripts *c* and *i*.

MS. 67 in the Vetus Latina notation is one of the more recently edited witnesses to the Old Latin version. It is a tenth-century palimpsest manuscript in the Cathedral library at León, Spain, containing Rufinus' translation of Eusebius' Church history. The under-writing is a seventh-century half-uncial of portions of the Scriptures, mostly in Jerome's Vulgate but with an Old Latin text of the books of the Maccabees, the Catholic Epistles (Jas. iv. 4–1 Pet. iii. 14; 1 John i. 5–3 John 10), and the Acts of the Apostles (vii. 27–xi. 13 and xiv. 21–xvii. 25). Bonifatius Fischer has provided a transcript of the text of Acts as well as an analysis of its textual affinities, which are definitely of the Western text-type and stand closest to the Spanish Liber Comicus.[2]

MS. 86 in the Vetus Latina notation refers to a manuscript in Biblioteca Capitolare at Monza ($\frac{i-2}{9}$), comprising fifty-five pages or fragments, which are all that survive of the second volume of a two-volume Bible written in Monza itself, or in Milan or its neighbourhood, about the beginning of the tenth century. Although Berger had referred to the manuscript in his *Histoire de la Vulgate*,[3] it appears to have been almost completely neglected until recently when Frede provided a transcription and analysis of its affinities.[4] In addition to several portions of the Old Testa-

[1] *JTS* i (1899–1900), 278 f.

[2] 'Ein neuer Zeuge zum westlichen Text der Apostelgeschichte', *Biblical and Patristic Studies in Memory of Robert Pierce Casey*, ed. by J. Neville Birdsall and Robert W. Thompson (Freiburg, 1963), pp. 33–63.

[3] pp. 139–40.

[4] Hermann Josef Frede, *Altlateinische Paulus-Handschriften* (*Vetus Latina; Aus der Geschichte der lateinischen Bibel*, iv; Freiburg, 1964), pp. 121–286.

ment in a form of text that agrees substantially with the Vulgate, the extant portions of the Pauline Epistles (Rom. i. 1–x. 2; xv. 11–xvi. 24; 1 Cor. i. 1–5; Eph. iv. 1–end; Col.; 1–2 Thess.; 1 Tim.; 2 Tim. i. 1–iii. 11) exhibit a pure Old Latin type of text. According to Frede it is a typical fourth-century Milanese text, belonging to his **I**-type, and standing very close to Ambrose. One of the peculiarities of this witness in Romans is the placing of the doxology at the end of chap. xiv and not at the very end of the epistle, a reading which, though well attested in Greek authorities, is extremely rare in Latin.

MS. 89 in the Vetus Latina notation is a newly discovered copy of the Pauline Epistles, with a commentary, dating from about the year A.D. 800 and identified as Codex latinus medii aevi 1 in the Hungarian National Museum at Budapest. According to its editor, H. J. Frede,[1] the text of the manuscript agrees in 86 per cent of its readings with the text of codex Claromontanus, our oldest witness to the Old Latin text of the Pauline Epistles.

Several comments should also be added concerning the Old Latin version in bilingual manuscripts. Scholars have sharply disagreed as to the independent value of the Old Latin version in such witnesses as codex Bezae (D, *d*), codex Laudianus (E, *e*), codex Claromontanus (D², *d*), and codex Boernerianus (G², *g*). For example, Hort declared in no uncertain terms that, with respect to these four bilingual manuscripts,

a genuine (independent) Old Latin text has been adopted as the basis, but altered throughout into verbal conformity with the Greek text by the side of which it was intended to stand. Here and there the assimilation has accidentally been complete, and the scattered discrepant readings thus left are the only direct Old Latin evidence for the Greek text of the New Testament which the bilingual MSS supply. A large proportion of the Latin texts of these MSS is indeed, beyond all reasonable doubt, unaltered Old Latin: but where they exactly correspond to the Greek, as they do habitually, it is impossible to tell how much of the accordance is original, and how much artificial; so that for the criticism of the Greek text the Latin reading has here no independent authority.[2]

---

[1] *Ein neuer Paulustext und Kommentar*; Band i, *Untersuchungen*; Band ii, *Die Texte* (*Vetus Latina; Aus der Geschichte der lateinischen Bibel*, vii, viii; Freiburg, 1973, 1974).

[2] B. F. Westcott and F. J. A. Hort, *The New Testament in the Original Greek*; [ii] *Introduction* [*and*] *Appendix*, 2nd edn. (London, 1896), pp. 82 f.

Quite other was the opinion of J. Rendel Harris, who revived the view of earlier critics (such as Mill, Wettstein, and Middleton), namely that 'the whole of the Greek text of codex Bezae from the beginning of Matthew to the end of Acts is a re-adjustment of an earlier text to the Latin version'.[1] As a consequence of what was taken to be Latinization of the Greek text of codex Bezae, Harris was unwilling to regard D as a distinct authority apart from *d*; instead one should 'regard D and *d* as representing a single bilingual tradition'.[2]

More recent scholars (with the exception of H. J. Vogels, who adopted Harris's views)[3] are persuaded, on what appears to be altogether solid grounds, that the Latin side of codex Bezae has been slavishly accommodated to the Greek text and is, consequently, of no independent authority.[4] It is only where the testimony of the Greek text of Bezae is lacking, either through erasure or mutilation, that *d* becomes a significant authority.[5]

With regard to other Greek and Latin bilinguals, the interlinear Latin version of codex Sangallensis (*Δ*, δ) appears to have been 'somewhat modified from the Greek, so that it is of little value'.[6] A notable feature of the Latin translation in this manuscript, as well as in codex Boernerianus (G, *g*), is the presence of alternative renderings for many Greek words; e.g. in *Δ* at Matt. i. 20 *uxorem vel conjugem* stands above γυναῖκα, and in G at Col. iii. 8 *furorem vel indignationem* is the rendering of θυμόν.

According to the most recent analysis of the text of the bilingual

---

[1] *Codex Bezae: a Study of the so-called Western Text of the New Testament* (*Texts and Studies*, ii. 1; Cambridge, 1891), p. 41. It goes without saying, of course, that the Latin text of the supplemental pages in codex Bezae has a different type of text; see J. Mizzi, 'The Vulgate of the Supplemental Pages of Codex Bezae Cantabrigiensis', *Sacris erudiri*, xiv (1963), 149–63.

[2] Ibid., p. 114.

[3] 'Codex Bezae als Bilingue,' *BBC* ii (1926), 8–12.

[4] The proof rests upon instances where readings of *d* not attested elsewhere in Latin correspond to readings of D that are shown by other evidence to be genuine Greek variants. On the ambiguity of certain other kinds of proof, see A. S. Wilkins, 'The Western Text of the Greek New Testament', *Exp*, 4th ser., x (1896), 389–92.

[5] So, e.g., J. H. Ropes, *The Text of Acts* (London, 1926), p. cxi; A. C. Clark, *The Acts of the Apostles* (Oxford, 1933), pp. 219–20; and M.-J. Lagrange, *Critique textuelle* (Paris, 1935), pp. 430 f.

[6] F. G. Kenyon, *The Text of the Greek Bible* (London, 1937), p. 102. On the other hand, J. Rendel Harris attempted to show that the Greek text of *Δ* was accommodated to the Latin text, which he regarded as a representative of the Old Latin version (*The Codex Sangallensis* (*Δ*); *a Study in the Text of the Old Latin Gospels* (London, 1891).

manuscripts that contain the Epistles of Paul,[1] the author concludes that they represent two branches of a common tradition: codex Sangermanensis (E, *e*) is a copy of codex Claromontanus (D, *d*), while codex Boernerianus (G, *g*) and codex Augiensis (F, *f*) are independent copies of a lost ancestor. Both branches derive ultimately from the archetype, which is to be dated about A.D. 350.[2] Both the Greek and the Latin texts, though independent of each other, belong broadly to the Western type of text, and the subsequent variations to which both were subjected in the bilingual tradition have exercised very little influence on the history of the text in monolingual witnesses.[3]

3. EDITIONS OF THE OLD LATIN VERSIONS

Although as long ago as 1690 Richard Simon[4] drew attention to the existence of Latin versions that pre-date Jerome's Vulgate, it was not until near the middle of the eighteenth century that the first efforts were made to gather the evidence of such texts into usable collections. The credit of assembling the relics of these pre-Jeromic versions of the Old and New Testament, so far as they were accessible at that time, belongs to the Maurist Pierre Sabatier, whose posthumously published work, *Bibliorum sacrorum Latinae versiones antiquae seu Vetus Italica*, 3 vols. (Rheims, 1743; also (with new title pages) Paris, 1751; repr. Munich, 1976), remains indispensable, for it includes the evidence of manuscripts that later were lost. On each page there is presented the text of the oldest continuous manuscripts of the Old Latin available to the editor, along with the evidence of fragments and quotations of Church Fathers.

Likewise in the mid-eighteenth century Giuseppe Bianchini (Josephus Blanchinus), a member of the Congregation of the Oratory, published his *Evangeliarium quadruplex Latinae versionis antiquae seu veteris Italicae*, 2 vols. (Rome, 1749). Each page gives in larger type the text of manuscripts *a* and *b*, and in smaller type

---

[1] Hermann Josef Frede, *Altlateinische Paulus-Handschriften* (Freiburg, 1964).

[2] Ibid., pp. 94–7.

[3] For a somewhat different assessment of the relationship among the several types of text, see Franz Hermann Tinnefeld, *Untersuchungen zur altlateinischen Überlieferung des 1. Timotheusbriefes: Der lateinische Paulustext in der Handschriften D E F G und in der Kommentaren des Ambrosiaster und des Pelagius* (*Klassisch-philologische Studien*, xxvi; Wiesbaden, 1963).

[4] *Histoire critique des versions du Nouveau Testament* (Rotterdam, 1690), pp. 23–9.

the text of *ff*[2] and of *f*, with supplementation from other Latin, Greek, and Eastern witnesses. Although limited to the Gospels, Bianchini's edition supplements Sabatier and provides a convenient tool for comparison of several important Old Latin witnesses. It was reprinted in Migne, *Patrologia Latina*, vol. xii.

By the beginning of the twentieth century more than one scholar felt acutely the need for a 'new Sabatier' that would incorporate evidence from the many additional Old Latin witnesses that had come to light. At the suggestion of Eduard Wölfflin, the principal founder of the *Thesaurus linguae Latinae*, one of his assistants, a parish priest named Joseph Denk (1849–1927), drew up plans and began to collect patristic quotations of the Old Latin Scriptures.[1] Before his death the tens of thousands of slips bearing Scripture citations which he had assembled were given over to the monastery at Beuron under the care of P. Alban Dold (1882–1960). One of the contributions that Dold made was the elaboration of a special process of reading palimpsests by means of photography with ultra-violet light. Subsequently, under the energetic leadership of P. Bonifatius Fischer, there was established at Beuron the Vetus Latina Institute.[2] In 1949 began the publication of *Vetus Latina; Die Reste der altlateinischen Bibel nach Petrus Sabatier neu gesammelt und herausgegeben von der Erzabtei Beuron*. Thus far the following volumes have been published:

Vol. i, *Verzeichnis der Sigel* (Freiburg, 1949); a second edition was issued as i/1 under the title *Verzeichnis der Sigel für Kirchenschriften* (1963). Five *Ergänzungslieferungen* were also issued (1964–70).

Vol. ii, *Genesis*, ed. by Bonifatius Fischer (1951–4).

Vol. xxiv/1, *Epistula ad Ephesios*, ed. by Hermann Josef Frede (1962–4).

Vol. xxiv/2, *Epistulae ad Philippenses et ad Colossenses*, ed. by Hermann Josef Frede (1966–71).

Vol. xxv, *Epistulae ad Thessalonicenses, Timotheum, Titum, Philemonem, Hebraeos*, ed. by Hermann Josef Frede (1975–).

---

[1] Heinz Haffter, 'Der Italaforscher Joseph Denk und das Thesaurus linguae Latinae', *ZNW* lviii (1967), 139–44.

[2] On 1 Jan. 1973, with the departure of Fischer for the Abbey of Mariendonk, the formal directorship of the Institute was taken over by Ursmar Engelmann, abbot of Beuron, while Dr. Walter Thiele has been taking charge *de facto* of the work at the Institute.

Vol. xxvi/1, *Epistulae Catholicae*, ed. by Walter Thiele (1956–69).

The volumes are monuments of meticulous and accurate scholarship. In the New Testament volumes the page is arranged in four registers, namely (1) the text-types identified by the editor and printed underneath the Nestle–Aland Greek text; (2) a verse by verse statement of which of the manuscripts are deficient, together with orthographic variants; (3) the apparatus proper; (4) the extant patristic quotations, set out in full. The amount of information presented is enormous. The seven verses of Phil. ii. 5–11, for example, require fifty-five pages for their presentation, a full forty-five of them being devoted to the apparatus of patristic citations. One single verse (vs. 7) requires twenty pages, with sixteen given to citations (those from Augustine alone run to almost three); close to 1,200 citations have to be reckoned with for certain single verses. Among features of the edition that have been criticized[1] is the multiplication of text-types identified in the first register, resulting in such a complicated presentation as to be a hindrance rather than a help. Another drawback is the adoption of a numerical system for the citation of all manuscripts, which introduces unfamiliar nomenclature into a traditional usage with no marked advantage.

A complete edition of the Old Latin manuscripts of the Gospels, begun by Adolf Jülicher, was published after his death by Walter Matzkow under the direction of the commission on Church Fathers of the Berlin Academy of Sciences (Volumes iii and iv and the second editions of the other two volumes have been under the supervision of Kurt Aland): *Itala: Das Neue Testament in altlateinischer Überlieferung nach den Hss herausgegeben*; i, *Matthäus-Evangelium* (Berlin, 1938; 2nd edn., 1972); ii, *Marcus-Evangelium* (1940; 2nd edn., 1970); iii, *Lucas-Evangelium* (1954; 2nd edn., 1976); iv, *Johannes-Evangelium* (1963).

Jülicher attempted to reconstruct the *versio Itala* and *Afra*, the latter represented basically by *k* and *e*. The later editors lamented that they were unable to determine at all times Jülicher's principles of recension, especially of the *Itala*, and that his subjective judgement seems to have been decisive in

---

[1] Cf. H. F. D. Sparks in *JTS*, n.s. viii (1957), 301–7; G. G. Willis, ibid., n.s. xvii (1966), 449–56; B. M. Metzger, ibid., n.s. xxii (1971), 209–11.

some cases.[1] Beginning with the Lucan volume the manuscripts themselves (or photographs of manuscripts) were examined; Jülicher had often relied on printed editions.

Another monumental project related to the Old Latin Bible, planned by the late Teófilo Ayuso Marazuela,[2] is *La Vetus Latina Hispana: origen, dependencia, derivaciones, valor e influjo universal; reconstrucción, sistematización y análisis de sus diversos elementos; coordinación y edición critica de su texto. Estudio comparativo con los demás elementos de la 'Vetus Latina', los padres y escritores eclesiásticos, los textos griegos y la Vulgata.* Of the eight projected volumes there have appeared thus far vol. i, *Prolegómenos, introducción general, estudio y análisis de las fuentes* (Madrid, 1953), and several volumes of the Old Testament.

The volume of prolegomena lists not only the Old Latin manuscripts of both Old and New Testaments but also the writings of nearly 1,000 ecclesiastical authors of the first seven centuries, as well as a bibliography of more than 5,000 titles of monographs and studies related to the Latin versions.

Editions of the more important individual manuscripts of the Old Latin Bible, as well as studies in Old Latin lectionaries, are published in several series: *Old Latin Biblical Texts*, 7 vols. (Oxford, 1883–1923); *Sacred Latin Texts*, 4 vols. (London, 1912–19); *Collectanea biblica Latina*, 13 vols. so far (Rome, 1912 onwards); and *Vetus Latina. Aus der Geschichte der lateinischen Bibel*, 8 vols. so far (Freiburg, 1957 onwards).

4. LINGUISTIC AND TEXTUAL CHARACTERISTICS OF THE OLD LATIN VERSIONS

Augustine's lament concerning the great diversity among Latin translators of the Scriptures and the indifferent skill they possessed for the task,[3] is amply corroborated by the extant evidence. In Luke xxiv. 4–5, for example, the Old Latin manuscripts present no fewer than twenty-seven variant readings!

---

[1] Cf. Karl Th. Schäfer, *Die altlateinische Bibel* (*Bonner akademische Reden*, xvii; Bonn, 1957), pp. 18 f.

[2] For a descriptive account of the varied contributions of Ayuso (who had been Canónigo Lectoral at Zaragoza) to the textual criticism of the New Testament, see the present writer's *Chapters in the History of New Testament Textual Criticism* (Leiden and Grand Rapids, 1963), pp. 121–41.

[3] Besides the quotation cited above (see p. 290), Augustine also refers (*Retract.* i. 21. 3) to the 'endless variety and multitude of Latin translators'.

Furthermore, the style of the translation in pre-Jerome versions is totally lacking in polish, often painfully literal, and occasionally even of dubious Latinity.

It is not difficult to understand how such characteristics arose from interlinear renderings of the Greek text which sought to preserve the letter of the sacred text. Such concern led to many important consequences, the first being a strong exotic quality in both vocabulary and syntax. The traditional literary convention of the times frowned upon promiscuous borrowings from foreign languages. There is no hesitation, however, in introducing Greek terms (and even a few Hebrew ones, such as *pascha, amen, alleluia*) into the language of the first Latin Christians. Most of them were to become permanently established, such as *apostolus, baptisma, blasphemia, diabolus, ecclesia, episcopus, eremus, laicus*. Others persisted alongside native Latin words; for example, *diaconus* and *minister, ethnici* and *gentiles*. Complete figures are impossible to give because of the lack of information, but we may suppose that more than half of the Greek words imported into Latin Christian usage date from this first period of translation, that is, from the second century.

Parallel with the adoption of Greek words there went the creation of many neologisms in Latin. These were made with no concern for the purity of the language, especially in the case of nouns in *-tio, -tor*, and verbs in *-ficare*. Mlle Christine Mohrmann[1] has observed that Greek terms were kept on the whole for the concrete aspects—institutions (e.g. *eucharistia, baptismus*) and the hierarchy (e.g. *episcopus, presbyter, diaconus*)—while Latin neologisms were created, or old words used in a new sense, to express abstract or spiritual ideas like redemption and salvation. Examples include *sanctificatio*, a new word translating ἁγιασμός, and *confessio*, an older word taking on a new sense to correspond to the ἐξομολόγησις of the Septuagint, and no longer meaning simply 'declaration' or 'avowal', but 'recognition of the greatness of God; praise' and so 'affirmation of belief'.

In the case of syntax, the slavish word-for-word rendering of the early translations introduced a certain number of Graecisms, or at least some constructions unknown in the literary language.

[1] 'Traits caractéristiques du latin des chrétiens', *Miscellanea Giovanni Mercati*, i (*Studi e testi*, cxxi; Vatican City, 1946), p. 437. For other examples, see Walter Matzkow, *De vocabulis quibusdam Italae et Vulgatae christianis* (Berlin, 1933).

Particularly to be noted are noun-clauses introduced by *quod, quia, quoniam,* instead of the accusative and infinitive construction, corresponding to the Greek ὅτι clauses; *si* used in indirect questions for *num,* 'whether' (e.g. *videre si, interrogare si,* 'to see if, to ask if'); the infinitive of purpose, like *venimus adorare,* 'we have come to worship' (Matt. ii. 2); the codex Vercellensis even preserves for us an example (John vi. 52) in which this infinitive is preceded by *ad* (*dare ad manducare,* 'to give to eat'), which clearly betrays the popular character of the rendering.

Similarly one finds a certain fondness for lengthened words, especially those having sonorous endings. Thus *odoramentum* (Rev. v. 8; xviii. 13) is used instead of *odor,* and *deliramentum* (Luke xxiv. 11) for *delirium.* Beloved also are the endings *-arium* (as in *cellarium* and *pulmentarium*) and *-aneum* (*calcaneum* for *calx*).

Another feature of these early translations is the colloquial and sometimes vivid, down-to-earth character of the Latinity. We find such an example in the Western reading of two manuscripts at Matt. vi. 8 where, instead of the familiar words, 'Your Father knows what you need before you ask him' (πρὸ τοῦ ὑμᾶς αἰτῆσαι αὐτόν), codex Bezae (Greek text; Latin *hiat*) and *h* read πρὸ τοῦ ἀνοῖξαι τὸ στόμα, *antequam os aperiatis,* 'before ever you open your mouth'. Other instances of greater vivacity in the Old Latin are found in the parable of the Barren Fig Tree. In Luke xiii. 7, according to the commonly received text, the owner commands the vinedresser, 'Cut it down; why should it use up the ground?' In codex Bezae, however, both the Greek and Latin prefix the order with, 'Bring the axe', φέρε τὴν ἀξίνην, *adfers securem.* The answer of the vinedresser (vs. 8), suggesting a delay 'till I shall dig about it and dung it', gains immeasurably in colloquial vividness in codex Bezae and several Old Latin witnesses: 'I will throw on a basket of dung', βάλω κόφινον κοπρίων, *mittam qualum* (= *squalum*) *stercoris* (*d*), or *cophinum stercoris* (Old Latin *a b c f ff*² *i l q*).

Old Latin texts contain an abundance of superlatives as well as show a preference for participial forms—neither of which features was typical of classical Latin.[1] There is thus no denying

---

[1] Cf. W. Süss, *Studien zur lateinischen Bibel* (Tartu, 1932), pp. 86 ff.; J. Schrijnen, *Characteristik des altchristlichen Lateins* (Nijmegen, 1932); and 'Christian Latin', in L. R. Palmer, *The Latin Language* (London, 1954), pp. 183–205; as well as the literature cited in p. 288 n. 1 above. For a comprehensive bibliography on the Latinity of the Old Latin Bible, see Teófilo Ayuso Marazuela, *La Vetus Latina Hispana*; vol. i, *Prolegómenos* (Madrid, 1953), pp. 190–5.

an early fourth-century verdict that the style of such versions was 'commonplace and despicable . . . the work of ignorant and un-cultured men',[1] nor is one surprised that Augustine in his youth was repelled by their inelegance.

The textual affinities of the Old Latin versions are unmistakably with the Western type of text. Not infrequently noteworthy Old Latin readings agree with the Greek text of codex Bezae and the Old Syriac. On the whole the African form of the Old Latin presents the larger divergences from the generally received text, and the European the smaller. The diversity among the Old Latin witnesses is probably to be accounted for on the assumption that scribes, instead of transmitting the manuscripts mechani-cally, allowed themselves considerable freedom in incorporating their own and others' traditions. In other words, the Old Latin was a living creation, constantly growing.[2]

Noteworthy among the additions to the Old Latin text of the Gospels are the so-called Great Interpolations, such as Matt. xvi. 2, 3 (the signs of the sky), Matt. xx. 28 *fin.* ('Seek from little to increase'), Luke xxii. 43, 44 (the bloody sweat), John v. 3, 4 (the descent of the angel); and the story of the woman taken in adul-tery). 'Now the stronghold of these interpretations', as Burkitt commented long ago, 'is the Old Latin.' The comment continues:

As we trace the history of the text of the N.T. in other languages we find the earliest form is free from these interpretations. In Greek they are absent from B and its allies; in Syriac they are absent from the Sinai Palimpsest, a MS with a very different text in other respects from B. But they seem to form an integral part of the earliest Latin version. They are especially characteristic of the African text: a fact all the more remarkable, as the best African documents often side with א B in rejecting the harmonistic and other ordinary additions often found in most other authorities.[3]

Other additions of varying lengths to the Gospel text are present here and there in one or more Old Latin manuscripts, often with slight variations among the witnesses. Noteworthy examples include the statement that when Jesus 'was baptized, a

---

[1] Arnobius, *Adv. Gentes*, i. 58.

[2] So, e.g., Hans von Soden, 'Der lateinische Paulustext bei Marcion und Ter-tullian', *Festgabe für Adolf Jülicher* (Tübingen, 1927), p. 273 n. 1, and Hans H. Glunz, *History of the Vulgate in England* (Cambridge, 1933), pp. 14 ff.

[3] F. C. Burkitt, *The Old Latin and the Itala* (*Texts and Studies*, iv. 3; Cambridge, 1896), p. 16.

tremendous light flashed forth from the water, so that all who were present feared' (*et cum baptizaretur lumen ingens circumfulsit de aqua, ita ut timerent omnes qui advenerant*, Matt. iii. 15 *a* and, with minor variations, *g*¹).¹ The crucifixion narrative in the Gospels has been enriched by such additions as (1) the new accusation brought against Jesus by the chief priests and scribes, 'he alienates both our sons and our wives from us, for he does not baptize as we do' (*et filios nostros et uxores avertit a nobis, non enim baptizatur sicut nos*, Luke xxiii. 5 *c* and, with minor differences, *e*); (2) the names of the two robbers who were crucified with Jesus, *Zoatham* and *Camma* (Matt. xxvii. 38 *c*; in Mark xv. 27 *Zoathan* and *Chammatha*), or *Joathas* and *Maggatras* (Luke xxiii. 32 *l*; for the latter, *r* gives *Capnatas*); (3) the expanded description of lamentation of the multitudes that witnessed the crucifixion, who said, 'Woe to us, because of the things that have happened today because of our sins; for the desolation of Jerusalem has come nigh!' (*Vae nobis, quae facta sunt hodie propter peccata nostra, adpropinquavit enim desolatio Hierusalem*, Luke xxiii. 48 *g*¹);² and (4) the expansion of Mark's account of the resurrection, 'Suddenly at the third hour of the day there was darkness throughout all the land, and angels descended from heaven; and he rose in the brightness of the living God, [and] at once they ascended with him, and immediately there was light. Then they [the women] drew near to the tomb' (*Subito autem ad horam tertiam tenebrae diei factae sunt per totum orbem terrae, et descenderunt de caelis angeli et surgent in claritate vivi Dei, simul ascenderunt cum eo, et continuo lux facta est. Tunc illae accesserunt ad monimentum*, Mark xvi. 3 *k*).³

Despite the very considerable diversity of readings among the witnesses to the Old Latin, to which reference has been made earlier (see p. 322 above), attempts have been made with more or less success to classify the extant documents. These witnesses, according to Hort,⁴ fall into three main groups. (*a*) The earliest, which he named *African*, consists of texts which agree,

---

¹ A similar statement is included in Tatian's Diatessaron (cf. pp. 35–6 above).

² A similar statement is included in the Old Syriac (cf. p. 40 above), in the Diatessaron, and in the Gospel of Peter vii. 25.

³ The English rendering gives the general sense of the Latin, which is ungrammatical at more than one point and requires emendation. For a somewhat similar account, see the Gospel of Peter ix. 35–7.

⁴ F. J. A. Hort, in a letter to *The Academy*, 14 Aug. 1880, and in Westcott and Hort, *The New Testament in the Original Greek*; [ii] *Introduction* [*and*] *Appendix* (Cambridge, 1881), pp. 81 f.

on the whole, with the quotations of Tertullian and Cyprian. To this group he assigned *k*, *e*, and *h* in Acts and the Book of Revelation. (*b*) A slightly later group, designated *European*, circulated in North Italy and the West of Europe generally. To this category belong most Old Latin manuscripts, except those mentioned as belonging to the other two groups. (*c*) The third family Hort called *Italian*, a name derived from the famous passage in Augustine (see pp. 290–1 above), and assigned to it manuscripts *f* and *q*, along with one or two fragments. In the following years, as further analyses were made of the textual affinities of Old Latin manuscripts, Hort's basic outline was adopted, with elaborations, by some scholars and modified by others. By the early part of the twentieth century what could be called a consensus of scholarly opinion approved the following schema of Old Latin manuscripts and early Latin Fathers:

African: Tertullian Cyprian; Gospels *k e m*; Acts *m h*; Epistles *m* Priscillian; Apocalypse *h* Primasius Tyconius.

European: Gospels *b a c ff*^{2} *h i n o s t p r z* Irenaeus; Acts *g g*^{2} *p s* Lucifer; Catholic Epistles *ff*; Apocalypse *g*.

Italian: Gospels *f q*; Paul *r r*^{2} *r*^{3}; Catholic Epistles *g*; bilingual codices (influenced by the Greek) *d e f g*.

By the middle of the twentieth century, chiefly through the researches of Bover and Ayuso,[1] the lineaments of yet another group of Old Latin texts came to be clarified, the Spanish form of the Old Latin version. In fact, Ayuso found that it was not a single version but existed in several forms. These have been preserved in four types of sources: biblical manuscripts, marginal notes, the Mozarabic liturgy, and Hispanic Church fathers.

Among those who have rejected the classification of an Italian group of Old Latin manuscripts was Burkitt, who (as was mentioned earlier) thought that Augustine, in mentioning the Itala, was referring to Jerome's Vulgate. Burkitt characterized the textual idiosyncrasies of the two main groups of witnesses (the African and the European) as follows:

(1) The earliest Latin version contained a text of the Gospels enriched by additions, some of which go far beyond the mere

---

[1] Cf. 'Recent Spanish Contributions to the Textual Criticism of the New Testament', in the present writer's volume, *Chapters in the History of New Testament Textual Criticism* (Leiden and Grand Rapids, 1963), pp. 121–41.

inventiveness of scribes and most ultimately have been derived from independent historical sources. In this respect the African text has most faithfully preserved the original Latin version. (2) Another series of interpolations of a less bold type is especially characteristic of the European Latin. This series is less certainly based on independent sources and seems to be of a later origin, though from the comparatively small scale of each addition they were easily introduced into manuscripts and so are widely spread among various types of text. The comparative isolation of the African text, which has preserved the longer interpolations, has kept that text more free from these lesser interpolations than any other predominantly 'Western' text.[1]

It has also been observed that certain renderings are characteristic of each of the two main families. For example, as a translation of φῶς the African family prefers *lumen*, the European *lux*; and for δοξάζειν the African prefers *clarificare*, the European *glorificare*. Such preferences are obviously useful in determining the territorial affinities of a manuscript when patristic quotations[2] are scanty.

Not a little attention has been directed toward solving the problem of the kind of New Testament text used by Marcion, whose edition of the Gospel according to Luke and ten Epistles of Paul has been lost, except for the extensive quotations made by later writers. From a comparison of the scriptural quotations made by Tertullian in his *Contra Marcionem* with those in his other writings it may be deduced that in Africa in his time there was not only the catholic Latin translation of the New Testament but also a Latin version of Marcion's New Testament. According to von Soden's analysis of differing terminology in quotations from the Pauline Epistles, *serere, baptizare, peccatum* would be Marcionite, whereas *seminare, tinguere, delinquentia* would be catholic.[3] As might have been expected, the textual affinities of the Marcionite version are much closer to the European Old Latin family

---

[1] *The Old Latin and the Itala* (Cambridge, 1896), p. 52.

[2] For a comprehensive list of monographs (up to 1952) on scriptural citations in the writings of Western patristic authors, see Teófilo Ayuso Marazuela, *La Vetus Latina Hispana*, i (Madrid, 1953), 195–7.

[3] Cf. Hans von Soden, 'Der lateinische Paulustext bei Marcion und Tertullian', *Festgabe für Adolf Jülicher* (Tübingen, 1927), pp. 229–81, and A. J. B. Higgins, 'The Latin Text of Luke in Marcion and Tertullian', *VC* v (1951), 1–42. The latter refutes G. Quispel's opinion (*De bronnen van Tertullianus' Adversus Marcionem* (Utrecht, 1943)) that Tertullian's quotations from Marcion are translations he made *ad hoc* from Marcion's Greek New Testament.

than are the quotations of the catholic version used by Tertullian, a version that is an older form of the African Old Latin which Cyprian quoted in the following generation.[1]

The influence of Marcion's text upon the Latin Bible can be seen not only in textual corruptions which have infected the Western types of text but also—as many scholars think—in providing the Great Church with a set of Latin Prologues to the Pauline Epistles. Examples of the former include such omissions as those at Luke v. 39 and xxiv. 20, both of which are lacking in representatives of the Vetus Latina as well as the Vetus Syra, and such additions as καὶ καταλύοντα τὸν νόμον καὶ τοὺς προφήτας in Luke xxiii. 2 and ἀποστρέφοντα τὰς γυναῖκας καὶ τὰ τέκνα, vs. 5.[2]

Problems concerning the relation of Tatian's Diatessaron and Old Latin witnesses have engaged the attention of many scholars (see pp. 26–31 above). It is clear that readings of the former have contaminated the transmission of non-harmonized Latin texts.[3]

---

[1] G. J. D. Aalders's view that Tertullian did not use the African version directly (*Tertullianus' Citaten uit de Evangeliën en de Oud-Latijnsche Bijbelvertalingen* (Amsterdam, 1932), supplemented by his article, 'Tertullian's Quotations from St. Luke', *Mnemosyne*, 3rd ser., v (1937), 241–82), is refuted by Merrill C. Tenney, who comes to the cautious conclusion that Tertullian probably possessed one or more Latin translations and that he may have been influenced by the Marcionite text or translation in his renderings of the Greek in dealing with non-controversial points (see the abstract of his Ph.D. dissertation, 'The Quotations from Luke in Tertullian as Related to the Texts of the Second and Third Centuries', *Harvard Studies in Classical Philology*, lvi–lvii (1947), 257–60).

[2] For other examples of Marcionite influence on the textual transmission of Luke and Paul, see Adolf von Harnack, *Marcion: das Evangelium von fremden Gott*, 2nd edn. (Leipzig, 1924), pp. 242*–54*; H. J. Vogels, *Evangelium Palatinum. Studien zur ältesten Geschichte der lateinischen Evangelienübersetzung* (*Neutestamentliche Abhandlungen*, xii. 3; Münster in W., 1926), pp. 95–9 and 132; Daniël Plooij, 'The Latin Text of the Epistles of St. Paul', *BBC* xi (1936), 11 f.; E. C. Blackman, *Marcion and his Influence* (London, 1948), pp. 50–60 and 128–68; C. S. C. Williams, *Alterations to the Text of the Synoptic Gospels and Acts* (Oxford, 1951); and H. J. Vogels, 'Der Einfluss Marcions und Tatians auf Text und Kanon des Neuen Testaments', *Synoptische Studien Alfred Wikenhauser zum 70. Geburtstag dargebracht . . .*, ed. by Josef Schmid and Anton Vögtle (Munich, 1954), pp. 278–89. On the other hand, Lagrange (*Critique textuelle*, pp. 262–5) could find little or no Marcionite influence in the transmission of the canonical text in Greek and Latin.

[3] The question whether the earliest Latin translation of the Gospels known at Rome was in the form of a diatessaron, as was held by von Soden (*Die Schriften der Neuen Testaments*, I. iii (Berlin, 1910), 1544–72), Vogels (*Beiträge zur Geschichte des Diatessaron im Abendland* (Münster in W., 1919)), and Burkitt (*JTS* xxxvi (1935), 257), has not been satisfactorily resolved.

By way of conclusion, two other features of the Old Latin versions deserve special comment. Despite the many diversities as to readings and renderings, according to which it is possible to group the witnesses into groups and families, here and there one finds a surprising unanimity, suggesting a common archetype at least for one or another book of the New Testament. How is it possible to explain the transposition 'no one looking back and putting his hand to the plough' (Luke ix. 62) against all Greek manuscripts—except codex Bezae, where the Greek may well have been influenced by the Latin—unless on the hypothesis of a single primitive version? At Luke ii. 14 all Old Latin manuscripts read *hominibus bonae voluntatis* ('to men of goodwill') in opposition to numerous Greek manuscripts that read εὐδοκία. More striking still is the agreement between representatives of the African and European groups in reading at Mark ix. 15 *gaudentes*, a rendering which is due to misreading τρέχοντες as χαίροντες.

The other remarkable feature of the Old Latin versions is their longevity. Long after Jerome's revision had been disseminated far and wide, we still find evidence here and there of the use and transmission of the earlier versions. As late as the twelfth or thirteenth century three Latin manuscripts of the New Testament contain in one or more books an Old Latin text: codex Colbertinus (*c*), written in Languedoc, has an Old Latin text in the Gospels; codex Perpignan (*p*), written probably in South France, has an Old Latin text in Acts i. 1–xiii. 6 and xxviii. 16–31; and codex Gigas (*g*), written in Bohemia, has an Old Latin text in Acts and the Book of Revelation.

II. THE VULGATE[1]

1. JEROME'S EARLY TRAINING AND COMMISSION BY POPE DAMASUS

As we have seen in the previous section, various people, at various times and in various places, with varying degrees of

---

[1] This version did not receive the honorific title 'Vulgate' (in the sense of 'commonly accepted') until the end of the Middle Ages, when Faber Stapulensis appears to have been the first so to designate it; cf. E. T. Sutcliffe, 'The Name Vulgate', *Bib*, xxix (1948), 345–52, and A. Allgeier, '*Haec vetus et vulgata editio*. Neue wort- und begriffsgeschichtliche Beiträge zur Bibel auf dem Tridentum', ibid. 353–90.

success, had translated various parts of the Bible into Latin. The result was chaos. The different versions had become so mixed and corrupt that no two manuscripts agreed. Accordingly Pope Damasus (366–84) undertook to remedy this intolerable situation, and the scholar to whom he entrusted the arduous task was the great biblical scholar of the ancient Latin Church, Sophronius Eusebius Hieronymus, known to us today as St. Jerome.

Both the exact place and the date of Jerome's birth are uncertain. According to his own statement in the final chapter of his *Lives of Illustrious Men*, he was born in 'the city of Strido(n), which is on the border of Dalmatia and Pannonia, and was overthrown by the Goths'. Pannonia, as is well known, was the southern part of what is now known as Hungary, and Dalmatia was to the south of Pannonia and north of the Adriatic (part of Yugoslavia today). Precisely where Stridon was located has been debated. According to recent opinion, it is probably to be identified with the modern Grahovo-polje, Yugoslavia.[1]

The date of his birth has been placed either at about 330 or in the year 346 or 347. The earlier date rests upon Prosper of Aquitania's statement in his *Chronicon*, that Jerome was ninety years old in 420, when he died. This, however, is contradicted by Jerome's own statement (*Epist.* lii) that he was little more than a boy when, in 374, he wrote to Heliodorus (*Epist.* xiv). Furthermore, inasmuch as Jerome's literary activity began in 370, most scholars[2] prefer the later date for his birth.

Jerome's early training was calculated to fit him admirably for his great work as translator. The son of Christian parents who were moderately well-to-do, he received a first-class training in grammar and rhetoric at Rome under the illustrious teacher Aelius Donatus, of whom he always speaks with great respect,

---

[1] Cf. F. Bulić, 'Wo lag Stridon, die Heimat des h. Hieronymus?' *Festschrift für Otto Benndorf* (Vienna, 1898), pp. 276–80; L. Jelić, 'Das älteste kartographische Denkmal über die römische Provinz Dalmatia', *Wissenschaftliche Mittheilungen aus Bosnien und der Hercegovina*, vii (Vienna, 1900), 194 f.; F. Bulić, 'Stridone (Grahavo-polje in Bosnia), luogo natale di S. Girolamo, dottore massimo della Chiesa', *Miscellanea Geronimiana* (Rome, 1920), pp. 253–330; and Germain Morin, 'A-t-on retrouvé Stridon le lieu natal de Saint Jérôme?' *Strena Buliciana. Commentationes gratulatoriae Francisco Bulić* . . . , ed. by M. Aramić and V. Hoffiller (Zagreb–Alspalth, 1924), pp. 421–32.

[2] Not, however, Pierre Hamblenne ('La longévité de Jérôme', *Latomus*, xxviii (1969), 1081–1119), followed by J. N. D. Kelly (*Jerome; His Life, Writings, and Controversies* (New York, 1975), pp. 337–9).

calling him 'praeceptor meus'. Jerome applied himself with diligence to the study of rhetoric, and attended the law courts to hear the best pleaders of the day. He became familiar with the Latin classics and studied Plautus and Terence, Sallust, Lucretius, Horace, Virgil, Persius, and Lucan, with commentaries on them by Donatus and others.[1] These developed his feeling for literary style, and he became a follower of Ciceronian traditions.

In the Greek classics he was less thoroughly at home. Indeed, it appears that he did not learn Greek at all until he went to Antioch in 373–4, when he was about twenty-six years of age. He shows some acquaintance with Hesiod, Sophocles, Herodotus, Demosthenes, Aristotle, Theophrastus, and Gregory of Nazianzus.

His scholarly tools included also the Hebrew language. This he learned with great labour in his mature years, first from a converted but anonymous Jew during Jerome's five years' ascetic seclusion in the Syrian desert of Chalcis (374–9), and afterwards in Bethlehem (about 385) from the Palestinian Rabbi bar-Anina, who, through fear of the Jews, visited him by night. Although Jerome's knowledge of Hebrew was defective, it was much greater than that of Origen, Ephraem Syrus, and Epiphanius, the only other Church Fathers who knew Hebrew at all.

Such was the philological training of the man who was destined to fix the literary form of the Bible of the entire Western Church.[2] Even the great Augustine seems to have stood in awe of Jerome's immense knowledge of things biblical. Although he felt obliged more than once to disagree with the learned monk of Bethlehem, he wrote him, not in false humility but in simple honesty: 'I have not as great a knowledge of the divine Scriptures as you have, nor could I have such knowledge as I see in you.'[3] That Jerome himself agreed whole-heartedly with such praise may be gathered from his boast to his opponent Rufinus, that he was 'a philosopher, a rhetorician, a grammarian, a

---

[1] Cf. Arthur Stanley Pease, 'The Attitude of Jerome toward Pagan Literature', *Transactions and Proceedings of the American Philological Association*, l (1919), 150–67; Gerard L. Ellspermann, *The Attitude of the Early Christian Latin Writers toward Pagan Literature and Learning* (Washington, 1949), pp. 126–73; Harald Hagendahl, *Latin Fathers and the Classics (Studia graeca et latina gothoburgensia*, vi; Göteborg, 1958), pp. 89–328; and id., 'Jerome and the Latin Classics', *VC* xxviii (1974), 216–27.

[2] See K. K. Hulley, 'Principles of Textual Criticism Known to St. Jerome' *Harvard Studies in Classical Philology*, lv (1944), 89 ff.

[3] Migne, *PL* xxii, col. 912; xxxii, col. 247; cf. Kelly, op. cit., pp. 267–8.

dialectician, a Hebrew, a Greek, a Latin, three-tongued' (*vir trilinguis*).[1] Despite supercilious pride in his learning, Jerome was by all odds the most competent scholar of his age who could attempt the revision of the Latin Bible. His commission to do so came about in the following way.

In the year 382 Pope Damasus summoned Jerome from Constantinople to Rome as advisor at a synod (*Epist.* cviii. 6). After the synod had been held, during which Damasus learned to value Jerome's extensive erudition, he kept him at Rome as his secretary (*Epist.* cxxiii. 10). In the following year, though Jerome was probably no more than thirty-five years of age, Damasus commissioned him to produce a uniform and dependable text of the Latin Bible; he was not to make a new version, but to revise the texts which were in circulation, using for this purpose the Greek original.

Although we do not have the original request of the scholarly Damasus, who is known today chiefly for his metrical epitaphs in several Roman catacombs, we can judge from Jerome's Preface to his revision of the four Gospels, addressed to Damasus about 384, how he regarded the Pope's mandate. He writes as follows:

You urge me to revise the Old Latin version, and, as it were, to sit in judgement on the copies of the Scriptures which are now scattered throughout the world; and, inasmuch as they differ from one another, you would have me decide which of them agree with the Greek original. The labour is one of love, but at the same time both perilous and presumptuous; for in judging others I must be content to be judged by all; and how can I dare to change the language of the world in its hoary old age, and carry it back to the early days of its infancy? Is there a man, learned or unlearned, who will not, when he takes the volume in his hands, and perceives that what he reads does not suit his settled tastes, break out immediately into violent language and call me a forger and a profane person for having had the audacity to add anything to the ancient books, or to make any changes or corrections therein?[2]

There were two reasons, however, which prompted Jerome to incur such an amount of opprobrium. The first reason, as he goes

---

[1] *Apol. adv. Ruf.* iii. 6. His claim to be a philosopher may be questioned.

[2] For a critical edition of the Preface, see Wordsworth and White, *Novum Testamentum . . . Latine*, vol. i, pp. 1–4, or R. Weber, *Biblia sacra iuxta Vulgatam versionem*, vol. ii, pp. 1515 f.

on to say in the Preface, was the command laid upon him by Damasus, the supreme pontiff. The second was the shocking diversity among the Old Latin manuscripts. There were, in fact, as he says, 'almost as many forms of text as there are manuscripts' (*tot sunt [exemplaria] paene quot codices*).[1]

Jerome's apprehension that he would be castigated for tampering with Holy Writ was not unfounded. His revision of the Latin Bible provoked both criticism and anger, sometimes with extraordinary vehemence. According to Augustine (*Epist.* lxxi), during the reading of the Scripture lesson in a service of worship at Oea, a town in North Africa, when the congregation heard that Jonah rested under *hedera* ('ivy'), instead of the familiar *cucurbita* ('gourd') of the earlier Latin versions, such a fanatical tumult was raised that the bishop was nearly left without a flock!

For his part, Jerome defended his work with forthright vigour, referring on occasion to his detractors as 'two-legged asses' or 'yelping dogs'—persons who 'think that ignorance is equivalent to holiness'. In the course of time, however, opposition to the revision subsided, and the superior accuracy and scholarship of Jerome's version gave it the victory. It was a clear case of the survival of the fittest.

2. NOTEWORTHY MANUSCRIPTS OF THE VULGATE

In view of the exceedingly great number of manuscript copies of the Latin Vulgate (estimated to be in excess of 10,000), it is obvious that to enumerate even the most important is here impossible. All that can be done within the present context is to mention a few copies that represent each of the chief families of the Vulgate texts. They are listed in the following order of types of Vulgate text: (*a*) the Italian, (*b*) the Spanish, (*c*) the Irish, (*d*) the French, and the recensions of (*e*) Alcuin and of (*f*) Theodulf.[2]

---

[1] Curiously enough, 'of no passage is this judgment more true than of this actual sentence itself, which is hardly quoted in the same way in any three MSS.' (H. J. White in Scrivener's *Plain Introduction to the Criticism of the New Testament*, 4th edn., ii (London, 1894), 42. See the apparatus to Jerome's Preface in Wordsworth and White, op. cit., vol. i, p. 2).

[2] The classic monograph on the several types of Vulgate manuscripts is Samuel Berger, *Histoire de la Vulgate pendant les premiers siècles du Moyen Âge* (Paris, 1893; repr. New York, 1958); cf. also H. J. White's classified list of Vulgate manuscripts in Hastings's *Dictionary of the Bible*, iv (1902), 586–9. For recent discussions see

(a) Vulgate Manuscripts with an Italian Type of Text

Codex Sangallensis (Σ, Sangall. 1395, with a few leaves elsewhere) is the oldest known copy of the Vulgate Gospels. Written in Verona probably during the fifth century,[1] in the Middle Ages it was dismembered and its leaves were used as guard leaves in rebinding other manuscripts, which today are in St. Gall and other libraries. About half of the text of the four Gospels has survived.

Edited by C. H. Turner, *The Oldest Manuscript of the Vulgate Gospels, deciphered and edited with an Introduction and Appendix* (Oxford, 1931); supplements by P. Lehmann in *Zentralblatt für Bibliothekswesen*, 1 (1933), 50–76; A. Dold, ibid. 709–17, and *Bib*, xxii (1941), 105–47; and B. Bischoff, 'Neue Materialen zur Bestand und zur Geschichte der altlateinischen Bibelübersetzungen', *Miscellanea G. Mercati*, i (*Studi e testi*, cxxi; Vatican City, 1946), 407–36, and id., 'Zur Rekonstruktion der ältesten Handschrift der Vulgata-Evangelien und der Vorlage ihrer Marginalien', *Mittelalterliche Studien*, i (Stuttgart, 1966), 101–11.

Codex Fuldensis (F) was written for, and corrected by, Victor, bishop of Capua, who signed his name in it (making a blot from a spluttering pen in doing so) in the year 546. Later St. Boniface acquired the codex and in 745 gave it to the abbey of Fulda, whence it has taken its name ever since. The manuscript contains the entire New Testament with the Epistle to the Laodiceans, but the Gospels are in the form of a harmony which derives from Tatian's Diatessaron (see pp. 20–1 and 28–9 above).

Edited by Ernst Ranke, *Codex Fuldensis* (Marburg and Leipzig, 1868); cf. John Chapman, *Notes on the Early History of the Vulgate Gospels* (Oxford, 1908), pp. 78–161.

Codex Foro-Juliensis (J), of the sixth (or seventh) century, is a Gospels manuscript, portions of which are in three different collections. Matthew, Luke, and John (lacking xix. 24–40; xx. 19–21, 25) are in the archaeological museum at Cividale del Friuli, and were edited by G. Bianchini, *Evangeliarium quadruplex*

Bonifatius Fischer, 'Bibelausgaben des frühen Mittelalters', *Settimane di studio del Centro italiano sull'Alto Medioevo*, x (Spoleto, 1963), 519–600; Raphael Loewe, 'The Medieval History of the Latin Vulgate', in *The Cambridge History of the Bible*, ii, *The West from the Fathers to the Reformation*, ed. by G. W. H. Lampe (Cambridge, 1969), pp. 102–54; and Bonifatius Fischer, 'Das Neue Testament in lateinischer Sprache', *Die alten Übersetzungen des Neuen Testaments, die Kirchenväterzitate und Lektionare*, ed. by K. Aland (Berlin and New York, 1972), pp. 1–92.

[1] E. A. Lowe thought it possible that the manuscript could have been written during the lifetime of Jerome (*Codices Latini Antiquiores*, vii. 984).

Latinae versionis antiquae seu veteris Italicae, ii (Rome, 1749), 473 ff. Tattered fragments of the Gospel of Mark, scarcely legible, are in the Biblioteca Marciana at Venice. Another fragment, containing Mark xii. 21–xvi. 20, has been treasured at Prague, where popular legend had it that it was the veritable autograph of Mark himself! In the eighteenth century Dobrovský, the founder of Slavic philology, was thrust into acrimonious controversy by his first publication, a textual analysis proving that the fragment dates from a period long after the lifetime of St. Mark.

Josef Dobrovský, *Fragmentum Pragense Euangelii S. Marci, vulgo autographi* (Prague, 1778); reprinted (Prague, 1953), with an introductory essay by Bohumil Ryba (written in Czech, with résumés in Russian, French, and English), in which are related the circumstances in which Dobrovský wrote his monograph, the controversies which ensued upon its publication, and the history of the fragment itself (with photographic facsimile).

Codex Amiatinus (A), generally considered to be the best authority extant for the Vulgate text, is a magnificent copy of the entire Latin Bible (called a Pandect).[1] Containing 1,029 leaves of parchment, each measuring about 50 × 34 cm. (19½ × 13½ in.) in length and breadth, it is written in a regular and beautiful hand, with the first lines of each book in red ink. The text is divided into lines of varying length (called technically *cola et commata*) corresponding to breaks in the sense. It was written early in the eighth century in the north of England, either at Wearmouth or Jarrow, from manuscripts brought from Italy, perhaps by Theodore of Tarsus when he came to England to be archbishop of Canterbury in 669. In 716 Ceolfrid, abbot of Wearmouth, set out with it for Rome, intending to present it to Pope Gregory II, but he died at Langres on the way. Carried to Rome by some of his companions, it was subsequently given to the Cistercian monastery of St. Salvator at Monte Amiata, whence it derived its name. Recalled temporarily to Rome to be consulted for the Sixtine edition of the Vulgate (see pp. 348–9 below), in 1786 it finally found a home in the Laurentian Library at Florence.[2]

---

[1] Not until the time of Cassiodorus in the second half of the sixth century is there mention of a Latin 'Pandect'—a complete Bible with all the separate books bound within a single cover. On Cassiodorus, see Raphael Loewe, op. cit. (p. 334 n. 2), pp. 115–20, and on Pandects, see B. Fischer, 'Die Idee der Pandekten', *Die Bibel von Moutier-Grandval . . .* (Bern, 1971), pp. 59 f.

[2] On the history of the manuscript, see H. J. White, 'The Codex Amiatinus and

The complete text of the New Testament was published by C. von Tischendorf (Leipzig, 1850; reissued with corrections, 1854); in 1887 it was recollated by H. J. White and made the basis of Wordsworth and White's Oxford edition of the Vulgate.

Codex Lindisfarnensis (Y), the magnificent Lindisfarne Gospels rivalling even the Book of Kells in the beauty of the script and the richness of ornamentation, is now in the British Museum (Cotton MS. Nero D. iv). Dating from the late seventh or early eighth century, it was written by Bishop Eadfrid in honour of St. Cuthbert (d. 687) and is illuminated in the finest style of the Northumbrian Anglo-Celtic school. A table of festivals on which special lections were read shows that it must have been copied from a Bible used in a church at Naples, probably one brought to England by the Neapolitan abbot Hadrian, the companion of Archbishop Theodore. Its text, which is closely akin to that of Amiatinus, was provided with an interlinear translation into Anglo-Saxon about A.D. 950 by a priest named Aldred (see pp. 446–7 below).

Edited by J. Stevenson and G. Waring (Surtees Society, xxvii, xxxix, xliii, and xlviii; 1854–65), and by W. W. Skeat, *The Holy Gospels in Anglo-Saxon, Northumbrian, and Old Mercian Versions* (Cambridge, 1871–87); facsimile edition prepared by T. K. Kendrick, with introduction by T. J. Brown, R. L. S. Bruce-Mitford, and A. S. C. Ross, *Evangeliorum quattuor codex Lindisfarnensis* . . . , 2 vols. (Olten and Lausanne, 1956, 1960).

(b) Vulgate Manuscripts with a Spanish Type of Text[1]

The history of the Spanish Vulgate begins with Jerome himself, who in the year 398 supervised the work of scribes sent by Lucinius Baeticus from Spain to copy his texts.[2] It is perhaps not surprising that (contrary to Ayuso's views), no extant Spanish texts derive from Lucinius' without contamination.

Codex Cavensis (C), one of the two most important representatives of the Spanish type of Vulgate text, is a superb specimen of calligraphy, 'perhaps the finest manuscript ever

its Birthplace', *Studia biblica et ecclesiastica*, ii (Oxford, 1890), 273–309; G. Schmid, 'Zur Geschichte des Codex Amiatinus', *TQ* lxxxix (1907), 571–84; A. Mercati, 'Per la storia del Codice Amiatino', *Bib*, iii (1922), 324–8; and Bonifatius Fischer, 'Codex Amiatinus und Cassiodor', *BZ*, N.F., vi (1962), 57–79.

[1] For a discussion of the Spanish types of Old Latin and Vulgate manuscripts, see Teófilo Ayuso Marazuela, *La Vetus Latina Hispana*; i, *Prolegómenos* (Madrid, 1953), 313–535.

[2] *Epist.* lxxi. 5 and lxxv. 4.

penned by a Spanish scribe' (Lowe). Containing the whole Bible in a small, round Visigothic hand, it was written in the ninth century by a scribe who, in a colophon to the Lamentations of Jeremiah, identifies himself as 'Danila scriptor'. Today the manuscript is in the Benedictine abbey situated near La Cava in the province of Salerno. The text of the Gospels shows signs of being a revision, being mingled with Old Latin elements. It contains the *comma Johanneum*,[1] 1 John v. 7 *after* vs. 8.

E. A. Lowe, 'The Codex Cavensis, New Light on its Later History', *Quantulacumque, Studies Presented to Kirsopp Lake* . . . , ed. by Robert P. Casey *et al.* (London, 1937), pp. 325–31.

Codex Complutensis I, a copy of the entire Bible dating from the tenth century (completed A.D. 927), was used by Cardinal Ximenes in editing the Complutensian Polyglot Bible. During the Spanish Civil War (1936–9) it was almost totally destroyed; the little that still remains is in the Library of the Facultad de Filosofía y Letras in Madrid (Bibl. Univ. Cent. 31). The Benedictines of the monastery of St. Jerome in Rome possess a photocopy of the entire manuscript. It was one of the most important Visigothic manuscripts, which in portions of the Old Testament presents an Old Latin version. In the New Testament the text is Vulgate, but with Spanish characteristics; the Epistle to the Laodiceans follows Hebrews.

M. Revilla, *La Biblia Polyglota de Alcalá* (Madrid, 1917); and R. Miquélez and P. Martínez, 'El códice complutense o la primera Biblia visigótica de Alcalá', *Anales de la Universidad de Madrid, Letras*, iv (1935), 204–19.

Codex gothicus Legionensis ($Λ^L$), a copy of the entire Bible, was written and illuminated in A.D. 960 by a scribe named Sanctius (Sancho) in Valeránica, near Tordómar (Burgos). Since the twelfth century the manuscript has belonged to the collegiate church of San Isidoro de León. There are a large number of Old Latin variant readings in the margins, especially in the Old Testament. It was collated for the Sixtine edition by Bp. Francisco Trujillo (and by him called codex Gothicus); the collation is preserved in the Vatican (Lat. 4859). Ayuso's opinion that the manuscript is a faithful reflection of the edition of the Bible prepared by Peregrinus in the fifth century was challenged

---

[1] Cf. Mateo del Álamo, 'El "comma Joaneo" ', *EB*, seg. ép., ii (1943), 75–105 (with wide-ranging bibliography), and Walter Thiele, 'Beobachtungen zum Comma Johanneum', *ZNW* l (1959), 61–73.

by Fischer, who shows that it belongs to a group of codices that originated in the tenth century in Castilla.

Cf. Teofílo Ayuso Marazuela, *La biblia de Oña. Notable fragmento casi desconocido de un códice visigótico de la biblia de San Isidoro de León* (Saragossa, 1945), and articles by Ayuso in *Estudios bíblicos*, seg. ép., ii–vii (1943–8); Bonifatius Fischer, 'Algunas observaciones sobre el "Codex Gothicus" de la R. C. de S. Isidoro en León y sobre la tradición española de la Vulgata', *Archivos leonenses*, xv, nos. 29–30 (1961), 5–47.

Codex Toletanus (T), apparently written at Seville and now in the National Library in Madrid (MS. Tol. 2. 1, vitr. 4), is a copy of the entire Bible, dating from the tenth century (completed A.D. 988).[1] It contains the characteristic Spanish form of Vulgate text, second only to codex Cavensis, and has the text of 1 John v. 7 in the same location (after vs. 8) as that manuscript. The manuscript was collated for the Sixtine revision by Chr. Palomares, whose work is preserved in the Vatican (Lat. 9508); the collation, however, was not used in that revision, as it reached Cardinal Caraffa too late.

Published by Giuseppi Bianchini in his *Vindiciae Canonicarum Scripturarum, Vulgatae Latinae editiones* . . . , i (Rome, 1740), pp. xlvii–ccxvi, and reprinted by Migne, *PL* xxix, cols. 915–1152.

(c) *Vulgate Manuscripts with an Irish Type of Text*[2]

Codex Kenanensis (Q; the famous Book of Kells) is an eighth- or ninth-century copy of the Gospels, with the most elaborate and beautiful Celtic decorations. Named from Kells or Kenanna, a monastery in County Meath, it was given by Archbishop Ussher to Trinity College, Dublin. The text, of the Irish type, shows a peculiar fondness for conflate readings.

[1] Cf. E. A. Lowe, 'On the Date of Codex Toletanus', *RBén*, xxxv (1923), 267–71; L. F. Smith, 'A Note on the Codex Toletanus', ibid. xxxvi (1924), 347; and A. C. Millares, *Contribución al 'Corpus' de códices visigóticos* (Madrid, 1931), pp. 94–130.

[2] Cf. Lemuel J. Hopkins-James, *The Celtic Gospels, Their Story and their Text* (Oxford, 1934); L. Bieler, 'The New Testament in the Celtic Church', *Studia evangelica*, ed. by F. L. Cross, iii (*TU* lxxxviii, Berlin, 1964), 318–30; id., 'Der Bibeltext des hl. Patrick', *Bib*, xxviii (1947), 37–58, 235–67; A. Cardoliani, 'Le texte de la Bible en Irlande du Ve au IXe siècle', *RB* lvii (1950), 3–39; Louis H. Gray, 'Biblical Citations in Latin Lives of Welsh and Breton Saints Differing from the Vulgate', *Traditio*, viii (1952), 389–97; H. J. Frede, *Pelagius. Der irische Bibeltext. Sedulius Scottus* (Freiburg im. Br., 1961).

A collation is included by T. K. Abbott in his edition of Codex Usserianus (Dublin, 1884). A facsimile edition, *Evangeliorum quattuor Codex Cenannensis*, 3 vols., was prepared by Ernest H. Alton and Paul Meyer (Bern, 1950–1).

Codex Lichfeldensis (L) is traditionally ascribed to St. Chad and was written in the seventh or eighth century. Belonging formerly to the church of St. Teliau at Llandaff, Wales, the manuscript was brought to the chapter Library at Lichfield in the tenth century. The writing and ornamentation are very beautiful, and resemble the Book of Kells. The manuscript contains the text of Matthew, Mark, and Luke (as far as iii. 9; the second volume has been lost) and has been thought to show traces of occasional correction from the Greek.

Edited by F. H. A. Scrivener, *Codex S. Ceaddae Latinus Evangelii SSS Matthaei, Marci, Lucae ad cap. III. 9 complectens* . . . (Cambridge, 1887).

Codex Rushworthianus (R), known also as 'the Gospels of Mac Regol' from the name of the scribe, who died in A.D. 820, contains the Gospels with an interlinear Old English gloss, Matthew in the Mercian dialect, the other Gospels in Northumbrian (see p. 447 below). The text, which has frequent inversions of order of words, especially in Matthew, has been thought to show corrections from the Greek.

Edited by J. Stevenson and G. Waring (*Surtees Society*, xxviii, xxxix, xliii, and xlviii; 1854–65), and by W. W. Skeat (Cambridge, 1871–87).

Codex Dublinensis (D; the Book of Armagh), now in the Library of Trinity College, Dublin, is a copy of the New Testament written in A.D. 807 in a small and beautiful Irish hand, by a scribe named Ferdomnach. It has the Epistle to the Laodiceans after Colossians, and the Book of Acts after the Apocalypse. It shows signs of having been corrected from Greek manuscripts akin to the Ferrar group (fam. 13).

Edited by John Gwynn, *Liber Ardmachanus. The Book of Armagh* . . . (Dublin, 1913).

(*d*) *Vulgate Manuscripts with a French Type of Text*[1]

Codex Sangermanensis, the second half of a Bible (Paris, Bibl. Nat. 11553) of the ninth century, contains portions of the

---

[1] On Vulgate manuscripts of the French type, see especially Samuel Berger, *Histoire de la Vulgate pendant les premiers siècles du Moyen Âge* (Paris, 1893; repr. New York, 1958), pp. 61–111.

Old Testament and the entire New Testament, of which the text of Matthew is Old Latin (g^1). Used in Robert Estienne's *Biblia sacra* (1540), as well as in the Wordsworth–White and the Stuttgart editions (siglum G), it is one of the more important witnesses to the French type of Vulgate text. The order of books of the New Testament is Gospels, Acts, Catholic Epistles, Apocalypse, and Pauline Epistles, followed by the *Shepherd* of Hermas (as far as *Vis.* iii. 8). The margins of the Gospel of John contain a remarkable set of *sortes sanctorum*, used for purposes of divination.[1]

Codex Beneventanus (British Museum add. 5463) is a carefully executed and well-preserved copy of the Gospels, written *per cola et commata* in an uncial script which Berger dated to the beginning of the ninth century. According to the same scholar the text contains a mélange of Spanish and Irish readings which appear to form the basis of the French type of the Vulgate Gospels.[2]

Codex Colbertinus (Paris, Bibl. Nat. 254) is composed of two different manuscripts; the first contains the Gospels in an Old Latin type of text (*c*), and the second, in another hand, the rest of the New Testament. It is dated by Berger on palaeographic grounds to the second half of the twelfth century; the archaic character of its illustrations indicates that it was executed in the south of France. The Acts of the Apostles is followed by a note, written in smaller script, on the passion of St. Peter and of St. Paul, analogous to that found in two ancient Spanish manuscripts (Leg.[1] and Compl.[1]).

(e) *Manuscripts of Alcuin's recension of the Vulgate*

When Charlemagne became sole ruler of the Franks (A.D. 771) he found several types of text of the Vulgate Bible current in his dominions. In the interest of both accuracy and uniformity of text he issued more than one edict bearing on the copying and revision of the sacred books. In a capitulary issued in 789 (*Admonitio generalis*) he ordered that there should be 'in each monastery and parish good copies of the catholic books . . . , and the boys must not be permitted to deface them either in reading them or by

---

[1] On the *sortes sanctorum* in codex Sangermanensis, see J. Rendel Harris, *AJP* ix (1888), 58–63.

[2] So Berger, *Histoire de la Vulgate*, p. 92. For bibliography on the manuscript, see Lowe, ii. 48, no. 162.

writing on them; and if there is necessity for writing [i.e. copying] a Gospel, a Psalter, or a Missal, men of maturity are to do it, using all care (*perfectae aetatis homines scribant cum omni diligentia*)'.[1]

Among the more scholarly efforts at bringing some order out of diverse and carelessly written copies of the Vulgate the name of Alcuin is prominent. Born about 730 in Northumbria, he was educated in the famous cathedral school of Archbishop Egbert of York, of which he became master in 766. After meeting Charlemagne at Parma in 781 he was made his adviser in religious and educational matters, and upon becoming abbot of Tours in 796 he established there an important school and library. In a letter written at Eastertide, 800, to Gisela and Rothrude, Charlemagne's sister and daughter, Alcuin says that he is busy with the king's charge (*praeceptum*) to emend the texts of both testaments.[2] Most scholars have taken the words to imply a specific injunction to Alcuin alone to make a uniformly revised text from the best Latin manuscripts available. Whether such an interpretation is justified, or whether, as Fischer has argued with considerable cogency,[3] no more is implied than that Alcuin was working, like others, within the framework of the Emperor's general directive, it remains true that a good many of the superb Carolingian manuscripts, as they are called, which are found in libraries throughout Europe, contain Alcuin's revision.

Alcuin, who was oblivious to the problems of textual criticism, made no attempt to restore the readings of Jerome. He aimed rather at the production of a text which should follow a grammatical norm and serve as a standard for monastery and school throughout the king's dominions. Editorial activity was limited to the purgation of errors in punctuation, grammar, and orthography.[4] For this work Alcuin obtained manuscripts from his

---

[1] *Capitularia regum Francorum*, ed. by A. Boretius, i (*Monumenta Germaniae historica*, Legum sectio ii; Hannover, 1883), p. 60, lines 2–7.

[2] *Epistolae Karolini aevi*, ed. by E. Dümmler, ii (*Monumenta Germaniae historica*, Epistolarum, iv; Berlin, 1895), pp. 322 f.: 'Totius forsitan evangelii expositionem direxerim vobis, si me non occupasset domini regis praeceptum in emendatione veteris novique testamenti.'

[3] Bonifatius Fischer, *Die Alkuin-Bibel* (*Vetus Latina; Aus der Geschichte der lateinischen Bibel*, i; Freiburg im Br., 1957); 'Bibeltext und Bibelreform unter Karl der Grossen', *Karl der Grosse, Lebenswerk und Nachleben*; ii, *Das geistige Leben* (Düsseldorf, 1965), 156–216; and 'Die Alkuin-Bibeln', *Die Bibel von Moutier-Grandval* (Bern, 1971), pp. 49–98.

[4] Of existing Vulgate manuscripts, the famous codex Vallicellianus (see p. 343 below) is often regarded as most nearly representing Alcuin's text.

native Northumbria, the scene at the beginning of the eighth century of the production of the magnificent codex Amiatinus and the Lindisfarne Gospels. It can be understood, however, that the prototypes used by Alcuin have not survived.[1]

Manuscripts belonging to the Alcuinian family—which textually shows a remarkable constancy—are designated by the siglum Φ (Alcuin having borne the sobriquet *Flaccus*). Among many copies extant today, the following may be singled out for special mention.

The St. Adelbert codex of the four Gospels (Gniezno Chapter Lib. MS. 1) appears to have been written during the third quarter of the ninth century. Lacking Matt. vi. 5–27; xxvi. 56–xxviii. 20; Mark i. 1–v. 32; Luke i. 1–iii. 38; and John i. 1–v. 38, the manuscript is considered by Gryglewicz to preserve a purer form of the Alcuin recension than has been thus far identified in any of the other Alcuin codices.

Felix Gryglewicz, 'The St Adelbert Codex of the Gospels', *NTS* xi (1964–5), 256–78; B. Bolz, *Najdawniejszy kalendarz gnieźnieński według kodeksu MS 1* (Posńan, 1971).

Codex Vallicellianus (V or Φ^v), considered by many to be the best specimen of the Alcuinian Bible, is in the Library of the Oratorians (B 6), near the church of Sta Maria in Vallicella, sometimes called the Chiesa nuova of Rome. Dating from the ninth century, it is a carefully written copy in three columns (a format which is rather rare for Alcuinian Bibles, which are usually in two columns). The manuscript was used in making corrections in the Sixtine edition of the Vulgate.

Codex Carolinus or Grandivallensis (K, or Φ^G) is a ninth-century manuscript from the abbey of Moutiers Granval, near Basel, but since 1836 in the British Museum. Written in Tours about 834–5, it is splendidly illuminated, and has been published in a facsimile edition.

Die Bibel von Moutier-Grandval. British Museum Add. MS. 10546 (Bern, 1971).

Codex Paulinus (Φ^P), a ninth-century manuscript preserved in the Library of St. Paul without the Walls, was written for

[1] For a chart showing such putative prototypes, see Hanz Glunz, *Britannien und Bibeltext; der Vulgatatext der Evangelien in seinem Verhältnis zur irisch-angelsächischen Kultur des Frühmittelalters* (Leipzig, 1930), facing p. 177.

Charles the Bald. Produced probably in northern France, it shows Saxon influence in its rich ornamentation.

Codex Bambergensis (B), now in the Staatliche Bibliothek in Bamberg (MS. 1),[1] is a handsome specimen of Carolingian art produced at Tours within some thirty years after Alcuin's death; it contains his portrait. The manuscript lacks the Book of Revelation.

(ƒ) Manuscripts of Theodulf's Recension of the Vulgate[2]

About the time of Alcuin's work of grammatical and orthographic revision of the Vulgate, another reviser began work along somewhat different lines. This was Theodulf, a Spaniard of Visigothic descent born near Zaragoza about 750. One of the leading theologians of his day, he was appointed both abbot of Fleury and bishop of Orléans (788–821). As bishop he carried out many reforms, including the introduction of parish schools and raising the standards of worship. He favoured especially the production of manuscripts of the Bible and sought to purify the text of the Vulgate.

Theodulf's text of the Vulgate (which he was at pains to improve continuously) is a precursor of modern editorial methods in respect of using sigla in margins to identify the sources of his variants, such as $\bar{a}$ for the Alcuinian reading and $\bar{s}$ for the Spanish recension. Unfortunately Theodulf's edition, though scholarly, was easily corrupted by careless scribes, who occasionally introduced marginal readings into the text. Copies of the Theodulfian recension, which are fewer in number than the Alcuinian, include the following.

Codex Theodulphianus (Θ), the property successively of the cathedral of Orléans, the family of the Mesmes, and the Bibliothèque Nationale at Paris (Lat. 9380), contains the whole Bible. Written in a beautiful and minute minuscule, the manuscript has been thought by Berger[3] to have been actually prepared under Theodulf's direction, the many marginalia being the result of his

---

[1] See F. Leitschuh, *Aus den Schätzen der königlichen Bibliothek zu Bamberg* (Bamberg, 1888), plates i–iv.

[2] Cf. Léopold Delisle, 'Les Bibles de Théodulfe', *Bibliothèque de l'École des Chartes*, xl (Paris, 1879), pp. 1–47; Raphael Loewe, op. cit. (see p. 334 n. 2), pp. 126–9; and E. A. Lowe, *Codices Latini Antiquiores*, vi, p. xx.

[3] *Histoire de la Vulgate*, pp. 149–76; E. A. Lowe dated the manuscript to the eighth–ninth century (*Codices Latini Antiquiores*, v. 576).

own editorial work. The Psalms and the Gospels are written on purple parchment in letters of silver (initials are in gold).

Codex Aniciensis, now in the Bibliothèque Nationale (4 et 4²), is a ninth-century Bible, written under the direction of Theodulf, which so closely resembles the preceding codex that, as Delisle commented, many pages look almost like proofs struck from the same type. It bears a strong resemblance also to the following codex. The scribe committed not a few blunders, such as writing *nomen* for *semen*, Rom. iv. 8.

Codex Hubertanus (H), formerly in the monastery of St. Hubert in the Ardenne, now in the British Museum (Add. 24142), is assigned by Wordsworth and White to the ninth or tenth century. It is written in three columns (a format of which there are relatively few examples), and breaks off at 1 Pet. iv. 3. The text shows affinities with the Northumbrian text of Amiatinus, traceable to the dependence of each on south-Italian archetypes, while the corrections (inserted by erasure) present a Theodulfian type of text.

The crowning glory in the transmission of the Vulgate during the Carolingian renaissance was the production of *de luxe* copies of the Scriptures, written on purple parchment with gold and silver ink, often with elaborate illumination.[1] Among such works of art what has been called one of the finest, if not *the* finest, of purple manuscripts in existence is the Golden Gospels now in the Pierpont Morgan Library of New York (M. 23). Written entirely in letters of burnished gold on purple parchment, this sumptuous codex contains the Gospels in a Vulgate Latin text with Northumbrian and Irish affinities. Previously considered to date from the close of the seventh or the beginning of the eighth century, it has more recently been assigned to the tenth century.[2] The codex shows signs of having been made in some haste (sixteen scribes took part in the work). Apparently it was never read by a corrector, nor was liturgical use ever made of it. It obviously was

---

[1] For a list of such *de luxe* copies, see Berger, *Histoire de la Vulgate*, pp. 259–77, and, with more recent bibliography, H. Höpfl, *Introductio generalis in sacram scripturam*, 6th edn. by L. Leloir, i (Naples and Rome, 1958), 388 n. 4.

[2] The earlier date was advocated by Wattenbach, de Rossi, Gregory, and its editor, H. C. Hoskier (*The Golden Latin Gospels in the Library of J. Pierpont Morgan* (New York, 1910)); the later date was proposed by E. A. Lowe, 'The Morgan Golden Gospels: The Date and Origin of the Manuscript', *Studies in Art and Literature for Belle da Costa Greene*, ed. by Dorothy Miner (Princeton, 1954), pp. 266–79.

made at short notice as a gift for some special occasion, perhaps a royal visit.

During subsequent centuries the Alcuinian recension suffered the same fate that befell other earlier attempts at purifying the Vulgate text. Its favour and reputation created a demand that outstripped the capacity of the writing school at Tours to produce accurate copies. Within a few generations, therefore, complaints of corruption of the text were heard once again, and other efforts were made to arrest the decline in purity of the text. One such effort was undertaken by Lanfranc, archbishop of Canterbury (1069–89), who is said to have worked at correcting all the books of the Old and New Testaments, and also the writings of the Fathers, *secundum orthodoxam fidem*.[1] None of his corrected manuscripts, however, is known to survive.

In the early part of the twelfth century Stephen Harding, third abbot of Cîteaux, made a similar revision. The four volumes of his corrected Bible, written in 1109, are still preserved in the public library of Dijon (MS. 12–15). He purged the text of a large number of interpolations, partly by collating good Latin and Greek manuscripts, partly with the aid of several learned Jewish scholars whom he consulted as to suspected passages in the Old Testament.

In the thirteenth century the task of clearing the Vulgate Latin text of scribal corruptions was taken up more fully and systematically by societies of scholars who united their efforts to produce 'correctories' (*correctoria*, or, more properly, *correctoriones*).[2] These were books listing variant readings, citing the testimony of Greek and Latin manuscripts as well as of Church Fathers. The principal *correctoria* are (1) the *Correctorium Parisiense*, produced probably about A.D. 1226 by theologians at the University of Paris; (2) the *Correctorium Sorbonicum*; (3) the *Correctorium* of the Dominicans, prepared under the auspices of Hugo de St. Caro about 1240; and (4) the *Correctorium Vaticanum*, prepared, it is thought, by the Franciscan William de Mara, who had spent nearly forty years in compiling the work. The last mentioned is

---

[1] So the *Vita* of Lanfranc by Milo Crispin, ch. xv (Migne, *PL* cl, col. 55).

[2] Cf. H. Denifle, 'Die Handschriften der Bibel-Correctorien des 13. Jahrhunderts', *Archiv für Literatur- und Kirchengeschichte des Mittelalters*, iv (Freiburg im Br., 1888), 263 ff., and 471 ff.; E. Magenot, 'Correctoires de la Bible', *Dictionnaire de la Bible*, ii (Paris, 1899), cols. 1022–6, and Gotthold Prausnitz, 'Über einige Bibelkorrectorien des 13. Jahrhunderts', *TSK* ciii (1931), 457–64.

the best of the *correctoria*, and it is cited by Wordsworth and White as *cor. vat.*

The custom of referring to chapters when quoting from the Scriptures was rare before the twelfth century.[1] The development of the lecture and *reportatio* method, however, must have shown the convenience of such a practice. The chief difficulty to its adoption arose from the lack of one generally agreed-upon system, for several systems of chapter-division from late antiquity and the early medieval period were current. The diversity was felt most acutely at the University of Paris, where the international provenance of the student body showed most clearly the absolute need for a standardized system of capitulation,[2] as well as a standardized canonical order of scriptural books.[3]

Uniformity was introduced amid such chaotic conditions by the Paris scholars, notably, as it appears,[4] by Stephen Langton (d. 1228), then a doctor of the University of Paris, afterwards archbishop of Canterbury and leader of the barons in the struggle which gave birth to the Magna Carta. His system, which is substantially the one in use today, was adopted in the earliest printed editions of the Vulgate. The chapters were at first subdivided into seven portions (not paragraphs), marked in the margin by the letters a, b, c, d, e, f, g, reference being made by the chapter number and the letter under which the passage occurred. In the shorter Psalms, however, the division did not always extend to seven. The present verse division of the New

---

[1] Cf. O. Schmidt, *Über verschiedene Eintheilungen der heiligen Schrift* (Graz, 1892), and A. Landgraf, 'Die Schriftzitate in der Scholastik um die Wende des 12. zum 13. Jahrh.', *Bib*, xviii (1937), 74–94.

[2] On the diversity of earlier chapter divisions, see the tabulation of differences in P. Martin, 'Le texte parisien de la Vulgate latine', *Mu*, viii (1889), 444–66, and ix (1890), 55–70, and especially the important monographs by De Bruyne, *Sommaires, divisions et rubriques de la Bible latine* (Namur, 1920); for a summary of part of De Bruyne's research, see Patrick McGurk, *Latin Gospel Books from A.D. 400 to A.D. 800* (*Les Publications de Scriptorium*, vol. v; Paris–Brussels–Amsterdam, 1961), pp. 110–21.

[3] For a list of 284 different sequences of scriptural books in Latin manuscripts, see Berger, *Histoire de la Vulgate*, pp. 331–9; and for a list of twenty different sequences of the Pauline Epistles in Greek, Latin, and Coptic manuscripts, see H. J. Frede, *Vetus Latina*, xxiv/2, 4te Lieferung (Freiburg, 1969), pp. 290–303, and id., 'Die Ordnung der Paulusbriefe', *Studia Evangelica*, vi, ed. by E. A. Livingstone (*TU* cxii; Berlin, 1973), pp. 122–7.

[4] On the ambiguous evidence supporting the attribution to Langton, see Beryl Smalley, *The Study of the Bible in the Middle Ages*, 2nd edn. (New York, 1952), pp. 222–4.

Testament was introduced by Robert Estienne (Stephanus) in his Greek and Latin New Testament published at Geneva in 1551.

3. NOTEWORTHY PRINTED EDITIONS OF THE VULGATE[1]

Johannes Gutenberg's invention of printing with movable type enabled books to be produced more rapidly, more cheaply, and more accurately. The first book printed by this method in Europe was the Latin Scriptures—the splendid Mazarin Bible (so called from the circumstance that the first copy which attracted attention in later times was that in the library of Cardinal Mazarin), issued at Mainz about 1456. But this edition, and many others which followed it, merely reproduced the current form of text, without revision or comparison with the best manuscripts.[2]

The first really critical edition of the Latin Vulgate was that published in 1528 by Robert Estienne (Stephanus) on the basis of three good manuscripts of the Paris recension. It was revised several times by himself, the fourth edition, in which seventeen manuscripts are quoted, being issued in 1540. On 8 April 1546, the Council of Trent not only decreed the Vulgate's authority but also required that it be printed 'quam emendatissime' (i.e. with the fewest possible faults).

No authoritative edition, however, was forthcoming until the accession of Pope Sixtus V in 1585. This Pope took up the matter vigorously, both by appointing a committee of scholars to undertake the work, and by devoting himself strenuously to the task of revision. Good manuscripts were used as authorities, including notably the codex Amiatinus, and in May 1590 the completed work was issued from the press in three volumes.

The edition, however, was short-lived. On 27 August Pope Sixtus V died, and on 5 September the college of Cardinals stopped all further sales, bought up and destroyed as many copies as possible, and made preparations for another edition. Although the pretext for this action was the inaccuracy of its printing, it is thought that the attack against the edition had been instigated by the Jesuits, whom Sixtus had offended by putting one of Bellar-

---

[1] Cf. Jean Gribomont, 'Les éditions critiques de la Vulgate', *Studi medievali*, 3rd ser., ii (1961), 363–77.

[2] H. Schneider, *Der Text der Gutenbergbibel* (*Bonner biblische Beiträge*, vii; Bonn, 1954), pp. 79–102.

mine's books on the 'Index', and took this method of revenging themselves.

In any case, another edition, differing from the 1590 edition in about 3,000 places, was issued by Pope Clement VIII on 9 November 1592, with a preface written by Cardinal Bellarmine. The misprints of this edition were partly eliminated in a second (1593) and a third (1598) edition (the latter contains also an Index corrigendorum).[1] The Clementine Vulgate remains the official Latin Bible text of the Roman Catholic Church to the present day.[2]

A noteworthy edition of the Vulgate New Testament was issued by Karl Lachmann in connection with his Greek New Testament (2 vols., Berlin, 1842–50). The two texts are printed together, the upper part of the page containing the Greek and the lower the Latin, with the authorities between them. For the Latin his authorities, though good, were limited to codex Fuldensis and codex Amiatinus—and the latter, unfortunately, was accessible to him only in an imperfect collation.

About 1877 John Wordsworth of Brasenose College, Oxford, began work on what was destined to become a definitive, not to say monumental, edition of the Vulgate New Testament.[3] After Wordsworth became bishop of Salisbury in 1885, the chief part

[1] In the twentieth century the widely used and dependable editions of the official Vulgate text prepared by A. Grammatica (Milan, 1914; 2nd edn., 1922) and by M. Hetzenauer (Regensburg and Rome, 1914) have been followed by several other editions, viz. those prepared by G. Nolli, *Biblia sacra Vulgata editionis iuxta PP. Clementis VIII decretum*, 4 small vols., of which vol. 4 contains the New Testament with the Greek text edited by A. Merk on facing pages (Rome, 1955); L. Turrado and A. Colunga, *Biblia sacra juxta Vulgatam Clementinam* (Madrid, 1957); and J. Leal, *Novum Testamentum DNJCh juxta editionem Sixto-Clementinam* (Madrid, 1960).

[2] Cf. A. Maichle, *Das Decret 'De editione et usu sacrorum librorum', seine Entstehung und Erklärung* (Freiburg im Br., 1914); W. Koch, 'Der authentische Charakter der Vulgata im Lichte der Trienter Konzilsverhandlungen', *TQ* xcvi (1914), 401–22; xcvii (1915), 225–49; 529–49; xcviii (1916), 313–54; A. Allgeier, '"Authentisch" auf dem Konzil zu Trent', *Historisches Jahrbuch der Görres-Gesellschaft*, lx (1940), 142–58; R. Draguet, 'Le maître louvaniste Dreido, inspirateur du décret de Trent sur la Vulgate', *Miscellanea historica in honorem Alberti De Meyer* (Louvain and Brussels, 1946), pp. 836–54; J. M. Vosté, 'La Volgata al concilio di Trento', *Bib*, xxvii (1946), 310–19; E. T. Sutcliffe, 'The Council of Trent on the *Authentia* of the Vulgate', *JTS* lix (1948), 35–42; and B. Emmi, 'Il Decreto Tridentino sulla Volgata nei commenti della prima (seconda) polemica protestanticocattolica', *Angelicum*, xxx (1953), 107–30, 228–72.

[3] *Novum Testamentum Domini Nostri Iesu Christi latine secundum editionem S. Hieronymi ad codicum manuscriptorum fidem*, 3 vols. (Oxford, 1889–1954).

of the work fell upon the shoulders of his young collaborator, Henry Julian White (born 1859). After twelve years of work the first fascicle, that containing the Introduction and the text of the Gospel According to Matthew, was published by the Clarendon Press (Oxford, 1889), while another nine years were required for the completion of the text of the four Gospels, together with elaborate *prolegomena* and an *epilogus*. The printed text is based upon the celebrated Northumbrian codex Amiatinus, written at Jarrow at the beginning of the eighth century. Textual evidence from nine other manuscripts (several of them fragmentary) is cited. In 1905 the Book of Acts was published.

Not long afterward the British and Foreign Bible Society opened negotiations with Bishop Wordsworth and with the Clarendon Press for the production of an *editio minor* of the Vulgate New Testament, the text of which was to be that of the Oxford critical edition. Since the text of the latter, however, had not been definitely settled beyond the Epistle to the Romans, the editors were compelled to determine the text for the remaining books by a rather summary induction from the manuscripts which experience had shown to be of the highest value. This convenient edition, the work chiefly of H. J. White, was published in 1911, and is furnished with an apparatus of variant readings from seven manuscripts of the whole New Testament, along with two others of the Gospels.[1]

In subsequent years fascicles of the larger edition appeared at irregular intervals. Volume ii, containing the Pauline Epistles, began with Romans in 1913 and closed with Hebrews in 1941. Volume iii, containing the Catholic Epistles (1949) and the Book of Revelation (1954), was edited by H. F. D. Sparks, assisted by A. W. Adams. Thus, after seventy-seven years (sixty-five years after the first fascicle had appeared) the undertaking was brought to a successful close.

It is not surprising that, in a project which extended for two-thirds of a century, a certain inner development in the edition can be detected. Wordsworth's primary interest was the creation of a critically established text, and only marginally in the history of the text. On the other hand beginning with the apparatus for Luke, White began to introduce, in ever greater number,

---

[1] For information concerning the relation of the *editio minor* to the *editio maior*, see H. J. White, *JTS* xiii (1911–12), pp. 207 f.

variant readings from the Old Latin manuscripts. From the Book of Acts onward increasing numbers of citations from the Church Fathers were introduced. In the case of certain Old Latin and patristic witnesses, the edition has been criticized for relying upon inferior and/or inaccurate editions.[1]

The most recently published critical edition of the Vulgate is that issued in 1969 by the Württembergische Bibelanstalt, under the supervision of both Roman Catholic and Protestant scholars.[2] The text is printed *per cola et commata* according to the ancient manuscripts and without punctuation. The editors have collated certain manuscripts not hitherto utilized by previous editors, such as N (fifth century) and S (first half of fifth century). The resulting text differs not only in many passages from the Clementine Vulgate, but also, here and there, from the large Oxford edition and from the manual edition of White (whose text differs from the Oxford edition only in 1 and 2 Cor., Gal., and Eph.). For Ephesians, Philippians, and the Catholic Epistles the editors have frequently adopted readings identified as Vulgate by the editors of the *Vetus Latina* against the Oxford edition. In agreement with the Oxford edition and the *Vetus Latina* the new edition rejects the *comma Johanneum* of the Clementine Vulgate. In 1 Thess. ii. 7 the editors adopt the reading *lenes* supported by certain Greek manuscripts, apart from any Latin evidence.

Finally, although nothing of the New Testament has thus far been issued, mention must be made of the work of the so-called Vulgate commission. In order to fulfil the mandate of Trent— which the Clementine edition did not really satisfy—and in view of important advances made since then by research into the history of the Bible text and its ancient versions, under the auspices of Pope Leo XIII a new critical edition of the Vulgate was planned. In 1907 Pope Pius X commissioned the Benedictine Order to undertake an extensive search, especially in Spain, for manuscripts hitherto unexamined and to produce as pure a form as possible of Jerome's original text. Since 1933 the work of

---

[1] For these and other criticisms of the edition, see Bonifatius Fischer, 'Der Vulgata-Text des Neuen Testamentes', *ZNW* xlvi (1955), 178–96; cf. also F. Lo Bue, 'Old Latin Readings of the Apocalypse in the "Wordsworth–White" Edition of the Vulgate', *VC* ix (1955), 21–4.

[2] *Biblia sacra iuxta Vulgatam versionem*, adiuvantibus Bonifatio Fischer OSB, Iohanne Gribomont OSB, H. F. D. Sparks, W. Thiele, recensuit et brevi apparatu instruxit Robertus Weber OSB, 2 vols. (Stuttgart, 1969; 2nd edn. 1975).

the commission has had its quarters, most appropriately, in the newly established St. Jerome abbey in Rome. Only the revision of a number of Old Testament books has so far appeared.

4. PROBLEMS CONCERNING JEROME'S WORK AS REVISER

Three main questions arise concerning Jerome's work as reviser of the New Testament. They are the following: (*a*) What was the type of Old Latin Text that Jerome made the basis of his revision of the New Testament? (*b*) Can we identify the type of text in the ancient Greek manuscripts that he says he consulted in correcting the Latin? (*c*) How much of the New Testament Vulgate is really due to Jerome's work?

(*a*) Obviously we cannot evaluate the work of Jerome as reviser of the New Testament until we know the form of the Old Latin text upon which he worked; only then can we estimate how much he contributed in revising it to produce the Vulgate. Wordsworth and White were among the first scholars to seek to identify the basic Latin text of the Gospels that was revised Jerome. They concluded, as was mentioned earlier, that by the sixth-century codex Brixianus (*f*) represents this type of text.[1] About four-fifths of Brixianus is identical with the Vulgate, and a large part of the remaining fifth in which the Vulgate diverges from it is explainable as corrections introduced by Jerome.

This theory of Wordsworth and White, however, was severely shaken by F. C. Burkitt, who showed that Brixianus is largely indebted to, and dependent on, the Gothic manuscript codex Argenteus.[2]

Another attempt to decide what form of Old Latin text underlies Jerome's work on the Gospels was made by Alexander Souter.[3] He examined the quotation of a score of verses (Luke xv. 11–32) which Jerome included in a letter to Pope Damasus (*Epist.* xxi. 4). The letter was written before Jerome finished his revision, and the length of the quotation is too long to be made from memory. On the basis of an analysis of this material Souter concluded that codex Vercellensis (*a*) reproduces the basic Old Latin text that Jerome revised.

---

[1] *Novum Testamentum Domini Nostri Iesu Christi latine secundum editionem sancti Hieronymi,* i (Oxford, 1889–98), 653 ff.

[2] 'The Vulgate Gospels and the Codex Brixianus', *JTS* i (1889–1900), 129–34.

[3] 'The Type or Types of Gospel Text used by St. Jerome', *JTS* xii (1911–12), 583–92.

Souter's conclusion, however, was unable to survive the criticism that H. J. Vogels levelled against it.[1] In the first place, he showed that Vercellensis and the quotation in the letter to Damasus are not as closely related as Souter maintained. Secondly, a comparison of the Lucan text of Vercellensis with that of the Vulgate reveals so many differences which cannot be explained as corrections as to exclude the former as the sole *Vorlage* of the Vulgate text.[2] Furthermore, Vogels found that three other Old Latin manuscripts approach the Vulgate text closer than does Vercellensis, namely Corbiensis II (*ff*²), Veronensis (*b*), and Vindobonensis (*i*). Vogels's conclusion is that the basic Old Latin text used by Jerome cannot be found preserved in any one manuscript.

Instead of seeking for a single manuscript, Vogels maintained that one must search for several manuscripts which together witness to the type of text lying behind Jerome's work of revision. He concluded that Jerome used now one type of Old Latin and now another type, represented chiefly in five Old Latin manuscripts which show least influence of the Vulgate, namely Vercellensis (*a*), Corbiensis II (*ff*²), Veronensis (*b*), Vindobonensis (*i*), and Monacensis (*q*). On the basis of these and several other witnesses Vogels attempted to reconstruct the manuscript Jerome used as the foundation of his revision. Vogels concluded that Jerome changed the text before him in about 3,500 places in the four Gospels,[3] either to correct evident mistranslations or to obtain stylistic improvements or to bring the text before him into harmony with the Greek.

If we compare these five codices with the Vulgate Gospels, we can learn something of Jerome's translational procedures. We learn, for example, that at the start of his work he was more exacting than during the later part of his work. Thus in Matthew he introduces changes which are of no importance and which he later neglects. For example, in the earlier part of his work he introduces very frequently the participial construction into the Vulgate, in accord with the Greek idiom, to replace the Old Latin finite verb. Later, however, he neglects to do this. Again, if

---

[1] *Vulgatastudien. Die Evangelien der Vulgata untersucht auf ihre lateinische und griechische Vorlage* (Münster in W., 1928), pp. 14–18. [2] Ibid., pp. 19–23.

[3] In the opinion of others, however, Vogels exaggerated the number of changes that Jerome made; cf. Fischer, 'Das Neue Testament . . .' (p. 334 n. 2 above), pp. 62 f.

we compare the parable of the Wicked Husbandmen in the three Synoptic Gospels (Matt. xxi. 33–44; Mark xii. 1–11; Luke xx. 9–18) we see that in Matthew Jerome consistently corrects the Old Latin *colonus* into *agricola* (both are translations of the Greek γεωργός); that in Mark he sometimes introduces the change and sometimes retains the Old Latin; and that in Luke he no longer bothers to make the change. Another example that shows Jerome's indifference to consistency is his translation of ἀρχιερεύς, which in Matthew is rendered *princeps sacerdotum*, in Mark *summus sacerdos*, and in John *pontifex*.

Such examples do not necessarily indicate that Jerome did his work with less care later in his task. It may be that he, like other translators, had, at the outset of his work, regard for negligible details which he later disregarded because they were unimportant. In any case, it is clear that Jerome did not submit the Old Latin to a thorough linguistic revision, but left much that approximated the Greek untouched. In comparing the Old Latin with the Vulgate we see how very few words he introduces into his version. He coins no new words for his revision, and has often eliminated neo-Latinisms coined by the Old Latin translators in imitation of the Greek.[1] He corrects, indeed, with care the errors or the barbarisms of the Old Latin, but retains any word or expression that comes close to expressing the Greek. At times he is meticulous in his alterations. Thus, John's Gospel usually places the enclitic με after the verb πέμπειν. Curiously the Old Latin texts reproduce this in the inverted order, *me misit*. Jerome has altered all but four of these instances, showing how much attention he paid to detail.[2]

By way of conclusion it can be said that, despite a certain unevenness and even an occasional error[3] in Jerome's work as

[1] Cf. G. Q. A. Meershoek, *Le Latin biblique d'après saint Jérôme* (*Latinitas Christianorum Primæva*, xx; Nijmegen, 1966).

[2] For other examples, see Vogels, *Vulgatastudien*, pp. 48–55.

[3] Here and there an erroneous reading in the Old Latin escaped Jerome's vigilant eye and so secured a place in the Vulgate; for example, Matt. v. 41, *vade cum illo et alia duo*, where the Greek says nothing of two 'other' miles; Mark i. 44, *principi sacerdotum* instead of *sacerdoti*; Luke ix. 44, *cordibus* instead of *auribus*; John vii. 25, *Hierosolymis* instead of *Hierosolymitis*.

On the other hand, in John x. 16 there is a notorious instance in which Jerome introduced an error where the Old Latin text is correct; in defiance of the meaning of the Greek original (μία ποίμνη) Jerome, succumbing (as it seems) to an advancing ecclesiasticism, replaced the Old Latin *grex* ('flock') by *ovile* ('fold'). In fairness

reviser, the general standard of his labours is high. The Vulgate represents the solid judgement of a competent and careful scholar, passed on textual materials as old (or in some cases older) than those available to textual critics today.

(*b*) The second problem confronting the investigator of Jerome's revision of the New Testament is to determine what type of Greek manuscripts were used in correcting the Old Latin *Vorlage*. Wherever Jerome changed the text without changing the meaning of the Old Latin we may be sure that he was influenced by the Greek copy before him. Thus there are several hundred passages in the Gospels where Jerome has altered the word-order of the Old Latin without changing the sense. Some of these alterations may indeed be due to the rhetorician's feeling for style, yet many of them may be used as an aid in identifying the type of Greek manuscript that was before him at that time.

Here, however, we meet with great diversity of opinion among modern scholars. To adopt a phrase of Jerome's, there are almost as many opinions concerning the textual character of these Greek manuscripts as scholars who have investigated the problem. Wordsworth and White concluded that he used the type of text represented by B, ℵ, and L.[1] According to von Soden, Jerome made use of a type of Greek that was the archetype of the three great recensions, *I*, *H*, and *K*.[2]

Vogels rejected these conclusions and held that Jerome utilized what modern scholars call the Koine or Byzantine type of Greek text.[3] Indeed, Vogels believed that Jerome was generally opposed to a certain type of reading. Inasmuch as many of the Old Latin readings that Jerome rejected are found only in codex

---

to him, however, it should be mentioned that in his *Comm. in Ezech.* xlvi. 19–20 (Lib. xiv. 46), Jerome writes of John x. 16: 'Et alias habeo quae non sunt ex hoc *atrio* . . . et fiet unum *atrium* et unus pastor'; 'hoc enim Graece αὐλή significat, quod Latina simplicitas in *ovile* transtulit.' Whether this implies that Jerome knew of Greek manuscripts which read μία αὐλή (as H. F. D. Sparks supposes, *The Bible in its Ancient and English Versions*, ed. by H. Wheeler Robinson (Oxford, 1940), p. 126 n. 2), or whether the existence of such a reading in Greek involves a 'most improbable conjecture' (as John Chapman declares, *JTS* xxiv (1922–3), 50 n.) need not be decided here.

[1] Op. cit., pars prima, pp. 655–72; cf. also Wordsworth and White, 'On the Question of What Greek MSS., or Class of Greek MSS., St. Jerome used in Revising the Latin Gospels', *Academy*, 27 Jan. 1894, pp. 83–4, where they are less certain that the *Vorlage* of the Vulgate can be ascertained.

[2] Hermann von Soden, *Die Schriften des Neuen Testaments*, I. iii (Leipzig, 1911), 1524–32.   [3] *Vulgatastudien*, pp. 75–8.

Bezae, Vogels concluded that either Jerome regarded the Western readings in codex Bezae to be wrong and therefore removed them from his Latin, or he did not know them. In other words, such Western readings were either rejected or unknown to a skilled textual scholar of the fourth century. In either case, it may be argued, Western readings cannot be valued very highly.

Vogels's analysis was subjected to criticism by both Burkitt and Lagrange. The former denied that Jerome consulted only one type of Greek text, and held that he depended upon at least two, one similar to that found in B and the other similar to that found in A.[1] Lagrange also believed that Jerome availed himself of more than one type of Greek text, but thought that, besides codices resembling A and B, Jerome was influenced by the type of text represented in F even more than by that in A.[2]

As for the text of the Acts of the Apostles, Wordsworth and White collected a series of readings which they interpreted as showing that Jerome's Greek text differed somewhat from any known to us.[3] After a close scrutiny of the readings, however, J. H. Ropes rejected their conclusion, holding that the Vulgate text of Acts is substantially the translation of an Old Uncial text of the general type of B, ℵ, A, C, 81.[4] Of these five manuscripts, the Vulgate agrees most often with A, but also preserves a certain number of Western readings derived from the Old Latin.

(*c*) At this point in the discussion of the Greek text underlying the Vulgate it will be appropriate to consider the question how much of the New Testament Vulgate is really Jerome's work. The commonly accepted opinion has been that, having finished his revision of the Gospels in 384, Jerome performed his work on the rest of the New Testament in a much more cursory manner, leaving much of the Old Latin as he found it.[5] During the twen-

---

[1] *JTS* xxx (1929), 408–12; see also ibid. xxvii (1926), 48–50, and xxx (1929), 411. [2] *Critique textuelle*, pp. 287 ff.

[3] Wordsworth and White, *Actus Apostolorum*, pp. xii f.

[4] *The Text of Acts*, p. cxxvii; and J. H. Ropes and W. H. P. Hatch, 'The Vulgate, Peshitto, Sahidic, and Bohairic Versions of Acts and the Greek MSS', *HTR* xxi (1928), 69–95, especially 73 ff. On the problem of the relation of Jerome's work to the Old Latin, Ropes follows closely Adolf Jülicher's study, 'Kritische Analyse der lateinischen Übersetzung der Apostelgeschichte', *ZNW* xv (1914), 163–88.

[5] Sometimes it is assumed that this part of the Old Latin New Testament had been less corrupted than the Gospels and Acts and so required less attention from Jerome; so, e.g., Chapman, 'St. Jerome and the Vulgate New Testament', *JTS*

tieth century, however, this view was vigorously opposed by several Roman Catholic scholars. The Benedictine Donatien De Bruyne proposed the astonishing thesis that what is commonly taken to be Jerome's Vulgate text of the Pauline Epistles is none other than the work of Pelagius.[1] The arguments advanced in support of this opinion are chiefly two: (a) in his commentaries, Jerome very frequently quotes with approval a form of the text of the Pauline Epistles which he himself rejected in the Vulgate; and (b) Pelagius not only cites the text of the Vulgate but knew Greek well enough to produce such a version. Next, the Dominican M.-J. Lagrange, while not accepting the role of Pelagius in the production of the Vulgate, argued in such a way as to lead readers to conclude that he denied that Jerome had any part in producing the Vulgate text of Romans and Galatians.[2] A few years later, the Jesuit Ferdinand Cavallera went beyond De Bruyne and denied that Jerome had any part in making the Vulgate text of Acts, the Epistles, and the Apocalypse.[3]

As would be expected, these views did not lack opponents who just as vigorously upheld the traditional view; notable among them were Buonaiuti,[4] Mangenot,[5] Chapman,[6] and Souter.[7] In

xxiv (1922–3), 282, and Tricot in A. Robert and A. Tricot, *Initiation biblique, introduction à l'étude des Saintes Écritures* (Paris, Turin, and Rome, 1939), pp. 266, 267.

[1] 'Études sur les origines de notre texte latin de saint Paul', *RB*, N.S. xii (1915), 358–92.

[2] 'La Vulgate latine de l'Épître aux Romains et le texte grec', *RB*, N.S. xiii (1916), 225–35; 'La Vulgate latine de l'Épitre aux Galates et le texte grec', ibid. xiv (1917), 424–50.

[3] 'Saint Jérome et la Vulgate des Actes, des Épîtres et de l'Apocalypse', *Bulletin de littérature ecclésiastique* (Toulouse), 1920, pp. 269–92.

[4] Ernesto Buonaiuti, 'Pelagius and the Pauline Vulgate', *ExpT* xxvii (1915/16), pp. 425–7.

[5] E. Mangenot, 'Saint Jérôme reviseur du Nouveau Testament', *RB*, N.S. xv (1918), 244–53. In his rebuttal of Mangenot, Lagrange says that it was his intention to show that Jerome had begun to use for his commentaries a text which approached that which he was to issue later as the Vulgate, but which had not yet been freed from as many Old Latin traits as the Vulgate; 'La révision de la Vulgate par S. Jérôme', *RB*, N.S. xv (1918), 254–7, and *Critique textuelle*, p. 503.

[6] 'St. Jerome and the Vulgate New Testament', *JTS* xxiv (1923), 33–51, 113–25, 282–99; 'Pelage et le texte de S. Paul', *RHE* xviii (1922), 469–81; xix (1923), 25–42.

[7] 'The Character and History of Pelagius' Commentary on the Epistles of St. Paul', *Proceedings of the British Academy*, 1915–16, pp. 261–96, esp. 264–74; 'Pelagius and the Pauline Text in the Book of Armagh', *JTS* xvi (1915), 105; and *Pelagius's Expositions of Thirteen Epistles of St Paul*; i, *Introduction*; ii, *Text and Apparatus Criticus*; iii, *Pseudo-Jerome Interpolations* (*Texts and Studies*, ix. 1–3; Cambridge, 1922–31), esp. i. 155–8.

opposition to De Bruyne, Chapman maintained that, at the time Pelagius wrote his commentaries on Paul, he knew no Greek and proposed no Greek variant readings. Furthermore, Souter found reason to believe that the scribe of MS. Augiensis cxix (see below) of Pelagius' *Expositions* had replaced the original lemmata with the text of Jerome's Vulgate. The chief proof that Jerome was then reviser of the entire New Testament, according to Chapman, is the uniformity of the principles according to which the Vulgate text as a whole differs from the Old Latin. In refutation of the argument based on the circumstance that Jerome approves in his commentaries what he rejects in his translation, Chapman argued that: (*a*) Jerome found reason to change his opinion on certain textual details during the interval between writing his commentaries and the time that Chapman thought he completed his final revision of the Vulgate (A.D. 391); and (*b*) in other cases Jerome was simply inconsistent in his literary work.

The most recent debate concerning the precise nature of Pelagius' text of the Pauline Epistles involves a statistical analysis of his quotations as transmitted in two divergent manuscripts of his works, namely MS. Augiensis cxix of the Landesbibliothek at Karlsruhe, on the one hand, and, on the other, MS. 157 of Balliol College Library, Oxford, which presents readings related to Old Latin witnesses. Nellessen[1] and Borse,[2] both students of Karl Theodor Schäfer,[3] hold that the Balliol manuscript presents the most reliable guide to Pelagius' text of the Pauline Epistles, a text which is not yet *the* Vulgate, but *a* vulgate text dating from the end of the fourth century, still characterized by Old Latin readings.

A contrary view, developed by H. J. Frede[4] and Walter Thiele,[5] is that the divergent text in the Balliol manuscript, instead of

---

[1] Ernst Nellessen, *Untersuchungen zur altlateinischen Überlieferung des ersten Thessalonicherbriefes* (*Bonner biblische Beiträge*, xxii; Bonn, 1965), and 'Der lateinische Paulustext im Codex Baliolensis des Pelagius-kommentars', *ZNW* lix (1968), 210–30.

[2] Udo Borse, *Der Kolosserbrieftext des Pelagius* (Inaugural-Dissertation; Bonn, 1966).

[3] Cf. Schäfer, 'Pelagius und die Vulgata', *NTS* ix (1962–3), 361–6.

[4] Hermann J. Frede, *Pelagius. Der irische Paulustext. Sedulius Scottus* (*Vetus Latina. Aus der Geschichte der lateinischen Bibel*, iii; Beuron, 1961), pp. 9–47; 'Der Paulustext des Pelagius', *Sacris erudiri*, xvi (1965), 165–83; and 'Epistula ad Colossenses', *Vetus Latina*, xxiv/2 (1969), 277–84.

[5] Walter Thiele, 'Zum lateinischen Paulustext, Textkritik und Überlieferungsgeschichte', *ZNW* lx (1969), 264–73.

being a stage in the development towards the Vulgate, is in reality Jerome's Vulgate text which has become contaminated by Old Latin readings. As a corollary, such an interpretation regards the Vulgate as too homogeneous and too systematic a revision to be the result of progressive modification.

In any case, it appears that the most that can be said with certainty is that the Vulgate text of St. Paul's Epistles came into being in the closing years of the fourth century at the latest. Its author is unknown, although he is to be identified with the man who gave to the Vulgate at least the Catholic Epistles and perhaps the whole of the New Testament apart from the Gospels. If it be asked why Jerome, having begun with the Gospels, did not continue with the rest of the New Testament, it may well be that Jerome's zeal for the *Hebraica veritas* led him to abandon, after the Gospels, his project to revise the entire New Testament.[1]

After this survey of research on the question how much Jerome had to do with the revision of the whole New Testament, we may return to investigations concerning the type of Greek text that lies behind the Vulgate in books other than the Gospels, whoever it was that was responsible for producing the version.

The most recent investigations of the textual complexion of the Vulgate text of the Pauline Epistles is summarized by Fischer as follows:

The Vulgate is a revision according to a Greek text which was predominantly Alexandrian, but which nevertheless presented also several readings of the Koine and the Western texts. The Latin *Vorlage* stood close to the D-type with a mixture from the later stage of the I-type (pseudo-Augustinian Speculum, MS. 86, and especially MS. 61).[2]

It thus appears that, as Lagrange suggested,[3] Jerome reacted against the predominance of the Western type of text, and deliberately sought to orientate the Latin more with the Alexandrian type of text.

For the Catholic Epistles of the Vulgate, there exists a type of text entirely distinct and of the greatest importance for the textual

---

[1] So Jean Gribomont, *La Maison-Dieu*, lxxiii (1960), 48 n. 27.

[2] Bonifatius Fischer, 'Das Neue Testament in lateinischer Sprache', in *Die alten Übersetzungen des Neuen Testaments, die Kirchenväterzitate und Lektionare*, ed. by K. Aland (Berlin and New York, 1972), p. 68; cf. also p. 21 n. 66.

[3] *Critique textuelle*, pp. 501 and 509.

critic. In a study of these Epistles, Harnack[1] translated the Vulgate of Wordsworth and White into Greek and then compared it with the Greek text of four modern critical editions, namely those prepared by Tischendorf, Westcott and Hort, B. Weiss, and von Soden. In so doing he identified thirty readings which, though not approved by a consensus of the four modern editions, Harnack believed to be the 'definitive' text. Although Harnack's reconstituted Greek text is interesting, it is (as Vogels[2] and Kümmel[3] point out) a text which never existed, for the Vulgate is a revision of the Old Latin according to the Greek, and it therefore contains variants which need not have existed at all in the Greek.

Harnack also applied the same method of investigation to the Epistle to the Hebrews.[4] Here he found that before Jerome's work of revision there existed at least two Latin translations of this Epistle, one represented today by the bilingual codex Claromontanus (*d*), and one which was used by Augustine and Capreolus of Carthage, of which considerable fragments exist today in the Freising codex (*r*). These two types he assigned to the early part of the third century, and thought that Jerome depended directly on the *d*-type, but also, in the interests of greater accuracy as well as the improvement of style, made use of the *r*-type. On the question whether Jerome consulted a Greek manuscript of Hebrews to aid him in his task, Harnack concluded that he did not, an opinion which has found few supporters.

One of the most valuable features of Harnack's textual studies was the stimulus he provided for other investigators. In particular there must be mentioned the work of E. Diehl[5] and Karl Theodor Schäfer.[6] The former, on the basis of a deliberately restricted induction of data, came to the conclusion that the Old Latin

[1] Adolf von Harnack, *Zur Revision der Prinzipien der neutestamentlicher Textkritik; die Bedeutung der Vulgata für den Text der katholischen Briefe und der Anteil des Hieronymus* (*Beiträge zur Einleitung in das Neue Testament*, vii; Leipzig, 1916).

[2] *Handbuch der neutestamentlichen Textkritik* (Münster in W., 1923), pp. 118–19.

[3] Werner G. Kümmel, 'Textkritik und Textgeschichte des Neuen Testaments, 1914–37', *ThRu*, N.F., x (1938), 316–17.

[4] 'Studien zur Vulgata des Hebraerbriefs', *SbBer*, 1920, pp. 180–201; reprinted with an extensive addition in *Studien zur Geschichte des Neuen Testaments und der alten Kirche*; i, *Zur Textkritik* (Berlin and Leipzig, 1931), 191–234.

[5] E. Diehl, 'Zur Textgeschichte des lateinischen Paulus'; I, Die direkte Überlieferung', *ZNW* xx (1921), 97–132.

[6] *Untersuchungen zur Geschichte der lateinischen Übersetzung des Hebräerbriefs* (*Römische Quartalschrift*, xxiii Supplementheft; Freiburg im B., 1929).

witnesses as a group depend upon the *d*-type, and that this type goes back to the early third century. The latter scholar, after thorough study, confirmed the twofold division of the Old Latin versions of Hebrews, but maintained that Jerome knew nothing of the *r*-type, which flourished in Africa and which was made perhaps by Augustine.[1] Subsequently, however, the Vulgate text was corrupted by mixture with the *r*-type.

Recent analysis of the Latin text of the Catholic Epistles discloses little that applies to all of them in the same way. Thiele's research[2] shows that the Vulgate of these Epistles is the result of an irregularly executed revision of a Latin *Vorlage* of the T-type (i.e. broadly European) by a Greek text which corresponded generally to that of codex Alexandrinus. The text of the Epistle of James exhibits markedly different characteristics from that of the other Catholic Epistles, particularly in the fluidity of the boundary between the Vulgate and the Old Latin texts. In 1 Peter the Latin *Vorlage* contained a considerable number of readings of the S-type (i.e. Spanish), while all that can be said of the basic Greek text is that it belonged to neither the Koine nor the type of text in Vaticanus.

The most important study of the Vulgate text of the Apocalypse is that by Vogels, who drew attention to the resemblances of the Vulgate to codex Sinaiticus.[3] At the same time he refused to admit that Jerome based his work on this type of text, for Vogels was convinced that the ancestors of Sinaiticus were influenced by the Old Latin. Lagrange also observed the close connection between the Vulgate of the Apocalypse and the Old Uncial type of text, and believed that not only did the Old Latin base of the Vulgate belong to this general type, but that so far as

---

[1] De Bruyne worked out this hypothesis still further in his 'Saint Augustin reviseur de la Bible', *Miscellanea Agostiniana*, ii (Rome, 1931), 521–606, holding that Augustine revised, for the Old Testament, the Latin text of the Psalms, Wisdom, the Heptateuch, and Job, and for the New Testament, the Gospels and the Pauline Epistles (including Hebrews, which he translated directly from the Greek). The work by C. H. Milne, *A Reconstruction of the Old Latin Text or Texts of the Gospels used by St. Augustine* (Cambridge, 1926), is an incomplete and ill-digested collection of data, some of which are irrelevant to the subject; see Burkitt's strictures, *JTS* xxviii (1927), 101–5.

[2] For a full account of the textual affinities of each of the Catholic Epistles, see Walter Thiele's introductory essay in *Vetus Latina*, xxvi/1, *Epistulae catholicae* (Freiburg, 1956–69), pp. 57*–101*.

[3] *Untersuchungen zur Geschichte der lateinischen Apokalypseübersetzung* (Düsseldorf, 1920), pp. 19 ff.

Jerome revised the Old Latin it was still further in the direction of the Old Uncials.[1] It is easy to see, therefore, why the Vulgate possesses an importance for the recovery of the text of the Apocalypse which the textual critic dare not overlook.

III. LIMITATIONS OF LATIN IN REPRESENTING GREEK

by Bonifatius Fischer[2]

In order to assess rightly the testimony of the Latin New Testament for the Greek text and its variants, it is necessary to pay attention to the history and evolution of the Latin Bible. It is rather evident that not all differences within Latin itself play a role here, but only the specific contact which has taken place with a Greek text. In this regard three things should be noted.

(1) A Latin text-type is normally but one witness for the Greek *Vorlage*, no matter how many single Latin witnesses represent the text-type. Consequently, the Fathers who quote the Vulgate are not independent witnesses for the Greek; *r* (64) and Augustine are only one witness in Paul's letters, just as *d* (75), *g* (77), and Lucifer stand together; similarly *g* (51) and Lucifer in Acts, *k* (1) and Cyprian in the Gospels, etc. This holds true also when the individual Latin witnesses are numerous. On the other hand, a Latin text-type cannot be ignored if only a single witness happens to be extant,[3] for in that case important text-types would be neglected; e.g. **K**, when represented only by *k* (1) or *e* (2) or Cyprian, or **F** in James, for which usually only manuscript *ff* (66) is available. Isolated witnesses must, of course, be examined most strictly in order to ascertain whether they really represent a text-type or whether they merely present an individual error. The larger the number of witnesses at one's disposal the greater is the certainty concerning the reading of a text-type. Only from this

---

[1] *Critique textuelle*, p. 615.

[2] Translated, with permission, from the concluding section (pp. 80–92) of Fischer's contribution 'Das Neue Testament in lateinischer Sprache', in *Die alten Übersetzungen des Neuen Testaments, die Kirchenväterzitate und Lektionare*, ed. by K. Aland (Berlin and New York, 1972), pp. 1–92. The bold-face letters signify text-types within the history of the transmission of the Latin Bible (cf. ibid., pp. 24–39).

[3] Such a proposal was made by E. C. Colwell in *Studies in the History and Text of the New Testament in Honor of K. W. Clark* (*Studies and Documents*, xxix; Salt Lake City, 1967), p. 8.

point of view is it in some measure justifiable to quote individual Latin witnesses in the apparatus of a Greek text. But the user of the apparatus goes astray if he values the cited manuscripts as a plurality of witnesses instead of merely an indication of the degree of certainty of the text-type in question.

(2) The Latin testimony relates to the place and time where contact with the Greek has taken place rather than to the place and time of the individual witness; hence it normally applies to the origin of the Latin text-type or of a variation within the type influenced by the Greek. When Gregory the Great quotes the Vulgate text of the Gospels, he witnesses to the Greek *Vorlage* of the revision undertaken by Jerome in Rome in A.D. 383; *r* (64) and Augustine witness to a Greek *Vorlage* not in North Africa at the time of Augustine but rather in upper Italy *c.* A.D. 370. The Latin is thus a witness for a second-century Greek text only if we can make contact with the original translation. The Old Latin testimony has a different weight in a Greek apparatus, one which wholly depends upon the nature of its text and which cannot be gathered simply from its individual witnesses.

(3) The development of the Latin version was influenced again and again through contacts with Greek texts. This caused not only varieties of readings, but also some varieties of renderings. If a second Latin text-type presupposes the same Greek *Vorlage* of a particular passage, this may be caused by the circumstance that the Greek text of the passage was not consulted afresh; then the second text-type is not a second witness for the Greek. But if the Greek really was consulted and the agreement ascertained, then we have a second independent witness for the same Greek text. On the other hand, the consultation of the passage may have been so superficial that a difference either was overlooked or was, for one reason or another, not taken into account; in such a case again we have no new witness for the Greek. Often it cannot be decided which of these cases has really occurred. When, however, through its choice of words the Latin text-type attains closer assimilation to the Greek, the second case is assured, and thus we have a second, independent witness for the same Greek text.[1] Likewise, this second case is demonstrable

---

[1] See the cautious judgement by H. J. Frede in *Vetus Latina*, xxiv/2, pp. 33, 34 f. (List V, 2) and 37 f. as well as 281 f., concerning the Greek *Vorlage* of the Vulgate.

when an original faulty translation has been corrected in the course of development;[1] sometimes, to be sure, it is difficult to decide whether what is involved is a misunderstanding by the translator or an inner Latin corruption. With names special care is necessary: only by reverting to the Greek do 'Caiphas' and 'Scarioth' become 'Caiaphas' and 'Iscariotes'; but with, e.g., 'Istrahel/Israhel' and 'Isac/Isaac' one cannot be certain whether the spelling reflects the original translation or whether it is a correction representing the Greek text. It must also be taken into account that Jerome occasionally changed the Latin text of the Gospels without having a corresponding Greek *Vorlage*.

How very closely the value of a Latin witness depends upon knowledge of the history of the Latin text is disclosed by comparing the view of Adolf Jülicher concerning the development in the Acts of the Apostles and Walter Thiele's view concerning the Catholic Epistles. Jülicher supposes one primitive translation from the Western text, practically represented by the African text, which was subsequently totally transformed according to the normal Greek text, but is preserved today only in four European text-types, each of which has again incorporated Western elements. So far as these do not arise from Latin contaminations or are new translations of the extant Greek manurcripts D and E respectively, we should have to judge all Latin text-types as being witnesses for the Western text quite independent of each other and from different times and places. Thiele, on the contrary, in the Catholic Epistles takes for granted Latin transformations of the African text with its Western readings. Accordingly all extant text-types constitute only one witness, representing usually the primitive translation, even where the African text itself is no longer extant but has been supplanted by European transformations.[2]

Certain limitations involved in the Greek and Latin languages

---

[1] 'Primitive misreadings and misunderstandings' is what A. V. Billen calls them (see his *Old Latin Texts of the Heptateuch* (Cambridge, 1927), pp. 161–5; examples are given of an original defect having been corrected by Cyprian, on the one hand, and, on the other hand, having a long after-life).

[2] One must first of all classify Latin witnesses like MS. 67 in the history of the Latin text before assessing their value as witnesses for the Western text of Acts. This is preferable to a direct comparison with the Greek, Coptic, and Syriac tradition, where the same must naturally be demanded for the Coptic and Syriac witnesses as for the Latin. This has not been sufficiently grasped by E. J. Epp in *JBL* lxxxiv (1965), 173.

themselves must be observed if one wants to evaluate rightly the witness of the Latin in terms of its Greek *Vorlage*. Above all, we must take into account the fact that the relation between writing and speaking was different in the ancient world from what it is in our modern time. Today the written form of a word is standard; in former times it was often only a rough and ready expedient for conveying sound in speaking, the main thing being the spoken word. Interest may have been focused on the correct pronunciation of a word, but never on its correct spelling—a circumstance that holds for Latin just as much as for Greek.

In summary we can therefore say that as concerns all the peculiarities and variants of sound and accidence of the Greek New Testament as dealt with in §§ 8–126 in Blass–Debrunner,[1] nothing can be concluded from the Latin versions. This also holds true for those cases in which the Greek text, though interpreted in a certain way, is nevertheless ambivalent in its written form as concerns word division, punctuation, accent (μένει/μενεῖ John xiv. 17), breathing mark (αὐτοῦ/αὑτοῦ), forms with or without iotas subscript (i.e. differences between nominative or dative), change of αι and ε in words like καινόν/κενόν (John xix. 41) or in certain forms like ἀπέχεσθαι/ἀπέχεσθε (1 Pet. ii. 11) and ἀποθέσθαι/ἀπόθεσθε (Eph. iv. 22), or of ω and ο (difference between indicative/subjunctive and present/future).

Although the Latin language is in general very suitable for use in making a translation from Greek, there still remain certain features which cannot be expressed in Latin. The aorist and the perfect tenses cannot be differentiated, so both ἐλάλησα and λελάληκα must be rendered *locutus sum*.[2] The same holds true for different forms of the imperative, e.g. αἰτεῖτε/αἰτήσασθε (John xvi. 24); also for the double negative (οὐκ ἐρωτήσατε οὐδέν John xvi. 23), which in Latin would be rendered by a literal translation,[3] as generally for the different forms of the Greek negative particle οὐ, οὐκ, οὐχ, οὐχί, μή, οὐ μή, μὴ οὐ. That *non* as well as *nonne* can be used for the interrogative οὐχί is involved in the inner

[1] F. Blass and A. Debrunner, *A Greek Grammar of the New Testament and Other Early Christian Literature*, translated and revised by R. W. Funk (Cambridge and Chicago, 1961).
[2] For the preference of the African text in rendering the Greek imperfect by the Latin perfect, see below.
[3] But in Latin two negatives produce an affirmative statement!

development of the Latin language. In Jas. iii. 3 εἰ δέ/ἴδε/ἰδοῦ iotacism also is involved.

In the Latin language there is no definite article. When it has a certain syntactical function in Greek, its absence in Latin is confusing and often necessitates various expedients. By way of examples one can refer to Acts xxiv. 25 τὸ νῦν ἔχον = *quod nunc adtinet* in the Vulgate, *nunc* in g (51); 1 Pet. i. 10 οἱ περὶ τῆς εἰς ὑμᾶς χάριτος προφητεύσαντες is rendered *qui de futura in vos gratia dei prophetaverunt* in text-type **C**, *qui de futura in vobis gratia prophetaverunt* in the Vulgate, *qui futuram gratiam in vobis prophetaverunt* and *qui venturam in vobis gratiam prophetaverunt* in two citations by Pseudo-Vigilius; in the following verse the two translations *qui in eis erat spiritus* of text-type **T** and merely *in eis spiritus* of the Vulgate both stand for τὸ ἐν αὐτοῖς πνεῦμα. As the examples show, the usual expedient in Latin is to render the article by a relative clause; the same can also occur where a clause would not be necessary, as in Col. i. 26 *quod absconditum fuit*.[1] Under special circumstances the article is occasionally rendered by the demonstrative pronoun, above all in the expression *hic mundus* or *hoc saeculum*. On the other hand, the New Testament very seldom employs the construction that is frequent in the headings of certain Psalms (*ipsi David* = τῷ Δαυίδ) in order to make the dative of indeclinable proper names recognizable.[2]

For the substantives that are *pluralia tantum*, a true plural is missing; other substantives normally form no plural (see below, section (d)). Latin verbs lack the perfect active participle and

---

[1] In Col. i. 26 this literal translation changes the Greek construction in the Latin, because everyone takes the following finite verb *nunc autem manifestatum est* to be the continuation of the relative sentence. See the different Latin translations in Hermann Josef Frede, *Vetus Latina*, xxiv/2, pp. 385 f., and, as a further example, the renderings of τοῖς ἔμπροσθεν (Phil. iii. 13). Concerning the complications which result by rendering the Greek article with *qui*, and specifically in connection with the present participle, cf. J. Svennung, *Untersuchungen zu Palladius und zur lateinischen Fach- und Volkssprache* (Uppsala, 1935), pp. 435 f.; S. Eklund, *The Periphrastic, Completive and Finite Use of the Present Participle in Latin* (*Acta Universitatis Upsaliensis, Studia Latina Upsaliensia*, 5; Uppsala, 1970), pp. 144–53.

[2] For the earliest stages and the beginnings of the Romance article, cf. the comments and copious literature in J. B. Hofmann and A. Szantyr's *Lateinische Syntax und Stilistik* (*Handbuch der Altertumswissenschaft*, 2. Abt., 2. Teil, 2. Band; Munich, 1963, 1965), pp. 191–4 (§ 106). For special consideration of the Latin biblical texts, see also F. Abel, *L'Adjectif démonstratif dans la langue de la Bible latine; Étude sur la formation des systèmes déictiques et de l'article défini des langues romanes* (*Beiheft zur Zeitschrift für Romanische Philologie*, cxxv; Tübingen, 1971).

present passive participle, deponents lack the entire passive system, and all verbs lack the middle. If therefore the Greek participial construction is retained, the time relationship must often be sacrificed; otherwise one must alter the construction. One can easily see this happening in the most diverse ways when one examines some verses in the edition of the *Vetus Latina* or in the Nestle–Aland edition of the Greek–Latin New Testament and observes the rendering of the participles.[1] Therefore, in Acts xxviii. 6 one cannot decide with certainty whether the *Vorlage* was μεταβαλόμενοι or μεταβαλλόμενοι for the *convertentes se* of the Vulgate or for the *conversi* in *g* (51). Especially difficult for the translator is the task of rendering a participle like ὤν, which is non-existent in Latin. For example, in Acts xxvii. 2 one finds various free renderings of ὄντος σὺν ἡμῖν Ἀριστάρχου, such as *erat autem cum nobis Aristarchus* (*s* [53]), *ascendit . . .* (*h* [55]), *navigabat . . .* (*g* [51]), and *perseverante . . .* (Vulgate). In James iii. 4 *esse* is preserved in the translation, and in spite of that we have for τηλικαῦτα ὄντα the renderings *quae tam inmensae sunt* (**S**), *tam magnae sunt . . . autem* (**F** [the participle is resolved into the main co-ordinate clause]), and *cum magnae sint* (Vulgate). The Latin translator encounters similar problems with the Greek infinitive, whether with or without the article and with or without a preposition; they are resolved with more or less skill.[2] We are

---

[1] The first possibility is that of changing participles in co-ordinate main clauses by connecting them with *et*; e.g., 1 Pet. ii. 20, κολαφιζόμενοι (κολαζόμενοι) ὑπομενεῖτε . . . πάσχοντες ὑπομενεῖτε, *punimini et suffertis . . . patimini et sustinetis* (text-type **C**), against *colaphizati suffertis . . . patientes sustinetis* (Vulgate), where the participles are introduced, paralleling the Greek. But this is an exact rendering only with *patientes*, since it happens to be a deponent, not with *colaphizati*, which should not be perfect tense. More complicated is the co-ordination of two participles and the connection of the following main clause with *autem* in the text-type **F** in James iii. 4 (see the edition at the passage). According to the context one can naturally employ *et* and *autem* as well as *atque, sed*, and other words for such a co-ordination. The other possibility is that of converting different kinds of subordinate clauses by means of *cum* (Jas. i. 12 text-type **V**; 1 Pet. i. 8 text-type **C**), *dum* (Jas. i. 12 text-type **T**), *quia, qua, quando* (all in different witnesses at 1 Pet. iv. 3), and most frequently in relative sentences, yet not exclusively when the article is present; the infinitive can also occur (1 Pet. iv. 4 text-types **T** and **A**). For different usages of the present active participle, which can lead to difficulties in both languages, cf. the entire book by Sten Eklund (p. 366 n. 1 above).

[2] The best way of expressing the final infinitive is to render it with *ut*; e.g. 1 Pet. ii. 15 **C** and **V**. Yet 1 Pet. ii. 5 can show still other possibilities, where we find for ἀνενέγκαι the following translations: *offerre, afferre, offerentes, offerte, ad offerendas, ut offeratis*. The reader who consults *Vetus Latina* xxvi/1 on 1 Pet. v. 8 will be at his wits end to decide which Greek reading the different Latin readings at the end of the

content to conclude with a combined example from Matt. v. 13, εἰ μὴ βληθὲν ἔξω καταπατεῖσθαι, which in the Vulgate reads *nisi ut mittatur foras et conculcetur* (cf. also Jülicher–Aland on the passage).

Normally there were difficulties with reciprocal pronouns such as ἀλλήλων, though in these cases the difficulties proceed more from the complicated development in Latin.[1] Certain Greek synonyms, such as καταγγέλλειν and ἀναγγέλλειν, οἰκεῖν and κατοικεῖν, are not precisely differentiated in Latin.[2] Especially great is the uncertainty with prepositions like ἐκ and ἀπό, ἀπό and ὑπό, ἐν and ἐπί, and in Latin prepositions like *a*, *de*, and *ex*.[3] Indeed, already in Koine Greek εἰς and ἐν generally overlap in meaning. The same development in vulgar and late Latin results in the favouring of the accusative (especially where it is differentiated from the ablative only by a final *m*) and its gradual development into the universal case which alone remains in the Romance languages. This uncertainty is not limited to instances

verse really presuppose. Almost as varied is the situation concerning infinitives with a preposition; e.g. James iv. 15 ἀντὶ τοῦ λέγειν ὑμᾶς, *et non dicitis* (S), *propter quod dicere vos oportet* (F), *pro eo ut dicatis* (V) (striving for the most exact rendering!), *quam ut dicatis* (Cassiodorus), *pro eo quod debeatis dicere* (Jerome). Only by chance is the rendering of Phil. i. 7 διὰ τὸ ἔχειν με more uniform, *eo quod habeam* (D, I, V), *propterea quod habeam* (A); cf. also James iv. 2 *propter quod* for διὰ τό. On the other hand, *ut* usually serves not only for the plain infinitive but also when it is connected with the preposition εἰς τό (Phil. i. 10 *ut* and *in hoc ut*) or πρὸς τό (Eph. vi. 11) instead of *ad* with the gerund and gerundive respectively. With certain verbs like *esse* or *posse* any other Latin translation is scarcely possible; e.g. Eph. vi. 11 πρὸς τὸ δύνασθαι ὑμᾶς, *ut possitis* (variant *ita ut possitis*); in Eph. vi. 13 it renders ἵνα δυνηθῆτε. If, as we shall see, the inference from a Latin preposition to the Greek *Vorlage* is generally uncertain, much more does this apply to prepositions before an infinitive in Greek; in fact, the question arises not merely which preposition was used, but whether any preposition at all stood in the *Vorlage* (e.g. Phil. i. 23 εἰς).

[1] Cf. J. B. Hofmann and A. Szantyr, op. cit. (p. 366 n. 2 above), pp. 176–8, and the literature mentioned there.

[2] Neither from *habitare* nor from *inhabitare* can one infer which one of two Greek words stood in the *Vorlage*; cf. H. J. Frede, *Vetus Latina* xxiv/2, p. 280.

[3] H. von Soden, *Das lateinische Neue Testament in Afrika zur Zeit Cyprians* (Leipzig, 1909), p. 155, says rightly: 'The range of meaning of a preposition differs very much in different languages, and it is not feasible to translate literalistically.' A clear example is ἐπί+the genitive, the natural translation of which is *super*; in temporal usage before proper names, however, it can scarcely be rendered otherwise than by *sub* (cf. Mark ii. 26; Luke iii. 2; iv. 27); and *in veritate* is a natural way of expressing ἐπ᾽ ἀληθείας. Cf. also A. V. Billen, *The Old Latin Texts of the Heptateuch* (Cambridge, 1927), pp. 150–5. This uncertainty in the rendering of prepositions is the more deplorable since they are so frequent and are words especially suitable for statistical studies; see the remarks by R. Morgenthaler, *Statistik des neutestamentlichen Wortschatzes* (Zürich, 1958), p. 160.

where actual variants are present in the corresponding Greek;[1] in other instances they certainly could have perished in the ongoing stream of the textual transmission.

In general the translation technique of the Latin Bible is very literal; nevertheless a certain freedom is maintained. The translator does not always render the same Greek word by the identical Latin word. On the whole, the development in the Latin goes from a freer translation to an ever closer correspondence to the Greek. For example, the Old African text-type favours *illius* etc. instead of *eius* for αὐτοῦ etc., and *fuit* instead of *erat* for ἦν.[2] When we try to classify the kinds of freedom involved in translation, we can differentiate the following:

(*a*) Word order.[3]

(*b*) Various particles: δέ is rendered not only by *autem* or *vero* but also by *sed, et, -que, igitur, itaque, ergo,* and *enim*; τε καί by simply *et*. Instead of *sed* or *at*, adversatives like *nam* can also stand for ἀλλά. *Enim* and *autem* are easily exchanged in Latin, so that reversions to δέ or γάρ are very uncertain. As regards the usage and meaning of the particles, the various developments of late Latin are to be observed.[4] Often inner Latin variations occur, such as *sed* and *sed et,* or *sicut* and *sicut et.*

(*c*) Various pronouns. In addition to the aforementioned forms of *ille* for αὐτός, one finds the intensifications of personal pronouns such as *me, memet, me ipsum, memet ipsum,* and the like. Personal pronouns that accompany the Greek infinitive are usually expressed in Latin by the form of the verb.

(*d*) Usage of singular or plural in some words, such as *lignum, caro,*[5] *aqua, ventus,*[6] *sanitas* (Acts iv. 30), and especially *manus.* Some neuter plurals change to feminine singular, as *gaudia* to Italian *gioia* and French

---

[1] The following are examples of such variation in Greek: ὑπέρ / περί with genitive (John i. 30); περί with genitive / ἐπί with dative (John xii. 16); ἐπί with dative / ἐν (John xi. 6); ἐπί with accusative / ἐν (John iii. 15); εἰς / ἐπί with accusative (John xxi. 4); πρός with accusative / εἰς (John xi. 32; Jas. iii. 3); πρός with dative / ἐν (John xx. 11); ἐκ / παρά with genitive (John xvi. 28) or ἀπό with genitive (John xi. 38).

[2] Cf. also the examples cited by Walter Thiele, 'Probleme der Versio Latina in den Katholischen Briefen', in *Die alten Übersetzungen des Neuen Testaments, die Kirchenväterzitate und Lektionare,* ed. by K. Aland (Berlin and New York, 1972), pp. 96–115.

[3] Cf. the statement by Adolf Jülicher, '. . . especially does [the Latin] abandon the word-order of the Greek innumerable times, even without adequate reason' (*ZNW* xv (1914), 178); cf. the examples cited by Thiele, op. cit., pp. 97 f.

[4] See J. B. Hofmann and A. Szantyr, op. cit., pp. 473–515.

[5] Cf. A. V. Billen, op. cit., p. 146.

[6] The plural *venti* in Acts xxvii. 7 (*s* [53]) could come from Acts xxvii. 4; see the example in section (*g*).

joie; therefore in biblical texts, for example, the inner Latin variants *opera/operam* or *retia/retiam* are not infrequent.

(e) The preference for stronger expressions shows itself, for example, in the use of *eicere* for ἐξάγειν or *pessimus* or *nequam* for πονηρός. Generally the Latin superlative can stand for the positive degree in Greek.

(f) Latin constructions, such as *intrare* (*ingredi*) with or without *in* with the accusative or the ablative, and *egredi* with or without *ex* or *de*, *adire* (*ad*), etc.

(g) Words or passages difficult to render: e.g. the word μέλλειν or the passage μὴ προσεῶντος ἡμᾶς τοῦ ἀνέμου (Acts xxvii. 7), which reads *cum venti essent contrarii* in *s* (53), *et non admittente nos vento* in *g* (51), and *prohibente nos vento* in the Vulgate. In Acts xxvii. 15 the Vulgate reads *data nave flatibus* for ἐπιδόντες over against the simple *laxantes* in *s* (53).

(h) Stylistic formation: e.g. ἔθεντο βουλήν (Acts xxvii. 12) is rendered *statuerunt consilium* in the Vulgate, *consilium fecerunt* in *g* (51), and *habuerunt consilium* in *s* (53).

(i) Special meanings of words in late Latin: e.g. *periculis* for θανάτων (2 Cor. i. 10); cf. also section (e).

(j) Minor additions suggest themselves, such as the auxiliary word *esse* or some object; such variations may originate in Greek, or in Latin, or in both languages.[1]

(k) Omissions of particular words which in Latin are scarcely rendered, like ἄν, or which, in view of their frequent usage, are contrary to Latin idiom, as is the case of μέν; or the omission of other words, especially in difficult or overloaded constructions.[1]

In such cases a Greek variant reading is ordinarily not to be inferred or reconstructed from the Latin. This is still more evident when it is a question of inner-Latin corruptions; e.g. Cyprian substitutes *ut suscitentur* for *ut iudicentur* in 1 Pet. iv. 6, and Augustine substitutes *et videte* for *et vitae* in 1 Pet. iii. 7. Such corruptions in Latin usually give good sense, a circumstance which has favoured their origin and preservation even when deviating far from the original; e.g. *descendentium* (Luke xix. 37) and *discumbentium* (John xxi. 12) for *discentium* = *discipulorum*. James iii. 7 is strange; there the error can have originated in Greek (ἄλλων instead of ἐναλίων) just as well as in Latin (*ceterorum* instead of *cetorum*).[2] Developments of syntax in late Latin, such as the previously mentioned preference for the accusative and the change

[1] For examples of (j) and (k), see Thiele, op. cit. (p. 369 n. 2), pp. 98 f.

[2] Cf. also Col. ii. 7 *abundantes/ambulantes* and περισσεύοντες/περιπατοῦντες, in all cases following after Col. ii. 6.

in meaning of different words (cf. section (*i*) above), need to be mentioned only in passing.

Finally, various peculiarities of phonetics as well as scribal peculiarities must be mentioned. The letters *ae* and open *e*, frequently written as *ę*, fall together phonetically; hence there are confusions between *caedere* and *cedere*, *maerere* and *merere*, *hebdomadae* and *hebdomade*, *novissime* and *novissimae*, etc. This confusion is to be observed particularly with names, especially when a similar phenomenon occurs also in Greek.

The sounds *au* and *o* indicate different linguistic orbits. Already in Cicero's time the patrician Claudius changed his name to Clodius because he wished to become a tribune of the people; consequently *claudus* and *clodus* stand side by side in the Stuttgart Vulgate.

The letters *b* and *v* are very often interchanged,[1] not only in Spain, where that is customary even today, but also frequently in sixth-century Italy; uncertainties between the perfect and the future tense occur in forms ending -*avit* or -*abit*, -*evit* or -*ebit*.

The letters *b* and *p* are sometimes interchanged. Thus, owing to a certain etymological manner of writing, *scribtum* and *scribtura* frequently appear in good manuscripts.

The letters *c* and *ch* also alternate in purely Latin words (*mihi* and *michi*); in foreign words such as *raca*, however, one cannot draw conclusions as to the orthography of the *Vorlage*.

The letters *d* and *t* change especially in the terminal sound; *inquid* is in late Latin a legitimate way of writing, as is *ad ubi* (which in *scriptura continua* is not differentiated from *adubi*) for *at ubi*.

Especially the closed *e* often exchanges with *i*, producing uncertainty between the present and the future tense in verbs of the third conjugation, such as *dicit* and *dicet*.

Thel etters *f* and *ph* are used entirely indiscriminately, especially in foreign words.

The letters *g* and *i* can sound the same between two vowels; that makes an error like *magis* instead of *maius* possible, and vice versa.

Since *h* had long since disappeared in the pronunciation of Latin, here the spelling is especially uncertain. Between vowels

---

[1] Stated more precisely, *b* between vowels is pronounced like *v*, while *v* as initial and after *r* and *l* is pronounced like *b*.

(especially *a* and *e*) *h* is likely to be inserted so as to prevent pronunciation as a diphthong *ae* (e.g. *Israhel*). One may question whether this is the only basis for *Iohannes*, or whether a remembrance of Jewish origins in the Hebrew comes into play here.

As regards *i*, the long *i* or double *ii* can be written with an apex not only in inscriptions but also in certain fifth-century manuscripts, where it appears as *í*. Consequently the converging of the perfect and the present tense yields forms like *abit* and *abiit*, as also the difference involving *venit* exists only in the pronunciation of the *e*.

One recalls that *m* had been practically silent at the ending of a word, and that it was often abbreviated in writing by means of a stroke; thus the confusion between the accusative and the ablative was furthered still more.

The letter *n* made itself perceptible after vowels only as a nasalizing of the vowel, which favoured confusions of the type *timens/times*, *ignorans/ignoras*, and *ignorantes/ignoratis*. Forms like *praegnas* and *praegnans*, as well as *formosus* and *formonsus* therefore stand side by side in Latin biblical texts.

The long *o* is also written as *u*, just as the short *u* can become *o*. *Epistula* and *epistola*, *parabula* and *parabola*, and *diabolus* and *diabulus* stand side by side. Therefore, *fulgur* ('lightning') and *fulgor* ('splendour') are often not differentiated, in spite of a different Greek *Vorlage*.

The letter *p* in the combination *-mpt-* is uncertain. Certain fourth- and fifth-century manuscripts prefer to write *promtus* instead of *promptus* or *temtatio* instead of *temptatio*. The existence of the alternative forms *volumtas* and *volumptas* gives rise to frequent confusion between the different words *voluntas* and *voluptas*.

Plain *p* also stands in place of *ph*, as in names like *Iosep*; that the letter was so pronounced is shown by the Italian 'Giuseppe'.

With *s* the uncertainty between single and double consonants is especially frequent.[1] There is hardly any difference in pronunciation since Latin knows only the voiceless *s*; therefore *abscisus* (from *abscido*) is identified with *abscissus* (from *abscindo*). When medial *s* is involved with other consonants, *t* is inserted, as in the form *Istrahel*. Prefixing a vowel to *s*+consonant at the

---

[1] This is true not only in Irish manuscripts, even though their special predilection for this kind of error cannot be denied.

beginning of a word is known to have lived on in the Romance languages; e.g. *Stephanus* becomes 'Estienne' ('Étienne') and 'Esteban'; on the other hand, through 'hyperurbanismus', instead of (*H*)*ispania* only *Spania* is written.

Confusion of *t* and *th* is usually harmless; in the case of proper names, however, one cannot draw conclusions concerning the orthography of the *Vorlage*.

Simple *u* also takes the place of double *uu* or *ú* with an apex; consequently, the form *manum* can also stand as the genitive plural.

The letter *x* coincides in pronunciation with *s*; one therefore encounters *milex* written instead of *miles* and *res* for *rex* as well as vice versa.

The letter *z* seldom takes the place of *s*, yet often replaces *di* before a vowel in forms like *zabulus* (instead of *diabulus*), resulting in possible confusion with *Zabulon*.

Some manuscripts designate the thousands by a stroke over the numerals, while others as a rule differentiate all numerals by a similar stroke;[1] according to the manuscripts, therefore, at Matt. xxvi. 53 the numeral $\overline{\text{XII}}$ means either *duodecim* or *duodecim milia*. Whereas in Greek the difference consists likewise only in the manner of making the stroke, here we have to do with parallel developments, a subject which will presently be discussed. Similarly, in the case of haplography and dittography of letters and syllables (arising from homoeoteleuton), we find assimilations of word-endings to the preceding or following word; cf. Rev. vi. 6 *animalium dicentem* (*dicentium*) or Rev. iv. 1 *vox . . . tamquam tubae* (*tuba*) *loquentis*.

As for uncertainties that are occasioned both by Greek and by Latin, we must mention instances where biblical texts in both languages exhibit parallel developments, so that one cannot decide whether the variants originated in Greek, or in Latin, or in both languages independently of one another. This uncertainty exists whether or not the corresponding variant is

---

[1] Old manuscripts normally place a full stop before and after the numeral, as also often before and after names, in order to signify in such cases the separation of words despite *scriptura continua*. Marichal, in an investigation of a Latin fragment of the third or fourth century, calls the overlining 'in principle irregular, but ancient and frequent' (see G. G. Archi, M. David, E. Levy, R. Marichal, H. L. W. Nelson, *Pauli Sententiarum fragmentum Leidense* (*Studia Gaiana*, iv; Leiden, 1956), p. 40).

actually attested in Greek. The case of εἰς and ἐν has already been mentioned. Some additional examples are the following:

(*a*) The omission or the addition of the auxiliary verb.[1]

(*b*) The omission or the addition of pronouns as subject;[2] the special case of personal pronouns with the Greek infinitive has already been mentioned.

(*c*) The adjustment of constructions in terms of congruence in gender and number, especially with two or more subjects and verbs.[3]

(*d*) The adjustment of tenses; e.g. Mark vii. 37 πεποίηκεν . . . ποιεῖ (πεποίηκεν W), *fecit . . . fecit* in the *Vetus Latina*. But the Vulgate has *fecit . . . facit*, even though most manuscripts make use of the same form *fecit*.

(*e*) The interchange of nouns and pronouns; cf. Col. i. 18 in the *Vetus Latina*, xxiv/2.

(*f*) The addition, especially by way of amplification, of titles in liturgical fashion; e.g. *Dominus noster Iesus Christus*. Generally to be kept in mind is the fact that confusions between *Dominus* and *Deus* in all forms (which are regularly shortened as *nomina sacra* and therefore little differentiated in written representation) are reflected in almost every text-type in at least some manuscripts.

(*g*) The influence of parallel passages when one cannot derive a Greek original from the different wording in Latin.[4] This kind of contamination occurs especially easily when the corresponding passage is given in the margin of the manuscript, as frequently occurs in the case of parallels in the Gospels as well as Old Testament citations throughout the entire NewTestament.

---

[1] Cf. Blass–Debrunner, §§ 127–8, and the example of 1 Pet. iv. 14 *beati estis*, μακάριοι+ἐστέ 255 1838.

[2] Cf. Blass–Debrunner, §§ 129–30.

[3] For *constructio ad sensum* and even stronger incongruences, cf. Blass–Debrunner, §§ 131–7.

[4] See the discussion of Walter Thiele, op. cit. (p. 369 n. 2), pp. 103–9.

VIII

The Gothic Version

I. THE INTRODUCTION OF CHRISTIANITY AMONG THE GOTHS AND THE TRANSLATION OF THE NEW TESTAMENT

THE Gothic[1] version of the New Testament is notable for several reasons. Besides the fact that we know who made it and the approximate date when it was completed, this version is of considerable cultural significance as being by several centuries the earliest surviving literary monument in a Teutonic language. The ancient Goths founded an extensive empire north of the lower Danube and the Black Sea. Two great tribes lived on opposite sides of the Dniester River: on the east the Ostrogoths and on the west the Visigoths. It was the latter who first became acquainted with Christianity, which they subsequently carried to their eastern kinsmen.

Already in the middle of the third century we hear of the success of evangelistic efforts on the part of Christian priests taken captive by the Goths following their invasions which ravaged Asia Minor during the reigns of Gallienus and the emperors who succeeded him.[2] According to Philostorgius,[3] in A.D. 264

---

[1] Gothic, as every linguist knows, is a dead language. Less well known is the fact that Gothic has been bequeathed to us in a limited corpus of texts which take up no more than roughly 280 pages. Except for fewer than ten pages, the texts are translations of various books of the New Testament, plus about three pages of Nehemiah, fragments of Genesis v, and Psalm lii. 2, 3 (two half-verses only). Well over half the total corpus consists of the Gospels, the text of which is preserved essentially in one source, the famous codex Argenteus at the University Library in Uppsala. For a convenient tabular arrangement of the several extant manuscripts of the Gothic Bible, see Elfriede Stutz, 'Das Neue Testament in gotischer Sprache', in *Die alten Übersetzungen des Neuen Testaments, die Kirchenväterzitate und Lektionare*, ed. by K. Aland (Berlin and New York, 1972), pp. 376 f.

A useful bibliographical tool for the study of Gothic is Fernand Mossé's 'Bibliographia Gotica; a Bibliography of Writings on the Gothic Language, to the end of 1949', *Mediæval Studies* (Toronto), xii (1950), 237–324. Supplements appeared in subsequent years: ibid. xv (1953), 169–83; xix (1957), 174–96 (prepared by James W. Marchand); xxix (1967), 328–43 (prepared by Ernest A. Ebbinghaus); and xxxvi (1974), 199–214 (Ebbinghaus).

[2] Sozomen, *Hist. eccl.* ii. 6 (Migne, *PG* lxvii, col. 949).

[3] Philostorgius, *Hist. eccl.* ii. 5 (ed. Bidez, p. 17 f.).

the grandparents of Ulfilas were deported to Dacia (modern Rumania) from Sadagolthina in Cappadocia. Ulfilas, born about 311, was probably the son of a Cappadocian mother and a Gothic father, who gave him a typically Gothic name, a diminutive formed from *wulfs*, meaning 'little wolf'.[1] Although Christianity had already made itself felt among the Goths (a Gothic bishop named Theophilus attended the Council of Nicaea in 325),[2] Ulfilas well deserves the sobriquet 'Apostle of the Goths'. At the early age of thirty, Bishop Eusebius of Nicomedia elevated him to the episcopate, and thereafter until his death in 381 (or 383) Ulfilas laboured among his people both as bishop and as temporal leader.[3]

Ulfilas' greatest accomplishment was the creation of an alphabet[4] (composed primarily of Greek and Latin characters, but including elements of Gothic runes) and the translation of the Scriptures into his native tongue.[5] In theology Ulfilas was

---

[1] The old historians wrote it Οὐλφίλας, Οὐρφίλας, Ulfila, Wulphilas, Vulfila. On the relation of the popular spelling Ulphila(s) with that involving an initial *w*, see Axel Koch, 'Zur Frage nach dem Namen des gotischen Bibelübersetzers', *Arkiv för nordisk filologi*, N.F. xxxvi (1924), 314–19. Cf. also H. J. Graf, 'Syrisch Aurophila(s) = Wulfila. Eine bisher unbekannte Nachricht über Wulfila', *Beiträge zur Namenforschung*, N.F. vii (1972), 79–80 (in Michael the Syrian's *Chronicle*); ibid., p. 290.

[2] Cf. Heinrich Gelzer, Heinrich Hilgenfeld, and Otto Cuntz, edd., *Patrum Nicænorum nomina* (= *Scriptores sacri et profani*, ii; Leipzig, 1898), p. 70. It is, however, not certain whether Theophilus was a Visigoth from north of the lower Danube or an Ostrogoth from the Crimea; see E. A. Thompson, *The Visigoths in the Time of Ulfila* (Oxford, 1966), p. 164.

[3] For a recent discussion of problems relating to the conversion of the Goths, see Piergiuseppe Scardigli, 'La conversione dei goti al cristianesimo', *Settimane di studio del Centro italiano di studi nell'alto medievo*, xiv (Spoleto, 1967), 47–84 and (discussion of the paper) 471–84.

[4] Cf. Joseph Boüüaert, 'Oorsprong en vorming van het gotisch alphabet', *Revue belge de philologie et d'histoire*, xxviii (1950), 423–7 and James W. Marchand, 'Über den Ursprung des gotischen þorn-Zeichens', *Beiträge zur Geschichte der deutschen Sprache und Literatur*, lxxvii (1950), 490–4. The 'working hypothesis' proposed by Siegfried Gutenbrunner, that Ulfilas merely revamped a previously existing Gothic alphabet ('Der Ursprung des gotischen Alphabets', *Beiträge zur Geschichte der deutschen Sprache und Literatur*, lxxii (1950), 500–8) is refuted by James W. Marchand ('Hatten die Goten vor Wulfila eine Schrift?' ibid. lxxxi (1959), 295–302).

For extensive bibliography on the Gothic alphabet, see Larry A. Viehmeyer, 'The Gothic Alphabet. A Study and Derivation' (Diss., University of Illinois at Urbana-Champaign, 1971). Viehmeyer concludes that the Gothic alphabet was based primarily upon common Germanic futhork (*Dissertation Abstracts*, xxxii (1971–2), 4597A).

[5] The commonly accepted traditions concerning the part played by Ulfilas

hospitable to Arianism (or semi-Arianism) ; how far his theological views may have influenced his translation of the New Testament, or whether indeed there was any influence, has been debated.[1] Perhaps the only certain trace of the translator's dogmatic bias is found in Phil. ii. 6, where reference is made to the pre-existent Christ in terms of being *galeiko guda* (= 'similar to God'), whereas the Greek ἴσα θεῷ should have been rendered *ibna guda*.

About a century after the death of Ulfilas the Ostrogothic chieftain Theodoric invaded northern Italy and founded a mighty empire, the Visigoths being already in possession of Spain. Since the use of Ulfilas' version can be traced among the Goths of both countries, it must have been the vernacular Bible of a large portion of Europe. Many manuscripts of the version were certainly produced during the fifth and sixth centuries in the writing schools of northern Italy[2] and elsewhere,[3] but only eight copies, most of them quite fragmentary, have survived until the present time. One of them, codex Argenteus of the early sixth century, was executed in *de luxe* format, being written on purple parchment in silver and some gold ink. Not only this feature but also the artistic style and quality of the workmanship suggest that the manuscript was made for a member of the royal household, perhaps King Theodoric himself.

as creator of an alphabet and as translator of the Bible have been (unsuccessfully) challenged by N. Akinian, who attributed the Gothic alphabet to St. Mesrop ('Der Ursprung des gotischen Alphabets' (in Armenian, with a German résumé), *HA* lxiii (1948), cols. 312–40; 441–3; 449–96; 621–32; cf. also *OC* 4th ser., iii (1955), 110–11), and by A. A. Leont'ev ('K probleme avtorstva "vul'filianskogo" perevoda', *Problemy sravnitel'noj filologii. Sbornik statej k 70-letijy člena korrespondenta AN SSSR V. M. Žirmunskogo* (Moscow–Leningrad, 1964), pp. 271–6). I owe this last reference to the kindness of Professor E. A. Ebbinghaus.

   [1] Cf. W. L. Krafft, *De fontibus Ulfilae Arianismi* (Bonn, 1860) ; Friedrich Kauffmann, 'Der Arianismus des Wulfila', *ZDP* xxx (1898), 93–112; H. A. van Bakel, 'Het Credo van Wulfila', *Circa sacra, Historische Studien* (Haarlem, 1935), pp. 86–113; Elfriede Stutz, *Gotische Literaturdenkmäler* (Stuttgart, 1966), pp. 5–7; and Thompson, op. cit., pp. 107–10.
   [2] A Gothic calligrapher named Viliaric (Wiljarith) lived and worked at Ravenna in the first half of the sixth century. For the suggestion that it was he who produced the famous codex Argenteus, see Jan-Olof Tjäder, 'Der Codex Argenteus in Uppsala und der Buchmeister Viliaric in Ravenna', *Studia gotica. . . . Vorträge beim Gotensymposion . . . Stockholm 1970*, ed. by Ulf Eric Hagberg (Stockholm, 1972), pp. 144–64.
   [3] James W. Marchand ('The Original Home of Our Gothic Manuscripts', *JEGP* lvi (1957), 217–19) and Elfriede Stutz (*Gotische Literaturdenkmäler* (Stuttgart, 1965), p. 21) think that several surviving Gothic manuscripts may have been the product of writing schools in the area of Toulouse in south-west France.

The Ostrogothic kingdom in Italy was of relatively brief duration (A.D. 488–554), and by the middle of the sixth century it was overthrown, succumbing in sanguinary battles to the power of the eastern Roman Empire. The survivors left Italy, and the Gothic language disappeared leaving scarcely a trace. Interest in Gothic manuscripts was completely lost. Many of them were taken apart, the writing scraped off, and the expensive parchment was used again for subject matter regarded as more appropriate to the time. Codex Argenteus is the only surviving Gothic manuscript (in addition to a double leaf of Gothic and Latin found in Egypt) that did not suffer this harsh treatment.

II. THE GOTHIC MANUSCRIPTS OF THE NEW TESTAMENT

The following is a list of all the extant manuscripts and fragments of the Gothic New Testament.

(1) The codex Argenteus contains the four Gospels written, as was mentioned above, on purple parchment in silver and some gold ink. Of the original 336 leaves, measuring 19·5 cm. wide and 25 cm. high (7⅝ by 9⅞ inches), 188 have survived—one leaf having turned up as recently as 1970 (see below). The order of the Gospels is the so-called Western order (Matthew, John, Luke, Mark), like that of codex Brixianus and other Latin Bibles containing an Old Latin type of text. Golden letters lend special splendour to the first three lines of each Gospel. They are also used for the beginnings of the different sections, as well as for the abbreviations of the names of the Evangelists in the four concordance tables at the bottom of each page. The silver ink, now dark and oxidized, is very difficult to read against the dark, mulberry-coloured background of the parchment. The photographic reproduction of the script of Matthew and Luke differs from that of the script of John and Mark, suggesting the use of different kinds of silver ink (that used to copy John and Mark had more silver in it than that used to copy Matthew and Luke).[1]

The fate of the 'Silver Codex' during the first thousand years of its existence is veiled in obscurity. At the middle of the sixteenth century Antonius Morillon, Cardinal Granvella's secretary, saw

[1] Cf. G. W. S. Friedrichsen, 'The Silver Ink of Codex Argenteus', *JTS* xxxi (1929–30), 189–92, and Michael Metlen, 'The Silver Ink of Codex Argenteus', *JEGP* xxxvi (1937), 244–5.

the manuscript in the library of the monastery of Werden on the Ruhr in Westphalia. He transcribed the Lord's Prayer and some other parts, which were afterwards published, as were other verses copied soon after by Arnold Mercator, the son of the illustrious cartographer, Gerhard Mercator. Subsequently two Belgian scholars, George Cassander and Cornelius Wouters, having learned of the existence of the manuscript, brought it to the attention of the learned world, and the Emperor Rudolph II, who admired *objets d'art* and manuscripts, took the codex to his favourite castle, the Hradčany in Prague. In 1648, the last year of the Thirty Years War, it was brought to Stockholm as part of the spoils of war, and presented to the young Queen of Sweden, Christina. After her abdication in 1654 her learned librarian, the Dutchman Isaac Vossius, acquired the manuscript, which then set out on a new journey when Vossius returned to his native land.

Chance now arranged for the manuscript to be seen by expert eyes. Vossius' uncle, Franciscus Junius (son of the Reformed theologian of the same name), had made a detailed study of the old Teutonic languages. To Junius it seemed to be an act of Providence that his nephew should provide him with access to this unique document, and from a transcript of the text made by a scholar named Derrer he produced the first printed edition of Ulfilas' version of the Gospels (Dordrecht, 1665).[1] Before the edition had come from the press, however, the codex had changed owners again, having been purchased in 1662 by the Swedish Lord High Chancellor, Count Magnus Gabriel De la Gardie, one of the country's most illustrious noblemen and patrons of art.

The precious manuscript was almost lost for ever when, during a blinding storm, the ship which was carrying it back to Sweden ran aground on one of the islands in the Zuider Zee. But careful packing protected it from the effects of salt water and the next voyage on another ship was completed successfully.

Fully aware of the historic worth of the codex, in 1669 De la Gardie gave it to the Library of Uppsala University, after having ordered the court goldsmith to prepare for it a magnificent

---

[1] For information concerning Junius' edition (which contained also an edition of the Anglo-Saxon Gospels; see pp. 452 f. below), as well as concerning the history of Gothic research in the Low Countries until the end of the eighteenth century, see R. G. van de Velde, *Die studie van het Gotisch in de Nederlanden* (Ghent, 1966), pp. 130–65.

binding of hand-wrought silver. Here it became the object of intensive research, and in subsequent years a number of editions of its text were made. From a philological point of view the definitive edition, with a beautiful facsimile, was produced in the nineteenth century by Anders Uppström (Uppsala, 1854; supplemented in 1857 by ten leaves of the Gospel of Mark which had been stolen from the manuscript between 1821 and 1834, but which were restored by the thief upon his death-bed).

In 1927, when Uppsala University celebrated its four-hundred-and-fiftieth anniversary, a monumental facsimile edition of the manuscript was produced. A team of photographers, using the most advanced methods of reproduction,[1] succeeded in producing a set of plates of the entire manuscript which are more legible than the faded parchment leaves themselves, while the editors of the edition, Professor Otto von Friesen and Dr. Anders Grape, then the Librarian of the University, presented the results of their investigations of the palaeographic characteristics and adventures of the manuscript through the centuries.[2]

The romantic story of the fortunes of this famous codex had yet another chapter added when, in 1970, in the course of the renovation of St. Afra's chapel in the cathedral of Speyer, the diocesan archivist Dr. Franz Haffner discovered in a wooden chest of relics a manuscript page which upon examination turned out to belong to the codex Argenteus. The leaf preserves the concluding verses of the Gospel according to Mark (xvi. 12–20).[3] A significant variant reading is the absence of Gothic representation of the participle περιπατοῦσιν in vs. 12. The presence of the word *farwa* ('appearance, form') in the same verse contributes an additional item to that which had been previously known of the total Gothic *Wortschatz*.[4]

---

[1] Cf. The Svedberg and Ivar Nordlund, *Fotografisk undersokning av Codex Argenteus* (*Uppsala universitets årsskrift*, matematik och naturvetenskap, no. 1; Uppsala, 1918).

[2] *Codex argenteus Upsaliensis jussu Senatus Universitatis phototypice editus* (Uppsala, 1927). Friesen and Grape also present their researches in Swedish in *Om Codex Argenteus, dess tid, hem och öden* (*Skrifter utgivna av Svenska litteratursällskapet*, no. 27; Uppsala, 1928).

[3] The underlying Greek text is reconstructed by Elfriede Stutz, 'Ein gotische Evangelienfragment in Speyer', in Kuhn's *ZVS* lxxxv (1971), 85–95, and 'Fragmentum Spirense—Verso', ibid. lxxxvii (1973), 1–15.

[4] For this and other grammatical and lexical features that are disclosed by the leaf, see, besides the articles by Dr. Stutz mentioned in the previous footnote, Piergiuseppe Scardigli, 'Unum Redivivum Folium', *Studi germanici*, N.S. ix (1971), 5–19; Oswald J. L. Szemerényi, 'A New Leaf of the Gothic Bible', *Language*, xlviii

(2) Near the beginning of the twentieth century a parchment leaf from a bilingual Gothic–Latin manuscript was discovered at Sheikh-ʿAbâde, a village close to the site of ancient Antinoë in Egypt.[1] Dating from the sixth century[2] it contained mutilated portions of several verses from the end of the Gospel of Luke (xxiii. 11–14; xxiv. 13–17). Unfortunately the fragment was completely ruined in 1945 by undetected seepage of water from the Lahn River into a bank vault in Giessen where it had been stored for safekeeping during the Second World War.[3]

All the other Gothic manuscripts are palimpsests, thought by many scholars to have been rewritten at the monastery of Bobbio.[4]

(3) In 1756 Franz A. Knittel discovered, and in 1762 published, four leaves of a codex at Wolfenbüttel (no. 4148), containing some forty verses of the Gothic text from Rom. xi–xv.

(4) The codices Ambrosiani, four in number, were discovered in the Ambrosian Library of Milan by Cardinal Mai in 1817. Two of them preserve portions of all the Pauline Epistles (only 2 Cor. is complete); a third contains parts of Matt. xxv–xxvii; and the fourth, parts of Neh. v–vii.[5]

(5) Codex Taurinensis consists of portions of four badly damaged leaves that once belonged to the same manuscript as one of the codices Ambrosiani. Found in 1866 by Reifferscheid in

---

(1972), 1–10; B. Garbe, 'Das Speyerer Codex-Argenteus-Blatt', *Indogermanische Forschungen*, lxxvii (1972), 118 f.; id., 'Die Verso-Seit des Speyerer Codex-Argenteus-Blatts', *ZDA* ci (1972), 325 f.; and H. Pollak, 'Weiterer Kommentar zum Fragmentum Spirense', *ZDP* xcii (1973), 61–5.

[1] Paul Glaue and Karl Helm, 'Das gotisch-lateinische Bibelfragment der Grossherzoglichen Universitätsbibliothek Giessen', *ZNW* xi (1910), 1–38; with a photograph. On Gothic–Latin bilingual manuscripts, see Henss (p. 386 n. 6 below).

[2] The date is assigned on the basis of Latin palaeography; cf. E. A. Lowe, *Codices Latini Antiquiores*, viii (Oxford, 1959), no. 1200.

[3] James W. Marchand, *JEGP* cvi (1951), 213–15.

[4] According to Charles H. Beeson ('The Palimpsests of Bobbio', *Miscellanea Giovanni Mercati*, vi (Vatican City, 1946), 162–84) at Bobbio Gothic texts were reused earlier than classical texts. Michiel van den Hout, however, thinks that the rewriting of the Gothic manuscripts was done before they came to Bobbio ('Gothic Palimpsests of Bobbio', *Scriptorium*, vi (1952), 91–3).

[5] The manuscripts have been most recently edited, with facsimiles, by Jan de Vries, *Wulfilae codices Ambrosiani rescripti epistularum evangelicarum textum goticum exhibentes* (Turin and Florence, 1936). Cf. also Charlotte T. Zietlow, 'The Gothic Text of Romans; a Decipherment, Edition, and Translation', Diss., University of Michigan, 1969 (see *Dissertation Abstracts*, xxx (1969), 2009A).

the binding of a manuscript at Turin, they preserve brief portions of Galatians and Colossians.[1]

No portion of Acts, the Epistle to the Hebrews, the Catholic Epistles, or the Apocalypse has survived. The standard edition of what remains of the Gothic Bible (with the exception of the recently discovered leaf of codex Argenteus) is that of Wilhelm Streitberg,[2] who provides a reconstruction in Greek of the presumed *Vorlage* translated by Ulfilas (see also the caution expressed below, p. 388).

III. CHARACTERISTICS OF THE GOTHIC VERSION

The Gothic version of the Gospels is severely literal. Ulfilas appears to have done his work of translation on a word-by-word basis, in which the order of the Greek is almost always retained, often against the native Gothic idiom.[3] Another marked characteristic of the style of the Gothic Gospels is the uniformity Ulfilas achieved in translating any word in the Greek by the same Gothic word, provided the sense allowed.[4] Thus, λέγειν appears as *qiþan* in 504 occurrences out of 508, and λαλεῖν is rendered by *rodjan* in all but two of the eighty passages where it occurs.[5] Furthermore, the translation technique that Ulfilas followed sought to represent in Gothic every word of the Greek text (except the definite article), even particles like μέν, δέ, ἄν, and others which, being peculiar to Greek, are unidiomatic in another language.[6]

At the same time it must also be observed that Ulfilas chose his

---

[1] Edited with facsimile by de Vries (see preceding footnote); cf. also Joan Mary Martin, 'The Gothic Version of Paul's Epistle to the Galatians: A Decipherment, Edition and Translation', Diss., University of Michigan, 1970 (cf. *Dissertation Abstracts*, xxxi (1970), 2368A).

[2] *Die gotische Bibel*; 1. *Der gotische Text und seine griechische Vorlage. Mit Einleitung, Lesarten und Quellennachweisen sowie den kleineren Denkmälern als Anhang*, 5te, durchges. Aufl. (Heidelberg, 1965). For a critique of passages where Streitberg has corrected the Gothic text, see Hans Pollak, 'Zur Überlieferung der gotischen Bibel', *ZDP* xci (1972), 49–58.

[3] So Georges Cuendet, *L'Ordre des mots dans le texte grec et dans les versions gotique, arménienne et vieux slave des Évangiles*, Iᵉ partie, *Les Groupes nominaux* (Paris, 1929), and Michael Metlen, 'What a Greek Interlinear of the Gothic Bible can Teach Us', *JEGP* xxxii (1933), 530–48.

[4] For such study there is now available J. R. Puryear's 'Greek–Gothic Lexicon and Concordance to the New Testament', Diss., Vanderbilt University, 1965.

[5] So G. W. S. Friedrichsen, *The Gothic Versions of the Gospels; a Study of its Style and Textual History* (Oxford, 1926), p. 23. For other examples of uniformity of rendering, see Friedrichsen, op. cit., pp. 15–68. [6] Ibid., p. 15.

renderings of individual words with care and discretion, so that his version possesses not a little individuality and colouring. For example, of the sixty-four Greek or Semitic words that have been taken over in transliteration into the Latin Vulgate, only twenty-eight occur in the Gothic version of the Gospels.[1] Thus in the individual renderings the version is faithful to Gothic vocabulary. In fact, based on an examination of the Gothic rendering of Gal. v. 7 and 8 and Luke iii. 23, Ulfilas has been judged 'to be a competent translator of Greek, more so than either Erasmus or Luther'.[2]

Concerning the question whether Ulfilas followed a systematic stylistic device for the repetition of words, sentences, syllables, alliteration, and homoeoteleuton, opinion is divided, Kauffmann,[3] for example, arguing affirmatively and Friedrichsen[4] negatively. In any case, however, it is agreed that his work is characterized by competence and faithfulness to such a degree that it is relatively easy, at least in the Gospels, to ascertain the wording of the underlying Greek.[5]

More than once the question has been raised whether Ulfilas was assisted in translating the Bible into Gothic.[6] As evidence that there was more than one translator some have pointed to the correspondence of two Gothic priests, Sunnias and Fretela, with Jerome[7] about the true readings of certain passages in the Psalter

---

[1] Ibid., pp. 35 ff. Cf. also C. Elis, *Über die Fremdwörter und fremden Eigennamen in der gotischen Bibelübersetzung* (Göttingen, 1903).

[2] So Hermann Collitz, 'Zwei Hapax Legomena der gotischen Bibel', [G. O.] *Curme Volume of Linguistic Studies* (Philadelphia, 1930), pp. 60–83.

[3] Friedrich Kauffmann, 'Der Stil der gotischen Bibel', *ZDP* xlviii (1920), 7–80; 165–235, 349–88; xlix (1923), 11–57.

[4] Op. cit., pp. 28 ff., and *The Gothic Version of the Epistles; a Study of its Style and Textual History* (Oxford, 1939), pp. 144 ff.

[5] For additional examples illustrating how slavishly literal the rendering is, and therefore how valuable the Gothic is for recovering the *Vorlage*, see Hans Steubing, 'Miscellen zur gotischen Bibelübersetzung des Ulfilas', *ZKG*, 4te Folge, lxiv (1952–3), 137–65.

[6] e.g. in the nineteenth century Eduard Sievers (*Encyclopaedia Britannica*, 9th edn., vol. x, s.v. 'Goths', p. 852) and J. Wright (*Primer of the Gothic Language* (Oxford, 1899)), and, more recently, Michael Metlen, who finds among the Gospels differences in the Gothic rendering of participles (*Does the Gothic Bible Represent Idiomatic Gothic?—An Investigation Based Primarily on the Use of the Present Participle in the Gothic Bible; with Some Corroborating Facts Drawn from Other Materials* (Abstract of Dissertation, Northwestern University, Evanston, 1932), pp. 22–3). Metlen's evidence, however, is interpreted differently by G. W. S. Friedrichsen, *The Gothic Version of the Epistles; a Study of its Style and Textual History* (Oxford, 1939), p. 259 n. 1.

[7] Jerome, *Epist.* cvi. An English translation is provided by Metlen in his article

some twenty years after the death of Ulfilas. Their queries, however, may be interpreted on the supposition that the priests were engaged on a revision of the Gothic Psalms.[1] In the case of the New Testament certain divergencies in translational technique can be detected when the four Gospels are compared with one another. Such a comparison reveals, according to a recent summary, 'a greater uniformity of vocabulary, a simplicity of diction, and a more primitive translation technique in Matthew, and to some extent in John, as against the other two Gospels'.[2]

Most scholars, however, regard the differences, at least those in the New Testament, as insufficiently marked to warrant the supposition of different translators. Rather, the differences in technique seem to be best accounted for either (a) as arising from the relaxation of meticulousness of method as the translator went on, or (b) as resulting from the greater influence in Luke and Mark of the Old Latin version and subsequent revision.[3]

IV. TEXTUAL AFFINITIES OF THE GOTHIC VERSION

The general textual complexion of the extant Gothic version is not difficult to determine. All investigators agree (e.g. Westcott and Hort,[4] von Soden,[5] Streitberg,[6] Nestle,[7] Streeter,[8] Kenyon,[9]

---

[1] 'The Letter of St. Jerome to the Gothic Clergymen Sunna and Friþila Concerning Places in Their Copy of the Psalter which had been Corrupted from the Septuagint', *JEGP* xxxvi (1937), 515–42. The view of Donatien De Bruyne that the entire 106th Epistle is a fabrication and that the two Gothic priests are, so to speak, phantoms ('La lettre de Jérôme à Sunnia et Fretela sur le Psautier', *ZNW* xxviii (1929), 1–13), has been sufficiently answered by Jacques Zeiller ('La lettre de saint Jérôme aux Goths Sunnia et Fretela', *Comptes rendus de l'Académie des Inscriptions et Belles-Lettres* (Paris, 1935), pp. 238–50).

[1] So, e.g., Ll. J. M. Bebb, 'The Gothic Version', Hastings's *Dictionary of the Bible*, iv (Edinburgh, 1902), 861.

[2] M. J. Hunter, 'The Gothic Bible', in *The Cambridge History of the Bible*; vol. 2, *The West from the Fathers to the Reformation*, ed. by G. W. H. Lampe (Cambridge, 1969), p. 344. Hunter's statement is based on data and analyses published by Friedrichsen.   [3] So, e.g., Hunter, ibid.

[4] *The Text of the New Testament in the Original Greek*; [vol. ii,] *Introduction*, 2nd edn. (Cambridge, 1896), p. 158.

[5] *Die Schriften des Neuen Testaments*, II. ii. 1469.

[6] Op. cit. i (1908), pp. xxxvii–xxxix.

[7] Eberhard Nestle, 'The Gothic Version of Ulfilas', *New Schaff–Herzog Encyclopedia of Religious Knowledge*, ii (1908), 134.

[8] B. H. Streeter, *The Four Gospels* (London, 1924), pp. 113–14. Streeter observes that according to tradition Ulfilas was consecrated as bishop at Antioch, implying that here he acquired the typically Syrian type of Greek text.

[9] *The Text of the Greek Bible* (London, 1937), p. 149.

Friedrichsen,[1] *et al.*), that it is basically a Syrian or Antiochian form of text which in the Gospels agrees generally with the group containing E F G H S U V, and in the Pauline Epistles with K L P, that is, with the text which Chrysostom used. It is, therefore, the oldest extant representative of the Lucianic or Antiochian type of text. At the same time not a few Western readings are embedded in this Antiochian base, many of which agree with Old Latin witnesses and some of which support isolated readings in codex Bezae.[2] In detailed analyses of the text-type of the Gothic version, von Soden was unable to find a precisely similar mixture of K and I readings, but he observed that its affinities seem closest to the K^a type.[3]

That there are, nevertheless, not a few primitive readings preserved in the Gothic is revealed by Friedrichsen's analysis of 157 readings of the Greek text of Luke, in which he tabulated only sixteen agreements with the Syrian or Koine type of text, as compared with sixty-eight agreements with pre-Syrian types of text, and thirty-two agreements with isolated uncial manuscripts against the Syrian type of text.[4] In the Pauline Epistles there is a curious coincidence of a Gothic reading which agrees with the Peshitta Syriac and the Syriac version of Eusebius' *Ecclesiastical History*, III. iv. 8, and with no other known witnesses. In 2 Tim. iv. 10, instead of the generally accepted reading Κρήσκης, one of the two Gothic witnesses reads *Krispus*, which is a confusion with Κρίσπος in 1 Cor. i. 14. In view of the absence, so far as we know, of direct influence from Syriac sources on the Gothic version, it seems best to regard the coincidence as due to chance.

The chief problem which confronts the scholar who wishes to go behind the extant Gothic witnesses concerns the origin of the Old Latin element. Did Ulfilas work with an Old Latin version at his elbow as well as a Greek text (so Lietzmann),[5] or was the

---

[1] G. W. S. Friedrichsen, *The Gothic Version of the Gospels; a Study of its Style and Textual History* (Oxford, 1926), and especially *The Gothic Version of the Epistles; a Study of its Style and Textual History* (Oxford, 1939), p. 257.

[2] For such readings see Paul Odefey, *Das gotische Lukas-Evangelium* (Diss., Kiel, 1908), p. 26.

[3] *Die Schriften des Neuen Testaments*, I. ii (Berlin, 1907), 1469.

[4] G. W. S. Friedrichsen, 'The Greek Text Underlying the Gothic Version of the New Testament. The Gospel of St. Luke', *Mélanges de linguistique et de philologie; Fernand Mossé in Memoriam* (Paris, 1959), pp. 161–84.

[5] Hans Lietzmann, 'Die Vorlage der gotischen Bibel', *ZDA* lvi (1919), 249–78, especially 276.

Latin tradition present already in a mixed Greek text which Ulfilas used (so Jülicher),[1] or has the Gothic version suffered Latinization in the course of its transmission (so Kauffmann,[2] Dobschütz,[3] Streitberg,[4] and Friedrichsen[5])? Since all of the manuscripts are later than the migration (A.D. 410) of the West Goths from the Balkans to North Italy, and since most of the manuscripts are connected with the Lombard region of North Italy, external factors appear to favour the view that many, if not most, of the Old Latin elements entered the Gothic version after it left the hands of Ulfilas. A fourth possibility, however, deserves to be investigated further—namely, how far Latin manuscripts may have been revised from the Gothic. Burkitt, for example, was able to collect a number of readings in the Old Latin manuscript Brixianus (*f*) which differ from both the Old Latin and the Vulgate and agree with the Gothic.[6] In short, there still remains not a little to be done in unravelling problems connected with the textual complexion of the Gothic version.[7]

After account has been taken of contamination of the Gothic text by Old Latin elements, a subsidiary problem remains in discriminating among variant readings in Greek witnesses. The Greek *Vorlage* in Streitberg's edition, for example, is especially open to question, as Friedrichsen points out,

when it happens that either of the alternative readings would have resulted in the same Gothic rendering, and when the readings differ

---

[1] Adolf Jülicher, 'Die griechische Vorlage der gotischen Bibel', *ZDA* lii (1910), 365–87, especially 379.

[2] Friedrich Kauffmann, 'Der Stil der gotischen Bibel', *ZDP* xlviii (1920), 7–80, 165–235, 349–88; xlix (1923), 11–57.

[3] Ernst von Dobschütz, 'The Bible in the Church', Hastings's *Encyclopædia of Religion and Ethics*, ii (1910), 585a; and id., *Nestle's Einführung in das griechische Neuen Testament*, 4te Aufl. (Göttingen, 1923), pp. 47–8.

[4] Op. cit. i (1908), pp. xl and xlv.

[5] *The Gothic Version of the Gospels*, p. 223, and *The Gothic Version of the Epistles*, pp. 40–3.

[6] F. C. Burkitt, 'The Vulgate Gospels and the Codex Brixianus', *JTS* xii (1911), 583–93. Friedrichsen also finds a relationship between the Gothic and the Old Latin manuscript *e*; cf. his article 'The Gothic Text of Luke in its Relation to the Codex Brixianus (*f*) and the Codex Palatinus (*e*)', *NTS* xi (1964–5), 281–90; cf. also Walter Henss's study, 'Gotisches jah und -uh zwischen Partizipium und Verbum finitum. Zur Herleitung der got. und altlat. Version des NT', *ZNW* xlviii (1957), 133–41.

[7] For a suggestive discussion of some of the problems, see Elfriede Stutz, *Gotische Literaturdenkmäler* (Stuttgart, 1966), pp. 34–42.

only by the presence or absence of a particle, or by the different renderings of introductory particles or conjunctions such as καί, δέ, οὖν, γάρ, the representation of which in the Gothic text especially of St. John seems to be subject to irresponsible variation.[1]

For further discussion and selected examples, see pp. 389 and 393 below.

There are several subordinate sources of information concerning the Gothic version. Eight palimpsest parchment leaves, divided between the Ambrosian and Vatican libraries, preserve a very early Gothic commentary on the Gospel of John. Since H. F. Massmann, the first editor of all eight pieces (Munich, 1834), the work has been called *Skeireins* ('interpretation, explanation', adopted from 1 Cor. xii. 10, xiv. 26). Owing to the unsatisfactory state of the palimpsest leaves, most investigators of the text have felt the need to propose here and there a wide variety of emendations—which by now number about fourteen hundred! The most recent edition of the material is that of William Holmes Bennett,[2] who, distrusting the multiplication of emendations, attempts to make sense of the text of the manuscript witness itself. As for the much-debated question whether the *Skeireins* is a native composition or a translation of some Greek or Latin commentary, Bennett inclines to the belief that 'the commentary, like the Gothic Bible, derived its Greek features from Greek and its Latin features from Latin. Assuming a Gothic original leaves most of the facts unexplained.'[3] The task of making a retroversion of the text of the *Skeireins* into Greek has been accomplished by Friedrichsen,[4] who provides many valuable philological and text-critical side-lights.

Another subordinate source of information concerning the Gothic version comes from the Veronese manuscript LI (49), which contains the Latin text of twenty-four homilies on the Gospels by the Arian Bishop Maximus. Most of these are furnished with marginal notes in Gothic, thought to be contemporary with

[1] G. W. S. Friedrichsen, *Gothic Studies* (= *Medium Ævum Monographs*, vi; Oxford, 1961), p. 2.
[2] *The Gothic Commentary on the Gospel of John: skeireins aiwaggeljons þairh iohannen, a Decipherment, Edition, and Translation* (New York, 1960).
[3] Ibid., p. 42.
[4] *NTS* viii (1961–2), 43–55 (leaves i–iv); x (1963–4), 368–73 (leaf vi); 499–504 (leaf viii); xvi (1969–70), 277–83 (leaves v and vii); cf. also id., 'Notes on the Gothic Bible', ibid. ix (1962–3), 44–55.

the Latin text of the fifth or sixth century, giving a brief indication of the subject of the homily. Twelve of these annotations are still more or less legible. Friedrichsen has discussed them in comparison with the τίτλοι of the κεφάλαια concerned, along with the relevant *capitula*.[1]

The ancient recension of the Pauline and Catholic Epistles, divided into thought-lines and attributed variously to Euthalius, to Evagrius, and even to Pamphilus, seems to have influenced, at least to some extent, the Gothic version. A preliminary study by James W. Marchand indicates the need for 'a thorough reinvestigation of our Gothic manuscripts with a view to determining with certainty their witness as to Euthalian matter'.[2]

Finally, caution should be observed in the use of Streitberg's reconstructed Greek text, which professedly represents the *Vorlage* of what remains of Ulfilas's version. The reconstruction is doubtless adequate for securing a rough and ready impression of the underlying basis of the version, but the textual critic must beware against taking the Greek as reflecting in every case exactly either the original Gothic or the Gothic text of the surviving manuscripts.[3]

V. LIMITATIONS OF GOTHIC IN REPRESENTING GREEK[4]

by G. W. S. Friedrichsen

The following notes are based on Friedrichsen's *Gothic Studies* (abbreviated *GS*).[5] This work covers the whole of Streitberg's

---

[1] *NTS* ix (1962–3), 39–43; corrected and supplemented by J. W. Marchand, ibid. xix (1972–3), 465–8.

[2] 'The Gothic Evidence for "Euthalian Matter" ', *HTR* xlix (1956), 159–67.

[3] In the second edition of *Die gotische Bibel* Streitberg himself expressed dissatisfaction with his Greek text: 'Der griechische Text ist unverändert geblieben. Hätte ich freie Hand gehabt, so würde ich ihn an manchen Stelle umgestaltet haben' (Vorwort (1919), pp. xi f., which remains unchanged in the 5th edition (1965, durchgesehnt von Ernst A. Ebbinghaus)). Cf. also the judicious comments of André Wilmart, 'Les Évangiles gothiques', *RB* xxxvi (1927), 46–71, esp. 51 f.

[4] Cf. also, chiefly from the standpoint of lexicography, B. T. P. Regan, 'The Differences between Greek and Gothic Vocabularies; an Analysis of the Use of Certain Words in the New Testament with a View toward Discovering the True Meaning of Corresponding Gothic Words in Ulfila's Gothic Bible', Diss., New York University, 1970 (see *Dissertation Abstracts*, xxxii (1971–2), 3981A) and id., *The Gothic Word; New Interpretations in the Ancient Biblical Translation* (Albany, 1972).

[5] *Medium Ævum Monographs*, vi (B. H. Blackwell, Oxford, 1961).

critical apparatus relating to Matthew, John, Luke, and 1 Corinthians, and should provide a representative sample of the Gothic renderings which could normally result from either of two Greek variant readings. In some passages, e.g. John xvi. 21, Luke v. 28, xviii. 7, xix. 22, one of the Greek variants is 'accepted' as the original with good reason, but these are nevertheless included in the following lists because the Gothic rendering could equally well represent either variant.

Gabelentz and Loebe[1] were well aware of this phenomenon and of the resulting doubt in deciding which of two Greek variant readings to adopt; cf. their *Prolegomena* (p. xxx); 'Inveniuntur quidem loca, ubi haereri possit, utram lectionem Gothus sequutus sit, quia eadem forma gothica duabus graecis respondet . . . aut particulae graecae diversae a Gotho non satis diligenter sunt distinctae, uti δέ et γάρ, δέ et καί, καί et οὖν; in his satius erit Gothum codices eos secutum dicere, cum quibus conspirare fere solet.' A note on the rendering of the Greek particles will be found below.

It is especially in the verbal forms that a Gothic rendering may represent two Greek forms of mood, tense, etc., which can be verified in the *Grammatik* of Gabelentz and Loebe and that of Streitberg;[2] here it is only necessary to record the fact. The Gothic, like the parent Germanic, has no future form, but uses the present tense with future meaning; thus κρίνει and κρινεῖ would both be rendered by the one form, *stojiþ*. Then the Gothic usually prefers the singular form of the demonstrative pronoun, even where the Greek has the plural, as in John xii. 16 ταῦτα δέ = *patuh þan*, and so in 2 Cor. xii. 19 τὰ δέ = *patuh þan*. If the Greek had the singular as a variant, it would be impossible, on linguistic grounds alone, to decide which variant the translator had before him.

To every item in the following lists the comment applies, 'The Gothic would equally well represent either of the Greek variants.' Further comment is provided where needed. The Gospels are cited in their Western order, Matthew, John, Luke, and Mark.

---

[1] H. C. von der Gabelentz and J. Loebe, *Ulfilas*, 2 vols., (Leipzig, 1843–6); available also in Migne, *PL* xviii, cols. 455–1560.

[2] W. Streitberg, *Gotisches Elementarbuch* (Heidelberg, 1920).

I. GREEK VARIANTS OF MOOD AND TENSE

Matt. vi. 5: προσεύχησθε . . . ἔσεσθε : προσεύχῃ . . . ἔσῃ] *bidjaiþ . . . sijaiþ*. The subjunctive would be required for either reading. See *GS*, p. 7.

Matt. xxvii. 1 : ὥστε θανατῶσαι : ἵνα θανατώσουσιν] *ei afdauþidedeina*. See *GS*, p. 9.

Matt. xxvii. 49: σώσων : σῶσαι] *nasjan*. See *GS*, p. 9.

John vi. 40 : ἔχῃ ; ἔχει] *aigi*.

John vi. 45 : (ὁ) ἀκούων : ἀκούσας] (*sa*) *gahausjands*. See *GS*, p. 18.

John vi. 58 : ζήσει : ζήσεται] *libaiþ*.

John vii. 27 : ἔρχηται : ἔρχεται] *qimiþ*. The Gothic indicative for the Greek subjunctive is here normal. See *GS*, p. 30.

John vii. 35 : εὑρήσωμεν : -σομεν] *bigitaima*, the Gothic subjunctive being appropriate in either case.

John viii. 12 : περιπατήσῃ : -σει] *gaggiþ*.

John x. 5 : ἀκολουθήσουσιν : -σωσιν] *laistjand*.

John xii. 18 : ἤκουσαν : ἤκουσεν] *hausidedun*. Collectives may take a singular or (as often) a plural verb. See *GS*, p. 31.

John xii. 40: (ἵνα) . . . ἰάσωμαι : ἰάσομαι] (*ei*) . . . *ganasidedjau*.

John xii. 40 : πεπώρωκεν : ἐπώρωσεν] *gadaubida*.

John xii. 47: κρίνω : κρινῶ (*judico, judicabo*) *stoja*.

John xii. 48: κρίνει : κρινεῖ] *stojiþ*.

John xv. 24 : πεποίηκεν : ἐποίησεν] *gatawida*.

John xvi. 13 : ἀκούσει : ἀκούσῃ] *hauseiþ*.

John xvi. 21 : τίκτῃ : τίκτει] *bairiþ*. See *GS*, p. 23.

John xvi. 21 : γεννήσῃ : γεννήσει] *gabauran ist*.

John xvii. 2 : δώσῃ : δώσει] *gibai*. See *GS*, p. 32.

John xvii. 24: ἔδωκας : δέδωκας] *gaft*.

Luke iii. 10, 12, 14: ποιήσωμεν : -σομεν] *taujaima*. See *GS*, p. 45.

Luke v. 28: καταλιπών : καταλείπων] *bileiþands*. The first reading is accepted; see *GS*, p. 54.

Luke vi. 34: δανείζητε : -ετε] (*jabai*) *leihwid*. See *GS*, p. 52.

Luke vii. 16: ἐγήγερται : ἠγέρθη] *urrais*. For the aorist, etc., see *GS*, p. 45.

Luke x. 19: (οὐ μή) ἀδικήσῃ : -σει] *ni gaskaþjiþ*. The first reading is accepted.

Luke xvii. 4: ἀφήσεις : ἄφες] *fraletais*. See *GS*, p. 46.

Luke xviii. 7 : μακροθυμῶν : -μεῖ] *usbeidands ist*. See *GS*, p. 46.

Luke xviii. 7 : ποιήσῃ : ποιήσει] *gawrikai*. The first reading is accepted. See *GS*, p. 53.

Luke xix. 22 : κρινῶ (*judicabo*) : κρίνω (*judico*)] *stoja*. The first reading is accepted.

2. VARIATION IN VOCABULARY

Matt. vii. 16 : σταφυλάς : σταφυλήν] *weinabasjo*. See *GS*, p. 9.

Matt. ix. 6 : σου τὴν κλίνην : τὸν κράβαττόν σου] *pana ligr peinana*. See *GS*, p. 9.

Matt. xi. 23 : Καπερναούμ : Καφαρναούμ] *Kafarnaum*, which is from the Latin, as is often the case with proper names.

Matt. xxvi. 71 : τοῖς ἐκεῖ : αὐτοῖς ἐκεῖ] *du paim jainar*.

John viii. 38 : ἃ (ἠκούσατε) : ὃ (ἑωράκατε)] *patei* (*hausidedup*). See *GS*, p. 13.

John x. 26 : ὅτι οὐκ : οὐ γάρ] *unte ni*. See *GS*, p. 14.

John xii. 32 : ἀπό : ἐκ] *af*. Cf. Luke ix. 54.

John xv. 14 : ὅσα ὅ] *patei*. Cf. John viii. 38. See *GS*, p. 22.

John xviii. 28 : πρωΐα : πρωΐ] *maurgins*.

Luke i. 37 : παρὰ τῷ θεῷ : παρὰ τοῦ θεοῦ : τῷ θεῷ] *guda*. The third reading has as good a claim as the first or second. See *GS*, p. 44.

Luke ii. 37 : καὶ αὐτή : καὶ αὕτη] *soh pan*. *Soh* may properly represent αὐτή, αὕτη, or ἥ. See *GS*, p. 45.

Luke iv. 41 : κράζοντα : κραυγάζοντα] *hropjandeins*.

Luke iv. 42 : ἐζήτουν : ἐπεζήτουν] *sokidedun*.

Luke vii. 11 : ἐν τῇ ἑξῆς : ἐν τῷ ἑξῆς] *in pamma afardaga*.

Luke vii. 24 : πρὸς τοὺς ὄχλους : τοῖς ὄχλοις] *du manageim*. Gothic *du* may represent the plain dative of the Greek. See *GS*, p. 52.

Luke vii. 44 : θριξίν : θριξὶν τῆς κεφαλῆς] *skufta*. Gothic *skuft* (O.N. *skopt*) means the hair of the head, and would probably not tolerate the addition of *haubidis*.

Luke viii. 5 : ἑαυτοῦ : αὐτοῦ] *seinamma*.

Luke viii. 34 : τὸ γεγενημένον : τὸ γεγονός] *pata waurpano*.

Luke ix. 52 : πρὸ προσώπου ἑαυτοῦ : πρὸ προσώπου αὐτοῦ] *faura sis*. See *GS*, p. 52.

Luke ix. 54 : ἀπό : ἐκ] *us*. Cf. John xii. 32.

Luke xiv. 21 : ὁ δοῦλος : ὁ δοῦλος ἐκεῖνος] *sa shalks*. The pronoun *sa* renders ἐκεῖνος but also the definite article.

Luke xv. 28 : ὁ δέ : ὁ οὖν] *ip*. The first reading is accepted, but *ip* = both δέ and οὖν : see below.

Luke xix. 41 : ἐπ᾽ αὐτήν : ἐπ᾽ αὐτῇ] *bi po*.

3. VARIATION IN WORD ORDER

John vi. 21: λαβεῖν αὐτόν: αὐτὸν λαβεῖν] *ina niman*. The first reading is accepted, but the Gothic could represent either. See *GS*, p. 18.

John xix. 13: τούτων τῶν λόγων: τῶν λόγων τούτων] *þize ⟨waurde⟩*. See *GS*, p. 32.

Luke i. 59: ἐν τῇ ἡμέρᾳ τῇ ὀγδόῃ: ἐν τῇ ὀγδόῃ ἡμέρᾳ] *in daga ahtudin*. Ordinals may stand before or after the noun. See *GS*, p. 37.

Luke xiv. 27: εἶναί μου μαθητής: μου εἶναι μαθητής] *wisan meins siponeis*. See *GS*, p. 53. This is not a matter of word-order, but of emphasis. Cf. next example.

Luke xiv. 33: εἶναί μου μαθητής: μοῦ εἶναι μαθητής] *wisan meins siponeis*. See *GS*, p. 42, and cf. preceding example.

Luke xv. 1: αὐτῷ ἐγγίζοντες: ἐγγίζοντες αὐτῷ] *imma nehiajandans sik*. See *GS*, p. 53.

Luke xvii. 25: πολλὰ παθεῖν αὐτόν: αὐτὸν πολλὰ παθεῖν] *manag gaþulan*.

The pronoun is not represented in the Gothic, therefore it is not possible on linguistic grounds alone to decide which of the Greek readings should be selected.

4. VARIATION IN QUANTITY

Matt. xxvii. 42: ἐπ᾽ αὐτῷ: αὐτῷ] *imma*. The first reading is accepted. See *GS*, p. 9.

John xviii. 39: βούλεσθε οὖν ἵνα: om. ἵνα] *wilwidu nu ei*. The presence or absence of ἵνα is not decisive: *ei* regularly introduces a final clause.

Luke xv. 21: οὐκέτι: καὶ οὐκέτι] *ju þanaseiþs*; but this could be from Luke v. 19 in the Gothic text. Also *ju = καί* in Mk. ix. 13, after Matt. xvii. 12.

Luke xvii. 3: ἐάν: ἐὰν δέ] *jabai*. See *GS*, p. 43.

Luke xx. 5: διατί οὖν: διατί] *aþþan duhwe*. See *GS*, p. 44.

APPENDIX I: PASSAGES FROM I CORINTHIANS

The material brought together in *GS* (pp. 65–89) for the Greek text underlying the Epistles includes fourteen passages in I Corinthians in which the Gothic rendering would properly represent either of the Greek readings given under Group I (77 readings, pp. 79–83).

i. 16: λοιπόν: τὸ λοιπόν] *pata anþar*.

v. 13: κρινεῖ: κρίνει] *stojiþ*.

vii. 5: σκολάζητε: σκολάσητε] *uhteigai sijaiþ*.

vii. 13: αὐτός: οὗτος] *sa*.

ix. 6: τοῦ μὴ ἐργάζεσθαι: om. τοῦ] *du ni waurkjan* (*du* would be needed in either case).

ix. 21: κερδήσω: κερδάνω] *gageig* ⟨*aidedj*⟩ *au*.

xi. 5: αὐτῆς: ἑαυτῆς] *sein*.

xii. 11: τὸ ἕν: ἕν] *ains*.

xiii. 3: καυθήσωμαι: -σομαι: καυχήσωμαι] *ei gabrannjaidau*.

xv. 7: εἶτα: ἔπειτα] *þaþroþ-þan*.

xv. 24: παραδῷ: παραδιδῷ] *anafilhiþ*.

xv. 50: κληρονομεῖ: -μησει] *arbjo wairþiþ*.

xvi. 17: τὸ ὑμέτερον: τὸ ὑμῶν] *izwarana*.

xvi. 17: οὗτοι: αὐτοί] *þai*.

APPENDIX II: THE RENDERINGS OF καί, δέ, οὖν, AND γάρ IN GOTHIC

These renderings have been treated, for the Gospels and the Epistles, in *GS*, pp. 90–111, to which the reader is referred for the copious details there provided. For the present purpose it will suffice to reproduce the summary table (p. 102), which shows that numerically the greatest amount of duplication exists in the Greek originals, either δέ or οὖν, of the Gothic *iþ* and *þan* (*aþþan*).

		δέ					οὖν		
	Matthew	John	Luke	Mark		Matthew	John	Luke	Mark
iþ	51	89	96	95 (Ep. 146)		0	10	0	0
þan	31	41	164	39 (Ep. 30)		1	36	4	1
aþþan	10	11	17	11 (Ep. 152)		0	1	2	2
þanuh	1	2	5	1		0	36	0	1
þaruh	0	3	16	4		0	28	0	0
nu	0	1	0	0		12	10	12	2 (Ep. 51)
jah	1	1	5	0		0	0	0	0

IX

The Old Church Slavonic Version

I. THE INTRODUCTION OF CHRISTIANITY AMONG THE SLAVS AND THE TRANSLATION OF THE NEW TESTAMENT

THE introduction of Christianity among the Slavic peoples is shrouded in the mists of semi-historical legends. According to an account dating three hundred years after the event, the first deliberate attempt to evangelize the Slavs was undertaken by the Emperor Heraclius (c. 575–641), who in this case seems to have been moved as much by political considerations as by religious zeal. In the sixth century hordes of a fierce Asiatic people, the Avars, appeared prominently on the frontiers of the Roman Empire. After they had ravaged the Balkan territories of the Eastern Empire, coming up even to the very walls of Constantinople, Heraclius considered it necessary to Christianize the Croats, who then would serve as a buffer preventing further incursions and predatory raids. Consequently, according to an account given by Constantine Porphyrogenitus (905–59), Heraclius decided to bring priests from Rome, and made of them an archbishop and a bishop and elders and deacons, and baptized the Croats.[1] Later in his narrative Constantine comments concerning the same emperor's attempt to evangelize the Serbs, again with the help of elders brought from Rome.[2]

How far one should give credence to Constantine's account has been widely debated. On the one hand, many historians reject his statements outright, since it is generally held that Byzantium and Rome were not on good terms and that, if Heraclius had desired to introduce Christianity into the Balkan peninsula, he would have sent Byzantine missionaries. On the other hand, it is necessary to recall—as Dvornik points out[3]—that Byzantium and

---

[1] *De administrando imperio*, chap. xxxi, ed. by Gy. Moravcsik and R. J. H. Jenkins (Budapest, 1949), p. 149.   [2] Ibid., chap. xxxiv, pp. 153–5.
[3] Francis Dvorník, 'Byzantium, Rome, the Franks, and the Christianization of the Southern Slavs', *Cyrillo-Methodiana. Zur Frühgeschichte des Christentums bei den*

Rome were not always quarrelling, and that, until A.D. 732, the whole of Illyricum was subject ecclesiastically to the Roman patriarchate. In any case, however, even if one accepts Constantine's statements concerning the missionary efforts of Heraclius, unfortunately we have no further information that would answer questions concerning the extent and success of such efforts at evangelization during the first half of the seventh century.

During the ninth century another mission to the Slavs was undertaken, and of this one, happily, history has preserved a somewhat fuller, though not entirely unambiguous, account. It is clear, in any case, that few events have had such a profound influence on the cultural development of so many nations as had the Byzantine mission to Moravia (in what is now central Czechoslovakia). Although the mission failed in the country for which it had been destined, the work eventually produced unexpected results among the Bulgarians, Serbians, Croats, and Eastern Slavs, and became the basis of the oldest Christian Slavic culture. Information concerning the Moravian mission has come down to us most fully in two Slavonic sources (the so-called Pannonian legends)[1] entitled *Vita Constantini* and *Vita Methodii*.[2] Although the broad historical reliability of these documents, composed, as it appears, not long after the events which they record, is now generally accepted, their limitations, arising from the vicissitudes of their transmission[3] as well as from their

Slaven 863–1963 (Slavistische Forschungen, ed. by M. Hellmann and R. Olesch, Band 6, Cologne–Graz, 1964), p. 88, and idem, *Byzantine Missions Among the Slavs; SS. Constantine-Cyril and Methodius* (New Brunswick, N.J., 1970), pp. 5 f.

[1] The traditional designation 'Pannonian' is due to a mistaken nineteenth-century theory that Old Church Slavonic was a Pannonian dialect.

[2] The standard edition of the two lives is that of P. A. Lavron, *Materialy po istorii vozniknovenija drevnejšej slavjanskoj pis'mennosti* (Leningrad, 1930; repr. in *Slavistic Printings and Reprintings*, ed. C. H. van Schooneveld, lxvii; The Hague, 1966). A French translation is given by Fr. Dvornik, *Les Légendes de Constantin et de Méthode vues de Byzance* (Prague, 1933; repr., with additional notes in English, by Academic International, Hattiesburg, Mississippi, 1969), pp. 349–93; a German translation with commentary, is given by Josef Bujnoch, *Zwischen Rom und Byzanz* (Graz–Vienna–Cologne, 1958), pp. 19–100; and a Latin translation is included in F. Grivec and F. Tomšič, *Constantinus et Methodius Thessalonicenses, Fontes* (Radovi Staroslavenskog instituta, 4; Zagreb, 1960).

[3] The manuscript tradition of the two *Lives* is very different. According to Horace G. Lunt, 'The *Vita Methodii* is known only in eight copies, all Russian, and none of the later seven (fifteenth–eighteenth centuries) offers readings that enable us to reconstruct anything of importance not found in the oldest, a clear

occasional lack of precision, leave the historian more than once in despair. When, however, the *Vitae* report details that agree with the ancient and shorter Latin account entitled *Legenda italica*, otherwise known as *Vita cum Translatione S. Clementis*,[1] most scholars feel fairly confident of their accuracy.[2]

From these sources the following can be gleaned concerning the 'Apostles to the Slavs',[3] as they came to be called. The two brothers were native Greeks of Thessalonica, Methodius being

and rather archaic copy from the end of the twelfth century. . . . The *Vita Constantini* has survived in some thirty copies of importance, none earlier than 1450. There are two major redactions, a South Slavic and an East Slavic one, the latter subdivided into a number of groups. Thus our text of VM is at least three hundred years removed from the original, and that of VC has undergone at least five centuries of copying and editing' ('The Beginning of Written Slavic', *SR* xxiii (1964), 213). Cf. also Natalino Radovich, *Le pericopi glagolitiche della Vita Constantini e la tradizione manoscritta cirillica* (Naples, 1968).

[1] The *Translatio*, as it is commonly called, describes Cyril's discovery of what were taken to be the bones of St. Clement of Rome, who, according to one legend, had been banished to the Crimea in the reign of Trajan and forced to work in the mines. The document is edited in the Bollandist *Acta sanctorum*, 9 Martii, vol. ii, pp. 20–2, and is available also in F. Grivec and F. Tomšič, op. cit. According to Paul Devos and Paul Meyvaert, the first edition of the *Translatio S. Clementis* was made probably as early as the middle of 879 ('La date de la première rédaction de la 'Légende italique', *Cyrillo-Methodiana* (see p. 394 n. 3 above), pp. 57–71). On the question of the bones of St. Clement, see Ambrosius Esser, 'Wo fand der hl. Konstantin-Kyrill die Gebeine des hl. Clemens von Rom?' *Cyrillo-Methodiana*, pp. 126–47.

[2] On the agreement between Eastern and Western sources, cf. V. Jagić in his classic essay 'Conversion of the Slavs', *Cambridge Medieval History*, iv (Cambridge and New York, 1933), 215–29.

[3] Much has been written in modern times concerning SS. Cyril and Methodius; a rich literature on their history and accomplishments is available in all Slavic languages, in German, French, Italian, and recently also in English. For Cyrillo-Methodiana scholars are fortunate in having two useful bibliographical tools: G. A. Il'inskij, *Opyt sistematičeskoj Kirillo-Mefod'evskoj bibliografii*, edited with additions by M. G. Popruženko and S. M. Romanski (Sofia, 1934), and M. G. Popruženko and S. M. Romanski, *Bibliografski pregled na slavjanskite kirilski iztočnici za života i dejnost'ta na Kirila i Metodija* (Sofia, 1935). In the former volume there is indexed in comprehensive fashion literature on the life, activity, and significance of the Apostles to the Slavs. The second volume is a survey of the sources for the life and activity of the two saints. The authors cite Slavic sources which are written in Cyrillic and the libraries in which these manuscripts are found, as well as works which treat of these sources. For literature on Cyril and Methodius since the date of publication of these two works, reference may be made to Emil Georgiev, 'Die bulgarische Literaturwissenschaft in den Jahren 1929–1939', *ŽSP* xvii (1940–1), 171–5, and to the bibliographical sections which appear regularly in *ByzŽ* and *Byslav*. Bibliographical guidance in the wider area of Slavic theological literature in general is supplied by *Slavorum litterae theologicae*, being *Acta Academiae Velehradensis*, i (1905), and succeeding volumes.

born, it seems, about the year 815, and his younger brother, christened Constantine, born in 826 or 827. Their father Leo was a high-ranking officer (drungarios), a rank nearly as high as that of colonel.[1] Since masses of Slavs had settled in the neighbourhood of Thessalonica, which was an important outpost of the empire and the second city after Constantinople, the two brothers were acquainted from childhood with the Slavic dialect spoken in the district. The younger brother, having completed his university education at Constantinople, took orders and became Librarian (*chartophylax*) of Santa Sophia. He also began to teach philosophy and theology, and eventually, as the successor of Photius at the University of Constantinople, came to be known henceforth as the Philosopher. He is said to have travelled into Mohammedan territory to debate with the inhabitants.

Later, about 860–1, and accompanied by his brother Methodius, Constantine engaged in a religious mission to the non-Christian Khazars in Russia, a Finno-Turkic tribe on the Sea of Azov. While they were spending some months in Cherson, the Byzantine possession in the Crimea, Constantine is said (*Vita*, chap. viii) to have acquired a thorough knowledge of the Hebrew language in preparation for his encounter with certain Jewish scholars of that district. His biographer likewise declares that after Constantine had had discussions with a Samaritan, he was able to learn enough of that language to read Samaritan books (perhaps of the Old Testament). How much of this account of Constantine's linguistic accomplishments should be taken *cum grano salis* is debatable; in any case, the *Translatio* is more moderate at this point and refers to his learning only one language in Cherson, that of the Khazars.

The author of the *Vita* also states that while in Cherson Constantine 'found there [a copy of] the Gospel and the Psalter written in "rus′skymi" letters and a man speaking that language'. Since we have no definite evidence of the previous existence of any developed Slavic script (although there may have been a runic script among certain Slavs),[2] this passage has given rise to quite diverse theories. Vasiliev argued that these letters were Gothic.[3]

---

[1] See Ihor Ševčenko, 'On the Social Background of Cyril and Methodius', *Studia palaeoslovenica* (Prague, 1971), pp. 341–51.

[2] Cf. V. Jagić, 'Vopros o runax u Slavjan', *Ènciklopedija slavjanskoj filologii*, iii (St. Petersburg, 1911), 1–36.

[3] A. A. Vasiliev, *The Goths in the Crimea* (Cambridge, Mass., 1936), pp. 113 f.

Vernadsky suggested a mixture of Armenian and Georgian characters adapted to the local Slavic dialect.[1] Vaillant[2] proposed an emendation which was endorsed by Grégoire,[3] elaborated by Jakobson,[4] and subsequently adopted by Lunt[5] and Dvornik,[6] namely that instead of reading роусьскыми письмєны ('Russian letters') the adjective should be altered slightly to read соурьскыми ('Syriac'). In support of the emendation is the circumstance that elsewhere in the manuscripts of the *Vita Constantini* exactly the same metathesis has occurred between *Suri* ('Syrians') and *Rusi* ('Russians').[7] Furthermore, the presence of Syriac books in Cherson at this time is probable in view of the circumstance that the Crimea was then under the ecclesiastical jurisdiction of Antioch, i.e. the Syrian Church.[8]

The chief work of Constantine and Methodius was still to be accomplished. Shortly after the middle of the ninth century a Moravian prince, Rostislav,[9] sent a petition to the Emperor Michael III ('The Drunkard') of Constantinople, for missionaries

---

[1] George Vernadsky, *Ancient Russia*, i (New Haven, 1943), 349–50.

[2] André Vaillant, 'Les Lettres russes de la Vie de Constantin', *RÉS* xv (1935), 75–7.   [3] Henri Grégoire, *Byzantion*, x (1935), 771.

[4] Roman Jakobson, 'Saint Constantin et la langue syriaque', *Annuaire de l'institut de philologie et d'histoire orientales et slaves* (Université libre de Bruxelles), vii (1939–44), 181–6. A decade later Jakobson reopened the questions whether Cyril may not have known Syriac (see also p. 424 n. 4 below) and, if so, whether 'he had looked into the Syriac *Diatessaron*' (*HSS* ii (1954), 69–70). Essentially the same point of view was taken by Karel Horálek in an article entitled, 'Sv. Kirill i semitskie jazyki', which he contributed to the Festschrift *For Roman Jakobson, Essays on the Occasion of his Sixtieth Birthday* . . . , compiled by Morris Halle *et al.* (The Hague, 1956), pp. 230–4. In fact Horálek went so far as to assert that Cyril knew various Semitic languages and sometimes used the Syriac and Aramaic (!) versions when translating the Gospels into Old Slavonic (see also the French summary of Horálek's article by A. Dostál in *Byslav*, xix (1958), 391). This problem, it need scarcely be mentioned, is quite different from the presence of Hebraisms in the Slavonic Old Testament; see Metropolit Ilarion [Ivan Ohijenko], 'Die Hebraismen in der altkirchenslavischen biblischen Sprache', *Münchener Beiträge zur Slavenkunde, Festgabe für Paul Diels* (1953), pp. 163–78. By a curious coincidence the Ostromir Lectionary represents the Cry of Dereliction (Matt. xxvii. 46) by *azav'tanii* (fol. 190) and by *azav'tani* (fol. 200), reproducing the Hebrew עֲזַבְתָּנִי (Ps. xxii. 2); see Pavel Vyskočil in *Slavia*, xxxii (1963), 395–7.

[5] Horace G. Lunt, 'The Beginning of Written Slavic', *SR* xxiii (1964), 217 f.

[6] Francis Dvornik, *Byzantine Missions Among the Slavs; SS. Constantine-Cyril and Methodius* (New Brunswick, 1970), p. 66.

[7] Chap. xvi (cf. Grivec and Tomšič, op. cit., p. 136, note on xvi. 8).

[8] My attention was called to this fact by Professor Lunt.

[9] The spelling Rastislav, preserved in *Vita Constantini* xiv, is South Slavic; since, however, Rostislav was a West Slav, the spelling with 'o', preserved in *Vita Methodii*, is to be preferred.

to instruct his people. The emperor, more noted for his dissipation than his piety, acceded to Rostislav's request, and, perhaps after consulting with the Patriarch Photius, sent Constantine, accompanied by his brother Methodius. Arriving in Moravia about 863, the brothers were received with honour and began the instruction of pupils who were confided to them. At this time, according to the *Vita Constantini* (chap. xv), Constantine translated 'the ecclesiastical order' (*crъkovnyj činъ*, perhaps 'order of service(s)') and some of the other liturgical books into Slavonic, and also started to train Moravians for the clergy.

Soon afterwards a controversy developed over the introduction of the Byzantine rite, sung in the language of the Slavs, into a land over which the bishops of Passau and Salzburg claimed spiritual sovereignty. The 'theological' base of the argument was that only Greek, Latin, and Hebrew had the right to serve as liturgical languages. Behind the cry of heresy in using any other language as the vehicle of worship, it is not difficult to understand that German priests would look with jaundiced eye upon a movement which would probably lead to Slavic independence of German ecclesiastical control. In spite of machinations against Constantine and Methodius, eventually two popes—Hadrian II and John VIII—gave approval for the use of the Slavonic vernacular in divine services. There was, however, one requirement that both pontiffs imposed: the Scripture lessons were to be read first in Latin and then in the Slavonic translation.[1]

---

[1] For the order of Pope Hadrian II, see his letter of 869 to Rostislav and two other Slavic princes, Svatopluk and Kocel (preserved in the *Vita Methodii*, chap. vii): 'Unus vero hic servandus est mos, ut in missa primum Apostolus et Evangelium legantur lingua Romana, postea Slovenica', *Monumenta Germaniae historica, Epistolae*, vi (Berlin, 1925), 764; see also Ph. Jaffé, *Regesta pontificum romanorum* . . ., ed. sec.,i (Leipzig, 1885), 368 (no. 2924). The genuineness of this letter has been doubted, e.g. by Ernst Perels (*Mon. Germ. hist., Ep.*, vi, p. 763 n. 1), Gerhard Ficker and Heinrich Hermelink (*Das Mittelalter*, 2te Aufl. (Tübingen, 1929), p. 54), and V. Sl. Kiselkov, 'Kiril i Metodij v Rim i papa Adrian II', *Istoričeski Pregled*, iii (1946–7), 98–105). On the other hand, Milko Kos ('O pismu papeža Hadriana II knezom Rastislava, Svetopluki in Koclju', *Razprave Slovenska akademija znanosti in umetnosti* (Ljubljana), ii. 12 (1944), 269–301), F. Grivec, ('Sláva na výsostech Bohu', *Slovanské studie; Sbírka statí, věnovaných . . . J. Vajsovi k uctění jeho životního díla* (Prague, 1948), pp. 45–51), and Bogo Grafenauer ('War der Brief Hadrians II. an die slavischen Fürsten: echt, verfälscht oder Fälschung?' *Cyrillo-Methodianischen Fragen, Slavische Philologie und Altertumskunde. Acta Congressus historiae Slavicae Salisburgensis (Annales Instituti Slavici*, I/4; Wiesbaden, 1968), pp. 63–77) argue on the basis of certain characteristics of diplomatic style found in contemporary papal documents that the *Vita Methodii* preserves a more or less faithful abridgement of

After a sojourn in Moravia, which the *Vita Constantini* declares to have been forty months and the *Translatio* four and a half years, the two brothers set out for Rome. According to both *Vitae* as well as the *Translatio*, Constantine fell ill while at Rome and, sensing that his end was approaching, took monastic vows and assumed the name Cyril. Fifty days later he died (14 February 869) and was buried in the basilica dedicated to St. Clement. Subsequently Methodius returned to Pannonia (in what is now western Hungary) as archbishop of Sirmium (including, probably, Moravia as well), a province which had lapsed at the time of the Avar invasion in the sixth century. Methodius' new authority came into direct conflict with the Bavarian hierarchy, and the ensuing polemics resulted in his imprisonment for two and a half years.[1] In 863 the Pope (now John VIII), having become aware of the situation, saw to it that Methodius was released, and the Slavonic liturgy was reinstated in Moravia. Upon the death of Methodius in 885, however, the German clergy renewed their efforts to forbid the use of the Slavonic liturgy in Moravia, and the disciples of Methodius were brutally expelled from the country and in some instances sold into slavery. Thus, extinguished in its first home, Slavonic Christianity was carried by these refugees to other Slavic lands.

a genuine letter of Hadrian II. In any case, however, the information which it supplies regarding the use of the two languages in the reading of the Scriptures must be correct; if it were not, the falsehood would be so obvious to anyone who attended the Liturgy in Slavic lands as to discredit the letter totally. The only uncertainty, if the letter be spurious, concerns the date at which the custom of the two-fold reading was instituted.

For the order of Pope John VIII (which, in spite of the scepticism of, e.g., Leopold K. Goetz, *Geschichte der Slavenapostel Konstantinus (Kyrillus) und Methodius* (Gotha, 1897), pp. 58–71, is undoubtedly genuine, cf. V. Jagić in *The Cambridge Medieval History*, iv (1923), 228), see his letter of 880 to Svatopluk: 'Jubemus tamen ut in omnibus ecclesiis terrae vestrae propter majorem honorificentiam, Evangelium Latine legatur, et postmodum Sclavonica lingua translatum in auribus populi Latina verba non intelligentis, annuntietur sicut in quibusdam ecclesiis fieri videtur', Migne, *PL*, cxxvi, col. 906c, and *Mon. Germ. hist., Ep.*, vii. 222. For further texts and bibliography, see Heinz Lowe, *Der Streit um Methodius. Quellen zu den nationalkirchlichen Bestrebungen in Mähren und Pannonien im 9. Jahrhundert* (Köln, 1947), and F. Grivec, *Konstantin und Method. Lehrer der Slaven* (Wiesbaden, 1960), pp. 241–61.

[1] Cf. P. J. Alexander, 'The Papacy, the Bavarian Clergy, and the Slavonic Apostles', *SEER* xx (1941), 266–93; A. Ziegler, 'Der Slawenapostel Methodius im Schwabenlande', *Dillingen und Schwaben, Festschrift zur Vierhundertjahrfeier der Universität Dillingen a. d. D.* (Dillingen a. d. D., 1949), pp. 169–89; and V. Burr, 'Anmerkungen zum Konflikt zwischen Methodius und den Bayerischen Bischöfen', *Cyrillo-Methodiana* (see p. 394 n. 3 above), pp. 39–56.

Intensive cultural activity in Bulgaria and Macedonia toward the close of the ninth century and throughout part of the tenth century provided a suitable context in which the Christian faith found root. Particularly in Bulgaria under Czar Simeon (893–927) there was a blossoming of literature which was to form the basis of the medieval Slavonic literature of the Orthodox Church. The latter part of the tenth century, however, saw a number of setbacks to Christianity in the Balkan peninsula, and thereafter the chief creative centre of Slavic culture was in Russia, where Christianity became the state religion as a result of the baptism of the ruling prince, Vladimir, in A.D. 988.

Our attention must now turn to the invention of the Slavic alphabets and the earliest translation of the Scriptures into Slavonic. According to the *Vita Constantini*, supported by the *Translatio*, before leaving for Moravia Cyril devised an alphabet for the writing of Slavonic and began the translation of the Gospel,[1] commencing (says the *Vita*) with the passage, 'In the beginning was the Word, and the Word was with God, and the Word was God.' A treatise entitled 'On the Letters',[2] composed some years later by a learned monk named Khrabr, tells us that Cyril's alphabet consisted of thirty-eight letters, and was as well suited to the needs of the Slavs as the Greek alphabet was for the Greeks. The difficulties that the modern philologist faces, however, arise from the circumstance that the extant Old Church Slavonic manuscripts present us with two distinct alphabets, the Glagolitic and the Cyrillic. Which of the alphabets Cyril

---

[1] Actually *Vita Constantini* (chap. 14) merely states that Cyril started writing down (not translating, though this is doubtless what is meant) *beseda evangelьskaja* (literally, 'the Gospel wording'). But exactly what the expression implies is a philological puzzle, since *evangelьskaja*, being an adjectival modifier, says nothing about the number of Gospels Cyril translated, and, in fact, since *beseda* normally means spoken word or even conversation (it translates, so Professor Lunt informs me, λαλιά Matt. xxvi. 73, John viii. 43, and διαλογή Ps. ciii. 34, etc.), it is conceivable that all that the biographer states is that Cyril wrote down a homily on the text of John i. 1.

On the question of the existence or non-existence of Slavonic letters before Cyril made preparation for his Moravian mission, see, respectively, G. Sotiroff, 'Y a-t-il eu une écriture autochtone en terre slave avant le temps de Cyrille et Méthode?' *Revue canadienne d'études slaves*, i (1967), 79–94, and Robert Auty, 'Slavonic Letters before St Cyril: the Evidence of the *Vita Constantini*', *Studia palaeoslovenica* (Prague, 1971), pp. 27–30.

[2] The treatise is variously entitled in different copies, the earliest of which dates from 1348; for a list of editions of the text, see A. P. Vlasto, *The Entry of the Slavs into Christendom* (Cambridge, 1970), p. 373 n. 87.

invented, the relationship of the two alphabets to each other, and their antecedents, are questions to which widely divergent answers have been given. Today, however, there is widespread agreement that the alphabet invented by Cyril to take to the Moravian Slavs was that now called Glagolitic. Many attempts have been made to demonstrate the affinity of the Glagolitic with a wide variety of other alphabets (including Hebrew, Samaritan, Gothic, Ethiopic, Armenian, and Georgian), but none of them can be regarded as successful.[1] It appears that Cyril, taking as a model the increasingly flamboyant Greek minuscule script of the ninth century, and perhaps adopting also several Latin and Hebrew (or Samaritan) signs, used his inventive powers to devise an assortment of stylized and symmetrical characters made up of little quadrangles, triangles, and circles, with appendages.[2]

The Cyrillic alphabet is, as most scholars agree,[3] of later provenance than the Glagolitic and is, without doubt, based on the Greek uncial script of the ninth and tenth centuries. This alphabet, which is considerably less individualistic than the Glagolitic, may have been devised by St. Kliment, a pupil of Cyril and Methodius and an active missionary in Bulgaria. After some amount of local variation, in 893 a great Bulgarian council held at Preslav not only decreed the general use of the Slavic

[1] An attempt has even been made to prove that Glagolitic is a cryptographic alphabet for use as a script that could be kept secret from the Franks, i.e. a script made up of zodiacal, alchemistic, and other esoteric signs; cf. E. È. Granstrem, 'O proisxoždenii glagoličeskoj azbuki', *Trudy otdela drevnerusskoj literatury Instituta russkoj literatury AN SSSR*, xi (1955), 300–13.

[2] According to the Finnish scholar Georg Tschernochvostoff, Cyril devised the Glagolitic characters from the three sacred symbols—the circle (representing eternity), the triangle (representing the Trinity), and the cross; cf. Valentin Kiparsky, 'Tschernochvostoffs Theorie über den Ursprung des glagolitischen Alphabets', *Cyrillo-Methodiana* (see p. 394 n. 3 above), pp. 393–400, and Michael Samilov, 'Das glagolitische Alphabet', *Das heidnische und christliche Slaventum (Annales Instituti Slavici*, II/2; Wiesbaden, 1970), pp. 98–104.

[3] Cf., e.g., Horace G. Lunt, *Old Church Slavonic Grammar*, 6th edn. (The Hague, 1974), pp. 14 f.; J. Kurz, 'Význam činnosti slovanských apoštolů Cyrila a Metoděje v dějinách slovanské kultury', *Slavia*, xxxii (1963), 315–18; Ihor Ševčenko, 'Three Paradoxes of the Cyrillo-Methodian Mission', *SR* xxiii (1964), 235 f.; and Wilhelm Lettenbauer, 'Bemerkungen zur Entstehung der Glagolica', in *Cyrillo-Methodiana* (p. 394 n. 3 above), pp. 401–10. An attempt (dictated, as it appears, more by political than linguistic considerations) to prove the priority of the Cyrillic alphabet was made by the Bulgarian scholar Emil Georgiev in his monograph *Slavjanskaja pis'mennost' do Kirilla i Mefodija* (Sofia, 1952); the argument is summarized in Georgiev's article 'Pis'mennost' rossov' in *Cyrillo-Methodiana*, pp. 372–81.

language in the Church, but also finally codified the Cyrillic alphabet, making it official for both ecclesiastical and secular use.[1]

The very earliest Old Church Slavonic manuscripts, preserving biblical, liturgical, and theological texts, are written in Glagolitic script. It must be observed, however, that no manuscript conveys to us directly the language of Cyril and Methodius, for by the tenth and eleventh centuries—the date of our earliest manuscripts—the extant texts already show dialectal variations, reflecting the area in which their originals were written.

It is impossible to determine with certainty what portions of the Bible were translated by Cyril and Methodius themselves. The *Vita Methodii* (chap. xv) tells us that the brothers together translated from the Greek the Gospel and the Apostolos. In this context the word Gospel (*evangelie*) is ambiguous. It may refer to a copy containing the full text of all four Gospels (a tetra-evangelium) or to a lectionary, a book of pericopes appointed to be read on the several days of the ecclesiastical calendar. After the death of Cyril, Methodius, with the help of two (or three[2]) priests serving as scribes, is said to have completed the translation of the whole Bible from Greek into Slavonic, omitting only the books of the Maccabees. According to the *Vita Methodii* the work took eight[3] months, from March to 26 October 884. This complete translation seems to have been soon lost, which, as Vlasto remarks, 'is hardly surprising if there were only one or at most two copies, in the turmoil which followed Methodius' death'.[4] Of course copies would have been made of the Psalter and of most of the New Testament books (the Book of Revelation, not being included in the Orthodox lectionary, had not been translated). Since only excerpts from the Old Testament are required in the Eastern Church, it is perhaps not surprising that the first complete collection of biblical books in the Church Slavonic language originated in Russia only during the last decade of the fifteenth century. It was made by Archbishop Gennadius of

---

[1] Cf. Vlasto, op. cit., pp. 41 and 174–5.

[2] The reading 'two' produces garbled syntax, whereas if the text is emended by reading 'three' the syntactical problems disappear.

[3] The text of the *Vita* reads six months; a Glagolitic numeral has been misread.

[4] Vlasto, op. cit., p. 78.

Novgorod, the New Testament being based upon the Old Church Slavonic Version, and the Old Testament being translated partly from the Septuagint and partly from the Vulgate.[1] Today Church Slavonic is a dead language, used only in the lessons and liturgy of the Church.

II. MANUSCRIPTS OF THE OLD CHURCH SLAVONIC VERSION

Since none of the Old Church Slavonic manuscripts is dated, scholars must determine their approximate age by considering not only palaeographic and iconographic features but also the presence or absence of archaic phonetic features.[2] Besides the Old Church Slavonic texts *per se* there are also later national 'recensions'[3] of Church Slavonic in which the language took on local colouring according to the areas in which it was used.[4] Thus, orthographical and grammatical differences help to characterize a Bohemian, a Croatian, a Serbian, a Bulgarian, and a Russian 'recension' of Church Slavonic.

In the following list of New Testament manuscripts, which has been drawn up to accord with the texts listed as *Fontes* in the Czech Academy's *Lexicon Linguae Palaeoslovenicae*,[5] mention is made, when appropriate, of the national recension of the Church Slavonic text. The sigla are those used by the *Lexicon*.

---

[1] The book commonly known as 2 Esdras (called 3 Esdras in the Slavonic Bible) was translated from the Latin Vulgate (where it is called 4 Esdras).

[2] For a discussion of criteria for determining the date of Old Slavonic manuscripts, cf. H. G. Lunt, 'On Slavonic Palimpsests', *American Contributions to the Fourth International Congress of Slavicists*, Moscow, Sept. 1958 (The Hague, 1958), pp. 191–209; cf. also N. Molnár, 'The Calques of Greek Origin in the Most Ancient Old Slavic Gospel Texts', *SS* x (1964), 99–146, especially 99 ff., and Marshall Winokur, 'An Orthographical Study of Toponyms and Names of Inhabitants in Old Church Slavonic', Ph.D. dissertation, University of Pennsylvania, 1973.

[3] By 'recension' is to be understood the linguistic structure of the Church Slavonic without reference to the history of textual transmission.

[4] At the same time, as Lunt points out, 'there is no clear-cut set of features which differentiate the language of the manuscripts called Old Church Slavonic from the oldest of the texts termed simply Church Slavonic, but the relatively "correct" usage of certain letters and the relatively high occurrence of certain morphological forms which comparative evidence shows to be old give us some criteria', *Old Church Slavonic Grammar*, 6th edn. (The Hague, 1974), p. 5.

[5] *Slovník jazyka staroslověnského*; fasc. ii, *Úvod* (Československá Akademie věd, Slovanský ústav; Prague, 1959), pp. lxii f.

A. GOSPELS

(1) Codex Zographensis (Zogr), a Glagolitic tetraevangelium of 288 folios,[1] was written in Macedonia perhaps as early as the end of the tenth century.[2] The manuscript takes its name from the Zographou Monastery on Mount Athos, whose monks presented it in 1860 to the Russian Tsar Alexander II. Today it is in the Saltykov-Shchedrin Public Library at Leningrad (Glag. no. 1). The initial folios of the manuscript are missing, and the text begins with Matt. iii. 11. Folios 41–57, containing Matt. xvi. 20–xxiv. 20, are replaced, having been written in a rough Glagolitic hand dating from the late eleventh or early twelfth century.[3] The language of Zographensis is a good reflection of the earliest Old Church Slavonic, except that the jers are assimilated. The manuscript was edited (in Cyrillic transcription) by V. Jagić, *Quattuor evangeliorum codex glagoliticus olim Zographensis nunc Petropolitanus* (Berlin, 1879; repr. Graz, 1954).[4]

(2) The Codex Marianus (Mar) is a Glagolitic manuscript of 174 folios, which, according to Auty,[5] was probably written in Macedonia in the late tenth or early eleventh century. Although in the form of a tetraevangelium, it has been clearly influenced by a lectionary, for it often includes incipits which are introduced very awkwardly.[6] In 1845 the manuscript was taken by the Russian scholar V. Grigorovič from the monastery of the Holy Virgin on Mount Athos to Russia. Unfortunately the first folios are lost, and so the text of Matt. i. 1–v. 22 is lacking.[7] Today the

[1] The Gospel translation ends with fol. 288; there follows a Cyrillic synaxarion (calendar of saints' days with indication of the Scripture lesson for the day) of later date.

[2] So Robert Auty, *Handbook of Old Church Slavonic*, Part ii, *Texts and Glossary* (London, 1965), p. 50.

[3] See Horace G. Lunt, 'On Old Church Slavonic Phonemes: the Codex Zographensia', *Word*, vii (1952), 326 f.

[4] Jagić's publication of the manuscript unfortunately leaves something to be desired, for the edition contains numerous errors in the reproduction and placement of supralinear and punctuation marks, the failure to indicate ligatures, instances of incorrect word-division, and various omissions and misreadings of letters. A re-examination of the manuscript was made by Leszek Moszyński (*Ze studiów nad rękopisem Kodeksu Zografskiego* (Wrocław–Warsaw–Cracow, 1961)), who provides seventy-four pages of corrections of Jagić's errors and omissions.

[5] Op. cit., p. 34.

[6] For this information, as well as for other details concerning several of the other manuscripts described in the list, I am indebted to Professor Lunt.

[7] Smaller lacunae are at Matt. ix. 7; xii. 42; John i. 1–23; xviii. 13–29; xxi. 18–25.

first two folios, which contain Matt. v. 23–vi. 16, are in the Nationalbibliothek in Vienna, while the rest of the codex (containing Matt. vi. 17–John xxi. 17) is in the Lenin Library in Moscow (*Φ* 87, no. 1689). The definitive edition of Marianus, with a glossary and an analysis of its language, is that of V. Jagić, *Quattuor evangeliorum versionis palaeoslovenicae codex Marianus glagoliticus* (Berlin and St. Petersburg, 1883; repr. Graz, 1960).

(3) The Dečani tetraevangelium (Deč), formerly of the Dečani monastery in Serbia and now in the Public Library in Leningrad (Gilf. 4), is a thirteenth-century copy of the Gospels in the Bulgarian recension of Church Slavonic. Jagić used this manuscript for his edition of codex Marianus in order to fill out the text of Matt. i. 1–v. 22, which is lacking in Marianus; see no. 2.

(4) The codex Assemanianus (As), a Glagolitic manuscript of 158 folios, is a Gospel lectionary, followed by a calendar of saints' days (fols. 112ᵇ–158).[1] It is usually dated to the eleventh century, but Vajs argued for a date in the tenth century. Inasmuch as the menology commemorates several Macedonian saints, including Methodius' disciple St. Climent of Ochrid, the manuscript is presumed to have been copied in Macedonia. In 1736 it was bought from Orthodox monks in Jerusalem by the Syrian Christian Joseph S. Assemani, whose nephew Stephan E. Assemani left it to the Vatican Library, where it is now preserved. Two nineteenth-century editions of the manuscript (by F. Rački in 1865, and by I. Črnčić in 1878) were not altogether satisfactory and have been superseded by the handsome edition of Josef Vajs and Josef Kurz, *Evangeliarium Assemani. Codex Vaticanus 3 slavicus glagoliticus. Editio phototypica cum prolegomenis, textu litteris Cyrillicis transcripto, analysi, annotationibus palaeographicis, variis lectionibus, glossario*; i, *Prolegomena, Tabulae* (Prague, 1929); ii (Prague, 1955).

(5) The Ostromir lectionary (Ostr), a Cyrillic manuscript of 294 folios, was written in 1056–7 by the Deacon Grigorij for Ostromir, the *posadnik* (mayor) of Novgorod; it is now in the Public Library in Leningrad (F *Π* I 5). The earliest dated Slavic manuscript, according to Auty[2] it is without doubt a copy of an original of east-Bulgarian provenance, but the native Russian of

---

[1] Fol. 29, containing John xiv. 1–21, is by a different scribe from the one responsible for the rest of the manuscript.   [2] Op. cit., p. 83.

the scribe has overlaid the original language. The lectionary is of the 'short' type (see p. 428 below). The edition of Aleksandr Vostokov, *Ostromirovo evangelie, 1056–57 g.* (St. Petersburg, 1843; repr. Wiesbaden, 1964), must be supplemented by the photo-lithographic reproduction (made at the expense of the St. Petersburg merchant Ilja Savinkov), *Ostromirovo evangelie* (St. Petersburg, 1883 and 1889).

(6) The Cyrillic manuscript known as Savvina Kniga (Sav), dating from the eleventh century, is an incomplete copy which originally may have contained about 200 folios. Of the extant 166 folios, only 129 are the work of the original scribe, a certain 'popŭ Savva'. The text, according to Lunt, is presumably east-Bulgarian Old Church Slavonic and preserves many singular readings, including several odd displacements of individual lections; e.g. Sunday of the seventh week of Luke is transposed with Sunday of the sixth week, in company with Ar[1] (see p. 410 below). Originally preserved in a monastery near Pskov, today the manuscript is at Moscow in the Drevnekhranilishche Tsentrarkhiva R.S.F.S.R. The edition of V. N. Shchepkin, *Savvina kniga* (St. Petersburg, 1903; repr. Graz, 1959), is provided with a glossary.

(7) The Ochrid Folia (Achr) are two leaves of a Glagolitic lectionary, discovered at Ochrid by V. Grigorovič in 1845; they contain several lessons appointed to be read from Tuesday after Easter to Monday of the following week. Written probably in the eleventh century, the leaves today are in the University Library at Odessa. Among several editions the best is G. A. Il'inskij, *Oxridskie glagoličeskie listki. Otryvok drevnecerkovnoslavjanskogo evangelija XI v.* (Pamjatniki staroslavjanskogo jazyka, III. 2; St. Petersburg, 1915), printed in Cyrillic characters.

(8) The Fragmenta Undol'sky (Und) comprise two folios of a Cyrillic lectionary written in the eleventh century. Preserved in the Lenin Library in Moscow (Φ 310, no. 961), it was edited by E. F. Karskij, *Listki Undol'skogo; otryvok kirillovskogo evangelija XI-go veka* (St. Petersburg, 1904).

(9) The Fragmenta Kuprijanivii (Kupr) are two folios of an eleventh-century Cyrillic lectionary, with some Russian elements. Now in the Public Library in Leningrad (F Π I 58), it was edited by F. V. Kaminskij, 'Otryvki evangelskix čtenij XI v.', *Izvestija*

otdelenija russkogo jazyka i slovesnosti Akademii nauk, xxviii (Leningrad, 1924), 273–6.

(10) The tetraevangelium Nicolai (Nik), dating from the beginning of the fifteenth century and formerly in the Serbian monastery of St. Nicholas, was transferred in the nineteenth century to the Belgrade National Library. It was edited by Dj. Daničić, *Nikolsko jevandjelje* (Belgrade, 1864).

B. OTHER BOOKS OF THE NEW TESTAMENT

(11) The Christinopolitan Praxapostolos (Christ) is a twelfth-century manuscript in the Russian recension of Church Slavonic. Formerly in the Christinopolitan Monastery in Galicia, it is now in the Library of the Stauropigian Institute of L'vov. It was edited by Ae. Kałużniacki, *Actus epistolaeque apostolorum palaeoslovenice ad fidem codicis Christinopolitani* (Vienna, 1896). Where the codex is defective the editor has supplied material from the Hil'ferding codex and two Moscow codices; see nos. 12, 13, and 14.

(12) The Apostolos of the Hil'ferding Collection (Hilf), now Gil'f. 14 of the Public Library at Leningrad, is a fourteenth-century Church Slavonic manuscript of the Serbian recension. It was used by Kałużniacki to fill out lacunae in Acts and 1 Peter of the Christinopolitan Apostolos; see no. 11.

(13) An Apostolos (Mosk[a]) written A.D. 1220, formerly no. 7 of the Moscow Synodical Library and now in the Library of the Historical Museum, presents the Russian redaction of Church Slavonic. It was used by Kałużniacki to fill out portions of 1 Corinthians lacking in the Christinopolitan Apostolos; see no. 11.

(14) A fifteenth-century Apostolos (Mosk[b]), formerly no. 18 of the Moscow Synodical Library and now in the Library of the Historical Museum, presents the Russian recension of Church Slavonic. It was used by Kałużniacki to fill out portions of several Pauline Epistles lacking in the Christinopolitan Apostolos; see no. 11.

(15) The Grškovićiana Fragments (Grš) are four leaves of an Apostolos dating from the end of the twelfth or the beginning of the thirteenth century and written in Croatian Glagolitic. Now in the Yugoslav Academy of Sciences in Zagreb, they were edited by

V. Jagić, 'Grškoićev odlomak glagolskog apostola', *Starine Jugo-slavenske akademije znanosti i umjetnosti*, xxvi (Zagreb, 1893), 46–53.

(16) Praxapostolos Achridanus (Ochr) is a twelfth-century manuscript presenting the Bulgarian recension of Church Slavonic, now in the Lenin Library at Moscow (Φ 87, no. 1695). It was edited by S. M. Kul'bakin, 'Oxridskaja rukopis' apostola konca XII veka', *Bulgarski starini*, iii (Sofia, 1907).

(17) Praxapostolos Slepčensis (Slepč), a twelfth-century manuscript of the Bulgarian recension of Church Slavonic, gains its name from having been at the Monastery of Slepče, near Prilep in Macedonia. Today the greater part of the codex is in the Public Library at Leningrad (*F II* I. 101, 101a), while stray leaves from it are in several other libraries. The text of the codex was edited by G. A. Il'inskij, *Slepčenskij apostol XII veka* (Moscow, 1912).

(18) Praxapostolos Macedonicus (Mak), a twelfth-century manuscript of the Bulgarian recension of Church Slavonic, is in the Library of the National Museum in Prague (no. IX E 25).

(19) Praxapostolos Šišatovacensis (Šiš), a manuscript of the Serbian redaction of Church Slavonic, was written in 1324. It was edited by F. Miklosich, *Apostolus e codice monasterii Šištovac palaeo-slovenice* (Vienna, 1853).

(20) The Mihanovićiana Fragmenta (Mih) are two leaves of a Glagolitic praxapostolos, written at the end of the twelfth or the beginning of the thirteenth century. Preserved in the archives of the Yugoslavian Academy of Sciences, they were edited by V. Jagić, 'Gradja za glagolsku paleografiju', *Rad Jugoslavenske akademije znanosti i umjetnosti*, ii (Zagreb, 1868), 1–35.

(21) Pagina I Foliorum Kijevensium (Kij[b]), written in Croatia at the beginning of the twelfth century, contains part of the Epistle to the Romans (xiii. 11–xiv. 3). It was edited by V. Jagić in *Glagolitica* (Vienna, 1890).

(22) The Book of Revelation is preserved in Codex Hval (Hval), a fifteenth-century Church Slavonic manuscript of the Serbian (Bosnian) recension. Now at Bologna, the manuscript was edited by Dj. Dančić, 'Apokalipsa iz Hvalova rukopisa', *Starine Jugoslavenske akademije znanosti i umjetnosti*, iv (Zagreb, 1872), 86–109.

Besides the manuscripts listed above, which are (as was mentioned earlier) utilized in the Czech Academy's Old Church Slavonic Lexicon, there are two or three other Slavonic texts that, for one reason or another, deserve to be described here.

The Archangel Gospel Lectionary, written in 1092 in the Russian recension of Old Slavonic, was copied by two scribes from lectionaries of differing types. The part known as Ar[1] comprises seventy-six folios containing Saturday and Sunday lessons from the fifth Sunday of John up to Lent, but with significant lacunae. Ar[2] comprises folios 77–174 and presents Saturday and Sunday lessons for Lent, as well as daily lessons for Holy Week and the menologion. According to an analysis made by L. P. Žukovskaya,[1] the textual witness of Ar[1] is earlier and much superior to that of Ar[2]; the latter is from the 'full' lectionary of the Mstislav type. A facsimile was published at Moscow in 1912 by the authorities of the Rumjancev Museum.

The Miroslav Gospel lectionary, dating from the close of the twelfth or the beginning of the thirteenth century, is a magnificent illuminated Cyrillic manuscript which, according to Lunt, manifests no sign of use. It was written by Serbian scribes for a Serbian prince; the text shows evidence of having been derived from a Russian Old Slavonic redaction. The object of many studies and monographs,[2] the manuscript was published in a facsimile edition by Lj. Stojanivić, *Miroslavljevo jevandjelje* (*Odlomci*) (*Spomenik Srpske kralj. akademije*, xx; Belgrade, 1893). A study of the relation between the system of the weekday lessons in Mi and the system represented in a small group of Greek lectionaries isolated by William D. Bray[3] was published by Mrs. Yvonne Burns.[4]

An apostolos lectionary in Old Bulgarian, dating from the

---

[1] 'Novye dannye ob originalax russkoj rukopisi 1092 g.', *Istočnikovedenie i istorija russkogo jazyka* (Akademija nauk, Institut russkogo jazyka; Moscow, 1964), pp. 84–118.

[2] For a thorough study of problems posed by the manuscript, see Josip Vrana, *L'Évangéliaire de Miroslav; Contribution à l'étude de son origine* (The Hague, 1961).

[3] *The Week Day Lessons from Luke in the Greek Gospel Lectionary* (Chicago, 1959). On the two forms of Bray's work, see Metzger, 'Greek Lectionaries and a Critical Edition of the Greek New Testament', *Die alten Übersetzungen des Neuen Testaments, die Kirchenväterzitate und Lektionare*, ed. by K. Aland (Berlin and New York, 1972), pp. 489 f.

[4] 'Raspored nedeljnih perikopa u Miroslavljevom jevandjelju, *Zbornik narodnog muzeja*, vi (Belgrade, 1970), 259–86, with a brief English résumé.

eleventh century, came to the attention of scholars through a fortuitous discovery. In 1960 at the village Enina in the Balkan mountains, an ancient church which had been unused for many years was being restored as an 'archaeological' monument. In a rubbish heap in the churchyard someone by chance picked up a nondescript clod, dirty and covered with lime; it turned out to be portions of thirty-nine parchment leaves of a Cyrillic codex that must have at one time contained about 215 or 220 leaves. The badly preserved remains have been published in convenient format by K. Mirchev and Ch. Kodov, *Eninski apostol. Staro-bŭlgarski pametnik ot XI v.* (Sofia, 1965), in which the photographic reproduction and the diplomatic transcription occupy facing pages. Many of the folios have been damaged and are illegible. The leaves that remain preserve portions of Acts xvii. 16–22; Rom. vi. 3–11; xiii. 11–xiv. 4, 19–26; 1 Cor. i. 18–ii. 2; v. 6–14; vi. 12–20; viii. 8–ix. 2; xi. 23–32; Gal. iii. 13–14; iv. 22–30; Phil. iv. 4–9; Col. iii. 12–16; 2 Tim. ii. 4–10, 11–19; Heb., portions of all chapters; and 1 John iv. 12–19.

What is perhaps the oldest known manuscript of the Book of Revelation in Slavonic is a fourteenth-century copy which presents the text in the Russian recension of Church Slavonic. Its text is considered inferior to the younger Hval codex (no. 22 above). Now in the Lenin Library in Moscow (Φ 256, no. 8), it was edited by Archimandrite Amphilochij, *Apokalipsis XIV veka Rumjancevskogo Muzeja* (Moscow, 1886).

Besides the New Testament manuscripts listed above, several other Old Church Slavonic manuscripts contain excerpts of the Old and New Testaments. One of the more noteworthy of these is codex Suprasliensis, a Cyrillic manuscript of which 285 folios are extant.[1] Its name is derived from the monastery of Suprasl near Białystok in north-east Poland, where it was found by M. I. Bobrovskij in 1838–9. It was subsequently broken up, and fols. 1–118 were sent to Ljubljana, where they are now in the University Library; the remainder (with the exception of the first sixteen folios, which are now in the Saltykov-Shchedrin Library in Leningrad) found their way to the Zamojski Library in Warsaw. Codex Suprasliensis, which is the longest of the extant Old

---

[1] The first edition of Suprasliensis, made by Miklosich in 1851, has been superseded by that of S. Sever'janov, *Suprasl'skaja rukopis'* (St. Petersburg, 1904; repr. in two volumes, Graz, 1956).

Church Slavonic documents, contains a menology for the month of March, comprising twenty-four lives of saints or other sacred legends, twenty-three sermons, and a prayer. Another book of homilies in Old Church Slavonic is the Glagolita Clozianus, which survives today in only fourteen folios of Glagolitic text. Formerly the property of Count Paris Cloz (d. 1856), two of the folios are now in the Ferdinandeum at Innsbruck, the other twelve in the Museo Civico at Trento in northern Italy. The most recent edition is that by A. Dostál, *Clozianus. Codex palaeoslovenicus glagoliticus tridentinus et oenipontanus* (Prague, 1959). Although most of the homilies parallel those in Suprasliensis, one of them which does not has been thought to be a sermon composed by Methodius himself.[1]

Both Suprasliensis and Clozianus contain many quotations and allusions to the Old and New Testaments which the textual critic can identify with relative ease by consulting the indexes to biblical passages drawn up by Nikolai Durnovo[2] and by André Vaillant.[3]

Finally it should be mentioned that the date of the Slavonic translation of the Book of Revelation is not known with certainty. How much earlier than the oldest known manuscript (see p. 411 above) the book was translated is disputed. In a thorough and cautious study of the question Oblak came to the conclusion that the translation was made no later than the twelfth century and

---

[1] So A. Vaillant, 'Une homilie de Méthode', *RÉS* xxiii (1947), 34–7.

[2] 'K voprosu o drevnejšix perevodax na staroslavjanskij jazyk biblejskix tekstov. Suprasl'skaja rukopis'', *Izvestija otdelenija russkogo jazyka i slovesnosti, 1925 g.*, xxx (Akademija nauk SSSR; Leningrad, 1926), pp. 353–429. The index of New Testament quotations and allusions, cited in full from Suprasliensis, extends from p. 373 to p. 406.

[3] 'Les citations des Écritures dans le Suprasliensis et le Clozianus', *Slavistična revija*, x (1957), 34–40. Vaillant, who was apparently unaware of Durnovo's index, lists only the biblical references of direct quotations in the two manuscripts. Lunt, who kindly brought the indexes of Durnovo and Vaillant to the present writer's attention, makes the following comment: 'Old Church Slavonic patristic translations are no help in establishing a Cyrillo-Methodius text. The translations of the homilies and saints' lives that are found in the two OCS collections (the extensive Suprasliensis and the fragmentary Clozianus) do not with certainty date back to the Moravian Mission, and Su in any case has undergone extensive linguistic revisions. What is more important, the translators apparently treated even long and obvious Gospel citations as part of the work they were translating. (For example, all forms in Matt. iv. 19 remain plural in Su, though they are properly dual in Zo Ma.) Coincidences with one or another variant of the five chief witnesses are random'.

might well (in the light of certain 'Pannonian' features in grammar and lexicography) be somewhat earlier.[1] In any case, the book has been generally neglected by the official Orthodox Slavic Churches (just as no lesson from the Apocalypse is included in the lectionary of the Greek Orthodox Church). On the other hand, the Bogomils of Bulgaria and the Patarines of Bosnia, as might have been expected, made considerable use of the book to support their views.

III. SURVEY OF RESEARCH ON THE OLD CHURCH SLAVONIC VERSION[2]

Apparently the first[3] editor of the Greek New Testament to cite evidence from the Slavonic version was Christian Friedrich Matthaei, a Thuringian scholar who at various times taught classical literature at Moscow, first in a gymnasium and later in the University. While in Russia Matthaei added considerably to the knowledge of the textual basis of the New Testament by collating many Greek manuscripts hitherto unknown to Western scholarship.[4] During the course of the publication of his rambling, twelve-volume edition of the Greek New Testament, he indicates that it occurred to him to cite evidence also from the

[1] V. Oblak, 'Die kirchenslavische Übersetzung der Apokalypse', *ASP* xiii (1891), 321–61, especially 346 and 357. Cf. also V. Peretc, 'Drevnejšij spisok slavjanskogo tolkovogo Apokalipsisa', *Slavia*, ii (1923–4), 641–4. Peretc was unaware of Oblak's study. Josip Hamm ('Apokalipsa bosanskih krstjana', with a résumé in French, *Slovo* (Zagreb), ix–x (1960), 43–104), on the basis of three Bosnian manuscripts of the Apocalypse, reconstructed the form of the text which hypothetically was current in round or semi-round Glagolitic letters of the eleventh or twelfth century, several of which he supposes were confused by later copyists.

[2] The material of section III is taken, with modifications and additions, from the present writer's discussion in his *Chapters in the History of New Testament Textual Criticism* (Leiden and Grand Rapids, 1963), pp. 77–90.

[3] Gregory indeed states that at earlier date J. J. Wettstein had cited Slavic evidence (Caspar René Gregory, *Textkritik des Neuen Testamentes*, ii (Leipzig, 1902), 734), but he supplies no references by which to verify this statement, nor does Wettstein discuss the Slavonic version in the Prolegomena to his edition (Amsterdam, 1751–2).

[4] It appears that Matthaei was, moreover, guilty of purloining from Russian libraries many Greek manuscripts of both the Classics and the Fathers. Some of these he kept in his own library, others he sold to various libraries in Germany and Holland. For an account of his life with incriminating evidence of his brazen thievery, see Oscar von Gebhardt, 'Christian Friedrich Matthaei und seine Sammlung griechischer Handschriften', *Centralblatt für Bibliothekswesen*, xv (1898), 345–57, 393–420, 441–82, and 537–66.

Slavonic version. (The only other version represented in his edition is the Latin Vulgate, based upon a single manuscript at Moscow, now lost, codex Demidovianus; see p. 302 above.) In an appendix to his edition of the Book of Revelation, Matthaei lists ten Slavonic manuscripts which he had seen in Russia. He contented himself, however, with collating the text of Revelation given in the folio edition of the Slavonic Bible published at Moscow in 1762. This evidence is given in Latin, the collation having been made against the Vulgate manuscript previously mentioned.[1]

Franz Karl Alter, a Jesuit from Silesia who was professor of Greek at Vienna, was the first editor of the Greek New Testament to incorporate evidence from Slavonic manuscripts themselves. In his cumbersome and inconvenient edition of the Greek Testament, he chose to print a thirteenth-century Greek manuscript in the Royal Library at Vienna (Greg. 218; von Soden, δ 300), which he corrected by substituting the text of Stephanus' first edition (1546). A list of readings thus modified is given at the end of each volume. On the basis of this oddly constructed text, Alter supplied in separate appendixes evidence from twenty-four other manuscripts in the same Library, including three Slavonic codices collated for him by Fortunatus Durich.[2] Unfortunately, however, most of the Slavonic evidence can be used only by one who is acquainted with that tongue, for the variants are cited by a transliteration of the Slavonic words in Roman letters.

The first textual critic who can be said to have made really serious use of the Slavonic version was Johann Jakob Griesbach. At his request Josef Dobrovský, the founder of Slavic philology

---

[1] Christianus Fridericus Matthaei, *Ioannis apocalypsis graece et codicibus nunquam antea examinatis . . .* (Riga, 1785), Appendix ii, 'De versione slavonica apocalypseos', pp. 343–88.

[2] Franciscus Carolus Alter, *Novum Testamentum ad codicem Vindobonensem graece expressum*, i (Vienna, 1787), 1122–56, 1157–94; ii (Vienna, 1786), 968–1039. The three manuscripts are numbers 101, 355, and 356, dating from the fifteenth or sixteenth century. Alter refers to these in his Preface as follows: 'Solum tres codices slavonicos eo consilio perlustravi, ut eruditos viros ad hanc utilissimam versionem (verbo venia sit, kralitzam, id est, reginam versionum appellarim) attentos redderem . . .' (vol. i, p. vii).

In addition to these three manuscripts, which are completely collated in the Gospels, Alter also supplied Slavonic evidence from a fragment containing Luke xxiv. 12–35 (vol. i, pp. 1008–11) as well as a collation of the printed text of John i–xiv in the Slavonic edition published at Moscow in 1614 (vol. i, pp. 403–11; see also p. 1202).

(1753–1829), collected noteworthy readings from nearly a score of Old Slavonic manuscripts.[1] Griesbach incorporated this evidence in the second edition of his Greek New Testament,[2] which remained for several generations substantially the only source of information concerning Slavonic variants. In fact, in 1869–72 Tischendorf borrowed the fruit of Dobrovský's labours from the pages of Griesbach, and Gregory reproduced Dobrovský's catalogue of Slavonic manuscripts of the New Testament.[3]

At the close of the last century, Voskresenskij began preliminary work in classifying Slavonic manuscripts of the New Testament.[4] He divided them into four families which represent, he thought, four recensions. The oldest recension is preserved in the south-Slavonic manuscripts, to which group most of the famous codices belong. The second recension is preserved in the oldest Russian manuscripts, dating from the eleventh and twelfth centuries. The other two recensions belong to the fourteenth and fifteenth centuries. Voskresenskij believed that he had shown that, in the Gospels, the Old Slavonic version agrees with the type of Greek text used by Photius, Patriarch of Constantinople.

It was not until well on in the twentieth century that the Old Church Slavonic version began to receive more sustained attention from a text-critical point of view. In a painstaking study of permanent value on the translation technique of the Old Church Slavonic version of the Gospels, Grünenthal devoted some attention to the textual affiliation of the more important

---

[1] Cf. Josef Dobrovský, 'Über den ersten Text der böhmischen Bibelübersetzung, nach den ältesten Handschriften derselben, besonders nach der Dresdener', *Neuere Abhundlungen der Königlichen böhmischen Gesellschaft der Wissenschaften*, diplom.-hist.-litt. Theil, iii (Prague, 1798), 260.

[2] J. J. Griesbach, *Novum Testamentum graece*, ed. sec., i (Halle and London, 1796), pp. xc–xci, xcvii, cxxvii–cxxxii; ii (Halle and London, 1806), pp. xix–xxi and xxxii–xxxix.

[3] C. R. Gregory, *Prolegomena* (Leipzig, 1894), pp. 1113–17, and *Textkritik des Neuen Testamentes*, ii (Leipzig, 1902), 736–8.

[4] G. A. Voskresenskij, *Drevne-slavjanskij Apostol. Poslanie Svjatogo Apostola Pavla k Rimljanam; po osnovnym spiskam četyrex redakcij rukopisnogo slavjanskogo apostol'skogo teksta s raznočtenijami iz pjatidesjati odnoj rukopisi Apostola XII–XVI vv.*, Part i (Moscow, 1892); *Evangelie ot Marka po osnovnym spiskam četyrex redakcij rukopisnogo slavjanskogo evangel'skogo teksta, s raznočtenijami iz sta vos'mi rukopisej Evangelija XI–XVI vv.* (Moscow, 1894); and *Xarakterističeskie čerty četyrex redakcij slavjanskogo perevoda Evangelija ot Marka po sto dvenadcati rukopisjam Evangelija XI–XVI vv.* (Moscow, 1896). For information concerning the first two of these works, cf. [Ll. J. M. Bebb], 'The Russian Bible', *CQR* xli (Oct. 1895), 203–25.

manuscripts of this version.[1] He found that the text of codex
Marianus frequently agrees with the Constantinopolitan (or
Lucianic) type of text found in the Greek manuscripts E F G H
K M S U V, while the text of codex Zographensis offers more
often a Western type of reading, agreeing with D, the Old Latin,
and Vulgate text. Grünenthal also observed that although the
Old Church Slavonic lectionaries, Assemanianus, and Savvina
Kniga may present the same Gospel pericope twice at different
places in the same manuscript, yet occasionally in Assemanianus
and frequently in Savvina Kniga one can discern a different type
of text[2] as well as a different translation technique.

A few years later the veteran Slavic philologist Vatroslav
Jagić published a thorough study of the fourteenth-century codex
Matica-Apostolus, containing the Acts, the Catholic Epistles, and
the Pauline Epistles.[3] Jagić found that in all its parts this manu-
script shows a close dependence upon the older forms of the
Byzantine text, and even reveals sporadic agreements with pre-
Byzantine texts.

In 1922 Andrej Snoj, professor of Sacred Scripture at Ljubljana
(Laibach), challenged the preliminary analyses made by Voskresenskij.[4] On the basis of more detailed study, Snoj discovered
not a few readings which had previously been overlooked where
the Old Slavonic version agrees with the Egyptian (or so-called
Hesychian) text in opposition to Photius. The chief object of his
brief report was to plead that the Old Slavonic version, which
contains old readings, should not be neglected by textual critics.

The scholar in the twentieth century who, more than any
other, gave sustained attention to the Old Slavonic version was

[1] O. Grünenthal, 'Die Übersetzungstechnik der altkirchenslavischen Evangelienübersetzung', *ASP* xxxi (1910), 321–66, 507–28; xxxii (1911), 1–48. For other
analyses of the translation technique, from a semantic rather than a text-critical
view, see the several contributions on the subject by E. M. Vereščagin listed in
footnote 1 of his article, 'Cyrills und Methods Übersetzungstechnik: drei Typen
der Entsprechung zwischen griechischen und slavischen Wörtern', *ZSP* xxxvi
(1972), 373–85.
[2] Exactly the same phenomena occur in Greek lectionaries.
[3] Vatroslav Jagić, *Zum altkirchenslavischen Apostolus*; I, *Grammatisches und Kritisches*,
in *SbWien*, Band cxci, Abh. 2 (1919). For a list of other Slavonic apostoloi, see
F. V. Mareš, 'Rokycanský rukopis církevněslovanského Apoštola', *Slavia*, xxvii
(1957), 180–91.
[4] Andrej Snoj, 'Veteroslavicae versionis evangeliorum pro critica et exegesi sacri
textus momentum', *Bib*, iii (1922), 180–7. His book, *Staroslovenski Matejev evangelij*
(Ljubljana, 1922), was not available to me. See also p. 420 below.

Professor Josef Vajs of Prague.[1] In considering the more significant of his many contributions to the subject one may begin with
the first volume of his 'Critical Studies of the Old Slavonic
Biblical Text'. This is an edition of the Slavonic text of Mark
with the Greek Textus Receptus printed on opposite pages.[2]
Vajs summarizes his research into the textual complexion of the
Old Slavonic as follows:

> An attentive examination of the Gospel of St. Mark has revealed
> that the Slavonic version belongs chiefly to the Syrian (or Constan-
> tinopolitan) recension, with numerous pre-Syrian readings of two
> kinds, Western and Alexandrian. The Greek manuscript from which it
> was translated was therefore a mixed manuscript; by reason of the
> numerous pre-Syrian elements which it contains, the Slavonic version
> is as worthy of attention as some other manuscripts or groups, such
> as the Ferrar group, Lake's fam. 1, or the manuscript 565. . . . Among
> the pre-Syrian variants, the Western readings are more numerous
> than the Alexandrian; but the majority of the pre-Syrian readings,
> being common to the two groups, Western and Alexandrian, it is
> difficult to discover their origin.[3]

Two years later Vajs published an article[4] in which he reveals
that, of about 2,500 variant readings that he had found in Old
Slavonic tetraevangelia, about one-half belong to the Byzantine
or Antiochian recension, about a fifth to the Western, and an
even smaller proportion to the Alexandrian.[5]

Continuing his study of the nature of the prevailing Byzantine
element in the Old Slavonic Version, Vajs discovered that it
comes closest to von Soden's K^i and K^a families, particularly the
latter.[6] (According to von Soden, the K^a family has manuscripts
A K Π at its head, with about one hundred others in more or
less close relationship, of which A is the oldest and Π the best
representative.) The Old Slavonic version, Vajs declared, 'like

---

[1] For an appreciative survey of Vajs's work, published on the occasion of his
seventieth birthday, see Josef Kurz's article in *Byslav*, vi (1935–6), 221–35 (with
a picture of Vajs). A bibliography of 168 items is included; very many of these
deal with the Old Church Slavonic version.

[2] *Evangelium sv. Marka a jeho poměr k řecké předloze* (*Kritické studie staroslovanského
textu biblického*, i; Prague, 1927).   [3] Ibid., p. 127 (French résumé).

[4] 'Byzantská recense a evangelijní kodexy staroslověnské (German résumé, 'Die
byzantinische Rezension und die altkirchenslavischen Evangelienkodexe'), *Byslav*, i
(1929), 1–9.   [5] Ibid., p. 8.

[6] 'Byzantská recense a evangelijní kodexy staroslověnské, II' (German résumé,
'Die byzantinische Rezension und die altkirchenslavischen Evanglien-Kodexe'),
Byslav, iv (1932), 1–12.

the K^a family, (a) retains in many passages the word order of the Western text, and (b) in still more passages agrees with Western additions or even omissions'.[1]

Vaj's next publications grew out of a proposal made at the meeting of the First Congress of Slavic Philologists, held at Prague in 1929, namely that the Old Slavonic text of the Gospels be reconstructed. As a preliminary step in editing such a text, Vajs published a study of certain noteworthy characteristics of the earliest manuscripts of the Old Slavonic version.[2] After classifying and assessing the relative worth of the manuscripts, Vajs concluded that 'since the Old Slavonic Lectionary was certainly the first literary work of St. Constantine-Cyril, in the reconstruction of the Gospel text one must proceed from the oldest Lectionary (Assemani)'.[3]

Furthermore, Vajs found that in a relatively recent manuscript of Bogomil origin, the tetraevangelium Nicolai (no. 10 in the list above) from the beginning of the fifteenth century, 'the Alexandrian and the so-called Western variants are present in much greater number than in the other manuscripts. This circumstance leads us necessarily to the conviction that this codex is to be regarded as a fairly accurate copy of a Glagolitic original, especially with reference to textual criticism.'[4]

The fruits of Vajs's studies in the Old Slavonic version were published during 1935 and 1936 in four volumes.[5] In each volume he prints his reconstructed text of the Old Slavonic version on one page and on the opposite page gives the Greek which inferentially lies behind the Old Slavonic.

In the introduction to his volume on Mark, Vajs presents statistics regarding the frequency of the Constantinopolitan (Koine) and the Western variants contained in his reconstructed Old Slavonic text.[6] These figures are as follows:

---

[1] 'Byzantská recense a evangelijní kodexy staroslověnské, II' (German résumé, 'Die byzantinische Rezension und die altkirchenslavischen Evanglien-Kodexe'), *Byslav,* iv (1932), p. 11.

[2] 'K characteristice nejstarších evang. rukopisů staroslověnských' (German résumé, 'Zur Charakteristik der älteren altslavischen evang. Handschriften'), *Byslav,* v (1933-4), 113-19.   [3] Ibid., p. 119.   [4] Ibid.

[5] *Evangelium sv. Matouše. Text rekonstruovaný* (Prague, 1935); *Evangelium sv. Marka. Text rekonstruovaný* (Prague, 1935); *Evangelium sv. Lukáše. Text rekonstruovaný* (Prague, 1936); and *Evangelium sv. Jana. Text rekonstruovaný* (Prague, 1936). These are vols. iii, iv, v, and vi respectively of the series *Kritické studie staroslovanského textu biblického.*   [6] *Evangelium sv. Marka,* p. xii.

	Matthew	Mark	Luke	John
Constantinopolitan	306	291	319	169
Western	292	200	289	210

As can be seen, in each Gospel, except that of John, the number of Constantinopolitan readings exceeds the Western. For Matthew the percentages are: Constantinopolitan = 51·25 per cent, Western = 48·8 per cent; for Mark, Constantinopolitan = 57·3 per cent, 42·7 per cent; for Luke, Constantinopolitan = 52·4 per cent, Western = 47·6 per cent; for John, Constantinopolitan = 44·6 per cent, Western = 55·4 per cent.

Concerning the question what significance is to be found in the circumstance that the Gospel of John has the highest percentage of pre-Syrian variant readings, while the Gospel of Mark has the highest percentage of Byzantine readings, another Slavic scholar, Josef Kurz, suggested that the answer is related to the historical background of the making of the Old Slavonic version from a lectionary text.[1] In a standard Eastern Orthodox lectionary almost the entire text of the Gospel of John is represented (90·6 per cent of the Gospel), whereas only about one-fourth of the text of Mark is included (27 per cent). Obviously, therefore, the Greek lectionary text which lay behind the extant Old Slavonic version had proportionately more Western variants than did the non-lectionary Greek original which, probably at a somewhat later date, was used to supplement all the Slavonic Gospels (but chiefly Mark) in making a non-lectionary Slavic text.

Noteworthy among reviews of Vajs's Old Slavonic Gospels was a critique prepared by Robert P. Casey and Silva Lake.[2] Restricting themselves to the Gospel of Mark, they conclude that Vajs, having followed von Soden's faulty grouping of New Testament Greek manuscripts, was in error in thinking that the Old Slavonic text belongs to family K^a. On the basis of a more highly refined analysis of family relationship in two chapters of Mark (chaps. vi and xi), Casey and Mrs. Lake made 'the

---

[1] *Byslav*, vi (1935–6), 238 and 242. A few years earlier, on the basis of an examination of linguistic phenomena, Nicolaas van Wijk had proposed the same explanation; see his brief note, 'Evangelistar und Tetraevangelium', *Slavia*, v (1926–7), 677.

[2] Robert P. Casey and Silva Lake, 'A New Edition of the Old Slavic Gospels', *JBL* lv (1936), 195–209. For a briefer statement, see Casey in *New Testament Manuscript Studies*, ed. by M. M. Parvis and A. P. Wikgren (Chicago, 1950), pp. 78–80.

tentative suggestion that possibly von Soden's I^π text lies behind the original Slavonic version. This is the text which he believes to have been that of the Cappadocian fathers, Basil, Gregory of Nyssa and Gregory Nazianzenus, and is extant in N, Σ, Φ, and ד. This suggestion is, however, most tentative. . . .'[1]

Casey and Mrs. Lake comment also upon Vajs's method of reconstructing the Old Slavonic version. As a working rule, Vajs apparently favoured the reading that diverges from the later Byzantine type of text. On the one hand Casey and Mrs. Lake acknowledge that 'within very definite limits this method is undoubtedly sound',[2] but at the same time they rightly point out that a wooden application of such a rule produces a quite distorted 'original' text. They conclude their study by expressing appreciation of Vajs's preliminary work, while acknowledging that 'the text of the Slavonic still remains one of the most obscure problems in the history of the text of the New Testament'.[3]

After the publication of his reconstructed text, Vajs gave attention to various intra-versional problems unearthed during his previous study. For example, continuing Grünenthal's preliminary analysis, Vajs rightly concluded that, despite the superiority of codex Marianus in accidence and vocabulary, because it so frequently exhibits later (Constantinopolitan) readings it can scarcely be regarded as preserving a primitive form of the Old Church Slavonic version.[4] On the other hand (as Vajs had pointed out in an earlier study), the late Bogomil manuscript Nicolai preserves a proportionately larger number of the older Western readings.

In a subsequent brief study, Vajs rejects Snoj's view that the Alexandrian type of text exerted an influence upon the Old Slavonic version, and reiterates in still more sharply defined terms his own view, namely that Cyril and Methodius used a Byzantine manuscript of their own age, containing an extraordinary number of non-Byzantine variants which were predominantly Palestinian in origin.[5] Vajs refers to von Soden's I^π

---

[1] *JBL* lv (1936), 208.

[2] Ibid., p. 206.

[3] Ibid., p. 209. Casey (in Parvis and Wikgren, op. cit., p. 79) is less satisfied with Vajs's standards of completeness and accuracy.

[4] 'Kladné a záporné výsledky kritického bádání v staroslovanském evangelním textu' (with a German résumé), *Byslav*, vii (1937–8), 149–57.

[5] 'La recensione bizantina e la versione paleoslavia dei Santi Vangeli', *Studi bizantini e neoellenici*, v (*Atti del V congresso internazionale di studi bizantini*; Rome, 1939), 560–4.

group as an example of such a mixed text. This subdivision of the *I*-text includes, according to von Soden's judgement, manuscripts U, 213, 443, 1071 (except Matthew), 1321 (only in John), 1574, 2145.

The next contribution[1] chronologically marks a retrogression in reliable conclusions. Joseph Schweigl published what, at first sight, appears to be a careful and sound investigation regarding the Slavic Textus Receptus of the liturgical form of the Gospels.[2] Here he concluded that the lectionary text in common use to-day in Slavic lands, namely the Liturgical Gospel published at Moscow in 1905, 'approaches closely to the *H*-type of text (Egyptian–Alexandrian), and therefore greatly excels the Old Slavonic (Glagolitic) version of the ninth century, which in many passages reveals a dependence upon the Palestinian–Caesarean recension'.[3] It is, however, only by a most perverse and uncritical evaluation of the significance of his evidence that Schweigl can come to this conclusion. The long lists of citations of passages that he has labelled Alexandrian[4] are made up of examples such as the following.

Matt. xi. 19, the Slavonic lectionary supports τέκνων with C L Ψ 33, 892, *al.*, whereas ἔργων is read by B* ℵ W 788, 2145, *al.*

Mark x. 29, the Slavonic lectionary adds καὶ γυναῖκα with C Ψ 28, 33, 597, 892, *al.*, whereas the words are lacking in B F D, *al.*

Luke xxii. 64, the Slavonic lectionary supports ἔτυπτον αὐτοῦ τὸ πρόσωπον with Ψ 33, 579, 892, *al.*, whereas the phrase is lacking in B ℵ K L M T Π, 209, *al.*

To identify these lectionary readings as Alexandrian is to display ignorance of the most elementary knowledge of New Testament textual criticism. The extraordinary number of presumed

---

[1] No account is taken here of the edition of the Old Slavonic Gospels published at Rome in 1943 (the first Slavic edition to receive general approval from the Holy Roman Apostolic See), inasmuch as it was professedly framed not on critical but on 'practical' principles and designed for liturgical services; see Schweigl's review in *Bib*, xxv (1944), 240–3.

[2] 'De textu recepto slavico evangelii liturgici', *Bib*, xxiv (1943), 289–303. In an earlier article, 'La Bibbia slava del 1751 (1756)', *Bib*, xviii (1937), 51–73, Schweigl refers to several bibliographical items of historical interest. It may be mentioned also that much curious information regarding the Old Slavonic Scriptures and early Bibles printed in Russia can be found in Ebenezer Henderson's *Biblical Researches and Travels in Russia* (London, 1826), pp. 60–135.

[3] *Bib*, xxiv (1943), 294; cf. also 303.

[4] Ibid. 292–4.

Alexandrian readings that Schweigl supposed he had discovered in the liturgical Slavonic Gospel is gained by labelling as Alexandrian any variant that may be supported by even *one* Alexandrian manuscript, irrespective of the character of that manuscript or the weight of the evidence for the contrary reading.

Mention must also be made of the debate regarding the question of possible influence on the Old Slavonic version from the Latin and the Gothic versions. So long ago as 1853, the philologist Šafařík expressed the opinion that the Old Slavonic text of the Gospels exhibits a certain influence from the Vulgate.[1] In 1925 Pogorelov worked afresh on the problem and found what he believed to be additional examples of Latin influence upon the Old Slavonic version.[2] Having scrutinzed Pogorelov's examples Vajs concluded that they were insufficient to prove his thesis.[3] The noted linguist Meillet also weighed Pogorelov's hypothesis and found that his examples prove no more than that the old Slavonic vocabulary which Cyril and Methodius used had already been influenced by certain Latinisms, and that these are quite insufficient to prove any influence of the Vulgate upon the Old Slavonic version as such.[4]

In the following year the Polish scholar, Słoński, in a much more detailed discussion, concluded that apparent agreements with the Vulgate text against the presumed Greek original, so far as they do not rest upon hitherto unknown Greek variants, may be explained best by postulating a certain critical independence on the part of the Slavonic translator in making the version.[5]

In a subsequent article Vajs[6] made several small concessions to Pogorelov's thesis by admitting that there are a few passages which can scarcely be explained apart from reference to the corresponding Vulgate renderings. These are Matt. xxiii. 4, which involves a misunderstanding of *colligunt* and *alligant*; John

[1] P. J. Šafařík, *Památky hlaholského písemnictví* (Prague, 1853), pp. xxiv, xxxvi ff. (referred to by van Wijk in *Byslav*, iii (1931), 89).

[2] Valerij Pogorelov, 'Iz nabljudenij v oblasti drevne-slavjanskoj perevodnoj literatury; i, Latinskoe vlijanie v perevode Evangelija', *Sborník filosofické fakulty University Komenského v Bratislavě*, iii. 32 (6) (1925), 209–16.

[3] 'Jaký vliv měla latinská Vulgáta na staroslovanský překlad evangelií', *Slavia*, v (1926–7), 158–62.

[4] A. Meillet, 'L'hypothèse d'une influence de la Vulgate sur la traduction slave de l'Évangile', *RÉS* vi (1926), 39–41.

[5] Stanisław Słoński, 'O rzekomym wpływie łacińskiej Vulgaty na starosłowiański przekład ewangelii', *Slavia*, vi (1927–8), 246–64.   [6] *Byslav*, i (1927), 9.

vi. 23, which rests on a misinterpretation, *gratias agentes* (instead of *agente*) *Deo* (instead of *Domino*) : εὐχαριστήσαντες τοῦ κυρίου; and Matt. vi. 11, *nasǫštьny*, which is a literal translation of Jerome's *supersubstantialem* for ἐπιούσιον. According to a critique by Rozov, however, each of these examples is susceptible of a different explanation which does not involve the supposition of influence from the Vulgate.[1]

Nicolaas van Wijk introduced a new element into the discussion by suggesting that the Old Slavonic rendering of συνέλεξαν in Matt. xiii. 48 as *izbьrašę* ('they chose') reveals dependence upon Tatian's Diatessaron (via the Latin Vulgate *elegerunt*).[2]

In 1942 the Croatian scholar Hamm proposed the theory that the Gothic version influenced the Old Slavonic.[3] He recognized that, according to all that is known of the Goths and their literature, it is unthinkable that the Gothic Bible could have influenced Cyril and Methodius in the second half of the ninth century. On the strength, therefore, of supposed parallels between the two versions, Hamm went so far as to transpose the beginnings of the Old Slavonic version to an earlier period, as early as the sixth or seventh century. Such a theory, if it is to be proposed at all, must be supported with the strongest kind of evidence. Instead of this, however, Hamm's examples are of the most trivial sort, which if valid, could be used to prove, *mutatis mutandis*, that the Authorized English version is dependent upon the Old Slavonic! In subsequent studies Vajs[4] and Janko[5] refuted Hamm's opinion, the former by showing that the underlying type of text represented in the Gothic version is markedly different from that of the Old Slavonic version, and the latter by considering the question from the standpoint of linguistics.

---

[1] Vladimir Rozov, *Slavia*, ix (1930–1), 620–1.

[2] 'Eine Vulgatalesart im slavischen Evangelium (Mat. XIII, 48)?' *Byslav*, iii (1931), 89–91.

[3] Josip Hamm, 'Über den gotischen Einfluss auf die altkirchenslavische Bibelübersetzung', *ZVS* lxvii (1942), 112–28.

[4] 'Je-li staroslověnský překlad evangelií a žaltáře nějak závislý na gotském překladu Vulfilově?' (with a French résumé), *Byslav*, viii (1936–46), 145–71. Vajs also supported his contention indirectly in another article, 'Které recense byla řecká předloha staroslověnského překladu žaltáře (with a French résumé), ibid., pp. 55–86, where he indicates, on the basis of an examination of 500 readings in the Old Slavonic Psalter, that 449 are pure Lucianic and the others are influenced by the Vulgate. None shows Gothic influence.

[5] Josef Janko, 'Měl-li Wulfilův gotský překlad bible vliv na překlad starocírkevněslovanský?' *Časopis pro moderní filologii*, xxviii (1942), 29–42, 121–34, 254–68.

A decade after Hamm's misguided article appeared, Ferdinand Liewehr, in a brief study which reveals little knowledge of previous literature on the subject, attempted to show that Cyril, while in Cherson, became acquainted with Ulfilas' translation of the Scriptures.[1] He confined his attention to the phrase 'Russian letters' in the *Vita Constantini*,[2] interpreting it to mean 'Gothic letters'. Liewehr was answered in a richly documented article by Dietrich Gerhardt,[3] who had no difficulty in showing the improbability of Cyril's contact with Gothic.[4] From yet another side, Hamm's theory was given the *coup de grâce* by the Germanist scholar Leopold Zatočil, who, on the basis of a minute analysis of the first five chapters of the Gospel of Mark, proves that the Gothic and Slavonic versions have nothing in common.[5]

In a posthumously published essay by Pechuška, edited by Kurz, attention is given to the Old Slavonic text of Acts as preserved in manuscripts of the twelfth and thirteenth centuries. According to the author, this text was based on a Greek original of mixed characteristics, belonging principally to the Constantinopolitan recension with pre-Syrian elements of two types, the Alexandrian and Western. Of these the Western readings predominate.[6]

---

[1] 'Wie Konstantin-Kyrill mit Wulfilas Bibelübersetzung bekannt wurde', *Beiträge zur Namenforschung*, iii (1951–2), 287–90.

[2] See pp. 397–8 above.

[3] 'Goten, Slaven oder Syrer im alten Cherson?' *Beiträge zur Namenforschung*, iv (1953), 78–88.

[4] At the same time Gerhardt supposes that Cyril was acquainted with the Syriac, suggesting that he, 'with the textual critical interest of a missionary preacher, could have studied their version [i.e. that of the Syrian merchants of Cherson] of the Scriptures exactly as Charlemagne on the very last day of his life corrected the Gospels *cum Graecis et Siris*' (p. 85; this comment concerning Charlemagne is found in Thegan, *Vita Hludovici Imperatoris*, § 7 (Migne, *PL* cvi, col. 409)). But, in view of the difficulty that Charlemagne had in learning to write ('temptabat et scribere . . . sed parum successit labor praeposterus ac sero inchoatus', Einhard, *Vita Karoli Imperatoris*, § 25 (= *Monumenta Germaniae historica, Scriptores*, ii. 457, lines 2 ff.)), Thegan is probably to be understood as meaning no more than that Charlemagne asked Greeks and Syrians questions regarding the Gospels. In any case, the incident has nothing to do with the question whether Cyril knew Syriac and used Tatian's Diatessaron.

[5] 'Zum Problem der vermeintlichen Einwirkung der gotischen Bibelübersetzung auf die altkirchenslavische', *Sborník prací*, Filosofická faculta, Brněnské universita, xiii (A 12) (1964), 81–95.

[6] Fr. Pechuška, 'Řecká předloha staroslovanského textu Skutků apoštolských', *Slovanské studie; Sbírka statí, věnovaných . . . J. Vajsovi k uctění jeho životního díla* (Prague, 1948), pp. 60–5.

Attention must now be directed to several studies by the Czech scholar Karel Horálek, who has argued that a progressive stylistic deterioration marks the textual transmission of the Old Slavonic text of the Gospels. What he terms the exquisite style of the original translation has suffered, he thinks, from the mechanical work of the scribes who replaced many a free but happy turn with a servile imitation of the Greek model, going so far as even to adopt the Greek order of words.[1] Horálek also distinguishes among the special characteristics of various Old Slavonic text-types. In the Balkans the Slavonic translation was subsequently harmonized with the official Greek text of the Byzantine Church. The Bogomil Gospel texts have a rather pronounced archaic character; relatively well preserved from the lexical point of view, they reveal nevertheless a syntax which is strongly Hellenized. The Croatian Glagolitic texts bear traces of a revision resting upon the Latin Vulgate.[2]

In a wide-ranging volume entitled 'The Lectionaries and the Four Gospel Manuscripts; Contributions to the Textual Criticism and History of the Old Slavonic Version of the Gospel',[3] Horálek takes as his starting-point the generally accepted view that Cyril translated a Greek lectionary of the shorter variety. Subsequently the text was completed by additions taken from a tetraevangelium. During the production and transmission of this text two types of modifications were introduced, those that reflected variant readings in Greek manuscripts and those that were merely stylistic and due to the translator(s). Horálek is pessimistic regarding the possibility of determining exactly the archetype of the Old Church Slavonic text, particularly since the transmission of the text discloses Slavonic readings which find no parallel in previously collated Greek manuscripts.

In an article entitled 'La traduction vieux-slave de l'Évangile — sa version originale et son développement ulterieur',[4] Horálek

---

[1] This had been pointed out earlier, e.g., by Georges Cuendet, *L'Ordre des mots dans le texte grec et dans les versions gotique, arménienne et vieux slave des Évangiles*; Ière partie, *Les Groupes nominaux* (Paris, 1929) ; compare also Vaillant's article mentioned in p. 412 n. 3 above.

[2] K. Horálek, 'K dějinám tekstu staroslověnského evangelia' (with a Latin summary), *Acta Academiae Velehradensis*, xix (1948), 208–29.

[3] *Evangeliáře a čtveroevangelia. Příspěvky k textové kritice a k dějinám staroslověnského překladu evangelia* (Státní pedagogické nakladatelství, Prague, 1954), with a résumé in Russian.

[4] *Byslav*, xx (1959), 267–84, being essentially an expansion of Horálek's article,

examines selected renderings in several Old Slavonic manuscripts, and reiterates his view that copyists made alterations in the Old Slavonic version, so that little by little it lost its pure Slavonic character and more and more imitated turns of expression in the underlying Greek. There is also a marked difference, he finds, between the characteristics of the Slavonic text that was translated originally from a Greek lectionary and those supplementary portions that were added later from Greek manuscripts of the four Gospels.

IV. THE PRESENT STATE OF RESEARCH ON THE OLD CHURCH SLAVONIC VERSION[1]

The present state of research on the Old Church Slavonic version leaves something to be desired. As was mentioned earlier in describing the earliest manuscripts of the version, not all of them have been made available in published editions. Furthermore, among the hundreds of later manuscripts that embody in a more developed stage the several dialectal forms of the Slavonic,[2] only a beginning has been made in the task of systematically cataloguing their contents, to say nothing of the collation of their text. As regards one of the later Slavonic versions, the Old

'K dějinám tekstu staroslověnského evangelia', *Acta Academiae Velehradensis*, xix (1948), 208–29. For a subsequent survey by the same author, see 'Zum heutigen Stand der textkritischen Erforschung des altkirchenslavischen Evangeliums', *ZSP* xxvii (1958–9), 255–74.

[1] For a comprehensive survey of the present state of research on the Old Church Slavonic version, see Christian Hannick, 'Das Neue Testament in altkirchenslavischer Sprache; der gegenwärtige Stand seiner Erforschung und seine Bedeutung für die griechische Textgeschichte', in *Die alten Übersetzungen des Neuen Testamentes, die Kirchenväterzitate und Lektionare*, ed. by K. Aland (Berlin and New York, 1972), pp. 403–35; for a brief summary, see Hannick, 'The Old-Slavonic Version of the New Testament', *BibT* xxv (1974), 143–6 and 353. Cf. also K. Logachev, 'The Work of Prof. I. E. Evseyev on the History of the Slavonic Bible', *Journal of the Moscow Patriarchate* (English edn.), 1972 (8) pp. 76–8.

[2] According to a census made earlier in the twentieth century, there are 4,101 Biblical manuscripts in a variety of Slavic dialects, dating from the eleventh to the seventeenth century, found in various libraries; see I. E. Evseyev, 'Rukopisnoe predanie slavjanskoj biblii', *Xristianskoe čtenie* (1911), pp. 436–50, 644–60 (brief summary in Latin in *Acta Academiae Velehradensis*, ix (1913), 89). J. Vašica and J. Vajs have catalogued the Old Slavonic manuscripts which are in the National Museum at Prague; see their *Soupis staroslovanských rukopisů narodního musea v Praze* (Prague, 1957).

Bohemian (which Tischendorf cited occasionally), in 1926 James Hardy Ropes lamented with a degree of justification:

A complete knowledge of the Old Bohemian Acts might yield results of much importance for the 'Western' text of Acts. Such a knowledge would not be difficult to secure, and it is not to the credit of New Testament scholarship that nearly a century and a half have passed [since Dobrovský] without any use being made of sources easily accessible in Germany and Bohemia.[1]

A start, however, has been made in the long-overdue work of classifying more distinctly the several kinds of Slavonic lectionaries. The preliminary work of Vrana in his study of 'The Types, Redactions, and the Mutual Relationships of the Old Slavonic Gospels',[2] in which he sets forth in convenient tabular form statistics concerning characteristic variations in seven of the more important Old Church Slavonic manuscripts, has been carried much further by the Russian palaeographer, L. P. Žukovskaya. Concentrating on cataloguing and classifying the several kinds of Slavonic lectionaries or *aprakos* (the term, used for both the singular and the plural, is derived from the Greek expression ἄπρακτοι ἡμέραι), Madam Žukovskaya has collected information concerning 506 Slavic manuscripts of the Russian redaction. She has found that *aprakos*, which predominate over tetraevangelia by a ratio of about five to two, fall into three main classes:[3]

(*a*) The full *aprakos*, giving lessons for each day of the year

---

[1] *The Text of Acts*, being vol. iii of *The Beginnings of Christianity*, Part I, *The Acts of the Apostles*, ed. by F. J. Foakes Jackson and Kirsopp Lake (London, 1926), p. cxli. That a certain amount of work, however, has been accomplished on this version can be seen from the admirable surveys by Josef Vraštil, S.J., 'Conspectus recentiorum de antiqua bibliorum versione bohemica litterarum et consilia', *Acta Academiae Velehradensis*, ix (1913), 31–44, and by J. Vašica, *Staročeské Evangeliáře*, being No. 68 of the *Rozpravy české akademie věd a umění*, iii (Prague, 1931).

[2] Josip Vrana, 'O tipovima, redakcijama i meďusobnom odnosu staroslovjenskih evanďelja', *Slavia*, xxvi (1957), 321–36; cf. also idem, 'Makedonska redakcija staroslavenskih evanďelja', *Simpozium 1100-godišnina od smrtta na Kiril solunski*, ii (Skopje, 1970), 51–64 (Eng. résumé, 'Macedonian Redaction of the Old Slavonic Gospels', pp. 65–6).

[3] Lidiya P. Žukovskaja, 'Ob obeme pervoj slavjanskoj knigi, perevedennoj s grečeskogo Kirrillom i Mefodiem', *Voprosy slavjanskogo jazykoznanija* (Moscow), vii (1963), 73–81; id., 'Nekotorye dannye o gruppirovke slavjanskix rukopisej polnogo aprakosa XII–XIV vv.' (with a German résumé), *PS* xvii (80) (1967), 176–84; and id., 'Tipologija rukopisej drevnerusskogo polnogo aprakosa XI–XIV vv. v svjazi s lingvističeskim izučeniem ix', *Pamjatniki drevnerusskoj pis'mennosti. Jazyk i tekstologija*, (Moscow, 1968), pp. 199–332.

except during Lent. There are, in fact, several variant forms of the full *aprakos*, differing as to the selection of the Scripture lessons.

(*b*) The short *aprakos*, providing lessons for all days of the period from Easter to Pentecost, but only those for Saturdays and Sundays during the rest of the year.

(*c*) An uncommon type which supplies only the Saturday and Sunday lessons and those for Holy Week (Russian *voskresnoe evangelie*).

Much work still needs to be done in tracing relationships among copies of *aprakos*, as well as seeking their ancestry in the several types of Greek lectionary manuscripts.[1] In the future more care must be taken in describing the contents of *aprakos*, not only as to the choice and sequence of lessons but also as to determining how far variant readings reflect a Greek *Vorlage* or have arisen through dialectal variation.[2]

Vajs's critical edition of the four Gospels in Old Church Slavonic, with the presumed Greek *Vorlage*, serviceable though it is in the absence of anything better, is satisfactory neither in scope nor execution. The casual user of the edition is likely to receive the impression that the reconstructed text rests throughout on the evidence of the thirteen manuscripts quoted in the apparatus. Such an impression, however, would be quite erroneous, not only because several of the manuscripts are defective, but also because Vajs provides an incomplete citation of evidence from the manuscripts he professes to use.

---

[1] A beginning has been made by Mrs. Yvonne Eileen Burns, 'A Comparative Study of the Weekday Lection Systems found in Some Greek and Early Slavonic Gospel Lectionaries' (Ph.D. diss., University of London, School of Slavonic and East European Studies, 1975), who distinguishes three types of Greek week-day lectionaries, as well as several sub-groups, and discusses their relationships to one another and to several Slavonic lectionaries. Cf. also her paper, 'The Canaanitess and other Additional Lections in Early Slavonic Lectionaries', read at the Third International Congress for South East European Studies, Bucharest, Sept. 1974.

[2] On the relation between the two types of analysis, see Josip Vrana, 'Über das vergleichende Sprach- und Textstudium altkirchenslavischen Evangelien', *WS* v (1960), 418–28; cf. also Leszek Moszyński's lexical investigations of the text of *aprakos* in his article, 'Staro-cerkiewno-słowiański aprakos', *Studia z filologii polskiej i słowiańskiej* (Warsaw), ii (1957), 373–95, a study which was followed a decade later by Moszyński's attempt to trace the ancestry of the long form of the *aprakos* ('Pokrewieństwo najstarszych staro-cerkiewno-słowiańskich tekstów ewangelijnych w świetle statystyki słownikowej', *Slavia Occidentalis*, xxvii (1968), 153–8).

While recognizing the limitations of Vajs's edition, one can nevertheless gain from it at least a partial representation of the textual complexion of the version, especially if one pays attention to evidence of individual witnesses in the apparatus. Using a collation of chapter viii of Vajs's Slavonic text of Luke against the Greek Textus Receptus,[1] the present writer collected the following data.[2] Sixty-three variant readings involving the reconstructed text and/or one or more Slavonic manuscripts find support among non-Slavonic evidence as follows: one or more of the Old Latin witnesses agree with Old Slavonic readings twenty-three times; the Syriac Peshitta agrees eighteen times; אֲ, X, and 1 agree sixteen times; L, Θ, and the Latin Vulgate agree fourteen times; D and 33 agree thirteen times; 69, 157, 213, and 1192 agree twelve times; 1071 and the Curetonian Syriac agree eleven times; B and 124 agree ten times; C, 13 and the Harklean Syriac agree nine times; R, W, 22, 118, 1012, and 1241 agree eight times. Each of eighty-five other witnesses exhibits fewer than eight agreements with the Old Slavonic. Finally, it should be mentioned that fifteen variants from the Greek Textus Receptus have no support from non-Slavonic witnesses. More than half of these variants, however, involve Slavonic renderings which might find an explanation in terms of idiomatic considerations without reflecting a different Greek original.

It is clear from these data that the Old Church Slavonic possesses textual elements derived from several distinct families. The basic text is, as one would expect, the Byzantine or Koine. This, however, is not any of the later varieties, but seems to be a development of that earlier form of the Koine that also lies behind the Syriac Peshitta[3] of the fifth century. This latter, as is well known, is a text which on the whole ranges itself with the Constantinopolitan or Koine type, yet not wholly, having a considerable intermixture of readings characteristic of the β and δ texts.[4] The proportion of Western readings normal to this form

---

[1] The collation was made in 1951 by Professor Giuliano Bonfante, at that time at Princeton University.

[2] For a more detailed account, see Metzger's *Chapters in the History of New Testament Textual Criticism* (Leiden and Grand Rapids, 1963), pp. 92–6.

[3] More than a century ago the Russian scholar K. I. Nevostruev discussed the question of influence from the Peshitta Syriac version in the Old Church Slavonic Gospels; cf. *Kirillomefodievskij sbornik* (Moscow, 1865), pp. 209–34.

[4] See pp. 418–20 above.

of the Koine is, in the case of the Old Slavonic, considerably heightened by the admixture of a Western strain similar to that which appears in the Old Latin, the Vulgate, and D. One is not surprised, therefore, to find that the Old Church Slavonic agrees not infrequently with ℵ, L, X, and Θ, all of them being witnesses that oscillate between the β and δ texts.

The question of the origin of the Western readings in the Old Church Slavonic has been debated more than once and is still *sub judice*. Their presence may well be the result of the papal requirement that, though the Byzantine liturgy might be used, the Scriptures should be read in Latin before they were read in Slavonic (see p. 399 above). What recension of the Vulgate was current in Moravia in the late ninth century may be difficult to determine with precision, but undoubtedly the way was open for a certain number of Vulgate (i.e. Western) readings to be introduced into the Old Church Slavonic version.

Whether, in addition to such accidental contamination with Vulgate readings, the Old Church Slavonic also had from the beginning a dual parentage of both Greek and Latin *Vorlagen* has been answered recently by Horálek in a qualified affirmative: 'The general situation speaks rather clearly for the use [by Constantine and Methodius] of the Latin *Vorlage* at least as a *Hilfsmittel*.'[1] At the same time, the continuing debate over individual passages that are presumed to exhibit Latinisms seems to be without end—and without conclusive proof.[2]

In assessing the value of the Old Church Slavonic version for the textual critic today, it goes without saying that this version, originating as it did in the ninth century, has little or no significance so far as an attempt to ascertain the original text is concerned.[3] On the other hand, however, besides providing welcome

---

[1] K. Horálek, 'Zur Frage der lateinischen Einfluss in der altkirchenslavischen Bibelübersetzung', *Cyrillo-Methodianische Fragen, Slavische Philologie und Altertumskunde* (Wiesbaden, 1968), pp. 29–42; quotation from p. 41.

[2] In addition to the literature mentioned above (pp. 422–3) the continuing debate has been carried on by N. Molńar, 'The Calques of Greek Origin in the Most Ancient Old Slavic Gospel Texts', *SS* x (1964), 108–16; D. G. Huntley, 'Is Old Church Slavonic "Lead us not into temptation. . . ." a Latinism?' *Slavia*, xxxv (1966), 431–5; and Heinz Wissemann, 'Die altkirchenslavischen Versionen der vierten Bitte des Vaterunsers', *WS* xiv (1969), 393–405.

[3] A different view is taken by most Russian Orthodox scholars, who consider the Byzantine recension to preserve most nearly the original text of the New Testament; cf. R. P. Casey, 'A Russian Orthodox View of New Testament Textual Criticism', *Theology*, lx (1957), 50–4, a series of articles in the *Zhurnal Moskovskoj*

information concerning the history of later stages in the transmission of the text, the version is useful in supplying fuller information concerning the development of the several divergent patterns among Greek lectionaries that served as models for the Slavonic *aprakos*.

V. LIMITATIONS OF OLD CHURCH SLAVONIC IN REPRESENTING GREEK

by Horace G. Lunt

The Moravian Mission of Cyril and Methodius produced a Slavic translation of the entire Bible, except Maccabees, in the period 863–85. Much of this was lost immediately, and only the Gospels and the Psalter have come down to us in relatively archaic south-Slavic manuscripts preserving the language defined as Old Church Slavonic. The four properly O.C.S. Gospel codices[1] probably date from shortly after A.D. 1000, give or take a decade or two; palaeographic dating is pure guesswork, and linguistic dating rests on a series of unprovable hypotheses. The four show all kinds of linguistic and textological variants, but it is possible to discern the outlines and some major details of the early translation and its language.[2]

The surface structures of O.C.S. and Greek coincide in nearly all major features. The form-classes are generally the same: verbs (conjugated for several tenses, with person–number desinences), substantives (nouns and adjectives, including participles, declined for case and number), pronouns (personal, demonstrative,

---

Patriarkhiï by A. Ivanov and K. I. Logachev (for summaries see Hannick, 'Das Neue Testament in altkirchenslavischer Sprache', op. cit., pp. 432 f., and Erich Bryner in *BibT* xxv (1974), 327 ff.), and K. I. Logachev, 'The Problem of the Relationship of the Greek Text of the Bible to the Church Slavonic and Russian Text', ibid. xxv (1974), 313–18.

[1] The Zographensis and Marianus are tetraevangelia, while Assemanianus and Savvina Kniga ('Saba's Book') are lectionaries (called 'short' in recent Russian scholarship, for they provide no week-day lessons from Pentecost to Holy Week).

[2] The witness of the oldest dated Slavic manuscript, the Ostromir, an East Slavic 'short' lectionary of 1056, is often cited for textological purposes, although important phonetic details cause most scholars to exclude Os from linguistic descriptions of O.C.S. A number of fragments and somewhat younger manuscripts must be brought in for textological investigations, but for the present discussion the five manuscripts are sufficient.

interrogative, relative; declined for gender, case, and number), numerals (declined), prepositions, adverbs, a variety of conjunctions, and particles. Syntactical devices are closely comparable and even word formation follows the same general patterns. So close were the two languages that a reasonable translation often could be achieved by a word-for-word rendering. In every manuscript there are examples of undue literalism, but on the whole the translation appears to have been made by people who had mastery of both languages and who aimed at reproducing the spirit and the meaning of the Greek while keeping very closely to the original wording. To judge in detail just what is too literal and therefore un-Slavic, and what is grammatically correct but somewhat unidiomatic is a perilous task, for we have no original O.C.S. writings to serve as a measure of 'normal' usage. In the vast literature on this topic[1] the successful parts of the translation (and scholars are by no means agreed as to what constitutes success here) are usually attributed to the original work of Cyril, perhaps with his brother,[2] and the misunderstandings or over-literal passages are blamed on later copyists and 'correctors'.[3]

Three of the manuscripts (Zo Ma As) are written in the Glagolitic alphabet, surely invented in 863 for the new translation, while Sa and Os use the probably misnamed Cyrillic, which is simply Greek uncials with extra letters for specifically Slavic sounds. The phonetics of proper names and loan-words reflect current Greek pronunciation. Thus *i* stands for ι, η, $\epsilon\iota$; *e* for ϵ, $\alpha\iota$; while upsilon (and its special Glagolitic equivalent) reflects both

---

[1] The most useful general assessment is still Otto Grünenthal, 'Die Übersetzungstechnik der altkirchenslavischen Evangelienübersetzung', *ASP* xxxi (1909–10), 321–63, and xxxii (1910–11), 1–48.

[2] The most ambitious attempt to represent the 'original' Cyrillo-Methodian translation was published in Prague by the late Mgr. Josef Vajs, who printed his O.C.S. reconstruction facing his reconstruction of *the* Greek text the early translators allegedly used. (Matthew and Mark came out in 1935, Luke and John in 1936.) Vajs's concept of the complexity of the problems was much too simple; his philological practice was uneven, to say the least. The convenient format still leads scholars to refer to Vajs for quick answers, despite detailed and severe criticism of his work, and I therefore offer a few illustrative cautionary remarks in subsequent notes.

[3] The gradual evolution of the original translation is a fascinating topic, worthy of detailed study. Scribes and more authoritative editors constantly referred to various Greek and Slavonic manuscripts, producing many new families of text. Yet none of the waves of reform resulted in anything that could be called a new translation until modern times.

v and $o\iota$, with variants u and i (*Sürija, Surija, Sirija* for $\Sigma\acute{v}\rho\iota\alpha$). The omega of both alphabets is used as the equivalent of ordinary o. Cyrillic uses Greek psi and xi appropriately; Glagolitic simply juxtaposes *ps* and *ks*. A special Glagolitic letter, transcribed *ǵ*, appears for γ before a front vowel. Glagolitic provides for theta and phi, but the corresponding sounds were obviously foreign to Slavic and *t* and *p* may be used instead in either alphabet, e.g. *Vithleemъ* or *Vitleemъ* $B\eta\theta\lambda\acute{\epsilon}\epsilon\mu$. Fluctuations such as *Nazaretъ* and *Nazarethъ* thus are unreliable clues as to whether the Greek had $Na\zeta a\rho\acute{\epsilon}\theta$ or $Na\zeta a\rho\acute{\epsilon}\tau$. The scribes had the usual difficulties with proper names, particularly in the genealogies, but on the whole variants parallel Greek variants. It is a curiosity that expected *Vith(ъ)saida*[1] or *Vit(ъ)saida* are minority spellings for more usual *Vid(ъ)saida* $B\eta\theta\sigma\alpha\ddot{\imath}\delta\acute{a}$.

The native character of the translation is guaranteed by the appropriate use of the dual in all possible conjugated and declined forms; it reflects the Greek plural. The O.C.S. supine, expressing purpose after a verb of motion, is generally used correctly, although it can be replaced by an infinitive.

The use of cases and of prepositions in the O.C.S. Gospels is generally native and idiomatic, despite occasional oddities and a considerable amount of variation which can be credited to differences in the local dialects of our unknown scribes and their predecessors. Thus Luke viii. 43 $\iota a\tau\rho o\hat{\imath}s$ / $\epsilon\hat{\imath}s$ $\iota a\tau\rho o\acute{v}s$ can be expressed only by the dative *vračemъ*. Matt. xiii. 52 $\mu a\theta\eta\tau\epsilon v\theta\epsilon\hat{\imath}s$ $\tau\hat{\eta}$ $\beta a\sigma\iota\lambda\epsilon\acute{\iota}a$/$\epsilon\hat{\imath}s$ $\tau\grave{\eta}v$ $\beta a\sigma\iota\lambda\epsilon\acute{\iota}av$ has to be *naučъ sę cěsarъstvъju*, for the O.C.S. verb requires a dative complement.[2] The Greek instrumental ($\acute{\epsilon}v$) $\pi v\epsilon\acute{v}\mu a\tau\iota$ $\dot{a}\gamma\acute{\iota}\omega$ always results in the O.C.S. instrumental case *duxomъ svętyimъ*, but the fact that baptism ($\acute{\epsilon}v$) $\mathring{v}\delta a\tau\iota$ is rendered by the instrumental *vodojǫ* except in John i. 31 *vъ vodě* (As has pl. *vъ vodaxъ*) does not guarantee that the underlying Greek had no preposition except in this last instance. In Matt. xiii. 1 $\acute{\epsilon}\xi\epsilon\lambda\theta\grave{\omega}v$ $\acute{o}$ $'I\eta\sigma o\hat{v}s$ ($\dot{a}\pi\acute{o}/\acute{\epsilon}\kappa$) $\tau\hat{\eta}s$ $o\grave{\iota}\kappa\acute{\iota}as$ O.C.S. must use a

---

[1] O.C.S. had few possible consonant clusters and no geminates. In foreign names and words ъ or ь (presumably representing short, lax *u* and *i* in native words in the early period) often occurs between letters making up intolerable clusters; e.g. Mark xiv. 32 $\Gamma\epsilon\theta\sigma\eta\mu a v\acute{\iota}$ *gethsimanii* Os, *getъsimani* Sa, *ǵedsimani* Ma, *ǵedъsimani* As, *gen'simani* Zo; Matt. i. 15 $Ma\theta\theta\acute{a}v$ *Mattanъ* As, *Matъthanъ* Sa. There is some evidence that this was purely graphic, but it is possible that in some Slavic traditions these letters were sometimes pronounced in such cases.

[2] O.C.S. spelling is normalized in this paper (except for the preceding footnote), even in citations of individual manuscripts.

preposition, *isъdъ Isusъ iz domu.*[1] Other examples of the inadequacy of O.C.S. in reflecting the Greek cases and prepositional phrases occur below in the discussion of other features.

The O.C.S. pronominal system agrees at every major point with the Greek, and there seem to be no important passages where the Slavic text allows for more than one Greek reading.[2]

Old Church Slavonic lacks an explicit definite article, and thus fails to reflect the presence or absence of the Greek article before a personal name or unmodified noun. Therefore in Mark iii. 1, preposition plus noun *vъ sъnъmište* represents εἰς συναγωγήν or εἰς τὴν συναγωγήν. In Matt. xxvi. 27, participle plus accusative *priimъ čašǫ* is a literal translation of either λαβὼν τὸ ποτήριον or simply λαβὼν ποτήριον.[3]

Adjectives and participles may express definiteness by means of the long or compound declensional forms, which usually correspond to a Greek syntagma containing a definite article. Thus Mark i. 4 *Ioanъ krъstę* shows no Greek article, Ἰωάννης βαπτίζων,[4] but vi. 14 *krъstęi* surely reflects ὁ βαπτίζων. Grünenthal found *duxъ svętъ* ten times for πνεῦμα ἅγιον, in clear contrast to *duxъ svętyi* for πνεῦμα τὸ ἅγιον eleven times.

Unfortunately, however, there is a series of complications. Certain adjectives, whether for formal or semantic reasons, apparently were used only in the long form. In Matt. xix. 30, *bǫdǫtъ prъvii poslědъńii i poslědъńii prъvii,* ἔσονται πρῶτοι (οἱ) ἔσχατοι καὶ (οἱ) ἔσχατοι πρῶτοι, the adjective 'last' contains a formant *-ъń-* that requires the compound declension, while the substantivized 'first' seems to require definition here in the same way English does.[5] Thus neither long form requires us to look for

---

[1] This is one of many cases where we have no basis for making a selection from among reasonably common Greek variants. Vajs arbitrarily prints ἀπό.

[2] e.g. in Luke ii. 22 τοῦ καθαρισμοῦ (αὐτῶν/αὐτῆς) Sa omits the pronoun, with some Greek witnesses, while the other texts attest αὐτῶν: the dual *eju* demonstrates that the translator had in mind specifically Mother plus *either* Child *or* husband, but not both.

[3] This sort of ambiguity is not hinted at by Vajs. He offers the articles in both these cases and the similar instances that abound in the Gospels. His decisions affecting the articles before names, particularly (ὁ) Ἰησοῦς, are based purely on his preference for certain types of texts.

[4] The O.C.S. stem *Ioan-* had surely been domesticated, though *Ioann-* occurs. O.C.S. is no guide to the Greek Ἰωάννης vs. Ἰωάνης, cf. p. 433 n. 1 above.

[5] Similarly, English must say '*the* Holy Ghost/Spirit': Grünenthal found definite *duxъ svętyi* five times for anarthrous πνεῦμα ἅγιον, but no discrepancies in the other direction.

a Greek variant with article. The extant spellings of many O.C.S. words can be taken as indefinite or as phonetically contracted compound forms (Mark vii. 23 τὰ πονηρά: Zo as expected *zъlaja vs.* Ma *zъla*). Possessive and locational adjectives apparently serve as definiteness-markers even in short form, but the relationship to Greek definite articles is ambiguous (cf. Grünenthal). Some expressions consistently fail to agree with the Greek, e.g. φωνὴ βοῶντος never adds τοῦ, but O.C.S. has the definite *glasъ vъpijǫštaego*. It is well known that the details of usage of definite articles or other definitizers may differ among closely related dialects; it is not surprising that O.C.S. has considerable internal variation and that we cannot equate fluctuating Greek usage to specific O.C.S. variants.

The Greek article with prepositional phrases tended to be translated by an O.C.S. adjective, but occasionally it is rendered by means of a relative pronoun, e.g. Matt. vi. 23 τὸ φῶς τὸ ἐν σοί *svĕtъ iže vъ tebĕ*. This construction is rare in the Gospels, and it was probably felt as an elliptic relative clause, with the copula omitted. In John xix. 38 *Iosifъ iže otъ Arimatheę* (As) surely reflects (ὁ) Ἰωσὴφ ὁ ἀπὸ Ἀριμαθαίας, while *Iosifъ otъ Arimatheę* (Os) more likely shows (ὁ) Ἰωσὴφ ἀπὸ Ἀριμαθαίας (along with all witnesses to Mark xv. 43). Yet O.C.S. ordinarily does not tolerate equational sentences without copula,[1] so John xix. 38 in Zo Ma have *Iosifъ iže bĕ otъ A*, in retroversion (ὁ) Ἰωσὴφ ὃς ἦν ἀπὸ A. Similarly Luke viii. 45 ὁ Πέτρος καὶ οἱ σὺν αὐτῷ (or μετὰ αὐτοῦ) has been expanded to a relative clause with the appropriate imperfect form of 'be' (= ἦσαν): *Petrъ i iže sъ nimъ bĕaxǫ*. Given this information, however, it seems likely that Luke v. 7 *pričęstъnikomъ iže bĕaxǫ vъ druzĕmъ korablji* reflects the Greek variant with article before the prepositional phrase τοῖς μετόχοις ἐν τῷ ἑτέρῳ πλοίῳ. On the other hand Mark v. 27 *slyšavъši o Isusĕ* is ambiguous, ἀκούσασα (τὰ) περὶ (τοῦ) Ἰησοῦ.

The O.C.S. verb distinguishes a present tense and two simple preterites (the imperfect and aorist) which specify person and number (singular, dual, plural), plus an active resultative participle used with the auxiliary 'be' to form perfect, pluperfect, and conditional-hypothetical tenses which also specify gender. Further, there are active and passive present and

---

[1] Compare Mark xii. 16 *čii estъ obrazъ sъ* τίνος ἡ εἰκὼν αὕτη, or Luke iv. 36 *čъto estъ slovo se* τίς (ἐστιν) ὁ λόγος οὗτος, where evidence for ἐστιν is very weak.

preterite participles which function as determined or non-determined adjectives plus the verbal meaning.

Most O.C.S. verbs occur in pairs that are formally distinct but semantically identical except for the grammatical category of aspect: one is perfective and presents the action as a whole (usually completed), the other is imperfective and has no explicit reference to the wholeness of the action. Generally speaking, O.C.S. perfectives correspond to Greek aoristic forms.

On the whole the intersection of grammatical form and category in the two languages makes it possible to predict correspondences with a high degree of exactness, so that literalistic translation is possible. Yet in fact such expectations are often disappointed, for obviously the details of the two systems did not coincide fully. A translator was sometimes forced away from literalism by syntactic and semantic requirements of O.C.S. In other cases the Greek offered a choice of interpretation and the translator chose one that is, at this distance, unexpected. In short, good translation into O.C.S. itself becomes a limitation in deciding on possible Greek variants.

The Greek present, imperfect, and aorist regularly correspond to O.C.S. present, imperfect, and aorist. Yet the O.C.S. aorist is the usual narrative tense, and it may take over from a Greek narrative or historical present[1] or perfect. While the meanings of the O.C.S. and Greek perfects appear to be very similar, the translators, puzzlingly enough, did not equate the two. The O.C.S. perfect is rare in the Gospels, and it may render a Greek aorist or perfect. Thus, for aorist, John vii. 46 *nikoliže tako* estъ glagolalъ *člověkъ* οὐδέποτε οὕτως ἐλάλησεν ἄνθρωπος; for the perfect, inconsistently, John xvii. 22 κἀγὼ τὴν δόξαν ἣν δέδωκας (or ἔδωκας) μοι δέδωκα αὐτοῖς *i azъ slavǫ jǫže* dalъ esi (perf.) *mъně* daxъ (aor.) *imъ*; with hesitation, Luke xv. 30 ἔθυσας αὐτῷ τὸν μόσχον zaklalъ *emu* esi *telъcъ* (perf., As) but zakla *emu telъcъ* (aor., rel.). Therefore Mark i. 38 *izidъ* (aor., morphological variant *izidoxъ*) does not allow us to choose between ἐξελήλυθα and ἐξῆλθον[2] while *prodastъ* Matt. xiii. 46 could reflect the unusual ἐπώλησεν (D) as

---

[1] Mark iii. 13 *vъzide* literally equals ἀνέβη, but it is a good translation for ἀναβαίνει.

[2] The *prid(ъ)* 'I came' of As probably shows unprefixed ἐλήλυθα or an unrecorded v.l. ἦλθον, since the O.C.S. prefixes ordinarily correspond closely to those of Greek when the meaning is concrete. Vajs here incorrectly attributes *izidъ* to As, and he automatically follows the Textus Receptus in giving only ἐξελήλυθα. This sort of procedure is common in his work and it renders his statistics meaningless.

well as normal πέπρακεν. Mark vi. 14 *vъsta* is closest to ἀνέστη, but quite good for ἐγήγερται or ἠγέρθη. John xii. 40 τετύφλωκεν . . . πεπώρωκεν/ἐπώρωσεν comes out with aorist *oslěpi* but perfect *okamenělъ estъ*.

The O.C.S. pluperfect is extremely rare, but when it occurs it is fully appropriate, though it has little to do with the Greek; e.g. John xx. 12 *ideže* bě *ležalo* *tělo*, lit. 'where the body had been lying' ὅπου ἔκειτο τὸ σῶμα. Luke v. 17 ἦσαν ἐληλυθότες is literally rendered *běaxǫ prišъli*, but the same O.S.C. stands in John xi. 19 for ἐληλύθεισαν.

The O.C.S. conditional reflects a variety of Greek forms. Let one sentence suffice: John xviii. 36 *ašte otъ sego mira* bi *bylo* (1) *cěsarъstvo moe, slugy ubo moę* podvizaly sę bišę (2) *da ne* prědanъ bimь bylъ (3) *ijudeomъ* εἰ ἐκ τοῦ κόσμου τούτου ἦν (1) ἡ βασιλεία ἡ ἐμή, οἱ ὑπηρέται ἂν οἱ ἐμοὶ ἠγωνίζοντο (2), ἵνα μὴ παραδοθῶ (3) τοῖς Ἰουδαίοις. O.C.S. offers no way to distinguish Greek subjunctive from indicative forms: ποιήσῃ and ποιήσει, ποιήσωμεν and ποιήσομεν will be translated alike.

O.C.S. is no real help in sifting out cases where Greek perfects and presents are in competition, for Slavonic is likely to choose the present. Thus in John i. 26 *stoitъ* 'stands' may either be good translation for ἕστηκεν or a literal rendering of στήκει. In John xx. 23 ἀφίενται/ἀφέωνται appears as a perfective present *otъpustętъ sę* which may indicate a single act completed in future time or a timeless completed action; the following κεκράτηνται comes out imperfective present *drъžętъ sę*, surely expressing general validity. In Mark vii. 37 καλῶς πάντα πεποίηκεν/ποιεῖ, καὶ τοὺς κωφοὺς ποιεῖ/πεποίηκεν O.C.S. generally has present *tvoritъ* both times, though As has the perfective aorist *sъtvori* '(has) made' for the second. This gives no information about the underlying Greek.

O.C.S. has no future tense. The most usual equivalent of a Greek future, which is aoristic and hence 'perfective', is a perfective present, e.g. Matt. xix. 16 τί ἀγαθὸν ποιήσω *čьto blago sъtvorjǫ* (cf. John xiv. 31 οὕτως ποιῶ *tako tvorjǫ*).[1] This remains the case in some types of subordinate clauses, e.g. John xx. 31 perfective *věrǫ imete* probably assures πιστεύσητε. In a specific condition a present may be excluded, as in Matt. v. 39 ὅστις σε

---

[1] A Greek present with implied future meaning may become O.C.S. perfective present: Matt. xii. 45 τότε πορεύεται καὶ παραλαμβάνει *togda idetъ i poimetъ* (perf. pres.).

ῥαπίζει/ῥαπίσει εἰς/ἐπὶ τὴν δεξιὰν σιαγόνα σου,[1] *ašte kъto tę* udaritъ *vъ desnǫjǫ lanitǫ* with the perfective verb as the only possible equivalent for either Greek variant. On the other hand, a completely general statement or condition is ordinarily in the imperfective present: Matt. xii. 50 *iže bo ašte tvoritъ* (pres.) could represent any of the four Greek variants ποιήσῃ/ποιήσει/ποιῇ/ποιεῖ.

Futurity is made clear in rare instances by the addition of an auxiliary 'begin': Mark xiii. 25 *zvězdy naчъnǫtъ padati* 'the stars will start to fall' for οἱ ἀστέρες πεσοῦνται.[2] Sometimes, especially in the presence of negation, the translators employed an auxiliary 'have' plus infinitive, which may also render μέλλω: the line between simple future, imminent action, and various modal expressions is obliterated; e.g. Luke xviii. 22 *imēti imaši sъkrovište* ἕξεις θησαυρόν; Matt. v. 20 *ne imate vъniti* οὐ μὴ εἰσέλθητε; Matt. xxiv. 6 *uslyšati že imate* (Ma As Os; Sa *uslyšite*, perfective pres.) μελλήσετε/μέλλετε δὲ ἀκούειν; Matt. x. 19 *kako ili чъto imate glagolati* (As Os; Zo Ma *vъzglagoljete*, perfective pres.) πῶς ἢ τί λαλήσητε.

O.C.S. clauses introduced by *da* are very close to a variety of ἵνα-clauses, but no sure guide. Since a *da*-clause may represent a Greek infinitival clause (Mark vii. 27 ἄφες πρῶτον χορτασθῆναι τὰ τέκνα *ostani da prъvēe* nasytętъ sę čęda), in Mark x. 36 *чъto xošteta da sъtvorjǫ vama* may represent the usual τί θέλετε ποιήσω ὑμῖν (Zo omits *da*), or the variant with ἵνα, or even one of the variants with ποιῆσαι. *Da* may further represent ὅπως, ὥστε, or various prepositions plus articulated infinitive, and with negative μή, μηδέ, εἰ μή, etc. O.C.S. is much poorer in means for expressing nuances of subordination than Greek.

O.C.S. is therefore inconsistent in rendering many kinds of Greek subordinate clauses. The O.C.S. dative absolute is so close in function to the Greek genitive absolute that some scholars believe it to be a special syntactic borrowing. Yet it may translate an articulated infinitive, though such an infinitive may also be rendered with a finite verb. Luke xviii. 35 ἐγένετο δὲ ἐν τῷ ἐγγίζειν αὐτόν ('Ιησοῦ in lectionary incipit) is reproduced liter-

---

[1] O.C.S. gives no help with the preposition, but shows omission of σου.

[2] Some consider the O.C.S. a felicitous free translation (perhaps influenced by Matt. xxiv. 29) of the somewhat odd but impeccably attested ἔσονται πίπτοντες, well represented in early non-O.C.S. codices with the literal *bǫdǫtъ padajǫštę* 'will-be falling'. Vajs gives the usual Greek without comment.

ally in the lectionaries, *bystъ približiti sę Isusovi*, but becomes finite 'when he approached' in the tetraevangelia, *bystъ že egda približi sę*. In Matt. ix. 10 ἐγένετο αὐτοῦ ἀνακειμένου the O.C.S. dative absolute is appropriately used in most texts, *bystъ emu vъzležęštu*, but Sa has the infinitive, *bystъ vъzlešti emu*. In the parallel Mark ii. 15, where Greek has (ἐν τῷ) κατακεῖσθαι, O.C.S. codices agree in the dative absolute. In Mark ii. 2 ὥστε μηκέτι χωρεῖν μηδέ has both literal and expanded translations: *jako kъtomu ne vъměštaaxǫ sę* (3 pl. imperfect, Zo Ma Os), but *vъměštati sę* (inf., As).[1]

Aspect in the infinitive and imperative is governed by the same general principles in Greek and Slavic: action regarded as a complete unity or as terminated is expressed by Slavic perfective and Greek aorist, and action not specifically so regarded is expressed by the Slavic imperfective and Greek present. The principles leave a good deal of room for choice, however, and one cannot expect the two languages to agree in every case. In Matt. x. 28 καὶ μὴ φοβεῖσθε/φοβηθῆτε . . . φοβεῖσθε/φοβήθητε δὲ μᾶλλον O.C.S. has perfective *ne uboite sę* both times, except that Ma has imperfective *ne boite sę* the second time. In Mark iv. 3 ἐξῆλθεν ὁ σπείρων (τοῦ) σπεῖραι, O.C.S. has *izide sěęi sějatъ* (imperfective supine), just as in Luke viii. 5, while the τοῦ σπείρειν/σπεῖραι of Matt. xiii. 4 also comes out imperfective, but with a finite clause *da sěetъ*.[2] In the subsequent verse (Mark iv. 4), for ἐν τῷ σπείρειν, O.C.S. keeps to the imperfective (a finite clause *egda sějaaše* in Mark and Luke, but dative absolute in Matt.). It would appear that the verb 'to sow' offered no suitable perfective form in O.C.S. Examples of this sort can easily be multiplied.

O.C.S. has no formal equivalent of the Greek middle and passive. Passive may be expressed explicitly by means of the past passive participle plus an auxiliary 'be', and passive and middle by the so-called reflexive. For example, Matt. xxvi. 2 ὁ υἱὸς τοῦ ἀνθρώπου παραδίδοται εἰς τὸ σταυρωθῆναι *synъ člověčьskъ prědanъ bǫdetъ* (ppp+'will-be') *na propętъe*[3] in As Os Ma, but *prědastъ sę*

---

[1] Further in this verse, for τὰ πρὸς τὴν θύραν, O.C.S. predictably has no equivalent for the article. Zo Ma Os have *prědъ dvъrъmi* 'before (in front of) the door', while As has the less specific *pri dvъrъxъ* 'at the door'. Incidentally, the O.C.S. noun is *plurale tantum* and could stand for a Greek plural, as in Matt. xxiv. 33 ἐπὶ θύραις *pri dvъrъxъ*. Therefore Mark i. 33 *kъ dvъrъmъ* allows no choice between τὴν θύραν and τὰς θύρας.

[2] This sort of clause may represent a Greek final infinitive or ἵνα-clause. The O.C.S. supine expresses purpose but is restricted to position after a verb of motion.

[3] The Greek passive infinitive here is rendered by a verbal noun 'crucifixion'.

(perfective pres. reflexive) in Zo. The reflexive is more frequently used, particularly if the agent is not named. Another device for rendering a Greek passive, however, is a third-plural verb with no explicit subject: e.g. Matt. xiv. 11 καὶ ἠνέχθη ἡ κεφαλὴ . . . καὶ ἐδόθη *i priněsǫ glavǫ . . . i dašę* 'and they brought . . . and gave'. Therefore in Matt. xii. 22 *privěsę emu běsьnujǫštь sę* literally corresponds to προσήνεγκαν αὐτῷ δαιμονιζόμενον, but could also represent προσηνέχθη αὐτῷ δαιμονιζόμενος (as Vajs assumes). A passive infinitive may simply become active: Matt. xiv. 9 ἐκέλευσεν δοθῆναι (αὐτῇ) *povelě dati* (*ei*).

O.C.S. has a series of particles that the translators used as close equivalents of Greek particles. Thus Mark ii. 24 *i farisei* reflects καὶ οἱ Φαρισαῖοι, but Sa has *farisei že*, implying reference to a Greek text with οἱ δὲ Φαρισαῖοι. However O.C.S. usage is varied enough so that it is no sure guide to the Greek.

The word order in the O.C.S. Gospel texts overwhelmingly follows the Greek as faithfully as is possible, and deviations usually turn out to coincide with known Greek variants. We may wish to assume that the original O.C.S. version had independent and native word order, but the O.C.S. codices offer only hints as to what it may have been. A few examples will suffice as illustrations: Matt. xxvii. 34 ἔδωκαν αὐτῷ πιεῖν ὄξος (or ὄ. π.) *piti ocьtь* Zo As Os, but *ocьtь piti* Ma Sa. Matt. xviii. 26 καὶ πάντα ἀποδώσω σοι (or σ. ἀ.) *vьzadzmь ti* Ma (and Vajs) but *ti vьzdamь* As Sa Os.[1] Matt. xxii. 46 καὶ οὐδεὶς ἐδύνατο ἀποκριθῆναι αὐτῷ (or αὐ. ἀπ., or αὐτῷ omitted) *otьvěštati emu* Ma vs. *emu otьvěštati* Os Sa vs. simply *otьvěštati* Sa. On the whole, then, O.C.S. word order is an advantage for establishing the Greek text, rather than the limitation one might expect it to be.

O.C.S. vocabulary is rich and flexible, but often cannot help us to select Greek variants, as some examples above have already suggested. The single verb *ljubiti* (with perfective *vьzljubiti*) stands for ἀγαπάω, ἐράω, and φιλέω.[2] Occasionally O.C.S. does

---

[1] The latter seems to me the neutral Slavic order, and I would suspect Ma here of Hellenization. How risky this sort of judgement is, is well demonstrated by the extensive and often polemic discussion of variants in word order (and many other features) in Karel Horálek, *Evangeliáře a čtveroevangelia* (Prague, 1954). His chief opponents are also Czechs, whose general 'feel' for the material might well be closer to Horálek's than the reactions of a native speaker of a different Slavic language, let alone those of a non-Slav.

[2] For a judicious selection of instances of thoughtful and idiomatic renderings, see the classic article by Erich Berneker, 'Kyrills Übersetzungskunst', *Indoger-*

offer a decision, however, as in Mark iv. 37 *jako juže pogręznǫti xotěaše* (*ei*), which indicates rather ὥστε ἤδη βυθίζεσθαι (αὐτῷ) than the usual ὥστε αὐτὸ ἤδη γεμίζεσθαι that Vajs prints.[1] On the other hand, common verbs like βάλλω and τίθημι are translated by many different O.C.S. verbs, each appropriate to its context. It is not uncommon for the O.C.S. witnesses to vary among themselves, surely because of scribal emendations to adapt vocabulary to local usage.

Apart from these questions of the nature of the difference between Old Church Slavonic and Greek, and the fact that O.C.S. evidence yields at best a ninth-century text, there remains a major drawback in using O.C.S. evidence to represent Greek variants: it is that the O.C.S. codices do not speak with one voice, as examples I have cited above demonstrate. The Slavic Church lived in the shadow of the Greek Church for centuries. Especially in the first decades of Slavic Christianity, when the texts were being intensively worked on and multiplied for the use of the many new parishes and monasteries, most of the Slavic clergy constantly heard and probably read the Greek Church books. Generation after generation, Greek manuscripts were referred to in order to verify the O.C.S. wording and 'correct' it in the light of local Greek authority. The original O.C.S. translation had little prestige; it was modified whenever and wherever a scribe saw fit to make a change. Therefore in verse after verse our five ancient Slavonic witnesses offer several disparate variants, usually coinciding with major or minor known Greek variants, and the picture becomes more bewildering as soon as more twelfth-century Slavonic manuscripts are consulted.

A major task before Slavic scholarship is to examine more closely the differences between the O.C.S. lectionary text—not as a whole, but lection by lection—and the full tetraevangelion version. Heretofore comparisons of O.C.S. codices have been made on the assumption, surely false, that the original translation,

---

manische Forschungen, xxxi (1912), 399–412. Horálek (see preceding footnote) also discusses vocabulary. The anniversary celebrations of the Moravian Mission (863) and the death of Cyril (869) called forth a mass of O.C.S. vocabulary studies in the Slavic countries, but none, in my opinion, is based on realistic hypotheses that survive after a careful textological examination of Greek sources.

[1] The addition of *xotěaše*, an equivalent of ἤμελλε, makes this infinitival clause finite and renders the sense of danger much stronger. Ma has an equivalent of αὐτῷ, Zo does not.

and indeed all later emendations, were made from a Greek tetraevangelion. It is vital now to recognize the independent tradition of the Greek lectionary and to compare O.C.S. lections with Greek lections. An indispensable preliminary is that many details about ninth- and tenth-century Greek lectionaries be made available for Slavists. The history of the known O.C.S. and other early Slavonic Gospel manuscripts is still very obscure.

X

Minor Western Versions

THE minor Western versions of the New Testament made before A.D. 1000 that fall to be considered in the present chapter are the Anglo-Saxon,[1] certain Old High German, and the Old Saxon (Old Low German) versions. Whether a version in the Thracian language ever existed is problematic; in any case, no copy is known to survive today.[2]

I. THE ANGLO-SAXON VERSION

1. THE INTRODUCTION OF CHRISTIANITY INTO BRITAIN AND THE TRANSLATION OF THE NEW TESTAMENT

The arrival of Christianity in Britain is shrouded in the mists of legend. The most circumstantial account is a late tradition preserved in an expanded version of William of Malmesbury's *On the Antiquity of the Church of Glastonbury*,[3] to the effect that in the

---

[1] On the debate whether 'Old English' or 'Anglo-Saxon' should be used in describing the literature produced in England before the Norman Conquest, see George K. Anderson, *The Literature of the Anglo-Saxons*, revd. edn. (Princeton, 1966), pp. 40–2.

[2] Despite confident assertions to the contrary, patristic testimonia thought to bear on the question of the existence of a Thracian version of the Gospels are either irrelevant or ambiguous; for a discussion of the evangelization of Thrace and the conversion of the tribe of the Bessians, see the present writer's contribution to the forthcoming Festschrift in honour of Arthur Vööbus, edited by Robert H. Fischer, to be published at Louvain in 1977.

[3] *De antiquitate Glastoniensis ecclesiae* (Migne, *PL* clxxix, cols. 168 ff.). On the basis of internal considerations as well as comparison with William's other historical writings, it is generally agreed that the original form of the treatise attributed the introduction of Christianity into Britain to the preaching of SS. Phagan and Deruvian, who were sent by Pope Eleutherius about A.D. 166 at the request of Lucius king of the Britons. Subsequent scribes, however, embellished the account and declared that when these two holy men came to the Isle of Avalon they found the ruins of the church that had been built the previous century by the hands of the disciples of Christ, etc. See William W. Newell, 'William of Malmesbury on the Antiquity of Glastonbury', *Publications of the Modern Language Association of America*, xvii (1903), 459–512; J. Armitage Robinson, *Somerset Historical Essays* (London, 1921), pp. 1–25; idem, *Two Glastonbury Legends: King Arthur and St. Joseph of*

year 63, at the instigation of St. Philip, Joseph of Arimathea with twelve companions arrived in Britain from Gaul, and, having settled near what came to be known as Glastonbury, built an oratory of twisted wattles and daub in honour of the Blessed Virgin.

Other less detailed notices concerning the beginnings of Christianity in Britain start with brief comments made by Tertullian and Origen. The former,[1] writing *c.* 200, speaks of parts of Britain, inaccessible to the Romans, which had yet been conquered by Christ, and the latter,[2] writing *c.* 240, alludes to the Christian faith as a unifying force among the Britons. Despite the rhetorical exaggeration of the two authors, Harnack considered it 'quite possible that Christians had arrived in Britain and laboured there by the end of the second century',[3] while Miss Toynbee thinks that the two reports, brief though they are, 'testify to a well-established Christian community, capable of at least some missionary effort, and to a fairly widespread diffusion of the faith, in the province by about the year 200'.[4]

The first Christian in Britain whose name is recorded is Alban, a layman of the Roman city of Verulamium, who, according to

Arimathea (Cambridge, 1926); Margaret Deansley, *The Pre-Conquest Church in England*, 2nd edn. (London, 1963), pp. 1–19; and R. F. Treharne, *The Glastonbury Legends: Joseph of Arimathea, The Holy Grail and King Arthur* (London, 1967).

[1] Tertullian, *Adv. Judaeos* vii: 'Britannorum inaccessa Romanis loca Christo vero subdita.' On this passage John T. McNeill comments: 'Allowing for the exuberance of Tertullian, we must also remember that he was one of the best-informed persons of his time. His "Britannorum inaccessa Romanis loca" is a studied phrase. It may well represent a report he had heard from a Christian traveler, conceivably one who had been himself displaced from somewhere in the Scottish lowlands where the Romans had then recently lost a wide territory to the Picts' (*The Celtic Churches, a History A.D. 200 to 1200* (Chicago, 1974), p. 19).

[2] Origen, *Homil.* iv. 1 *in Ezek.* (Migne, *PL* xxv, col. 723), 'quando enim terra Britanniae ante adventum Christi in unius dei consensit religionem?'

[3] Adolf Harnack, *Die Mission und Ausbreitung des Christentums in den ersten drei Jahrhunderten*, 4te Aufl., ii (Leipzig, 1924), 886 f. (Eng. trans., *The Mission and Expansion of Christianity in the First Three Centuries*, 2nd edn., ii (New York and London, 1908), 272).

[4] J. M. C. Toynbee, 'Christianity in Roman Britain', *Journal of the British Archaeological Association*, 3rd ser., xvi (1953), 1–24; quotation from p. 2. Frend is inclined to regard Origen's statement about Christianity being a unifying force among the Britons as having little basis in fact, for 'Christianity in Britain was not in the first place an indigenous movement' (W. H. C. Frend, 'The Christianization of Roman Britain', *Christianity in Britain, 300–700, Papers presented to the Conference on Christianity in Roman and Sub-Roman Britain . . .*, ed. by M. W. Barley and R. P. C. Hanson (Leicester, 1969), pp. 36–49; quotation from p. 37).

Bede,[1] had given shelter to a Christian priest fleeing from his persecutors. During the following days, while the priest remained in hiding, Alban learned of the Christian faith and was converted. When the soldiers came to arrest the fugitive, Alban, wearing the priest's hooded cloak (*caracula*), gave himself up, and was condemned to death and martyred at the hill where the Abbey church of St. Albans, Hertfordshire, now stands. The date is generally assumed to have been about 304 or 305, during the persecutions under Diocletian.

By the early part of the fourth century Christianity must have spread rapidly in the British Isles, for the Church was sufficiently organized and established to send three bishops to the Synod of Arles in 314, one from London, one from York, and one from Lincoln (though the name of this locality is uncertain). In the second half of the fifth century, however, the coming of Anglo-Saxon invaders submerged Celtic culture and drove Christians into the western parts of Britain, and the new faith suffered a temporary eclipse. The conversion of the Teutonic pagan conquerors was subsequently undertaken from two sources, one by the labours of Celtic missionaries from monasteries of Ireland and Scotland and the other by the mission headed by St. Augustine sent in 596 from Rome by Pope Gregory the Great. The two traditions, Celtic and Roman, differed in a number of matters, one of which was the date when Easter should be celebrated. Even after the Synod of Whitby in 664, when an agreement was effected in favour of Roman customs, an independent Celtic Christianity lingered on in Wales and Ireland for many years.

The earliest translations of portions of the Scriptures into Anglo-Saxon were made in the seventh and eighth centuries. Unfortunately, however, neither the metrical paraphrases ascribed to Caedmon (died *c.* 680), a layman serving as cowherd at the monastery at Whitby,[2] nor the translation of the Gospel according to John, which the Venerable Bede is credited with finishing on his death-bed (A.D. 735),[3] has come down to us. According to

---

[1] *The Ecclesiastical History of the English People*, ed. by Philip Hereford (London, 1935), Bk. I, chap. vii (pp. 11–14).

[2] Ibid., Bk. IV, chap. xxiv (pp. 239–43).

[3] So the *Epistola Cuthberti de obitu Bedae*. Unfortunately nothing certain is known of the author, recipient, or date of composition of this letter; for a discussion of theories, see Alan S. C. Ross, 'A Connection between Bede and the Anglo-Saxon

William of Malmesbury, at the close of the ninth century an attempt to translate the Psalter was made by King Alfred, who, however, died when he had 'barely finished the first part'.[1] Whether this can be identified with the prose version of the first fifty psalms in the eleventh-century bilingual Paris Psalter[2] is a question on which scholars are not in agreement.[3]

The oldest extant New Testament material in Anglo-Saxon is in the form of interlinear glosses to a Latin text—for glossing was a feature of Old English pedagogy. While such glosses give a rendering of (almost) every word in the text, they naturally follow the Latin order instead of the Anglo-Saxon, and would therefore require to be rearranged, and frequently made more idiomatic, before they could serve as an independent translation. In fact, they were not intended to take the place of the Latin text, but to help the reader understand it. One of the most note-worthy of these interlinear manuscripts is the famous Lindisfarne Gospels, a superb example of the art of the medieval scribe (cf. p. 337 above).[4] The Latin original dates from about the year 700 and was written by Eadfrid, bishop of Lindisfarne, in honour of St. Cuthbert (d. 687). During the tenth century the manu-script was transferred to Chester-le-Street, near Durham, and there, before 970,[5] an interlinear gloss in the rather rare literary

Gloss to the Lindisfarne Gospels?' *JTS*, N.S. xx (1969), 482–94. Ross suggests that what Bede did was to dictate a gloss rather than a straightforward translation of the Gospel of John (ibid., p. 493).

[1] *Gesta regum Anglorum* ii. 123, 'Psalterium transferre aggressus vix prima parte explicata vivendi finem fecit.'

[2] The Paris Psalter (Bibliothèque Nat. MS. fonds Latin 8824) presents the re-maining Psalms in a metrical version of Anglo-Saxon alliterative verse. The manu-script was edited by Benjamin Thorpe, *Libri Psalmorum versio Latina cum paraphrasi Anglo-Saxonica, partim soluta oratione partim metrice composita, nunc primum e codice MS. in Bibliotheca Parisiensi adservato* (Oxford, 1835). A facsimile edition was published by Bertram Colgrave as vol. viii of the series *Early English Manuscripts in Facsimile* (Copenhagen, 1958).

[3] For a survey of the debate see John I'a. Bromwich, 'Who was the Translator of the Prose Portion of the Paris Psalter?' in *The Early Cultures of North-West Europe*, ed. by Sir Cyril Fox and Bruce Dickens (Cambridge, 1950), pp. 289–303, and Minnie C. Morrell, *A Manual of Old English Biblical Materials* (Knoxville, 1965), pp. 139–47.

[4] A handsome facsimile edition of the Lindisfarne Gospels was prepared by T. D. Kendrick *et al.*, 2 vols. (*Evangeliorum quattuor codex Lindisfarnensis* . . . (Oltun and Lausanne, 1956, 1960)).

[5] On the date of the gloss, see Marco K. Minicoff, 'Zur Altersfrage der Lindis-farne Glosse', *Archiv für das Studium der neueren Sprachen*, clxxiii (1938), 31–43; Alan S. C. Ross, *Studies in the Accidence of the Lindisfarne Gospels* (Leeds, 1937),

dialect of Old Northumbrian was added under the supervision of a priest named Aldred.[1] Another famous Latin manuscript, the Rushworth[2] Gospels (cf. p. 340 above), written in an Irish hand of about A.D. 800, was glossed in the latter half of the tenth century. The gloss on Matthew is in the rare Old Mercian dialect, which was spoken in the central part of England, while that added to the other three Gospels is a form of Old Northumbrian.[3] The work was done by two men: a priest named Farman,[4] of Harewood in Yorkshire, who glossed all of Matthew, Mark i. 1–ii. 15, and John xviii. 1–3, and a scribe named Owun, who worked on the rest of the Gospels. Farman's portion (except the part from Mark, where he generally follows the Lindisfarne gloss) is marked by considerable freedom of translation, whereas Owun was content to base his part of the work on the Lindisfarne gloss.

As distinct from interlinear glosses, which tend to be wooden and unidiomatic, the first attempt at producing a separate and more freely rendered version of the Gospels in Anglo-Saxon dates from no later than the second half of the tenth century, being related, as is generally thought, to the so-called Benedictine Reform.[5] At the close of the last century the question of the

17–25; and idem, Book 2, 'The Anglo-Saxon Gloss', in *Evangeliorum quattuor codex Lindisfarnensis . . .* , ii (Oltun and Lausanne, 1960), 32.

[1] On Aldred, who seems to have begun to insert the gloss himself from John v. 10 onwards, see N. R. Ker, 'Aldred the Scribe', *Essays and Studies*, xxviii (1943), pp. 7–12 and 106. On the question whether Aldred followed other Latin manuscripts while glossing Lindisfarne, see Alan S. C. Ross, 'On the "Text" of the Anglo-Saxon Gloss to the Lindisfarne Gospels', *JTS*, n.s. ix (1958), 38–52. There appears to be some evidence that Aldred made use of Bede's translation of the Gospel of John; see Constance O. Elliott and A. S. C. Ross, 'The Linguistic Peculiarities of the Gloss on St. John's Gospel', *English Philological Studies*, xiii (1972), 49–72, and Ross, 'Supplementary Note', *JTS*, n.s. xxiv (1973), 519–21.

[2] The name is given to the manuscript because, at the time of its first historical appearance, it was in the possession of a deputy clerk of the House of Commons in the Long Parliament by the name of John Rushworth.

[3] Uno Lindelöf, *Die südnordthumbrische Mundart des 10. Jahrhunderts* (*Bonner Beiträge zur Anglistik*, x; Bonn, 1901).

[4] On the question how far Farman may have depended upon an earlier gloss, see Robert J. Menner, 'Farman Vindicatus', *Anglia*, lviii (1934), 1–27, who concludes that Farman probably did his work independently of an older gloss.

[5] On the Benedictine Reform (which was less a reformation than a refounding of monastic life in England after the Danish invasions) and its stimulus in the production of manuscripts, see David Knowles, *The Monastic Orders in England* (Cambridge, 1949), and Eleanor S. Duckett, *St. Dunstan of Canterbury: a Study of Monastic Reform in the Tenth Century* (New York, 1955).

authorship of the version was investigated by Allison Drake, who concluded that 'the authorship of the West Saxon Gospels is at least dual, and probably triple; more explicitly, that the Matthew is by one translator, the Mark and Luke by another, the John by a third (unless possibly the translator of the Matthew)'.[1] These conclusions are based on an evaluation, from Gospel to Gospel, of such linguistic data as the use of the weak form of *heofon*, of *underfōn* as a synonym for *onfōn*, of *willan* after *þaet* to express purpose, and several similar features. Although Drake's arguments persuaded several other investigators,[2] Bright and others[3] considered the evidence to be insufficient, pointing out that he had not taken into account either the differences in style of the Gospels in the original, or the translator's gradual modification of stylistic traits as he proceeded in his work.

The Anglo-Saxon version of the Gospels exists in several closely related manuscripts, none of which is the original. To judge from the dialect, the version was made in the south-west of England, in the region known as Wessex. Whether more of the New Testament besides the Gospels was translated we do not know; in any case only the Gospels in West Saxon have survived. The following is a list of all the known manuscripts.

2. ANGLO-SAXON MANUSCRIPTS OF THE GOSPELS[4]

(1) Cambridge, Corpus Christi College, MS. 140, dating from the eleventh or twelfth century (so Ker; others date it about A.D. 1000), is generally considered the principal authority for the West Saxon Gospels. A scribal note at the end of Matthew (fol. 45ᵛ) associates the manuscript with Bath Abbey: 'Ego Ælfricus scripsi hunc librum in Monasterio Baðþonio et dedi Brihtwoldo preposito.' Each Gospel is in a different hand, except that Mark xii. 26–38 is in the same hand as Luke. The initials, in green, blue, or red (two shades), are well drawn and often slightly

---

[1] *The Authorship of the West Saxon Gospels* (Diss., New York, 1894).

[2] e.g. O. Brenner in *ES* xx (1895), 297, and G. Sarrazin in *ZDP* xxix (1897), 139.

[3] James W. Bright, *The Gospel of Saint John in West-Saxon* (Boston and London, 1904), pp. xxv sq.; Hans Glunz, *Die lateinische Vorlage der westsächsischen Evangelienversion* (Leipzig, 1928), pp. 60–2 and 82 f.; and George K. Anderson, *The Literature of the Anglo-Saxons*, revd. edn. (Princeton, 1966), p. 351.

[4] For palaeographic and codicological information concerning the manuscripts, see N. R. Ker, *Catalogue of Manuscripts Containing Anglo-Saxon* (Oxford, 1957). The manuscripts described by Ker are as follows: (1) is Ker's no. 35; (2) is no. 20; (3) is no. 312; (4) is no. 181; (5) is no. 325; (6) is no. 245.

decorated with a crescent ornament. The manuscript was bequeathed to Corpus Christi College by Archbishop Parker.

(2) Cambridge University Library MS. Ii.2.11, is 'a handsome regular hand of the "Exeter" type' (Ker), with red, blue, or green initials, and is generally dated to about A.D. 1050. The text of the Gospels is valuable for its accuracy in grammatical forms and the purity of its West Saxon orthography. The rubrics relate the Gospel text to the openings of the liturgical lections throughout the Church's year. According to an inscription the manuscript was given by Bishop Leofric (d. 1072) to his cathedral church at Exeter, just after the Conquest. Another inscription records the gift of the book by the dean and chapter of Exeter to Archbishop Parker in 1566, who gave it to Cambridge University in 1574. In addition to the four Gospels, the manuscript contains the apocryphal Gospel of Nicodemus and the Embassy of Nathan the Jew to Tiberius Caesar, both in Anglo-Saxon.

(3) Bodleian MS. 441, dating from the first half of the eleventh century, lacks about a dozen folios (those that contained Mark i. 1–iv. 37; xvi. 14–end; Luke xvi. 14–xvii. 1; xxiv. 51–end; John xx. 9–end); these were restored on new parchment in the sixteenth century, supposedly under Archbishop Parker's direction, the text being taken from the Corpus manuscript (no. 1 above). The first edition of the Anglo-Saxon Gospels, published by John Foxe in 1571, was printed from this manuscript.

(4) British Museum Cotton MS. Otho C. i, dating from the middle of the eleventh century, was severely damaged by fire in 1751. Because of the fire, as well as accidental loss of folios, the manuscript today lacks all of Matthew; Mark i. 1–vii. 21; Luke xxiv. 7–29; and John xix. 27–xx. 22. A scribal note at the end of the Gospel of John reads: 'Wulfwi me wrat.'

(5) British Museum MS. Royal I A. xiv, dating from the latter part of the twelfth century, has the four Gospels in the order Mark, Matthew, Luke, John. Each Gospel begins on a new quire. The manuscript lacks the text of Luke xvi. 14–xvii. 1; and the concluding words of Mark (from xvi. 14 'nehstan'), Luke (from xxiv. 51 'þa he') and John (from xxi. 25 'awritene') were originally omitted and have been supplied by another hand. That all four omissions correspond to omissions due to the loss of folios from Bodleian MS. 441 (no. 3 above) shows that the latter is an ancestor

of this manuscript. Initials are alternately in red and green, and both colours are employed in the larger initials at the beginning of each gospel. Linguistic forms are Kentish. The manuscript once belonged to St. Augustine's Abbey, Canterbury, and subsequently to Archbishop Thomas Cranmer, whose name is on fol. 1.

(6) Bodleian MS. Hatton 38, dating from the twelfth or thirteenth century, contains the four Gospels in the order Mark, Luke, Matthew, and John. Each Gospel begins a new quire. In the sixteenth century the text of Luke xvi. 14–xvii. 1, which is missing on fol. 61^v, was supplied on fol. 62. The omission shows that the manuscript is a descendant of the Bodleian MS. 441 (no. 3 above), from which a leaf with these contents is missing. According to Ker, the translation of the last verses of Mark, Luke, and John is like that in British Museum MS. Royal I A. xiv (no. 5 above) and unlike that in other copies. Probably therefore this manuscript is a copy of Royal I A. xiv, which is itself a copy of Bodley 441. The Latin Gospel-texts added in the margins of Bodley 441 are here part of the text, as in Royal I A. xiv.[1] The initial letters are alternately red and blue, with ornamentation in the other colour. A third colour, green, is used in the larger initials at the beginning of each Gospel. The linguistic forms are Kentish. The manuscript once belonged to the Revd. John Parker, son of Archbishop Thomas Parker, and later to Lord Hatton, when it was used by Thomas Marshall for the edition of the Gothic and Anglo-Saxon Gospels which he and Francis Junius published in 1665 (see p. 379 above). It was acquired by the Bodleian with other Hatton manuscripts in 1671.

Numerous studies have been made of the interrelation among the principal witnesses to the West Saxon Gospels. Skeat drew up the following stemma:[2]

Original MS. (now lost)

Corpus (I) = Bodley (III) = Otho C. i (IV)   Cambridge (II)

Royal (VI)

Hatton (V)

---

[1] N. R. Ker, *Catalogue*, p. 387.

[2] Walter W. Skeat, *The Gospel According to St. Luke in Anglo-Saxon and Northumbrian Versions* . . . (Cambridge, 1874), p. x.

Contrary to earlier views that the Gospels in the vernacular may have existed in more than one version and have been fairly numerous, Skeat concludes:

When we consider . . . that, out of the six MSS. now existing, it is absolutely certain that MSS. I., III., and IV. scarcely differ in a single letter (due allowances being made for variable spellings); that MS. V. is copied from MS. VI. and from nothing else, and that MS. VI. is copied from MS. III. and from nothing else, we are almost irresistibly led to conclude that perhaps *not* very many of the copies perished, and that they may *never* have been very numerous, and that there is at present not the faintest trace of any *other* version.[1]

On the other hand, the recently published study by Grünberg[2] of the Gospel of Matthew in the West Saxon manuscripts has cast a measure of doubt on the validity of Skeat's simplified stemma. It appears that the complexities of the textual data make the exact relationship of the manuscripts more difficult to determine than had been previously supposed. According to Grünberg, 'It does not seem doubtful that the relation between Corpus and B[odley], B[odley] and R[oyal], and R[oyal] and H[atton], is only indirect.'[3]

Besides the six principal manuscripts mentioned above, a few stray folios from other Anglo-Saxon Gospel manuscripts are known to have survived. They are the following (with their numbers in Ker's *Catalogue*).

(7) Part of a leaf belonging to the collection of Major J. R. Abby (Ker's no. 1), dating from the eleventh century, contains the text of Mark i. 24–31, 36–42.

(8) Bodleian MS. Eng. Bib. C. 2 (Ker's no. 322) comprises four leaves from a manuscript dating from the eleventh century and preserving John ii. 6–iii. 34 and vi. 19–vii. 11. The leaves were discovered by Napier in a volume of charters, deeds, and other documents, which the Bodleian acquired from the library of W. H. Crawford, of Lakelands, County Cork, Ireland. The division of the paragraphs is the same as in no. 3 above; the text is related to that of no. 2 above, both being 'independently derived from a copy that is not directly represented by any other

[1] Ibid., p. xi.

[2] M. Grünberg, *The West-Saxon Gospels: a Study of the Gospel of St. Matthew, with Text of the Four Gospels* (Amsterdam, 1967).

[3] Ibid., p. 364.

of the extant manuscripts'.[1] The leaves came to the Bodleian in 1891 and in the same year were edited by Napier,[2] whose edition is reprinted in an appendix to Bright's edition of John's Gospel in West-Saxon.[3]

(9) One leaf (fol. 87) of a miscellany of theological pieces in British Museum MS. Cotton Vespasian D. xiv (Ker's no. 209, article 30), dating from the middle of the twelfth century, contains the text of John xiv. 1–13.

3. NOTEWORTHY EDITIONS OF THE ANGLO-SAXON GOSPELS

In 1571 the *editio princeps* of the Anglo-Saxon Gospels came from the press of the well-known Elizabethan printer John Daye; it bears the following title: *The Gospels of the fower Euangelistes translated in the olde Saxons tyme out of Latin into the vulgare toung of the Saxons, newly collected out of auncient Monumentes of the sayd Saxons, and now published for testimonie of the same.* The Preface is signed by John Foxe, the martyrologist, and is addressed 'To the most vertuous, and noble Princesse, Queene Elizabeth'. In it Foxe discourses on the theme implied on the title-page, namely the testimony of antiquity in favour of the Scriptures in the 'vulgar tongue'. It does not appear what further share Foxe may have had in the volume, which was prepared under the sponsorship and financial assistance of Archbishop Parker. The text, which is in Anglo-Saxon characters, is a more or less faithful reproduction of the Bodleian MS. 441 (no. 3 above), with some slight use of the Cambridge manuscript (no. 2 above), from which the rubrics are also taken. The Anglo-Saxon occupies two-thirds of the width of the page, and the remaining third is filled with an English version in small black-letter type, which is chiefly from the Bishops' translation of the Bible (1568), here and there conformed to the Saxon.

The first edition to include philological and textual comments on the Anglo-Saxon Gospels was the diglot edition of the Gothic (see p. 379 above) and Anglo-Saxon texts prepared by Francis

---

[1] So James W. Bright, *The Gospel of Saint John in West-Saxon . . .* (London and Boston, 1904), p. xxxix.

[2] A. S. Napier, 'Bruckstücke einer altenglischen Evangelienhandschrift', *Archiv für das Studium der neueren Sprachen,* lxxxvii (1891), 255–61.

[3] Op. cit., pp. xxix–xxxvii.

Junius, entitled *Quatuor D. N. Jesu Christi Evangeliorum versiones perantiquae duae, Gothica scil. et Anglo-Saxonica . . . ,* 2 vols. (Dordrecht, 1665). The notes on the Anglo-Saxon texts, written by Thomas Marshall, rector of Lincoln College, Oxford, provide *inter alia* not only variant readings from the four manuscripts used in the preparation of the edition (nos. 1, 2, 3, and 6 above), but also Anglo-Saxon readings which differ from the Vulgate and agree with codex Bezae, as well as readings which represent a misunderstanding of the Latin.

The standard edition of the Old English Gospels is that of Walter W. Skeat, which brings together within one cover the separate publications of the individual Gospels that appeared between 1871 and 1887. The title indicates the scope of the work: *The Holy Gospels in Anglo-Saxon, Northumbrian, and Old Mercian Versions, synoptically arranged, with collations exhibiting all the readings of all the MSS.; together with the early Latin Version as contained in the Lindisfarne MS., collated with the Latin Version of the Rushworth MS.* (Cambridge, 1871–87; repr. Darmstadt, 1970).

The most recent edition, with detailed analyses of the spelling, language, and style of the translation of the Gospel of Matthew, is that of Madeleine Grünberg, *The West-Saxon Gospels: a Study of the Gospel of St. Matthew, with the Text of the Four Gospels* (Amsterdam, 1967). Grünberg provides (pp. 33–5) a list of more than sixty errata (mostly minor) in the transcription of the Anglo-Saxon text in the earlier editions of Skeat and Bright.

4. CHARACTERISTICS AND TEXTUAL AFFINITIES OF THE ANGLO-SAXON VERSION

The literary characteristics of the Old English version have been described in the following terms: 'It is earnest, sincere, straightforward, and pedestrian, and it shows a willingness to speak out in vernacular speech which is not too grossly inclined to fall back upon its Latin original. In other words, it is, considering the time and the environment, authentic English writing.'[1] The translator generally avoided using terms which in other versions are adopted from Hebrew, Greek, and Latin, and chose to utilize indigenous Anglo-Saxon compounds, so descriptive as

[1] George K. Anderson, *The Literature of the Anglo-Saxons*, revd. edn. (Princeton, 1966), p. 351.

to be intelligible to every reader. Several examples will be sufficient to show this feature, and the compositive power of the Anglo-Saxon language. For centurion the translator sometimes used *hundred-man* (similar to the Latin *centurio*) and sometimes *hundredes ealdor* ('chief of a hundred'); disciple is *leorning-cniht* ('a learning youth'); a man with dropsy is called *waeter-seoc-man*; parable, *biyspel* ('a near example'); repentance, *daed-bót* ('an amends-deed'); resurrection, *aeríst* ('a rising again'); sabbath, *reste-day* ('a day of rest'); scribe, *bóc-ere, bóc-wer* ('a book man'); synagogue, *gesamnung* ('a congregation'); treasury, *gold-hórd* ('gold-hoard').[1]

The competence of the translator as a Latinist has been variously estimated. It is generally recognized that a considerable number of mistaken renderings are the result not only of haste and carelessness, but also of misapprehension of meaning.[2]

The question of the textual affinities of the Anglo-Saxon version of the New Testament is difficult to answer. Even a cursory comparison of the version with the apparatus in Wordsworth and White's *editio maior* of the Latin Vulgate is sufficient to show that it rests upon no one of the Latin manuscripts whose readings are reported in that edition. In general it is clear that the *Vorlage* contained a noticeable strain of the Irish type of Vulgate text, though this is only one of several constitutive elements. A large amount of continuing strains of Old Latin readings, including some that Marshall long ago detected in codex Bezae, produced a composite in which Alcuin's recension of the Vulgate and the Irish type of text predominated. It may even be, as Peters has argued,[3] that the Anglo-Saxon version preserves a Tatianic element via the Old Latin. In any case, the opinion which Harris[4] and Bright[5] advocated, that the type of text represented in Matthew differs from that in Mark and Luke and both from that

---

[1] These examples are cited by Joseph Bosworth and George Waring, *The Gothic and Anglo-Saxon Gospels in Parallel Columns...*, 4th edn. (London, 1907), p. xvii.

[2] For lists of various kinds of mistaken renderings in the Anglo-Saxon Gospels, see Robert Handke, *Über das Verhältnis der westsächsischen Evangelien-Übersetzung zum lateinischen Original* (Diss., Halle a. S., 1896), pp. 26–32, and Lancelot M. Harris, *Studies in the Anglo-Saxon Version of the Gospels*; Part I, *The Form of the Latin Original and Mistaken Renderings* (Diss., Baltimore, 1901), pp. 35–52.

[3] Curt Peters, 'Der Diatessaron-Text von Mt. 2, 9 und die westsächsische Evangelienversion', *Bib*, xxiii (1942), 323–32.

[4] Op. cit., pp. 30–4.   [5] Op. cit., pp. xxvii f.

in John, is based on an inadequate induction of data, and the thorough investigation undertaken by Glunz[1] revealed no marked differences of type of text among the four Gospels.

The search for the Latin manuscript that most nearly matches the Latin *Vorlage* of the Anglo-Saxon Gospels has engaged the attention of more than one scholar. The suggestion thrown out by Max Förster,[2] that Wordsworth and White's 'O', the seventh-century Bodleian MS. 857 (Auct. D. 2.14) formerly belonging to St. Augustine's Library at Canterbury, may well lie behind the West Saxon Gospels, has been challenged by Glunz,[3] who proposed as *Vorlage* Wordsworth and White's 'W', the thirteenth-century British Museum MS. Reg. I. B. xii.

From what has been said above, the limitations of the Anglo-Saxon version in representing the Greek text of the Gospels will be obvious enough. The chief value of the version for the textual critic is its contribution to the task of tracing the history of the transmission of the Latin Bible.

II. THE OLD HIGH GERMAN VERSIONS

The baptism of Clovis I, king of the Franks, on Christmas Day 496 marked the effective beginning of Christianity among the Germanic peoples dwelling along the middle and lower courses of the Rhine. Unlike the east-Teutonic tribes, however, who were provided with a translation of the Bible in the fourth century as part of Ulfilas' missionary efforts (see the Gothic Version, pp. 375–7 above), the west-Teutonic tribes had to wait several centuries longer before being able to read the Scriptures in their own dialects. Those that have survived[4] are the Monsee Matthew, the German Tatian, and Otfrid's *Liber Evangeliorum*, which are described below. Nothing further, however, is known of the *Evangelium Theudiscum* which, in 876 with other books, was included in a list of bequests made by Heccard, count of Authun,

---

[1] Hans Glunz, *Die lateinische Vorlage der westsächsischen Evangelienversion* (Leipzig, 1928), pp. 60–2 and 83.   [2] *ES* xxviii (1900), 430.

[3] Hans Glunz, op. cit., pp. 103 f., and *Britannien und Bibeltext; der Vulgatatext der Evangelien in seinem Verhältnis zur irisch-angelsächsischen Kultur des Frühmittelalters* (*Kölner anglistische Arbeiten*, xii; Leipzig, 1930), pp. 175 f.

[4] In addition to glosses in Latin Bibles; see the collection made by E. Steinmeyer and E. Sievers, *Die althochdeutschen Glossen*, vol. i, *Glossen zu biblischen Schriften* (Bonn, 1879).

Mascon, and Châlon in Burgundy, to certain churches and pious individuals.[1]

1. THE MONSEE FRAGMENTS

The oldest portion of the Bible in a west-Germanic tongue is probably the Gospel of Matthew produced at the Benedictine monastery at Monsee (Bavaria) and dating, as it seems, from the eighth or ninth century.[2] The fragmentary remains of the manuscript, which preserve portions of treatises by Isidor and Augustine besides part of Matthew, comprise thirty-nine leaves in Vienna and two in Hanover.[3] The manuscript, which is bilingual with Latin on the left-hand page and a form of Old High German on the right, preserves parts of Matthew, chaps. viii–x, xii, xiii, xviii–xxviii. According to the thorough philological examination undertaken by Hench, the language of the version is a mixture of Rhine Frankish, the dialect of the original from which the surviving fragments were copied, and certain Bavarian intrusions.[4] The Frankish translator evidently strove after an idiomatic rather than a literalistic rendering, though the order of words sometimes tends to reflect the Latin original.[5] Occasion-

[1] The list of bequests is cited by Estienne Pérard, *Recueil de plusieurs pièces curieuses servant à l'histoire de Bourgogne* . . . (Paris, 1664), p. 26; cf. Paul Lejay, 'Catalogues de la Bibliothèque de Perrecy', *Revue des bibliothèques*, vi (1896), 228. According to Pérard (p. 22) Heccard was the founder of the priory of Perrecy.

[2] The manuscript is dated by Eberhard Nestle to the year 738 (*Urtext und Übersetzungen der Bibel in übersichtliche Darstellung* (= *Realencylopädie für protestantische Theologie und Kirche*, 3te Aufl., iii; Leipzig, 1897), p. 121); to the year 789 by Rudolf Sonnleithner ('Die Mondsee Bruckstücke der ältesten hochdeutschen Evangelienübersetzung', *Festschrift der Nationalbibliothek in Wien* (Vienna, 1926), p. 801); and to the beginning of the ninth century by Hench (see the following footnote) and Wilhelm Braune (*Althochdeutsches Lesebuch*, 10te Aufl. (Halle (Saale), 1942), p. 145). According to W. B. Lockwood, 'the date of the translation cannot be precisely established, but it could be prior to 800' (*The Cambridge History of the Bible*; ii, *The West from the Fathers to the Reformation*, ed. by G. W. H. Lampe (Cambridge, 1969), p. 417).

[3] They were edited by George A. Hench, *The Monsee Fragments. Newly Collated Text with Notes and a Grammatical Treatise and an Exhaustive Glossary, and a Photo-Lithographic Fac-Simile* (Strasbourg, 1890). The same material, without the glossary and facsimile (pp. 143–212), was presented as a Dissertation at Johns Hopkins University (Strassburg, 1890). Reproductions of specimen folios are included in Wilhelm Walther, *Die deutsche Bibelübersetzung des Mittelalters* (Braunschweig, 1889–92), frontispiece in Part iii, and in H. J. Vogels, *Codicum Novi Testamenti specimina* (Bonn, 1929), pl. 51.   [4] Hench, op. cit., p. 139.

[5] So Walther, op. cit., col. 442, and Elias Steinmeyer, 'Isidor und Fragmenta Theotisca', *Prager deutsche Studien*, viii (1908), 147–63.

ally the Latin was misunderstood, as at Matt. xxi. 4 where the translator took *altilia* to mean *daz hohista*, and at xxvii. 2 where *Pontio* may have been abbreviated in such a way as to suggest *Pontico*, for he translates *demo pontischin herizohin pilate*.

An analysis of the textual affinities of the version discloses occasional intrusions of Western elements. A notable instance is the lengthy addition following Matt. xx. 28 ('But seek to increase from that which is small . . .'), found also in codex Bezae and several old Italian witnesses.[1]

2. THE GERMAN TATIAN

Another German rendering of the Gospel story was produced about A.D. 830 in Fulda, then the most significant monastic centre in the northern half of Germany. The rendering, which is in the east-Frankish dialect, was not made from a tetraevangelium, but from a Latin manuscript of Tatian's Diatessaron written about 540 for Bishop Victor of Capua (see p. 335 above). The German Tatian,[2] as it is called, is preserved in several manuscripts, the chief of which (according to Sievers) is MS. 56 of the Stiftsbibliothek at St. Gall, dating from the second half of the ninth century.[3] The text is presented in two columns, the left-hand in Latin, the right-hand in German; the latter follows the Latin closely, even as to word order. The unity of the translation has been questioned by Sievers, who held that the presence of varying expressions (particularly conjunctions) in different parts of the work can be explained only by the hypothesis that the German rendering was produced by several translators—as many as seventeen or eighteen! As could be expected, Sievers's opinion provoked a variety of reactions, some in support and some in opposition.[4]

---

[1] Cf. Klaus Metzel, 'Der lateinische Text des Matthäus-Evangeliums der Monseer Fragmente', *Beiträge zur Geschichte der deutschen Sprache und Literatur*, lxxxvii (1965), 289–363; for the text of Matt. xx. 28, see pp. 294–300 and 305–21.

[2] The standard edition is that of Eduard Sievers, *Tatianus. Lateinisch und Altdeutsch* (Paderborn, 1874; 2nd edn., 1892).

[3] According to P. Ganz, however, the Bodleian MS. Junius 13 preserves in some cases a more original wording of the German Tatian (*Beiträge zur Geschichte der deutschen Sprache und Literatur*, xci (1969), 28–76).

[4] In support of Sievers, e.g., the review by E. Steinmeyer (*Zeitschrift für deutsche Philologie*, iv (1877), 474–8); Friedrich Köhler, *Zur Frage der Entstehungsweise der ahd. Tatians Übersetzung* (Leipzig, 1911); and Taylor Starck, 'Der Wortschatz des ahd. Tatian und die Übersetzerfrage', *Studies in Honor of Hermann Collitz* (Baltimore, '

Among idiosyncrasies of the German rendering we find that, instead of 'Jesus', with a few exceptions, the translator generally prefers 'the Saviour' (*ther heilant*), even at Matt. i. 21. At Matt. xxvii. 2 the same error occurs as in the Monsee Fragments (it occurs also at Luke iii. 1), where *Pontico* is read instead of *Pontio*, resulting in *themo Pontisgen grauen Pilate*. In John i. 13 the translator must have read *volu(m)ptate* instead of *voluntate*, since he wrote *son fleiskes luste*.[1]

3. OTFRID'S *LIBER EVANGELIORUM*

In the ninth century Otfrid, a German poet in the monastery at Weissenburg in Speyergau (Lower Alsace), composed the *Liber Evangeliorum*,[2] comprising 7,416 lines of rhyming couplets in the south-Rhine Frankish dialect. From the presence of dedications it is known that the work was finished between 863 and 871.

Although often referred to as Otfrid's Gospel Harmony, the poem is not properly a harmony, for the writer was guided in his choice of selections from the Gospels, as it seems, by an ecclesiastical lectionary. He also incorporated material from the Apocrypha, the Church Fathers, and early medieval theologians, the latter especially in the moralizing, the mystical, and the spiritual interpretations of events recounted in the Scriptures. The work is divided into five books, professedly for the purification of the five senses. The first book is devoted to the birth and baptism of Christ; the second to his life from the temptation to the healing of

---

1930), pp. 190–202. For what can be said against the multiplicity of translators, see Walther, op. cit., cols. 446–55; E. Arens, 'Studien zum Tatian', *ZDP* (1897), pp. 63–73, 510–31; and George Baesecke, *Die Überlieferung des althochdeutschen Tatian* (*Hallische Monographien*, 4; Halle, 1948).

[1] For a discussion of other readings in the German Tatian, see Wilhelm Wissmann, 'Zum althochdeutschen Tatian', *Indogermanica, Festschrift für Wolfgang Krause* (Heidelberg, 1960), pp. 249–67; Anton Baumstark, *Die Vorlage des althochdeutschen Tatian*, ed. by Johannes Rathofer (Cologne–Graz, 1964); and Rathofer's contributions to *Literatur und Sprache im europäischen Mittelalter, Festschrift für Karl Langosch* (Darmstadt, 1973), pp. 256–308, and to *Zeiten und Formen in Sprache und Dichtung, Festschrift für Fritz Tschirch* (Cologne–Vienna, 1972), pp. 337–56.

[2] *Otfrids Evangelienbuch*, ed. by Oskar Erdmann and Ludwig Wolff, 4te Aufl. (*Altdeutsche Textbibliothek*, nr. 49; Tübingen, 1962). For a detailed bibliography from 1880 (the date of Paul Piper's edn. of Otfrid) to 1937, see Cornelis Soeteman, *Untersuchungen zur Übersetzungstechnik Otfrid von Weiszenburgs* (Rotterdam, 1939), pp. 127–32.

the leper after the sermon on the mount; the third to selected miracles until the decision of the high priest to put Christ to death; the fourth to the passion; and the fifth to the resurrection, ascension, and last judgement. Otfrid attached less importance to the deeds of Christ than to their symbolic interpretation and the dogmatic questions derived from them. Whether therefore the work deserves to be regarded as a New Testament version is open to question.[1]

After years of toil on his opus, Otfrid had a clean copy of the poem prepared by two scribes, which he then revised with his own hand and provided at the same time with two accent marks in each half verse to indicate the syllables that should receive the stress. This autograph copy, which is the earliest extant Old High German composition in rhyme, is preserved at Vienna (codex Vindobonensis[2]), and is the parent of codex Palatinus at Heidelberg (eighth century) and also of codex Frisingensis at Munich (copied soon after 900). Fragments of a fourth manuscript (codex Discissus) are in Berlin, Bonn, and Wolfenbüttel.[3]

III. THE OLD SAXON (OLD LOW GERMAN) VERSION

The Old Saxon *Heliand*[4] ('Saviour'), a poem of 5,983 verses written at the order of Charlemagne's son, Louis the Pious (d. 840), for the benefit of his Saxon subjects recently converted to Christianity, is sometimes reckoned as a New Testament version.

---

[1] Cf. Donald A. MacKenzie, *Otfrid von Weissenburg: Narrator or Commentator? A Comparative Study* (*Stanford University Publications, Language and Literature*, vi, 3; Stanford, 1946), and Wolfgang Kleiber, *Otfrid von Weissenburg. Untersuchungen zur handschriftlichen Überlieferung und Studien zur Aufbau des Evangelienbuches* (Berne and Munich, 1971), pp. 334–40.

[2] A facsimile edition, with an introduction by H. Butzmann, was published as vol. xxx of *Codices selecti phototypice impressi* (Graz, 1972).

[3] Cf. H. Herbst, 'Neue Wolfenbüttler Fragmente aus dem Codex Discissus von Otfrids Buch der Evangelien', *Zeitschrift für deutsche Geistesgeschichte*, ii (1936), 131 ff., reprinted with additions in *ZDA* lxxiv (1937), 117–25; and H. Hempel, 'Bonner Otfridsplinter', ibid. 125–9.

[4] Although the Heliand was discussed by Francis Junius in the seventeenth century, it was not edited until the nineteenth, when J. A. Schmeller published the *editio princeps* (Munich, 1830), and a critical apparatus as 'Lieferung 2' (1840). Other editions were prepared by Eduard Sievers (Halle, 1878), Paul Piper (Stuttgart, 1897), and Otto Behaghel (Halle, 1882; 7th edn., 1958).

Since, however, it is based on Tatian's harmony[1] (see pp. 21–2 above) with supplementary and explanatory additions taken from later ecclesiastical literature,[2] the work scarcely qualifies to be regarded as a version in the ordinary sense. Furthermore, inasmuch as the author chose to write in alliterative verse, he was compelled to take certain liberties in paraphrasing.[3] As a consequence the colouring of the poem is entirely Teutonic, and the personages are essentially Germanic in character, as are the descriptions of natural phenomena, feasts, and ceremonies (e.g. Christ is depicted as the liege-lord, and his apostles as his loyal vassals, to whom he gives rings).[4]

The poem survives complete in a tenth-century manuscript in the British Museum (Cotton Caligula A. VII);[5] a ninth-century manuscript at Munich has two lacunae. Smaller fragments are found in two ninth-century manuscripts at Prague and the Vatican, the latter also containing two portions of an Old Saxon version of Genesis in the same style but by a later poet.

[1] For a recent discussion of the relation of the Heliand to Tatian, see G. Quispel, *Tatian and the Gospel of Thomas; Studies in the History of the Western Diatessaron* (Leiden, 1975), pp. 26–77.

[2] Cf. Ernst Windisch, *Der Heliand und seine Quellen* (Leipzig, 1868); G. Keintzel, *Der Heliand im Verhältniss zu seinen Quellen* (Hermannstadt, 1882); Juw fon Weringha (known also as J. J. van Weringh), *Heliand and Diatessaron* (*Studia Germanica*, 5; Assen, 1965); and Wolfgang Huber, *Heliand und Matthäusexegese. Quellenstudien insbesondere zu Sedulius Scottus* (Munich, 1969).

[3] Cf. Gottfried Berron, *Der Heliand als Kunstwerk* (Würaburg–Aumühle, 1940), and Johannes Rathofer, *Der Heliand; theologischer Sinn als tektonische Form. Vorbereitung und Grundlegung der Interpretation* (Cologne, 1962). For an English translation which reproduces the kennings and alliterative features characteristic of the original, see Marina Scott, *The Heliand, translated from the Old Saxon* (*University of North Carolina Studies in the Germanic Languages and Literatures*, 52; Chapel Hill, 1966).

[4] Cf. Gustav Ehrisman, *Geschichte der deutschen Literatur bis zum Ausgang des Mittelalters*, 2te Aufl.; i, *Die althochdeutsche Literatur* (Munich, 1959), 164–8.

[5] Robert Priebsch, *The Heliand Manuscript Cotton Caligula A VIII in the British Museum* (Oxford, 1925).

APPENDIX

Addenda to the Check-list of Old Latin Manuscripts of the New Testament

After reading the page proofs of the chapter on the Latin Versions (Chap. VII above), P. Bonifatius Fischer kindly brought to the author's attention information concerning a score of additional Old Latin manuscripts as well as several bibliographical references. This material, comprising the following addenda, will supplement the check-list on pp. 295–311 above.

THE GOSPELS

λ (J^Lk 2nd edn.). Fragmentum Rosenthal, saec. viii–ix, at San Francisco, owned by Bernard M. Rosenthal, contains Luke xvi. 27–xvii. 8 and xviii. 11–16, 18–26; ed. by Aland in Jülicher (2nd edn.); text and script are most similar to *r²* (see B. Fischer, 'Das Neue Testament in lateinischer Sprache', op. cit. (see p. 362 n. 2), p. 30 n. 87).

μ (J^Mt only). Fragmentum Monacense, saec. v, at Munich, Bayerische Staatsbibliothek, Clm 29155^G, contains Matt. ix. 17, 30–7; x. 1–10 with lacunae, palimpsest; ed. (provisionally) by Jülicher.

ρ (24). Also A. Dold, *Das Sacramentar im Schabcodex M12 sup. der Bibliotheca Ambrosiana* (*Texte und Arbeiten*, i. 43; Beuron, 1952), pp. 39–45 and 25*.

41. Also H. J. Vogels, 'Codex VII der Cathedralbibliothek von Verona (b²)', *Colligere Fragmenta. Festschrift Alban Dold*, ed. by B. Fischer and V. Fiale (Beuron, 1952), pp. 1–12.

Codex Vindobonesis, saec. v, at Vienna, Nationalbibliothek, cod. lat. 563, fols. 122–77, contains fragments of Matt. xxvi. 56–xxviii. 2, palimpsest, ed. by G. Philippart, 'Fragments palimpsestes latins du Vindobonensis 563 (ve siècle?). Évangile selon s. Matthieu, Évangile de l'Enfance selon Thomas, Évangile de Nicodème', *Analecta Bollandiana*, xc (1972), 391–411.

Codex Laudunensis, saec. ix¹, at Laon, Bibliothèque Municipale 473 *bis*, contains the same citations of the Gospels in Eusebian Canon Tables as nos. 39 and 40; see B. Fischer, *Karl der Grosse, Lebenswerk und Nachleben*; ii, *Das geistige Leben* (Düsseldorf, 1965), p. 188.

ACTS OF THE APOSTLES

(67). Also B. Fischer, 'Ein neue Zeuge zum westlichen Text der Apostelgeschichte', *Biblical and Patristic Studies in Memory of R. P. Casey*, ed. by J. N. Birdsall and R. W. Thompson (Freiburg, 1963), pp. 33–63; *Vetus Latina*, xxvi/1, *Epistulae Catholicae*, ed. W. Thiele; for specimen of script, see Lowe, xi, no. 1636.

r (62). Also P. K. Kelin, 'Date et scriptorium de la Bible de Roda. État des recherches', *Les Cahiers de Saint-Michel de Cuxa*, iii (1972), 91–102.

69 = τ^{69}. Liber comicus Legionensis, saec. xi², at Léon, Archivo Catedralicio 2, contains Old Latin readings in lessons from Acts, Pauline and Catholic Epistles, Revelation; ed. by J. Pérez de Urbel and A. González y Ruiz-Zorrilla, *Liber Commicus*, 2 vols. (Madrid, 1950–5) (Cod. L); *Vetus Latina*, xxiv/1; xxiv/2; xxvi/1.

70 = τ^{70}. Liber comicus Aemilianensis or of S. Millán, saec. xi², at Madrid, Academia de la Historia, Aemil. 22, contains Old Latin readings in lessons from Acts, Pauline and Catholic Epistles, Revelation; ed. by J. Pérez de Urbel and A. González y Ruiz-Zorrilla, *Liber Commicus*, 2 vols. (Madrid, 1950–5) (cod. E); *Vetus Latina*, xxiv/1; xxiv/2; xxvi/1.

72 = τ^{72}. Missale Toletanum, saec. ix–x, at Toledo, Cabildo 35-4, contains Old Latin readings in lessons from Acts, Pauline and Catholic Epistles, Revelation; ed. by J. Pérez de Urbel and A. González y Ruiz-Zorrilla, *Liber Commicus*, 2 vols. (Madrid, 1950–5) (cod T_2); *Vetus Latina*, xxiv/1; xxiv/2; xxvi/1.

73 = τ^{73}. Missale Silense, saec. x–xi, at London, British Museum, Addit. MS. 30846, contains Old Latin readings in lessons from Acts, Pauline Epistles, Revelation; ed. *Vetus Latina*, xxiv/1; xxiv/2.

74. Fragmentum Sinaiticum, saec. ix–x, at Mount Sinai, St. Catherine, Arab. MS. 455, fols. 1 and 4, two leaves of an epistolary contain Acts x. 36–40; xiii. 14–16, 26–30; Revelation xx. 11–xxi. 7 as pericopes; ed. by E. A. Lowe, 'Two New Latin Liturgical Fragments on Mount Sinai', *RBén*, lxxiv (1964), 252–83.

262. Missale Toletanum, saec. ix–x, at Toledo, Cabildo 35-5, contains Old Latin readings in lessons from Acts, Pauline and Catholic Epistles, Revelation; ed. *Vetus Latina*, xxiv/1; xxiv/2; xxvi/1.

271 = τ^{271}. Missale Toletanum, saec. x, at Toledo, Cabildo 35-6, contains Old Latin readings in lessons from Acts, Pauline and Catholic Epistles, Revelation; ed. *Vetus Latina*, xxiv/2; xxvi/1.

Missale Silense, saec. x, at London, British Museum, Addit. MS. 30844, contains Old Latin readings in lessons from Acts, Pauline and Catholic Epistles, Revelation.

THE PAULINE EPISTLES

w (B M) = *gue* (T) (79). Also A. Dold, 'Die Provenienz der altlateinischen Römerbrieftexte in den gotisch-lateinischen Fragmenten des Codex Carolinus von Wolfenbüttel', *Zentralblatt für Bibliothekswesen, Beiheft* lxxv (1950), 13–29.

x_2 (T) = O (W). Also E. S. Buchanan, *The Epistles of S. Paul from the Codex Laudianus* (*Sacred Latin Texts*, ii; London, 1914); J. Wordsworth, H. J. White, *Novum Testamentum* . . . , vol. ii. This manuscript is a copy of Würzburg,

Universitätsbibliothek, M.p.th. f. 69; see H. J. Frede, *Vetus Latina*, xxiv/1, p. 17* f., and xxiv/2, p. 18.

61 = D (W). See 61 in list of Acts manuscripts; the Pauline Epistles are Old Latin.

68 = τ^{68}. Fragmenta Toletana libri comici, saec. ix–x, at Toledo, Cabildo 35–8, contain Old Latin readings in lessons from Pauline and Catholic Epistles; ed. by J. Pérez de Urbel and A. González y Ruiz-Zorrilla, *Liber Commicus*, 2 vols. (Madrid, 1950–5) (cod. T); *Vetus Latina*, xxiv/1; xxiv/2; xxvi/1.

69 = τ^{69}. See 69 in list of Acts manuscripts.

70 = τ^{70}. See 70 in list of Acts manuscripts.

71 = τ^{71}. Fragmenta Parisina libri comici, saec. viii–ix, at Paris, Bibliothèque Nationale, lat. 2269, fols. 17–48, palimpsest, contain Old Latin readings in lessons from Pauline and Catholic Epistles; ed. by A. Mundó, 'El commicus Palimpsest Paris Lat. 2269 amb notes sobre litùrgia i manuscrits visigòtics a Septimània i Catalunya', *Liturgica I, Cardinali I. A. Schuster in memoriam* (*Scripta et Documenta*, vii; Montserrat, 1956); *Vetus Latina*, xxiv/2; xxvi/1.

72 = τ^{72}. See 72 in list of Acts manuscripts.

73 = τ^{73}. See 73 in list of Acts manuscripts.

83. Fragmenta Waldeccensia et Marburgensia, Graeco-Latin, saec. xi (Beu[1]), x–xi (Beu[24]), x ex. (Beu[25]), at Mengeringhausen in Waldeck, Stadtarchiv; Marburg, Hessiches Staatsarchiv, Best. 147, contain in Latin 2 Cor. xi. 33–xii. 14; Eph. i. 5–13 and ii. 3–11; Titus i. 1–iii. 3; the 2 fols. at Mengeringhausen with text of Eph. ed. by V. Schultze, *Codex Waldeccensis* ($D^{W\ Paul}$). *Unbekannte Fragmente einer griechisch-lateinischen Bibelhandschrift* (Munich, 1904). This manuscript is a copy of d (75); see H. J. Frede, *Vetus Latina*, xxiv/1, p. 13*; xxv, pp. 28 f.

88. Fragmentum Basilense, saec. x, at Basel, Universitätsbibliothek, B.I. 6, fol. 21, contains 2 Cor. vii. 3–x. 18; ed. by G. Meyer, 'Ein neuer Zeuge des e-Typus der Vetus Latina im zweiten Korintherbrief 7, 3–10, 18', *RBén*, lxxv (1965), 40–53.

89. Codex Budapestiensis, saec. viii–ix, at Budapest, National Museum, Clmae 1, contains the Pauline Epistles with a commentary; ed. by H. J. Frede, *Ein neuer Paulustext und Kommentar*, 2 vols. (*Vetus Latina. Aus der Geschichte der lateinischen Bibel*, vii–viii; Freiburg, 1973–4).

262. See 262 in list of Acts manuscripts.

271 = τ^{271}. See 271 in list of Acts manuscripts.

Missale Silense (London, British Museum, Addit. MS. 30844), see last item in list of Acts Manuscripts.

Missale Silense, saec. x, at London, British Museum, Addit. MS. 30845, contains Old Latin readings in lessons from Pauline Epistles and Revelation.

THE CATHOLIC EPISTLES

32. See 32 in list of Gospels manuscripts.

68. See 68 in list of Pauline manuscripts.

69. See 69 in list of Acts manuscripts.

70. See 70 in list of Acts manuscripts.

71. See 71 in list of Pauline manuscripts.

72. See 72 in list of Acts manuscripts.

91, 92, 93, 94, 95. See *Vetus Latina*, xxvi/1, p. 17*.

262. See 262 in list of Acts manuscripts.

271. See 271 in list of Acts manuscripts.

London Add. MS. 30844. See last item in list of Acts manuscripts.

THE BOOK OF REVELATION

69, 70, 72, 73, 74, 262, 271. See these items in list of Acts manuscripts.

330. Psalterium Reginense, saec. viii med. (Beu Lo), at Rome, Biblioteca Apostolica Vaticana, cod. Regin. lat. 11, contains (as a liturgical canticle) an Old Latin text of Rev. xv. 3–4; ed. by G. Morin, 'Un texte pré-hieronymien du cantique de l'Apocalypse xv, 3–4', *RBén*, xxvi (1909), 464–7; for specimen of script, see Lowe, i, no. 101.

I. Index of Names and Subjects

Q

II. Index of Versional Manuscripts of the New Testament

III. Index of Passages of the New Testament